THE ABZs OF
SENSUALITY, SOCIETY,
AND SEX

THE ABZs OF SENSUALITY, SOCIETY, AND SEX

Magno J. Ortega, M.D.

Library of Congress Control Number: 2015919475
ISBN: Hardcover   978-1-5144-2838-2
                  Softcover   978-1-5144-2837-5
                  eBook   978-1-5144-2836-8

Print information available on the last page.

Rev. date: 01/29/2016

To order additional copies of this book, contact:
Xlibris
1-888-795-4274
www.Xlibris.com
Orders@Xlibris.com
716081

CONTENTS

INTRODUCTION

Let me introduce myself, me as rememberer, writing about what I have done, how and when, seldom why.

This book is written as a docudrama in parts, in others as poems and excerpts of commentary, or assonant rhythms. Formal in content or informal in context, each part contributes to a totality greater than the sum of their separate insights. (So will yours be larger than their total by the end of your journey through these pages.)

The reader may find its central character too different from popular ones ranging all the way from heroes to antiheroic intellectual hypochondriacs. In order to understand, he seldom asks why instead of why not and more often demands why now. Sequence, not causes, decides outcome.

This is a theory for the practice of transcultural psychiatry that connects life with both art and science in absolute relativity by a clinical senso-social-sexual rationalysis of becoming, believing, and begetting.

This triadic, sex-differentiated but value-free rationalysis of becoming, believing (to belong), and begetting is based on absolute relativity in the triad of anthropology, biology, and cosmology, even if some of their beginnings are still obscure or just beginning to be revealed.

This is not just the science of history that Jared Diamond recommends in *Guns, Germs, and Steel* (1997) to understand "the fates of human societies" from their geographical distribution and the flora and fauna that they can handily domesticate, but also a history of science to plot its uneven and spotty progress through time.

It is unscientific to treat life as a singularity. It is self-serving to explore space for life-forms.

As we keep growing, we learn that the whole cosmos is a closed system, that everything that happens to it, whether of our doing or another's, affects everything else one way or another to a greater or lesser extent, largely unpredicted by the doer and lost on the bystander.

Great civilizations, now dead, never accepted this emotionally. In this postindustrial age, what we know to be ecologically true, we can now simulate electronically; but, whether we know our history or not, are we doomed to repeat its mistakes?

Copernicus changed the landscape in cosmology, Darwin in biology, Einstein in physics. I want to build on their discoveries to make psychiatry a modern science.

My students and patients and their parents and mine and my grandchildren helped. Try to separate what is informative or disruptive from the comfortably old or acceptable. (Can you all see where you entered our world's history? If bogged down, switch thinking gears to get out of rediscovered mental ruts.)

To study human life, I have singled out our alphabet so that—like Aristotle in his A=A—what one stands for, from A to Z, cannot be confused with what another has been assigned to designate. Mathematics does the same, using numbers (instead of Roman numerals) and fractions (ratios) for convenience. (Fractions quantify but do not compare what ratios can.)

When we pray, it is to ask for (A) what we wish or want. When we meditate, it is to listen to (B) our inner reptilian unconscious. When we think, it is to (C) remember and recognize what we have recently heard or read. When we compare, we (D) contrast wishes with wishes, silence with silence, words with words, and deeds with deeds. When we (E) create, we juxtapose what is conscious against what is unconscious with or without words, or hitherto unrelated events that belong together.

Our database consists of a kaleidoscope of "periscope sightings" from the past and present by my personal and professional family, looking back to animals, sideways at us, and ahead with computers. Unlike Marx, who wants not to understand "reality" but only to change it, I do not think much of it is up to us. I have no vested interest in my synthesis (more comprehensive than eclectic), though I can defend it. It is not even mine (though the words are). It is nature's behavior that triggered it.

The basis for this compendium is largely empirical (inductive and heuristic), not inferential (deductive or epistemological); the process itself is less (C) conceptual (or metaphorical) or analytical (dependent on logic), more simile than analogy, and more (D) postlogical (historical and evolutionary), using homology (genealogy) rather than ontology.

Only when professionals rely on (C) deductive logic (untestable certitudes) instead of (D) comparative study, do they reenter the Dark Ages of Aristotle and St. Thomas Aquinas and cease to be post-Renaissance scientists.

Who among us are still pre-Hippocratic, pre-Copernican, pre-Cartesian, pre-Darwinian, or pre-Pavlovian?

We can forever chip away at tradition as mental ramparts defending against intellectual onslaught. Instead, I have used it as a natural catapult to leap to higher ground for a wider panoramic view of more distant scientific horizons.

In a world overloaded with information and teetering on chaos, an attempt to systematize what is new and reconcile it with the old produces a testable synthesis that we have called the theory of absolute relativity for the practice of a new psychiatry. Solidly grounded on the *ABCs* of cosmology, biology, and anthropology, we use the ABZs of life in the clinical rationalysis of sensuality **(A to E)**, society **(F to O)**, and sex **(P to Z)**.

We have discovered and are exploring the growing polarity between biology and beliefs.

The seeds for this book were planted in the Philippines—by bipeds and quadrupeds, large and small—on a farm which the author left to attend kindergarten. (Cities foster anthropocentrism [*human racism*].) It blossomed in Manila during a Pacific congress on transcultural psychiatry, with my redefinition of "transcultural" as "transcending all cultures" and therefore common to many animals rather than uniquely human.

Our new definition required an old pyramid from the New World to illustrate its implications. It illuminated the *ABCs* of art and science for New Renaissance artists and scientists and underlies the confluence of all life, art, and science.

Most of the human race may be biased against other species. Some psychiatrists may still be biased against animals, even if they favor the body over the brain because of earlier familiarity with it in medical school.

It is not often that we question what fascinates us, favors us, and sets us apart. Nonetheless, if we are also curious about the guiltiest and greediest of all species, as well as the most skilled but not the best prepared nor the wisest but the wordiest, we can all share and learn from that fascination, and then sort it out.

With animals as a bridge between mind and matter, it is equally important to deal with nature. If we struggle to compensate for our natural weaknesses as bipeds that cannot fly, can understanding nature itself assist us to cope? How does our nature surrender its self-conscious and social defenses to sex, as other animals unquestionably do?

Because psychiatrists are expected to consider a wider and wilder range of behavior than other scientists, it behooves them to tie in even the most unnatural or supernatural account of personal experiences with biological, and therefore natural, events. Nature includes matter, animate and inanimate. Material, animal, and human behavior are here explored without favoring one or the other against the rest. Keeping this extraordinarily broad scope in mind can help us connect what seems, on first reading, to be disconnected (irrelevant).

Are we more than the sum of global attributes shaped by the past as we slowly evolved from being puny to proud to painfully puritan to puffed up to pushy to predatory to planet-conscious? Can these conversions gain extra credits for each convert?

I started out less innocently than other non-fiction writers. I thought that if psychiatrists are to be consulted privately about society and sex, they must at some point present credentials about personal, social, and sexual experiences.

Increasingly, it became obvious that behavior can only be comprehended by comparing across cultures and species. And so, to what is already known, I added what I have learned from actual experience with animals, mostly mammals, which have been under direct observation in their natural habitat for years and years in Paradise Found, my hillside country home.

If we are each a microcosm of our universe, are our orbits decided by the centers of force or influence that we cannot leave behind? Are all of us not interdependent elements in an interlocking system? Can we change what happens outside such spheres in our life cycle even while it decays and we burn out before reaching our prime during the half-life span we spend in the corner of space that we live in? To explore this, we need to open our hearts as well as our minds.

First chronologically, and then alphabetically, we discuss cosmology (*I*, all matter in motion), biology (*II*, all life), and anthropology (*III*, all humanity, becoming, believing, and begetting), subdivided into (*i*, A to

E) sensuality and liberty *(ii,* F to O), society and equality, and *(iii)* sex and *erotica* (P to Y) until (Z) virtual androgyny for WoManly grandparents.

It took the genius of Freud to see what is oral, anal, or genital. We can compare our experiences among *H. sapiens, domestici,* and *metropoli* with his sexology, Erikson's sociology, Piaget's senso-cognitive epigenesis, and Maslow's humanism in order to arrive at a senso-socio-sexual rationalysis of all human behavior.

We still don't know how life began, what all its arbitrary rules are, and when it will end; but I can show you its contours. Dying cannot stop our sweating, nor do our hair and nails stop growing, even after we are buried.

I cannot, therefore, promise you closure nor meaning. Meaning requires both imagination and frustration, just as purpose is sought whenever energy is surrounded by obstacles. (Questions should then focus on frustrations or obstacles, not abstractions.)

Your destination will still be up for grabs. I can only lead you in directions you may or may not have taken on your own, sooner or later.

1.00 a/A Periodic Table of Elements of Behavior in Clinical Rationalysis: A NEW PSYCHIATRY

There are vital signs that show we are alive under sub-cortical control. Without their control, we die. There are also essential developments that tell us while we are alive and growing that we will endure. They are under more collective control. Without them, we face extinction as a species. Will we survive in the long run, or just prevail in our own lifetime, while engaged in becoming, belonging and/or begetting?

There is the ABC (Anthropology, Biology, and Cosmology) of a New Science of (I-III) Absolute Relativity, and the ABZs of a new psychiatry of (i-iii) Clinical Rationalysis of senso- (A -> E)- socio (F-> O)-sexual (P -> Z) behavior

Which came first, fission or fusion, violence or sex? All behavior found in (I) nature, (II) animals or (III) humans can be classified as (i) liberation or libertarian, becoming free or sensual, with or without violence, (ii) egalitarian, believing in equality or social parity, with or without merit, or (iii) eroto-sexual, begetting kin, with or without intimacy, within each orbit under observation.

Operationally, doubting rather than certitude is built into this culture-free strategy of absolute relativity. All that science needs to advance are healthy doses of doubt and penetrating questions to ask. No subject, sacred or profane, is taboo or safe from scrutiny in this New Psychiatry, as long as we agree with Hippocrates to "do no harm" in our clinical practice of senso-socio-sexual rationalysis.

We live these sub-cycles (i-iii) and stages (A-Z) in varying ratios as we age. How do we now use them to understand history and ourselves? It is not that nothing is irrelevant but that everything is relative by being related to something or other under similar but not identical circumstances. This is the central controlling and defining nature in any given time or place of both sub-atomic (electro-chemical) and subliminal events. Which also allows us, as in chemistry, to create a "periodic table" of behavior, but in a tri-dimensional and more pyramidal shape.

Stages of human growth and development are co-terminous as in physical evolution. We start with feelings — (we are more e-motional the less mobile we are as animals who are not rooted to the spot like plants, which themselves send distress signals when threatened), — and then, like hydrogen, feelings are bonded to more evolved behavior — (e.g., "fear of ghosts" becomes "awe of spirits" and gaseous hydrogen becomes an unseen God) — beyond touching, tickling, or being moved to cry or giggle.

In our personal and private lives, we just need to touch and be touched, to signal intention and reception. Only in our public life are spoken or written words inevitable. But they can be like loose cannon if used carelessly, unless they are treated as symptoms pointing in a general direction. Catch words like (A) "vulnerability" and (B') "commitment" signify different stages of life.

The only advantage of spoken words over sign language is in their alliteration, as in "rigid, frugal and punctual" to define "anal". To the deaf, the same sign may signify "church" (righteous: "I'm right to hate"), "pious" (puritan) and "narrow-minded" (tunnel-vision), but the defensive lyrics to the same music when the subjects are stressed cannot be alliterated. Unstressed, "baby talk" suffices at any age. (Sign language is acquired by children of deaf parents earlier than speech by peers.)

Tables

(You will want to refer back to the tables in
this chapter as you read the book)

SENSO-SOCIO-SEXUAL RATIONALYSIS

Table 1
SENSO-SOCIO-SEXUAL RATIONALYSIS in 26 Stages of Personal Development

The steps in this New World pyramid are steeper
where sensual development is concerned.

A: Affectionate or emotional, passionate or passive, good or bad (A-)
B: Bold or bashful, willing or willful or decisive, right or wrong (B-)
C: Contemplative, logical or rational (ratio-minded, true or false (C-)
D: Discriminating or comparative, fact or fiction, more or less
E: Experimental or creative, *avant garde* or traditional, new or old

The social steps face south but are easier to climb.

F: Spiritual or animistic, gnostic or agnostic, atheistic or cynical (F-)
G: Political or patriotic, xenophobic or receptive, prideful or not
H: Commercial or barter-minded, money-mad or fraternal or not (H-)
I: Individualistic or psychological, consciousness driven or not (I-)
J: Group-minded or sociological, community-minded or not (J-)
K: Mechanical or technology-driven, progress-oriented or not (K-)
L: Humanistic or anthropocentric, community conscious or not (L-)
M: Ecological or nature-loving, planet-conscious or globe-minded
N: Ethological or animal-lover, instinct- or physiology-conscious
O: Cybernetic or computer-smart, simulation-guided vs ratio-driven

The female faces east, the male faces west, they meet north or south.

FEMALE	MALE
P: Narcissistic or self-worshipping	Auto-erotic or self-stimulating
Q: Tomboyishness (assertiveness)	Fetishistic (hoarding)
R: Homo-erotic (slumber parties)	Voyeuristic (Tom-peeping)
S: Play-nursing (role-,orroring)	Exhibitionist ("hard"-selling)
T: Spouse-shopping (mate-finding)	Bestiality (pet-"thing")
U: Child-swapping (baby-sitting)	Playing doctor (pedophilia)
V: Child-bearing ("heavy"-dating)	Homosexuality ("buddy"-body)
W: Empty-nesting (client-saving)	Driven-mating (rapaciousness)
X: Adult-swapping (adult-mixing)	Sensuous coitus or monogamy
Y: Cradle-snatching (menopausal)	Proud fathering (meta-pausal)

ANDROGYNY

Z: Grand-mothering (social)	Grandfathering (virtual)

Table 2
(i) SENSO- (ii) SOCIO- (iii) SEXUAL PYRAMID OF BEHAVIOR

```
                          .......
                          : Z :
                       ....:.....:....
                    E : f Y m : O:
                ..........:...........:....:....
              :     : m X f:      N:
           :.......:.................:............:.
           D :      : f W m :        M:
        .......:...............:...........:......
        :           : mV f     :          L:
       :...............:.................:.......:....
        C :     :     :f U m:      :      K:
      ....:........:..........:..............:......
        :      :      : m T f :      :      J :
      :.......:...............................:......:....
        B     :     : ::f S m:     :     :      I:
     ..........:........:.........:..........:......:......
        :     :     :     :m R f    :     :     H:
    :...........:........:...........:.........:.......:...
      A :     :     :     :f Q m:     :     :     G:
   ..........:........:..........:..........:......:....
     :     :        :        :m P f :        :        F:
   ........:........:..........:..........:......:......:.........
  :Pavlov :Jung  : Freud  : Ortega  : Piaget  : Maslow  : Erikson:
  :..........:.........:.........:..........:.........:........:....
```

(i, A-E) sensual self   **(iii, P-Z) sexual kin**   **(ii, F-O) social clan**
moral virtues, virtuosity   erotic intimacy   ethical values

Table 2A
OUR SENSO-SOCIO-SEXUAL DEVELOPMENT

In (i) becoming sensual we go from lonely (A, emotional) to wanting to go it alone (E, creative), in (ii) believing to belong, from social slavery (F, spiritual) to mastery of machinery (O, electronic) and to (iii) beget sexually, from (P) self-stimulation to (Z) grandparenthood (which Jung left out).

PERSONAL LIBERTY Senso-moral	PUBLIC EQUALITY Socio-ethical	PRIVATE EROTICISM Male/Female sexuality	FREUD Psycho-sexual
A) feel: Good/Bad taste/touch	F)aith in Pa X'Mas or a God	P: autoerotic or narcissistic	ORAL
suck/grasp How soon?	G)overn the weak	Q: asserting or collecting	ANAL
B) act: Right/Wrong grab / reject	H)ustle: barter or trade tokens	R: curious or peeping	OEDIPAL
push/pull How much?	I-centered: ego-centric	S: exhibiting or flirting	LATENCY
C) think: True/False reason/beg	J)oiner: ethnocentric	Tmf,Uf: pedophilia/	
seek/yield Who? Why?	K)in to machines L)over of humans	baby-sitting Um, Vf: gay or promiscuous	
D) compare:Test or no? fit/discard	M)a Earth now: geocentric	Wf, Vm: adoptive or bestial	GENITAL
find/explore When? Where	N)aturalist: ethnocentric	Wm, Xf: rapist or adulteress	
E) create: New or not? venture/see		Yf, XYm: divorced or monogamous	
change/wreck How? What	O)verclever bio-chips	parenthood Z: grandparenthood	
D' to A': Entropy decay -> die	N' to F': Ideology = bigotry	V' to R': Retrogressve "perversions"	

Freud and, until recently, Erikson, also ignored grandparenthood. Nobody saw anyone who is not a grandparent as being handicapped, yet no one can say one has been fully challenged until one meets one's grandchildren. Then one rises to meet their needs or fails.

Table 3
(i) SENSUAL FACE in BEHAVIOR PYRAMID

....

: E : creative: skills:

..........:...............:......................:.........:.......

: D : comparative : expertise :

.....:...............:...............:......... .....:...............:.........:.......

: C : pre-conditioned :to seek purpose:

............:.......:...........................:..:......

: B: intuitive grasp: or try and see: problem solving:

....:.............:...................:...............:...............:......:.......................

: A : emotional approach: to need-satisfaction: and data collection:

:.....:...:...........................:...........................

(i) BECOMING

Table 4
SENSO-PERSONAL VIRTUES AND VIRTUOSITIES

You are evolving from one column to the next, from left to right. (If senescent, you may be returning to your second adolescence and/or childhood back to the first column in your life-cycle.)

Pre-logical stage/period

A for affect-prone, awe-inclined assistance/acceptance: "Children and patients come before adults and associates." [Emotional: (A) adualistic, "affective", baby, caring, feeling, good, infancy, mood, taste, touch; (A') bad, impulsive, vulnerable]

B for bashful or brash volitional initiative: "Give me more space or another chance." [Intuitive: (B) childhood, choice, commitment, "conative", doing, correct, fair, juvenile, motivation, right, stamina, territoriality, toddler, trying, willful, willing; (B') temper tantrums, unwilling, urchin, voluntary, wrong, wrong-doing]

Table 4A
A to B: SUB-SEQUENCES OF SENSO-MORAL DEVELOPMENT

SIGN:	[A]re you mine?	[B]elieve in me.
ERAS:	Adualistic	Pre-logical
AGES:	INFANTILE	JUVENILE
a STAGES	Taste / feel	Grab / Push
b MENTAL	"Affective"	"Conative"
c SENSES	Somesthetic	Kinesthetic
d ACTION	Child-like	Brash or bashful
e DEEDS	Suckle/bite	Choose or reject
f TRAITS	Cooing/crying	Mobility
g STYLE	Echo / regurgitate	Barter / blame
h HINTS	Hungry	Greedy
i NEEDS	Care-givers	Buddies, enemies
j ALLIES	Lull(b)abies *(sic)*	Prejudices
k TOOLS	Taste buds / trust	Sphincters/order
l RISKS	Starve/fall	Poverty/slavery
m GOALS	Satiety	Safe passage
n WEAPONS	Suck/Grasp reflex	Disown the bad
o SET	Gut reactions	Peer approval
p SETTING	Familial/parental	Tribal/communal
q ISSUES	**Good or Bad**	**Right or Wrong**
r FOCUS	What is offered?	What is fair?
s STAKES	Appetitive	Trade or take-over
t VALUES	Security	Property/privilege
u HAZARDS	Thumb-sucking	Advancement
v REPUTE	Clinging	Driven
w DEFENSE	Intellectualized	Rationalized
x SYMBOLS	Food, music	Money, power
y SAMPLES	Gourmands	Profiteers
z QUERIES	How soon?	How much?

The ages (infantile, juvenile, adolescent, etc.) do not describe you as a person, but under each are listed what each of us, sooner or later, goes through in the process of growing old, not up. (Some of us grow older more slowly at certain stages in the process. Some of us are precocious from the start.)

[Each column in the transitional tables which follow each developmental stage just shows what to expect as we age at heart, slowly or prematurely. (We age in our mind as we live only to believe in age-old beliefs around us.) Did FDR's "infantile paralysis" allow him to swim with children without self-consciousness?]

Table 4B
B to C: Senso-Moral URCHINHOOD and ADOLESCENCE

	[**B**]elieve in me.	[**C**]orrect it.
SIGN:		
ERAS:	Pre-Aristotelian	Pre-scientific
AGES:	JUVENILE	ADOLESCENT
a STAGES:	Grab / Push	Digest / Purge
b MENTAL:	CONATIVE	COGNITIVE
c SENSES:	Kinesthetic	Apperceptive
d ACTION:	Bold or shy	Questing
e DEEDS:	Choose / reject	Accept / search
f TRAITS:	Mobility	Idealism
g STYLE:	Barter / blame	Ruminate / think
h HINTS:	Greedy	Convinced
i NEEDS:	Buddies, enemies	Answers
j ALLIES:	Prejudices	Dogma, symmetry
k TOOLS:	Sphincters / order	Reason / logic
l RISKS:	Poverty / slavery	Martyrdom
m GOALS:	Safe passage	Meaning
n WEAPONS:	Disown the bad	Seek the good
o SET:	Peer acceptance	Loud consensus
p SETTING:	Tribal / communal	Sectarian
q ISSUES:	**Right or Wrong**	**True or False**
r FOCUS:	What is fair?	What is fact?
s STAKES:	Trade or take-over	Yield or pray
t VALUES:	Property / privilege	Timely rewards
u HAZARDS:	"Ass"-licking	"Screwing"-up
v REPUTE:	Driven	Converted
w DEFENSE:	Rationalized	"I believed"
x SYMBOLS:	Money, power	God, utopias
y SAMPLES:	Profiteers	Professors / Confessors
z QUERIES:	How much?	Who, Why ever?

Logical stage/period

C for cleverly "critical", confrontation-shy, conflict-conscious, compromise-susceptible, conclusion-grasping, closure-seeking, cognitive-dependent timid search for true meaning: "My mind is my pride and joy." ["Rational": (**C**) abstraction, adolescence, analogy, analytical, answers, idealistic, introspective, logic, meaning, philosophy, reasoning, recognition, reductionistic, reflective, seeking, thinking, true; (**C'**) double-take, false, unconstructive]

Table 4C
C to D: Senso-Moral PUBESCENCE and ADULTHOOD

SIGN:	[C]orrect it.	[D]ata / desire
ERAS:	Philosophical	Post-logical
AGES:	ADOLESCENT	POST-PUBESCENT
a STAGES:	Digest / Purge	Test -> Discard
b MENTAL:	COGNITIVE	CORRELATIVE
c SENSES:	Apperceptive	Comparative
d ACTION:	Questing	Exploring
e DEEDS:	Accept / search	Re-search / remodel
f TRAITS:	Idealism	Skepticism
g STYLE:	Ruminate / think	Refute / re-examine
h HINTS:	Convinced	Reserved
i NEEDS:	Answers	Questions
j ALLIES:	Dogma, symmetry	Null hypotheses
k TOOLS:	Reason /logic	Ratiocination
l RISKS:	Martyrdom	Re-cognition
m GOALS:	Meaning	Gaps, omissions
n WEAPONS:	Seek the good	Expose falsehood
o SET:	Praise /promise	Silent consensus
p SETTING:	Sectarian	Secular / collegial
q ISSUES:	True or False	Testable or not
r FOCUS:	What is fact?	What is fanciful?
s STAKES:	Yield or pray	Disprove or try
t VALUES:	Timely rewards	Opportunity
u HAZARDS:	Screwing-up	Burning out
v REPUTE:	Converted	Critical
w DEFENSE:	"I believed"	"Need more cases"
x SYMBOLS:	God, utopias	Lab or library
y SAMPLES:	Professors / Confessors	Professionals
z QUERIES:	Who, Why ever?	Where, Why now?

Post-logical stage/period

D for data-insistent, decision-wary, disproof/correlation of claims / contradictions: "Numbers speak louder than words." [Constructively critical: **(D)** "comparative", compeering, correlating, exploring, homology, post-logical, post-pubescence, questioning, research, testing]

E for enduring creativity, excellent originality, precocious or not: "Life is too short." [Inventive: **(E)** "alogical", artistic (crea-teasing, crea-tickling), combining, connecting, "creact-ive" (crea-trying), creative, discovering, experimenting, imagination, non-random, novel, original, precocity, pre-senescent, scientific, talented, venturesome]

Further familiarity with the clusters of behavior that combine together in each period of development will show you what makes one a dreamer **(A)** or a doer **(B)**, a talker **(C)** or explorer **(D)**. What decides whether one depends more on **(A)** taste or **(B)** tests or **(C)** analogy or **(D)** homology? What makes you fall back on **(C)** rationalization rather than rely on **(D)** ratiocination? What differentiates a deist **(A+F)** from a theist **(C+F)**, and atheist **(AxF')** from an agnostic **(D/F)**?

Table 4D
D or E: Senso-Moral PRE-SENESCENCE or PRECOCITY

"Sequence" is not synonymous with "chronology":

SIGN:	[D]ata/desire	[E]xcel in it.
ERAS:	Post-logical	Post-Cartesian
AGES:	POST-PUBESCENT	OR PRECOCIOUS
a STAGES:	Test -> Discard	Discover +/ Destroy
b MENTAL:	CORRELATIVE	CREATIVE
c SENSES:	Comparative	Adventurous
d ACTION:	Exploring	Venturing
e DEEDS:	Re-search / remodel	Fuse / synergize
f TRAITS:	Skepticism	Enthusiasm
g STYLE:	Refute / re-examine	Imagine / Change
h HINTS:	Reserved	Inspired
i NEEDS:	Questions	Inventions
j ALLIES:	Null hypotheses	Syntheses
k TOOLS:	Ratiocination	Homologies
l RISKS:	Re-cognition	Analogies
m GOALS:	Gaps, omissions	Perspective
n WEAPONS:	Expose falsehood	Iconoclasm
o SET:	Silent consensus	Con-nexus
p SETTING:	Secular / collegial	Idiosyncratic
q ISSUES:	Testable or not	Couth or not
r FOCUS:	What is fanciful?	What is new?
s STAKES:	Disprove or try	Old assumptions
t VALUES:	Opportunity	Challenge
u HAZARDS:	Burning out	Dissonance
v REPUTE:	Critical	Different
w DEFENSE:	"Need more cases"	"It was there"
x SYMBOLS:	Lab or library	Study or studio
y SAMPLES:	Professionals	Artists, Scientists
z QUERIES:	Where, now?	How, Why not?

Our tabulation is a gentle introduction to the way (**i**) our senses, muscles and intelligence (**A, B, C**) develop to become receptive and then freer to be resistant to indoctrination (**ii**). Its implications are further ruthlessly systematized as we unfold the evolution of *"Homo domesticus"* in *hir* (**ii**) socio-ethical and (**iii**) eroto-sexual sub-cycle.

[(**A**) Emotionally to (**B**) experience their (**C**) conceptual (**D**) permutations will clarify personal or international crises and interpersonal and gender relations.]

Indoctrination *(ii)* in religion (**F**) is rooted neither in thinking (**C**) as crude philosophy, nor in action (**B**) as primitive morality, but in feelings (**A**) of absolute dependence.

August Comte (1798-1857) saw religion (**F**) as appropriate to the (early) childhood (**A**) of man, to be replaced first by philosophy (**C**), and then by science (**K, M, N, O**) which advances by making comparisons and testing its suspicions.

Frazer in the "Golden Bough" (1890) substituted ethnography for Comte's historical approach to explain ritual kingship (**G**), fertility rites [to serve (**H**)], and human sacrifice [ignoring (**I**)]. Durkheim (1857-1917) claims that religion exists to cramp self-serving impulses of "individuals" and therefore allows society to exist. (The Elementary Forms of Religious Life, London, 1915)

Robert Coles more recently divided intelligence into emotional (**A**), cognitive (**C**), and moral (**A**<**B**<**C**).

[Durkheim thinks **F** / **I** = **J**. In Comte's view, art is **A** x **E** or the marriage of taste and creativity.]

Table 4E

COMPARATIVE TABULATION of SENSUAL DEVELOPMENT DURING OUR LIFE-CYCLE

	[A]re you mine?	[B]elieve in me.	[C]orrect it.	[D]ata/desire	[E]xcel in it.
SIGN:					
Eras	Adualistic	Pre-Aristotelian	Syllogistic	Post-logical	Post-Cartesian
AGES	INFANTILE	JUVENILE	ADOLESCENT	POST-PUBESCENT or	PRECOCIOUS
a STAGES:	Taste/feel	Grab/Push	Digest/Purge	Test->Discard	Discover+/Destroy
b MENTAL:	"Affective"	CONATIVE	COGNITIVE	CORRELATIVE	CREATIVE
c SENSES:	Somesthetic	Kinesthetic	Apperceptive	Comparative	Adventurous
d ACTION:	Child-like	Bold or shy	Questing	Exploring	Venturing
e DEEDS:	Suckle/bite	Choose/reject	Accepts/search	Re-search/remodel	Fuse/synergize
f TRAITS:	Cooing/crying	Mobility	Idealism	Skepticism	Enthusiasm
g STYLE:	Echo/regurgitate	Barter/blame	Ruminate/think	Refute/re-examine	Imagine/Change
h HINTS:	Hungry	Greedy	Convinced	Reserved	Inspired
i NEEDS:	Care-givers	Buddies, enemies	Answers	Questions	Inventions
j ALLIES:	Lull(b)abies (*sic*)	Prejudices	Dogma, symmetry	Null hypotheses	Syntheses
k TOOLS:	Taste buds/trust	Sphincters/order	Reason/logic	Ratiocination	Homologies
l RISKS:	Starve/fall	Poverty/slavery	Martyrdom	Re-cognition	Analogies
m GOALS:	Satiety	Safe passage	Meaning	Gaps, omissions	Perspective
n WEAPONS:	Suck/Grasp reflex	Disown the bad	Seek the good	Expose falsehoods	Iconoclasm
o SET:	Gut reactions	Peer acceptance	Loud consensus	Silent consensus	Con-nexus
p SETTING:	Familial/parental	Tribal/communal	Sectarian	Secular/collegial	Idiosyncratic

	Good or Bad	Right or Wrong	True or False	Testable or not	Couth or not
q ISSUES:	What is offered?	What is fair?	What is fact?	What is fanciful?	What is new?
r FOCUS:	Appetitive	Trade/take-over	Yield or pray	Disprove or try	Old assumptions
s STAKES:	Security	Property/privilege	Timely reward	Opportunity	Challenges
t VALUES	Thumb-sucking	"Ass"-licking	"Screwing"-up	Burning out	Dissonance
u HAZARDS:	Clinging	Driven	Converted	Critical	Different
v REPUTE:	Intellectualized	Rationalized	"I believed"	"Need more cases"	"It was there"
w DEFENSE:	Food, music	Money, power	God, utopias	Lab or library	Study or studio
x SYMBOLS:	Gourmand	Profiteer	Professor/Confessor	Professional	Artist, Scientist
y SAMPLER:	How soon?	How much?	Who, Why ever?	Where, Why now?	How, Why not?
z QUERIES:					

Table 5
(i-ii) SENSO-SOCIAL STEPS/FACES in the PYRAMID of BEHAVIOR

E: innovative	**O**: cybernetic:
	N: animalistic
D: comparative	**M**: naturalistic
	L: humanistic
C: intellectual	**K**: mechanistic
	J: ethnocentric
B: volitional	**I**: self-centered
	H: money-mad
A: emotional	**G**: power-mad
	F: God-minded

III: Pavlov	Jung	Freud	Ortega	Piaget	Maslow	Erikson
II: Watson	Darwin	Miller	Pasteur	Goodall	Wallace	Crick
I: Einstein	Heisenberg	Copernicus	Galileo	Newton	Kepler	

[(**I**) Con-natural, (**II**) Con-vivial, and (**III**) Con-familiar Pioneers]

Table 6
(ii) SOCIAL FACE in BEHAVIOR PYRAMID

```
           ...........................
           : O : electronics :
           ...............................:....
           : N : animal : studies:
         ...:.....:.........................:....
           : M : ecological: integrity:
        ....:.........:...................................:.....
         : L : humanitarian: obsessions:
        ..:.....:...................................:......
         : K : technological: preoccupations:
        ......:.....:...................................:.....
         : J : sociological : special-interest: lobbies:
        ...:.....:.................:.............:.............:.....
       : I : individual, : self-centered : consciousness :
      .......:.....:.................:....................:.............:...
      : H : economic, :capitalist or: communist,: enterprise:
      ..:.....:.................:.............:.............:....
    : G : government,: selected or:elected by all,: the elite:or God :
    :...:.................:...................:...................:..........:
  : F : spiritual awe: of unknown,: mysterious, :or unclear, : phenomena:
  :...:.................:.............:...................:.............:
```

As you can see, the lower steps are available to everybody. This also explains the power of those who exploit emotions, religious faith, political privileges and economic resources. Nearer the peak are those who are relatively autonomous, neither master nor serf, who are creative, cybernetic, or post-parental as grandparents.

If creativity is inherited it may be precocious. All other stages co-evolve step-by-step. Adjacent steps in each pyramid are shared by the same kin, clique, clan, class, culture, etc., and they must cross each other's paths of senso-social development (above) to meet the opposite sex:

Table 7
(iii) GENDER-DETERMINED male and female SEXUAL DEVELOPMENT

Zenith of Andro-gyny

fatherhood	**mYf**	divorce
monogamy	**mXf**	adultery
rapaciousness	**mWf**	child-saving
bestiality	**mVf**	promiscuity
homosexuality	**mUf**	baby-sitting
pedophilia	**mTf**	baby-wanting
exhibitionism	**mSf**	spouse-shopping
voyeurism	**mRf**	homo-eroticism
fetishism	**mQf**	assertiveness
auto-eroticism	**mPf**	narcissism
Uni-sex	(in the first trimester)	Zero

(ii) BELIEVING

Table 8
PUBLIC ETHICAL RESPONSIBILITIES and SOCIALLY EQUAL OPPORTUNITIES

Pre-historic stage/period

F for faith in Father Almighty: "God we trust more than Santa Claus." [Spiritual: (**F**) animism, creationism, cross, deism God, magic, mercy, religion, souls, supernatural, theism, "theocentric", theology, theopathic, worship; (**F'**) Devil, evil]

G for government intervention: "My country, right or wrong." [Political: (**G**) clan, clemency, colonialism, country, democracy, government, "jingo-centric", law, patriotism, sword; (**G'**) anarchy]

H for high finance: "Money makes the world go round." [Financial: (**H**) barter, class, conglomerates, communists, cost-efficient, dollar, "econo-centric", economics, grace period, market, money, multinational corporations, tokens; (**H'**) profiteering, usury]

Pre-scientific stage/period

I for individualism: "One does not live by bread alone." (Psychological: "psycho-centric", self-examination)

J for joint advocacy: "People who need people are the luckiest people." (Socio-logical: collectivism, "ethno-centric")

Technological stage/period

K for know-how: "Progress is our most important product." (Industrial: manual, mechanical, "techno-centric", technocracy)

L for lover of mankind: "God is dead but that's O.K." (Humanistic: anthropocentrism, secular)

M for Mother Nature: "Earth is our home, sweet home." [Ecological: (**M**) environmentalism, "geo-centric"; (**M'**) pollution]

N for natural intelligence: "Animals deserve to be totems." (Ethological: animalism, "ethocentric")

Post-industrial stage/period

O for ominous artificial intelligence, oft-repetitive automation: "Robots will make us redundant." [Electronic: (**O**) artificial intelligence, "circu-centric", computers, cybernetics, robot; (**O'**) idiot savant]

Table 8A.
OUR SEPARATE EROTO-SEXUAL ODYSSEYS According to M. ORTEGA and S. FREUD

(iii) EROTO-SEXUAL (Amoral, sexist or not)	FREUD (Psycho-sexual+)
(P-f, Play-m) narcissism or autoeroticism	0-1+ Oral (swallow/bite) (id/ego)
(Qmf) "fetishism" or assertiveness	-2 Anal (collect/hoard) (superego/id)
(Rmf) voyeurism or curiosity	3 Oedipal (covet/cower) (superego/ego)
(Smf) exhibitionism or flirting	5 Latent (wait/sublimate) (ego ideal/ego)
(Tmf,Uf) pedophilia or baby-sitting	
	13 Genital (date/mate) (ego/superego)
(Um,Vf) homo-eroticism or promiscuity	[Freud thought man was a
(Vm,Wf) "petting" or adopting	boy who had been afraid he
	cannot keep his penis, and
(Wm,Xf) rapaciousness or driven mating	girls were boys without one
(Xm,Ymf) sensuous sex or child-swapping	but just a poor substitute.]
(Z) androgyny of grandparenthood	
(V' to R') retrogressive "perversions"	+meta- or menopausal

(iii) BEGETTING

Table 9
PRIVATE EROTO-SEXUAL PRACTICES AND PERVERSIONS

Pre-reproductive stage/period

"oral"
P for playing, or loving one's self: "Secret shame is for sharing." (Auto-eroticism/narcissism)

"anal"
Q for quivering possessiveness: "I know what I like." (Assertiveness/fetishism. Cf: feminism)

"urethral"
R for restrained sexuality: "A beautiful body is everything." (Homo-eroticism/voyeurism. Cf: lesbianism)
S for strip-tease eroticism: "If you have it, flaunt it with pride." (Exhibitionism/flirting)

"genital"
T for tempter or temptress: "Thank God for little girls and sugar-daddies." (Pedophilia/baby-wanting)
U for udder-programmed denial/grasping, nurture or symbiosis: "Men are — almost/all alike/I like." (Homo-sexuality, baby-sitting)
V for variable pet-thing/contraception: "My privates are mine/My body is my private property." (Bestiality/abortion, promiscuity)

Populative stage/period

W for willingness to adopt or rape: "Teats are for tots." (Adoptive/rapacious)
Y for x-perimental or x-purgated sex: "It only takes two to tango." (Adultery/monogamy)
Most animals never see their fathers, but our species even get to know grandparents.

Special Stage with Increased Longevity
Z for zenith: "Kids will be kids." (Grandparenthood. Cf: asocial, asexual, androgyny, DNA)

Table 9a.
COMPARING SOCIO-SEXUAL DEVELOPMENT

ERIKSON (Psycho-social)	(iii) EROTO-SEXUAL (sexist or not)
0-1+ Oral / sensory:	(P-f,Play-m)
trust / mistrust = optimism	narcissism or autoeroticism
-2 Anal / muscular:	(Qmf)
autonomy / doubt = willfulness	"fetishism" or assertiveness
3 Locomotor / genital:	(Rmf)
initiative / guilt = purpose	voyeurism or curiosity
5 Industry / inferiority =	(Smf)
competence	exhibitionism or flirting
11 Identity / loyalty =	(Tmf,Uf)
emancipation	pedophilia or baby-sitting
	(Um,Vf) gay or promiscuous
18 Intimacy / isolation =	(Vm,Wf) "pet" or adopt
commitment	(Wm,Xf) driven mating
21 Generativity / stagnation =	(Xm,Ymf) sensuous sex or
productivity	"child-swapping"
60 Integrity / resignation or	(Z) androgyny of grandparenthood
wisdom / despair = faith / trust	(V'to R') non-reproductive retrogression
	to "old perversions"

Table 10
COMPARING SENSO-SOCIAL DEVELOPMENT

Try covering any column above and below to see if it hides or adds to what you already know but do not find in what remains (+signs precede what I have added, e.g., internal proprioception which governs the amplitude of any movement to flee, fight, feed or fornicate, to Maslow's columns in Tables 2a and 2b.)

MASLOW: Humane:	Senso- personal	PIAGET: Cognitive:	Socio-cultural
PHYSIOL:	(A)	SENSORI-MOTOR:	(F)
Air			
Water			
Food			
+Warmth		OPERATIONAL:	
+Stimulation		Preconceptual	(G)
Sleep			
Sex			
+Proprioception	(B)	Intuitive	
+Movement			
SECURITY:			
Property		Concretistic	
+Patrimony			
Person			
+Privacy	(C)	FORMAL ABSTRACTIONS:	(I)
		+Logicentric	(J)
PEERS:		reductionism	
Friends			
Lovers			(K)
ESTEEM:	(D)	+RATIOCINATION:	(L)
Self		+Postlogical	
Group		thinking	(M)
Guild			
EXPRESSION:	(E)	+Scientific	(N)
Technical/		artistic	
+Cathartic		pioneering	(O)
+PATHOLOGICAL:	(D'-	+artful self-	(N'-
Alienation	A')	realization	F')
Mysticism		+introspection	

Once we get used to using letters instead of words, we can say it had been enough for (F) to know about (A), (G) about (B) and (C) and (H) about (A) and (E) -- or for churches to learn what is evil from what is good or bad, for courts to determine guilt on the basis of what is right or wrong and what is true or false and for corporations to profit from what is (A) wanted or (E) new. But as we (D) compare more facts, we can (E) create more enduring alternatives.

Table 11
COMPARING PHYSIO-SENSUAL DEVELOPMENT

According to A. Maslow and M. Ortega

MASLOW (Humanistic+)	(i) SENSO-PERSONAL (Asocial, free or not)
PHYSIOLOGY	(A): EMOTIONAL:
Air, water, food	Good or bad?
+External stimuli	(taste / feel:
Sleep / +dreaming	suck / grasp)
+Warmth / +grooming	How soon?
+Proprioception	(B): VOLITIONAL:
Sex	Right or wrong?
SECURITY	(choose / reject:
Property	grab / push)
+Patrimony	How much, when?
+Movement	(C): RATIONAL:
Person	True or false?
+Privacy	(think / reflect:
PEERS	yearn / accept)
FriendsWho, why?	
Lovers	(D): COMPARATIVE:
ESTEEM	Testable or not?
Self	(fit or discard:
Group	prove / explore)
Guild	How, why now?
EXPRESSION	(E): CREATIVE:
+Cathartic	Different or not?
+Soulful	(change/destroy:
Aesthetic	venture / discover)
Mechanical	Where, why not?
+PATHOLOGY	(D' to A')
Alienation	Entropic decay
Superstition	Timely or not?
(Faith sedates.]	(decline / die)

For the *cognoscente*, this revision may already be redundant: Models are for playing/testing.

All of Maslow's, Piaget's, Freud's, and Erikson's stages of development can be seen as proceeding from the purely subjective to the objective, from the emotional (**A**) to the intuitive (**B**) to the more reflective (**C** or "rational") to the comparative (**D**) or more impersonal (**E**) and post-logical.

To study ourselves, we must get away from simple numbers which ignore nuances, and resort to letters, for our brain can only "choose" between those two. Numbers alone restrict explorations for other explanations, letters permit processing of permutations and post-logical ratiocinations.

We slowly evolve from the purely subjective to the more objective in our three-pronged *(i - iii)* con-vivially sensual (even plants suffer distress), con-naturally social (electrons tend to orbit), and con-sensually sexual but separate development for each gender.

As in chemistry, this periodic progression in behavioral stages of development is testable.

Ideally, *homo sapiens* should be $\underline{E > (D > C) > (B > A)}$, $\underline{O > F}$, and $\underline{Z > P}$ whenever possible.

We progress from *(i*, **A** -> **E**) "solipsistic" infant to inspired inventor, *(ii*, **F** -> **O**) awe of an omniscient God to computerized subservience, and **P** -> **Z**) auto-erotic or narcissistic male or female to grandparenthood.

In *(ii)* our social evolution (from religious to economic to electronic), we repeat the same process of being more "objective".

In *(iii)* our sexual maturation (from autoerotic narcissism to homosexuality to genital promiscuity), males and females repeat the same journey towards "object-relations".

Table 12
COMPARING PHYSIO-MENTAL DEVELOPMENT

MASLOW:	free/unfree:	PIAGET:	unequal/equal
PHYSIOLOGICL	A) feel:	SENSORIMOTOR	(F)aith in: Pa X'mas or a God
	Good/Bad: taste / suck, touch / grasp How soon?	OPERATIONAL Preconceptual	(G)overn the weak
SECURITY	B) act: Right / Wrong: pull / push, grab / reject How much?	Intuitive	(H)ustle: barter or trade tokens
PEERS	C) think: True / False: reason / beg, seek / yield Who? Why?	Concrete FORMAL ABSTRACTIONS	I-centered (J)oiner: ethnocentric (K)indred Machines
ESTEEM	D) compare: Test or not? fit / discard, prove / explore When? Where?		(L)ove of us: humanistic speciesism (M)other Earth now geocentrism
EXPRESSION	E) create: Differ or no? change / wreck, venture / find How? Why not?		(N)aturalistic: ethocentric (O)ver-clever bio-chips: *Deus ex machina*
+PATHOLOGICAL	D' to A': Entropy: decay -> die		N' to F': Ideology =bigotry

Table 13
COMPARING OUR SENSUAL EVOLUTION
According to M. ORTEGA and J. PIAGET

(i) SENSO-PERSONAL	PIAGET
(free or not)	(Cognitive+)
(A): EMOTIONAL:	0-2 Sensori-motor
Good or bad?	
(taste / feel:	(2 to 12 Concrete operations):
suck / grasp)	
How soon?	2 preconceptual
(B): VOLITIONAL:	-4 intuitive
Right or wrong?	
(choose / reject:	
grab / push)	
How much, when?	-7 concretistic
(C): RATIONAL:	12 Formal abstractions
True or false?	(Logicentric reductionism
(think / reflect:	can mislead.)
yearn / accept)	
Who, why?	
(D): COMPARATIVE:	+Ratiocination
Testable or not?	(ratio/logic)
(fit or discard:	
prove / explore)	+post-logical
How, why now?	thinking
(E): CREATIVE:	+original or
Different or not?	artistic or
(change / destroy:	scientific
venture / discover)	pioneering
Where, why not?	experiments
(D' to A')	+artful "self-
Entropic decay	realization"/
Timely or not?	"scientific"
(decline / die)	introspection

Does analogy mislead the blind about elephants? As you can now more clearly appreciate, separable stages in development for

EveryWoMan clarify what makes one more of a dreamer (**A**) than a doer (**B**), more reductionist (**C**) than heuristic (**E**), what decides whether we depend more on (**A**) taste or (**B**) tests or (**C**) analogy or (**D**) homology. What makes us fall back on (**C**) rationalization rather than relying on (**D**) ratiocination, what differentiates a deist (**A+F**) from a theist (**C+F**), sexual atheist (**AxF'**) from agnostic (**D/F**)? (Saints can reach more people than scientists in our life-cycle from **A** to **Z** to **A'**.)

Table 14
PERSONAL LIBERTY and SOCIAL EQUALITY

Sensual	Cognitive: PIAGET	Consensual	Psychosocial: ERIKSON
(**A**)	SENSORI-MOTOR:	(**F**)	ORO-SENSORY: trust / distress = +optimism
	OPERATIONAL Preconceptual		ANO-MUSCULAR: autonomy / doubt = +willfulness
(**B**)	Intuitive	(**H**)	GENITO-MOTOR: initiative / guilt = +purpose
	Concretistic		INDUSTRY / inferiority = +competence
(**C**)	FORMAL ABSTRACTIONS: +Logicentric reductionism	(**I**) (**J**)	IDENTITY: emancipation / loyalty = +treason
(**D**)	+RATIOCINATION: +Postlogical thinking	(**K**) (**L**) (**M**)	INTIMACY: isolation / commitment = +nihilism
(**E**)	+Scientific / artistic pioneering	(**N**) (**O**)	GENERATIVITY / stagnation = +productivity
(**D'- A'**)	+artful self- realization +introspection	(**N'- F'**)	INTEGRITY: despair / wisdom = resignation

Table 15
PSYCHOSOCIAL EVOLUTION OF EQUALITY
According to M. ORTEGA and E. ERIKSON

(ii) SOCIO-CULTURAL (Asexual, equal or not)	ERIKSON (Psycho-social+)
(F)ather Almighty: After Santa Claus, "in God we trust": theo-centric	0-1+ Oro-sensory: trust / mistrust = +optimism
(G)overnment-led: "My country, right or wrong": nationalistic	-2 Ano-muscular: autonomy / doubt = +willfulness
(H)igh Finance: barter of tokens of of entitlements: trade-centered	3 Genito-motor: initiative / guilt = +purpose
(I)ndividualistic (psycho-centric)	5 Industry / inferiority = +competence
(J)ointly-active (ethno-centric)	
	11 Identity / loyalty = +emancipation
(Kindred machines (mechano-centric)	
(L)over of mankind (anthropocentric) (human racism or speciesism)	18 Intimacy / isolation = +commitment
(M)other-naturized (geo-ecological)	
	21 Generativity / stagnation = +productivity
(N)ative animality (etho-comparative)	
(O)ver-intelligent (with bio-chips) *(Deus ex machina)*	
(N' to F'): return to ideology (beliefs = bigotry) dogmatism returns ="born again"	60 Integrity / resignation: wisdom / despair

Table 16
THE THREE SUB-SPECIES OF *HOMO SAPIENS SAPIENSIS*

[Freudian or not, is *H. sapiens* more "genital", *H. domesticus* more "oral", *H. metropolus* more "ano-urethral", whatever their gender? (N. Gingrich, futurist wannabee President, complained of leaving Air Force One by the back door.) Some recent effort has been made to understand male and female differences (e.g., men are Martians, women Venusians). Because co-existence is needed for species survival, the differences have to be overcome. As to the sub-species in above classification, every line can be rearranged and the column which has captured the most and the least in each case would be the kind most difficult for that person to co-exist with.]

Our bio-sexual development into Wo-Manhood is separate (XX and XY) and unequal: more advanced in females (the "weaker" sex who survives her older mate):

1. Female genital anatomy separates reproductive from urinary channels (her vagina from the urethra), whereas males continue to micturate and ejaculate through a common orifice which, in less evolved species like fishes, reptiles and birds, is called a cloaca for passing urine and feces. There is probably an engineering rather than an epigenetic explanation for "le difference". Which is why there are separate specialists for urology and for obstetrics and gynecology.

2. Females will constitute virtually another species once they can reproduce by themselves virginally, which may come sooner than men can accept.

3. In fact, are there two sexual sub-species of *Homo sapiens sapiens*, the male "Manimachineroticus", still an experimental model, and its evolutionary superior in anatomy and physiology, the female "Womanimachineroticus"?

4. If they are married to each other, will the marriage last? That depends on how long their parents stay married, and their birth order in the family. First-borns quarrel a lot over territorial rights, second-born tends to give way oftener, last born tends to expect more.

[No entry can be used separately from related others. "Uncircumcised" (in infancy) is differentiated from early religious "ritual" among

H. domesticus or a castration-"threatened" (penis-envious) *Homo metropolus*.]

We can make a tentative inference that *Homo sapiens* are more sexual and sensual than social, that *Homo domestici* are more social than sensual or sexual, and *Homo metropoli* are less social and sexual than sensual.

The following non-dichotomous tabulation also tests linearity, circularity, absolutism and relativity. Today, human sub-species very roughly and uncleanly differentiate or change in varying degrees into:

H. sapiens	*H. domesticus*	*H. metropolus*
skeptoptimistic	superstitious, meek	suspicious, assertive
open-minded'	afraid	pressured
unintimidated	prayerful	pugnacious
non-literal	strident	legalistic
animalistic	moralistic	ethical
intuitive or counter-intuitive	"tender loving care" advocate	"the logical choice" analyst
unconforming	virtuous	value-ridden
uncircumcised	ritualistic	threatened
"hip"	"square"	"yuppie"
alert	frustrated	bitter
looks	blushes	leaves
alogical	logical	logistical
comparative	absolutist	dichotomist
agnostic	deist	theist
fit	obese	hyperkinetic
opportunistic	passive	planful
inventive	parrot-like	copy-cat
data	dogma	ideology
loner	lonesome	lonely
marriage-shy	abuse-prone	divorce-prone

loving	beloved	lover
receptive	obligated	committed
pragmatic	unworldly fears	pessinic
questioning	law-abiding	materialistic
process-centered	progress-oriented	prosperity-nut
territorial	utopian	celebrity-keen

2.00 b/PREVIEW

INTRODUCTION

> Science proceeds more by what it has learned to ignore than
> what it takes into account.
>
> —Galileo

Words are double-edged swords. Fanatics are often the victims of phonetics. Without words, human behavior can be coded from **A** to **E** for persons, from **F** to **O** for groups, and from **P** to **Y** for the sexes until both achieve the (**Z**)enith of human development as grandparents. (Grandparents live two lifetimes. Only in knowing the fruits of our seeds beyond the second generation are we different from other sexually reproductive animals.)

This nongenetic coding from **A** to **Z** is the behavioral equivalent in the postindustrial world of the periodic table of chemistry from the Industrial Revolution (*Tables 1, 2A*).

Psychopharmacology is transcultural because of the periodic table of elements in chemistry. I hope psychiatry will not need the adjective "transcultural" to become an integral part of modern medicine.

As (**i–ii**) senso-social preoccupations change—postwar American, British, French, German, Italian, Japanese, Russian, and other youths are more like each other than their elders—domestication (virtue and value/sensuality and liberty) compete with breeding, and (**iii**) sex has become more recreation (domestication/breeding) than procreation (breeding/domestication) (*Tables 3, 5, 6, 7*).

GLOBAL VILLAGE PSYCHIATRY

Culture means kinships and traditions. Psychiatry deals with what is different or deviant, *(b/1)* that which seems more and more disconnected from the rest of the world. What is local is political, not transcultural. Transcultural psychiatry, unlike cross-cultural psychology, is value-free.

Training doctors from every continent except Australia to practice a value-free psychiatry showed us how culture can be set aside except as family history. Family heredity and family prejudices do not carry the same weight in helping the mentally ill. Prejudices run deep, but they defend what is wrong rather than create what is right. Defenses are symptoms, not diseases. History shows how defenses fail.

It is not necessary to probe how culture makes its own people different from its neighbors. All we have to ask is how our traditions affect our autonomics. If a house has rugs or carpets, how is the toddler affected? How they are housebroken just to protect floor coverings tells us how their autonomics are domesticated to protect costly rugs and carpets. Without such protectionism, capitalism cannot win. But at what cost to our children!

We are socialized humanimal life-forms that can be subdivided into different subspecies.

We need to distinguish between lifestyles in families (hippie, yuppie, etc.) and the life cycles that evolve in succeeding generations. These life cycles (the ABZs of sensual liberty, social equality, and eroto-sexual carnality) have resulted in different adaptations, not only to changing habitat (geography and climate) but also to the changing times ("liberated" men are now called "enlightened"). If the adaptations endure in varying degrees but uniformly enough for a large enough group, we may have evolved into three different subspecies from the prototypical *Homo sapiens sapiensis.*

Three human subspecies (like primary colors), *Homo sapiens* (blue-violet), *H. domesticus* (red) and *H. metropolus* (green), go through life with different ratios in their senso-socio-sexual sub-cycles. We have used mythical beasts (unicorns, centaurs and androgynes) to bring senso-socio-sexual subcycles to life.

Child care and early socialization that may produce varying degrees of compliance, circumspection, withdrawal, or alienation by sensual and sexual deprivation differentiate the subspecies.

(1) How Our Personal History Changes Our World

With the union of our parents' chromosomes, we started our life's journey. If our father's contribution was the Y chromosome, we lose—like some of our "liberated" sisters had to give up—the chance for motherhood.

Unlike birds, we are all female in the first six weeks of life. Afterward, males return to an amphibian cloaca, but women keep their vaginas tilted forward—leaving them vulnerable to rape—unlike other primates. (Sex decides for men and women.)

We are lucky, if during pregnancy, our mother did not smoke tobacco or drink alcohol. But because we are going to be born of a human mother, we are going to have the biggest headache known to man.

So we need taking care of from birth more than other animals. Do our mothers stay with us and nurse us?

(We can observe different species without trying to domesticate them. Domestication is designed to interfere with the autonomic nervous system and convert our cortex into a composer who cannot conduct what it composes. It is not too late to see this conversion as both unnecessary and injurious to health. We only have to look at how we have translated the functions meant to be regulated below the cortex.)

If our parents are no longer self-sustaining *Homo sapiens* but have become timid *Homo domesticus*, our genitals may also be hurt by ritual circumcision or clitoridectomy without our consent. (Some think our history is a diary of mindless superstitions and pointless rituals.)

So we got hurt without having done anything at all. Later, we will try to explain why we were hurt through no fault of our own, but it would be too late to do us much good.

With acute birth trauma of varying but significant severity and infantile genital *abuse*, we are ourselves going to be timid *Homo domesticus* or counterphobic *Homo metropolus*. We will then try to undo, without success, what we have suffered, using the help of others like us who were equally handicapped from infancy: the blind leading the blind and relying on strange strangers, unmet and unseen.

With such initial handicaps, we need a mother who is a saint. She must stay with us and feed us whenever we get hungry. She has to be a virtual marsupial. But if she is a liberated *Homo metropolus*, she'll feed us cow's milk and leave us in a child-care center most of the day.

If she is like the mothers of luckier *Homo sapiens*, we will grow up to be (**A**) optimistic. If not, we'll be (**A'**) pessimistic about our chances.

Optimistic toddlers (**B**) try and try again.

(Anthropologists feel indebted to the author for drawing attention to the better mothering as an infant of all optimists. Optimists have faith without belief to sustain them.)

Pessimistic children (**B'**) give up after a few false starts or blame others for being (**A'**) bad. Those who (**B**) succeed with their muscles are more free to (**C**) think more (**A**) fearlessly. Those who (**B'**) fail with their muscles think with timidity and, after failing (**B'**), blame others for not caring (**A**) or not helping (**B**) enough. These (**A'**) timid (**B'**) losers become *Homo domesticus* instead of ingenious *Homo sapiens*. If their frustration is contagious enough, they form the nucleus of *Homo metropolus* who use machines to assist weak muscle power and erratic brainpower. They were benefited by the Industrial Revolution and by postindustrial robots and computers. They are now members of a more ingenuous "me too" generation.

Children are also abused by being asked to give up their vocalizations in order to talk like adults. And then to think the way adults do, mostly with only their left brain.

They call this left-brain thinking "logical" or "linear" thinking. Natural or nonlinear thinkers depend more on their right brain.

Homo sapiens who are not copy-cat thinkers can (**D**) compare facts rather than borrow (**C'**) dreams. With (**E**) inspiration, they become our pioneers in innovation. (Dreams commit copycats [**C'**] to agendas for their unsuspecting progeny.) *Homo domesticus* is intimidated by (**F**) God, (**G**) queen, or (**H**) money as servant, subject, or employee. *Homo metropolus* is more (**I**) egocentric, needs (**J**) popular approval, trusts (**K**) machines more than people, and thinks that (**L**) humanity deserves a better (**M**) Earth mother who can recognize its inherent superiority over (**N**) naturally intelligent animals and (**O**) artificial intelligence.

Homo domesticus is more procreative than *Homo metropolus*, who thinks less-developed nations should strive for zero population growth. They see themselves as role models in putting careers ahead of families.

But their own conspicuous consumption of finite, non-self-sustaining natural resources is three times that of second-world countries. As world population drops, viruses, bacteria, and insects gain ascendancy, despite vaccines, antibiotics, and pesticides. (In fact, germ warfare is the only weapon left to third-world countries to fight against super-powerful, strong-willed, and wrong-headed enemies.)

Transcultural psychiatry tries to clarify how these different aims and lifestyles influence our lives more than established traditions or kinships. Only after transcending cultural boundaries can we cope with global changes.

"Mind" is not the master of behavior; it serves more often as a public relations consultant when we need to put a spin or a different slant to our actions. Psychiatry must be less "psychological" as the study of the mind, and more competent in dealing with both the brain and nervous system outside the spinal cord, namely the autonomics, which works even when we are asleep or unconscious (vegetating). Instead of domesticating our instincts with borrowed dreams of heaven, utopia, conspicuous consumption, etc., we need to "mind" how dreams become agendas for us to hand down to our legitimate but unsuspecting children.

Split-brain experiments show that the animal modular brain is less erratic in judging outcome than the lateralized specialization of the human brain, where the left hemisphere is more erratic from trying to impose order on a sequence of randomized events. The more literary of the hemispheres also probably imposes the sense of false unity as "mind" in a structurally modular organization of neurons. Without this false sense of unity, "consciousness" itself would merely be "minding," instead of "mind."

Our genetic DNA is less than 1% different from other primates. There is only one human race of three subspecies. Our body can stay alive even after brain death. Our mindless instincts are the only intelligent life-support system that we have.

After separating the development of men from women, I was suddenly struck by the fact that some families produce henpecked husbands (the opposite of roosters routinely ruling the roost). And then it occurred to me that we have a subspecies that behaves like henpecked husbands.

Homo domesticus tames the parasympathetic when it comes to eating, drinking, grooming, and fornicating.

My patients who are henpecked put up with their wives by reassuring themselves that their wives really love them more than we give them credit for.

It dawned on me that this is the same reassurance that we give ourselves once we are domesticated by intimidation. When fate has been cruel to us, we claim that it's for our own good, that God really loves us more than we give Him credit for.

The model for *Homo domesticus* is, therefore, the timid wimp of a henpecked husband.

But now a newer betrayal of our fearless and self-sustaining *H. sapiens* has come upon the global stage. An ingenuous *H. metropolus* evolved in reaction to timid *H. domesticus*.

Homo metropolus perverts the sympathetic about whom to fight or flee from.

If the henpecked husband is the model for *Homo domesticus*, then the model for *Homo metropolus* is the militant feminist against male oppression. Since the victim mentality—like the colonial mentality of the intimidated and converted *Homo domesticus*—is also not gender-based, men now outnumber women among the new *Homo metropolis*.

(*H. domesticus* is more oral and intimidated. *H. metropolus* is "ano-urethral" or competitive *[Table 16]*. Especially numerous in Washington, they tried to unseat their oppressor. But as an alpha male, all he is doing is simply and fully enjoying his pecking order perks to eat and fornicate more than the chance to fight or retreat. [*Homo metropoli* of both sexes do not get enough sex, no matter how much they diet.])

In our global village, the industrial revolution has given *Homo domesticus* some relief from hard work, and the postindustrial personal computer has drawn *Homo metropoli* closer together than the automobiles of the industrial era. Modern transcultural psychiatry must work with all races and all classes and both sexes who are less and less as wise as the old *Homo sapiens*. Ratios between right and left brain activity show who can adapt to unexpected changes or just believe old lies. (Superstitions back opinions that pass for conventional wisdom.)

We can go back to what made ingenious *Homo sapiens* different from animals. Our thumbs helped build the first fire, and our tongue helped us work together to survive natural threats to life, not just any fancied "paper tigers." But now we ask not only to survive but also to conform, even if it makes us less fit as a species.

We cannot legislate equality. We are all different, like snowflakes. We are not like mud, which is homogenized. For us to coexist with joy and optimism, we must also like being different from the other subspecies.

Homo sapiens are more ingeniously self-sustaining than *H. domesticus* or *H. metropolus*. But to be wiser than both is not enough. We need to understand them better.

To be optimally optimistic, we must begin life unhurt when we are born and get groomed and fed on time and learn to control our sphincters and speak another language at our own pace. (Psychotherapy cannot elicit memories before the child learned how to talk like his/her elders. We have to depend on their art or nightmares to get a glimpse of those years.)

Early physical and social abuse, well intentioned or superstitious, can make *Homo sapiens* retreat, disown parents as well as their animal ancestry, or become domesticated or disconnected as self-exiled expatriates. Because or since *Homo domesticus* and *metropolus* are untested neophytes whose origin is traceable to early infancy, we can raise more of our young to be *Homo sapiens* for the future of the entire human race. To be scientists (+) (below), they need to be postlogical.

(a) Moral Stages (-) in the History (+) of Science

-1) If you are pre-Hippocratic *(b/2)*, you tend to blame violent seizures or their gentler sister afflictions on spells of divine displeasure. You also think *(b/3)* on the basis of (**A**) good or bad (evil) or blasphemous (whose accessible source must be cleansed with soap, as part of early brainwashing with "cleanliness is next to godliness").

-2) If you are pre-Copernican, you still think that the sun exists for our convenience (to serve our needs, etc.). You also think on the basis of (**B**) right or wrong and damnable (unless somehow exorcised).

-3) If you are pre-Cartesian, you cite authorities to judge what is (**C**) true or false or heretical (a candidate for burning with holy fire).

-4) If you are pre-Darwinian, you can be a "human racist" (**L**) in insisting that human beings have a special mission (to save their souls [**F**], etc.).

-5) If you are pre-Pavlovian, you still pretend to choose even when already willing or just willful. You still think you can decide on the basis of (**A**), (**B**), or (**C**) instead of (**D**) comparing them to learn what you (**A**) feel, (**B**), or (**C**) "recognize" as reflections from another era in the mirror of your mind.

Unwittingly, all philosophers who have misheard "cogito" as "cognitio" or "cognition" still depend on logic or rhetoric. They are (-3) pre-Cartesian, at the same developmental stage as thoughtful but inexperienced adolescents. For them, "Cogito, ergo sum," is more welcome as "I think, therefore I am" than its accurate translation, which is "I cogitate or doubt, therefore I exist." If only doubting cannot be doubted, solipsism becomes pure sophistry.

Aristotelian logic (-3) just defends what is understood or "chosen" (-5), even if selective consciousness limits choice to options. DNA also curtails freedom of choice. An option, to a well-domesticated mind, can be an obsession that soon enough becomes a firm commitment.

As doctors, we cannot be (-1) pre-Hippocratic and charge for learning how to take care of both body and soul. As psychiatrists, we cannot afford to be (-5) pre-Pavlovian and separate minds from bodies.

No matter how uncritical the mind of a true believer is (for whom ignorance is bliss), we cannot split any such person's mind from the body or the environment that it minds.

The more we suspect that we might be living on forgotten memories or superstitions about divine displeasure—in a world that has changed a lot since Hippocrates—the more open we will be for post-Cartesian doubting. To "re-cognize" that we cannot doubt that we doubt is the beginning of (**C**) reflection or cognition. Reflection (or intellectual masturbation) merely mirrors the past in our mind. Correlating and predicting can (**D**) sort out and separate human fantasies from scientific facts.

Sorting identifies contradictions to be resolved beyond the mind as (**E**) discovered paradoxes in nature. They must be explored by talented artists and scientists. Today, what both postlogical (**D**) science and (**E**) art do—but not to please (consumers beware!)—may make the world we all share seem illogical or odd until we get used to it. (What is original will often be ignored by closed minds, before it is adjudged a classic in inspired creativity.) Talent may be precocious but can be tracked, if we think less like human racists to be more humanimal.

On the eve of our third millennium, we have two new scientific tools to bring art, science, and life together:

(1) Postlogical thinking: philosophers argue from concepts; scientists create from context.

(2) Postideological, nonrhetorical alphabet (**A** to **Z**) for nongenetic electronic transmission and retrieval of information about behavior in a postindustrial society.

(b) First Seven Ages (+) of Amoral Science

The first stage in our amoral, professional development began with Hippocrates finding that we do not get sick because God is mad at us.

We can now be

(+1) post-Hippocratic (nonjudgmental). We cannot dehumanize offenders and then try to rehabilitate them.

(+2) post-Copernican (nonevangelical). We cannot condemn those who are different from our teachers.

(+3) post-Cartesian (skeptical). We cannot cite the dead (who cannot change what they have written) as authorities in modern living.

(+4) post-Darwinian (irreverent). We cannot claim superiority (with only five imperfect senses) over all animals.

(+5) post-Pavlovian (forgiving), since most of our programming is not conscious but conditioned.

(+6) post-Freudian (unblaming), since unconscious or automatic and defensive forgetfulness stored as repressed memories (selective remembering eliminates recollection of shame) deforms and falsifies all choices.

(+7) postlogical (what is valid does not have to be understood except by finders and their peers). Doubt what you still believe even if it is defensible by logic. Ratios, not reason, decide everything in the cosmos. *(b/4)*

Can this simple dating system allow us to review or revise some of our undergraduate courses in college where we sit, (**C**) read, and regurgitate? And to start questioning what critical (unconstructive) thinkers, dead poets, and literary luminaries (e.g., Graham Greene) left behind are just biographies (e.g., of a Russian roulette gambler), not advanced learning for those who are well read but inexperienced for being sedentary or untraveled?

(+8) We are now apprehensively but inexorably approaching (+8) the asocial postideological age of science—beyond aggressive amateurism (like George Bernard Shaw calling the speed of light the most obvious lie he had ever heard)—in our collective evolution toward professional competence.

In psychiatry, this simply means using the same tools that medicine does, regardless of culture. What our close relatives among animals can do, we should be able to, if we are not sick. To decide what to do, we need the equivalent of the periodic table of chemical elements from the Industrial Revolution.

Because we are dealing with behavior, we need to be able to divide it into stages that are called periods in the table of chemical elements. And to predict what is missing but, once found, would fit where it belongs.

All of these criteria are met by the postindustrial alphabet of behavior that we call the ABZs of Life. It can be coded and traced along genetic lines, even if not inherited like DNA or creativity. We now have a nontabular four-faced senso-socio-sexual pyramid of behavior *(Table 2)* that is truncated to leave more room at the top. The sexes face each other.

Incidentally, once senso-socio-sexual ratios are used, it also works the same way that Crick and Watson's DNA codons transmit information. ("Codons" in the DNA coda are 3-nucleotide sequences—from the four available that change the instruction inherited in DNA templates for replication—which inform the cells as they divide and grow.)

There are comparable sensual, social, and sexual codons (from "code" + "-on"). These senso-socio-sexual codon combinations can be identified as nongenetic fingerprints in extended treatment case reviews that show where other pioneers, without its use, only partly grasped the problems of very difficult patients *(see case study in chapter 19).*

Our "sensor-dons" are coded **A** or pre-Hippocratic, **B** or pre-Copernican, **C** or pre-Cartesian, **D** or post-Darwinian and postlogical, and **E** or precocious and postideological.

Our "socio-dons" are coded **F** to **O** (from an absentee [**F**] Father Almighty to an omnipresent electronic [**O**] Overseer as Big Brother or Solicitous Sister, virtual or digital).

F to J are prehistorical (**F** to **H** are preliterate, **I** to **J** are more literate), **K** and **L** are industrial (**L** is more metaphorical), **M** to **O** are postindustrial (**O** is less postlogical and more linear without "fuzzy logic," now used for "smart appliances").

The personal and public senso-social codons combine with more private male or female codons ("sexo-dons") from P (autoerotic narcissism) to Z (grandparenthood).

The gender-based sexo-dons—except for **Z**, which is familial (postparental)—are **P** to **R** or pregenital (visual or tactile), **S** to **V** or genital (primary or secondary), **X** and **Y** or procreative (with or without love: romanticized linkage in marriage is like making trade agreements conditional on human rights).

DNA says there are no races, just cultures that exploit skin color or birthplace. Many would rather think of themselves as white, American, English, Irish, Jew, or Palestinian, rather than humanimal, sharing 98%+ of the chimpanzee's DNA.

And, because civilization is man-made, it can be understood without genuflection.

C. P. Snow genuflected before the two cultures of art and science. In America, there sometimes seems only two parallel worlds of black and white races. Increasingly, the colors are more widely separated by immigration.

And so we have any number of universes, depending on culture. But there is only one human race. This is what transcultural psychiatry would like to clarify.

Transcultural psychiatry would like to erase self-serving human racism, which discriminates against all other animals.

As in the Olympics, there are levels of difficulty. For EveryWoMan, the first level of difficulty is studying ourselves as sensual, unequal, and carnal human beings. For professionals, the second level of difficulty is learning the *ABCs of Absolute Relativity (1984)*. This new synthesis says nothing stands by itself in anthropology, biology, and cosmology.

All of twentieth-century medicine is transcultural, but they do not use that word for it. They just call it modern medicine. Why do we need a separate adjective for psychiatry?

Modern medicine starts with the cell. Tribal medicine begins with the soul. Transcultural psychiatry, like psychopharmacology, should start with the equivalent of Mendeleev's periodic table of elements in chemistry.

Before Mendeleev, there was Eckhart's alchemy, which claims all metals want to be gold. If Mendeleev had suffered from gold fever, would Au be elsewhere in his table of elements? Mendeleev starts from hydrogen to complex carbons, to radioactive elements. We start with feelings (**A**, emotion), which allows us to develop more bonds beyond imprinting in the unsuspecting, until **Z** (grandparenting).

Language itself evolved from trying to please (groom or purr) and then to belong (befriend to bond).

Historically speaking, psychiatry is now where alchemy was before we learned our chemistry. We left alchemy behind when we found out that gold is just another metal.

What we prize and worship today, like gold then, has no intrinsic value beyond what we give it. But for the worshipful, social value—mistaken for personal virtue in *The Book of Virtues* by an ex-drug czar—still wins debating points for privileged treatment.

We also seem to worship history and logic, both of which are man-made. When we see two patients who claim they are Jesus or Napoleon, we expect one to give up his claim. We expect him to think that logically there cannot be two of the same thing at any one time. We forget that both people are long dead. This makes the freedom to (**D**) compare a hostage to history's legacy for those inclined to genuflect.

We must be ourselves; we cannot just be copycats, ruled by ancient images and idols. By not worshipping heroes, we can think of Jesus as representing (**F**) faith, and Napoleon as representing (**G**) government. Then we can expect our faithful paranoid to be more chronic than another who claims to be a secret agent for the government. Divine rule is more ancient than imperial rule. ("Iran first, then Islam" is Iran's new slogan for better relations with Americans who are not cult worshippers.)

Clinically, the intractability of a delusion depends on the seniority of the idol. We can even predict that a patient who is afraid that (**H**) Communists are under every bed will get better faster than someone who thinks the FBI suspects him of being a traitor. Anticommunism (**H'**) among Americans in the post-McCarthy era is not as idiosyncratic as sedition (**G'**).

If religion (**F**) is older than patriotism (**G**), and nationalism is older than materialism (**H**)—trade routes recently became another national security consideration—do we find behaviors among older primates that correspond to ours?

Apes can (**A**) feel, (**B**) move, (**C**) abstract (gorillas invent words by sign language), and (**P, m**) masturbate (in zoos), but do they practice (**F**) religion, (**G**) politics, and (**H**) profiteering?

I knew about **A, B, C, G,** and **P, m** among animals long before computer-aided sign language research symbols. **F** was predictable from how my paranoids recovered or improved but exceedingly hard to verify in animals. Then I heard about a captive chimpanzee behaving suspiciously in Stanford where I send some doctors for their electives. Finding my missing link, I almost jumped for joy.

(**F**) Because sounds are invisible, they are scary. A captive chimp started making ungodly noises without apparent provocation, until a plane flying overhead was belatedly seen by his audience with inferior hearing. He tried harder to drown its noise, rattling the bars of his cage and increasing the decibel of his protests. Almost godlike, such mock display against intruders produced the desired results: The plane left our chimp's territory. After the plane's noise faded away, the chimp started posturing, strutting around, thrusting his chest out, and beating it with both hands, like Tarzan, King of the Apes, our sterilized version of an alpha male. (We applaud the use of power, but not in the service of sex, not for Tarzan or for Clinton.)

This vignette illustrates magical thinking, which is what (**F**) religion offers. (The same self-hypnosis and delusions of adequacy about the power of ritual is demonstrated.) Listed after **F** are (**G**) territorial imperialism and (**H**) trading or barter, as below.

(**G**) We also have wild chimpanzees who make war on others who have left the herd for greener pastures.

(**H**) Others in captivity pay with computer tokens for sexual favors from outnumbered females in a primate lab. (Our oldest profession is no longer uniquely ours.)

(2) ABCs of Sex and Violence

"Innovations in psychiatry" can be more than just a laundry list of what's new. The papers should stimulate exploration as well as trigger discoveries. I try to exaggerate enough to strain credulity. I don't want you to believe what I say. I want you to test what it means.

In what follows, I will simplify sex and violence without stigmatizing either, in a new truly transcultural practice of psychiatry.

The ABCs of anthropology, biology, and cosmology impose absolute relativity. Primal violence and driven sex made us what we are. What keeps us going are our instincts, the only intelligent life-support system that we have to the extent that our brain leaves them alone. Drugs of all kinds disturb homeostasis to produce allostasis.

Beliefs in big lies are addictive. Nouns, like God, queen, and money are toxic to this autonomic life-support system.

(Without early brainwashing about sin, godlessness or undelayed gratification and religious bureaucracies promising to save our souls would starve. "If it feels good, don't do it right away! Sex, especially if it is good, is bad!")

We use language to hide our nakedness, as if to be naked makes survival problematical. (Only the mind can break your heart or write tragic love stories for the gullible hypochondriac [with an exposed soft belly].) When we make love the condition for feeding and loyalty the reason for fighting, we corrupt our oldest friend in life. Our autonomics can help override speech centers in our left brain.

Words, Meaning, Symptoms

The cost of peace at any price is lust for life, lost by denying our instincts, in domesticating the autonomics. "Live" is "evil" spelled backward. To keep us from enjoying life, we have a Tower of Babel that keeps growing taller. Words excuse or discourage our autonomics in the four f's of living.

The four *f*'s of life are all gerunds from verbs: feeding and fornicating, fighting and fleeing.

For gerunds, we substitute nouns that excuse genocide and enslave us all our lives.

We still use euphemisms for body parts and functions, as if they are to be ashamed of.

And only human beings will blow themselves up to kill unmet enemies of their friends. Being human can result in inhumanity.

Our women are also unique in being abused or raped by the opposite sex and in asking to be their equal. Their vagina, unlike that of other mature primates, remains tilted forward. Vulnerable like a child, the law allows abortion after incest or rape.

To depend on our newest organ, the neocortex, and what it says about being human or man and woman instead of male or female, we are going to have problems that modern medical science, but not traditional psychiatry, escapes.

If words override the parasympathetic in feeding and fornicating, then we have *Homo domesticus.* They identify with aggressors, whether they are (**F**) divine, (**G**) local or (**H**) fiscal colonialists.

(In America, they are called religious accountants or right-wing Republicans. They feel preempted by New Democrats who steal some of their fearful fantasies for political debating points. In good economic times, they are more libertarian than egalitarian.)

If to prevail, nouns distort whom we must fight or flee from, then we become *Homo metropolus.* When men become feminists and worry about what Bill is doing to Hillary Clinton, then we have an oppressed *Homo metropolus* who is jealous of a testosterone-richer alpha male animal's privileged (charismatic) access to more females than him.

> (In psychoanalysis, this is called "penis envy" for both sexes. Prosecutorial curiosity about sexual performance by other males is called latent homosexuality. FBI under Hoover kept promiscuous JFK and Martin Luther King under close surveillance.)

We have famous men whom we call ex-presidents. Can they be divided according to their autonomics as fighters or fornicators? Jefferson, at age 60, bought Louisiana and, at 65, sired a son by a mulatto. Roosevelt prevailed in war if not in bed, so did Truman and Eisenhower. Kennedy and Johnson prevailed in bed more than in war. Nixon in neither. Nor did Ford, but Carter failed ignominiously against Iran as a protagonist. As a result, he did not get reelected. He lost to Reagan and Bush.

Lincoln once shared the same bed with another man for two years before he went to Washington. But no connection has ever been made between this (**U, m**) and his stormy marriage (**W, f; X, m** [m=male, f=female]).

Both Reagan and Bush, unlike Roosevelt and Truman, went to war over insubstantial, if not implausible, pretexts with third country nations that they predictably overwhelmed with ease. Reagan invaded Grenada, Bush Panama and, with Thatcher's help, defeated Iraq. Thatcher had previously prevailed in the Falklands. *(b/5)*

President Clinton gets good marks in (**A**) caring and (**B**) trying but was accused of (**C'**) lying. He also received good marks for love of (**F**) God, for (**H**) reducing the budget deficit, and supporting (**J**), (**K**), (**L**), and (**O**) or, respectively, community, technological, environmental, and electronic access. But he is faulted for (**G'**) dodging the draft and (**W, m**) compulsive heterosexual promiscuity at age 50.

Those who want Clinton impeached also do not want him to have fun as an alpha male, which they are not. (This is why democracies flourish—they cater to the mediocre: when their leaders win more than what got them elected, they are unceremoniously thrown out of office, like Winston Churchill and George Bush as war leaders.)

Alpha males protect their brood, which a commander-in-chief will, but not as cannon fodder. Using his flock for cannon fodder to continue as commander-in-chief is betrayal of trust by the elder. He is then as bad as former imperialists who cannot fight their own battles.

Frustrated by being shortchanged in love or work or sex, we suicide or abuse those who are more helpless. Among these are animals who have been adopted as pets or our own children and wives and others who are dependent on us. Alpha males don't do these cruel things! High testosterone produces dominance and forthright behavior in animals, not violent or high-handed and criminal or underhanded conduct from men or women in power.

Below are twenty strings of answers to questions—that animals do not dream of asking—about how our corrupted cortex stresses our body parts and alienates us. Which answers we gamble on may dominate our lives and make each day more hellish on earth than it needs to be. Which column do you prefer? Left (autonomic) or right (cortical)?

AUTONOMICS (INSTINCTUAL LUST FOR LIFE):

Visceral Lifestyle -> Ideological Abstractions or Intellectual Hypochondriasis

The parasympathetic nervous system mediates (1) lust for fornication, (2) play to develop fitness to survive, (3) hunger, feeding, and storing or hibernating, and (4) love as grooming.

Our neocortex enjoins *Homo domesticus* to add to

(1)	fornication ->	(a) marriage		
(2)	play ->	(b) losing ->	(c) shame	
(3)	feeding, storing ->	(d) greed ->	(e) hoarding	
(4)	love, grooming->	(f) charity ->	(g) mercy ->	(h) heaven

The sympathetic nervous system evolved for (5) sexual rivalry, territorial (6) fighting, (7) alliances and (8) competition, (9) ferocity and (10) violence, or (11) fleeing and (12) fearing or freezing and "playing possum."

The new cortex enjoins *Homo metropolus* to add to

(5)	sexual rivalry ->	(i) envy ->	(j) jealousy	
(6)	territorial fighting ->	(k) heroism		
(7)	alliances ->	(l) allegiance		
(8)	competing->	(m) courage ->	(n) chivalry	
(9)	ferocity ->	(o) hate ->	(p) contempt	
(10)	violence ->	(q) murder ->	(r) vengeance->	(s) justice
(11)	fleeing->	(t) cowardice ->	(u) revulsion ->	(v) horror
(12)	fear->	(w) terror ->	(x) awe ->	
		(y) prayer->	(z) adoration	

In health, our autonomic nervous system leads a balanced life together, as yin (cold) and yang (hot).

Unhealthily, the domesticated neo-cortex adds to

(13) co-existence ->	(14) control	
(15) failure ->	(16) regret ->	
(17) self-pity ->	(18) remorse ->	(19) "sin"

and to suspicion of self-absorption or sinfulness by "choice" according to cultural "consensus"

->   (20) "hell"

If we are not humanimal enough (cf. *Neo-etho-sexology*) to live an unfettered life as *Homo sapiens*, our personal evolution is more domesticated, and we belong to the subspecies *Homo domesticus. (Table 16)*

And if we are more covetous than competitive in our domesticity, more militant for equality than freedom-loving, then we have evolved into Homo metropolus.

Our parasympathetic nervous system makes us fornicate as well as feed ourselves and the life inside us. (Women can give up needed calcium to the unborn. Thus, the parasympathetic is the seat of love, sexual and maternal.) Sees to what is sexual and maternal.

All animals are equipped to flee or fight ("sympathetically"), fornicate or feed (parasympathetically).

To the original instinctive four *f*'s, *Homo sapiens* has added fantasy to the parasympathetic nervous system, and *Homo domesticus* and *Homo metropolus* have added fanaticism to the sympathetic nervous system.

Fantasy leads to creativity, fanaticism to ideology. Fantasy comes from the right-brain thinking and dreaming; fanaticism is facilitated by the left-brain talking and believing.

The creative *f*'s of **(A)** Feeling, **(B)** Forcing, **(C)** Framing, **(D)** Fitting, and **(E)** Finding ensure enough joy, even without our joining with others once the instinctive *f*'s of routine feeding and fornicating, and adaptive fighting and fleeing give us endurance to thrive:

A (emotional): Feeling inarticulate but expressive with music, painting, etc.

B (volitional): Forcing forms and shapes in architecture and sculpture and exploiting movement in dance and sports and with prostheses manufacture

C (intellectual): Framing agenda-driven myths, slogan-spinning philosophy, and cliché-ridden rhetoric

D (postlogical): Fitting theories to clarify and explore, research to disprove and discard, paradoxes to reconcile

E (extracurricular): Finding the unknown, discovery of the unfamiliar, unique interpretations of the absurd.

We can make a tentative inference that *Homo sapiens* are more sexual and sensual than social, that *H. domestici* are more social than sensual or sexual, and *H. metropoli* are less social and sexual than sensual.

PREVIEW HISTORY OF ABSOLUTE RELATIVITY

Science proceeds like a more subtle cross-examination of nature than the pyrotechnics of the courtroom. However, the yields from both come from a relentless pursuit of contradictions that come out of/during discovery as facts that need to be connected and summarized in words to be understood. In some cases, their unfolding may even have to be staged to be appreciated, with or without rehearsed histrionics. Further exploration is then up to the interested parties.

Witnesses / Dramatis Personae
(not necessarily in order of appearance in the world as a courtroom or stage)

Act I includes Aristotle, Bohr, Copernicus, Einstein, Heisenberg, Kepler, Newton, Planck, Plato, Ptolemy, etc.

In Act II we have Adam, Darwin, Eve, Goodall, Lilith, Mendel, Pasteur, and burrowers, climbers, stalkers, etc.

In Act III, we start with Satan and continue with Hippocrates, Pavlov, and Freud (who happen to be physicians but are not all healers).

As peers, contemporaries, and accessible subjects, we sample US Supreme Court Justices (bench sitters, and nominees [benchwarmers], bureaucrats, doers, dreamers, philosophers, pleaders, and preachers. We meet preceptors (for learning by thinking), and professors (for teaching by professing), teachers (for learning by telling), tutors (for learning by doing), and writers who simply fantasize. We get to know prisoners, parrots, and perverts, and reincarnations of Adolf Hitler and Helen Keller. Their grandchildren among us are human unicorns, centaurs and androgynes who may, respectively, want to be more (**i, A -> E**) free sensually, (**ii, F -> O**) equal socially, and (**iii, P -> Z**) erotic sexually. (They climb up and down a dream pyramid of uneven stages/steps in life's ABZs of becoming, believing, and begetting human beings.)

From what our selected cast in such a three-act play say, we might learn more about (**I**) nature, (**II**) life, and (**III**) people that we can immediately use but must also study further.

ABZs of Life, from violence to freedom, parity, and carnality

To help us with some of the questions that we ask about life, sex, violence, etc., we also need to recognize the limits of talking with feeling, our role when we do not know how problems first arose, etc.

In trying to be more global and accurate, we have substituted "parity" for "equality," which spawns slogans that beg questions, e.g., about "affirmative action."

Does it mean a talent search among minority groups or special treatment for them? Is "artificial selection" more benign than Hitler's? ("Racists" feel threatened by their "inferiors," including their own children, and will not tolerate encroachment.)

The superior who is secure in their superiority does not hate or advocate. Only those who feel inferior want equality.

(Freedom and equality bring opportunity both to the free and for the equalizer.) Or should we scale down our scenario?

Can animals (**B'**) doubt? If not, are they more (**K**) mechanical (like believers) than adventurous? And can we take them apart like machines, even in experimental (**N'**) vivisection.

And is this why we are inhumane toward those who (**ii**) believe but believe differently from us? And are those who are inhumane mechanical in their inhumanity?

Violence and sex were around long before we got here, but man has perverted both more than his predecessors. ("Man" comes from "manus" or "maker" as in "manufacture." Toolmaking was originally thought to be a uniquely human talent, until a hungry chimpanzee was observed stripping leaves from twigs to "fish" for termites inside their nests.) *(b/7)*

Raw sex and violence are expectable in nature. To orchestrate either is both human and foolhardy. Those who are wise, including animals, do not choose between them. (Love among/between people produces tension; sex and violence end it.)

Violence is the sudden unilateral expansion or multilateral confrontation of opposing forces, as in thunderstorms. "Matter" was born out of violence with a big bang at least 15 billion years ago. From quasars (quasi-stellar radiation sources) have evolved 50 billion galaxies, each with a billion stars like our sun, whose interdependent behavior toward us we can anticipate only during solar eclipses.

Nature is all that is around and inside us. About three billion years ago, Nature produced life. Life started as simple irritability. After plants have produced enough oxygen—which, unless we are near freezing, we cannot do without for more than five minutes—animals evolved. (Some plants later became meat eaters.)

For two billion years, there was only cell division for multiplication without procreation. Sex is the periodic reunion of male and female seeds, each containing half the normal number of instructions for living and adapting. Cross-pollination by plants started about one billion years ago, before animals acquired the drive and joys of sexual reproduction. *(b/8,9)*

Mankind's evolution spans about five million years. Humanity is but a tiny fraction of nature or of life all around us. To put us ahead of nature is to shun what is known. We cannot defy, alter or control, or ignore nature indefinitely.

Before we learned of our ancestry, many thought that Satan alone or his assistants could make us betray our destiny. (Limping away from an eight-story fall, a survivor thanked his God, not for saving his life but for not letting him die in sin! This is *Homo domesticus* par excellence.)

We have learned by now that we are perfectly capable of substituting myth for instinct. Working against instinct is like working against nature; we do so at great risk to ourselves and to our planet and end up as our own worst enemies in hot pursuit of promises and purposes that are alien to all other animals.

Human Use, Misuse, Abuse of Sex and Violence

The cerebral cortex invents concepts. Concepts create convictions in the weak or sick. Shared convictions become traditional beliefs. Medicine based on traditional beliefs is tribal medicine. Modern medicine is based on science, not beliefs. Tribal medicine begins with the soul or spirit, modern medicine with the cell, two of which receive, jointly according to doctrine, one soul after union in the zygote.

Not only is modern medicine based on science, but it also cannot be fully assimilated by believers. Comparison is the basis of all scientific knowledge. Beliefs handicap observers when comparing what they see through tinted, tainted, or stained glasses.

Does the esoteric anatomy of acupuncture exploit the yin and yang principle and stimulate or depress the autonomics outside the central nervous system? And is its demonstrability more difficult for the West to accept because we treasure our neocortex too much?

Knowledge is what remains after disproving what seems merely logical. We preserve our planet by disproving that it is unmoving and learning that it does not make others move around it, that it is insignificant in size but not likely to disappear soon even if, out of pride and ambition, we cannot be as animals again.

Fantasied free will or freedom of choice—which is factually demonstrable only as an option that is open to actors who also change their names with every role—may theoretically explain to the unsure why sin earns hell for the soul.

But even in the role that actors try to recreate from a script, they are at the mercy of their autonomic nervous system, over which they have little conscious control. (When the script takes over and the drabness of their lives fades away as their adrenaline starts pumping, their sympathetic nervous system honestly speaks in body language to their audience with a deeper "truth" than they can articulate. But note that such "truth" is still someone's fiction.)

Choice is the proverbial white elephant that comes with exercising control, which often loses to consensus by education. Can we control hereditary or habitual addiction to stimulants or sedatives (alcohol, cigarettes, debates, drugs, gambling, etc.)? Free will dies unsung when personal responsibility cannot be accepted. *(b/6)*

Data make irresponsible decisions entirely unnecessary. Leaders who are wiser than decisive share additional information that leads to the best course of action. Leaders act, thinkers guess. Actions can be corrected more easily than precious guesses. Guessing is costly. Only when we cannot wait for needed data do we have to jump the gun! Forewarning may be foreclosed.

Violence and sex remain separate below the brain, and also because both sympathetic and parasympathetic autonomic nervous systems are more proprioceptive than tactile and more mesodermal than ectodermal (intellectual or verbal). Chickens can run with their heads cut off.

[Luigi Galvani had shown (unpublished) a long time ago, that headless frogs respond to electrical stimuli.]

After more than three million years of evolution, can it pay to be stubborn (willful)? Conflicted sex and violence arise from interference in their expression by the human brain, which becomes more erogenous and violence-prone than other animal brains. Only if we do not take ourselves seriously can we be tender or tough and play joyfully or laugh rowdily.

Even elephants shed tears, mourn, or drive scavengers away from their dear departed.

If adult play or laughter (which is supposed to heal the soul) make us human, are those without playfulness or a sense of humor less human or hopeful or more willful and accountable?

Living among animals throws a different perspective on ethology—with or without sex—and on violence among humans. (More than money, sensual and sexual experiences produce pleasure and happiness in man and animals. Social mobility results in chaos more than peace.)

The ABCs of Science: Anthropology, Biology, and Cosmology

Cosmologists hold that violence scattered matter with a Big Bang into galaxies made of stars. One such star is our sun, around which planet Earth revolves.

Biologists know that the sun feeds life on Earth through photosynthesis. Plants keep an eye open for the sun, to convert gas and salts into food. Oxygen as a by-product becomes available for animals to evolve and breathe, eat plants, and breed to help the wind cross-pollinate more randomly. (Mongrels adapt better to changing conditions than inbred pedigrees.)

Ethologists find that animals also form their own food chains. They become violent (a) with others to protect their lives or loved ones, (b) within their group in male rivalry only to reproduce their kind, and (c) kill the nurslings of other males in order for their mother to stop nursing and go into "heat" or oestrous sooner.

Anthropologists see how infertile sexuality, family violence, and sensual skills combine to make human beings more problematical than other animals. *Homo metropoli* are the worst.

Cosmology is thus the study of primeval violence; biology and ethology accept violence and sex as legitimate means and ends, while classic anthropology and old-school psychiatry still vainly look for ways to invalidate both sex and violence as to their primacy and legitimacy. A new breed of psychiatrists can use a more radical, dogma-free, three-pronged senso-socio-sexual scrutiny to (1) arrive at stages of growth and development of (i) self, (ii) clan, and (iii) kin and (2) ask better questions or (3) test different solutions to heretofore (a) unsorted or (b) distorted impulses that, respectively, are dangerous and deadly to us and our planet.

In our New Psychiatry, we have only just begun to study our genealogy beyond past generations. It begins to cast a different light on our relationships with (I) nature, (II) animals, and (III) humankind. These relationships we can study as behavior beyond the reasons that we use to explain them.

A recent perverse but well-reasoned distortion of this web of relationships is that we are to behave as self-appointed custodians of nature as if a tail can ever tell a dog where to go.

If the heretofore indivisible atom as the virgin mother was split after a big bang into galaxies including our Milky Way, can the mother bomb breed monster mutants that we may not welcome as siblings or in-laws?

(Can "true" believers study nature's mysteries or just resign themselves as *Homo domestici* or limit their search as anthropomorphic cosmologists to wondering aloud at or puzzling over God's "creativity"? If the world is a stage, is God the theater owner or just its usher? One or the other, are there other stages? Actors?)

Because dead civilizations, primitive cultures, and modern societies all have gods, guardian angels, ghosts, spirits, ideologies, philosophies, and prophesies or hopes for a future elsewhere, are these needed to assist our senses in making sense of our sensations?

Acculturation (**F–O**) goes hand in hand with individuation (**A–E**) and erotization (**P–Z**):

a) As we grow, we leave (**F**) monolithic theology for (**G**) multiparty politics. Thusly, do we disregard revelations or "divined intelligence"?

b) Politics or "elected intelligence" can, in turn, raise more questions. We turn to economics for answers. Commerce uses bartered intelligence to trade in free-enterprise markets.

c) With money from (**H**) business, we pursue self-knowledge in (**I**) individual psychology, group intelligence in (**J**) special-interest sociology, and know-how in (**K**) consumer-oriented technology.

d) As human intellect fails at every turn to solve its self-created problems, (**L**) humanism also fails, and (**M**) defensive ecology is embraced by Earth First activists, natural animal intelligence is studied by (**N**) ethologists, and artificial intelligence developed by (**O**) cyberneticists.

We live in a universe of (**I**) con-naturality. In nature there is a world of (**II**) con-viviality in air, land, and sea. On land, there is global (**III**) con-familiarity. Wherever we are, we have mineral, biological, and human attributes, and (**i**) family, (**ii**) cultural, and (**iii**) gender-based relationships that shape our personal, public, and private lives at senso-moral, socio-ethical, and eroto-sexual levels, respectively.

What we mind that matters only to us in a world of matter may make us timid or fretful or sinful or sick. This is the hidden assumption behind the practice of transcendental meditation. The brain is a manager of muscle and a monitor of its surroundings and—with endocrine organs—of our interior life (like air movement on breathing during meditation). "Mind" is a working brain, dreaming of utopia to increase self-esteem. If mind evolved from matter and muscle, should it be the master? Or the servant? *(b/8)*

Do not animals serve plants by sowing their seeds even as vegetarians? Is it not preposterous to hold that plants preceded animals in order to be their diet? Did grandchildren produce grandparents to be babysitters? (Pets raise their masters like children their parents.) To see patterns rather than purpose in the emergence of behavior is not teleological, but scientific, thinking. *(b/9)* Do we need to add romance and religion (to dignify remorse or self-pitying sinfulness) to the four *r*'s of recreation and reproduction, remembrance and regret (or sorrowful embarrassment)?

How This Theory Evolved

(An encyclopedic mind does not think like a writer.)

We use analogy (functional) and allegory (poetic) to consider strange ideas and arrive at new destinations. For verification, we rely on homology (structure) and genealogy (origins).

Consider our body. It is composed of many different organs and parts. It took eons of trial and error to put more and more specialized organs together before they could work in reasonable harmony. We are sometimes still "all thumbs," especially under stress.

Tardier than the thumb in evolving, our brain is no different from any other newcomer who does not yet know the "system" and will therefore bring a different perspective that old-timers automatically discount. But nothing in the world ever remains a misfit for long and survives—not even brainy cynics—except inside our own minds. (Paradoxically, even the ideas in our dreams and nightmares cannot be mutually exclusive, once we take the time to examine them without mental reservations. This requires absolute relativity.)

And despite what our "mind"—which is a strictly human perversion of "minding" or the monitoring of our environment—insists or fears, none of the subsequent developments has been inimical to the ones that preceded it, from which they had also evolved. (Some may outgrow their usefulness, like our appendix or small toe, but we do not reject them for being obsolete: the ABZs of life is nonjudgmental.) *(b/10)*

Nor are additions just strung together randomly. Would our alphabet of life from (**A**) to (**Z**) be more difficult to use than our fingers and toes? Our fingers and toes continue to fit into each other's contours. Seldom do we use any of the digits separately, except perhaps to accuse or to poke.

(When we favor one digit over the others to point or penetrate, are we just thumb-sucking or substitute-seeking oro-anal reductionists who are simply excluding what we cannot trust?)

Likewise, in order to cope—as our (i) sensual capabilities (e.g., memory storage), (ii) social skills (e.g., with practice and euphemisms), and (iii) sexual potency (i.e., reproductive ability) continue to grow—we seldom just depend on what any one stage of development alone can do.

If you designed your own body, would you have dared to put as many organs all jammed up together and expect immediate coexistence? With time, is this mutuality what the alphabet eventually achieved so that now none of the 26 letters is expendable? (Of course, other alphabets have more than 26 letters, and we combine some of ours to speak their language.)

In time, maybe not soon enough for our students, our 26 (A–Z) stages of human growth and development will be understood by all. The early preliterate (A–C, F–H) and oral (P) stages are already shared with other animals. Even the later developments get along fairly well, crowded together—like the clenched digits of our fists—especially tightly on both sides of each stage during crises (before we regress and retreat until we are fit).

Just as we do not use the alphabet by stringing its letters sequentially to form words, so are the stages not chronological from A to Z. Each milestone in our dictionary of behavior in becoming, believing and begetting human beings begins with letters from stages in our (i) sensual growth (A -> E), (ii) social learning (F -> O), and (iii) sexual orientation (P -> Y) until we again become more sensual than social or sexual as grandparents (Z).

In our schema, we do not outgrow any stage altogether but are always welcome to stay on at any time as long as we wish, or to return with or without notice later and still feel at home. (Indeed, home is where they must keep us warm and cozy, like it or not: Keeping the home fires burning goes beyond simple housekeeping.) If we are not yet ready to leave home to further our development, can we stay put without starving?

Before reaching the (Z)enith of grandparenthood, we lead three lives at the same time, as (A -> E) sensual, (F -> O) social, and (P -> Y) sexual human beings. Only in our sexual lives do we need to separate males (m) from females (f). In a fourth life that some lead as (Z) grandparents, we can also omit socially valued gender distinctions.

Our separable selves can be

i) free and (**A** -> **E**) more sensual and personal or moral than social or public and sexual or private,

ii) "cultured" (**F** -> **O**), less sensual or sexual and more consensual and ethical while repeating the history of our social struggle for valued equality (before God, Caesar, sellers, etc.) by consensus, or

iii) carnal (**P** -> **Y**) and less sensual or social, as we grow more privately erotic and able to appreciate the biosocial differences between the sexes, e.g., women look at stockings, men see legs. (**Z**) is reserved for more androgynous grandparenthood, whose breed has again increased since the deluge drowned all but Noah et al. in the first total ethnic cleansing of unbelievers ever recorded.)

The terms that we use are bound to overlap and must always be understood in context until replaced by a better vocabulary. Even separable senso-socio-sexual divisions overlap, as well as each subdivision with the adjacent subsection.

To discover their continuity, we must know the similarities that the divisions and subsections share, and then the differences between each subdivision to understand why they are identified separately.

All stage names may change, literally speaking, but their interrelationships tend to remain constant, just like that between individuals in both teams covering complementary areas in a good game of basketball, football, volleyball, etc.

Our separate (**i**) personal and (**ii**) social evolutions are listed together side by side by topological and chronological order, from prelogical to postlogical, in sensual growth and cultural progress:

(i) SENSUAL

(ii) SOCIAL

HUMANIMAL

A) affectionate
    or emotional,
    passionate
    or passive,
    good or bad
B) bold or
    bashful,
    willing or
    willful or
    decisive,
    right or wrong

HUMAN

C) contemplative,
    logical or
    reflective,
    true or false

PRELITERATE

F) spiritual
    (animistic)
G) political
    (patriotic)
H) commercial
    barter-minded)

LITERATE

I) psychological
    (individualistic)
J) sociological
    (group-conscious)

INDUSTRIAL

K) technological
    (mechanical)
L) humanistic
    (anthropocentric)

POSTLOGICAL

D) discriminating
    or comparative,
    factual or not
E) experimental
    or creative,
    new or old

POSTINDUSTRIAL

M) ecological
    (nature lover)
N) ethological
    (animal lover)
O) cybernetic
    robot lover)

Religion was originally humanimal. Transcultural animism is, in fact, as preliterate as politics and economics for many primates. Claims of unique human needs are not scientific but somersaults of self-deception or monumental tautologies.

(It is comforting for many to know that an uncaused cause thought enough of us to cause us to be.)

(iii) Species-Wide Sexual Maturation

1) Biological (Unisexual) Stage
(true only for the first trimester)

2) Biosexual Genito-Erotic Stages

	Female (**f**): Girl -> Woman	Male (**m**): Boy -> Man
P)	narcissism	autoeroticism
Q)	tomboyishness (assertiveness)	fetishism (hoarding)
R)	homoeroticism (pajama "orgies")	voyeurism ("window-shopping")
S)	play nursing (role-modeling)	exhibitionism ("hard-selling")
T)	spouse-shopping (mate-finding)	playing doctor (pedophilia)
U)	child-swapping (babysitting)	homosexuality ("buddy body")
V)	childbearing (heavy dating)	bestiality ("pet-thing")
W)	child-losing (client-saving)	driven mating (rapaciousness)

X) "hubby-switching"   sensuous coitus

Y) cradle-snatching   proud fathering
        (after menopause)   (until metapause)

3) Final Stage of Biosexual Maturation

Z) virtual androgyny (grandparenthood)

Both typologically and topologically, all categories are created equal, without the ageism of seniority. (Viagra may delay **X, f** and **Y, m**. Was Adam [before/and Lilith and Eve] autoerotic to begin with?)

Behaviorists who are not creationists (closet animists) should borrow a page from the book of evolution and consider that what is transcultural (across tribal boundaries) may be equivalent in function or physiology to what has common origins in form or anatomy among different species.

(i) What is sensual is largely con-vivial or shared with all living things.
(ii) Just as electrons con-naturally keep within certain orbits, whatever is social is also shared in its early evolution with some animals in the state of nature: Intelligent life in the universe, here or elsewhere, includes animals. While some people are more intelligent than others, so are some animals more intelligent than some people.
(iii) What is sexual is con-specific (con-familiar) or special to our species (the family of man).

Robots have sensors and can process data better than we can think. They can be programmed to reproduce asexually, like some plants and animals. Other animals are less eroticized. Humans are uniquely "AniMachinErotic."

Neo-Etho-Sexology for a New Psychiatry

Editor (Ed)
Author (Au)

Ed: Everybody knows what sexology means, but what is new about your ethology?

Au: It compares different species and studies different kinds directly. Doctors dissected cats before they studied cadavers, but no psychiatrist ever observed cats during life in a group of several families living together to compare them with their own extended families.

Ed: Hemingway had a hundred cats take up an entire floor of his house in Havana. How do you distinguish them from each other?

Au: We give them descriptive names, like Tiny Kitty for the runt of the first litter. She in turn had one more kitten than she had nipples and her sister, Pretty Kitty, helped nurse Little Bit. (Only grandmother cats [menopausal?] and those in the middle of pregnancy [fetus-conscious?] did not want the young nursing, rooting, or "horsing" around them. "Matriarchs" among cats would, however, rather take care of offspring other than their own.)

Ed: Mother cats permit weaned kittens to knead their nipples, but have you seen male cats indulge themselves that way?

Au: Yes, and I have seen cats near term invite newly born kittens to suckle even if they have no milk, but only if their uterine contractions are weak.

Ed: Are they instinctively maternal?

Au: Some are better mothers than others, just like some of our mothers.

Ed: Do they abort their young?

Au: No, but they eat the stillborn, like they do their placenta or afterbirth.

Ed: Do subhumans commit adultery? Do they even achieve orgasm?

Au: Of course, and noisily with alpha males, but noiselessly yet with the same contorted facies during clandestine "dates" behind bushes in open-air zoos.

Ed: Is there also a double standard of morality among chimpanzees? Is their sexual life conducted under different rules than their sensual or social activities?

Au: I did not raise the question of a double standard of morality among animals until we had a second peacock. He is still too young to sport a full complement of tall tail feathers. My wife would feed him behind the back of the dominant peacock, and he would surreptitiously take what is clandestinely offered. Are they coconspirators?

Ed: Is there a different standard for males and for females? The alpha males are not covert about coveting other females. Is covert action a confession of weakness?

Au: I would admonish my wife against setting the dominant peacock against the usurper, but she persisted even when he already had his dandy feathers up to warn the younger against encroachment. And then it dawned on me that she thought the younger one was still a baby, not a rival, and that she must "mother" it.

Ed: Are females more interested in social equality and males more interested in personal freedom?

Au: The question is not only anthropomorphic but begs another question.

Ed: Are females in other species as competitive or envious as all-too-nosey Mrs. Jones?

Au: It would seem so, even among birds who are less promiscuous than other animals. Hens are more so, but only women henpeck their mates. No other male animal is so treated.

Ed: Is it because he overstays his welcome?

Au: Or we are too monogamous for our own good.

Ed: Why do not multiple births demand more parents?
Au: Need for better care for the young came with less mature brains at birth.

Ed: And our brains kept growing bigger than our mothers' birth canals.
Au: Until just before they got too big to get out, and so we were born without fully developed brains.

Ed: And mothers now need a village.
Au: At least some help to feed the family.

Ed: What have you learned from studying animal behavior?
Au: Chimpanzees have been seen by Jane Goodall inserting sticks in termite nests and licking the termites that stick to them. They were then thought to be the only animals besides us who can use tools.

Ed: And they are not?
Au: We often open one of our sliding glass doors wide enough for kittens to slip through but not their mothers. One of our cats, Shaggy Kitty (SK), reached in and worked the doormat between it and the jamb and pulled it partly out, just enough to slip in herself.

Ed: Could it have been an accident?
Au: Some discoveries are serendipitous.

Ed: Will others use the same technique?

Au: Many simple solutions have to be rediscovered over and over again. Once soon after its signal success, the doormat slipped through too smoothly without serving as a wedge. SK proceeded to chew on it in anger—as even we ourselves tend to vent our frustration on tools that fail us.

Ed: So now we have three species able to use tools or improvise but not invent.

Au: All inventions are improvisations from available materials. (Beetles carve balls out of elephant dung to roll away and store elsewhere for their use.) The difference between Jane Goodall's chimp and SK is the engineering sophistication of economically employing a wedge to drive a wider gap between adjacent walls. It ranks with the discovery of the fulcrum, wheel, and keystone for arches (which gave architecture its name and eventually allowed larger spaces than the interior of the Parthenon to be unbroken by pillars).

Ed: Architecture, therefore, cannot be the mother of all arts?

Au: Its own name derives from a later technology.

Ed: Are cats cleverer than chimps?

Au: Even birds use stones as tools. Brains got bigger after Stone Age australopithecine. Our brain is about four times their size or 1400 cc, but Neanderthals had an even bigger brain (1500 cc).

Ed: That dates the use of tools as far back as the emergence of birds and mammals and maybe to the age of dinosaurs! Are you sure about this? Should we now change our name to Homo-pomposus?

Time Travel as Science "Faction"

Did Noah need dowels for his ark and did the deluge drown all life that had evolved above sea level? We can now embark on a voyage of discovery and start exploring what we have overlooked about ourselves.

Time travelers can look forward to journey's end. Before returning home, for rest and relaxation after our tour, we have arranged a short debriefing stop at a reconstruction of a truncated pyramid built by a civilization that had invented the best calendar in our history.

> The only heliport in the island of New Z. is at the top of this New World pyramid. The steps are wide enough to pitch a tent or hold a picnic. What levels you choose to share with compatible companions constitute part of your own debriefing.

Our truncated pyramid was modeled after the steps you took upon disembarking at each tour stop, which is named after the initial of each time zone that you visit. The cornerstones of the reconstructed pyramid were laid by Freud, Erikson, Maslow, Ortega, Pavlov, and Piaget (all of whose contributions will be compared as they become relevant) on the solid foundation provided by giants of basic science.

From a bird's-eye view of our dream pyramid, you can see the four facades facing toward the four points of the compass.

Facing the north are steeper steps to greater freedom. The southern facade has twice the number of steps. It is easier to be more equal in short steps than to be free. (You may have heard that the more southern climes are inhabited by easygoing, dawdling natives who even drawl in their speech, which is more lilting than the staccato of their northern neighbors.)

The sexes meet on the north steps or on the opposite side to lead a less fragmented and contrived life than in fraternities or sororities. The men have come from out west where they roam, and the women from the east where the sun rises to nourish life.

Grand Tour of Post-Diluvian Settlements

Even long, long after the great deluge—which inundated the flat earth of the Fertile Crescent near Mt. Ararat and hidden antediluvian Eden from view—we can now only visit what was left dry after the floodwaters subsided: some tiny islands, a small subcontinent, and a huge land mass with different time zones.

We will travel through three settlements. Their inhabitants may, at first glance, collectively look alike—like we do to the Chinese—at least until we get to know each other better.

The natives speak different dialects and tell time differently. Their time zones are thus designated differently and variously.

As with early settlers everywhere, most natives still prefer to be near the water. Only later does testing replace tasting and trusting, and think tanks and test labs get built. If they are not commercialized, we may have to use fat snow tires to reach their time zones in the hilltops of the highlands.

Pretend at each stop as if you have already arrived at your destination, e.g., **E.**, the Paris of Ernest Hemingway, Gertrude Stein, and other expatriates in search of creative fellowships.

[No one who, in fantasy, attempted this guided tour of arbitrarily segregated settlements ever wanted to live all their lives in any of the time zones. They are only interesting places to visit for those more interested in a well-rounded life.

Have you been to **(A)** Gauguin's Tahiti, **(B)** old Sparta, **(C)** ancient Athens, **(D)** modern think tanks, **(E)** artists' colonies, **(F)** monasteries and nunneries, **(G)** the company town we call Washington DC, **(H)** Wall Street's stock exchange, **(I)** Beverly Hills' introspection canyon, **(J)** California's encounter groups, **(K)** Detroit's assembly lines, **(L)** Esalen's human potential workshops, **(M)** Buckminster Fuller's seminars, **(N)** Konrad Lorenz's geese farm, **(O)** Silicon Valley's chip shops, and **(P-Z)** your friends' friend's private retreat like **(U, m)** Polk Street in gay San Francisco, etc.?]

Imagine you're a modern Darwin visiting a giant Galapagos archipelago, tarrying in the temples of morality, culture, and fertility, sorting out the sights and sounds that suggest the origins, not of our species, but of some of our subspecies and present dilemmas. We will thus reach the roots of human behavior at its source.

More temples are to be found in the time zones of our early sensual and social life cycles, which are governed by **(A)** taste and **(F)** faith, unlike our sexual life. They are therefore rich in amphitheaters and cathedrals in plain view, while sexual club life tends to go underground.

(i) Subcontinent of Sensuality

A unicorn and the Statue of Liberty tower over visitors to the Subcontinent of Sensuality. Both stand for love of freedom to (**A**) feel, (**B**) try, (**C**) think, (**D**) compare data with, and (**E**) deviate from obsolescing computers made of meat, meaning their egalitarian "friends" across the ocean.

> We are free / To try / Even prayer,
> To fail / Even to pray,
> And to play / Even at praying.

Slow climbers take one "step" at a time and know that what is (**A**) good is not necessarily (**B**) right or (**C**) true or (**D**) tested or (**E**) new. Chronic backsliders impatiently claim that whatever is old (**E'**) is good, right, and true: they have never learned to (**D**) compare and always insist that the new (**E**) is ugly or (**A'**) bad, (**B'**) wrong, and (**C'**) false.

(The lower steps are worn out in the middle by dissidents. It is literally a slippery slope for failed artists and scientists. It is a favorite with backsliders who, at home, use the banisters instead of the stairs except for climbing.)

The five time zones of the Subcontinent of Sensuality go from **A** to **E**, which are respectively better suited for indulging (**A**) pre-Hippocratic passion or passivity or emotion; (**B**) pre-Copernican action or activity or motion; or (**C**) pre-Cartesian reflection or abstract reasoning; and, for the skeptical and experimental, encouraging (**D**) Darwinian correlation of data or Pavlovian testing of theories, or pushing (**E**) new ideas to replace traditional superstitions that their cultured egalitarian "friends" cherish but dare not or cannot verify.

Our hosts are proud to call themselves libertarians, compared to the egalitarian "five-year planners" of the Continent of Culture, whose social values seem to accuse libertarians of elitism.

Below Licentious Lady Libertine—which is what her egalitarian "friends" call her—is inscribed:

> "Come ye all who are hungry but proud and erect and I shall not ask what you can do for me, but what I can do for you."

(**ii**) Continent of Culture

Another statuesque woman astride a centaur greets visitors to the Continent of Culture.

The plane lands above a welcoming plaza and the visitor descends by progressively wider steps to reach it. The middle of the last three steps are also worn smooth with constant use by robber barons who can climb to riches but cannot reach the higher levels of culture. They tend to be defensive and to use earlier slogans to protect their baronial status. They have been known to retort, "They also help who help themselves" to criticize both (**I**) the egocentric and (**J**) the civic-minded who have risen higher. And they justify their wealth (**H**)—just as early royalty did their sovereign privileges (**G**)—as part of the divine design (**F**).

Instead of the Torch of Liberty, the Icon of Culture holds aloft a scale to balance competing claims and, in the other hand, a sword. But she is blindfolded!

Below Liba—or the Lady of the Impossible Balancing Act, which is what libertarians call her—is a line of graffiti someone scrawled to taunt her, could she but see. It is enclosed in quotation marks, as if to attribute what it says to her: "My brothers are my keepers, I am their Big Sister." Her sword points to another longer and more officious inscription that leaves libertarians cold or guilt-ridden:

> "Can you get rich without robbing the unwary? Can you be both egocentric and civic-minded? Can you use machines without contempt for human weakness? Can you love nature and yet domesticate animals? Can you use computers to run robots instead of people?"

As egalitarians, our hosts advocate equality before God, government, and granaries, as individuals, groups, technocrats, or humanists, for plants and animals as well as for robots that are insured against injury, just like everybody is insured "from the cradle to the grave."

Their poet laureate defends the right of all to "equal guarantees":

> Don't plants exploit animals / As beasts of burden,
> To sow the same "wild oats" / That all pubescents must,
> Because the wild wind / Does not always succeed?
> Are we expected to multiply / To help plants spread?
> Is this our purpose, / Or our built-in program

That vegetarians / Seek to sustain?
Can our philosophies explain, / Or our eyes deny,
That cloning started with trees / For their own benefit?
Gardeners hate "weeds" / But cannot eliminate them

In the Continent of Culture, their ten time zones go from **F** to **O**, which are progressively suited to the institutionalization (as temples, palaces, banks, etc.) of different value systems: spiritual (the church), political (the state), economic (the estate), psychological (the self), sociological (the group), technological (the machine), humanistic (our species), ecological (the environment), ethological (all animals), or electronic (the robot). But habits of thinking lag behind historical changes in cultural fads. And so robot and God (a "Goferobot" at our beck and call) coexist in a Pollyannish mismatch.

(iii) Archipelago of Eros

The denizens of the Archipelago of Eros do not have icons or totems to welcome visitors or warn them about what to expect or what is expected of them, what to worship or what to fear. But they are not less intolerant than the libertarians or more liberal than the egalitarians.

At the wharf, the sexes embark separately. They arrive in the time zones of Eros (**P** to **Y**), which are also designated according to gender (**m** or **f**) in various sexual stages of development for procreation, including rapaciousness without foreplay (**W, m**), or postpubescent perversions for recreation. (The tourists and their hosts often crisscross between the tiny islands at night.)

Most islanders think that their own neighbors in the rest of Eros are queer or interesting. Besides their gender gap, there are Erosian neighborhood battles of all the sexes between the young inverts and the old perverts while closet heterosexuals hide in the dark.

I have not yet succeeded in persuading the Erosians to designate a separate time zone as **Z** for grandparents because "coupling is no longer arranged by parents" to ensure survival of their seed. Modern marrieds now decide between recreation (**iii + ii/i**) and procreation (**iii x i/ii**).

But, unlike Freud, the theoreticians of Eros continue to separate the sexes in the same time zone (as we do in our boarding schools) because "their preoccupations do not always coincide in content" (which may explain both their gender gap and erotic preferences that puzzle sexually unsophisticated adults). Instead of just engraved inscriptions or prosaic graffiti, their minor poets become lyrical on paper:

Men hunt for fun, / Females kill for kin,
Men are dispensable, / Women are invincible,
Men must have sons, / Athletes have "Mom,"
Men have to produce, / Females must reproduce.
Predators need hard data, / Women feast on feelings,
Males must penetrate, / Females need not perform,
Man trails behind, / But the view is better.

Most amateur sexologists touring the archipelago who insist that sex could be both traumatic and fun are told to visit the museum displaying the books of de Sade and Masoch. They are both fiction writers, not practicing clinicians, who have emigrated to the Isles of Eros as famous expatriates from the Continent of Culture.

(For those who cannot visit or do not like to read, and to the less squeamish, we recommend that they closely scrutinize explicit scenes in adult films to see if sadomasochism arouses the actors where it counts.)

Bondage may physiologically heighten emotional arousal, since we become more passionate when we cannot act.

That's why absence makes the heart grow fonder, and familiarity breeds not only contempt, but more violence in families than among strangers.

Actual strangulation and air hunger will, of course, also physiologically, if not pathologically, produce visible erections or tangible turgidity, which made lynching men thoroughly dependable as public entertainment. (Women were not hanged but bound and guillotined or burned at the stake.)

[Which may be how "Vive le difference" got started. Its modern-day mourners are those who beat it and eat it. Did zero-population zealots (Domestication/Breeding or **iii**) schedule AIDS

and abortion in their human husbandry agenda? (Domestication =
society/sensuality or **ii/i**.)]

(None of us expect to live as long as Noah. Did he carry an
AIDS-like sexually transmissible disease in his ark?)

Any sexual aberration can end up as recreation or addiction
depending on the range of opportunities that are available. "Only their
doctor knows."

> Some chronic alcoholics, drug addicts, and transsexuals may
> be so predisposed by their genes or hormones. Transvestites may
> just be hedonic exhibitionists or fetishists. (Whether they are or
> not makes a great deal of difference only to them, their family, and
> their doctor.)

Nor is there, unlike in other sexologies, a separate time zone in
the Archipelago of Eros for incest. The natives think actual incest is
strictly a family affair as opportunistic sex between partners living
in close proximity before both have reached the legal age of consent.
When stepchildren are molested, it may technically be child abuse, but
certainly not incest.

> Where have my blinders gone
> In the land of the blind?

The Erosians, however, agree: "Incest fantasies belong to children of
the Subcontinent of Sensuality."

> Society was not founded / On the graveyard of incest
> But spread far and wide / On the shoulders of exogamy
> Borne by soldiers or traders / (But not by visionaries)
> Leapfrogging local heredity / Outside animal husbandry.

> Agrarian island communities / Accommodated incest without fuss,
> Denied circumcision until necessary, / When
> performed, it was permission
> To be promiscuous without supervision, /
> While thoroughbreds on the farm,

Slated to be inbred for excellence, / Were
carefully deprived and supervised.

(For Freud the explanation for incest is sexual, for Erikson
social, for Piaget cognitive, for Maslow physiological. The author
thinks they are explaining the taboo against forgiving it. If it is not
impermissible, why ostracize the players at all? To be consistent,
miscegenation—which denies imprinting or leaves one's childhood
behind for good—should be equally welcome. Sanctions are directed
at what is natural that society fears.)

In the suburbs, cherishing the young is the next best thing to finding
the Fountain of Youth. Child-care centers are separated in every direction
from estranged parents' town houses. You'll find visiting grandparents
cavorting with their grandchildren, undistracted by competition for
their favors that guilty parents—who are competitive in their careers—
engage in every time they visit their progeny.

"**Z**" or Zenith

The island of New **Z**., which has been artificially reclaimed from the
sea, is your last stop.

You must take a helicopter because the only place to land is at the top
of its pyramid. You will be greeted by the statue of an ancient androgyne
to indicate that at the zenith, all will have achieved or dismissed social
equality and need not struggle to win it, after winning sensual and
sexual parity that are enjoyed without guilt or haste. Time travelers who
have paid their dues to get this far are debriefed:

Before reaching their (**Z**)enith, grandparents on their first date had to
climb around to and down or up the steps of senso-social development,
so as to meet their mate who is often chronologically behind or ahead
in their separate and asymmetrical sexual development.

Absent (**i**) sensual seduction (auditory titillation or courting, or
tactile attention or foreplay, which is called "grooming" or "imprinting"
among less romanticized animals), they may have achieved (**ii**) social
union with the help of (**F**) spiritual sanctions (all marriages are made
in heaven), (**G**) political alliances (nepotism), (**H**) economic assistance
(bribes in the form of dowries), etc.

Of course, this makes both newly betrothed very strange—and more socially suited than sensually compatible—bedfellows. Until they share personal secrets, private intimacy is delayed. They can (1) remain subtotal strangers or (2) learn to abort the battle of the sexes (a) by redundant communication across the gender gap or (b) by much more physical struggle or communion in their ascent to the zenith of androgyny.

[Sex-linked characteristics are easier to understand if sex chromosomes are distinguishable and labeled differently with seldom used letters (**X, Y**) of our alphabet. But their carriers are not sold on, or marketed by, such labels. Adults are either erotic or narcotic with each other, narcotic with children, and erotic or educative or both with students.]

If the first question asked about every newborn is whether it is a girl (**XX**) or a boy (**XY**), does gender make for a separate asocial (sic) sensual (**i**) or sexual (**iii**) development?

Monkeys and apes immediately inspect the genitalia of the neonate. So do we, in the barnyard or under our roof, counting their digits only if they are fingers and toes.

It is noteworthy that domesticated puritans, who hide their genitals but not their breasts, permit premarital orality (dining out) but not premarital sex (making out).

If men are dressed to kill and women use "war paint" on their faces as part of rites of passage to manhood or maidenhood, is (**S, m**) exhibitionism and (**T, f**) flirting more mature than (**P, f**) narcissism and (**R, m**) voyeurism—and less mature than (**Wf, Ym**) parenting—as higher and lower steps in the sexual facades (**iii, f** or **m**) of our New World pyramid, even for different cultures?

We cannot expect the genders to be objective while still caught up in coping with the drive to reproduce, or until they are reconciled to the uniqueness of their separate and unequal eroticism. I shall later tell you more about what (**Z**) grandparents can do when sex gets mixed up with sensuality and society.

(*Footnotes*, a best seller in the late nineties, started with T. Tune reflecting, "I never had a grandfather.")

Fertile and productive, you can retire earlier to the truncated "peak" of the pyramid as asocial, androgynous, but sensual, grandparents who have time to smell the roses, unperturbed by the din of battle between the sexes and the bustle of social hustlers. You will have risen above sexual differences by acknowledging the uniqueness of each gender in every culture, and above social skirmishes by giving each ideology the benefit of the doubt in their own subculture.

Living by Life's Pyramid of Freedom, Opportunity, and Omnisexuality

[The author distinguishes moral brainwashing (personalized) from ethical brain-stuffing (socialized), and domesticated perversions (desexualized) from eroticism and breeding. Are the lowest steps in our pyramid those in which there is preoccupation with the four g's of (A) goodness, (F) godliness, (G) government, and (H) go-betweens? Old beliefs (F -> H) are the least perfectible.]

Our nonlinear life cycle can be plotted like the periodic table of elements in chemistry.

All of us have personal preferences, social styles, and erotic orientations.

As you can see from the model pyramid, no one has to ascend many public steps to inhabit a monastery or nunnery (F), or to get along in Washington (G) or Wall Street (H) today. Nor need it take long. But it is not easy to stay on without burning out. More and more are forced to quit. (In Washington, habitués have to worry about prayer and politics without separating church from state unless the moral majority (F + G) agrees with their (H) fiscal policies.)

There is no reason why everyone should have to go above the lowest three social stages on the pyramid that other primates likewise inhabit. [Animals also know what is (A) good for them and (B) right for their own sake.] After all, not everyone wants to scale Mt. Everest or walk on the moon.

If we learned to speak before we could (C) think or (D) compare, are freedoms of speech, thought, or dissent different and separable steps in the pyramid of life that we try to climb? If we worshipped before we experimented, is (F) religion more universal than (E + D) science?

If we live in the ivory tower of academia that is supported by religious endowments or government subsidies, we have to pay lip service to our patrons (**H**) even if, in our own psychological development (**I**), once our daily bread is assured (**A**), we see both spiritualism (**F**) and nationalism (**G**) as obsolete ideologies.

In community psychiatry, we have to deal with many more diverse ideologies from the various subcultures, especially (**J**) minorities interested in equal access. If current (**K**) technocracy fails to help them, we try to be reassuring, if not resourceful, as hypersensitive (**L**) humanists. Then, as we later become oversensitized to impurities, we can become (**M**) ecology-minded, even if we continue to commute and pollute. (The true "**m-f**" is the corporate polluter of Mother Earth.)

When we are less invested and protective (committed) and more resourceful, we have turned to (**N**)aturally ingenious animals and to (**O**)verintelligent computers for more helpful insights in the practice of a sex-aware, culture-free etho-psychiatry.

The ABCs of Absolute Relativity

Like pioneers who settled the New West, we have used the letters of the alphabet as our wagon train, led by **Z**, to arrive at a postdiluvian vista point.

From here the distant horizon beckons. But it will continue to recede with each step.

And whatever territory we leave behind in our journey of discovery can later be explored at greater leisure forever after by those who follow in our footsteps.

Shall we briefly look back before we start?

There is a hefty prize offered in England awaiting the inventor of a new alphabet. How would you start one?

By age nine, we have learned a new word every hour. For me, it was easier to convert the existing alphabet to a pyramid of behavior like Mendeleev's periodic table of elements in chemistry. His was a series that started with the simplest element (hydrogen) that led to carbon, etc., as the cosmos evolved. So do (**A**) feelings lead first to imprinting all the way to the complex bonds of (**Z**) grandparenting. Because behavior is nonlinear, I needed a different graphic and used a truncated pyramid, from whose steps anyone can meet anybody else.

[The Greeks claimed that without courage, what is (**i**) virtuous or good, right, and true will be lost. Which is why the freedom to (**A**) feel, (**B**) try, and (**C**) think must be cherished even by those who are not scientists (who must be free to compare, **D**) and artists (who must be free to be different, **E**).]

[Virtues are different from (**ii**) values that value (**F**) Father Almighty, (**G**) government, (**H**) hoarding, etc. More and more, values that are used to accuse and blame need guns that the virtuous must do without. Values also need luck and pluck to beat the odds.]

Our brain is a younger organ than our muscles, our thumb, or our tongue. We cannot mistake it for our mind.

Our mind is a pretender, traitor, or dictator who wants greater jurisdiction over our body which produced it and is wiser by far. As a younger appendage than our thumb or our tongue, it is like an adolescent who thinks it knows more than its parents. It is especially repressive as a bureaucrat over our genitals. *(b/11)*

For a person to identify with his mind is like an executive giving blanket authority to his clerk.

For me, my left brain is a computer-aided filing system. My right brain keeps it occupied with paradoxical findings.

I also tend to see the more serious left brain as the talking brain and the more playful right brain as the thinking brain.

Cerebral hemorrhage in my left brain will handicap me less than it might those who talk and write.

The mind is a monocentric, reductionist abstraction. Linear thinking is not open-minded. Open-mindedness is not intolerant, but tolerance as condescension is no substitute for science. Science does not need to apologize to the tolerant and intolerant for what it discovers.

We have now set a postdiluvian stage scenario for you before exploring the ABCs of anthropology, biology, and cosmology as the essential con-naturality of all objects in the universe (moon-rocks are made of the same material as ours), the con-viviality of the living (we grow like all plants and animals), and the con-familiarity of humankind beyond outdated cultural relativism. This road to Absolute Relativity is now open for travel, and life's vista points from A to Z have been sign-posted. *(b/12)*

From hereon in, during a longer debriefing from past time travel-ing after the deluge, we cannot take anything for granted, even from the mental giants of old. We will learn, though not without mental reservations, more about our childhood as a species (humanimal) and ourselves (self-conscious) in groups. We can also answer (**i**) our "moral" (**A–C**) and asocial (**D–E**) questions as we are growing up so that we do not confuse (1) what is (**A**) good with what is (**B**) right and (**C**) true before (**D**) testing and (**E**) venturing, as well as (2) with what is natural to all (**ii, F–O**) social animals (bonding with or without bellyaching) enamored of totemic solutions that invite (**F**) a self-created animistic God into (**G**) the political pecking order and (**H**) the checks and balances of barter (trading with tokens), or (3) with (**iii, P–Y**) our sexual maturation beyond the **P**'s (solitary grooming behavior) and **Q**'s of eroticism on the way to (**Z**) virtual asocio-sexual androgyny.

The basic problem for our future children (humankind's own "bottom line"), in more manageable terminology, is the ongoing battle (family civil war, hopefully **ii/i** = -1) between

Homo domesticus + Homo metropolus (or indoctrination for belonging + socialization of reputation) and *Homo sapiens* (or procreation/recreation). Our species is doomed when civilization/breeding = >1.

Domestication and gossip do not weed out the unfit while hunting misfits. Animals do not strive for zero population growth. They practice bioecology (carbon-dioxide recycling among animals, the air, and plants) without our asking, as we do, the reason for being "born . . . and then dying to be reborn."

2.00 b/PREVIEW

b/Chapter Notes Asides from Basic Conjectures, Defining Experiences

[b/1] A (1) sign of tolerance of "incest" or (2) defensive symptom against sex with father—either by counterphobic litigiousness about, or involuntary withdrawal from, failed fantasies, homosexual or normal—may be behind (a) disconnectedness as well as (b) preoccupation with "office Ovalitis."

[b/2] Hippocrates before the meltdown of deities into one showed that convulsions had natural instead of divine origins. Truly lying to yourself (oxymoronic "true faith") is true believerism at its best.

[b/3] Dichotomies (like good or bad, right or wrong, and true or false) breed absolutes, like beauty, time, and infinity that are obsolescent or obsolete.

Before "rational" became popular as rationalism, it did not mean "logical" but addressed itself to "ratios." Could or would academic observers or counselors, legal advocates, or watchdog reporters differentiate between "rationalization" and "ratiocination"?

Obsolescent as well are phraseologies that are oxymoronic by implication: there cannot be a "mathematics of calculus," only an inexact but exacting "physics" of relationships. Exactitude reassures insecure numerologists.

Even individual psychotherapy and monogamous marriage share electromagnetic force fields with phantom participants from both parties.

[b/4] Postlogical may be more methodical than logical but, if "logos" is intelligence or data, the uncertainty principle or requisite randomness in quanta, depending on observer/observation mix, makes postlogical less literally logical than postmethodical.

[b/5] New York ran out of the Monaco brand of lipstick that Monica wore when interviewed on TV. A past survey showed that 75% of American women had sexual fantasies about Clinton. This helps explain his reelection: no one fantasizes over a loser except his enemies.

(But it is easier to hate than to love for those who are unloved. And to fault a lover of another for lying. Locker-room stories are often about love and sex or kissing and telling. At least Clinton is not boasting.)

(If not for sex, what else is left to lie about? Getting away with lying started us doubting our parents and their omniscience. And trusting adults to tell the truth is naive or lazy. One only needs to trust when one is not equipped to check things out that matter a lot, like one's chances when desperately ill.)

(Psychiatrists who cannot abide lying are too lazy to check the facts and will not make good psychotherapists if what the patient says gets criticized. Lies disguise fear or counterphobic recklessness. A psychotherapist should not listen to words but should hear with a third ear what was missing or omitted out of shame or defensiveness; a psychiatrist should always attend to body language.)

If Gentleman Bill won't tell white lies about sex, can you trust him? Ideology imprisons believers who must trust those they don't know well except for their well-known knee-jerk principles, e.g., about adultery or abortion. (Abraham was not punished for adultery with a young slave girl though Jesus had to save a prostitute from being stoned.) To be married to a dogma is more monogamous than most marriages.

Both dogma and marriage are institutionalized. Do you want to be? Wealthy or not, doing what comes naturally is healthy. In an ideal world, all children should be "love children," as in the animal world—a natural offspring rather than a contrived product to realize its parents' ambitions, whether noble or, worse, self-serving.

[b/6] Communists believed in economic determinism, and China can only embrace capitalism if its benefits can be seen as a rising tide that lifts all boats, with collective responsibility, which makes an independent free will a drag.

[b/7] Birds have been around for more than 80 million years. (Evolution tends to defeat conformity by biological mutation and individual variations. Culture tends to erase these or be subject to change itself. Science, unlike religion, exploits variations and varies its own reach with new technology and pioneering experiments)

[b/8] A senso-socio-sexual study of becoming, believing, and begetting among human beings in a clinical rationalysis of freedom, parity, and carnality shows that what we are most proud of also evolved from behavior found among older life-forms.

Other primates have exhibited (1) animistic self-deception, (2) political acumen, and (3) economic entrepreneurship:

1.   Giambattista Vico (1668–1744) claimed that thunderclaps were the first accepted signs of a mysterious occult power.
2)   Jane Goodall saw chimpanzees fighting fire that lightning started even if it did not threaten them. She also found unbroken harmony in a tribe until it split up, and "imperialism" for "greener pastures" was born.
3)   In another primate lab, tokens awarded for computer literacy went, sooner or later, to female chimps in exchange for scarce sexual favors

[b/9] We have to develop our theory from our data. Yet it is axiomatic, as in modern quantum physics, that the theory as formulated decides what we can observe. Asymmetry between student and object is thus assured.

[b/10] There is no historical "dialectic process' in the evolution of the brain from inverted skin. Only the idle (Marx was unemployed) perversely speculate about a thesis producing an antithesis and arrives at a synthesis which is only a thesis in search of antithesis (Engle, Hegl).

[b/11] Outraged bureaucrats who are monogamous, jealous, or impotent wanted to impeach President Clinton for high crimes and misdemeanor. He denied under oath that he had a sexual affair with a young girl who voted for him, but they did not believe him! They also suspected him of trying to suborn perjury from the only other eyewitness. Suspicions are unvalidated but stubborn opinions. (Is truth in the eye of the beholder?)

[b/12] Visualizing the Evolution of Liberty, Equality, and Sexuality:

My interest in dead or endangered civilizations produced a truncated pyramid from the New World to represent the ascent of WoMan from embryonic unisexuality to the androgyny of grandparenthood. Are peak experiences transient or destabilizing, e.g., following marathon efforts with anoxia and endorphin intoxication? Life being a round trip, peaks are as inaccessible to us as the tip of a needle crowded with angels.

Those who ascend can see more from their higher vantage point, even if they were not unhappy where they were before. Unhappier are those who try to look over the shoulders of others on the same step instead of climbing to the next higher stage of their own pyramid. But to climb involves more than looking; it requires stretching and bending for all primates.

Our three senso-socio-sexual subcycles are unified in a four-faced pyramidal view of global evolution. The stages of human development are subcategorized as personal (**A** -> **E**), public (**F** -> **0**), and private (**P** -> **Z**). Absent genital hypochondriasis [a/4], sexual maturation (**P** -> **Z**) is the easiest part of growing up, personal growth (**A** -> **E**) most venturesome, and social conformity (**F** -> **O**) more rewarding.

3.00 c/Preface:
MORAL, ETHICAL, and EROTIC or
SENSO-SOCIO-SEXUAL BEHAVIOR

Behavior touches every one of us, our families, our communities, and our country. What I have to say, therefore, will touch all of us.

Are my mental patients more like us than different from us? In my experience, yes. Or maybe they are just more like me.

Are we ourselves, as people, more like each other than we are different? Definitely.

Psychiatrists see the mind as simply the relationship of the brain to its surroundings, both inside and outside our skin. If shared with others, our brain's behavior can be studied and observed, even when it is not valued.

Animal and human brains developed later than other organs in our evolution. Like bureaucrats, brains take over only after the organization has stopped growing. Is this why we naturally distrust bureaucracies? *(c/1)*

Brains and bureaucracies are bloated paper empires. Our brain is both a programmed computer and a copier. Our mental red tape gets longer with rumination about life as a philosophical proposition.

In life as in psychiatry, literature and logic (from George Bernard Shaw to Bertrand Russell) are necessarily gratuitous. *(c/2)*

We do not learn about ourselves or others by reading fiction or listening to rumors or accepting theories or abstractions. If we can learn by listening to experiences second- or thirdhand, psychiatrists would be the wisest of specialists, yet they vie with ophthalmologists in suicide-proneness. Psychiatrists using senso-socio-sexual rationalysis listen harder for what is not said, just as astronomers look for what should be visible but is not, in order to find black holes.

We need to look harder also at what we take for granted. *(c/3)*

We can cut down philosophical and literary red tape by (1) looking for the absolute relativity of all events, cosmic or microscopic, and (2) using rationalysis for humanimal behavior to derive the ratio of what is (a) natural or animal to what is (b) human or cultural. To reduce the risk of getting too personal in attempting to do this, I have used (i) unicorns, (ii) centaurs, and (iii) androgynes to illustrate that we are all three mythical animals, metaphorically, in our sensual, social, and sexual behavior, respectively.

Our animal instinct to be free can be inconvenient. Androgynes, except when in heat, are as asocial as the invulnerable loners that unicorns (and pandas) are.

To be untamed as a unicorn displeases us. When we raise animals to please us, they also behave differently from the rest of their species.

Invaders on horses looked like centaurs in early cavalry charges against foot soldiers.

As ingenious (1) *Homo sapiens,* we unwittingly forget our place in a world that we all share by trying, as (2) *Homo domesticus,* to exploit whatever we can, even at the cost of killing each other—including ancient neighbors of Israel as far back as biblical times (Numbers 31)—and, as alienated (3) *Homo metropolus,* by destroying our natural heritage in transporting fire and firepower. These last two recently evolved subspecies in our society can—but not forever, even with modern technology—indulge in wholesale slaughter of our enemies and continue wanton pollution of our planet, while ranting about the blessings of peace and goodwill and unpreserved natural foods. Once domesticated or disconnected, can they go back to animal ingenuity without human exploitation or environmental pollution?

Male or female—behaving freely, equally, and erotically as humanimal unicorns, centaurs, and androgynes respectively—we occupy, at different stages of development, different steps with different perspectives in the pyramid of life of our senso-socio-sexual life cycle.

Do we have time and energy to notice and study connections between real animals and human behavior? Do we have enough leisure to spare before it is too late to act on behalf of all at risk?

Other civilizations were quite advanced before they were overrun by genocidal hordes of enemies. Have we become envious or suspicious enough to terminate the history of our species? Tardily or not, we need to know this as scientists.

Are all of us more like animals than we like to think? I hope we all are, because no animal has ever risked extinction by its own behavior.

Creationists are still claiming a special pedigree for our anatomy. Egalitarians, on the other hand, deny that, by itself, anatomy decides their destiny. Who is more idealistic?

If our anatomy can be traced back to other animals, can we also trace our behavior back to them? This remains to be seen. We begin chronologically, from bacteria to fish to frog to beast to birds.

We started as bacteria (plants), developed fins (fish), reached land (frogs), lived like beasts.

Darwin held back for a quarter of a century before he dared to publish his findings for a select group of scientists. He knew what kind of a reception to expect from other groups that have never understood that science does not respect sensibilities. *(c/4)*

Evolution as a science is nothing if not biology and paleontology, or we would not have started as doctors to learn about the human body by first looking at frogs (amphibians) and cats (mammals) before examining cadavers.

Now, as students of behavior, we shall also want to learn about birds (avian), from parrots to peacocks (fowls), and examine our closer relatives among fellow primates.

Sensually, our ears and eyes are not as good as birds who also flock together and are more social. We use our intelligence to save our muscles just to sit around on our haunches. The evolution of human behavior has yet to produce its own Charles Darwin. I will try to climb on his shoulders to study our history better.

What I have found is that *Homo sapiens sapiensis* can now be (1) differentiated into three subspecies, *H. sapiens, H. domesticus,* and *H. metropolus.* Behavioral elements from all three and among animals (2) can be alphabetically encoded to complement the periodic table of elements in chemistry and, (3) approximate its usefulness for psychopharmacology in senso-socio-sexual rationalysis.

All evolution results from prior behavior, even of lifeless particles (from hydrogen to helium), or of petrified thoughts (from Heraclitus to Heidegger). We can examine them all.

In the story of creation, first there was light. In physics we call the beginning the Big Bang, lighting up the whole universe. In Genesis, other creatures preceded Adam, for each of whom he had a name but none of whom satisfied all his needs. In evolution, dinosaurs inhabited this planet long before we arrived to colonize it. Many species have died to be replaced by others, like we did the dinosaurs, but we still don't know all their names nor many of the new ones that have just evolved.

Names, even ours, also evolve. They are not one man's immaculate conception.

"Females" cloned themselves before there was sexual reproduction. In God's ghostwritten version of creation, Eve came from Adam (or first man). In Filipino folk tales, a beautiful woman (Maganda) preceded a strong man (Malakas). But neither could emerge from their bamboo cocoon until an eagle split it with its beak to set them free. In evolution, winged dinosaurs also preceded our ancestors, just as their wings foreshadowed our forelimbs.

FIRST. EVOLUTION DID NOT BEGIN WITH ANATOMICAL OPPORTUNISM

We live on a hill, and the first few times my granddaughter heard an airplane, she would scan the sky and point to it. But in pointing upward, she was also reaching up, standing on her toes; and because we were on a slope, she looked like she would take off and join the airplane in flight.

For birds' wings to evolve, form always followed function, but it never dawned on me before that our hind limbs can be used the way condors use theirs, to assist in getting air-borne. If bipeds are more alike than different, do we have other behaviors that birds that lay eggs also share?

The first time I started playfully thinking about comparing us with other species was when my grandchildren were visiting us at Easter years ago. I tried to explain to all three why there are Easter egg hunts. I said that Jesus liked children more than He ever liked adults and, on Easter Sunday, children look for eggs that might bring Jesus back among His friends. All three understood what I said, but their parents thought I was joking. So I had to remind my own children that all of us started as eggs, even if our mothers did not hatch them by sitting on us.

And that brought me back to when my own life started. A doctor had to use forceps to deliver me. Yet only recently—relatively speaking—a cat by itself delivered her litter on the sundeck outside our bedroom, and we did not even know she had kittens during the night.

It must be a different experience to be born alone from being born together with your brothers and sisters. Brain injury at birth must have helped me try to help people whose minds are not helping them. It must also be a way of reassuring myself that I am not a hopeless mental case. Isn't that just like hiring a cripple to coach the physically handicapped for marathon competition?

I am not the only one who arrived in the world crying, while other animals are born without a sound to mark their coming. Are we all so proud of our mind partly to reassure ourselves that it did not get damaged during delivery? Once you ask that question, a lot of things fall into place. Without such questions we have no open sesame to behavioral science.

A. We can define the very first freedom as (**A**) freedom to feel or to experience what is around us, but (**B'**) without the freedom to choose our own ancestors, who managed to give us only our thumbs and a tongue to make up for prolonged physical mediocrity.

B. Do animals have verbs to guide their actions? If they can hunt together, they must have invented verbs before we did. Here we speak of the freedom to move or pause, limited always by evoked willingness or provoked willfulness to act or react.

C. Can animals use nouns? If they can teach their young without pointing with their forelegs, they must also have common nouns to generalize from particulars with names called proper nouns. Now we speak of the freedom to think, which is the opposite of the right to believe what we are told when we doubt but cannot act. (Believing is denying that we are ignorant when we are unsure.)

D. Can animals think in orderly sequence? Because they always look before they leap, they can succeed where we often fail. That is their freedom to compare past experiences in order to face new challenges, instead of relying on others to warn them of old hazards.

By accident, a macaque monkey in Japan discovered that grain would float and sand sink in water so that it is easy to separate them after they get mixed together. Because the reward is more food for the clan, a whole colony of monkeys learned, without words, how to use the laws of gravity and density to retrieve grain that has been dropped on the beach.

E. If comparing and combining past experiences do not give us the solutions, we can ask new questions that open doors to new worlds, instead of repeating the answers to old ones that keep those doors closed. (All I ask of us is that we start doing this.) This is our freedom to invent that does not come with age (or by species). Both the young and the old can change old questions, and those who hear the new ones can look for different answers.

SECOND. THE BRAIN ACCEPTS IDEAS AND INVENTS IDEOLOGIES

F. As children, we used to ask, "Where did I come from?" as if suspecting that we had different parents. Theologians spend their whole lives trying to answer just such a query, out of the mouth of the innocent of all ages. They read what had been written and think about what they had read. I don't know how they learn that way, but most of them feel sure of their answers. (They hold that "God exists and Jesus lives" and that their slogan is less of a theory than the theory of evolution or of relativity.)

For a long time, I have been wondering what makes our paranoids sicker by believing what many of us still cannot immediately disown. (c/4, 5)

If humanism is a latter-day secular religion, is old-time religion a sacred ideology? Can animals believe in God or magical thinking, like some of my patients?

Paranoids who think that they are the second messiah got better more slowly than those who thought traitors have turned the FBI against them, or those who believe that there are communists under every bed. Those who always looked under their bed before going to sleep could return to better reality testing sooner.

Those who are afraid for their country got better more slowly. And slowest to recover are those who—like battered women or children—love and fear at once, and only tardily realize that, in self-defense, they must take over even from God. *(c/6)*

Battered wives and kids and disappointed believers take an inordinately long time to be disillusioned, especially if they have become used to living in fear but with love, growing up. Abused communists who love Mother Russia were slow to revolt for the same reason battered wives and children do not leave home: fear can coexist with love, as in most religions (animistic inventions). This is different from the mixed fascination and repudiation among bigots, whether homophobic or genocidal: wasn't Hitler (born Schicklgruber) anti-Semitic partly for being part Jewish? How can thoughtful people claim that their genetic heritage is unmixed?

THIRD. DEPENDENCY, JEALOUSY, AND MOBILITY CHANGE TOGETHER

All my deluded patients share an inherited anatomy yet believe differently from each other. Some can give up their delusions easier than others, but they are given up in a predictable pattern: paranoid patients who insist that they were son of God, savior of their country, or wanted by the Communists recover in reverse order their old sense of reality. (Our senses do not decide what is real except for ourselves.)

Like them but less and less, we once needed God more than country or money for our peace of mind. Our need for them during health diminishes, unlike that for air, water, and sleep. Why is the ratio of different human needs and dreams ideal as a measure of our mental health?

Is it because other animals have shorter periods of total dependency when they are young but spend more of that time with their mothers? They have to share her only with their brothers and sisters, with whom they can compete on more equal terms, instead of giving her up to their father even when they need her more.

In the West—just as nursing homes are used to separate generations who cannot stand each other—nurseries are added to houses *(c/7)*, and infants are immediately started on cow's milk instead of their mother's milk. They are fed through a rubber nipple and with a bottle. Less harassed mothers bottle-feed the infant when it is hungry. Mothers who run their lives by the clock also feed their children by the clock. No other animal runs its life on demand by a timekeeper.

Infants placed by their mothers on scheduled artificial feeding sleep alone with a bottle, instead of dozing off at the breast. Should biologists no longer think of such mothers as mammals? *(c/8)*

Some cultures have separate names for boys and girls. In the Philippines, at puberty, boys become *binatillos* and girls become *dalagitas*, in recognition of their coming of age. *(c/9)*

In America, pubescents, regardless of gender, are lumped together as teenagers. Does this clever generalization serve as a magical incantation to help society deny that their activated sexual hormones shake up the status quo? *(c/10)* (Begetting thus becomes problematical for the young.)

Can magical thinking create generation gaps in some societies? Does magical thinking also divide people in other ways?

FOURTH. ANIMALS CAN BE ANIMISTIC, POLITICAL, AND COMMERCIAL

Are animals capable of fanciful dreaming to preserve their peace of mind? The answer to this question about the universality of flights of fancy, appropriately enough, came out of the blue.

Our trainees rotate through different universities from my freestanding postgraduate four-year hospital residency program in psychiatry. On one of my visits to the Stanford campus, I was told of a chimpanzee who behaved like Tarzan.

He would start rattling his cage for no apparent reason, stop for no apparent reason, and then thump his chest in triumph. Sometime after he starts rattling the bars, a plane would fly overhead, but he still would not stop rattling them even if the plane could no longer be heard.

I was told about this to prove how good a chimpanzee's hearing is compared to ours. Any good clinician can also detect self-hypnosis in our primate's behavior.

But if a chimpanzee could think that rattling the bars of his cage would make a plane go away, don't we also think that way about the power of prayer? (At least our chimpanzee could document his success.)

A psychiatrist might also say that the ape thinking that he is another Tarzan could mean that he is suffering from delusions of grandeur in congratulating himself for fighting noise with noise and believing himself the winner. At least we give thanks to God and our parents for our blessings. Yet when we ask God for something that we expect thankfully to receive, we can speculate as to cause and effect when our prayers are answered, sooner or later. *(c/11)*

But our chimpanzee cannot wish away an unseen airplane and had to take over himself to make the ungodly noises overhead go away. Which also explains why—beyond the need for self-defense that is as old as plants wanting their own place in the sun—patients who thought they were Jesus stay in the hospital the longest: because old hopes favor enduring illusions.

G. If primates, including us, indulge in animistic thinking to overcome feelings of inferiority, how do they pick their superiors? Do they, like birds, also have their pecking orders? In the wild and in groups, animals soon come to know where they stand in their hierarchy, which provides a separate place in it for everyone by its rules. This is the politics of power. Our own government is our means of enforcing another pecking order. It started by protecting our property, and now it has also begun protecting people, even hardened criminals, although it must, in self-defense, protect itself, especially against secret enemies in its midst.

H. Having established that, like us, other primates have both animistic fantasies and political rituals; can we also expect some of them to have commercial aptitudes? What do captive chimpanzees do after they are rewarded with tokens for cooperating with their captors? In primate labs, their keepers found that the females seem to accumulate all the tokens. It turned out that the males were using their tokens to buy sexual favors, which are in short supply. If affluent chimps earn and barter tokens for sexual privileges, then what is still thought of as the oldest profession in the world is not even uniquely human.

"Lower" primates therefore already have at least the rudiments of religion, politics, and economics.

We take great pride in our theology, government, and commercial ventures. Are we not, in fact, just somewhat better in fantasizing about these preliterate social endeavors that, in actual practice, make us worse (**F**) animists, (**G**) governors, and (**H**) economists than "lower" animals who are never homeless?

We have more religious, political, and economic strife than all other animals combined. *(c/12)*

FIFTH. OUR HISTORY IS AN OBITUARY, AND PREDICTOR OF UTOPIAS

If the distinguishing feature of magical thinking in the behavior of primates is self-attribution without documentation, is this also the essence of belief in the supernatural? And the be-all and end-all of all believers in general? Is believing itself an act of faith? And when our faith is misplaced or unpopular, are we heretics or deluded? Are all strong beliefs or deep convictions virtual delusions? And are paranoids those persons who subscribe to socially unacceptable delusions?

My questions led me to see history as a laundered list of serially acceptable ideologies, from ancestor worship of the Heavenly Father of Moses or the earthly remains of Lenin and Mao, to faith in Big Government, Big Business or Big Science, to blind trust in substitute siblings like a stereotypically solicitous Big Sister or unquestioning awe of a modern all-seeing, all-knowing electronic Big Brother. *(c/13)*

In our ancient history, it was an easy step to go from God, as the only ruler of the world, to the divine right of all kings to rule. We left the feudal ages when we went from autocracies to democracies, including the dictatorship of the proletariat. We have since then been moving away from a possessive God to powerful governors to profitable global go-betweens.

> The financial success of the printing press by mass marketing to pilgrims of religious indulgences (old trading stamps) in the name of popular saints, prompted Martin Luther to engage in a propaganda war against the pope.
>
> Predictably, since recorded history tends to repeat itself, the pope as vicar of Christ on earth has recently just dedicated a whole year to the Virgin Mary as our pipeline to heaven.

Children of God all wish they had different parents. Neighborhood Big Brothers are welcome to those who had none. Sisterhood for victims is embraced by those who had disappointing siblings.

History often recycles magical thinking by inventing many go-betweens, to plead for greater equality before God, king, or money lenders. *(c/14)* Even nuclear powers try for parity in their ability to kill as many as they can reach with their technology. When there is envy between nations, natural animal territoriality is replaced by each ruler's imperial ambitions. Then imperiousness goes far beyond simple squatter's rights that other animals always insist on, and will fight to keep, but never die for.

Our behavior therefore varies, not because we are no longer animals but because we are brought up differently as children. Yet under our skin, we are no different in our programmed instincts.

I found our hidden humanimality in a very roundabout way when I stopped over in Mexico City during the Olympics on my way to a medical meeting. I got there without a ticket, but many Mexicans were also without tickets and were milling around the gates. I was in the middle of this milling throng when suddenly it surged forward to crash the gates. At first, I was worried that I might lose my camera in the melee, and then I became a part of the mindless crowd pushing forward. The experience I had must have been like that of being part of a stampede, forgetting everything except to go with the flow. I learned for the first time that I could be part of a herd and even grow to like it.

At lunchtime, there were not enough tables even in the best restaurants. I was told to wait while a headwaiter consulted a regular patron who had already been served. He agreed that I could share his table. But throughout his meal, he only looked at me sideways and did not seem to welcome my being there. By the time the waiter started to collect his empty plates, I was feeling like an intruder, but then he suddenly began asking me intelligent questions.

I decided that, even if his questions were those of a cultured aristocrat, his behavior was not unlike that of a dog threatened by another dog wanting what it has. In fact, because he had established squatter's rights to his table, he was only exercising natural animal territoriality, which was limited in scope even among all-male social pecking orders. (When I got home I thought of a simple test to see how far territoriality alone decides the behavior of males in particular, i.e., peacocks.) *(c/15)*

Babies at all ages of innocence, including our patients, are more likely to believe what they are told; and we must be truthful because they cannot check us out. Juveniles of all sizes are more likely to rebel, and adolescents of both sexes to be mystical, especially about love when they cannot have sex. We call this being romantic. Men need to want and women want to be needed.

[Few with milk-engorged breasts or with good erections have ever killed themselves. (In illegally assisting suicides, is Dr. Jack Kevorkian himself asking to be killed?") Males must mate, females nurture. Men must also produce (more cut off their penises, only one alcoholic his thumb while intoxicated)].

SIXTH. OUR SENSO-SOCIAL HERITAGE IS NOT UNIQUELY HUMAN

Unlike lower mammals, we are born alone, and we are therefore surrounded from the beginning with our kind who are all bigger than us. It is no wonder that when they hurt us, we turn to someone bigger than they to plead our case.

And by how much bigger the chosen judge, by that much higher ratio, can we be certain that when we win our case, the decision cannot be reversed later. So we prevail over our parents by calling on some other bigger father (never *n*-great-grandfather) to judge our case in our favor. *(c/16)*

When (**A'**) we feel trapped, we begin (**B'**) to doubt, and doubts make us (**C**) think and (**D**) compare before (**E**) taking a creative leap to a solution or (**A'**) giving up hope. Our sensual development that sentient and social animals share may have uniquely human social consequences that changes from culture to culture.

A or Emotional. If we used our tongue as an infant to decide what is good or bad for us, is taste the mother of virtue? Is beauty in the eye of the beholder? (Desmond Morris, who wrote about us in *The Naked Ape*, made money selling art that had been produced by hairier primates.)

B or Volitional. If, as toddlers, we insisted on freedom of movement, is liberty a reward for urchinhood? (Groups who seek sanctuary outside their countries seek lateral mobility, and minorities who have already found their sanctuaries seek upward mobility.)

C or Intellectual. If, as adolescents, we used our mind to give us answers, is logical thinking easier for the human brain than careful observation? Only philosophical questions can be answered logically. Can syllogism assist science? *(c/17)* Science defies all logic. What philosopher could have reasoned out that time itself can be warped by speed?

D or Comparative. If, as adults, we increased our scientific knowledge more by homology than by analogy, is comparing by assigning ratios the real meaning of rational science? To be truly rational one cannot be reasonable or logical. Ratiocination is more advanced sensually than rationalization or "moral excuses" for disregarding information.

E or Creative. If, whether young or old, we can be inspired to create, is the freedom to be original or different separate from growing up? The precocious among us cannot keep waiting for their elders to catch up.

Can we also locate ourselves in the pyramid of life both by the type of questions which we ask or the kind of answers that we like? Or by the jokes which we enjoy while we try to get out of the current social ruts that we are stuck in? *(c/13)* (Don't priests and psychiatrists have their favorite jokes?)

F or Spiritual. If we seek equality for our souls by living by the Word of God, are we conscious that we are flawed for life? We cannot really continue to blame a snake in the grass for our protracted exile from Paradise.

G or Political. If we seek equality before the law by living by the law of the land, are we confessing our need to be governed? We do not need leaders to stockpile bombs, as much as we need help to extricate us from conflicting claims.

H or Economic. If we work beyond subsistence levels, is it because we are afraid that our providers are fickle? Freud insisted that we could never find security in money that we did not enjoy during infancy. Animals store fat or squirrel nuts away to hibernate or save up for a rainy day in the foreseeable future. Among misers, fears from the past determine how much to hoard forever.

Can the light at the end of a tunnel be from a train? Is going up or down the steps of our truncated (imperfect) pyramid like stepping out of a cave for Plato or into a river for Heraclitus?

A-type behavior among infants asks, "Where did I or it (the newborn) come from?"
F-type theologians wonder or answer, "Where did we come from?"

B-type behavior among urchins asks or insists, "Why not?"

Even toddlers can demand, "Let us be" (e.g., to be unhampered by diapers). Urchins in the tropics can keep running around bottomless until kindergarten, with adults applauding and pointing to a boy's "bird" flying when he gets an erection. (In the West, you only point to his crotch if a man's fly is open.)

Where the climate is more inclement, children are bundled up in swaddling clothes at birth and kept in diapers until they have been trained to deposit what their parents don't want their guests to smell except in places especially reserved for it. These places are usually uncarpeted for easier cleaning.

G-type politicians answer, "I'll tell you why not!"

Rooms that are carpeted are not for children who are not yet housebroken. Which is probably better for them, because carpets can look clean without being clean. But the message children get is that they are unwanted and unclean. Another message is that their genitals must be hidden and controlled.

H-type economists caution, "We have to be self-reliant or reliable."

Religion, government, and commerce seek to satisfy only the questions raised by innocent infants and unangelic urchins. Atheists replace theology with stories about their version of Santa Claus and Cinderella. Lower primates, who grew up faster and did not have to rely on others as long as we did, do not kill each other over their magical thinking, pecking orders, or trading practices. Unlike them, we are doomed to listen to promises made by (**F**) preachers, (**G**) politicians, and (**H**) profiteers and to defend our beliefs in icons (e.g., a wooden cross), flag (of colored fabric) or gold (a malleable metal), in totemic, tribal, and trade wars.

C-type behavior of adolescents insistently asks, "Why?"
I-type individualists assert, "Because I am unique."
J-type joiners assume, "Because we belong together."
K-type technocrats declare, "Because progress is our most important product."
L-type humanists claim, "Because we are special among the species."

The freedom to think is the freedom to disbelieve any of the above. To believe is an unwillingness to accept any alternative, even if thinking itself does not require effort, or dying.

D-type behavior in adults only asks, "Why now?" (And sometimes, "Why then?")
M-type environmentalists reply, "We thought we were the custodians of what we surveyed."
N-type animalists assert, "All species are separate but equal."

Better practitioners get to the roots of clinical problems by meticulous history taking. Psychologists who want to preach and psychiatrists who think like witch doctors tend to believe that parents are responsible—like submissive Adam and seduced Eve—for what ails us.

E-type behavior in pioneers is mainly interested in "What? How?"
O-type cyberneticists expect only the best to program the behavior of the rest.

These sequential linkages between (**A–E**) sensual and (**F–O**) social questions and answers quite deliberately do not even attend to the empty query "Why?" which covertly demands (a) debate out of commitment to, or (b) dying for, cherished explanations.

"Why?" when meant as "Wherefore?" changes our quest: from (1) seeking a better understanding of, to (2) craving for the reason or meaning behind any sequence of events by (3) at once assuming that they constitute a purposeful curriculum or ordeal: is there a hidden agenda or happy ending in store for us, or just another bedtime storyline, like Cinderella's? *(c/18)*

We ask, not "Why it had to be so?" but instead, "Why now?" or "Why then?" in particular, or "What?" or "How?" as in "How what is" is, in general. (Only then do we find that stage-specific behaviors cluster together.)

The longer we tarry in the steps of the pyramid of life, the less panoramic will our perspective become from the fewer and lower stages that we have reached. All of us can be (**A**) emotional but not all will be (**E**) creative; few of us can (**C**) comprehend (**B**) the power of (**O**) artificial intelligence, but all of us share (**F'**) the fear of the unknown: even animals dread lightning crisscrossing the sky without warning.

Ratios between achieved sensual and social development, and between both, and stages in sexual development permit ratioanalysis of human behavior, with each person as his own control at any time or age or era.

If (**A**) good or bad was originally gustatory in infancy, (**B**) right or wrong originally locomotor during urchinhood, and (**C**) true or false is decided deductively, can the ABCs of virtue be just sensual residues from brainwashing by our early providers? Freud, an agnostic Jew, would go along with what the Jesuits claim, "Give me the child until he's seven, and I'll give you the man."

> Domesticated elephants do not, as adults, test their strength against the belief (which they acquired growing up as infant elephants) that the rope tying them to a tree is still strong enough to hold them, even if they can already uproot larger trees.

Believing means one was not quite weaned yet when won over. Is being reborn like finding another Santa Claus in Jesus Christ? (Infantile beliefs among adult zealots permit overkill with "elephant guns" by saturation bombing of "human gnats" from other childhood faiths.)

Science can study but not dictate. Society can suggest but not dispose. Where their spheres of influence encroach on each other, our image of nature can influence our image of ourselves as part of nature, but not vice versa.

To insist that nature reflect our ideals is to return to Ptolemy and geocentricity. There is no need to reconcile science with society. Both only need to know the limits of their respective jurisdictions.

SEVENTH. WHAT IS SENSUAL IS *NOT* NECESSARILY SEXUAL

What we do that is done in other countries is probably also within the abilities of other animals to do. Is mothering, even surrogate mothering, different from country to country? We have kittens who are looked after by their aunts, as in our extended families. (American surrogate aunts are called "baby-sitters".)

If we are not better as social animals, which of our in-house human family practices are shared by our ancestral relatives? Captive chimps, who *(sic)* do not have to keep looking for food, have been observed mothering the young in a way known as smothering. Like "kept" mother chimps, our human smotherers who are devoted to their children are different from their sisters who are devoted wives and mistresses, as well as from casual adulterers.

Is smothering a form of loving pedophilia? Do animals also practice pedophilia as a sexual perversion? Mammals "lower" than primates let "uncles" mount "nieces" still suckling from their common mother. On our sundeck, three generations of cats "play house" just as kids secretly make-believe like "doctor and nurse."

EIGHTH. WHAT IS EROTIC DOES NOT HAVE TO BE REPRODUCTIVE

Are there other so-called "perversions" that naturally occur among other mammals? Our first tomcat tried to make love to my wife's bare arm. Is this reverse bestiality on his part? Or love of his mistress? Probably both.

Cats and other mammals, of course, just as casually engage in autofellatio. Are they ever warned by anyone that hair will grow on their tongues? (Unless double-jointed, infants can only reach their thumbs.)

Female kittens also suck the nipples of male cats in true androgynous fashion. Would you suspect latent homosexuality? And precocious foreplay if the genders were reversed?

> Like all androgynes, men have nipples and women have breasts. That is because, unlike birds, we all start as females, and then among male fetuses, the female organs stop developing after the first trimester.
>
> Some people have more than two nipples. That is because we used to have litters, which we now call quadruplets, quintuplets, etc.

NINTH AND LAST. FREEDOM, PARITY, AND POSTERITY ARE NOT COVALENT

We have talked of what we share with other animals. Some cultures have a higher incidence of crime and mental illness and different problems with them. When this is so, that particular crime or mental illness does not make criminals or patients more or less like animals. They are unlike other animals because they were brought up differently as human beings.

> If intentional homicide is higher south of Canada and north of Mexico, then homicide is uniquely human. *(c/19)* If crime and punishment varies from place to place, then all penology is uniquely human. If psychoanalysis is more popular with certain groups, its promise of undoing past mistakes is uniquely human. *(c/20)*
>
> Highly condensed, above paragraphs introduce an alternative approach to behavior that we have started calling rationalysis. *(c/21)* We can now supplant with rationalysis the one-upmanship inherent in psychoanalysis, and with absolute or wholistic relativity the condescension of parochial or cultural relativism.]

What is an even more revolutionary discovery is that animals are more interested in liberty than human beings. *(c/22)* We are more interested in equality before the Last Judgment, the laws of the land *(c/23)*, the forces of commerce, etc. Plants and animals are more interested in sex, while human beings are more interested in *erotica*.

[A second-rate painter and better-known biologist, Desmond Morris, explains erotic behavior as pair-bonding techniques in order to keep a couple together to raise their children who are born serially instead of all at once. But birds pair off even if their eggs hatch at the same time while mammals with litters often do not.]

There is always conflict between liberty and morality, between (**A**) freedom to feel and being good, (**B**) freedom to try and being right, (**C**) freedom to think and being true to one's beliefs, (**D**) freedom to compare and being liked, (**E**) freedom to be original and being accepted. Judges cannot legalize, justify, or adjudicate morality. *(c/24)*

There is always conflict between societies about equality. Our history is a series of wars between competing forces with fanatical ideologies about who provides more equal opportunities before God, the law, the marketplace, etc.

The conflict between sex and eroticism is a measure of our ignorance about both. Sex is reproductive; eroticism is foreplay. This distinction is more acceptable to grandparents who have outlived the battle of the sexes than to many kids and adults who are still battling for sexual rights and privileges.

Plants are not very interested in sexual foreplay beyond displaying themselves in the best possible light. Animals practice grooming by licking each other with tenderness, but they do not forget that kissing each other is just foreplay, or getting better acquainted. To them neither is enough—consummation is requisite.

Even after they have been weaned, cats still suckle from their mothers' breast and knead them just as I did. With human beings, foreplay is what mothers themselves do with their infants sans milk. It is called love and care of the young to prepare them for love and care of their young to have whom they must have sex.

In psychiatry we need to distinguish between what is oedipal, which is foreplay in fantasy or fact, and incest which is sexual nepotism. At work, incestuous nepotism has been called, by rival interests, sexual harassment of the subordinate by *his/her* superior, even when confined to foreplay without possibility of consummation, where one cannot get pregnant, or they share gender. Is that because only men and women can be raped, which requires penile insertion without consent?

Homo domesticus would much rather be a matriarch than a mother. *(c/25)* Who would rather be patriots for the fatherland fighting for the flag than "matriots" for Mother Earth working to preserve the planet? *(c/26)*

No animal except *Homo metropolus* would rather become a patriarch than be a father to as many as he can sire, publicly or privately. *(c/27)*

If *Homo metropolus* are less like other animals, will this subspecies survive the pressure for parity in the pursuit of liberty through medical or surgical contraception and the technotronics of mass murder?

SUMMARY AND CONCLUSIONS

To summarize, whether as predator or prey, we are all born in essential harmony with our endowments and environment. Human life at any age, time, or place is a struggle also to harmonize sensuality with morality, society with equality, and sexuality with eroticism or procreation with recreation. In this we are unique as a species. No other animals strive for this highly artificial harmony.

All animals are born free. Human beings are born more dependent on others than other animals. No animals except human beings and some domesticated animals aspire to be equal to each other.

Egalitarian ideologies act like addictive drugs, infectious brain fevers, or sexually transmitted diseases, needing basic research to keep from spreading. Believing is toxic.

The ABZs of life shows us how domesticated we are as we give up our freedom for the sake of equal access to those who are superior to us in fact or fancy, whether it be a possessive Godfather (**F**) or powerful governors (**G**) or profiteering preserves (Swiss or Caribbean banks) (**H**) or any other special "establishment" *(c/13)* from (**I**) to (**O**) or automation.

Liberty and equality are reciprocal, each subtracting from the other; but both, like love and eroticism, should serve sex.

Instead of carefully domesticating those whom we condescend to breed, can clever *Homo sapiens* feed more people by scientific farming of barren lands and by aquaculture of even vaster stretches of water?

Only with domestication and breeding, after brainwashing and brain-stuffing, have *Homo domesticus* and *metropolus* succeeded in creating a temporary imbalance in the cosmos. But this is very temporary. The universe will eventually regain its equilibrium, with or without us, or the universe that we now know does not exist at all.

Can we turn back the clock of evolution? That would be an unnatural struggle for survival. But we can stop being pompous or pugnacious and punitive to prove that we are special.

Can we listen more closely to what our body has to say, since it has been around longer than our brain? Would it not be better for our planet if we treated our cortex as a bright but not very smart administrative assistant that we can train to procure essential supplies with ingenuity to reduce the wear and tear on our bodies?

Without brainwashing and brain-stuffing, and mental fornication and intellectual masturbation *(c/1)*, can we begin to see that needing to be free is instinctive, wanting to be equal is infectious, wishing to have sex and children is unselfish and learning to be erotic is self-indulgent foreplay? None of these is (**A'**) bad, (**B'**) wrong, or (**C'**) illusory. In the ABZs of life, that just happens to be the way it is, as human subspecies behaviors evolve.

In conclusion, I have discussed some sanitized discoveries in the evolution of universal and global behavior, which I now dedicate to a bold and brave, undomesticated and unenvious but venturesome generation. By disregarding Ptolemy, logic, etc.—and, as surviving *Homo sapiens,* interested in what is revolutionary, even at the risk of being destabilized—we have reached out to the moon. Some of our findings may be disturbing to *Homo domesticus* (believer in the status quo*)* and to *Homo metropolus* (who is prone to be jealous, like the prickly God of the Jews). *(c/6)*

We now know more about brains and bureaucracies, experimentation and scientific thinking, paranoids and physiology, mothering and mobility, becoming and begetting, nurseries and nursing, bedrooms and retirement homes, primates and mammals, pecking orders and prostitution, Godfathers and Big Brothers, history and recycling, territoriality and imperialism, smothering and pedophilia, masturbation and bestiality, sensual and social typology, cultural and absolute relativity, liberty and equality, recreation and procreation, oedipal foreplay and incestuous nepotism, matriarchs and matriots, patriarchs and patriots, natural order and artificial harmony.

Can you still grasp or pinch with your big toe and the next one to it like I can, just as we all can with an opposable thumb and index finger?

Can you see where we are more like each other than we are different, but that I am more like animals than I am like you?

3.00 c/PREFACE

c/Chapter Notes

[c/1] The brain is a bureaucrat. Bureaucrats sometimes silence their meddlesome brains with drugs or bullets.

Others who are convinced that their guts have dishonored their more gutsy ancestors commit hara-kiri with a sword in their belly, with or without assistance.

Our brain behaves like a bureaucrat when it reels off red tape by quoting dead writers or popular philosophers. This is not mind-jerking but a marriage of convenience with other minds embalmed in libraries. I call it mental fornication. It keeps the idle mind occupied but does not produce, just as masturbation passes the time but does not procreate. Fiction laced with pornography pays off.

Self-serving claims of authenticity (that only the claimants are genuine and spiritual but not supernatural) imply that others are inauthentic (spurious even if spirited). In fact both statements are synthetic (artificial but not unnatural) in being unoriginal.

[c/2] Psychiatrists who depend on either or both philosophy and fiction are wearing blinders. They try to fill the gaps in their experience with stories and the gaps in their knowledge with argument. Clinically, we can only compare our patients with real people—not with mythical heroes like King Oedipus—or the heroic with each other.

We can compare live "heroes" like Lt. Col. Ollie North (after he was fired from the US National Security Council) with the late Jimmy Ongpin of the Philippines (who stood tall against ex-president Marcos but committed suicide after resignation under pressure from President Aquino's cabinet). Both heroes were deeply religious and quite patriotic yet turned in different and opposite performances after they were displaced. Both had access to guns. Jimmy surprised his friends that he owned a gun and used it to destroy his brain. On the day of his suicide, he had lunch with cronies who did not notice any loss of enjoyment of food. His sensual and social life had not made them suspect suicidal tendencies. (Senso-socio-sexual rationalysis allows other questions to be asked: had he become impotent under stress?)

[c/3] A parrot once flew inside one of our state prisons. It almost triggered a riot among the inmates by its haunting, taunting chant: "I can talk. Can you fly?"

Before my grandchildren could talk, I noticed that whenever I repeated their vocalizations (which is what psychiatrists do when we do not want to interrupt a patient's trend of thought), they acted as if I understood what they meant.

This started me talking to birds in their language by whistling the sounds they make when I go to our mailbox a quarter of a mile downhill. By the time I get there and all the way back, more will have joined with their bird songs, and we can get a veritable concert going.

Don't you think it was a terrible mistake to ignore our children's early vocalization and replace it with verbalization? In psychiatry we cannot go back to the time before any of us learned our second language. Yet we know that preverbal experiences are more important than those we now have words for.

Though human intercourse specializes in talking, my fellow psychiatrists are often accused of not talking enough. We do not just listen to what is said but also try to hear what has been omitted, or wait to see what the body language says that the speaker denies outright or defends against automatically.

[c/4] Believing is like being an AIDS victim, seeking desperately to hold on against reality. (It is better to approve than to believe.) Smoking, like believing, is a sign of weakness. (Seventy-six percent who try to quit fail. The weak either succumbs to peer pressure, as in other forms of substance abuse, or finds other sources of reassurance right away, e.g., in religion or other ideology.)

[c/5] Philosophers are fond of arguing that God must exist by using the conventional analogy that all our watches also needed their makers. St. Thomas Aquinas carelessly accepted *causa efficiens* literally as "cause" when *poiesis* (as in "mythopoiesis" or mythmaking) was intended by the Greeks to mean "responsible for."

The modern watchmaker must, therefore, be held responsible for the digital clock that is made of synthetic materials ("indebted to" matter or *causa materialis*), digital in design or form (*causa formalis*) and more accurate (not "correct" or right) than grandfather clocks in keeping time (*causa finalis* or final cause).

Are we just clocks automatically ticking away?

[c/6] Only domesticated animals, children, and God learn to be jealous. In the West, where children don't even get to sleep with their mothers, their God who created them in His image is even more jealous than any Buddhist in the Orient can understand.

[c/7] Why are human beings the only animals who build homes for grown-ups? All other animals build nests only for their young.

[c/8] My mother and my wet nurse, between them, had four breasts for nursing me, hungry or not. As a kid, if my parents displeased me, I could go on a hunger strike like Mahatma Gandhi and consent to come to the table only after they made amends. This tactic cannot often succeed in countries where children are ordered to leave the table, and go to their room to sleep without dinner, whenever they cannot please their parents.

I am therefore neither surprised nor scandalized when there is widespread food abuse and misuse of sleeping pills.

If their early childhood refuge felt like a prison, where hungry children are sent when they are naughty, is it surprising that a great many—as soon as they can afford it—move around a lot, and later choose to retire as far from home as the coastlines will allow?

Or do they also want to be closer to the ocean where our old amphibian ancestors came ashore? Probably both.

Are those who live on the water, on houseboats or yachts, closer to their animal nature than those who live inland? And those who occupy high ground more like birds who must scan for prey below?

[c/9] In some cultures, if puberty leads to pregnancy, coming of age becomes juvenile delinquency. In any herd or flock, animal or human, "becoming" leads to "begetting" before "being."

[c/10] In California, I started designing houses for families with teenagers, in order to separate them from their elders. If their paths do not always cross when they need to hide something from each other, fantasies cannot feed on renewed suspicions, and many unnecessary domestic quarrels are avoided.

[c/11] Do all primates obey Auguste Comte's Law of the Three Stages of Intellectual Development? These are (1, 2) theological (or supernatural) and metaphysical (or ideal)—when they do not know the natural causes of things—and (3) natural (or phenomenological). Are thinking about (1) heaven, (2) utopia, and (3) nature the steps that believers, dreamers, and realists climb before they can be scientists without bias?

When God chooses to be passive, some of us wonder whether He is deaf or dead. Are comets missiles from heaven hurled in anger at a wicked world? Can Satan or theologians drive us insane?

How many at first (1) simply (A) attribute to things (B) wills like our own, in which case (C) theory becomes (F) theology unless (D) tested, then (2) metaphysically think that everything is derived from transformation of (i) fundamental energies or (ii) indispensable ("plausible") ideas, but do not (3) scientifically observe, (E) hypothesize, and (D) disprove?

[c/12] Can we teach other species or machines to be as literate as the least of us? Some gorillas have been taught the sign language for the deaf and can even invent names for fruits that they see for the first time. We can certainly program our computers to be more accurate than our children and employees.

[c/13] If our history is a perpetual calendar of oft-repeated but well-reasoned errors, we cannot learn from it. (Academics who teach history just fill in classroom time.) If history repeats itself, we cannot also learn from present perceptions unless we screen them for hidden agendas, or priorities decided by the past ("principles") rather than by emerging opportunities. Is pragmatic better than principled? (The principled are prisoners under agendas or priorities decided by the past ["principles"] rather than by emerging opportunities.) Is pragmatic better than principled? (The principled are prisoners under a life sentence, or slaves in indentured service to past masters.)

Then we must explore the developmental rut—which their rhetorical questions and favorite jokes disclose—where the principled simply stagnate.

Questions and jokes reveal pride in or fear of (F) God, (G) leaders, (H) wealth, (I) individuality, (J) race or subgroup, (K) skills or career, (L) origins or mission, (M) dependence or mastery, (N) other species, or (O) better-programmed machines.

[c/14] Many are still trying to resurrect the ghost of Virgin Mary, Mother of the Son of God, to intercede for them before an unreachable force. Like Freud who would deny that he was Freudian, Jesus never called himself Christ or Christian, or said he was a permanent member of the Holy Trinity. He claimed to have sole access to his Father but never that if Eve was our mother, his was a holy virgin. (He is both a demigod, and son and grandson [two votes], a trinity with God). Unlike Mohammed who proclaimed himself the only prophet, Jesus was always ambiguous about being God's messenger or the long-awaited Messiah, whenever he was asked directly.

[c/15] I lined up three piles of grain six feet apart, and sure enough, our dominant peacock started to chase away the nondominant one who had started feeding at the other end. But he stopped at the middle pile of grain and left the other alone in order to feed himself. He was hungry but not greedy. Only human beings can be consumed by greed, and then they are not only territorial but also empire builders. Imperialism feeds on human greed.

(Deprivation produces greed. We have two permanent bird-feed and watering stations aloft, five basins for fresh water for the unfeathered, sixteen dishes for cat food inside and five outside the carport "cathouse"— some do not like to share their plates—one deep milk bowl indoors for extra nourishment and a shallow one outdoors for treats besides diced cheese daily. Food and care can victimize and domesticate animals and people only if we expect payback. It is better just to give.)

[c/16] "I am not I but Am" is often quoted to imply "I am not only I but am your Father." Erikson was preoccupied with identity (identification) because he could not say, "I am not only I but also Erik's son."

Erikson never knew his father, only his father's son.

[c/17] Unthinking philosophers since Descartes have separated the mind from the body in order to (1) pose a dichotomy ("A is not not A, and never the "twain shall meet"), and then (2) exercise the deductive syllogism of the Greeks. [Indian logic from which it came is additionally inductive, and explores not just causes but sequences, processes or circuitry.]

Mistranslated everywhere, Cartesian cogitation (doubting) has been confused with cognition (thinking). [Sartre, a French existentialist, even divides doubting to prove the primacy of existence ("am") over essence ("I"): "Descartes had confused spontaneous doubt, which is consciousness, with methodological doubting, which is an act. 'I doubt, therefore I think' becomes 'I am aware (cognitive) that I doubt, therefore I am.'"]

[c/18] Life, like REM sleep, starts in the brain stem (which controls all our vital functions), but we assign it meaning just like that which we read into our dreams. (*Amer. J. Psychiatry*, article on the meaninglessness of REM dreams evoked more reaction than any in its history.)

Parasympathetic inhibition allows the heart to maintain its rate despite faster breathing during REM sleep and wet dreams.

Those who need to find meaning are bored with themselves or looking for something to interest them. To lose interest in anything is to find it meaningless. (Meaning is here used to mean significance or importance, not relevance.)

[c/19] If there was no law against fratricide in their lifetime, does Abel's death only teach us that Cain was not his brother's keeper? Or that the good die young (before they can go bad), and the bad live on to build a better life? (Cain in exile founded Enoch, the first city, from which we have derived the word "civilization.")

[c/20] Mothering without smothering is caregiving without caretaking or healing without leaning. Patients who need healing from caregivers become passionate (e-motional) when immobilized and cannot help themselves, but only caretakers need clients to lean on them.

[c/21] Rationalysis and its clinical findings and results were first presented before the Second Pacific Congress of Transcultural Psychiatry. At that time, "transcultural psychiatry" was thought to mean respect for cultural relativity, since patients from different cultures have to be treated with professional tolerance toward their cherished traditions.

The paper I presented was my first serious challenge to entrenched interests. I suggested that (1) "transcultural" (as distinguished from "cross-cultural") could be limited to imply "a learned ability to transcend culture itself, at any place, at any time." Even our belief systems are not exclusively con-specific (limited to our species). If they were elaborated by the forebrain in prehistoric man, they must have been shared by other primates and are not exclusively the product of human civilization. Simply (2) to accept all cultural traditions is to be personally condescending or clinically self-defeating, since all those with traditional values either covertly accuse others or say to them, "I'm okay."

Psychiatrists who were not also students of ethology, sociology, and anthropology could not accept my criticism of cultural relativity as being more self-serving than practical. It alienated them even more when I reported that in orienting physicians from all over the world to our postgraduate training program in psychiatry, I try quite literally but carefully, and indirectly, to "demoralize" them:

I caution our trainees not to expect from their patients what their friends before entering medical school had accepted as good or bad, right or wrong, or true or false. Or else the fees that they charge as clinicians will be earned by just being unlicensed proxies of their parents and their culture. Their immediate "demoralization" was therefore necessary to achieve the requisite deculturation for clinical rationalysis.

Love (**A**) is sold by the smug as a panacea and domesticated by the insecure who need it to live. Substitutes for love (**A'**) can (a) dominate our ability to (**B**) test limits, (**C**) think of alternative answers, (**D**) compare findings, and (**E**) be creative. Domestication by (**F–O**) beliefs in (**F**) God (the Santa Claus for adults) or (**G**) the state or (**H**) money or (**I**) autonomy or (**J**) associations or (**K**) technology or (**L**) humanity or (**M**) ecology or (**N**) ethology or (**O**) electronics can also (b) separately interfere with

(**P–Y**) breeding except in the practice of animal husbandry (eugenics), if not (c) deprive us altogether of (**Z**) grandparenthood.

[c/22] Because we live close to nature, I happened to catch a centipede as I was closing a sliding glass door. Before I could reopen it, he regained his freedom without begging by sawing himself in two. It was then that I realized what I did not like about Patrick Henry demanding from the British, "Give me liberty or give me death."

Our centipede knew that it is its own responsibility to stay free, not another's duty to provide unconditionally. (When can you drop which hero from your pantheon of heroes?)

[c/23] If we tend to hold the government answerable for our well-being, it may be to absolve both God and ourselves of any accountability. Growing up, we slowly learned that we are not responsible for what our parents do, unlike abused children who accuse themselves when their parents mistreat them or each other. But *Homo domestici* still tend to blame themselves, not God, for what he has wrought.

[c/24] What is (**A'**) bad (denying people what is yours that they need more) may not be (**B'**) wrong (denying them what is theirs that you need more), and what is wrong may not be (**C'**) false (claiming that they want only what you refused to return). Like absolute truth, falsehood is illusory, even if entombed in code or consensus. What is good or right or true may be mixed up with each other and with *(iii)* sex, just as *(i)* liberty (for minorities) is confused with *(ii)* democracy (majority rule).

[c/25] Animals never get pregnant against their wishes, because they are freer to flee or fly than we are. (Does this make a rapist proud in penetration and sex a source of shame for us?)

In the wilds, where *alpha* males corner the market for females, those who cohabit with nondominant males try not to make any sounds while they engage in illicit sex.

(Do animals experience shame or just don't want to risk retaliation with "their pants down"? Is shame more than prudence in the face of potential retaliation that fear of/or forceful rejection/ejection can produce?)

[c/26] To centralize decision-making in the human cortex—which is prone to take over anyway, like a bureaucrat—is to deprive the older parts of us of the autonomy that these organs had always enjoyed before inverted skin became ganglia and then a central nervous system.

[c/27] Was President Aquino's ex-mentor and first supporter, Jimmy Ongpin, who shot himself in the head, doomed by being bureaucratized into a social eunuch, compared to another hero, Col. Ollie North, who deftly defied bureaucrats? Or did Jimmy take his troubles home to bed? His last public act that has been posthumously known was the transfer of control of his wealth from his wife to his son.

4.00 d/GLOBAL OVERVIEW

Seek simplicity and distrust it.
—Alfred North Whitehead

Succinctness passes the taste test if it does not challenge what has previously been mastered nor include what has always been avoided.
—M. J. Ortega, MD

All About Behavior Across Time and Dogma

People are different from other animals in their ability to learn without thinking for themselves. This makes it easy to train them to talk, read, write, and copy. As copycats of what is saleable in stories, speech, slogans, fads, or fashion, people have no equal.

A few among animals are as creative as the exceptional among us, e.g., one macaque monkey who taught others to separate grain from sand by dumping them in water, or chimpanzees who have learned to fish for termites deep in their nests with twigs stripped of leaves to which they cling and from which they are plucked by the tongue, or our cat (SK) who "designed" a wedge out of a doormat to pry open wider a sliding door that had been left ajar.

We have, throughout the ages, substituted dogmas for animal instincts, and founded cultures on such doctrines. In modern times we have substituted slogans for older revelations. Through both, we convince ourselves that our shorter history surpasses that of older animals. How short our history turns out will decide if our conviction of superiority is deceptive illusion or simple self-serving delusion. Or whether there is a timeless difference between sentiment and science.

Past and Present Science Fictions?

After copyrighting *Absolute Relativity*, with the offhand aside that an alternative explanation for our common biochemistry is that chimpanzees might be our descendants, archeologists claim to have exhumed a 17-million-year-old skeleton of an orangutan in Africa. We have many more features in common with what the natives of Borneo call the man of the forest, but because we traditionally trace our origins to the African continent, we thought we belonged with the gibbons, gorillas, and chimpanzees, since orangutans were believed to have evolved after Africa was separated from the other land masses by water. Now it will be more respectable to wonder if the African apes and we are not descendants of orangutans.

(Chimps and orangs, like us, recognize their reflected image in a mirror with self-consciousness.) Which transforms our Oriental grandparents into the living fossils of Borneo. (Orangs also attempt rape.)

Then we can think of our African aunts and uncles as underdeveloped in their spiritual, political, and economic practices, and of ourselves as overdomesticated to the point of alienation. Instead of speciesism or human racism, which, like other "-isms," is plausible but fallacious, we can be more discriminating and speak of sub- and species differentiation to explain our cultural evolution.

It is scholarly but not helpful to cite *Homo habilis* (for Neanderthals) and *Homo erectus* (for Cro-Magnons) as predecessors (DNA-identical or not), once our brain got so large as to shorten pregnancy and prolong infancy beyond those of any other primate. (Computer storage capacity is likewise disproportionately larger than available or needed information.) This divergence has derailed natural selection at our expense—only temporarily, I hope—in favor of narrow parental and social bias that mandates puritan genital mutilation (early circumcision and clitoridectory), family brainwashing, and public brain-stuffing. We must now look *(see Table 16)* at three subspecies (Homo sapiens [ingenious and resourceful], *Homo domesticus* [intimidated and righteous], and *Homo metropolus* [ingenuous and litigious]).

(The following play antedated above discoveries of the African orangutan or the three human subspecies.)

Interactive Foreplay: A Conversational Chess Game

(As in traditional chess, all the pieces make predictable moves [speeches], but the outcome is not often expectable. You can insert comments to make the play go your preferred way as *H. sapiens*, *domesticus* or *metropolus*.)

"The world is a prop for all things, large or small."

On the stage are five armchairs arranged in a semicircle. Seated in the middle is the psychiatrist-moderator of a fictional panel of discussants about human evolution.

Psychiatrist: Good evening, panel and ladies and gentlemen. I am a psychiatrist and your moderator for this conference on the evolution of behavior. When we were growing up, we read of animals who talked in Aesop's Fables. Recently there was a startling report that plants also can communicate, especially in times of distress. Communication is especially important for those who are afraid of surprises, for whatever reason.

As adults, we heard a famous scientist claim that science is rooted in conversation. He is famous for discovering the uncertainty principle in nuclear physics, for which he won the Nobel Prize in 1932. He is no other than Werner Heisenberg, one of the founders of the quantum theory.

Heisenberg learned a lot from working with atoms. In *Brave New World* (1984), surely we can ask people and other animals what they think about, and even try to talk to atoms. Tonight we will ask the atom to speak first and let the other members of the panel introduce themselves before they speak.

Atom: Where did I come from?

Astronomer:　　I am an astronomer. We can now make some educated guesses. In the beginning there was just energy, but like all power, it needs elbow room, and so it expanded and created space and time. As it ballooned to bursting point, expansion was followed by explosion, which fragmented energy into particles of matter, large and small, scattered and suspended in space, and that's how you were born, out of violence.

Atom:　　I can take it from there. The Greeks thought I was the smallest indivisible particle when all I was is better described by what Americans call uptight. And then Einstein came along and wondered where all the cosmic energy went, and his American friends split me open to find out.

Animal:　　I am an animal, but we had evolved into many different species by the time of Einstein. Is he not one of our better mutations?

Individualist:　　I am an individualist. I think Einstein is one of the best, but not a mutant. Mutant or not, long before his conception, we had already sold the world on the human ideal of indivisible individuality.

Psychiatrist:　　And then biologists discovered that we were all just collections of individual cells.

Animal:　　Like me.

Astronomer:　　Each cell contains a nucleus that behaves like a star in a galaxy of cells.

Individualist:　　And now I am left with just my mind to separate me from animals.

Psychiatrist: And my colleagues in neurology, who still deign to speak to psychiatrists, tell me that the mind is only a working brain.

Animal: Don't I have a mind too?

Individualist: Can you appreciate truth?

Atom: What is that?

Astronomer: He does not know he only means facts.

Psychiatrist,   *smiling*: Before there was truth, there was only sex and virtue.

Individualist: I know all about you psychiatrists. Everything comes down to sex.

Psychiatrist,   *immoderately*: Only for sexual hypochondriacs who are mystical about sex being involved in nearly everything that we do. If I can now finish what I started to say, the story was that in the mythical Garden of Eden, there was only sex and virtue. And then God came visiting and made a virtue out of innocence and separated it from knowledge.

Atom: Who is God?

Animal: He invented sex so that we can multiply.

Individualist: He is also the Fountain of Knowledge.

Atom: Is he therefore far from innocent?

Astronomer: He is a connoisseur of all that is evil.

Psychiatrist: Anyway, nobody bothered to tell the Greeks that God hated dissenters, and so their philosophers kept on telling everyone who would stop to listen that virtue and truth were one and indivisible. Until I came along and discovered that good and bad sentiments and right and wrong conduct are different from true or false concepts.

Astronomer: That is important. God himself cannot judge facts because that would merely be validating his knowledge. It would be like checking your wallet when there are no pickpockets to suspect of theft. God can only judge what we call virtues and values, because they alone are man-made.

Psychiatrist: I don't even think we get to choose our virtues or values.

Individualist: I agree. We can be brainwashed into believing money is good value.

Astronomer,   *addressing moderator*: I suspect you have something up your sleeve about freedom of choice being different from the right to consume.

Psychiatrist: Well, Freud says we cannot even choose what to remember.

Animal: There goes the mind that my friend here (patting the individualist on his thigh) is so proud of.

Psychiatrist: We are all unique, but only in the singular. The bigger the grouping, the more we share.

Individualist: You are being coy.

Psychiatrist: It sounds that way, does it not? I am really waiting to hear in what ways animals surpass us.

Individualist: In what way do you think we are not like atoms and animals?

Psychiatrist: In a nutshell, we are con-substantial with atoms, con-natural with animals, and con-specific with prehistoric and modern man.

(Our terminology has since been changed to avoid the suggestion of "trans-substantiation". The author considered "con-materiality" and decided it was too materialistic. Because of his contempt for "-isms" and his respect, if not love, for nature, he decided to upgrade "con-naturality" and substitute "con-viviality" for it, to refer to all living plants and animals, with whom, as a human family, we are not con-familiar.)

Animal,   *addressing astronomer*: Did you understand what he just said?

Astronomer: Well . . . he's saying all of us have nothing that the atom does not have, except what is common between us and animals, and nothing between us and animals that they don't have except what is common between primitive and civilized men.

Individualist: Isn't that just another way of saying that we're superior to animals, and animals are superior to atoms?

Psychiatrist: If you like. But differences are definable and verifiable, while superiority is a matter of definition and ascription.

Animal: Wow! I can never imagine myself using words like that.

Atom,   *addressing the last speaker*: Remember, they are just
                   talking. When it comes to proving, they have to come
                   to you and me.

Psychiatrist: That's right, to find out if nature is biased toward
                   human beings.

Individualist: What other abilities do animals claim to have?

Animal: The moderator knew a cousin of mine who can make
                   noise from heaven disappear by rattling his cage.

Psychiatrist: His captors could hear an airplane overhead while he
                   rattled his cage, but he continued doing it even if they
                   could no longer hear the plane. And then he began
                   strutting about and drumming his chest like Tarzan,
                   as if to celebrate his success in silencing the ungodly
                   noise.

Animal: We can also play politics, including sexual politics,
                   and our sexual politics is as self-serving as your free-
                   market economy.

Astronomer: Now you have me thoroughly mystified. You have
                   political and economic impulses? Do animals also
                   believe in spirits?

Psychiatrist: If "spiritual" means a "lapdog mentality," yes. *(d/1)* But
                   I had two proud peacocks that refused to be pets and
                   cannot be treated like lapdogs of any god or deity. To
                   find out how autonomous they can be, I had to think
                   of the very simplest test of territoriality:

                   We always made sure that the less dominant peacock
                   does not starve, but once I felt inspired to put three
                   separate piles of grain in a straight line six feet apart.

As soon as the dominant one saw the other pecking at the furthest pile, he stopped feeding and started to chase him away but did not get past the middle pile, where he stopped to resume feeding. Territoriality can exist without greed or lust for power or followers.

We were lucky that no peahens were around for either peacock to impress, for then the economics of feeding, when hungry, would be contaminated by sexual politics, when horny.

Animal: Ordinarily the strongest male hoards our females to himself. But in captivity, our economics becomes politicized into a system of barter for sexual favors, and so we end up with the oldest profession in the world. Whoever has learned his computer instructions well and earned the most tokens to throw away gets any available female.

Psychiatrist: Among us, power bought with money does not appeal to women who are not greedy. Their lust is satisfied by pimps who are not power brokers but sex merchants. Women who do not need middlemen marry sugar daddies and have lovers. Those who are not lusty get fat or drunk. The saintly become mothers, and we owe them our very lives.

Animal: In your second oldest profession, we are also becoming adept. Caged and subsidized, the unpromiscuous among us tend to use their children as exclusive love objects and smother them with affection and expectations, like some Jewish mothers who cannot be adulterers. Now I am talking like our moderator. How about that?

Astronomer: It does make sense that different groupings produce different skills. And those who develop speech learn it while sitting in their mother's lap. Do boys who are mothered by smotherers and expected to be responsive grow up to be better talkers?

Psychiatrist,   *evasively*: A long time ago I tried to distinguish between communication of signals for hunting even among a pack of hyenas, and communion between the sexes who are face-to-face during sexual union *(d/2)*, unlike other primates. If there is no physical union, then we have the battle of the sexes.

Individualist,   *incensed*: Now you are trying to explain away our being the only species gifted with speech. Just because we talk to our mothers and to our loved ones during foreplay cannot altogether explain our ability to talk.

                   (While single-handedly building a multilevel tree house for his grandchildren, author added another motivation for talking: Resourceful ingenuity is much slower than coordinated teamwork from helping hands. Alone with pulleys and clamps, it took six months.

Animal: Without hyperbole, you can talk only because of your voice box. We ourselves can learn to communicate by sign language like the deaf who cannot hear sounds or like the mute with a silent voice box. Given the same opportunity, pound for pound in brain weight, I can communicate better than a child.

Astronomer: And now even computers can chatter to each other in our absence.

Atom: And so, with proper care and feeding, even atoms without natural intelligence are capable of intelligent conversation. In fact our conversation, if not our programming, is more intelligible than that of our moderator.

Animal: But even robots who can talk do not know that what they can see, which is not as dark as the rest of a wall, is a window. Whereas animals and children seem to have that knowledge already stored in their brain. Computers can only learn what can be transmitted by symbols.

Individualist: That is why robots can never equal us in intelligence.

Astronomer: Just like a child needs compulsory education, so can a chess-playing robot improve his performance with better programmers.

Animal: But all they can program are what can be translated into symbols by thinking about it. Yet most of our intuitions are untranslatable into language. That is why intelligence can be transferred (as in spying) but not as wisdom, which we learn only in the art of living.

Psychiatrist,   *smiling to himself*: I think this is a good place to stop, for now. We are back where we began. We can increase our intelligence by talking but not be any wiser afterward. Addiction to symbols is like being just drunk enough to keep looking for a dropped coin but only under a streetlight at night. Enlightenment is finding what is not lit up. Symbolic achievement is different but not superior, beliefs to the contrary notwithstanding.

What we have invented words for—to reach for the stars in our minds—atoms and animals do not need or want. We invented writing around 3,000 BC to help more of us talk about us, but has it kept us from making the same errors atoms and animal avoid without words?

Thank you, panel and ladies and gentlemen, for listening.

(Below is a more serious three-act play starring nature in the first, animals in the second, and people in the third.)

Act I. Observing Nature

Some speeches begin with an old joke but end with a new punch line. That is because information increases dissonance; only the familiar produces reassuring resonance. Familiarity is like a celebrity, welcome if recognized, irrespective of merit. This is why TV news feature celebrities. Thusly, does early morning news compete with the familiar, and late-evening TV is anchored by established comedians joking about the news to keep their viewers awake.

Information is better transmitted (1) chemically as in genetics (our brain also relies on neurochemical transmission), (2) electronically as in automation (or intelligence gathering by orbiting satellites), or by (3) written numeral or musical symbols, than by (4) animal vocalization, which can be used to mislead predators, or (5) oral verbalization and, least well, by (6) every backyard gossip, including investigative reports (for faceless strangers), which need only submit to the test of legal fiction for veracity or plausibility: testified beliefs (originally recited while holding the testes) count as court evidence and all precedent opinions as judicial decisions! *(d/3)*

There is both a reason and a remedy for communication being mistaken for information. We can diagnose and cure ourselves of this predilection for, and addiction to, unexamined redundancies as facts ("faction").

Psychiatrists do not listen as much as read between the lines to hear what is not said. That is how at first we inform ourselves about what is new, which we can later clearly communicate as old news . . . *(d/4)*

To bypass shored-up defenses against disturbing information, I have tried to be lyrical ("Cosmic Mothering," below, has been set to music)— about (**I**) nature and nurture (universal con-naturality), narrative about (**II**) living with other species (general con-viviality) and explicit about (**III**) teaching/learning by doing (specific con-familiarity).

Prose cannot succinctly encompass both (1) emotion and reason, (2) contentions and conclusions, (3) analogies and communication as persuasion, and (4) homologies and information as education. *(d/5)*

(The witty are often more wimpy than meaty.)

Can old reasons (fine vocal art-form as rhetoric) resist new rhymes?

Cosmic Mothering

The universe is deaf / Not indifferent:
It's a Super-Bowl / Not a Wailing Wall,
And our life in it / Just another noise,
That softly echoes / An older Big Bang.

Our cosmos dictates / How we all play,
But never to a tie, / Nor to win or lose,
Since we were born / To mate and beget,
By uniting to divide / Before we die,
Only to be reborn / With another cry.

Need we feel unwelcome / And forever lost
Because we were hurt / Before we could breathe?
As we sink or swim, / Does Mother Nature care?
If the cosmos does or not, / Should it really matter?

Our heads got too big for painless labor. Forcibly evicted from the cozy cocoon of a womb, some *Homo sapi*ens find themselves, head hurting, in a strange nursery, longing for their absentee mother unlike the newborn of other species: twin grizzly bears suckle on demand for thirty months or more.

To be alone for hours before one is wise enough to know what is missing, dooms one to (1) a chronic need to belong to, by believing in, very strange groups who need befriending—by offering one's heart and mind to be enslaved for the duration—and to (2) a longing to make a difference! Some *H. domesticus* believers become silent and closet bullies on the way to becoming *H. metropolus*. In the process, those believers who become bullies unwittingly abuse technology and pollute the environment by commuting in the privacy of a gas-guzzling car, now their secret cocoon.

By commuting and polluting with industrial-age machines—at a time when business can be taken care of at home with postindustrial electronic devices—they clog public highways with such substitute nurseries to get ahead of those who need nature more, like they did their own mothers as infants. In Silicon Valley, the computer capital of the world, concern over children's education is overshadowed by preoccupation with heavy traffic going to and from and past their satellite cities. (Other impotently envious pursuits are political journalism and art criticism. Cheering a sports team is tantamount to saying, "My father can beat your father" to a fellow bully.)

Is Mother Earth just a parent but not ours alone, nor the beginning or the end? Did the first light come right before the Big Bang went unheard? (There was light before there were receptors for visible light waves.)

Were protozoa created along with instructions for the construction of electron microscopes? (A droplet of seawater is cosmic in scale compared to our cells.)

Mothering Marathon (does Nature nurture?): From Sea to Cell to Child

A truly ideal mother / Hugs without squeezing, /
Grasps without gripping, / And lets go without losing.
The ocean was our Eden. / A protozoa our Eve, /
Pudgy "pseudo-pods" our feet, / Slender whips our fins.
Suspended in salty water, / A single egg ripens, /
To burst forth and meet / The swiftest sperm.

In an outside sac, / It had kept its "cool" /
Before forced eviction / Without warning.
Halved in genes, / It needed protection /
Before being cast out, / To mate or die.

Swimming upstream, / It left far behind, /
Millions of comrades, / Deformed, tired, or dying,
To rush deeper inside. / And bury its head in an egg, /
The child of their union / Left stranded afloat.

From this aquatic race / Run by Eve's sisters /
With unwritten rules, / A zygote results.

Unsexed for weeks, / A penis might show; /
Amphibious for months, / It is forced to breathe.
Crushed out of shape, / It cries out in pain and fear /
With its first breath / Under bright lights.
Codependent but alone, / Vulnerable outside its nest, /
Instinctively struggling as Homo sapiens,
Ready to submit as Homo domesticus,
Or fight its fate as Homo metropolus.

As *Homo sapiens,* taped recordings of blood circulating in the maternal womb from which they were prematurely torn quickly stop a newborn's fretting. Even as adults, we can still be soothed by the trickle or rush of moving water.

Lying suspended in saltwater (so that they do not sink) and wearing blinders in a soundproofed room can quickly drive *H. domesticus* and *metropolus* into misperceptions (or enlightenment from within). Both tense up without familiar sounds and sights—even primeval forests were not silent—keep their radios, TV, and telephones with them wherever they go, and sometimes invent explanations for what they could not see clearly or hear well, or else they begin to suspect others of talking behind their backs. Once the relative peace of the womb is shattered by eviction there from, they dream of utopias that lead nowhere. *(d/6)*

Act II. Studying Life-Forms

Are we mineral, vegetating, or animate? (Or more reptilian than spiritual during near-death experiences? *[d/8]*) We are not just any but all of these at once in ratios that vary with stimuli or input.

Philosophy as father and theology as mother have produced psychology. All three strive for internal consistency in drawing analogies. [Our "socialized" soul is weightless, but it weighs us down as we walk uphill after we learned to talk (sic). For *H. domesticus*, it is better to believe in angels when young and for *H. metropolus* to blame our guardian angels when we slip up and fall downhill. (Both err and talk the blame game.)]

Darwin did not take philosophy or religion seriously and did not know about psychology. Freud was not a psychiatrist but saw religion as pure illusion. Growing up, we forget what does not suit us, and some use logic and reason to rationalize or excuse what we have forgotten.

Our New Psychiatry has adopted evolution as its father and ethology as its mother. For these three sciences, homologous natural origins rather than formulation of sterile syllogisms is the crucial consideration. *(d/9)*

Armchair analogy advances our understanding by making what is unfamiliar familiar, but it has not increased our knowledge since logic was systematized in 350 BC.

Homology has done so, since 1555, when it was used in the scientific study of skeletons—while making the familiar unfamiliar—by connecting anew what we already know: apples and oranges are fruits, but they are so in order to succeed as seeds. (Do we take blind dates out to dinner because we are hungry or horny?)

Homology seeks the roots of what may be superficially dissimilar, amasses solid data, and surprises us with hidden answers; analogy depends on similarity of superficial characteristics and does not require detailed study, only a plausible opinion after consulting one's bias. (Armchair analogy would thoughtfully have denied us record players, airplanes, contact lenses, etc.) *(d/10)*

Linear thinking was enough after we left the trees and before we learned to throw stones. Now that we have learned to fly, can we give up flat-earth checkers and take up tridimensional chess? *(d/11)*

A Double Inspiration: Animal and Human Behavior

We meet most people by accident, and some meetings end in marriage. My adult life among animals also began by accident. Being in the right place at the right time—and observing, un-awed, but wondering—yielded new data and details for further global study of behavior.

If the sun is the mother of all living things, plants provide animals with sustenance. Roots make plants easier to track. Habitat and rivals, not creature comforts, select for fitness and endurance. To study the differences between problem-solving animals and conflict-ridden people, we need to share living space or spend a long time with both, which we do/did.

Nature warmly welcomes the "unliterate" with questions more than the articulate with answers. Absolutely nothing at all is taboo to wonder about. *(d/12)*

Paradise Found: "Fruits of the Tree of Knowledge"

(Ethopsychiatry from [A] to [Z])

This narrative account of events and related reminiscences— from more than a decade of observations comparing human and animal behavior—was unplanned. It was drafted on the return trip from a wedding ritual on the East Coast, when the in-flight movie was a rerun. That gave me time to write down all that I have started thinking through on the outbound flight after a glimpse of the Colorado River before its cleavage deepened into the Grand Canyon.

It occurred to me then that the origins of behavior (ethopsychiatry) is like the old river, and our own lives like the ever-changing panorama downstream that awes artists, dilettantes, and tourists more than wondering scientists.

We can now visit upstream tributaries where cold- and warm-blooded, scaly, furry, feathered, clawed, or horned life-forms still thrive. (We never got to know three wild foxes in the vineyards below our hilltop.)

From at least five tributaries of the "River of Life" that are inhabited by (**l, a–e**, see below) birds, (**2, f**) a centipede, (**3, g–x**) cats, (**4, y**) deer, and (**5, z**) fishes came hints/insights about:

(1) (a) power and greed, (b) rivalry and violence, (c) constitution and learning, (d) nest and shelter, (e) communion and communication, as well as learning and educational disabilities,

(2) (f) liberty and ideology, self-sacrifice and auto-mutilation,

(3) (g) mothering and fathering, (h) sensuality, society, and sex, (i) animal and human will, (j) having and caring, (k) incest and pedophilia, (l) wanting and needing, (m) orality and anality, (n) homosexuality and hanging on, (o) lust and rape, (p) bestiality, nudity, obscenity, and pornography, (q) fulfillment and satisfaction, (r) clinging, crawling, and smelling, (s) signaling and following through, (t) dying, defending, and expiring, (u) curiosity and ingenuity, (v) tool use and abuse, (w) growth and change, (x) security for kittens and salvation for nuns, cannibalism, and conscription,

(4) (y) intuition (immediate) about feuding and losing old enemies, and

(5) (z) speculation (cumulative) about finding allies and new friends from patterns of feeding and fasting, sitting, and overreaching.

The observer/ethopsychiatrist, however, cannot just be a listener but must have confidence that the mute (whether depressed, catatonic or autistic) or "dumb" (whether animal or infant) can communicate directly by behaving or vocalizing without the self-serving window-dressing provided by language.

(The periodic table of elements in chemistry was a revolutionary discovery during the industrial revolution. In this postindustrial age of computers, we can wordlessly separate stage-specific behavior of humanimal freedom-loving "unicorns," parity-seeking "centaurs," and eroticized "androgynes." They cluster together like elements by atomic weight. We simply use bracketed senso-socio-sexual markers from (**A**) to (**Z**) to store, retrieve, and then compare them intuitively, deliberately, or electronically for culture-free, color-blind but sex-aware con-familial rationalysis.)

How Older Species Live in the Same Space with Us

(1)

A peacock who happened to roost in the woods behind our house slowly made his way to our roof, which was higher than the hilltop. He was followed soon after by another younger peacock, and thus we were able to study basic dominance behavior. *(d/13)* Abuse of power, which did not turn out to be absolute, appeared only when hunger seeks surcease but never to assuage greed, which was demonstrably absent in the undomesticated.

(Lions can, but do not, deny their prey limited access to a watering hole when they are not hungry. Does socialization succeed only after initial sensory deprivation for *Homo domesticus*, that costly overcompensation by *Homo metropolus* never overcomes?)

(a)

To establish with some precision the parameters of dominance behavior, we set three piles of grain six feet apart in a single row, and as expected, the dominant peacock started feeding first. *(d/14)* The younger one went to the farthest pile at once. Sure enough, its elder stopped feeding and started to chase it away. But he hesitated at the second pile, hunger (as distinguished from greed among some beasts) won, he started feeding again, violence was avoided, and peace prevailed. (My headstrong wife would sometimes feed the younger peacock behind the other's back, but for purely maternal, not egalitarian, reasons.)

(b)

We do not know if peahens would have made a difference beyond expectable sexual competition. Were our peacocks in celibate exile as losers to an older rival or—by genetic accident—to one with more eyespots in his tail? Violence and sex do not coexist without a crowd of three or more of the same animal species; dyadic violence without sexual rivalry is expectable only from two different species except ours, where territoriality pits the sexes or parents and children against each other. *(d/15)*

(c)

Quails would also drop in and quietly queue up according to their pecking order (after both peacocks have finished feeding). Birds have been described as "nature's most eloquent expression." Can adult neurogenesis also explain their adaptive cultural evolution?

[Descended from dinosaurs whom we have yet to outdo in longevity (they reigned for 140 million years; we are only four million years old, but is to endure everything?), birds and those which came before them are able to regenerate their brain cells later in life! (F. Nottebohm, *Scientific American*, Feb. '89, p. 74; G. Montgomery, Discover, Jun '90, p. 48.)]

(d)

Birds' eggs serve to shield them from maternal stresses (fetuses often share maternal addictions).

Claims that we are more adaptive are made by adults who do not realize that we adapt at the cost of thoughtlessly changing how we look after our children: They are the neediest of all species but have to please two or more adults of kin or clan, few of whom sleep with their young. Their genitals stay soaked or soiled to defeat alleged benefits of prophylactic circumcision or clitoridectomy (to prevent itching and "self-abuse"). *(d/16)* Can one have castration anxiety (*H. domesticus*) or penis envy (*H. metr*opolus) without genital mutilation?

Better parents than ours are penguins who crow in triumph, like Tarzan, after chasing off predators from their nest and then take turns to keep eggs from freezing.

[Forsaking nesting for the young in favor of shelter for adults— and then mortgaging their own future to "own" bigger showplaces to impress strangers—thick carpets and throw rugs may keep our kids warm, but instead of feeling at home, they have to be housebroken before cavorting on floor coverings that their parents bought on credit.] *(d/17)*

[Today, the homeless in ever-greater numbers cannot even nest or rest in peace inside public parks.]

Territoriality ensures the survival outside the mother of the young among other animals.

(e)
Other birds to whom I call out, by whistling, reply in kind. Was I talking to them? If they were talking back in their native tongue, and not just parroting me, is it a form of child abuse—with more permanent consequences than forcing children to wear clothes to hide what we are ashamed of—to substitute a second language for our native tongue?

(In psychotherapy, the primary reason for not being able to share very early experiences is that we have forgotten our native tongue in the interim.)

[We suspect whatever is expressed in something foreign to us and insist (1) that foreigners speak our language in our presence, and (2) that our children tell the truth after they learn to speak ours even if—as Oliver Wendell Holmes of the US Supreme Court once pointed out—"pretty much all the honest truth-telling there is in the world is done by children" (at least until they become more like us in being less open).] *(d/18)*

In my family therapy practice, even if they are not yet toilet-trained, I hold toddlers who have not learned to talk loosely on my lap so that, whenever a family member is distressed—but ignored or unnoticed by the group, including me—they can leave me to commiserate in animal kinship, without words. *(d/19)*

"Dumb" animals have sometimes been used to bypass psychotherapeutic impasse. Is it because true learning disability only maps out for us (1) what is inaccessible to (2) the normally educated in (3) the normally intelligent? Do we, in fact, qualify as educationally disabled whenever we retreat from art and science to fantasies of utopia? (Animals who have left the water dream like us. Awake, do they also day dream of utopia?) *(d/20)*

(2)

(f)
After the peacocks, the next intruder into our sanctuary was a centipede. It must have been on its way out and got caught between the

jamb and the sliding door that I was closing. I did not see it in time and, before I realized that it was trapped, it used its jaws, like all carnivorous mammals with fangs—not its tongue to cry or beg for help—in setting itself free and escaping with its life.

It thus won its liberty sooner without waiting. Nor did it need to plead for self-destruction, which Patrick Henry publicly did with what, to some, sounded like an ultimatum: "Give me liberty or give me death!" Translated in animalese, this early American role model (Canadians to the north won their freedom without oratory) was begging, "Give me back my fangs or kill me now!" (He also pleaded for taxes for Christian morality.)

["Self-division" to continue creeping is different from automutilation by captive or drug-stimulated lab rats. (A. Favarazza, *Bodies under Siege*, Johns Hopkins Press, Baltimore, Md., 1987.)]

(3)

(g)
Our next encounter with a more evolved crawler snatched it out of death's jaws and away from extended exposure to the elements. On arrival late one night after vacationing in warmer climes, we heard strange noises from the thicket in front of our house. The sun came up before the sounds got too faint to investigate.

With a swimming pool net, we retrieved a tiny kitten, Baby Kitty (BK), who (sic), Eskimo-like, must have crawled deeper in search of insulation under a thick cover of foliage encrusted with early morning frost. (Cars below may have run over its mother.) We nursed the kitten with eyedroppers and by puncturing the tiny nipples of toy nursing bottles. It sucked dry whatever was soaked in milk.

(h)
In accepting, Eskimo-like, responsibility for BK's young life, we also resolved not to do what his mother would not. Uncastrated, he eventually had a harem of nubile cats serially in heat or oestrus arriving from near and far.

BK sired some kittens who stayed, and thus was born an extended study of another mammalian family's sensual, sexual *(d/21)*, and social life—negligible in cats, compared to dogs (domesticated wolves), which are claimed to be "the noblest beasts that God ever made."

(i)

By easily getting us to play his sensually challenging hide-and-seek game that he always won, BK by himself taught us that free will—his or ours—is merely our sense of willfulness or willingness to play at winning nothing at all. *(d/22)*

("Sensual" is the use of our senses, separately or together, simply because we can, not because we are socially rewarded for it.)

(j)

Multiplying as their sexual nature intended, many of BK's mates were better mothers in being more constant and comforting, predictable and protective, and less possessive or selfish than ours.

Their young did not cry out in pain on being born, unlike ours. *(d/23)* Blind and deaf for days after birth, they did not fear the future or distrust the unknown on the basis of early experiences (of perinatal and genital injuries).

Mothers (1) slept with their young (none of whom got smothered in their sleep: sudden infant deaths occur in cribs), (2) fed them on demand (without their having to clutch a bottle), (3) accepted nursing sisters as wet nurses (even for "rookie weanlings"), (4) left nurslings only to replenish their milk supply, (5) groomed them more neatly than our toilet training can hope to achieve (as children, we ran around dry but bottomless in our farm until kindergarten, but kittens bury their excretions), (6) showed them exactly how to stalk, when to pounce, and whether to kill or play, (7) chased away predators or distracted them when they could not be easily intimidated, and then (8) let each kitten go its own way before producing the next litter.

When three generations are offered milk in a bowl, the newly weaned can make the mother give up room for it, but "aunt" (sister) from the previous litter is excluded.

When a baby sleeps alone in its crib, it loses its mother's smell, the warmth of her proximity, the touch of her skin when it moves around, the sound of her voice when it cries while dreaming, etc. (I just dropped my notebook, and the noise made my 22-month-old grandson reach out for me in his sleep.)

Among us, not only must our young thrive (thus reducing infant mortality), but it must first, as a fetus, survive its parents' personal, public, and private ambitions. *(d/25)*

Is female liberation a social or human ambition? Two sister cats differed enough to typify human mothers who may be more filial (family-centered) or tribal (herd-oriented): One mother (GG) would leave her kittens but stay close to see if they would protest. Her sister (R) would leave hers for hours to be with peers, much as would a flighty female or social butterfly.

(My wife thinks of R as more a devoted wife to the alpha male from whom she is inseparable, not out of jealousy but in order to assert her dominance. Social butterfly or matriarch, she is quite distinguishable from sister GG) *(d/24)*

(k)

Though we never saw a son mount his mother, all sensual and sexual behavior among or with the young seemed to be socially tolerated. Mothers let uncles mount nurslings even while they suckled.

In prison, pedophiles are held in greater contempt, counterphobic or not, than rapists (who may have more "machismo," called "charisma" in those who are charming in their observations but just as penetrating).

In our farm, my father simply married off pregnant daughters of incestuous fathers to eligible bachelor tenants. (Mothers who may have been impregnated by incestuous sons were already married.)

(l)

Kittens suckle the dry breasts of pregnant aunts to start or stimulate late or weak uterine contractions at full term or during incomplete abortions with irregular or prolonged bleeding. (Young or old knead or suck breast or nipple, to nurse or not, for mutual sensual satisfaction, regardless of gender.)

Maiden aunts sometimes steal kittens. (My wife ensures the return only of stolen nurslings.)

Absent demands for ransom, children may be kidnapped for sexual abuse, but infants are often abducted out of purely maternal motives. (Males are usually not moved to adopt even lovable stepsons unless their mother is part of the transaction. Stepdaughters often seal the new deal sooner.)

(m)

Cunnilingus in cats may be more sensual (narcissistic grooming) than sexual. When nursing delays oestrus, autofellatio is a practical alternative for males (our primate relatives masturbate openly; boys and girls do not) but not anal intercourse.

With scheduled feeding of infants came early toilet training of toddlers, sometimes supplemented by enemas. Anal eroticism is common among conscientious adults throughout history.

Circumstantial homosexuality in prisons, soldiers' boot camps, and boys' boarding schools, and experimental group sex in girls' pajama parties are not unlike secret bestiality in isolated pastures. *(d/26)*

(n)

Cats seem more curious than concerned (like we are about highway accidents) when peers die. *(d/27)*

Some primates would not part with their stillborn for days. (When my father died, I clung to him long after rigor mortis had set in.)

(o)

As in a human cathouse, a male queue may form for a female in heat and a second male cat impatiently mount the first who has already mounted, but only to dislodge him rather than take advantage of his position for anal intromission.

Their awkward ménage à trois never became a gang bang by bullies forcing submission to a uniquely inevitable human perversion of normal sex and violence:

The evolution of erect ambulation tilted the vagina forward so that, spread-eagled, women cannot escape rape. *(d/28)* This, with inability to flee from swifter male predators, has forever colored their relationship with the opposite sex, even orangutans.

Does rape ensure survival of the fittest? A random genetic pool, coerced or contractual, has higher survival potential: Mongrels, including many bastards who somehow survive bungled infanticide thrive like weeds (sometimes rising to prominence or notoriety). Among teenagers, does sowing wild oats yield human weeds? *(d/29)*

(p)
Besides sensually being quite playful around us ([i], above), BK can also get sexually aroused and not discriminate even between species. (The Koran still permits bestial shepherds their pastoral perks or perquisites.)

(q)
BK would sometimes mount my wife's arm with his penis red and erect. Her sensual stroking would not elicit social purring nor reduce his sexual thrusting. *(d/30)*

Stroking does not separate snarling rivals or struggling combatants either.

Animal sex and violence must be more deeply muscular or proprioceptive than with us who are susceptible even to superficial strokes by touch or speech (more symbolic than substantive).

[Our tissues develop from three layers: ectoderm (skin and brain, etc.), mesoderm (muscles and tendons, etc.), and endoderm (organs and their linings, etc.) Deep tendons are the source of proprioception. Muscle memory, as in balancing on a bicycle, is lifelong.]

[Speech or reassuring sounds are selected by enfolded skin that we call our brain. (Can music soothe the beast that lurks in all hearts, or could just absence of the odor of danger be enough reassurance? If videoconferences cannot close deals, is it because— at greater cost in time and money—contractors must smell each other?)]

(r)
With me, Baby Kitty likes to snuggle close under my armpit, relax, and purr even without stroking. *(d/31)* He must separate my wife from me by smell, not by sex. *([s], below)* Males and females exude different odors, which perfumeries exploit for huge profits that make selling cosmetics second only to religion as a sure bet among so-called growth industries.

Are both industries the home of the gullible about original sin and body odor (as the Sure brand of deodorant claims?) Original sin was conceived and preached by the ritually circumcised without consent. Involuntary refugees seek clandestine sanctuary in "safe houses" that usually reek of the smell of fear. Are both groups vulnerable or susceptible to coercive threats or retaliatory acts by those who claim to be their superiors *(d/32)*? Which belongs to *H. domesticus* or to *H. metropolus*?

By not using deodorants, I avoid sending confusing signals to violent patients whose clinical management under minimum physical or pharmacological restraint I have taught for more than twenty years. An alumna of ours had no problem with prisoners until pregnancy altered her odor. (Did Jane Goodall leave her chimpanzees when she was pregnant? How do veterinarians cope with a wide range of scents in their practice?)

(s)

Pheromones, sexual or not, like colors, can seduce, threaten, reassure, disorient, or defend. Odor also goes directly to the old brain or archipallium, whilst looking is lateralized to the opposite brain hemisphere across from the seeing eye (which evolved later than the nose).

(A motion to ban perfumes from public buildings to reduce temptation or sexual harassment inside was recently tabled by a California county board of supervisors.)

When the reigning alpha or dominant male joins the other cats to welcome my wife home from work, he tries to reestablish his territorial rights by spraying her and sometimes succeeds.

During their screening, physicians applying to our four-year residency-training program in psychiatry may be greeted by an incontinent patient to help tell us by any involuntary grimace of displeasure whether early toilet training precludes their working with the untidy. (They must also interview the most disturbed patient in the hospital and do well to be accepted for training.)

(t)

BK had previously demonstrated his determination to live out his life even after his mother failed to return. *(d/33)*

I also thought that the will to live was very much alive in a dying weanling when it was able to keep a stalking cat at bay with a fierce and fearsome snarl. Its expiring right afterward made me question my theory about its not wanting to die before its time. It may have only smelled with its old olfactory brain or "rhin-encephalon," the scavenger's hunger for meat.

(u)
Curiosity in the cat is not only appealing but also opportunistic and practical. (Stifled in children by pat or promised answers, it has to be reawakened by good teachers.)

Curiosity is looking, expecting to find something. Adventure is looking just to be looking. Discovery is finding out for yourself. Exploring is looking hard at what you find.

Today, with the cosmos breaking all prescientific rules of logic left over from classic civilizations, curiosity attenuates rapidly in those who keep asking, "Why is that?" rather than "What now?" (Our lives are therefore more synthetic, filled with the results of other people's curiosities, without furthering personal discovery, exploration, or exploitation.)

Not only was BK's daughter, SK, curious, but she also displayed an uncommon intelligence akin to that of Archimedes. Besides pregnant cats and weanlings waiting to get canned liver, etc., no other cats are allowed inside our house unless they are at risk, sick, or dying. (d/34) SK, however, gained entry surreptitiously when we left a sliding door ajar once, by reaching in to pull the doormat out to make the narrow opening wider. Once inside, we could not evict her without first rewarding, with extra food and stroking, her ingenuity in rediscovering the idea behind, and then proceeding to use, the wedge that she designed.

By exploiting it, SK had equaled two separate scientific discoveries: the principle of the fulcrum—with which, given a long enough pole, Archimedes promised to move the world—and the more sophisticated use, much later on, of keystones to hold up buttressed arches to span vast spaces in post-Grecian "arch"-itecture. (The famous Parthenon is a forest of columns.)

Discoverers of both fulcrum and arch outshone their contemporaries, but they were not necessarily ahead of their time: prehistoric people used a pointed stick like a wedge to dig soil for planting in small temporary clearings. This led to wider use of the plow, which made them less nomadic (but made farmers more interdependent in fighting flash floods to preserve their commonwealth [sic]). This collective need along the Nile resulted in the first nation-state. *(d/35)*

(v)

What was also arresting was SK's reaction whenever the doormat failed to act as a wedge and slipped out too easily. Then, like us, she blamed the tool that did not work as she had expected, violently venting all her pent-up frustration by pouncing on it.

(w)

SK was also exceptional in being more sexually fulfilled when in heat than her peers: her postcoital writhing always lasted longer than theirs, from better senso-sexual development.

"Better" means better balanced or healthier, as in *Homo sapiens*; "sicker" means a greater imbalance in senso-sexual and social development: "orderly"—as distinguished from "balanced"—signifies a narrower "comfort zone" in *Homo domesticus* from subservience to superior forces, usually social. Discomfort from disorder in *Homo metropolus* implies fear of any change, imposed or unexpected, conservative or destructive.

"Change," rapid (as in "crisis") or not, means transitory or transitional disorder, with or without healthy outcome in growth or development: This is because, like plants, we grow by stages preprogrammed by DNA, not by incumbent social superiors. Any induced change or development outside these stages is disorganizing, and also destabilizing, for all animals.

Early sensual and sexual stages are shared with other mammals like cats; social stages (like animistic beliefs older than stars directing kings to a manger, pecking orders older than power politics, and barter practices older than capitalism) are shared with primates like hairier apes and other bipeds like quails and peacocks.

Many birds and a few animals combine sex with raising families, but none of them run mom-and-pop bakeries, etc., so that "making love" is separate from "making a living."

Both sex and money are also combined in legal houses of prostitution and in serial spouse-swapping (lawful hypergamy) through divorce courts. *(d/36)*

(x)

Our cats eat their stillborn as well as the afterbirth or placenta. Kittens, who die later on, are eaten by others not their mother. Some male cats, like lions, kill and eat the young sired by others so that their nursing mothers can go into heat or oestrus once they stop breast-feeding. *(d/37)*

Does this preemptive killing of another's offspring eliminate future rivals, or is this their version of bombing civilians? (The switch from bombing airfields to raiding London denied the Germans air superiority for the rest of the war. Bullies use muscles instead of brains.) Does not war, after all, exile the young of any era to distant places where they may die or stay and never return home to better or bother their doddering Establishment elders?

When partly eaten remains greeted us on coming home, we surmised that our protection was solicited. *(d/38)*

[Like nuns who "chose" to save their cherished souls instead, mother cats will sacrifice freedom outdoors to save their precious kittens from predatory tomcats. (For human females who are vulnerable to rape, there is less magical thinking or animism inside cloisters than for people outside who fear the unknown.)]

(4)

(y)

We were delighted when our gardener found a couple of deer antlers under the weeds that he was uprooting. I hung them low and upside down from a tree stump near the kids' picnic table so that they do not run into them when chasing each other. To inspect them, stags came very close to the house for the first time. Their timid does and fawns have been doing it for twenty years, watching me watch them as I drink my coffee. To what do we owe such unexpected recklessness?

> (Their tails—which rise in anticipation of fleeing—stayed down,
> and they have confidently and frequently come closer and stayed
> longer to lie on the grass, ever since.)

Did they instinctively recognize as an appeasement gesture my
hanging those old antlers upside down? Had I unconsciously buried
the proverbial hatchet? Since I did not know that I was doing any such
thing, was the impulse behind it subcortical, or archetypal, arising out
of the collective animal unconscious? Can carnivores like us appease
vegetarians like them? Are old or reptilian brains programmed alike?
(Some reptiles are older than mountains!)

> Or did they just not smell any threat even when they came closer out
> of curiosity? (My wife claims my hair standing on end on arising in the
> morning looks like a horn—which, like nails, are just hardened skin that
> molt like claws—while my grandchildren say it makes me look more like
> an infant and, in their eyes, automatically harmless.)

(5)

(z)

The last, for now, of my unsought discoveries (finding without
looking) came while feeding fishes in a pool that we had converted into
a pond in an attempt at aquaculture with carp and goldfish.

> (Should we just do what the dolphins did, ten million years ago,
> and fish the oceans to feed ourselves or can we learn to "farm" our
> lakes?)

Some of them, though I could not say whether they are the same
fishes each time, would stay with my shadow even after the breeze takes
the ground cat food—on which they thrived—to sunnier parts of the
pond. Can they identify my silhouette as friendly, separately from those
of predators hovering over their prey like kingfishers?

> Or are fish, like infants and other nonverbal animals, capable
> of silent gratitude that we mock with our ever-ready "thank you"
> for small favors? *(d/39)*

> Can fishes, safe from danger, live to befriend, breed, and feed
> but "not only on bread alone"? Harry Harlow's monkeys forsook
> "wire mothers" with milk bottles for "terry-cloth mothers" without
> milk after feeding or when scared.

Does safety ennoble the fish, once its security is secured, or is it suffering that ennobles victims?

(Do brains of lower species molt like skin from originally having been ectodermal? Does neural regeneration also make fish food good brain food?) *(d/40)*

New Questions, Other Observations of Strategic Implications

Nonverbal animals do not throw parties in the wake of death in the family. Instead, they eat whatever they kill without totemic rituals or fancied transubstantiation *(d/41)* for believers and bullies. Only human beings kill strangers for other strangers, even invisible ones whom they believe in, like God or Queen. (Fathers, not mothers, sacrifice their sons to strangers or trade them for slaves. Mothers groom children for social esteem.)

Were we more like animals, fat generals—once sated or satiated—will order earlier cease-fire in the killing fields. (With such a given, Hitler who was a vegetarian would not have his easy final solution to the Jewish "problem.")

What is far wiser than insisting that mass murderers eat their victims? (Big cats, except for cheetahs, which scavenger dogs trail after for their leftovers, bury and eat carrion.)

Instead of our killing and fastidiously not eating killers who— just as fastidiously—did not eat those whom they had killed, can we just exile them to a New Georgia more south than South America, where they can survive like Eskimos but not prevail or threaten anyone again? Initial outlay to provide more antifreeze may be higher, but burial costs, even of those who kill themselves, will be cut down to the bone by freeze-drying. (This nonutopian, uncouth but simple innovation only needs "biosocial imagineering" to implement.)

Do other parasitic relationships discriminate against the weak, like political or economic imperialism does? (Can we be democratic politically but not economically? Or "independent" [C] intellectually but not [B] volitionally or [A] emotionally?) And are other more symbiotic relationships less destructive to codependents? (Cleaner fish enters the open mouths of bigger fishes and emerges unharmed after cleansing them of harmful parasites.) Are animal alliances lethal to others of their own species or a mortal danger to another? Have we done more harm than dinosaurs during our shorter sojourn as the dominant beast?

Unlike insects and more like birds, once we stuck our noses in the air, we started to depend less on smell and more on our eyes and on colors more than odors. (Primates look before they leap to branches that are a healthy green, while we sell our foods sealed in sterile, pretty packages.) But birds can flee from danger by flying, unless the predator is swifter.

We cannot fly, women can be raped frontally, and our back can be broken by taskmasters who are stronger. (Wits can outwit only the witless and powerless.)

Some of us, scientist or not, still think that we are superior to other animals, if only because we can talk or repeat what we have read. (In New Guinea, the sick who cannot speak can be buried alive, because their souls are thought to reside in their throat.)

"Man" originally meant "handyman" and "ma-ma" came from "mammalian." When mothers pump their breasts so that their husbands can feed their baby, the adults may be happier but not the infant. When men use their brains to abstract instead of soiling their hands, society may profit, but not their manhood. (Lincoln, Churchill, Carter, and Reagan liked working with their hands.)

Act III. Life among Handicapped Human Racists

Without some kind of God, man is not even interesting.
—T. S. Eliot

When I was growing up, we had séances during which spirits of the dead picked out letters (arranged alphabetically in a circle on a table made without nails) to spell out their message. Is it uncalled for to be amazed that even the unlettered departed were all excellent spellers? (Is this less outrageous than expecting us to go through all of life's stages from **A** to **Z**?)

H. sapiens tries to catch up with animals who have been around longer by using wheels and sails, diving bells and jet propulsion, microscopes and telescopes, microphones and telephones, and radar and heat sensors. *(d/42)*

(*H. domesticus* hoards; *H. metropolus* complains of crawling in rush-hour traffic!)

The only nonprosthetic (time- or labor-saving) invention may be our turning night (darkness) into day. Daylight savings time is in the same class. Light boxes are now also used to return depressed patients to normal body rhythms without using drugs. *(d/43)*

But with tools to overcome disparity, believers and bullies are tempted to take advantage of the disadvantaged, including children out of school and women at home or at work, for being weak or provocative.

What makes believers and bullies different or alienated from other life-forms, domesticated or not, in our universe?

Whatever it is does not necessarily make us unique or special, except in our eyes. *(d/44)* Just thinking that we are unique and special—e.g., as (**J**) ethnocentric Nazi Aryan racist or Zionist xenophobic Jew or (**L**) anthropocentric humanist, etc.—even if (**iii'**) "sexist," like a lion with his pride, or a queen bee with her drones, can keep or stop us from asking how time ties into our behavior.

Specialists debate nature vs. nurture to win converts to their biology or sociology. We shall bypass this obsolete dichotomy and, instead, speak of growth of *H. sapiens* and development of *H. domesticus* and *metropolus*.

Growth is what happens inside and outside the uterus under DNA instruction. Development is what happens with influences outside one's own DNA.

> For the truly proper study of man (bioanthropology), a group of 700–800 people is necessary. Freud studied a smaller group and can guide only those who work with same-sized samples, and who, like him, afterward merely read about the rest of humanity.

Only from directly studying the problematical subjectivity of different groups can we see the natural pattern of human evolution.

Our history reveals strange permutations. It is as if (1) Helen Keller, who was blind but overachieved nonetheless, was our spiritual mother, and (2) Adolf Hitler, who found himself overextended by his belief in the supremacy of his race, had been our secular patriarch.

Their most famous "daughter" was Marie Curie who allowed us to see what is hidden from our eyes, and their most illustrious "son" might be Albert Einstein who made time intervals just another yardstick by which to measure our reach. Their more entertaining pair of "siblings" are Shakespeare and Mozart.

Are we the Helen Kellers of the cosmos or the Adolf Hitlers of the animal kingdom, or inextricably both simultaneously, or are we their "children"? *(d/45)*

Once our brain outgrew its exit route from the womb, its size became a mixed blessing. We begin life with a headache from brain trauma during natural birth and fear of pain from the unforeseen before we can think. And, to talk with our clan, we had to give up using the sounds we already knew. Compared to other species, we are also slow learners from sedentary living as virtual amputees for much longer than unhurt and stronger animals. This extended dependency (neoteny) of the puny cries out for dependable people and machines as prostheses. (Our need to belong even extends to being cheerleaders for sports teams with animal-sounding names.)

Artificially intelligent computers can assist us to think logically—in order, foolhardily, to predict with precious few new facts from fewer given premises—and slow us down further, because what we already comprehend still has to be translated into words to process or to protect as abstractions.

Great apes linger less, with undelayed gratification, on sensual stages **A** to **C** and social stages **F** to **H**, while we often burn out waiting and languishing, or digging ourselves deeper, down these ruts in our churches, courts, and corporations:

A (emotional): good or bad (from evoked taste or smell or feelings)
B (muscular): right or wrong (in lateral mobility, to comply or not)
C (cognitive): true or false (untested except by what-if questions)
F (animistic): security or salvation (is it sinful?)
G (pecking order): peace or chaos (is it illegal?)
H (barter): prosperity or scarcity (is it a bargain?)

Great apes and *Homo sapiens* can be (**F**) awed by the mysterious without engaging in genocide *(d/46)*, (**G**) make war and establish hierarchies (without ideologies to justify power plays and ploys), and (**H**) trade or commit larceny for goods or favors without middlemen, sometimes called pimps. *(d/47)*

There are two kinds of scarcity, that of goods or services, including labor, and that of capital or money. High finance (**H**) decreases wealth except for the few who use money in short supply to buy and sell companies that produce goods in order to make more money (rather than expand production). Paper money then becomes a profitable commodity rather than merely a convenient medium for exchange of originally bartered goods and services.

Puberty heralds sexual division of labor. We also expect girls to outgrow being a tomboy (**Q, f**) to be our mothers. Tomboys compete with their peers of both sexes (playfully among animals), mothers (**V, f**) protect their young (in deadly earnest, even against overwhelming odds).

All young animals start with (**A**) assistance in becoming free and (**P**) playful autoeroticism. *H. sapiens* and some chimpanzees are capable of (**E**) artistic self-expression and (**F**) fantastically magical thinking; other bipeds, including birds, are also (**G**) governed by pecking orders and (**H**) hoard decorations for nest building or trade lab tokens for sexual favors. *(d/48)*

Homo domesticus and *Homo metropolus* go on to (**F**) Father Almighty in our theology, (**G**) group together to govern and fight as political animals, and enthrone (**H**) High Finance to achieve conspicuous consumption. *(d/49)*

We generally specialize in problems which we have not yet outgrown. For peripatetic Aristotle (384–322 BC), equal access to (**F**) gods was not as important as (**AxH**) the good life that (**G**) politics can promote: **G/F = AxH**. *(d/50)*

Life crises or simple aging can make us revisit dichotomies of obsolete absolutes that still plague mellowed philosophers who are sedentary paraplegics, or intellectual idiot savants (wordy yet unwise but better at citing chapter and verse than the square roots of given numbers that true idiot savants have memorized). Aging also returns us to earlier milestones in erotosexual development that we call our second adolescence during metapause (male midlife crises) or menopause and, in our senescence before death catches up, we retreat to a more erotosensual second childhood.

We used to look to (**F**) God for help; these days we expect more from (**G**) politicians. We are also increasingly turning to (**H**) business but tend to stay away from domestic problem areas. Civilization used to be a source of pride for *Homo sapiens*; today our cities (civic centers) are a disgraceful shadow of our dreams. Yet captains of industry can now command their commander-in-chief to order his generals to rescue their locally threatened investments abroad.

There is a growing realization that war is not fighting but business. Those who spy for another country for (**A**) love of (**H**) money are more professional than those who spy for the enemy because they hate (**A'**) their leaders (**G**). *(d/51)*

Economics influence our lives more than politics, as politicians once did more than theologians. Economic harassment (even of Al Capone through the IRS) is getting more dangerous than political (sexual scandals in the candidate's history) or religious (grand inquisitions for heresies) persecution. Our cityscapes used to be dominated by (**F**) cathedrals, then by (**G**) city halls, and then by (**H**) bank towers taller than both. (Will museums replace them all?)

"Prisoners," "Parrots," and "Perverts"

> *The true, strong and sound mind . . . can embrace equally*
> *great things and small.*
> —Samuel Johnson

To be (**BB**) righteous or (**F'**) evil probably means you are abnormal, whether you are (**B**) right or not.

To be abnormal does not mean that you are (**B'**) wrong or (**A'**) bad or (**C'**) false.

What is normal, as long as it does not mean the absence of abnormality, cannot apply to the soul, which cannot get sick and die. Normal (functional) means elastic (flexible) adaptation to life and continued success and survival as a species. What survives and endures is seldom the statistical norm, though the majority (average) may prevail and prosper a while.

Across cultures, what is wrong with being functional (flexible or elastic, like steel)? Consensus (conformity to arbitrary or fixed standards) is not necessary in ratioanalysis if we can use changes in favorite (**i**) personal questions, (**ii**) social slogans, and (**iii**) sexual practices as reliable signs of advance or retreat from **A** to **Z**.

Our (**i**) sensual, (**ii**) social, and (**iii**) sexual growth and development may flow smoothly, swiftly—skipping some stages which we then disdain, e.g., rapacity (**W, m**)—or slowly (if we get in a comfortable rut).

Not uniformly imperfect, we are all unequally normal (**i**, sensually free), abnormal (**ii'**, socially arrested) or paranormal (**iii'**, sexually retarded); but we cannot be (**i'**) "prisoners," (**ii'**) "parrots," and (**iii'**) "perverts" all of our lives.

i: Children begin like unicorns and are free (**A**) to feel anger or fear until they become (**A'**) prisoners of what is good or bad. Juveniles are free (**B**) to fight or to flee until they become (**B'**) prisoners of what is right or wrong. Adolescents are free (**C**) to speculate or to wait until they become (**C'**) prisoners of what is true or false. Adults are free (**D**) to compile and compare until they become (**D'**) prisoners of what is testable or verifiable. At any age, we are free (**E**) to create or destroy, or become (**E'**) prisoners of the new or fashionable.

ii: "Parrots," like trained centaurs, repeat society's stock phrases without wondering why they reassure. All parrots must have teachers.

(Teachers who are not parrots are self-taught, like Buddha, Jesus, Freud, and Gandhi. [Freud and Gandhi, because they learned by doing, are also educators rather than just preachers of the untestable.] But if we use them as their own controls, they can still be minimum-security prisoners or short-term perverts at some stage of their sensual and sexual growth or, like some of us, occasionally detained in their own social development from [**F'**] fear of ever-absent, all-powerful God, to [**O'**] awe before ever-present, all-knowing computers. [Divine absentees are harder to deal with, especially if their presence is assumed.])

iii: "Perverts" cannot use all their natural androgynous endowments even when it is time to go on to the next stage of sexual development from **P** to **Z** (Perversion is like an acquired addiction, easily recognizable by withdrawal symptoms when progressively increasing need is unmet. It is different from being driven by biologically programmed need. Such needs can be satisfied periodically, whether for food [celebrities boast a lot about not having to wait for a table at popular restaurants] assistance, or sex. Perversions are more peculiar to human beings.)

DENOUEMENT

The first lesson to learn (**A**) emotionally, (**B**) actively, and (**C**) intellectually is that one of our principal imperfections is to be less proud of our parents—until we join their ranks ourselves—than of our race, sex, birthplace, and clannish beliefs, even as worker or guard bees or farmer or soldier ants, by proselytizing and bureaucratizing ideals into ideology for glory or profit. *(d/52)* (It is by pure accident that we share our race, sex, country, and ideology with our neighbors.)

But a worse double-standard error is to act as if we are the proud parents of thought experiments or lyrical writings left to us by the likes of Einstein or Shakespeare as their surviving if not deserving beneficiaries.

We are handicapped, like blind Helen Keller, compared to other animals. Yet we behave toward animals like Adolf Hitler toward non-Aryans. If our study of nature found us to be the tail wagging the dog, our survey of the animal kingdom shows up our believers and bullies as handicapped human racists who (like a workaholic) have compensated with their brain to overachieve, with an opposable thumb and overworked tongue.

The mischief and weapons (arms) that their tongue and thumb end up making have helped them outdo other species in reach, speed, and lethality. But their by-products are also the source of uniquely human conflicts.

H. domesticus and *H. metropolus* have not looked after our children like both now want to look after Mother Nature. They kill themselves and each other with work and from greed, envy, and hate, unlike other animals. In the name of self-serving delayed gratification, they frustrate and abuse those around them who depend on them, and think that helps natural selection. That is not what animals taught Charles Darwin.

We think we are wise (sapient) because we can think, but that is not what Rene Descartes said or meant with *cogito ergo sum* He discovered that only from doubting and cogitating can we ever be sure that we exist. Thinking, no matter how reassuring as "cognition" (cognitif), does not ensure anything. *(d/53)*

What decides whether we depend more on (**A**) taste or (**B**) tests or (**C**) analogy or (**D**) homology? What makes us fall back on (**C**) rationalization rather than relying on (**D**) ratiocination? What differentiates a deist (**A+F**) from a theist (**C+F**), and an atheist (**AxF'**) from an agnostic (**D/F**)?

What will be increasingly obvious—during our life cycle from **A** to **Z** to **B'** (second adolescence) to **A'** *(second childhood)*—is that separable stages in development for EveryWoMan can clarify what makes one more of a dreamer (**A**) than a doer (**B**), more reductionist (**C**) than heuristic (**E**), etc.

> Can one be free without every person being free? Yes, but it won't be fair. Can one be fair without being free? Only by self-sacrifice. Can one be equal and just at the same time? Only by self-denial. But self-deception is always easier than either self-sacrifice or self-denial.

We therefore have to reexamine our history and compare our behavior with that of Mother Nature and her animals to extricate ourselves from the conflicts that continue to plague humankind. Might information let us survive longer with our imperfections, or are they only tolerable with the help of delusions? Can we—without succeeding like a simplistic Adolf Hitler, only to fail in the end—prevail like a subtler Helen Keller and outlive our overcompensatory tendencies to be pompous, pugnacious (mean), punitive (mean-spirited), etc.?

Clinicians consistently find continuing trends, transtemporally, as we go through life from A to Z. And what we call senso-socio-sexual patterns of becoming, believing, and begetting seem to subdivide within each person and subspecies. A preliterate subculture is common to children and other primates, and cohabitation characterizes certain ages in both sexes. It is therefore not surprising that human beings become, believe, and beget in similar ways throughout history.

Transcultural psychiatry then begins with the business of spelling out what we mean by "mind." Literally, cross-cultural psychology should change its spelling to "mynd" or "myths of my mind" that cannot be tested. Ethopsychiatrists are better off thinking of it as "minding" what is going on and how it affects behavior.

Cross-species comparisons show us where we have erred because we are human. To control nature, domesticate animals, and socialize children is to abuse them to realize our dreams. The battle of the sexes is also human and recent. With sexual inhibition and genital hypochondriasis, the brain compensates as an erogenous zone.

Contrary to most creation myths, we all started out as Eve and, by the grace of dice or chance or God, some of us became Adam. (Nor did he have any choice, either, in what happens to his heirs.)

People tend to look up (to others, including God) or down (on others or themselves). Scientists try harder to look out for the unexpected and around for what is taken on faith.

(I was once taken for a miracle worker when I relieved a boy's distended bladder by immersing his hand in cold water, the reflex arc bypassing his cortex.)

Without a star or rhetoric of short and catchy sound bites to guide us on our journey to our destiny or destination, can we slowly if painfully be more context-centered, content-conscious, and conclusion-cautious? Can we separate critical thinking from constructive criticism, reasoning from fact-finding, our conceptions from our perceptions, our sensations from our sex, our virtues from our values, and our liberties from our rights, through tough times and over rough terrain in the next century? (d/54) Only to find that we are not special as a species?

Can we show we are not a singular aberration? We must forget everything that was taught before we learned about zero, all about the soul before we learned about the cell, all slogans before we learned about organs, and all about self before we learned about cycles.

English literacy needs an alphabet, 8 punctuation marks, and 10 numbers. Transcultural psychiatry needs 26 letters, 6 different Roman numerals, and < and > for clinical rationalysis.

Of the Roman numerals, *I* is for cosmology, *II* for biology, and *III* for anthropology; *i* is for sensual, *ii* is for social, and *iii* is for sexual. (There is not one self but changing ratios between our senso-socio-sexual selves.)

In addition, innovation needs new words: **(I)** con-natural, **(II)** con-vivial, and **(III)** con-familial.

Psychiatric practice that is limited to one specific group or cult or culture is a form of tribal medicine with its own magicians and vocabulary of incantations.

We can leave this ivory tower of Babel for a better alphabet for the next century.

ABZs of Life started out as a modern periodic table of elements of behavior to go with Mendeleev's and Meyer's independent but similarly radical discovery in chemistry. Our ABZ is the alphabet of nongenetic transmission of information.

DNA forms the organism; senso-socio-sexual growth and development shapes its own legacy. Can its senso-socio-sexual ratios now be used to understand us, like the four codons of Crick and Watson's DNA in basic biochemistry can explain how life continues from generation to generation?

Our (**E**) discovered nonlinear, ratio-driven patterns do not differ from other natural verifiable patterns that (**A**, e-motional) nonambulatory (**C**, logical) reductionism will not ever (**B**) endeavor or try to (**D**) test or explore.

We Live in Three Different Dimensions

What we feel, try, think, test, and make for ourselves is senso-moral; what we believe and share with others is socioethical; what we do to beget or not is erotosexual.

4.00 d/GLOBAL OVERVIEW

d/Chapter Notes

[d/1] Lapdogs obey and follow, attack dogs fight and lead, sheepdogs watch and listen, hunting dogs scout and chase, watchdogs bark and frighten, seeing-eye dogs look and guide.

Not all cultures nor all citizens become domesticated from (1) lapdogs of the gods to (2) attack dogs of politics, economics, individualists, and technocrats, to (3) sheepdogs of psychologists and sociologists, to (4) watchdogs for minorities, humanists, our environment. and other species, to (5) seeing-eye dogs of engineering and electronics, to (6) hearing-aid dogs of radar technology, all the way to (7) hunting dogs for science and with computers.

(Because of increasingly limited options, we develop the appropriate opportunistic mentality, whether it be that of a lapdog, attack dog, sheepdog, hunting dog, seeing-eye dog, or hearing-aid dog [e.g., as a psychoanalyst or psychotherapist].)

What more properly describes our best friend are roughly equivalent stages in idealization that we demand of our best friend's master.

To feel close as a lapdog, to act as an attack dog, or bark as a sheep dog to herd the timid together, to find the right path as a hunting dog, to compare clues as a watchdog, to assist as a seeing-eye dog, etc., are the stages that domestication demands.

We are, by now, in our progress through the history of our collective domestication:

1a) outgrowing the lapdog mentality of the unambitious as well as that of attack dog in the self-made WoMan,

1b) except as psychological aggression in sheepdog assertive training by simulated confrontations designed for the timid who has not succeeded: the model domesticated beast itself can be trained to herd sheep at the tender age of eight weeks, but would be handicapped as a hunting dog;

2) and moving into the arms of class-action, consciousness-raising groups for watchdog vigilance over institutional and dangerous concentrations of power.

With neo-etho-ethical consciousness, in which sensitive awareness more than concentrated vigilance is required to preserve endangered species, the watchdog mentality—needed by ecologists to publicize the unthinking abuse of applied science in changing the world to serve mankind—will now have to give ground to the seeing-eye and hearing-ear dog mentality.

The magic eye tells us about intruders or trespassers and in robots allows them to avoid obstacles just as a seeing-eye dog guides its master. Electronic eavesdropping allows us to monitor sounds the human ear cannot hear, from the nursery or from burglars if we are deaf or asleep or from callers if we are not home to answer the telephone.

Thus, we have the seeing-eye and hearing-aid dog models to increase our awareness and reduce our vigilance, and even a hunting-dog model that sniffs out smoke to warn us or our neighbors of danger when we are asleep or absent.

Our progress with technological prostheses has by now taken us from
(1) the domesticated lapdog for love and warmth, to
(2) (a) the attack dog for protection, to
      (b) the sheepdog to keep the herd together, to
(3) the hunting dog to lead us to niches that are rich in resources, to
(4) the watchdog for safeguarding our interests, to
(5) (a) the seeing-eye and
      (b) the hearing-aid dog, to keep us in touch with the world, away or awake or asleep, so that we can work, play, or dream without worrying.

For dog lovers, dogcatchers, and dog owners to be blessed with (1), (3), and (5) (a) and (b) is good preparation for eternal peace in a warm, dreamless sleep—at the end of our life cycle or of civilization itself—from which there is no awakening, whether or not we loved ourselves.

Is a reporter a privately hired pen? Does (s)he need to toe the editorial line like an ideological mercenary? Some newspapers are attack dogs (muckrakers), some are hearing ear dogs (echo-chambers), some are seeing-eye dogs (war correspondents on spying missions).

(Some psychiatrists are attack dogs [advocates], some hearing-ear dogs [analysts], and some seeing-eye dogs [visionary "gurus").]

The test of a good relationship, either with man's best friend or God or guns or goods or drugs or computers or anyone else, is whether you can take it or leave it.

1) To need it beyond your childhood or sickbed is pure and simple addiction.
2) Withdrawal symptoms may be mild or severe or heartbreaking, depending on your love for or addiction to your particular fetish, whether fantasied or real, animal or chemical.

We have thus progressed from (1) passively waiting to be loved, (2) (a) attacked, (b) assisted, or (3) exploited, to (4) active interaction (despite our human handicaps and reactionary racism) with the playful and purposeless whom we strive to domesticate.

In the process, we have gone from the purely symbolic, to the selfish, to the selfless, to the consumer, toward a "womanimalectronic" network of relationships,

(1) to be studied as well as
(2) indiscriminately enjoyed,
(a) independently (I) and collectively (J), but
(b) not without demanding correlations (D).

(My paranoids are as demanding as ideologues but more criticized.)

[d/2] In Khomeini's Iran, the prophet Muhammad is now claimed to have warned, "Refrain from speaking during fornication; otherwise, your child will have a troubled mind." How did he or other Shiite saints know? (Muhammad as numerologist, before menstrual cycles were known: "Avoid coupling on the first and fifteenth day of the month, lest woman and child be stricken with madness, leprosy, or faulty intelligence." Would orgasm, preventable by clitoridectomy, produce anoxia to hurt the brain?)

[d/3] Communication cannot be perfect, which is why it is essentially redundant, unlike information that must, technically speaking, be entirely brand-new. Knowledge yield may be minimal when information hurts those who have been slaves to dogma.

Communication needs open channels; information only needs attention. Assimilators need input, just as digestion requires food; integrators additionally demand coherence at their level. All animals digest information; not all integrate what they attend to.

[d/4] Whenever we are both surprised and moved deeply, we say, "I can't tell you how sad (or glad) I am." Body and nonverbal language do not deceive as much as verbiage. Written messages are not easily distorted, but oral transmission alters content cumulatively by the very process of repetition with different overtones and body language.

[d/5] Albert Einstein turned time around in his relativity theories, and very few scientists grasped their implications. James Joyce showed us language in a different light, but he is understandable to only a hundred academics around the world.

Ernest Hemingway, with his journalistic training, was easier to read in his use of short, terse sentences (sound bites) which characterize TV news reports that reserve time for sponsors' commercials. (Have you ever wondered how much you have missed in order for a TV or newspaper reporter to make a quick point?) News reports achieve clarity by sacrificing details that need mulling over.

[d/6] Spermatozoa are treated like foreign cells for having only half the usual number of chromosomes and need the protection of "nursing" or "sister" cells before "eviction." After ejaculation, brothers of the swiftest swimmer delay their rivals among later arrivals from overtaking it.

[d/7] Artistic license: Mothering—like Freemasonry (said to be an Asian legacy from Alexander the Great)—is antithetical to monotheism in Western patriarchal religions, which, like totalitarianism and organized extortion, exact obedience by the promise of protection. (Unlike Western theology in recognizing universal interdependence without demanding subservience. Oriental religiosity is also the antithesis of abusive husbands.) One God is, like Cosa Nostra, a single parent who is better able to look after animals who do not need prolonged care.

(God himself was willing to let his son die over stolen fruit from his Tree of Knowledge. [Militarism in Russia declined when mothers objected to the conscription of their sons to fight Afghanistans abroad. Against the Viet Cong, American draftees, not their mothers, endured the heavy hand of military and civil authorities in a democracy.])

(After Hiroshima, did Hirohito's disavowal of divinity as a living god affect other worshippers' awe of Lenin's wisdom in political science, an old oxymoron? [Or does money corrupt a new generation of commies as easily as it has our yuppies? Do we usually put our pocketbook prudently ahead of principles?])

[d/8] Around age nine, I had to be forcibly pulled up from the river bottom where I was close to drowning yet (1) behaving as if I could breathe underwater and (2) resisting being rescued by clutching at reeds that were within my grasp. (Could I have been virtually dehumanized by oxygen deprivation of my neocortex and taken over by my reptilian brain?) It was right after that near-drowning that I experienced my earliest sense of union with nature when I was surrounded by a sea of tall rice stalks swaying in the wind, and my hair, no matter which way I turned my face, kept flying in the same direction as the breeze. (Is this my reptilian brain talking?)

Only after entering medical school did I learn that, in fact, hair follicles (even among Hiroshima casualties) and nail cuticles in all animals did not die at the same time as their brain cells.

As expected with all acute, and therefore readily reversible, brain traumas, my grades started to pick up after initially falling off; and I was head of my class again until puberty. Thereafter, my grades were high only when I want to impress a teacher who attracted me or was attracted to me, in mind and body. (Some I dated after high school.)

My medical school professors mimeographed their lectures for a price, so I did not need to attend nonlaboratory classes in our preclinical years, when my girlfriends were unchaperoned all day. There were rooms close to the campus that can be rented cheaply for short trysts. (Creative, if not critical, thinking was encouraged by many old customs, like chaperoned dates.)

[d/9] Philosophy idealizes reason, psychology reasonableness (in a spirit of compromise). Both exalt responsibility only for rational or reasoned decisions, not for our parents, societies, or celebrities.

It is not that Greek rhetoric and logic have left us untouched. Many avoid them because they could not save Athens from losing out to its well-known enemies (even if Plato and, after him, Jurgens Habermas—in *Communication and the Evolution of Society*—argue that reason has a primordial universal transparency that, like murder, cannot be veiled by selfish interests forever).

The Renaissance (a cultural revival not much different from religious ones, like that of Eastern mysticism in the West) notwithstanding, we owe ancient Greece, more than anything else, the Hippocratic oath to do no harm. Beyond that dictum, nothing is taboo to those who came after him.

Second-hand students of Cartesian thought have labored under the misconception that *cogito ergo sum* meant "I think, therefore I am" when, in fact, cogitation from incertitude is the opposite of convictions arising from cognition. For Descartes, only the "re-cognition" of doubt when actually doubting cannot be doubted.

Critical flat-earth thinking does not close off debate on old questions and solves no problems; technology does but creates new ones. Debates only need clarity of vocabulary; problem solving needs new skills. Critical doomsday thinking is not constructive criticism, which specifies what can be done better now or later. Thinking simply produces opinions, not observations, and the intellectual (educated thinker) is just more opinionated and articulate than the skilled observer.

Intellectuals think of ideas as infrastructure. What is ignored is that infrastructures must be solid ideas, as mental models are fragile, even if objectified for worship as icons.

Computers can store, compare, categorize, and conceptualize symbols or patterns, but simulation is not experience or knowledge. (Chief Justice Earl Warren: "There is no such thing as a false idea.")

[d/10] Tennis players who blame external factors can be helped to lose by giving them an excuse.

[d/11] Can we learn more from comparing postwar USSR, not with the United States, but with postwar Japan? And Masada's martyrs with

Jonestown's mass suicide, or Jonestown's failure as a cult with Salt Lake City's financially successful Church of Latter-day Saints? Should going to the zoo remind us of Roman revelry at the expense of both Christian gladiators and captive lions?

[d/12] In the pre-Ptolemaic times when Genesis was written, to mark our days, the sun travelled across a flat earth, which can be drowned in a deluge to postpone doomsday. There are still flat-earth thinkers who use their left more than their right brain and are more linear and logical than spatial and graphic. How would chair-bound philosophers explain that not only is the earth round but that it spins at a speed that we cannot match while earth-bound?

[d/13] As in all science, luck usually steers our curiosity, and one cannot argue with luck. But like all scientists, I tend to look both very closely and from afar without consciously meaning to. The result is a kaleidoscope (chaotic for closed minds) of close-ups and wide-angle views of behavior.

[d/14] Across cultures, we also wait for authority figures to begin eating unless they are afraid of being poisoned.

[d/15] Two roving and starving pit bull dogs finally trapped both peacocks under our half-opened garage. Their tail feathers—which were worshipped in the past as divinely inspired icons for beauty and symmetry—interfered with flight and were all that were left behind.

Those tails also attracted our cats (who were themselves objects of ancient worship), whom the peacocks had to chase away when they try to play with their feathers.

[d/16] To be uncircumcised until puberty (and then accept a dorsal slit without loss of tissue rather than circumferential excision of the prepuce) can save one from untraceable castration anxiety.

[d/17] Parents become carpet custodians and car upholstery security police.

[d/18] My 31-week-old grandson—on waking up without crying, but needing to be fed and attended to—mouths *m* silently, clicks his tongue, and licks his lips, between exhaling and inhaling 31 syllables, some of which he repeats when I echo them incorrectly. He would additionally put his hand on my mouth, take my forefinger and bite, and snatch the notepaper I am jotting all of this on. He is asking, without saying so, for a change of diaper, a bottle of milk, and his teething ring along with the attention that comes with each.

When he wants me to pick him up, he would wave my thumbs away, instinctively sensing that he cannot pull up his 24 pounds by his hands, and keeps waving his hand until I lift him under his armpits, when he would touch/slap my face.

Dolphins, who have bigger brains per pound than people, are thought to have a culture of their own. The sounds they make are studied with the help of computers in order to establish direct communication with them. Aren't babies even more accessible as unprinted books from the past? Babies before their first birthday carry on long conversations in the dark. (Social scientists who still think "the proper study of mankind is man" but now agree that "the child is the father of the man" should, at least, begin with vocalizations that babies will teach, untaught.)

Gorillas can find new names for objects by using sign language. Elephants, orangutans (up to $3,000 per painting) and chimpanzees have produced art that connoisseurs have collected for enjoyment and profit. Primates and preschool children can manipulate computers for reward and enjoyment. Our only unique skill is decipherable scribbling on paper. That we excel in the use of symbols benefits us only in musical notations and scientific formulae. Concepts for other uses tend to cloud rather than clarify the issues that they address.

[d/19] On his first post-Christmas nonfamily gathering, my grandson did not want to be held by the host or hostess but surprised us by singling out a woman whom we hardly knew. It turned out that she had had two tubal pregnancies, the first of which nearly killed her. What this means is that she is undaunted about having babies. Did my grandson intuitively know without thinking that those who love and are not loved back suffer more during seasonal lovefests?

At this writing, he is 30 months old. That he senses suffering sooner than the person hurting I learned directly when he stayed next to me while I told the other grandchildren that, because of its size, the county building department did not want their tree house completed without a plan to follow. (But planning is nothing more than improvising on paper, and I can finish it unassisted.)

Does this mean that he is incapable of hurting anyone? He pokes at me with a retractable sword but today hit his next older cousin hard enough to hurt. He had to be asked to apologize to her by his sister. As I consoled his cousin, he joined us but merely said "Hi" offhandedly to her. He was, however, fully aware that he made her cry. He may only have reservations about the unilaterality of his role as contrite apologist but did not have the words to say so.

[d/20] Are animals dumb because, unclothed, they have nothing to hide or dress up with words. Are the articulate or more civilized dressed to kill and less civil for being ashamed of their nakedness?

[d/21] All that is pleasurable or painful that is not sexual is sensual, including foreplay or courting, verbal or nonverbal. Only male dogs can be trained to be better friends as lovers of their mistresses, which might explain why only castrating females are called bitches (female canines entrap by "vaginissmus"). Those who need to be loved keep dogs; those who need to love keep cats. (Ideally, people should progress from dogs to cats.)

[d/22] When mother cats hesitate about leaving their litter, they demonstrate that additional data are needed.

[d/23] Birth is the beginning and essence of life. Events before and since are more existential than essential.

[d/24] When R, matriarch or social butterfly, died along with the likely successor to the alpha male cat, there was chaos while the survivors jockeyed for positions in the pecking order. Less involved was W, who—more than properly maternal GG or industriously social R, both from another litter—stuck to her brood and seemed to need her kittens more than they need her, just like a smotherer or overprotective Jewish mother might. She immediately returns them to their condominium box before they can roam as far as their peers. (We are fondest of GG, but she'd leave as soon as her kittens can leave with her and not return until her next litter is due. Is friendship less necessary than protection?)

[d/25] Can husbands let wives be mothers first, and mothers be a bedfellow again after weaning, when dual parenting by selective attention replaces mothering? Bottle-feeding is as human and inhumane as nursing by appointment. Was scheduled breast-feeding the first step toward mammalian reproductive freedom? Today, silicone, more than mother's milk, makes for larger breasts in a million American women. This particular cosmetic gimmick must rank as one of our stupidest. I have even seen some postmastectomy statuesque specimens—like unabashed amputees—in sun-loving, dress-optional resorts, looking like legendary Amazon women warriors. (More useful, arguably, are our phallus-shaped space vessels that took man farther out of this world during the ball-shrinking Cold War.) Banning of toxic breast implants, after more than 2 million have been inserted, was staunchly resisted by many on the basis of the right to choose and use, but without forfeiting their standing to sue for suffering physical and mental damage that can exceed $7.3 million! (O. J. Simpson was assessed $8.5 million for the wrongful death, not of his wife, but of the man with her.)

[d/26] Exclusively human are (1) oral or anal homosexuality (shared narcissism or nonimmaculate contraconception), (2) actual or mental necrophilia (iconic and institutional denial of death for pharaohs, Lenin, Mao), (3) necrophobia (resurrection for Jesus Christ and reincarnation for Elvis Presley) among worshippers and fans, and (4) thanatophobia (neurotic fear of dying), "sublimated" among philosophers and theologians. All except shared narcissism are "anal" perversions or inventions, unlike immaculate conception ("undirty" begetting all by one's self). Parenting without partners was practiced by plants as apomixis and by insects as parthenogenesis.

[d/27] What is philosophy with its ultimately unanswerable questions if not a wake before there is a funeral? If philosophy is preparation for dying, is preoccupation outside the tropics with almost dying more prevalent wherever leaves fall from trees before long winters? And their theologians more puritan?

[d/28] Why is there so much fuss made about a wedding dress that is not meant to be worn for very long? White floor-length dresses that flare out at the waist suggest and promise purity and fertility in exaggerating the bride's thrusting pelvic movements during the wedding march to the altar and back.

Human eggs have to be fertilized with or without (1) foreplay or courtship, (2) public announcement of private intentions, or (3) surrender by the father of the object of oedipal fantasies in front of witnesses. Would bride and groom be much better off to elope and spend what is saved on a round-the-world honeymoon instead?

[d/29] Was Jesus faulted for befriending Mary Magdalene (who was not a nun), or—with his curly hair and skin color—for being an uppity male mulatto or both? (Even as Christ, he is only allowed to marry gentiles who must remain virgins as Christian nuns.)

Did an ex-nun who married Judge Robert Bork, a Jew, doom his appointment to the Supreme Court? (It is the height of arrogance to consummate an ex-widow's marriage to one's tribal casualty. Can a virgin just desert her Divine Husband to join the matrimonial lottery for an exclusive mate?) It is better if a Christian marries a Jewess (one who did got to be secretary-general of the United Nations.) Was anti-Semitism greater among righteous critics of Monica Lewinski and Clinton?

[d/30] A pubescent female kitten licks the same arm to obtain more scent for herself. Adam himself was bestial until Eve and Lilith but not "Bruce" were provided as better sexual partners. (If Noah can have two wives, why not Adam? Old paintings of biblical scenes show two women in Eden, but only Eve and Adam leaving. During the Renaissance, direct descent of American Indians from Adam was greatly doubted, because in woodcuts made at that time, they were unashamedly buck naked.)

In an electronic near lynching, a black female ex-employee against a black Supreme Court nominee who was married to a Caucasian had alleged vicarious bestiality. Had this "uppity nigger" (his own words) even verbally harassed a white woman with explicit details of lurid sexual scenes, his confirmation might have been derailed. (The first American Negro hero and heavyweight champion loved white women and was hounded out of the country. Was Jack Johnson miscegenophilic or bestial in reverse, like our sex-cited tomcat, toward his mistress?)

The Jewish nominee who married an ex-nun was also vainly investigated for pornographic interest! (For both nominees, miscegenophilia was an unspoken criticism from miscegenophobes who object to mixed marriages, even in fantasy.) Did their enemies know that the retiring token black justice was the first to arrive at a weekly screening of X-rated movies in the Supreme Court to decide whether they are obscene (scatological and offensive) or pornographic (aphrodisiacal and exciting)?

In their wisdom, the justices decided that if the goal of pornography is to stimulate erections, the impotent cannot legislate nostalgic regrets, and ruled that obscenity depended on the toilet training history of the community.

Dirt and sex are separable: Good or bad taste is "oral," obscenity more "anal," we are born nude but not necessarily exhibitionistic or "urethral," erectility is more "genital."

"Ano-urethral personalities" act as if their genitals get dirty under layers of garment and wash their hands after passing sterile urine. (Subordinates are also afraid of their odor offending their superiors, whose criticisms can "cut to the quick.") Those afraid of having been sexually injured during coitus reassure themselves visually afterward by lighting a cigarette to relax, or going to the bathroom, turning on the light, and emptying their bladders.

"Genital personalities" wash their hands before handling male or female genitalia or take a shower right after sexual intercourse.

[d/31] When my infant grandson snuggles close to the armpits of both parents, is it their familiar smell or—like penguins who are cold-blooded at birth—their body warmth that is sought by a reptilian brain, whose muscle memory traces make toddlers trying on "walkers" totter backward on limbs once used for crawling? Must the inebriated propel themselves forward to resist tendencies to crawl or teeter in the opposite direction? (The old brain directs us to crawl before we can walk, the new brain to talk before we can think.)

[d/32] Cults become reorganized as religions, not because their creed is persuasive but because, like the Mormons, their leaders are businesslike in their fund-raising. Catholics lose converts who use cosmetics because making the sign of the cross with fingertips moistened with holy water can leave unsightly streaks or spots in expensive facial makeup.

[d/33] As adoptive parents, we took our first cat wherever we went in a van that we had converted for sleeping, cooking, and bathing, and even smuggled him into hotels. When he failed to return home from a nocturnal jaunt, we suffered the fears that parents of missing children must live with about the likelihood of sexual abuse.

Only by castrating him can BK be kept indoors indefinitely.

The Arctic caribou can also be herded by castrating restless males and keeping the untouched stag on a leash to lead the herd to pasture. ("Liberation forces" isolate leaders who would not collaborate and keep quislings on a tight leash to insure against resistance to their liberators.)

An ancient civilization may have died, according to Mayan historians, from sacrificing its best young men to their chosen god. (They routinely and ritually left young bleeding hearts upon his reclining, sleeping or dying, graven image to replace his still or stone-dead heart, but any such crude attempt at cross-species cardiac transplantation was bound to fail.)

[d/34] We look after our cats the way dolphins of Denham, the westernmost beach in Australia, are taken care of by the natives. They come to be fed without any attempt at domestication.

[d/35] Disasters or imminent acts of God are what made mutual assistance groups necessary, and gave birth to group loyalties, even mutual admiration societies, which exclude outsiders in xenophobic fanaticism. (Should environmental impact studies include lists of loyalties that are weakened by avoiding community crisis?)

Groups are imperative only when the individual members are weak and can believe make-believe myths. Making group ideologies, including theology, denominators in the human equation makes better sense than giving them the primacy that old thinking accorded them. Personal sensuality—including passion (e-motion without action)—and private sexuality are the numerators of this equation in the practice of a New Psychiatry called clinical rationalysis of behavior: Becoming + Begetting/Believing. All three (sensuality, society, and sex) change, stagnate, and age.

Intelligence is inherited and ranges more broadly from species to species. Smart use of it is also hereditary and is called talent. To be talented is better than to be intelligent. Intelligence only indicates amount of memory stored, as in the idiot savant; talent may show itself before enough memory has been stored in the precocious, like Mozart. The intelligent can only be critical; the talented can be creative. But only a few are so far ahead of their time that they are dead before they are recognized. (In 212 BC, Archimedes himself burned Roman boats off the coast of besieged Syracuse by focusing the rays of the sun on their sails with mirrors.)

[d/36] Laws enforce institutionalized prejudices (dogma) that are therefore perpetuated by worship of precedents.

[d/37] A grasshopper can remove a rival's sperm from its mate and stay coupled while it lays its eggs from a second sex organ, even underwater for up to 15 minutes. A thin layer of air clings to their bodies to keep them from drowning. Cold-blood, they die in the fall. The next spring their nymphs are hatched, with gills.

[d/38] At one point, for their protection, we had three litters indoors. Territorial cats and canines devour bastards that some societies cast out. Is primogeniture the encoding of territoriality along bloodlines?

[d/39] My only jotting that possibly hints at animal gratitude goes back to what prompted our opening our doors to the sick and dying among our cats. We had friends looking after them on one of my trips abroad to give talks on the evolution of behavior. Two were very sick, and we called home to keep track of their progress. On our return, when my wife picked a recovering kitten up, it stretched its neck to touch hers. I was moved and I saw her brushing away a tear. I don't recall feeling as deeply under similar circumstances with those who express thanks in words.

The other sick cat whom we called LE has since died and its successor, EB, now would only eat baby food. Like Gandhi and me, it has learned to fast to get what it wants.

And we cannot deny its need, because my parents would also wait for me to join them at the table rather than trivialize the reason for my refusing, which I can, as a child, only assert by fasting. A short collective fast seems to bring the family closer together than prayer. So we all thought, except that on my camping honeymoon, the longer we drove to find an idyllic picnic setting, the more hypoglycemic and irritable we got.

I know now that feelings run high on an empty stomach but did not escalate if food to fill it is within sight and smell. (With psychiatric trainees, I make sure we meet before lunch, and with my faculty, during lunch: the quickest way to the brain is an empty stomach, to the heart a full one.)

[d/40] The "fishpond" was drained after LB drowned in it. We had been afraid that might happen and floated a raft in the middle where cats who overreached to drink or fish can dog-paddle to safety. LB did not make it because he had weak hind legs from having been the seventh in a litter whose mother had only six nipples.

Are runts more ambitious than their abilities warrant? Are they the prototypical Napoleonic personality with which overcompensates human racists (chauvinistic humanists) for being more inept physically than animals? (Younger by several years, we got our youngest grandchild his own smaller wading pool, separate from the deeper one for his sister and cousins who are rough with whomever is within reach.)

[d/41] It is next to impossible for someone who believes that the communion wafer is Jesus incarnate to disbelieve in heaven above us (there was still "up" and "down" when he died) after weekly soul cleansing by confession (to avoid hell below).

(Copernicus relocated earth from the center of the universe—which happens to have no center—and Newton's gravity removed "up" and "down" from the category of absolutes, though he continued as a deist to the end. Einstein in turn made time and speed relative, but remained a theist nonetheless. That their discoveries cast doubt on their beliefs makes them more honest scientists.)

[d/42] Art is also a way of taking advantage of popular technology (e.g., "fast" films) while waiting for the next scientific breakthrough (e.g., electron microscopy). Thusly does art appreciate science. On the other hand, science appreciates man a good deal less than art does. Both art and science now appreciate nature, though religious art and music interested early artists more, and science originally attempted to control nature for our own ends.

[d/43] Psychiatrists, police officers, ophthalmologists, and dentists are more suicidal than other professionals. Until I had a cataract removed, I did not know why. Now we can test whether the fact that they work in relative darkness, even when they use spotlighting, may have a common consequence. (The space I designed for housing us, my private practice, and group teaching has south-facing, 12-foot wide, three-story glass walls in the living room and no interior corridors to traverse in relative darkness.)

[d/44] Bears are truly unique in giving birth and nursing their young while still asleep during hibernation.

[d/45] You might note that, like philosophers, including Rousseau (1712–1778) and Nietzsche (1844–1900), no artist is listed as cofounder of the applied science of absolute relativity. (In our clinical conferences, I have always rejected the use of literary figures or clever ideas to support treatment strategy. Only amateurs use them.)

Like Shakespeare (1564–1616) of an earlier Elizabethan Age, both philosophers were pre-Darwinian—Nietzsche being hopelessly insane from syphilis of the brain by the time Darwin (1809–1882) achieved notoriety. (Was Hitler [G], though much less individualistic [I] than his hero, also syphilitic in his grandiosity about a race of supermen?) All are also definitely pre-Pavlovian in their worldview.

[d/46] Did fighting Native Americans hold up economic progress for American pioneers so that Australians have almost caught up even after a late start of almost a century and a half in settling their subcontinent, just from not engaging in genocide of aboriginal infidels?

[d/47] Hairy tailless apes may be small (gibbons and simians) or great in size or brainpower: "orangutan" means "man of the forest," gorillas can learn 500 words in sign language, and chimpanzees are closer to us and almost as dangerous to each other as we are.

[d/48] Precisely because religion, politics, and economics are preliterate in origin and specialization in them has not improved our HQ or happiness quotient, we have to ask one simple question: why are their fanatics so fanatical?

Assistance in becoming free of our parents is helped by the tooth fairy, Easter Bunny, and Santa Claus. All, nonetheless, can be replaced by Virgin Mary, Jesus, or their Father Almighty (his incestuous grandfather), to free us even from Mother Earth. Christianity itself, however, is a syncretic assimilation of older traditions, just like Australian cricket, which is played as *kasaya* by Trobriand Islanders.

[d/49] To exalt the elegance of expensive artifacts of old civilizations—that lost for its masses the dignity of civil disobedience to those enthroned—is to honor the masterful, not the masterless. Quality of life does not correlate with cost of possessions. It corresponds better with the quality of fornication (which must be discussed with couples in prescribing drugs with adverse sexual side effects). Wherever it is costly or least expensive to live is probably unhealthy, whether next to dense traffic or in a deserted ghost town.

[d/50] In the modern world, when (G) politicians try to justify their stand, they talk about what is (A) good or unseemly, (B) fair or wrong, and (C) true or false (even when there are no third-party witnesses, as in alleged sexual harassment of accuser by a controversial Supreme Court nominee).

Karl Marx (1818–1883) is proving to be farsighted in predicting that (H) economics is more decisive than (G) politics. (Canadians, Americans, and Mexicans may be equally patriotic; but the traffic across our north and south boundaries are dramatically different for economic reasons.)

We hope we can go beyond other primates and show that (K) knowledge, not (C) truth, is power, and that information spreads with (O) computer literacy so that (K x O) global networks can replace (G x K') balance of terror among (BB) imperious (G x H) superpowers.

[d/51] When faced by bullies, some go back to their childhood fantasies or seethe in silence. Those more frustrated by them, instead of becoming speechless, spit out terse but unquotable sound bites or sputter profanities and clichés to rail at villains or rally their victims.

(Others hire speechwriters to hide their endangered civility or suspected inferiority better.)

[d/52] Is "mind" more than a clerk for filing away memories and retrieving them from storage when needed? Environmentalists deny that their DNA decides their destiny; geneticists insist that it does. Can we program consciousness of alternatives or choice of options in a computer chip so that it can discriminate and select?

[d/53] There is a movement among intellectuals to emphasize critical thinking as practiced by Socrates and other philosophers. This will last until the Dark Ages of cold reason gives way to postlogical science. (If upon self-examination, Socrates decided that his life was not worth living, but on self-realization, he exclaimed, "I drank what?" did Socrates uselessly go through two stages of introspection: [1] self-examination [self-tasting] and [2] self-realization [test-tasting]?)

[d/54] To hear in a bird soaring above us the songs of Cyrano whose bill they surpass is as riveting as de Bergerac's biology: "Plucking the flowers will keep the plants in bloom."

5.00 e/Nature: ORIGINS and REVOLUTIONS of BEHAVIOR

Each unit of behavior, animate or inanimate, is an event in the present and a message from the past. We respond to it as part of our past and react to it as it involves us in the present.

Behavior, human or animal, if similar, no matter how subtle or complex, must have roots that are far-reaching in time and scope.

We will therefore continue to learn about historical and global correlations as long as we can be challenged by new explanations that transcend tradition and culture in living and dead civilizations.

(Without an outline or agenda, topics seem to fall into place nonetheless and naturally. This is not a story and therefore has no beginning or end, just a continuity which branches off, but not to suit the author.)

WoMan evolved from the same substance as matter in distant nebulae (con-naturally), as did other living things (con-vivially), like people before and during recorded history (con-familially).

We were not created equal, nor did we evolve and survive uniformly in the same eras until we invented tools. Since then our lifestyles (culture) seem to be converging, differing ideologies notwithstanding.

We have already achieved this uniformity in the practice of modern pharmacology, but not yet in medicine, including psychiatry (outside psychopharmacology) or older traditional medical practice with natural herbs and time-tested techniques like acupuncture.

ABZs of Life

It is how we change, not what we change into, that makes us healthy or unhealthy, whether (**i**) we, (**ii**) the clan, or (**iii**) our kin profit or not from the changes.

Before the (**Z**)enith of life, only a few can (1) find what is (**A**) good, bad or beyond judgment, (**B**) right, wrong, or unyielding, (**C**) true, false, or unchallenged, (**D**) provable or inaccessible or refreshing, and (**E**) original or traditional or retrofitted, and then proceed (2) without buying or denying that belief systems are addictive, to study (**F**) Father Almighty, (**G**) good governors, (**H**) hoarding, (**I**) individualism, (**J**) joint undertakings, (**K**) know-how, (**L**) love of mankind, (**M**) Mother Earth, (**N**) natural intelligence, or (**O**) overintelligent computers, while (3) developing (**P–Y**) sexually to earn (**Z**) grandparenthood.

Are We All Con-Natural? (Act I)

We shall now explore what we have in common with (**I**) the cosmos, (**II**) animals, and (**III**) humanimals (*Homo sapiens* more than *H. domesticus* or *metropolus*) (**i**) sensually, (**ii**) socially, and (**iii**) sexually.

(Sexual differentiation results in cohabitation. Partners who would rather work or write than fornicate are perverts, by definition. And those who would make the sexes equal as family caregivers have become ideologues. Fathers should be compared with other fathers of other species.)

Ionian Greeks were the first to ponder whether our planet revolves around a star, instead of occupying the exact center of the universe. Did their neighbors think they were odd? (Sometimes I had wondered if Imola, California, as a postgraduate training center, can be the new Ionia of the West.) Ionian intuition and astrophysics both imply that any examination of universal behavior during life in an open system (<—>) may be easier but not simpler than the study of inanimate substances in a closed but expanding (-> . . . <-) cosmos.

An open system like ours, unlike stars and other heavenly bodies, conserves energy and adapts environmentally while it is alive and healthy.

Our own convivial environment may be internal (given or genetic) and external (borrowed or social).

Because most plants are genetically rooted or immobile, their borrowed environment is easier to study than the socially active environment of more genetically animated matter that we call animals.

All living things, plants or animals, adapt to their con-vivial environment out of healthy self-interest, except during con-sensual reproduction. Then their "selfish genes" or parasympathetic autonomic drive them to multiply in order to perpetuate their species, even at the cost of their longevity.

(Because sex is older than animals, they do not have to be reminded to go forth and multiply. In both botany and zoology, a species is defined by its selfish genes alone, since reproductive incompatibility results in sterile mutants that biologists call monsters.)

Beyond the Big Bang

Are contributions to understanding large-scale changes beyond the boundaries of psychiatry? Must we confine ourselves to what we can examine minutely? Since philosophers, priests, politicians, profiteers, and other amateur social psychologists have not helped, where do we look? What can we ignore? Can we begin with what is touted to be the very beginning? Did "Let there be light!" produce the big bang? Or the other way around?

Tailored for humorless, color-conscious skinheads, our local story of creation—in order to explain how Filipinos got baked a golden brown instead of ending up overdone black or underdone white—claims that God in his oven (sic) had to try thrice to create us in his image (Zeus also looks Greek).

Another myth for all islanders explains how, surrounded by water, our own Adam and Eve emerged from giant bamboos: An eagle split one open and out came Malakas (Strong, not vainglorious but uncircumcised) and Maganda (Beautiful, not vain but orgasmic) *(e/1)* to enjoy our warm archipelago, which is neither as dry nor as icy as other Gardens of Eden. Our parents' good fortune they owe entirely to indigenous plants and other animals, not to some mysterious force or jealous idol who demands blind obedience. (The Darwinian theory of evolution agrees with their uninformed notion of trees being around and birds being ascendant before their local version of Adam and Eve appeared as a pair.)

(On a hillside in the Greek island of Patmos where St. John dictated his version of Divine Revelation to a devotee before he died, there is a church door on which is painted what is purported to be Paradise with two women in it.)

(In the Harvard Library archives, Eve and Lilith [who became God's consort] are contemporaries.)

Another Myth of Creation

Preamble *(e/2)*: Many accept our Constitution and the Bible at face value even if both reflect their writers' ignorance and bias, no matter how inspired. They would deny outright any suggestion that the framers of the Constitution made states equal to man in order to create a select Senate to protect the rich against one-man, one-vote. Likewise, our new myth of creation—originally captioned "From Tail to Thumb to Tongue to Tale" *(e/3)* (birth defects include embryonic gills and tails)—begun with "help" as the first word uttered and heard (to compensate for losing our first thumb, a prehensile tail, on becoming a great ape) but, since early idolatrous wordsmiths cannot ghostwrite biblical history around a verb, this later version is also noun-driven.

"The beginning was—not a divine dance as the Hindus claim, but—a Word, and the word was Alpha, which is the alias for Cosmos. He had two sons who complemented each other: a smart and/or sinister Satan and a jealous and/or covetous Jehovah. For them he produced Lilith and Eve. Lilith seduced Jehovah and Satan seduced Eve with the fruits of a Tree of Knowledge. Now occupied for the rest of their lives, Cosmos can let his sons' balancing act of 'yin' and 'yang' proceed without fine-tuning.

"Jehovah, with Lilith conniving, wanted the world for himself. Like a spoiled kid, he acted as if it was intended to feed his ego. Lilith had no children. Outsmarted and smarting from losing Eve, Jehovah accused her of freely (intelligently) committing 'original sin.' Inherited by sons from their fathers, it can be cleansed by circumcision with sharp tools after leaving the Stone Age behind. When one of her descendants seemed odd because of his dark skin (as seen in Black Nazarene icons) and hair like 'lamb's wool' (as described in the Bible), instead of calling him a 'mulatto,' they crowned him 'King of Kings' and crucified him to save all sinners without abolishing circumcision. (He can, since his resurrection, formally marry only gentile virgins forever looking for Mr. Right.)

"Magic fascinated Jehovah, and he blessed all who believed in holy ghosts and guardian angels, tooth fairies, and Santa Claus, and who expected miracles from him all their life as his subjects. Satan, on the other hand, delights in reminding Jehovah that Cosmos has natural laws that he cannot keep challenging with his supernatural powers. (Shrinks and siblings everywhere understand their rivalry.)

"With Eve's support, Satan encouraged skepticism and testing, and the physical sciences flourished. Her descendants lived longer than those immaculately conceived (John the Baptist and Jesus). But some have more talent than stomach for doubting. In times of increasing uncertainty, they turned away from Satan towards certitude.

"Those who doubted Jehovah were persecuted as heretics during a Grand Inquisition, which later drove Galileo Galilei into exile. (Eve's descendants by now had a first name and a family name.) He suggested that 'causal enquiries' lead nowhere. Today this underground 'witch hunt' is legitimized by Aristotle's metaphysical 'final cause,' which he argued as the be-all and end-all of all thinking: of course, Aristotle knew only about Zeus and nothing about zero, where everything begins and ends. *(e/4)*

"Werner Heisenberg did not hesitate to doubt and, for elevating 'uncertainty' to the status of a 'principle' in physics, he was awarded the Nobel Prize. But Sigmund Freud was not similarly honored— probably out of lingering respect for the ancient idea of a conscious free will (which the criminally insane can now legally disown to escape capital punishment)—when he showed how much both sensible and irrational behavior develop from past experiences which we have forgotten or cannot remember nor deliberately discount.

"Before Galileo or Freud, a monk called Nicholas Copernicus, who had been taught that man was an imitation of his Maker— suspected what few of us can accept: that 'never had Jehovah or Satan influenced Cosmos.' What this obviously implies is that the

Cosmos himself cannot change the blueprint for the beginning (BBB or Before Big Bang) or the end (GGG or Gone Gib Gnab) of the universe. Was its design fossilized when the Tree of Knowledge died and got buried with the dinosaurs?

"Gas or ash, many fragments of memory surface out of our collective past, as animal intuition reaching our reptilian brain, which instinctively takes over the moment all mammals are born. What naked primates recall then becomes prescient and prophetic mythology or short-lived metaphysics, and therefore more elegant and promising than helpful in coping: Plato thought geometric figures were memories of perfect forms. Virgil was claimed to have inklings of the Old Testament's prophesy of the coming of a Messiah.

"As Alpha's Omega, we were not privileged to witness the beginning, but as guests of honor, we will be invited to say good-bye before the world ends. However, who can wait forever to verify if there is no ending, because there may have been no beginning?"

Unlike older myths, this new one will not satisfy those who seek final certitude. Afraid to face facts, they substitute logical ("If, then") for methodical ("When, then") thinking. Afraid of deadlines and dying, they cannot abide loose ends as they prepare to meet their Maker. But our version should clarify what still confounds the curious who are not querulous. (Scientific testing and outer space vigil can help identify what makes our world tick and keeps it running, even at the risk of blowing up parts of it and ourselves, because it will not stand still for us to continue sitting on our ignorance.)

From Metaphysics with a Smirk to Physics and "Wisdom" with A Smile

The cosmos is 15 billion years older than all of us. Does it care about us enough to listen?

Energy is either light or heat or matter. Energy from matter produces light, heat, and explosion.

All physics and natural philosophy (what is not metaphysical or beyond physics) before zero was used in mathematics should be considered obsolete. Whitehead's and Russell's *Principia Mathematica* (1910) showed how all our familiar mathematical concepts and facts can be logically derived from certain very simple and primitive principles of reasoning, and rejected the notion of a perfect and omnipotent God.

Godel's incompleteness theorem (1931), five years after Heisenberg's uncertainty principle, doubts that rational thought can ever penetrate to the final ultimate truth. (That means there is none or reason is not meant to: what is meaningful to one can only be subjectively significant and may be meaningless except to fellow travelers.)

> I was born the same year that God died after the uncertainty principle first saw the light of day. Certitude about our central position in the universe had gone with Copernicus, and now even the exactitude of the physical sciences is disproved.

Confusing variables encouraged self-fulfilling bias until Kurt Godel proved in 1930 that mathematics is open-ended. (All it means is that mathematicians are also imperfect connoisseurs.)

Reader: Will progress always stop short of perfection?

Editor: I hope so. Otherwise, only one of us will be left to enjoy it.

Author: Or we'd only have clones of ourselves for company to bore or entertain us.

Continued doubting about clues drives more curious scientists to use nature studies (out-of-doors) or in-house (lab or zoo) observations.

> (Today's facts are just tomorrow's building blocks until newer ones fit better. To be scientific [Galilean], we need to ask questions [e.g., "Does weight or mass decide acceleration of free fall?"]; to be a legend we must provide answers (i.e., "Neither under experimental conditions in a virtual vacuum."); to be an explorer we must track history, to be a pioneer we must enter the unknown, to be wise we must not confuse proving with knowing and evidence with truth.)

What we need today is to be able to test all limits, provided it poses no risk to the helpless, i.e., our new science of absolute relativity in anthropology, biology, and cosmology must be applied boldly but "scienethically." Only those who learn to test reality by testing its limits will push art (as James Joyce did) or technology (as test pilots do) or human experience (as we do) to its limits.

(Buddha had warned, "Do not believe anything simply because it is found in your religious books . . . or merely on the authority of your teachers" [or gurus, even in science].)

For Uninvested Interests

Perhaps no man is an island, but inside our skin, we are all prisoners of our past with varying prison sentences for degrees of original sin or wrong thinking as defined by our critics (judgmental parents, peers, seers, etc.).

Chained to our culture, most of us are restricted to our intellectual neighborhood, like the old Soviets, who could not travel far without official permission. We also cannot think as freely once we are suspected of defecting. Very few of us carry a passport to travel away from truths preached in our home, clan, or ranks, whether tribal or professional. (Even expatriates seek congenial groups.)

(For those with conventional vested interests, the author uses humor ["God in his oven," etc.] to communicate, rather than expertise to inform. In driving home the distinction between choice and options, he usually describes himself as stubborn enough to refuse any summons from the Great Beyond but not for a house call from a dysfunctional family where stepfather and stepson are about to get into a fist fight.]

As in astronomy, our verified observations in nature studies cannot be tested experimentally, even among close relatives in the animal kingdom, but these experiences are often reenacted without being reported to those whose expectations may have been violated or disappointed. Silence encourages prejudice to spread.

Moon Rocks and Earth Sand

Dust thou art and to dust shalt thou return.
—Genesis 3.19

If the atom is a microcosm of the universe, and the universe is not anthropocentric, then we are essentially like the atom more than our ancient myths about it.

One of those myths is that the individual atom is indivisible. Only in our minds was it ever so. Fission and fusion was its lot as nearly and as early as we can tell. *(e/5)*

If, in fact, nature is our Virgin Mother and God is not our father, then the atom is our ancestor and animals our aunts and uncles.

If we begin life by closely resembling our aunts and uncles in utero, is death merely atavism and dying just a prelude to becoming our own ancestors again? (Atavis is Latin for great-great-great-grandfather.)

There's nature, then instincts, then ritual to continue tradition. There's natural law, moral law, and common law. There's physics, then morality, then ethics.

What is uncertain may be exciting, like a blind date, rather than an impending examination in a curriculum called living dangerously.

We all have a blind date with the future. Will it, like the movies, feature sex and violence?

Sex created us; violence (as in solar fusion) maintains us. We annihilate matter to produce energy, just like the sun does. But other animals think of watering holes and hunting grounds, not life and death.

We diminish life by being fearful for our lives and the fruits of our loins. Are our genes not good enough?

(If not, we only need our children to love us. If we are not lovable, they will be unborn. We used to choose what children we begot with arranged marriages. Hypergamy should distinguish between talent and resourcefulness. Romantic coupling with or for commoners no longer seeks to improve their genetic heritage: the poor need romance as much as the weak need God to keep them going in the face of adversity.)

Mind over Matter

George Bernard Shaw, informed that light travels at the speed of 186,000 miles per second, retorted that this was the most obvious lie he had ever heard. Many have felt that way about some of the things we will now try to set straight.

Astronomers used to think that what they discover must fit their earth-bound ideas. Others still think that our behavior today must be judged by old borrowed ideas of what mankind is all about.

> Ptolemy preached orbital symmetry,
> Newton professed provable perfection
> > in pure straight lines
> > of force and acceleration.
> Einstein proved neither knew enough
> > to understand our universe.
> Yet we use Einstein as an example
> > that we are a rational species.
> If we truly are, he must be a mutant
> > and we are the missing links
> To this changing civilization
> > still seeking symmetry
> > for the sake of equality.

Recurrent Errors and Suggested Remedy

Though Copernicus proved centuries ago that we are no longer the hub of the universe, the "headshrinker" in me can still see how all of our behavior, internal or invisible and external or tangible, mirrors all that the particles in the cosmos may be capable of.

Others have proposed an anthropic cosmological principle, which is more anthropomorphic. As such, its proponents must still be stuck in Stage (**L**) (anthropocentricity) of their development. This is one step lower than that of Archimedes, the first to theorize along the same lines, at a time when (**M**) geocentricity was the basis on which he argued that calculating the number of grains of sand in Sicily can give us the number of particles in the whole universe. (Accidentally or coincidentally, the number he arrived at is almost identical to the calculated number of nucleons by modern reckoning.) Anthropomorphism makes man the measure of what he measures, and what is measured is forever distorted by human handicaps. I wonder if a dog also judges its master by his attention to its well-being.

That our behavior is not peculiar to us should not insult us. All it means is that we are as much a part of the cosmos as we ever were in the days when we thought we were the hub of the universe and our species was the best that it ever saw fit to produce. But it also means that we may not be the finished product that we had thought we were.

(This is not to say that we are perfectible. Perfection precludes dying. Even our own star, which sun worshippers adore as their life-giver, is slowly dying. Appreciating it for its unfailing warmth will not keep it alive. [Nor does cherishing an old flame or an earlier civilization alter either.])

In the wider cosmic scheme, we are but innocent bystanders (kibitzers, like astronomers who have no moves of their own in a chess game between star players). Though we scratch when we itch, scratching is not the same as exercising wide-ranging, freewheeling initiatives willfully or willingly. (Itching includes looming deadlines, learned hatreds, uninvited inspiration, etc. Scratching includes writing about fact and fiction, and has a predictable pleasure/pain threshold.)

If we are at all different, it is from being more "AniMachinErotic." Animals are more "animasexual" and less interested in mechanical or sexual prostheses. (Chimps improvise tools but do not patent them.)

Our theory is not intended to make science comprehensible to the unschooled (like George Bernard Shaw who is more articulate than learned), or mysticism acceptable to skeptics, but simply to apply evaluation (valuation or devaluation) by senso-socio-sexual rationalysis to the behavior of scientists, artists, mystics, etc. In our "pyramid of life" the cornerstones were laid by proven clinicians like Freud more than by published playwrights or novelists.

Is it now timely to discard the concept of immortal soul or precious self (secret identity) and replace it with a group of selves ([i] sensual, [ii] social, and [iii] sexual), coevolving at different rates in different people (persons, not indivisible individuals), beginning at different ages and ripening according to concurrent opportunity?

Behavior of Stars in Heaven and of Humanimals on Earth

Nature is motion and matter. Because neither needs us, do we proceed to enslave both? How much less like nature, animals, and other humans do we behave when we try to live up to what we claim to be?

Unarguably, cosmologists denied geocentricity (our earth is not even a star), Darwin anthropocentricity (we may be superior to a few animals, but we are not special), Freud our logocentricity (very few of us are rational, and of those, some protest too much), and physicists atomic indivisibility (we can even convert matter into energy).

The study of behavior, like the study of the universe, involves details forever remote from our direct experience. Astronomy is doubly handicapped, because the object of its study is remote, both in space and in time. The study of behavior is only handicapped by the remoteness of its origins.

Yet students of the evolution of the universe are more confident than those who deal with behavior directly. Is it because they have better lenses than our rose-colored glasses?

[As a clinician, author insisted that his staff never refer to his patients as "disturbed" instead of disturbing. As an educator, his students cannot say "mind" instead of "minding," and as a biobehavioral scientist with or without a soul, he sees "God" (cop-out/scapegoat) as "Sol," since (s)he nurtures all of us and not just some of us.]

Young or old, we ourselves cannot easily outgrow what we have been taught too early to doubt. Repeated cross-examination of the basis of our certitude is needed. Are we not ready yet to grant that human behavior also obeys universal laws that we have already discovered in nature?

In astronomy, Ptolemy was superseded by Copernicus, and Copernicus by Kepler. Ptolemy made the planets go around the earth in perfect circles, and Copernicus discovered that they orbited around the sun instead. Kepler found that their elliptical orbits were not capricious.

Darwin discovered in isolated Galapagos that there was nothing extra-special about mankind except perhaps its ability to reason things out, not always to its own advantage, as Freud proved later.

Freud also discovered that human behavior, no matter how irrational, was not capricious. Can we now see that behavior may be unreasonable, even when rational in the eyes of another? Does distance change perspective and therefore vectors of convergence?

Newton discovered that apples fell, ripe or not, in accordance with the universal laws of nature, which are inexorable. Einstein found that even starlight bends in obedience to the laws that Newton formulated too narrowly.

But to go beyond present dilemmas, we have to go back in time, to the ancestry of human ideas about becoming, believing, and begetting, or about liberty, equality, and sexuality, as they apply in different ratios, to EveryWoMan.

(The next questions to be answered are the following: Is freedom to create inversely proportional to the right to believe? Does believing in order to belong interfere with begetting or caring? Humans sometimes choose autoeroticism, orifices, or owners; animals do not: an alpha male imposes its will on its rivals to monopolize the females, who are themselves receptive to others clandestinely when in heat and, as mothers, militantly prepared to defend their offspring against any enemy.)

5.00 e/NATURE

e/Chapter Notes

[e/1] Infantile circumcision for religious reasons exaggerates fear of the unknown in the puny; 90% of modern Egyptian women have undergone clitoridectomy in infancy as an obeisance to tradition.

[e/2] The Constitution had to be amended with a Bill of Rights for persons regardless of citizenship [human rights, because it originally sought only to delimit states' rights, to build a more perfect union (federation)].

[e/3] Without a tail, I was able to build a three-story tree house for my grandchildren, with just the help of my thumbs. Only once did I feel like using my tongue to ask for help. Then it dawned on me that if in the beginning was the Word, and the word was "help," it would not spawn fanaticism. Who could be fanatical about helping? Verbs and gerunds do not breed believers!

(The author proudly wore a coat with tails to present his younger granddaughter at her cotillion.)

[e/4] Starting with zero requires achieving simple superiority; without it, supremacy and idolatry are necessary.

[e/5] Is it also only in our minds that we insist on being individuals even if our own behavior constantly belies it? And then we explain it in terms of being conflicted, with our parents, with society, or about sex.

Is it not rather due to domestication that enslaves our minds? Is it any wonder that we accept/permit/legitimize abortion?

6.00 f/Life:
ARE WE ALSO CONVIVIAL? (Act II)

Any *global* examination of behavior among plants and animals in our planet during life in an open system is bound to be slightly different from the *universal* study of inanimate substances in a closed system (now decaying) until the ultimate demise of our sun.

[Having established our natural citizenship in the world of matter, can we also learn about being alive from plants which feed us and animals who suckled, then learned to taste and to touch and, from touching, to get more and more "sexcited"? And, having defined our continuity with other creatures, including our own creations (computer-programmed robots), can we reach out beyond Luther's two kingdoms and Snow's two cultures, to probe the soul as an idea like the heart of a lion, and our cultural heritage as the history of civilization?]

We inherit energy to move around, as do all other animals. Action is energy at work in the form of force exerted over distance. Friction restricts motion and produces accommodation. (We call it compromise, which sometimes leads to seething frustration and stomach ulcerations.)

Some of our prehistoric preoccupations are shared to some degree by some animals, domesticated or not, notably chimpanzees in captivity. And so I began to consider domestication as a factor in the institutionalization of ideas.

Delusional thinking has retraced the history of civilization, as more popular beliefs (ideology) reflected the retreat of the church from politics, after the divine right of kings to rule was replaced by rampant internationalism as communist or capitalist imperialism (through free-standing or subsidized multinational business conglomerates, e.g., of old Warsaw Pact member nations or the European Common Market).

But domestication, like all charity should, begins at home. And so, I must distinguish the civilizing influence of the home for *Homo domesticus* from the history of civilization.

Because animals already had some muscles and the nerves to coordinate them long before they evolved genitals, not only must I separate personal from social domestication of *Homo metropolus*, but also domestication itself from sexual development, which, for breeding purposes among *Homo sapiens*, remain independent of personal virtues (moral principles or excuses) and social values (religious, political, business or professional ethics, etc.). *(f/1)*

Neo-Ethology

All sentient animals perceive (senses are largely inherited and conflict-free)—some have better memories—and others are more able to combine bits of memory in a process called recognition or reflection or secondhand thinking.

Original ideas are rare and come from the gifted who may unwittingly evoke conflict. The conflicted who are talented can opt for sublimation rather than innovation. They are more self-expressive than creative.

With our overdeveloped civilization (here defined transculturally as the ratio of personal comfort to communal celebration) comes zero population growth or sexual but not erotic attrition as our senso-social pre-occupations change:

Threatened by psychological amputation without surgical castration in both religious circumcision or traditional clitoridectomy, domestication (virtue + value/sensuality + liberty) now competes with breeding (sensuality + sex/society) even in modern societies.

Sex must also compete culturally with biologically barren recreation from concentration on our secondary (breasts and lips, etc.) and tertiary (brain) erotic appendages, or else be penalized for socially unsafe procreation in using primary genital organs (testicles and ovaries).

Even our secondary appendages (nipples, penis, etc.) are being upstaged by our tertiary sit-down erotic organs (buttocks, brains, etc.), all of which are bigger than those of other species, pound for pound of body weight.

All nonprimary organs are also exploited sensually even when sexually unripe or inconvenient (outside oestrus or partnerships) and used more and more for just sedentary dreaming, fondling, kissing, rubbing, and sucking.

Our New Psychiatry seeks to understand man as an animal and as a person in a rat race deciding whether to produce or reproduce.

In fact, even sexual harmony for households with unemployed fathers and working mothers can benefit from studying animal behavior (comparative ethology):

The New Poor can be treated like a pride of lions in family therapy.

Data from animal and human experiments and experience have not been integrated before but needed to be. They were not, because of territoriality or tunnel vision in the narrow-minded.

We also tend to study animals that we can easily manipulate, just like prudent alcoholics who restrict their search for dropped coins to well-lighted streets.

Desmond Morris of *Naked Ape* notoriety made money from art produced by a chimpanzee but denied that elephants could sketch when, in fact, they are more spontaneously inclined to do so than even human paraplegics.

That abstract art sells means that beauty is in the eye of the beholder. But it also implies that what we behold may be more to our taste rather than the truth.

If only the articulate can represent their perceptions in words, can we only expect to get representational art from the left brain of the articulate?

After we teach sign language to chimpanzees, will they draw what they are told? Asked to draw a basketball, one scribbled three vertical lines. Children draw lawn mowers as circles. Both chimp and child "artists" seem to know what the objects do, and their art is the equivalent of gerunds in our grammar.

Elephants, chimpanzees, and children are all intelligent, territorial, and social. Gerunds internalize our perceptions and now have cult followers among existentialists whose philosophical position is "abstraction is the only evil."

Can gerunds prevail by institutionalizing their interpretation of Genesis that "in the beginning was a gerund" [the author thinks it was the verb "help" and that the only fruits of the Tree of Knowledge are generalizations. (Would a father disinherit his children for petty theft?)]

Furthermore, if neoteny's continuum goes from chimpanzee to human to Einstein, does the continuum for brain size per unit of weight go from baby elephant to human infant to baby chimpanzee?

Pygmies are not subject to as lengthy a neoteny as we continue to be to prepare for life in our subculture. They are adequately prepared sociosexually by age eight, whereas we continue to outgrow the average size of the helmets and suits of armor of our ancestors.

Culturally, unlike pygmies, we have needed school and vocational counselors to make it socially, and additionally undergo compulsory continuing postgraduate education to be professionally adequate, and marriage and family counseling along with sex therapy with or without surrogate partners to be sensually functional or erotically fulfilled.

We just might be neurologically handicapped from birth by getting too big for our mothers' breeches (sic). And have not become extinct like the Neanderthals, who may have had the same problem, because we have inhabited a safer niche, like the New World monkeys did after South America split from Africa.

Other animals outgrow the uterus: horses and elephants may be born with some foreleg weakness. Only human brains outgrow our mother's pelvic headroom.

Foreleg weakness is also not crucial for procreation: elephants attain puberty in 20 to 25 years. (They also try to bury fresh carcasses, or carry bones with them after examining skulls, as if to identify whether they were those of friends.)

(Any of the above that is taken personally telegraphs areas of inferiority among babes in the arms of their captors. To protest heavenly purpose is to escape a hollow feeling of emptiness.)

Child Ethology

If we want to study life as it unfolds, babies are as close to animals as we can get. That's why children and animals get along together better than children and their guardians.

We were like children when we are protective of stray dogs and alley cats and, later, of wild animals and other endangered species, domesticated or not, including man.

Our survival—more in doubt than that of other animals or our pets, including domesticated (nurturing) robots—depends on doing more than deliberating, in or out of the United Nations. (We also fear that robots, which we create in our image, will be as destructive.)

To study babies before they can use our symbols is to be a human ethologist. Only by comparing animals can we understand how human beings develop and how our culture evolved in captivity (domesticity).

(Because cats are not as easily domesticated as other pets, they are excellent subjects for protracted observation. But it was pure luck that we were able to study several generations of the same family.

To allow us scientifically to draw testable conclusions about behavior in general, (1) not only must we compare children with animals of their own social age, but (2) we must also compare social hang-ups with (a) our institutionalized procedures and (b) their domesticated victims whom we learn about, from the human dilemmas they muddle through, unsorted or distorted and therefore self-destructive or deadly.

Brooding on our limited mobility is what makes us think harder to get out of our prison, emotional (primarily mental) or physical (universally gravitational): the dream of flying is universal.

Only skydivers can understand why birds sing.

On a slope, as if attempting to escape the grip of gravity in order to join them, my granddaughter lifts herself up on her toes and takes the weight off of her Achilles' heel when pointing to birds or planes flying high above her head.

How many times have we wished that we had a fifth limb (a prehensile tail) until we eventually had to invent or buy a vise or climb a ladder to trim our trees because we had only two hands?

My big toe can still grasp like an opposable thumb (to my grandchildren's chagrin or delight, depending on what I pinch or pick). My wife, having worn stockings to keep her feet warm even in her crib, cannot.

Am I the missing link? And is this why I practice ethopsychiatry, as inherently one of the great apes whose n-great-grand-nephew I consider myself? (Are not all theories, including this, confessions if not alibiographies?)

In Wonder but Not Awestricken

Our life underwent another change more than two decades ago: We added a baby to our household. Heretofore, we have felt responsible only for two peacocks, feeding them on their regular visits from their roost on the crest of the hill behind our house. But we heard a kitten whimpering in the bushes one night and the next morning fished it out with a swimming pool net.

Having saved its kitten from fatal hypothermia, we now felt obliged to let it live its normal life span, as the Eskimos do with those they rescue. We tried feeding Baby Kitty milk with a medicine dropper, then by teaspoonfuls, but got more down its throat by soaking a piece of sponge shaped like a nipple in milk and letting it suck to its heart's content.

We learned that the Golden Rule does not apply because we cannot expect it to have the same appetites and distastes that we take for granted. It will nip the thumb or bite the hand that feeds it.

But that is because my wife does not chastise it even verbally. She exclaims "No!" in disappointment when it bites or nips her. Disappointment is too complex an emotion for the kitten to grasp.

When I say "No!" loudly when it started jumping into bed with us, it understood and behaved accordingly for as long as its memory served it.

We see our children's potential (from **A** to **E**) as promising human animals. Later on, we will look at man's best friend as a model of behavior (from **F** to **O**) for their sheepish "masters" stirring at the sound of an alarm clock, our version of the bark of a sheepdog.

[What is sensual (**A** to **E**: emotional, volitional, intellectual, rationalytic, and inventive) is more neurological than cultural, and therefore more apt to be an unequal, natural endowment than what is artificially decreed as equalizers and sold to the domesticated as valued social institutions (from **F** to **O**, God to computers).] *(f/2)*

Plants and animals have a virtually undeniable will-to-live, evangelists a will-to-save, politicians a will-to-power, entrepreneurs a will-to-riches, individualists a will-to-separate, collectivists a will-to-congregate, technologists a will-to-produce, humanists a will-to-accuse, ecologists a will-to-conserve, ethologists a will-to-share, and cyberneticists a will-to-automate.

Whatever we share with animals is natural (not man-made). And whatever is not just true only of small groups of people separated by water or mountain range is quite probably more animal than human.

(In groups, we are more suggestible, above and beyond our need for shepherds, from feeling helpless since the day we were born.)

Are animals capable of love? Do they have a tongue to lick your face? Do they feel envy? Do they look like they are smiling when snarling? Can they think? Do they have a brain that tells them what to do next? Are they capable of discrimination? Do they have eyes? Are they creative? Can they discover hidden connections? Do they believe in magic? Or take after their masters? Can fishes recognize shapes other than portents of danger? Do other species practice self-stimulation? Captive and domesticated animals do.

Are they able to save for a rainy day? Squirrels squirrel nuts away. Do they believe in "a show of strength"? They bluff and bark. Do they remember? Dogs know where the bones lie buried. Homing pigeons are reliable couriers.

Whatever is transcultural is quite probably not altogether human. The test is (1) whether we find the same behavior in dumb animals and very young children before they can talk or get brainwashed by their custodians and brain-stuffed by their teachers.

And that includes (a) self-examination in the mirror or reflectively looking at ourselves through the mirror of our mind.

(f/3) As well as (b) any behavior that is shared by a herd of suggestible animals, whether or not defending against or escaping from danger.

And, of course, (2) whether as young children, they are alert to differences between boys and girls. (Some animals inspect the genitals of their young as soon as they are born.)

In no instance are our children ahead of other two-footed animals who cannot fly on these tests. The only advantage we have is the same advantage children of developed countries have over the less fortunate: ours have more time to play and learn before they specialize in any one direction. As specialists, their abilities can again cross oceans and their technology get handed down to the next generation as easily as the color of their eyes. But without interchanging what they had learned while helpless. (Procreation is now encouraged for the elite who can afford the cost of wanting children or, if infertile, a designated surrogate.) In varying degrees, this is because all children, including my grandchildren, are taught by their parents to be different from animals.

ETHO-PSYCHIATRY

Only if we see behavior as a continuum can we understand that what seems paradoxical is more than merely human.

My grandson had his cousin pinned down to the floor when his mother admonished him to let her go when she resists. I said that that is precisely when she is at risk if he is not a predator. Animals won't strike a rival who is down. She said her son had not read my book. Yet both grandchildren were behaving as if they had. *(f/4)*

[The author thinks that we should accept responsibility for our grandchildren (and our parents for theirs). But only for them and for those whom we program ourselves (after they leave home, like our students) but are not our children (willingly sharing responsibility for them with their genetic grandparents).]

Needed behavior samples include fear of the unknown in animism, the politics of pecking orders, barter trading of tokens, self-examination in a mirror or in the mirror of our mind as memory permits, as well as group activity, which, among us, surpasses that of insects only during our World Wars.

Termites are such virtuosos
In very high-density living
As to put Amsterdam to shame.

Ants also share charitably;
Their own soldiers' loyalty
Amply protects each colony
Without need of any oratory
Or self-exile afar from wars.

Animals have evolved extensible tongues for feeding, but not arms. Words at least do not kill, only those who believe in abstractions do. Would that we have to eat what we kill for whatever 'reason'.

Although all started with a tongue (even our parody of anthropocentric human racism is symbolic phagocytosis, tongue-in-cheek), serial and intermediary steps (e.g., to our thumb in technocracy) in our evolution are different from those of animals.

Our theory will take us on a journey from (i) sensually (A) tasting and "tongue-ing" (lingo-gustatory) and swallowing (gullibility) and trusting, and (B) trying and (C) thinking and (D) suspecting (sorting) and (E) creating (assimilating) and destroying (excreting); to (ii) social experiences that are more and more independent of parental approval, and that are different from other animals only in our excursions between our thumb and technocracy; to (iii) the joys of breeding (sexual and proprioceptive).

With maturation comes more (i) precise sensual perception with (ii) vulnerable social gullibility and (iii) versatile eroticism, as an immature great ape (neotenous) who walks erect instead of swinging (brachiating) between trees. We are able to enjoy our muscles and gender-determined erogenous zones, until just before second adolescence or middle-age crises (metapause in males) and even after menopause. (Viagra extends sexual ambitions beyond normal involution.)

Clinical investigation in ethopsychiatry proceeds by triangulation from at least two related databases (sensual and social) that are transcultural or normal rather than normative models of domestication.

Ideally, we should become more and more independent of parent-peer (i) and social-self (ii) approval, at least until our second childhood.

When we do not do our best, it is because we can't; only when we fail have we tried our best.

The more universal the basis for any interpretation, the more valid it is.

DNA from our grandparents shape (1) our constitution, whether weak or strong, for breeding; parenting shapes (2) children's moral upbringing; and past history (3) our cultural gullibility.

Whatever we share with healthy animals is not sick or uniquely human but adaptive.

What is not is man-made and has not been tested long enough in the crucible of time to be depended on for survival.

> What primates find easy
> That man finds too hard
> Makes the person unhealthy,
> Whether it is climbing
> Or eating to keep going
> Or "knowing" without sinning.
>
> What the mind is
> matters not as much
> as minding does.
>
> Inability to mind
> in the strong or weak
> separates the sick.
>
> Unwillingness to mind
> for valid reasons or none
> defines the strong.
>
> Ability to mind the weak
> allows the weak to treat,
> the strong to succeed.

As with animals, the only fighting that should be allowed is hand to hand (the "manly" art of manual combat). Yet we are ready to ban boxing because it kills, even if ballyhooed as a sport. Is the objection to the name or the killing? *(f/5)*

The Holy Family Boxing Club in Northern Ireland prohibits its members from swearing, drinking, using drugs, or debating politics, and counts among its members the young from militants in the warring parties. It may be the observance of all rules even in the ring between boxers that allows the gym to outlast the troubles.

What we kill with man-made tools we should dispose of, like we did when we first invented tools, for feeding our kin and clan. Otherwise who might enforce gun control and a ban on weapons of mass destruction?

Misled, Mutant, or Mistaught

If the violent had been physically abused as children, should we elect those who were not so abused to avoid a push-button war? Are war-torn nations more likely to have and choose them as their leaders? Is that why war is perennial among abused nations? And why Truman can waste cities with the atomic bomb without being afraid for peace, and Kennedy can wield it like a big stick without hitting a weaker Russia during the Cuban crisis, and why Nixon had to court China after Russia armed itself (to prevent another humiliation and/or capitulation)?

Ptolemy, Copernicus, Galileo, Kepler, Newton, Darwin, Picasso, and Einstein have provided or proved testable large-scale hypotheses. Untestable are those by Freud, Descartes, Kant, and Marx. What remains is a record of excuses and assumptions that hide the apologies and alibis that their thinking contains, and accepts whatever others with the same needs will agree is enough to sustain them. Logic can be used as a weapon and reason as rationalization, not ratiocination, for justification.

Only the young Einstein in his precocity was objective but not adualistic, and he could well be a rare recessive mutation (more different from us than we are from animals).

Duality, for Einstein, one "imbibes with one's mother's milk." That's why he prefers expansion and constriction in a steady state universe, not the Big Bang.

All explanations are created equal. Only testing makes them unequal.

1) Our "moral" development (i) cannot be understood if we are unskeptical about teleology (even as a misreading of Descartes) and epigenesis (espoused by Piaget and Erikson).

In our schema (without contradicting the data on which Piaget's epigenetic theory of mental or cognitive development is based), animal intuition is visceral knowing (as in "carnal knowledge"), conception is mental (or maternal), and cogitation itself simply the agitation that we suffer deep inside (visceral) from doubting (thinking but not knowing).

[If we do not have mental indigestion from doubting, we would not even be conscious of conceiving, mentally (or maternally).

[Doubt is distressing: "I do suffer, therefore I exist" -> "I am now conscious (of suffering)" -> "I know (I mind), therefore I am."]

Descartes separated (B) cogitation or (1) "the fluctuating testimony of the senses" from (C) conception after (2) "intuition . . . which an unclouded and attentive mind gives us so readily and distinctly that we are wholly freed from doubt about that which we understand" and (3) convinces us that we, indeed, exist. In fact, *cogito ergo sum* only means "I can see, therefore I am awake (to data testified to by my senses*)."*

[To cogitate when in doubt brings "re-cognition" of the sensations as testimony (after oath-taking, before there was a Bible, by holding one's testes) to one's existence: "I can remember, therefore I was." Is this "cognitive"?]

Afraid of being charged with heresy, Descartes delayed publication of *The Treatise of Man* until 1664, 14 years after his death. Arthur Schopenhauer was thankful that Descartes placed reason on its own feet by teaching men to use their own, in place of which the Bible had previously served on the one hand and Aristotle on the other. (Both Descartes and Aristotle are still philosopher Adler's favorites under stress of skepticism.)

Intuitive certitude inevitably begets confidence in the powers of introspection among the autodidactic (self-taught or "in-tuitive").

2) Our historical development (ii) can be understood if we are conversant with, but not misled by, Aristotle and syllogism, Ardrey and imperial territoriality, and Einstein and celestial crap games.

Robert Ardrey is as instinctivist about territoriality being unlearned but maladaptive in the naked ape as Ashley Montagu is humanistic about nonterritorial altruism (acquired rather than sociobiologically adaptive).

3) Our sexual development (**iii**) was misunderstood in the writings of Freud (fantasied), de Sade, and Masoch (both fictional) as sensual. Why?

Sadism and masochism are enjoyable only until fight or flight responses are elicited by enough blood platelets breaking down. Observe more closely when that occurs in explicit films without special effects.

Is the Grafenberg spot recently reported in the anterior wall of the vagina in multiorgasmic women a recessive hereditary mutation?

4) Some misleaders (misinformed rather than mutants) are human racists, which is the best kind to be, if they or we have to be biased (bigoted or consciously prejudiced).

Their bigotry is no more than that of a majority of mediocre mutants who have survived because their socially (not biologically) protected or unthreatening mediocrity was normative (**i** and **ii**) rather than normal. [Mutants who cannot reproduce (**iii**) are called monsters.]

(We are, in fact, con-natural with other creatures. If we believed that we are all derived from clay and to ashes we shall return, then we are even con-substantial with all creation. If, con-substantially, we are all fragments of the same material, so are our civilizations over the ages fragments of universal behavior, elaborated by ideology as culture.)

If we were created equal, then our Creator would approve of equal time for all beliefs expressed in graven or spoken images of him in amulets and mantras, ritual and sacrifice, magic and witchcraft. (Does organized religion abet addiction to science fiction and horror movies?)

Without taxing them, Hindus have state-subsidized nursing homes for old cows.

We engulfed food as carnivorous plants and animals before we needed sexual partners, were parthenogenetic and animistic until we discovered muses and totems to worship, and less individualistic before we invented tokens for barter.

As mammals, we stole milk meant for calves from contented vegetarians. And, rootless as children of broken homes and unkept promises, we rush to "sink roots" or settle down but demand to die rather than vegetate. Why?

> For a long time / We moved around /
> Without danger / On "false feet."

> Suspended afloat, / We developed fins. /
> Grounded and heavy, / We crept away.

> Warm-blooded, / We swooped aloft /
> To perch on trees / Or skyscrapers.

> Or climbed higher / On space capsules /
> To pick moon rocks / Like lunatics.

As we grow older, do we appreciate liberty less, and love somewhat more, even under the shadow of another?

Our normal life cycle (beyond peak experiences when breathless and anoxic) is different from other animals (who have left the deep and their gills behind).

Twice, we left a tridimensional world of locomotion, as a fish, and as a monkey, able to swing from tree to tree by brachiation. Now we have nuclear subs to protect our shores, and space weaponry to guard us from diving birds of prey.

The quality of our lives is inversely proportional to the number of predators who prey on us, whether or not we have the means or endowment to bribe or buy them off. We therefore pray for them to be more like us. We have it made if we are (1) strong even if physically handicapped, (2) rich in money or family, and (3) confident mentally, wise or not.

(The best life is to have contingency plans for being richer, while enjoying the status quo without reservations.)

Predators must fight to live; prey must flee to survive. For creatures of prey, usually vegetarians, like rabbits and deer, the eyes are located on opposite sides of the head to enable it to monitor its surroundings. For hunters, the eyes are up front so that the visual fields overlap, providing stereoscopic vision of necessary depth for pouncing or grasping.

(Musk ox wheel around to form a ring of horns against invaders.)

Progress (domestication) comes from specialization of limbs and organs (like domestication of the mouth in a falcon or hunting dog), and of one hemisphere (the left brain), which monitors their special movement (uses), including that of the tongue in speaking.

Our left brain evolved with handedness and then with the use of language. Thusly has technology and information allowed our society to evolve further than other species.

Sensually, other animals can also (**D**) compare their observations and (**E**) invent tools, even if they do not talk about it.

Like animals, what we feel (**A**) like doing, if we can (**B**), we nearly always will, without (**C**) deliberation.

The only question is "When?" Yet life is Now, not When, nor Then.

Man has always preferred violence to explain or resolve dilemmas, from the Big Bang to the Gib Gnab of physics or the Great Deluge of the Bible to the Apocalypse of Judgment Day. Animals need no such explanations to coexist in nature.

Just as birds need no digital watches to check on estimated time of arrival because they can land on a dime, they do not need others to tell them what they ought to know.

But, as animals, are we not more (**C**) rational than other species, even close relatives, like the chimpanzees?

Not when it comes to (**F**) religion, (**G**) politics, or (**H**) economics, which they also practice as animism in established pecking orders, and with the use of tokens for barter.

1) Tribes of male chimps war with each other for territory (not for the power to oppress the vanquished or even to exploit their females sexually).

a) They differ from us in not hurting their own mates or offspring who, of course, never learned to talk back as an equal.

b) Sexually, we are unique in (1) (a) narcissistic expression (seven billion American dollars for cosmetics) and autoerotic titillation (seven million rented X-rated video cassettes nationally) and (b) some of our perversions and when (2) we (a) rape in concert (uncoerced, alley cats accept serial intromission) and (b) abort (though humanistic in our inhumanity).

2) Primates have been known to obtain sexual favors with lab tokens (but not to bribe overprotective mothers to keep them quiet).

(Female chimps in captivity practice the world's oldest profession (primate lab custodians find that tokens earned for learning computer symbols are used to buy sexual favors).

(In the second oldest profession, only chimpanzee mothers in captivity become smotherers of their young when bored from being well-fed with nothing else to do.

Our human smotherers are morally or mentally incapable of adultery. Boredom, of course, afflicts only the unimaginative.)

3) Captive primates have observable tendencies toward (**F**) animism or magical thinking, and are capable of (**G**) political power struggles and (**H**) commercial greed.

But after we invented the idea that there are different gods (animals act as if the awesome are identical), we have become less noble and sporting than horses.

4) If, like other animals, we eat what we kill, we can (**A**) enjoy a better social substitute for (**G**) war. (I enjoin my grandchildren not to kill insects unless they enjoy eating them, or else "kill the buggers" can creep into their vocabulary.)

Instead we have advanced toward mass worship (ecstatic orgasms), gang bangs, and sex orgies. (Only the intoxicated or inhibited have privately abused their dependents.)

5) We are even less rational than most animals (a) about sex and (b) in looking after our young.

a) The desperate battle of the sexes is between (1) men who buy sex for impersonal reasons without intimacy, and (2) women who buy emotional intimacy with sex for more personal reasons.

(Tame cats accept or solicit sexual overtures even when pregnant. Caged lions fornicate lying side by side. It is the enforced proximity and idleness that extends erotic receptivity, as in incest and for the duration of a blackout when power shortage blankets an area and deprives TV addicts of their scheduled entertainment.)

b) Between wet or soiled diapers and soaked or smeared carpets, adults choose to raise uncomfortable children and keep capitalism going.

The undomesticated multiplies without asking why, and is not awed enough to be heretical, nor irreverent enough to know how to be.

Is irreverence, but not about life itself, what Jehovah feared from the fruits of the Tree of Knowledge, or what gurus from Freud to Stalin disliked in ex-disciples like critical but gentile Jung and Slavic but unslavish Tito? Do we need to ask why before we multiply? (f/6)

When hoping becomes heroic, death is waiting in the wings. This heroism is the heritage of the "not yet" of childhood, when procrastination for adults and patience among their children is considered par for the course. Because it was imposed rather than rewarded, such heroic hoping becomes wishful thinking during crises. (f/7)

Close Encounters of the Natural Kind

Our senses are especially attuned to what we can reach. What they cannot sense, with or without prostheses, may as well not exist. We did not attend to our immediate surroundings as much until we first saw the light, or heard our parents making strange noises in the night.

There may, indeed, be (I) con-natural but (II') non-convivial and (III') unfamiliar universes all around us (not necessarily antimatter but batlike) of which we are unaware but on which our ecology must, in part, rely. But what we claim to be ours is large enough to keep us from being bored, and finite enough to keep us from being awed. Nonetheless we are both more awed and bored than other primates. They don't need drugs or cults as crutches.

Variety is the spice of life for the bored who cannot go to sleep, but for the enthusiastic, accidents arouse interest besides being serendipitous or unfortunate. (Genetic accidents also produce DNA variations.)

[We have just finished reviewing biocosmology (con-naturality and con-viviality) and can now look at the evolution of our fraternities and sororities. Our own three subcycles make us senso-socio-sexual personally, publicly, and privately.]

6.00 f/LIFE

f/Chapter Notes

[f/1] Virtues and values are asexual, even when sexist, e.g., toward correcting legal indifference to women. Is it because the fathers of our country were raised to be courteous (courtly) toward ladies like their mothers, but not to consult them about court business? Or is it because our male lawmakers were under assertive female teachers' thumbs in their most rebellious years?

Some of what I have studied professionally have been published (e.g. "A Psychiatric Odyssey of Personal Discoveries," in *VOICES*, the art and science of psychotherapy, Summer, 1974), but not what I have learned as a person (of many parts, of all seasons) and as a male (from boyhood to manhood) in a society where man are manly (macho).

[f/2] Our five freedoms, or "uncivil" liberties, are also stages in (**i**) our personal growth that allow us to be free (**A**) to feel good, bad, or beyond judgment; (**B**) to be right, wrong, or unyielding; (**C**) to think about what is true, false, or unchallenged; (**D**) to compare what is testable, unproven, or illuminating; and (**E**) to produce what is new, old, or refreshing.

Our ten civil, not constitutional, rights are stages of (**ii**) social development in our struggle for the opportunity to be equal (**F**) before God or (**G**) governor, (**H**) in the marketplace, (**I**) to anyone, (**J**) with any group, (**K**) in using machines (**L**) to benefit our species, (**M**) preserve our planet, (**N**) protect other animals, and (**0**) develop artificial intelligence.

[f/3] Socratic self-examination or reflection (not ratiocination or rationalysis) is supposed to result in insight that is personally useful but not beneficial to anyone else, which is why psychoanalysis outlasts several marriages. The gain from self-analysis can be compared to that from transcendental meditation.

[f/4] My youngest grandchild has a sword made of tubes that collapse into each other when used to poke solid objects like me, but he desists from using it when I am lying down, just as charging cavalry desisted from trampling Gandhi and fellow demonstrators lying prone on their faces in the dirt in South Africa. That lesson ("nonviolence is not injurious to your health"), once exported, eventually earned India its independence from England.

My granddaughters have also learned that they can preserve harmony after they start trading blows if one hits me instead of her cousin and I don't hit back at either of them. Statesmen invent foreign threats to preserve domestic tranquility.

[f/5] The logic-oriented, analogy-prone devil's advocate might ask first, "If you could only regulate one of two growth industries, would you regulate boxing or abortion?" The biology-oriented, homology-prone angel's advocate might ask next, "If you are in favor of abortion, do you also favor capital punishment?" The historian might ask who had benefited by abortion, boxing and capital punishment.

But not who may be protected. The victim may not get the chance to ask the question or demand an answer.

Our New Psychiatry would classify the first query as both (**C**) speculative and (**F**) puritanical, the second as (**E**) creative and (**G'**) antiestablishmentarian, and the third as (**D**) exploratory and (**H**) economic.

The answer, of course, depends on how we tend to deal with such questioners and their speculation, inclusiveness, or creativity about what is spiritual, political, and profitable.

Why were there more abolitionists in the North than in the slave-owning South?

An award-winning writer of recent fiction (Toni Morrison's *Beloved*) described her heroine as not having the right to kill her daughter but was right in choosing social euthanasia or postnatal abortion to save her from growing up a slave. This tale of mercy killing was inspired by a newspaper report of a mother who killed not just one, but all her children. Severe depression (remorse more than shame or regret) sometimes results in self-mutilation or mass homicide followed by suicide, where the body itself or the victims are seen as unforgivable parts of the patient. Euthanasia is a less punitive and more self-indulgent unwillingness to suffer the suffering of others, be they relatives or pets.

Mothers who sacrifice their male children (e.g., Susan Smith's two to win a new mate in a 1995 court case in South Carolina) on the altar of another marriage are asking to have still more children. (Seeds will not bud in a blizzard, and animals can cannibalize their unborn or stillborn during droughts. But only humans will abuse the living who barely squeezed through—battered with misshapen and swelled heads from not having to compete with littermates or even a twin—to be born a loner.)

(When the dependents are outnumbered by their seniors, they are vulnerable to their parents' whims. Litters and single parenthood save animals from intense indoctrination.)

[f/6] Between anticipated anarchy and potential extinction, the latter may be the lesser fantasied evil for the meek and faint-hearted who want to spare their unwanted progeny the struggle to survive, which had scarred their own lives.

[f/7] When some women become mothers, they take it personally when there is seeming neglect on the part of the child and its father, just as they did when still single and he was Mr. Right. Are those who worship an absent father not unlike those who keep daydreaming of Mr. Right and still picture God as a dreamboat?

7.00 g/Humanity: THEORY and STAGES of CON-FAMILIARITY (Act III)

Australopithecus

Homo Erectus

Homo Sapiens
Neanderthal

Homo Sapiens Sapiens
Cro-Magnon

[Even birds use stones as tools. Brains got bigger after Stone Age australopithecene. Ours is about four times their size or 1400 cc, but Neanderthals had an even bigger brain (1500 cc).]

(That dates the use of tools as far back as the emergence of birds and mammals and maybe to the age of dinosaurs!

From Hand (Thumb) to Mouth (Tongue)

It is scholarly but not helpful to cite *Homo habilis* (for Neanderthals) and *Homo erectus* (for Cro-Magnons) as predecessors (DNA-identical or not), once our brain got so large as to shorten pregnancy and prolong infancy beyond those of any other primate. (Computer storage capacity is likewise disproportionately larger than for available or needed information.)

This divergence has derailed natural selection at our expense— only temporarily, I hope—in favor of narrow parental and social bias that mandates puritan genital mutilation (early circumcision and clitoridectomy), family brainwashing, and public brain-stuffing.

Homo erectus descended from the trees to forage in savannahs more than 300,000 years ago. It discovered fire. (Its brain size was 700 to 1200 cc vs. our 1400 cc) Then came *Homo habilis*, whose hands had been freed to use stone tools and build fires. Our handyman was the first human suspected of engaging in collective ritual (substituting form for substance, words for deeds, promises for performance, ideology or "-isms" for "-ing" or gerunds).

(Is philosophy simply substituting "-sm" for "-ng"?)

This *proto-Homo domesticus* is an early primate in a mental, social, and sometimes sexual cage of its own making. [*H. sapiens neanderthalensis* also gave way to the Cro-Magnons (*Homo sapiens sapiens*) just 40,000 short years ago.]

We must now look *(Table 16)* at three subspecies out of Cro-Magnons *Homo sapiens* (ingenious and resourceful), *Homo domesticus* (intimidated and righteous), and *Homo metropolus* (ingenuous and litigious).

What I now call the subspecies *Homo sapiens* was described (as Semitic nomads) firsthand by the first *Homo domesticus* (Sumerian settlers) in T. Cahill's *The Gift of the Jews* (1998) as follows: "A tent-dweller, buffeted by wind and rain, he knows not prayers . . . has no house in his lifetime, is not brought to burial when he dies."

Dichotomy-driven (but insightfully, irreverently, or ironically), Cahill adds, "This is almost a description of an animal: without manners or courtesy—even toward the dead—without religion . . . Behind the description we can detect the prejudice of imperialists throughout history, who blithely assume superiority, moral as well as technical, over those whom they have marginalized and therefore their divine right to whatever is valuable, especially the land."

Homo domesticus can be as primitive as jungle tribes who perform ritual sacrifices and as modern as Jim Jones's suicidal cult of expatriates, or the Internet web designers in San Diego's Heaven's Gate.

The anatomy of the human brain reveals a natural selection for success in manual skills by our species. Whichever hand becomes more skilled also prompts language development in the hemisphere that monitors its muscles.

And, as in secondary bureaucracies outside the brain (which is their prototype and without which no powercrat can lead), the talker (reductionist) soon outdistances the doer.

Because my wife has less brute strength, she is better at figuring out labor- and time-saving shortcuts than I am and in imagining (rehearsing) time-motion scenarios beforehand. I'm more opportunistic ("logos" or data-driven) than methodical (what the Greeks call *methodos* but which we call "logical") and prone to trial-and-error ventures.

We know some facts about us before we were born. We ourselves acquire more data. Before we die, can we reconcile what seems to be a contradiction between facts and experiences by finding other connections than the obvious?

> We traced developments in physics and biology under the con-naturality of matter throughout the cosmos and the con-viviality of life-forms all over the globe. We will now trace the development of civilizations, dead or alive, in the human family wherever it settled or survived and prevailed or left traces. Materially or mentally, we have to assign ratios of sensual, social, and sexual maturation, not maturity.

Civilizations that we have fashioned tend to have a life cycle of their own that take them from promised paradise (utopia) to their poor approximations by proxies, from (**F**) faithful "Godoggie" to (**O**) predictable prosthetic performance by "goforobot." Our own human male role models have switched from the more heroic strong and silent type (Ulysses, John Wayne) to the sensitive, vulnerable antihero (Hamlet, Woody Allen). This is an atavistic regression toward the unsexed uterine life-form.

> (In the opposite direction, there is the return of Rambo as a one-man Green Beret avenger of patriots in a two-front battle, with trained guerrillas abroad and vocal peaceniks in a civil war at home.)

> [Modern female fashion models also have gone from thin, tomboyish figures to modern, broad-shouldered, mannish suits in socially ambitious "testis envy" (sexually, embryos start out as girls). Old Hera hated Hercules, and Lilith all of Eve's sons, who thereafter had to be circumcised.

Are We Special or Just Better-Trained Seals?

There's "humanism," which is anthropocentric; "humanimalism," which is anthropomorphic; and "animalism" which is ethocentric.

With animals, it is better to be ethocentric at the expense of being scientific; with children less anthropomorphic (do not expect them to be patient when their sense of time is not much better than that of our pets); and with adults more humanistic only and, especially, if we want to be their friends.

1) Animals are dumb, but they are smart. (Don't we say the same thing about blondes?)

2) a) If we love ourselves, we try to bring other animals to our level. That's called anthropomorphism. Because our observations are distorted by our love of ourselves, they are not very reliable.

   b) If we love animals, we don't avoid bringing ourselves to their level. I call that being animalistic. Our observations will be equally distorted by our love.

3) If we only love people we know, and not all of humanity, and love only the animals we have, and not the animal kingdom, we can observe better or relate what we see in people and animals that we know to those of others that we are not involved with. I call that neoethology, and the scientist an ethopsychiatrist:

   When his mistress (sic) picks up our first tomcat on arriving home, he stretches his neck to reach her face. On joining us in bed, he does the same to me. But he never mounts and humps my arm like he sometimes does hers, nor makes thrusting movements in an unmistakably sexual fashion.

   If then she reaches out to caress him, he does not welcome the distraction the way he usually accepts being stroked. He vocalizes his objections as he continues thrusting his pelvis, with his penis red, hard, and extended out of its foreskin, but without touching her arm. It is her smell that excites him, not her arm.

4) The more we deny our nose or hide its natural function, the more civilized we are.

5) a) Savage animals get along as well as do people who are tamed.

   b) Any society can survive both WoMan and beast thriving together without animosity or sanctions.

6) The earlier we are treated differently from other animals, the more human we will become.

This is also true of other animals: if they first see a human being after birth or hatching, they think of him as their mother and follow him as they would their mother, and will imitate even what is not natural to them if they possibly can, or at least parrot their teachers.

Our first cat was abandoned on our doorstep when it was but a few days old and now joins us as we walk the quarter mile to the mailbox, even if it is not a dog.

7) Disturbed patients can benefit from being treated as if they are natural animals:

There are not many psychiatrists who try to work with the most disturbed (disturbing) patients. I had to, in order not to be taught (supervised) by those who cannot deal with the biggest problem in mental illness.

(Drugs sedate them without helping them. When they are sedated, the staff can sleep on the job. But involuntary docility only increases hidden hostility.)

8) Human beings are unique among animals in being able to live with contradictions (e.g., "free will" and tobacco smoking). To do this they have to deceive themselves about one or the other half of the contradiction. Other animals can believe what they cannot directly test, but do not chronically deceive themselves.

Knowing what is common to all animals can (i) confer personal immunity of indefinite duration against moral epidemics, as well as (ii) increase social resistance against cultural conformity and (iii) enhance sexual liberation from popular stereotypes.

[The "liberated" who seeks relationships instead of sexual relations learned from her father that sex is not meant to make anyone a better partner, or even be more memorable. Only lust in general (rather than for the particular, which is a form of chronic fetishism) endures the passage of time and survives the decay of short-term memory in the elderly.]

But as long as we keep our mind or body going, we can comfort ourselves throughout our lives, solitary though we may be at the very end. Do we die happy or with dignity? (With incontinence our mind will prove practically useless, but will not mind. Our loved ones, if they love dignity more, will.)

When we are not conscious or do not complain of hunger, cold, or pain, etc., we are not human beings. In simply being, we lose our precious selves. We lose our humanity when satiated or drugged or anoxic or during contemplation. Habituation to all or anything that satiates or sedates or exults or exalts validates our humanity only during withdrawal, pangs of hunger from fasting too long, cramping from sitting stiffly, or overexposures to sun or snow and to glancing criticisms that reach our consciousness again.

(Because its own opiate is entirely natural for the poppy, it is no jollier than other plants even when it is in full bloom. Since there are human opioid peptides for all but "mu" receptors—which prefer poppy juice—are weed-sucking habitues of opium dens vegetating as denizens of the distant past in modern nurseries for "indoor poppies"? Are such addicts looking for their hidden being as human or vegetable?]

Unlike Jesus, Buddha begged for food, not for relief or forgiveness.

To be human and in pain is virtually to be possessed by the devil. Painkillers (even for emotional aches) that work are sought and bought to vindicate one's innocence. Drug merchants are our modern messiahs.

(If criminals are more sick than bad, and corporal punishment not retribution but exorcism, then they must be saved, not for heaven but for society. Since no children are born bad, why whip any? If deterrence deindividualizes to reach those who might be tempted to do what has been forbidden, then prisoners serve as examples only to the dehumanized.)

Can What's Different Make a Difference?

> *All the rivers run into the sea; yet the sea is not full . . .*
> *whence the rivers come, thither they return again . . . and*
> *there is no new thing under the sun.*
>   —Ecclesiastes 1:7–9

It's true we cultivate and domesticate, and we don't create except to combine or destroy what has been cultivated or domesticated. We have not only cultivated plants, we have domesticated them. We do not only have house pets, we have houseplants. (Does keeping them indoors keep them from multiplying?) We have cultured bacteria and DNA, to recombine soon even with our own or with computers which we have invented out of base metal that we have tamed.

But why must there be a different beginning other than the big bang, or an ending other than a gnab gib (the smallest black hole to swallow all black holes), or even a Big O (a moral orgasm to end all doubts, **B** -> **A**, by a political solution toward eternal oblivion, **G** -> **F**)?

We're all armchair travelers in the time machine that we call history, which concentrates on gods and kings and conflicts like today's soap operas.

We also do not know much about other nations, except in our imaginations. Yet we are as sure about the meaning of evil as we are about the meaning of the universe that we have not yet visited. *(g/1)*

If evolution begins as a successful alteration of structure, was Darwin as inevitable as God, and Gandhi as Hitler? If not, is it because we do not evolve socially except in our minds?

Human social evolution (unmediated by DNA) does not proceed at a uniform rate: there is hibernation and revolution (recycling).

The feudal stage returns but hides in indebtedness among credit card holders, while Marxism itself stagnates without large loans.

There are no universal values, only old and new, frail or durable, depending on the power of superior forces (seniority in the bureaucracy of the family or weaponry among fanatics), not on their merits. ("Thou shalt not kill" and "Go forth and multiply" were timely when there was enough food to go around.) *(g2)*

Our Senso-Socio-Sexual Life Cycle

(i) The Development of our Sensual Life (The Five Ages of Man)

Even if some are (A) content to (B') stagnate, others get hurt (A') falling down on running or jumping or climbing, yet go on (B) trying. We say we like to think (C) for ourselves but want more sex with others of similar tastes (A). Some of us soon look around (D) to see how the rest of the world behaves outside our mind. Even more rarely, we achieve what others cannot because they share the same world that looks different (E) to us.

(ii) The Evolution of our Social Lives (The Egalitarian Eras of Our History)

What is historical or cultural, including art, is consensual, even when institutionalized as suprapersonal or spiritual.

(iii) Our Sexual Life Cycles as Male or Female or Their Facsimiles.

What is sexual must differ from what is personally sensual if by it we mean what is privately erotic or genitally mediated between partners. The subcycles are different for each gender as early as six to twelve weeks after conception, when the fetal genitalia differentiate according to what the father had contributed. And so we must hereafter disregard traditional sexologies.

Keep in mind always that, depending on how and where we got started, senso-socio-sexual sources of frustration are closely linked, but not equal in impact.

Maverick development (e.g., **iii** x *i*/**ii**, or sexuality x liberty/equality), like radioactive mutation, may augur a change in direction or destination. If not monstrous (sterile and incapable of achieving momentum), does it matter whether the change is for the better (A), or that we will be better off (H) for it? Does it count if the change (A) appeals to us whether it is (B) right for us or (D) worth testing?

Just as in personal development (A -> E), all or any disappointing delays or retardation in our ideological development (F -> O) imply no more than simple arbitrariness (dictated by artificial deadlines), not

(1) abnormality (temporary disability), nor (2) deficiency (potential lethality):

1) a) Such slogans as "better red than dead" (**H**) or "the only good Communist is a dead one" (**G**) move only those whose wealth has not been or was already nationalized (**J**), respectively.
    b) Socialized medicine (**J** + **K**) is welcome among leprologists, phthisiologists, and alienists who are tax-supported in their respective leprosariums, tuberculosis sanitariums, and mental asylums.
    c) Competition for government funding of revolving-door psychiatric hospitals and community and university clinics has made more ivory-tower psychologists (**I**) suddenly very civic-minded (**J**).

2) Instead, we ought to think of each delay in development as simply a pause, a latency phase, whether it is restful or not.
    a) Arrest at any step encourages delusional thinking about what is dawning as the next stage.
    b) Believing is either (1) guessing without data and gambling a part of or one's entire life on one's guess, or (2) just lying to one's self and kindred spirits until the next rude awakening of civilization by new facts discovered through science, not logic.
    (Such white lies need not be confessed or, at worst, are venial sins. Lies or untruths which hurt others are racist, sexist, etc.)

3) It will soon become exceedingly easier than heretofore for ethopsychiatrists to
    a) compare (**D**) the values of one ideology with another,
    b) examine (**C**) their merits that have been "virtuously" parroted,
    c) "choose" (**B**) another more suitable (**A**), or
    d) invent (**E**) a new ladder or scale of different values to (**B**) climb or (**D**) weigh.

There is only the paradoxical "apathy" of inertia (reflex habits of judgment) to overcome. Others have proceeded to do so, once they see that values accuse without conscious bias or cautious discrimination.

We may have sensory organs, but what we experience is sensitivity. We may have senso-receptors, but what we can observe is receptivity.

There is no mind but "minding" makes us think there is.

We must deliberately separate change of mind—usually chaotic, often dictated by desire (A) rather than data (D)—from organismic growth, which is orderly and predictable (clocked by DNA). *(g/3)*

The good life is characterized by amused or mindless activity, as in other animals, bemused not at all by means or ends or style without spontaneity. It has class without struggle or strife, called animal grace, and the simple uncontrolled beauty of effortlessness.

Only human beings care whether the newborn has five fingers of unequal lengths on each hand. Animals just check its genitals. Today we even worry about whether each prospective child will need a lot of love to overcome inherited handicaps that other animals outgrow.

Acculturation patterns that we disapprove of do not get examined as to (1) antecedents, but only as (2) questions begging judgment as to (a) guilt over wrongdoing or (b) rewards for right conduct.

Some queries are answerable by (C) reasons that prompt the behavior, (B) right or (B') wrong.

To "examine our lives" in toto, we must also discover and explore what we can uncover and recover of those experiences that we share with animals but never thought we did.

In our personal development, this includes (A) passions and emotions, (B) instinctive motivations and intuitive decisions, preconceptual trial-and-error problem solving, and concrete testable solutions as well as (D) postlogical thinking about what we can (B) manipulate (e.g., sand and wheat separated by saltwater for monkeys who did not want sand in their diet), and (E) invention of tools as prostheses (animals find / design / use tools, e.g., a twig to reach termites deep in their burrows).

It does not include (C) formal abstraction by symbol representation and reasoning by analogy.

In our cultural development it includes belief in (F) magic and miracles, (G) political alliances, and (H) bartering of goods and marketing of tokens. It does not include obsession with (I) self or (J) society, (K) tools of production, (L) human perquisites, (M) ecological balance, (N) animal rights, or (O) robotic limits.

Bioanthropology

Bioanthropology studies all of life as it has been lived out down through the ages.

What we call preliterate civilizations evolved before recorded history. Their traces still influence our social evolution.

Civilizations, living or dead, whose mysteries are not accessible to exploration, we tend to call primitive cultures.

(This is how culture and civilization sometimes get mixed up.)

What Makes Us Civilized in Our Eyes?

Some equate civilization with literacy, others with art, and both groups with great poetry. Why? The Greeks would reply, because poetry is more interesting than words or pictures. Civilization then becomes an exploration of the mysterious, narrower than unbiased science.

(Goethe, though a humanist, once said, "The thrill of awe is the best thing humanity has." The author thinks astrologers would agree. Santayana, a historian, claims, "Perhaps the only true dignity of man is his capacity to despise himself.")

There were at least three Golden Ages in our history whose tarnished glitter might establish a different perspective for the reflective. Other crossroads errors have been noted earlier.

1)   The Golden Age of Greece: An abbreviated Oriental syllogism found its way to Greece from India. It started with (b) reason (teleological), followed by (d) application (logical) and (e) conclusion (essence). It omitted both (a) proposition (prediction) and (c) example (data). This resulted in Western deductive logic, which delayed inductive scientific research. (Aristotle, who had been a published naturalist, is now only remembered as a philosopher.)

2)   The Golden Age of Jerusalem: This was an escape from polytheism into reductionism. Monotheism was substituted for worship of the Golden Calf without questioning, even logically, why one is better than the other.

Professional: Both totems, of course, survive in more sophisticated forms of animism; and both Jehovah and the Golden Calf also provide the golden harvest of silence when asked any question, dumb or not.

Specialist: Except that those whose God is made invisible to his un-sainted children had also once believed in Santa Claus.

Generalist: Some now argue that there must have been a God for the world to function like clockwork. For many, it seldom does.

Moreover, the same argument holds true for those who offer that 2,000 New World monkeys with typewriters cannot match an Elizabethan genius, without even wondering why 2,000 modern critics with word processors have never produced a sonnet like Shakespeare's, nor the Elizabethan Age a woman of equal stature as a poet. Was Shakespeare a mutant but not a monster?

3) The Golden Age of Virginia: This produced the Declaration of Independence, where slave-owning Thomas Jefferson asserted (and the French believed, even during their Reign of Terror) that all men are created equal.

    (In his later correspondence, Jefferson acknowledged an aristocracy of talent, which is hereditary but rare.)

There are, of course, older civilizations with precocious science and ageless art, and more recent developments, with mixed reviews from civilized critics. Can only the uncivilized be unbiased about *Homo domesticus*?

Classical civilization had gone from alchemy to chemistry; modern civilization is going from petrochemical to biochemical and will go from biochemistry to bioengineering to bioelectronics.

Classical theo-philosophy is no more than the alchemy of the past transformed into anthropocentrism (human racism). Like base metals that were once believed to be convertible to gold, *Homo metropolus* hopes that today's raw human potential can yet be ennobled with some help from friends/drugs.

(An otherwise hard-headed scientist, Kurt Goldstein, also believed that all of us are seeking to realize our potential. Had he just stayed with his notion that brain injury constricts our venturesomeness in order not to fail where we used to succeed, our specialty would have been better served. He was our modern equivalent of Meister Eckhart, the thirteenth-century mystic who thought copper is restless until it becomes gold.)

(We then become self-appointed trustees of our patients' potential rather than their doctors trying hard to increase their mental competence and reduce infirmity.)

Civilizations are supposed to supply the mind and soul with food for thought and reflection.

If we have confused you by using literacy, art, civilization, culture, history, and social evolution as overlapping concepts, it is only so that you can anticipate the absolute relativity of abstractions, which is probably the most mysterious of paradoxes.

There is no contradiction in making a million of them dance on the tip of a needle, like angels, now that the angelic is suspect.

As a child, every Sunday, I accepted unleavened bread, as did Jesus at the Last Supper. (Protestants even sip red wine to drink his blood.)

[If their elders had ever believed that alchemy can turn base metal into gold (or the philosopher's stone prolong life), children could also believe that bread can be made flesh, without either group being found insane. The process is aptly called transubstantiation, from which con-substantiality was first contrasted (and because of which it has been dropped, and replaced by con-naturality).

The longer the antecedent history of the content of a doctrine, the more is it likely to be integral to human civilization, which is but an extension of our development as a person.

[In some ways, it is almost as a child that the author learned the grammar of cultural development. And like a child who cannot say how it learned the grammar of the language it speaks, the author cannot satisfactorily explain how he arrived at the grammar of cultural evolution, except that his patients' delusions seemed to indicate which ones antedated which, and are therefore more intractable, like the early accents in our speech.]

[The author can, however, pinpoint when he suddenly discovered that he could completely list them effortlessly in the order that they have emerged from patients' ideological hang-ups, and this compendium was born.]

How much of our lives are regulated by the spirit, our politics, economics, psychology, colleagues, technology, humanism, ecology, ethology, and electronics?

History offers New Psychiatrists excellent opportunities to compare spiritual, political, economic, and subspecies problems (questions) of a greedy upper class, a materialistic middle class, and a brutalized lower class.

Studied sampling of man-made behavior explains why (**F**) a Father Almighty but jealous God replaces Santa Claus even among paranoids in their religious delusions, yet does not need to be worshipped in school where we pledge allegiance to (**G**) our motherland against her mortal enemies. Would this sequence hold in other fields?

[The author's favorite sport, tennis, another man-made artifact like modern ideology, was embraced first by (**F**) monks and then by (**G**) monarchs.]

[Because their town has more courts per capita than any of the same size, without any waiting, he can play two sets of singles with his wife even on Sundays, amused that others go to church, synagogue, or mosque for their souls, when the body is said to be the temple of the soul.]

Discoveries about nature and civilization more often come from problem solving, rather than from sedentary theorizing.

The past is past, the present is upon us, but the future belongs to the bold. In the absence of immaculate perception, we must be fully alive to interaction with nature, silent or voluble. This is also to perceive more fully, but for perception to be profound, it must be lived with different kinds of pets, people, and other animals.

Are fishes different from frogs and birds from beasts because of the different environments that they inhabit? Is their habitat their handiwork or their prison?

Does diversity make us free or greedy? Do deadlines even in dying become our masters? Those in a hurry are afraid nobody will wait for them, or are suspicious of being disparaged behind their backs. Those always late know others will wait, critical or not. Only when time is our own to spend are we richer than the wealthy. Only then are we masterless.

Anthropology of Modern Societies

I enjoyed, as a boy growing up in a *barrio* or village, listening to bare-breasted women giggling over family secrets while gathered around our watering hole, bathing and washing dirty linen. Substitute experiences are now offered in TV talk shows, vaudeville routines by stand-up comedians and—to mimic milk-engorged breasts—silicone-augmented topless dancers entertaining older boys for a price.

The furniture in the various rooms that we inhabit changes with time. TV stands replace bookshelves, and now we receive more information on a computer screen than from the printed page. Adjustable vibrating beds replace curtained four-posters, and secular art has replaced religious artifacts on our walls.

Once upon a time there were just nests but only for the young, and lairs or caves at ground level or underground.

Today, we do not even have to open the front door to talk to outsiders; we just pick up the phone. And the phone has moved from room to room, from the common room to the kitchen to the bedroom, to the teenage dorm, and to the bathroom and patio, and away in more and more cars. Exclusive clubs ban portable phones.

Boats changed trading posts into settlements' wheels, inland villages into towns; roads, towns into suburbs; planes, suburbs into airports; and computers, bedroom towns into electronic cottage conglomerates processing and distributing a peculiar commodity called information.

The printing press was to Martin Luther God's last and greatest gift. It took the populace by storm just like TV and created instant celebrities, like Luther.

After skyrocketing to fame on TV, more and more celebrities crash to oblivion right away.

Before the First World War, half of the labor force still worked on the farm. In 1970, half of the product of labor was information. Magazines published more technical information than gossip in the '80s. (It is no longer enough to be literate as a talking head.)

Feudal cottage handicrafts that had given way to heavy industry now make room for the cottage economy of high technology in an information-marketing society.

Farmers accounted for 95% of our population in 1790. In 1970 it was 5%, and those engaged in the manufacture of goods was nearly halved between Orwell's 1948 and 1984.

Before there were caravans to trade or pillage abroad, man had to stay close to home to live out his life just doing what his family always did.

Generous GIs have now become cult heroes for some primitive tribes, and their airplanes are replicated as straw fetishes while the skies are scanned for their return since demobilization.

In Baghdad is a prototype of a battery that antedated the modern discovery of electricity by 2,500 years. Electricity did not wait for the steam engine to fail, and internal combustion did not develop because electricity was found wanting, nor was electronics (telecommunication) born out of the frustration of commuters.

[The same is true of popular art (modern or primitive), which will not bury classical art. It is not the intelligence but the talent of the artist or scientist that counts, not their will but the inspiration of the muse whom they serve, the artist depending on developed taste (**A**), the scientist on testing limits (**B**).]

We used to divide behavior into those we do lying down, sitting tall, or standing up.

(Partners who get along in at least two positions, one of which/ whom is lying down, tend to stay together.)

And then into what we do in the bedroom, the living room, and outside, including the outhouse and the courthouse. And then, as we became more fastidious, the bathroom, the kitchen, etc.

As we became affluent, the kitchen became a place to avoid. And as we spent our days away from home, the windows got less attention, and professional window washers now scale our high-rise air-conditioned offices so that we can look at other windows or other offices artificially lighted from the inside, even on sunlit days.

In epidemiology, we learn that AIDS affects mostly homosexuals in the New World but can also be found among heterosexuals in Africa. Hence, we have to revise our parochial bias about the disease. (The chances are that what helps American victims will also help African carriers.)

(Even in the young, age consciousness has been overtaken by AIDS wariness.)

Professional: To prevent desertion in Vietnam, it was thought that an American who begins to understand the inscrutable Oriental would soon need professional help.

Generalist: The same can almost be said of immigrants to America: the day they question its promise, they should right away seek the same assistance.

Specialist: Are those in favor of (**G'**) political and (**H'**) economic apartheid in South Africa the same group who wanted separate but equal accommodation and education in the Deep South? Are (**F'**) religious apartheid believers more intractable than (**G'**) or (**H'**) fanatics, just as they are among those deluded in fantasy or fanatical in reality?

(We can now help more of those who feel the need to understand some of the very old "answers" [social delusions], even in their faddish disguises.)

Will an ethopsychiatrist see a person successively developing (**A**) emotionally, (**B**) willfully, (**C**) thoughtfully, (**D**) comparatively, and (**E**) creatively during their time together?

Will the spiritual (**F**) succeed the political (**G**. even as sexual politics) after the economic (**H**, a starting point of negotiations in psychoanalysis), (**I**) egocentric, (**J**) ethnic, (**K**) technical, (**L**) humanistic, and (**M**) ecological ideologies (ethology and electronics not yet conflictful) fade in significance as dreams from which clients have awakened?

Will (**Y**) fathers or empty nesters become chaste or (**P**) autoerotic as potential partners become senso-socio-sexual risks?

[To be truly conservative (a conserver of tradition), must we recycle to (**G**) statism and (**F**) spiritualism or further back to our animal roots?]

(Recycling is not regression to more rigid patterns of behavior. Rigidity is arrest at an earlier level of development that is more congenial. Regression results when one retreats to what is no longer congenial and becomes symptomatic.)

We can now study our lifestyles as different subspecies, dominated by any one of our three life subcycles at any one time (e.g., sensual in our second childhood, sexual in our second adolescence).

7.00 g/HUMANITY

g/Chapter Notes

[g/1] We sometimes mistake reflection as more than a mirror of reality but as another window on the world. Inability to distinguish between mirror and window will confuse us about time and infinity, ourselves and others.

[g/2] While millions starve in underdeveloped countries, even those that don't (and the weaker sex) in overdeveloped areas kill others (especially during the "safe" first trimester), and older men everywhere send younger rivals to war or their pacifist peers to look after casualties. Only in our first foreign legion called the Peace Corps do they work for more food, at the behest of the youngest commander-in-chief to succeed an old World War II general.

[g/3] Proteins and DNA in the chromosomes divide mankind into Caucasian, African, Asian, and Australian, with the latter two evolving 39,000 years ago out of the former (100,000 years old). Does racial evolution explain the primacy of the Japanese in robotics? The oldest fossil of truly modern man came, not from Africa, but from Indonesia.

(Cross the Timor Straits and Asians reach Australia. Is this why non-Aboriginal white Australians dislike Orientals as much as Caucasians dislike African gorillas? Or are all values learned prejudices?)

More than just brothers and sisters, primates may also belong to different generations:

1) Is the generation gap what makes us think of gorillas as King Kong coveting a white woman?

2) Because gorillas are in fact less beastly than we are, is the sexually masterful gorilla fantasy a projection of early or unsatisfied bestiality (**V, m**) in our domesticated sexual development?

[Is agnosticism inversely proportional to neoteny among primates and birds, but not among amphibians and fishes which can depend on a soft landing for their heads after hatching? Can a pygmy and a postcesarean baby float in a warm pool and grow up less emotional (or hung-up)?]

(If **C** is rationalization and **D** is ratiocination, does **D** or **C** explain parts of this section on humanity?)

8.00 h/Liberty:
TRAVAILS of FREEDOM-LOVING "UNICORNS" (SCENE i)

(Sensuality should be explained to children as stages of development from good or bad to right or wrong to true or false, etc. if we are going to do better as *Homo sapiens*.)

To Be or Not to Be a Unicorn

> Can we be masterless / With effortless ease
> By scorning success / In travelling circuses
> Well-attended by cows, / But scorned by unicorns?

"Unicorns," who unite only briefly purely for procreation, promise a better future—for peaceful coexistence and personal fulfillment, if not shared happiness—than centaur teams, even of both sexes, can guarantee. Teamwork may be more convivial and familiar but less natural, except for the puny who need social fathering or mothering or a Big Brother or Solicitous Sister.

> [In the season of the rut (the unicorn) grows gentle toward the chosen female and they pasture side by side, but when this time is over he becomes wild again and wanders alone (From Aelianus, 2nd Century AD, *De Natura Animalium*)]

We are as unicorns when we are born, and then from *H. sapi*ens, some of us are domesticated into *H. domesticus* as centaurs to do the bidding of others, and as *H. metropolus* some become ladder climbers to equal status with those who have domesticated them. In the (**Z**) enith of our lives, more get less competitive and grow androgynous as grandparents.

> ["If God had not created the Unicorn, man would have invented him, for he has a form and nature that must exist . . . The second characteristic of the Unicorn which recommends him to mankind's love is his purity. He is pure because he is rare, distant, untouched. He is not rare from biological inadaptability or geographical accident. He is rare because it is the expression and fulfillment of his nature . . ." (From the introduction to *A Book of Unicorns* compiled by W. Poltarness, 1978.)]

Human freedom of/to dissent is often shackled by canons of taste and delimited by discomfort. Some words even acquire a taste and smell of their own.

> When we were children, we did not ask why our nose is called a nose. As we grew older, we learned that those who used their nose for other than breathing were called nosey, but most were not taught that—unlike our other sense organs—the nose is wired to the oldest part of our brain and on the same side, because it is still important, even when we are not aware of it, as when we are eating. In fact, odors cloud our judgment, if it offends our nose. Or when it is confused by other odors. *(h/1)*

Most postpubescent vocabulary is made up not of words, but of communicable ideas.

> Having become nosier, if less curious, than when we were children, the meanings we read into odors and words become important.

Are liberty and equality incompatible, irrespective of species? (Trapped animals make a last-ditch stand and sometimes survive.)

If rational, can you be a law unto yourself, restrained only by reason? If not, you are not reasoning as you should, despite all the tongue-wagging. (We are even reluctantly honest at our expense. The only exception to lying should be to patients and children, who are entitled to the truth, since they cannot disprove falsehood.)

The freedom to feel, freedom of movement, intellectual liberty, freedom to criticize, and creative freedom is personal, perhaps moral (more humane than humanistic), but rarely equal.

By "person" we do not mean individual, and by "personal" we do not mean (**I**) individualistic (psycho-centric).

By (**i**) "moral" we do not mean moralistic (proselytizing).

By "virtue" (personal and moral) we do not mean "value" (social and ideological).

By (**ii**) "social" we do not mean (**J**) socialistic (socio-centric) or (**H**) communistic (which is more economic).

By (**L**) "humanistic" we do not mean humane but anthropocentric.

By "personal (sensual) evolution," we do not mean personality (social mask) development.

A to E: Senso-Moral Evolution

	STAGES	JUDGMENT	ACTIVITY
A	E-mote/Feel	Good/Bad	Suck/Grasp
B	Act/Decide	Right/Wrong	Choose/Reject
C	Think/Guess	True/False	Yearn/Accept
D	Compare/Fit	Test/No	Prove/Discard
E	Create/Invent	New/Old	Change/Destroy
D'->	A' Decay/Fade	Early?	Decline->Die

[As babies we were more "into" feelings, as toddlers into "willing," as juveniles into "trying," as adolescents into "teasing" (to pieces in our minds what we think), as adults into "sizing" (quantifying or comparing), and, precocious or not, some of us succeed in creating theories or inventing prosthesis.]

All animals can (**A**) feel good or bad, (**B**) do right or wrong, and (**C**) be curious enough to think straight or not. But we must not confuse (**A**) e-motion with (**B**) action or (**C**) answers with (**D**) questions.

[Can immobilized robots "feel" trapped like invulnerable men coerced to commit themselves to something? Dreaming and hypnosis make the subjects more (A) e-motional for being immobile.]

Senso-moral development progressively goes by stages from (**A**) tasting to (**E**) creating by stages as
   (A) sensorimotor (infantile), then
   (B) operational, from preconceptual or trial-and-error to intuitive (leaps of insight), to concretistic or limit-testing among animals and toddlers, then
   (C) "rational" (formal abstractions and logical reductionism in early Western thought), to
   (D) comparative (disproving correlations postlogically or experimentally in modern science), and/without
   (E) creativity (precociously or not, because this is universally more a gift than a skill) discovering new, nonrandom connections, sooner or later or, often, never.

We can even be "creactive" (**E** + **B**) beyond ordinary reason (**C**), comparison (**D**), creativity (**E**), chivalry, and kinship.

SENSUAL DEVELOPMENTAL STAGES

A: FEELING (GOOD OR BAD): HOW DO I FEEL? ("WHERE IS MY MOTHER?")

On coming to America, I was surprised that families did not stay with their kids in pediatric units. Later, I found out that even their mothers did not stay with them in their nurseries at home.
   [In the animal kingdom and in the Orient, there is no legendary patricide (Freudian) or fantasied filicide (Laotian). Where fathers are rivals, they are more easily replaced by an Almighty, sooner or later.]

Narcissistic, nonerotic disorders are now more common because parents are more remote from their children. Our families are smaller, and fewer persons are at home. (Our visitors are more often electronic than corporeal.)

Mothering (even by fathers) requires both extended time (for nursing) and space (for nesting). Both are also needed in our second childhood. They are not found in "nursing homes" for the old and abandoned.

When working mothers lobby for child-care centers, are infants competitors for precious (quality) time in a tight money market where more dedication is demanded of their once braless mammas?

Mammals must suckle and infants, like pets, also have to be groomed. Eroticized grooming becomes sexual foreplay. Violent extremists (mean or mean-spirited or homophobic) have to have been orphaned or scared out of their boots or wits when they needed tenderness (caresses).

Birds still chirp, but we hurriedly take away from our babies their songs in their own natural dialect, which has become Greek to us. All is not lost if we sing them to sleep with lullabies, which even beasts find soothing, no matter how incoherent they sound except to the singer.

(Can those who find the incoherence of rock-and-roll lyrics distasteful defend what they liked in their adolescence as much more intelligible?]

Infants of all ages wonder about good or bad. On their own, they later let their acquired tastes decide unoriginally about art and beauty. As to "What is good?" outside aesthetics, the hidden question is "Who is the beneficiary?"

B: WILLING (RIGHT OR WRONG): WHAT CAN I DO? ("CAN I GET AWAY WITH IT?")

Like all other animals, we inherit energy to move around. (Action is energy at work in the form of force exerted over distance.)

But because man is puny and terrestrial, he is easily awed. Even insects (like guerilleros with small arms) are bolder than large beasts because of their mobility, and can inspire fear among children (and superpowers).

All animals are also curious. That's why children want to see everything in a new place, not because they're pests.

[To be bored, you have to be a child who cannot go where (s)he wants (animals who are not domesticated can) or an adult without much of an imagination to take hir (sic) away from hir immediate surroundings. Then the child sucks hir thumb and the adult drinks, snacks, smokes, reads, or watches TV instead of thinking and writing out hir own fantasies.]

Animal political instincts are surer because they are never expected to know their fathers and therefore do not yearn to follow their leaders, some of whom lead us to perpetrate "purges." *(h/2)*

Many concentration camp survivors think of memory as a shield; old people use theirs as a bank from which to draw a pittance when in need of sustenance. Both shy away from the mind as monitor.

So do those of us who are younger prisoners of our culture. We only remember more easily what is not alien to our comfort.

Toddlers of all ages wonder about doing what is right or wrong, and decide according to inclination (angle of incline in the path of least resistance), willfully or willingly (i.e., when agreeable to similarly inclined superior).

Otherwise, what is right is decided by "What is fair?" and the hidden question is "Who is the arbitrator?"

C: THINKING (TRUE OR FALSE): WHAT WILL I FIND? ("WHERE IS THE ANSWER?")

[Grecophiles think of Greece as the womb of Western civilization. It reached its peak in philosophy and the arts—not music or science—during the Golden Age of Athens. If you're a humanist or homosexual, Greek history pulls you in different directions: righteous repugnance for slavery or envious fascination with gay artistry, though Sappho, the first recorded lesbian (Stage **R, f**), was arguably but a minor poet.]

Philosophy became more formal introspection as theology (Stage **F**) until Descartes introduced doubt (**B'**, "cogitation") as the beginning of all thinking ("cognition"). [Or **F** -> **B** ->**C**]

More psychological introspection (Stage **I**) followed the separation of "mind" from matter. It spawned (**J**) groups which espoused the human potential movement (Stage **L**). Some members now (**C**) think our human consciousness is the altered state that entitles us to be (**BB**) righteous as (**M**) custodians of our corner of the cosmos. [Or **I** -> **J** -> **L** -> **C** -> **BB** -> **M**]

Wanton experimentation on lower animals had prompted advocacy of their rights (**N**) and other alternatives to vivisection. The lives of expendable but superior test pilots have been saved by computer simulation (**O**). Pilot projects involving other endangered species must not only have environmental impact studies but must project other possible injuries, by processing and correlating all available data electronically.

The seeker/answerer (Stage **C**) is not ready to (**D**) compare. (S) he is still—(**F**) religiously like Luther, (**G**) politically like the pope, and (**H**) economically like Hitler—seeking dogmatic relief or "the final solution," unlike the searcher/discoverer. (Stage **E** sometimes discovers by observation what had not before been expected.)

To ask "What is (**C**) true?" often becomes "What will (**B**) decide, (**A**) desire, or (**D**) data?"

Martin Luther thought Jews were inferior to Germans, and the pope himself did not protest against Hitler's atrocious experiments on non-Aryans.

Juveniles of all ages wonder about true or false, and adolescents seek the simple answer without searching, by introspection.

D: COMPARING (MORE OR LESS): WHAT IS PROVED? ("WHO VERIFIED IT?")

The researcher and explorer (who traverses the ground already trodden) is less suggestible than the seeker. He is also more skilled in his use of his senses but not as creative or original as the searcher/discoverer.

Adults who can compare but won't measure even in terms of "more or less"—which can be calibrated (e.g., in thermometers) as precisely as our inventiveness allows—are more interested in compromise: "Where does it fit?" ("Will others agree?"). They seek to preserve relationships or to reciprocate rather than answer in terms of absolute relativity or reciprocity.

To be comparative, we don't have to be morally virtuous. We cannot correlate if we want to be good, right, reasonable, or even logical. But we have to be sensible or rational (which originally referred to ratios, relative or reciprocal). To be reasonable and logical is to justify or excuse one's action by rationalization (which technically means that the speaker, the writer included, does not himself know when he is protesting too much).

Our conclusions can be received badly (rejected on emotional grounds), treated wrongly (misinterpreted), or adjudged falsely (misunderstood); but they cannot be faulted as long as we do not compare oranges with apples except as seeds. (We also cannot compare ideas as such but only the data on which theories are based.)

We can be mistaken if there are variables that we have neglected, but that is an honest mistake, not an atrocious crime. It is only in this sense that to err is human, because as a species we have only five senses, and some are neglected in favor of others. (Are other species also biased toward any given sensibilities?)

Facts are always of the past and can be correlated, forecast, and predicted to share the probability of their recurring in similar circumstances, without any guarantee that they will.

[If God does not gamble, it is because we discard events that we cannot correlate by calling them coincidences or miracles instead of being somehow related in ways that we cannot fathom.]

E: CREATING (NEW OR ANEW):
WHAT CAN I FASHION? ("WILL IT OUTLIVE ME?")

The faddish answers the question "What was created?" by "According to whom?"

Unlike Stages **A** to **D**, creative development can be precocious or prodigious, since it is more genetic: all talent is hereditary, only skills can be learned. With both, a virtuoso develops, but no matter how equally we may be endowed, which can happen with identical twins, all of us use our given talent (giftedness) differently. Some of us develop into articulate intellectuals or art critics, competent technicians (e.g., statisticians), skilled artisans (craftsWoMen), or scientists and artists.

[In this age of amateurs, we do not all have to be skilled: many just need determination and stamina].

[People who are untalented and keen on environmental determinants need to blame somebody else for their predicament more than those whose genetic heritage is better but are lazier (less militant). All controversy between them is based on their unacknowledged bias or ignorance (about utopias or eugenics).]

Creative people stay lost longer in a world not entirely their own, just like the sexually fulfilled in erotic abandon. They seem to be driven from inside or by a muse outside to do what they must then finish to their satisfaction. (Absolute relativity aside, all theories exclude the gifted as atypical. We do not!)

In the very act of creation, the truly talented are inaccessible. Their identity is transformed from the pedestrian to the sublime, but they are not mad. Only schizophrenics do not recognize the person they seem to have become when they break with their own reality. (Those who search for another identity seem to be more dissatisfied with themselves than misunderstood schizophrenics ever are.)

This losing oneself in untimed and often untimely feverish activity makes it more difficult to place creativity in a pigeonhole among (**i–iii**) coevolving stages of development in our senso-socio-sexual life cycle. Only if the artist and his art unite, and the potter and her pot come together, can the changes and stages validate each other.

Progress in the development of talent depends on the freedom to feel, freedom to act, freedom to think, freedom to correlate, and freedom to destroy, which society abhors.

TO THE YOUNG AND SENSUOUS

This is written for those of you whose world has not been bent out of shape by the dreams others have for you.

Dreams or visions direct or focus energy while neglecting other opportunities. Common goals oppress and enslave the community for the duration of the strife.

*You will quite naturally, learn first (**A**) good, and sometimes why something is bad.*

What is good for you, your body will naturally accept; what is not, it will simply refuse, and you might not know why until much later. What your body accepts, you also do not question right then, just as you don't question why the sun is shining, unless it is too hot on your skin. It is the same with parts of your body. You don't know you have a toe until you stub it. It is not (**B'**) wrong for you to stub your toe; it is merely (**A'**) bad for your foot.

*Next, you learn about (**B**) right and wrong.*

What is wrong, you usually find out from someone before you find out you were right in throwing a tantrum without knowing it. Again, what is right does not need as much explanation as what is wrong. And because explanations are always secondhand (or hand-me-downs), like all secondhand news (or gossip), why something is wrong is usually not (**C**) the truth.

*What is (**C**) true or false is the third step in learning as you grow up.*

Some people do not bother to judge what is true or false most of their days and live only on the basis of what is good or bad, which is how all animals decide for themselves. Animals also seldom use their sense of what is right or wrong except in respecting the right of another to a place if it got there ahead of them.

> Student: Is that why we planted our flag on the moon? And are we prepared to throw a temper tantrum to end all temper tantrums with *Star War* weapons over a mere planet? Will we allow anyone to enter our space without prior consent or conquest? Are early warning signs the signal that we are fit to be tied?
>
> Professional: Are we asking ridiculous questions? Will we get serious answers? The right ones from animals will not matter to the greedy who is armed to the teeth.

Because we do not often think of these three early stages of personal growth separately, I want to teach your teachers the **ABC**s of the very young growing up, and I'll put them down in a way that adults can recognize or refuse but not ignore.

FOR THE YOUNG AT HEART

A. "Affective" or Emotional Stage

When people ask "How do you feel?" they don't know that they're asking "How did your mother treat you?" Habitually smiling or frowning faces come from being treated differently. Those whom some call optimists smile more often than pessimists, who frown frequently.

> Optimists have more of the four *c*'s than most of us: They are caring and curious, and they are also considerate and cooperative. They are especially loyal and loving even when you don't feel lovable, tender (in medicine, what is tender is what hurts and needs tender caring), and trusting, yet quick to forgive when you disappoint them, which makes them the patient and easygoing caregivers.
>
> Pessimists, on the other hand, have only three *c*'s: They are cold, cross, or crabby and themselves need but won't take caring even if they complain a lot. Caregivers who are more careful than caring and expect to be asked for help in so many words are put off by pessimists in need.

Those who take care of you should be people who were well taken care of at your age. You can sense whether they have been or not, but adults need them to be described and given a name in order to recognize them. I simply call all of them "nurses," but those who cannot or will not nurse from their breasts call them "nurturing." When they think of themselves as members of the "helping professions," whether they are optimistic or pessimistic, their helpfulness varies with their outlook.

B. "Balancing" or Volitional Stage

When others ask "How do you do?" they may not know that they're asking how much space you could call your own as toddlers without insisting or screaming.

Those who get past this stage without feeling fenced in become leaders. They have the two *C*s in capital letters: they are Confident and Competitive. They also have two *d*'s: They are demanding and decisive. They can demand loyalty and keep your secrets or decide to give them away without your consent.

Toilet-trained parents raised gingerly on carpets usually buy and then protect them and help incite rebellion against routine among their children. Those who cannot express how they feel about being "second banana" to floor coverings may start wetting their beds. The chances are good that they become stutterers and grow to be dirty-mouthed leaders who will need speechwriters to clean up their language for carpet worshippers.

Leaders need followers who can be persuaded to work for them. Some followers are more willing than others. Those who are not are called willful and defend themselves by saying that they have the right to decide for themselves. They believe that everyone has to exercise the free will given to all human beings, which they claim makes them quite different from animals.

You can only believe that is so if you have not yet learned to smoke or have since been able to quit or you do not have animals around to make you doubt its alleged source. (Who tempted whom in Eden? Our first kitten "wills" us to keep playing hide-and-seek with him. He always wins because he does not make much noise when he moves and has a better sense of the best places behind which to hide.)

To your parents, I also want to add the following: Our free will is no freer than a free fall and for the same reasons. Nor can we blame not being free in both instances on mysteries or "weakness of the flesh."

C. "Cognitive or Rational Stage

Whenever people ask, "What do you think?" they do not know that they're also asking if you depend on opinions to make decisions like teenagers do.

Those who liked this part of their growing up we can call "examiners" because they carefully examine everything, even how they think about thinking. They eventually get into the habit of consulting themselves. (Those who make a living analyzing life but keeping the answers to themselves are often called philosophers.)

We can give them two Ds. They like Details but remain Detached from the decisions that are demanded once they finish their examination, which usually takes them a long time because they want to be sure.

In fact, they don't like making decisions and would rather give you several choices from which you must select. What you choose then becomes your decision, not theirs. That is how they distance themselves from blame if something goes wrong.

With the following later stages of development, adults will not quarrel. They can explain them to you if you are curious about them already.

D. "Distrustful" or Comparative Stage

When people ask "How's everything?" they may not intend to invite you to compare what you can. Only scientists must, by measuring, even just in terms of "more or less" of anything.

Those who enjoyed this part of growing up become science luminaries in their field because they are different from examiners or leaders. We usually call them "consultants."

Consultants may get paid better than A, B, or C. They also have two Cs in capital letters: They Criticize and Compare. They also practice two d's: They diagnose and disprove. They disprove what is not so and arrive at a diagnosis of what remains in order to recommend a remedy.

For instance, if D is consulted when one gets into trouble, he would recommend more attention for A; for B, more freedom to test and escape artificially set limits; for C, more time to decide about going to college or joining the armed services medical corps by negotiating indefinite delays in artificial deadlines; and for E, intelligent neglect: it is foolish to praise or push the Muse for fame or money.

E. "Exceptional" or Creative Stage

When friends ask "What's new?" they don't know that they expect you to judge what's different. If you are old before your time, you may already have made a difference that they can or cannot appreciate nor match.

This is the stage most people wish to reach so that they can be called "creative." You can be creative at any age because talent is inherited.

If you are precocious, they will describe you as inventive and unpredictable. If they do not like your invention, they will say you are irresponsible. If they cannot agree, it is probably because you are not too concerned about what they think. Sooner or later, three capital Is stick to you: Inventive, Insensitive, and Irresponsible.

"Irresponsible" means that you don't jump as soon as you are supposed to react, "insensitive" that you prefer to go at your own pace using a timetable that is dictated by inspiration or your Muse, and to exercise your initiative, to be "Inventive" or (**B + E**) "creative."

That's why those who are truly creative don't become science leaders until after they are dead, and fewer are even asked for advice while they're alive.

Because you are younger than your teachers, you can easily remember how old you were when you began to learn bad from good, wrong from right, and false from truth.

For your teachers, the following are the years when, very quickly or more slowly, normal children seemed to learn all three "moral" lessons:

> Stage A: Years 1–3, good or bad
> Stage B: Years 3–7, right or wrong
> Stage C: Years 7–17, true or false

As you grow older, especially if you took your time learning your ABCs, what is "good" and "right" and "true" get more mixed up because you want what is true to be right and what is right to be good, when they really have nothing to do with each other.

Your parents may have also learned their moral ABCs more slowly than children their own age and, in raising you, made no comments on what was wrong when you were not bad and did not point out what is false because you did not yet know right from wrong. *(h/3)*

Infants of all ages wonder about good or bad and let their taste decide.

Toddlers of all ages wonder about right or wrong and decide according to inclination. (Urchins are more formidable among these juveniles.)

Adolescents of all ages wonder about true or false and answer by introspection. (Toddlers allowed to test limits will be testing the truth after adolescence. Only those who learn to test reality by testing its limits will push as far out as James Joyce did as an artist or take technology further than their science teachers could.)

As a doctor, I know that your body decides what is GOOD for you; as a psychiatrist, I know your parents decided what is RIGHT for you, and as a scientist, I know nature decides what is TRUE of you and all that surrounds you, including us.

We recreate in our homes the prenatal paradise we lost, loving animals of older ancestry as pets, like Adam and Eve. We even keep them from some parts of our house, but unlike God, we forgive them all their trespasses. Because they are dumb, we don't feel offended by their behavior. "Dumb" blondes also do not offend us, yet they are as smart as animals.

(The implications of this for battered wives and abused children are discussed in the section on "Violence: Modern Dilemmas," to bite and digest which you need explicit or implicit permission from your parents or guardians, dead or alive.)

FOR OLDER, TALLER, BUSIER PEOPLE LOVERS

Infants of all ages divide reality into good or bad, and their instrument of judgment is personal taste, which they acquired before they could walk or visit art galleries and science museums.

Juveniles of all ages divide reality into right and wrong, and their judgment is based on experiences gained before they could run, whether motivated by good or bad intentions. Their instrument of judgment is consensual perception of actual wrongdoing, not the message it carries, whether of protest or anger. (Cops only police what is visible or audible and chase criminals or dissidents without discriminating between them.)

Adolescents of all ages divide reality into true or false, and their instrument of judgment is past authority. (Lawyers decide on the basis of what TV Sergeant Friday of "Dragnet" officiously intones: "Just the facts, ma'am." Judges decide on the basis of what is coded or accepted as precedent [in a hallowed or unholy past]).

Adults of all ages—until senility returns us to a second adolescence (middle-age crises) or childhood—decide reality on the basis of what is testable (objective) or not (subjective). Their instrument of judgment is all the prostheses of perception that allows us to observe and measure (quantify what can be objectified) so that we can share the results or improve on the tests and explore their implications.

Creative persons of all ages, precocious or not, divide reality into what is new or not. Their instrument of judgment is the unrecorded novelty of the event. The obsolete is not mourned. Creativity is out-innovating one's peers.

From the beginning, we all want to raise a good kid. This desire is as universal as doubting, which cannot be doubted. And so we praise the kid for being (**A**) a good baby. Then we want to raise (**B**) a decent kid. Later, we are content if our young will only be (**C**) truthful.

After outgrowing adolescence at any age, what else lies beyond the moral virtues of [**A**, **B**, **C**] goodness, righteousness, and truthfulness? Is tunnel vision a risk when all we ask is what is good, right, and true? Are there more "moments of truth"? Socrates and Hemingway took their own lives after thorough examination thereof.

Truthfulness also becomes a factor in psychological testing by truth worshippers, when errors are mistaken for falsehood, when being erratic may in fact be organic, mental (rather than moral) retardation.

Revelation ("truth" or **C**) to a self-selected prophet or chosen people is NOT (1) (a) testable by research into cherished coincidences (as in biblical "science") or (b) discoverable by connections independent of correlations (as in homology) BUT (2) defensible only by formal logic (analogy).

Reason (**C**) and rationalization (ideology, ii) result in ritualizations (**B'**) without ratiocination (**D**) or ratios of relatedness. (Literate worshippers of the Greek god of syllogism play word games with their left brain and produce tabulations. The right-brain processes sensory stimuli topologically and produces graphics.)

Evil is simply misunderstanding good, and therefore, as Sartre himself "divined" in rejecting even the Devil, abstraction is the only evil.

Like a child or robot, there is no predictably bad, delinquent, or devilish God (a superrobot), only a manhandled, misprogrammed machine (deus ex machina) in the bug-ridden prototype of a computer we call WoMan.

All of us, intelligent or not, are born ignorant, so we have to be taught. Sometimes we are taught we are naughty even if we are merely amoral and innocent of malice. When we protest with tantrums against such accusation, we are punished or admonished to be meek.

This makes us hire loudmouthed lawyers later in life and/or join demonstrations against unusual and cruel punishment.

Some of those for capital punishment believe that if you can't outdistance your pursuers, killing them is the next best thing to do, as in the wild, wild frontiers of the West or when wild animals are trapped by trappers.

In our farm, there are plants that shrink from our touch. Chickens have been known to keep running with their heads cut off. Uprooted by our limbs, we must be on the move and award prizes to the fleet of foot (four-minute milers, fictional Forrest Gump, tragic O. J. Simpson, etc.).

Our attitude then depends on how concerned we are about others' concerns, which unicorns do not share. The less concerned *Homo domesticus* are, the more their attitude, as *H. metropolis* becomes a false front. *(h/5)*

If we think of ourselves as sensual unicorns, we can see our development into social centaurs as **(i)** brain-washing and **(ii)** brain-stuffing rather than progress in personal growth, to become less *Homo sapiens* and more *H. domesticus* or, worse, *H. metropolus*.

It is easier to live as unicorns as long as we are healthy and away from centers of civilization. The closer we are to crowds, our "decisions" are limited to "choices" between "options" that others share but did not create. *(h/4)*

8.00 h/LIBERTY

h/Chapter Notes

[h/1] Odors are especially crucial when dealing with disturbed (disturbing) patients. I had always emphasized this in my teaching but had to repeat it for an alumna who got along well with a prison inmate until just before he was due for parole. And then he claimed that she was pregnant by him. He was confused by the different smells that pregnancy brings, rather than fearful of parole. Many parolees cannot stay out of prison for very long, but habitual lifestyle is not the only explanation.

[h/2] Stalin outdid Hitler in killing 10 instead of just 6 million for (**F**) religious, (**G**) political or national security, or (**H**) material or economic reasons.

[h/3] "Health care professionals" who are mixed up about what is good, right, and true are as likely to be mixed up also about (**A'**) loneliness, (**B'**) depression, (**C'**) unhappiness, (**D'**) frustration, and (**E'**) boredom.

1) (a) Loneliness is absent among gardeners, bird-watchers and animal lovers, (b) depression is guilt that is medically treatable but not legally punishable, and (c) unhappiness is not treatable or relieved by caring after others by one who feels deserving of something better and is bitter for not getting full entitlement.

2) Frustration is inability to enjoy coping with and comparing present and past dilemmas or with the record made by poets or peers. [The uncreative (**A**) cry-babies who attempt to compare may later wallow in (**A'**) self-pity; (**B'**) self-flagellation in (**BB**) the overachiever is a specialty only of the depressed]

3) Boredom is failure of imagination. Animals go to sleep instead of suffering boredom. Prolonged "sleep" is called hibernation among them. Among us, adaptive mental apathy in those institutionalized is misdiagnosed as "chronic" schizophrenia (cf. Ortega, Mental Hospitals, Professional Article of the Month, Dec. 1959.)

[h/4] LOVE AND LOSS OF LIBERTY

> Man's capacity for justice makes democracy possible, but
> man's inclination to injustice makes democracy necessary.
> —Reinhold Niebuhr

King Christian X of Denmark outflanked the Germans by threatening to wear a yellow armband with the Star of David if all Jews were ordered to wear one.

Liberty is an instinct that momentarily lives when we feel cornered or trapped and there seems to be no exit. The traps may be sprung by old, bad, or vague memories or new, bright, or explicit commitments. The more numerous they are that entrap us, the more we fight, openly or subversively, only to give in at the end (of entropy, below), when we settle for a small hole underground in which to rest in peace.

St. Augustine wanted to disregard the world (as psychoanalysts did everything except psychic reality): "Believe, then you'll understand." Today, if you understand something, then it's already obsolete as hindsight.

Certitude is a danger when light blinds the believer.

Our inalienable right to a natural life and the liberty to pursue happiness takes precedence over the right to any lifestyle among consenting adults, or to unilateral perversion (foreplay without partner), and "voluntary" abortion.

Liberty does not mean competition, but should include the freedom not to compete. If love is cooperation between siblings by blood or upbringing, so be it.

Liberty to do what is right (the temptation to do good) is no liberty at all, just as the freedom to agree is not the essence of our freedom to speak or sing.

Specialist: To call the freedom to do what is wrong—or to differ as "licentiousness"—is to accept censorship of verbal or nonverbal expression.

Professional: Dissenters may be punished for wrongdoing, but not prevented from being in the wrong.

[h/5] (Even centaurs may be domesticated with some difficulty, but unicorns resist—they are always "unattainable, unique, a distant flash of white among the trees, a vision of a firebird that can never be caught" (from *Animal Land* by M. Blount, 1975).

The first time both sexes were yoked together in science, Mme Curie teamed up with her less-enterprising husband, and both produced the first man-made radiation. If our mission is to understand nature in order to control it, we increase our chances of success by concerted group effort.

Dr. Oppenheimer, the coordinator of America's success in developing the first radioactive explosive, never completed an "individual" project. (Having usurped what Mother Nature reserved for herself, we now scare ourselves with a Mother Bomb in fear that we cannot abort the monstrous mutants that we may bring to life.)

9.00 i/Equality: GUIDED TOURS for HUMAN CENTAURS (SCENE ii)

> The roots of politics are older than humanity.
> —Frans de Waal, ethologist and author,
> *Chimpanzee Politics*, London, 1982

"Lower" primates can organize to bully the weak or nonconforming "unicorn" of its species into giving up territory that the group wishes to annex (the "eminent domain" exercise to evict timid *Homo domesticus*).

Without blinders, we can see how we have domesticated "centaurs" into centurions and trained dogs to guide the blind through city traffic. These are also the stages in the evolution of *H. domesticus*, some of whom turn into *H. metropolus*, defending hir (*sic*) rights instead of fighting to be free like "unicorns" (who never pause to listen to priests, politicians, profiteers, etc.).

When alone, we may be somewhat saddened that the Clone/clown/canine of our childhood had such a role to play in our new play. But we also know that many have left us enough old scripts and scrapbooks to keep us from forgetting "the good old days" and the way we were.

(Socialization for *Homo sapiens* is convivial, for *H. domesticus* and *metropolus*, self-centered and perverted.)

A UNICORN IS NOT A CLONE

Except for unicorns
Who resist taming
For show or racing,
Our world is a stage

Of children play-acting,
Or adults self-masking,
As personalities change
Self-hood into selves
By different stages.

Born as an animal
We can shed our shells
That have become our jails,
And outgrow our carapace
Of hard human conceits
And sail with the wind
With mankindly grace,
Unbowed by booing,
Uncowed by crowding.

We can all cease "cell" division
Just to build cancerous empires
With bugles and marching,
And let live without greed
But without starving
For food, warmth, love or space.

(A unicorn wanders alone except to mate, cannot bear being common or to be taken alive.)

We now have a few answers, some methods and tools for correlating data, and some graphs to guide us. We can plot our virtues and our values and show how brain-washing and brain-stuffing interferes with breeding mutants different from Animachinerotic clones.

FROM UNICORNS TO CENTAURS TO ANDROGYNES

We are elaborating on three separate, not subspecies, but subcycles in human evolution: The first is the origins of personal morality (virtues, not values) and liberty (also cherished by animals). The second is our ideo-ethical struggle for valued equality (before God, Caesar, Big Business, etc.) throughout history. The third is the socio-biological differences between the sexes from the unisex of the fetus to the androgyny of grandparenthood.

I will later talk more about sex, which is even more restricted by parents (like the movies rated R by their fellow parents).

FROM UNTAMED UNICORNS TO DOMESTICATED CENTAURS

(A centaur with hands bound behind and a cupid astride his back, torturing him with lust, inspired this "travelogue.")

Our behavior keeps evolving before domestication (virtuous or valuable) overcomes breeding and/or biological involution overtakes inherited creative and pro-creative potential. We can plot their topology and chronology.

We can divide our sensual growth and development (**i**) into prelogical, logical, and postlogical, the last of which may be precocious.

We can divide our social development (**ii**) into subgroups that started early (prehistoric), later (historic), and recently (current), many for some being still novel or new.

We can divide our sexual growth and development (**iii**) into pregenital, genital, and reproductive, the last two subgroups being precocious for some, ready or not. Some substages may be passed over at our peril though we may feel proud of the fact and try to take credit after the fact, e.g., of disdaining rapacity.

Virtues have not changed, but values have. Growth in virtue and the evolution of values have not gone hand in hand. (Lawyers can withhold the truth and still succeed.)

Many now value machines more than God who, for some of us, have no claim on our virtue.

ESCALATION of IDEOLOGY

What goes into domesticating humans? There are two stages, personal and social, both asexual, coevolving but in conflict with each other. *(i/2)* Our social subcycle is more mental than sensual (neurological) for being ideological (distorting data into dogma in order to be equal in the eyes of God, government, guilds, etc.). *(i/1)* It is also more human except for the first three substages but not less convivial than the sexual (which is itself the most erotic and expressive in the animal kingdom).

OUR OVERLAPPING SENSO-SOCIAL SUBCYCLES

(Time spans and successes can vary.)

i) SENSO-MORAL   ii) SOCIO-CULTURAL

A)	emotional, affectionate, passionate	**F)**	theocentric: spiritual
		G)	jingocentric: political
B)	willful, decisive, motivated	**H)**	econocentric: barter-prone
		I)	psychocentric: individualistic
C)	intellectual, reflective, abstract	**J)**	ethnocentric: groupminded
		K)	technocentric: progress-driven
D)	testing, comparing, exploring	**L)**	anthropomorphic: humanistic
		M)	geocentric: planet-conscious
E)	creating, venturing, discovering	**N)**	ethocentric: animalistic
		O)	circu-centric: cybernetic

There are two (**A** and **B**) vocal if (nonverbal and inarticulate) emotional and volitional stages in our preliterate personal (sensual, not socio-sexual) development. (Which is why both demand a mouthpiece or spokesperson for the illiterate to be heard and understood expeditiously or, in writing, adjudicated legally. Which is also how advocacy got started, by early ghostwriters of love letters.)

Both stages are prelogical and shared with other animals, just like three of our social preoccupations in the form of animism (**F** for faith), pecking order (**G** for gun), and hoarding (**H** for hustling) of tokens for barter (to be exchanged for sexual favors during captivity by resourceful lab animals or later left posthumously to others by successful but shortsighted misers).

(1) We're better than "lower" animals because we have a richer sign language vocabulary even as deaf-mutes, and (2) we can be as God once we use adjectives to shape reality, then (3) we can also be (a) ideagogues, or even delude ourselves as (b) ideologues.

We made great advances in helping the handicapped once we disregarded their brain except to help it manage their muscles, which is its mission.

We are (1) poor if we do not have everything we need as an animal, (2) ambitious if we do not have everything we want as a human being, (3) successful if we get what we want, and (4) rich if we are neither poor nor wanting in anything.

There are also, in our cultural development, at least five (**F** to **J**) prehistorical stages—religious, political, economic, psychological, and social—which are more metaphorical and axiom-ridden, like (**L**) irreligious Western Hemisphere humanism.

More scientific or theory-tolerant are (**K, M, N,** and **O**) technology, ecology, ethology, and electronics, which are also postlogical except for the last (so far) in our historical preoccupations.

(Computers, unless they use "fuzzy logic" that "smart" appliances do, are hyperlogical on an "all or none" basis and in-tolerant, like preachers and other dogma-driven believers, even when "user-friendly" or simpler to use.)

As innocent infants, we are both free to be (**A**) emotional and (**F**) eligible to join the angels in heaven.

As toddlers we would rather (**B**) play than cry except (**G**) to protest.

As juveniles, we worked (**H**) for a pittance to achieve (**I**) individual autonomy as (**C**) an adolescent.

As adults, we took care of (**A**) dependents (children) as their breeders or of clingers (clients) as (**J**) our civic responsibility.

At the zenith of some of our lives, we become (**Z**) grandparents.

With increased longevity, having children to perpetuate the species can now stretch to wanting grandchildren by your children or as your patients' or student's children, whom they are proud to present to you.

(This also averts middle-age crises for overachievers. Reborn Christians are the reincarnation of innocence without a second childhood.)

A SOCIAL PRIMER FOR ALL CHILDREN OF TENDER AGE

Given how you behave now, how will you make out later on? Not smoothly for some stages.

Older children can remember more than five letters; can you remember twice as many? You already know about what **A**, **B**, **C**, **D**, and **E** represent. Now we shall talk about the next ten letters of the alphabet.

If you do not remember them all, don't forget that even older people cannot recite the area or zip codes of their grown children's telephones or addresses.

When
(**AA**) helping others becomes saving souls, then we have (**F**) missionaries;

(**B**) persuading becomes (**BB'**) power grabbing, then we have (**G**) politicians;

(**B'**) saving carpets becomes investing to get rich, then we have (**H**) traders;

(**B**) demands are self-centered, then we have (**I**) egotists;

(**A**) caring becomes sharing, then we have (**J**) social workers;

(**E**) creating becomes producing, then we have (**K**) artisans;

(**C**) examining themselves ends with being proud to be human, then we have (**L**) lovers of mankind;

(**AB'**) loyalty becomes concern for the environment, then we have (**M**) conservationists;

(**AB**) helping children becomes protecting helpless animals, then we have (**N**) animal lovers;

(**CC**) logical thinking decides in terms only of black or white, or all or nothing, and 1 or 0 without overlapping or converging ("fuzzy") sets, then we have (**O**) computer programmers;

For all of the above, you need very little parental guidance (or "PG" as they say in the movies). The rest that I want you to know, now or soon, you must read with parental permission.

I am not sure parents would want you to know everything yet that you should know *(i/3)* or even that they themselves know what I am going to talk about in the rest of this section.

SOCIO-CULTURAL STAGES of DEVELOPMENT for OLD KIDS

F: Spiritual: Am I all alone? ("Where is my Father?")

In God we trust with all our heart but not with all our might, unless we are militant martyrs (terrorists, **F** x **G**. *(i/4)*. [Saddam Hussein: "God willing, God will be our ally!" (Sept. 1, 1996)]).

G: Political: What is my party? ("Who is my protector?")

There are those who measure success in life, not by rebirth unto the Lord, but by their access to earthly powers (sometimes decided by how much money they gave away as bribes or political contributions that cannot otherwise be spent before they die).

H: Economic: Where are my competitors? ("Who is my provider?")

If money is just a way of keeping score, scoring very high means you're afraid someone might catch up with you.

Historically speaking, real estate developers are the descendants of the pioneers of the untamed frontiers, mortgage holders today the settlers of yesterday.

New classes will compete for new territories as history unfolds, the last to date being "hackers" or the elite amateur/entrepreneur (the new robber barons in electronics (Stage **O**) versus their inferiors, the computer illiterates.

(The slow learner of our moral **ABC** sensually confuses what is good with what is right and what is true. We can also socially confuse the role of provider with that of protector in God the Father [Godfather], if we did not have [1] a good mother, aunt, or sister who provided needed care; [2] a strong father, uncle, or brother who had frightened bullies away; and/or [3] grandparents or relatives who offered sanctuary, protection, and provisions when needed. [Ancient forms of religion evolved from tribal ancestor worship.])

I: Psychological: Who am I? ("Who will play with me?")

There is no self (sole repository of the soul) but a series of selves, some discovered but not forgotten, others still latent and waiting in the wings to play a part in our lives.

Just as we can all have more than one name or middle initial (identity beyond family membership), we can have more than one career or credential (professional, not personal, identification).

Lonely persons languishing at this stage may be fonder of their pets than of their parents or peers and are, in fact, children of varying ages who secretly cherish their psychological "autonomy." Some have, however, lost it again as slaves of an inarticulate pet who personifies a demanding master/playmate/mistress.

(But they are not among other so-called "lost" souls who seek the "real" self as an "individual," presumably having lost touch with it in the past.)

(As unimportant intellectuals, the lost mourn their "inauthenticity" without finding that self-contradictory. Often idle and afloat without rudder or direction but with calories and money to burn, they feel purposeless without a plan [a favorite diet, etc.] and insignificant unless involved in something "meaningful" [a favorite charity, etc.].)

J: Sociological: Who are we? ("Where are my friends?")

Groups, identified by membership outside their immediate families, are different from crowds (which act like a herd that can stampede). Such special-interest groups behave more like a flock of birds. Their members share the same sources of pride and shame and define what might be regrettable as unethical or valueless.

Ethics is seen as a more purposeful and professional value system than virtuous moral principles, which are never seriously questioned. (Immorality unconsciously produces guilt and unremitting remorse rather than simple shame or brief regrets. Your guild can place you on probation for breach of ethics, but only you or the God you specify can forgive your "sins.")

K: Technological: What can we do? (What can man produce?)

After hunting and gathering evolved into herding and farming (and hunters became soldiers and gatherers became robbers), farmers still migrated in order for cultivated land to lay fallow and regain its fertility with the passage of time. Crop rotation and fertilizers made farming communities and agribusiness possible, and heavy farm machinery made settling down desirable (just as medical technology made group practice profitable and house calls inefficient and inconvenient). Seasonal crops abolished black slavery as an economic institution in Sunbelt plantations; technology enslaved us to machinery (and the farmer also to the bank that carries the mortgage on his land to secure loans to buy a tractor, etc.). Absent modern technology for seasonal harvesting in sunny California, we have Mexican braceros instead of African slaves toiling in the sun.

Competition for jobs (a) abolished child labor (for raising tobacco after Sir Walter Raleigh introduced Europeans to nicotine) and (b) instituted compulsory education to keep cheap competition out of circulation. (c) The minimum wage law keeps them "on ice," except in labor-intensive Third World countries.

Only citizens of more industrialized countries can afford the luxury of self-indulgence (including self-doubt) and a better life through chemistry (including pills for fasting or getting high). Elsewhere, the starving will share (J) only with kin (kids, pets, etc.), and the unemployed becomes less preoccupied with individual autonomy (I).

L: Humanistic: What are we doing? (Can we destroy ourselves?)

To be a humanist, we have to be both godless and "civilized" or inured to cities (suburbs are for children to romp about in the narrow green belts between neighborhoods much neater than inner-city slums).

Humanists, as well as ecologists, have forgotten that because of our puniness, we were better scavengers than predators until we trained our thumbs. As producers with our opposable thumb and our brain to coordinate the man-ufacture (*sic*) of prostheses, we tax the ability of the carbon dioxide cycle to recycle what we waste instead of consuming and thereby risk getting lung cancer within five miles of smog belts ("freeways"), from breathing tar, with or without nicotine.

Self-styled humanists now try to restore beauty to the ghettoes that are a blight to their cities, and amateur ecologists have begun to praise the glories of Mother Nature. Both see the halo of "civilization" and the rainbow in the sky, seldom the cesspools or the sinkholes.

M: Ecological: What are we losing? (Which is overkill?)

People who feel small are diminished by the immensity of the universe. Those who feel alone are lost in its vastness. Those who feel empty are drained by its endlessness. Those who are apologetic are awed by it, but fear the loss of awe from our own deliberate depredations of nature. Those who feel expansive are excited by its grandeur. Those who feel powerful share its majesty.

N: Ethological: Who are our kin under the skin? (Are we born this way?)

What is worrisome to us now—almost rivaling ancient anxieties about epidemics of plague (from germ-carrying vermin) and about periodic pestilence (from pests, like locusts)—is our own lethality. Man-made radioactivity (since Mme Curie) and defoliants are deadlier than locusts. We can ourselves soon outdo other "acts of God" (earthquakes, tidal waves, etc.) with electronically detonated explosives, which, so far, also defy our power to deploy where needed, just like our own children defy our well-intentioned demands.

> *Homo sapiens* are not meant to be middlemen, but just simple multipliers, untouched by AIDS. We do not have to be merchants and hustlers to survive.

Our fall from grace in paradise (Genesis 3:16–19) made us less plastic and therefore more like animals, who are not perfectible, which is reassuring. But what if like all animals we evolve (mutate) rather than self-destruct (become extinct)?

Is it the atomic explosion that we dread or the radioactive fallout that mothers strange mutants? Or does mutation or extinction both mean either rejection or repudiation by a God who can err or disown, even before innocent Adam was seduced by avaricious Eve to educate himself?

> If the truth be known outside our self-assigned niche (speciesism), what is especially human is that (1) we stopped using our nose to lead us to food that fire has not touched, and (2) we bury our dead both (a) to hide them from scavengers above ground and (b) to insure suffocation and prevent resurrection even before Christ returned to haunt us from behind the stones, closing off the cave where, like Lazarus, one does not suffocate. Do we also

(3) attend funerals and lynchings to see with our eyes the final disposition of those who have scared us?

O: Electronic: Where are the data? (Can we teach ourselves?)

Can we continue to be more intelligent than our robots? Are not our kids sometimes more intelligent than our parents because our spouse was more intelligent than theirs? If we cannot domesticate our kids at an early age, can we enslave a robot with artificial intelligence? Your answer will depend on your natural intelligence, whether you can master or program a small computer.

Are atheists doomed or likely to advance to agnosticism? (Can you believe anyone who insists that your parents were never any good and claims perfection for Oneself?)

Our ability to enjoy life will depend more on our personal development. Human or not, animals must be free to feel, try, think, compare and invent, but not all species are equally capable. Survival so far may be due to their social tools, e.g., among insects. (Did God make more of them and more stupid people because they are not as venturesome as Eve, who wanted to find out what His forbidden truth may be? Are we doomed to genocide because Noah was no Messiah? Is pork "non-kosher" because it tastes like human flesh and genocide has led to cannibalism?)

Each of us belongs with one of the periods of senso-socio-sexual development in any three adjacent stages at any time in our life cycle. Everyone, male or female, can settle for hirself which one is hirs (*sic*). All are roughly, but only roughly, chronological in emergence in our life or mankind's. "Arrest" at any step encourages "delusional thinking" with the dawning of the following stage. (*i/5*)

As *Homo sapiens*, we evolved as (**A–E**) a baby who first discovers its mouth, then its feet, then its mind, then that it could count, and then sort out or solve its problems. *Homo domesticus* can examine (**C**) intent or (**B**) motivation on the basis of new convictions/delusions (about mass movements or "-isms") as well as older ideals (ideology) and doctrines (dogma), but not in order to (**D**) compare behavior on the basis of what was cherished or is valued by whom, since when, or for how long (either rooted in tradition or radicalized as avant-garde).

Ideal solutions (**F–O**) that *Homo metropolis* evolved involved the cross, the crown, trading tokens, the self, society, machinery, humanism, ecology, ethology, and electronics.

To climb the ladder of values that they offer, if and when the opportunity presents itself *(i/6)*, *H. metropolis* exploits new gadgets or joins whichever handy or congenial establishment (old or recent institutionalized belief system) will advance their ability to do so:

They subspecialize as (**F**) theologian (**G**) politician, (**H**) self-employed entrepreneur or corporate bureaucrat, (**I**) psychologist, (**J**) social activist, (**K**) technician, (**L**) humanist, (**M**) ecologist, (**N**) ethologist, or (**O**) computer programmer. (*Homo domesticus* serves them.)

Ideologues, warts and all, depend socially on (F -> O) God, shoring up one's power or lining one's pockets or doing one's own thing or linking up with others or using other sources of energy or safeguarding the human race or the planet or learning from animals or relying on artificial intelligence. (In each case, hoping exceeds the rewards received.)

(Cults exert pressure and succeed as cultures, as other cults find pressure points that make cultures notice.

(We will have longer layovers at all the stage stops that cult followers made throughout our history, but we will just briefly visit each on this whirlwind tour. However, just because we have a dictionary, we do not have to use all the words from **A** to **Z**, but only what is necessary.)

ALTERED CONSCIOUSNESS -> DISTORTED REALITY

1. Image-sharing between totem and descendants is the "old-time religion": God is more like us than like His other creatures.
    a) Adjectives—e.g., willful (**B**) and "intelligent" (**C**), even if no longer comparative (**D**) nor creative (**E**) due to jealousy in both Him and us—can make man a God and impose what is "supernatural" on our vocabulary of ideas: macho archangels and archenemies (superpowers, the ultimate macho).
    b) Whether "satanic" or "secular", an adjective can, by verbal inventiveness, "recreate" reality.
2. Nor does an adjective have to be a "Word." It can be creactive (*sic*) behavior that discloses (describes) what the actor ascribes to hirself (*sic*).

As a captive chimp in an experimental lab, aspiring to alpha-malehood (over his air space by temper tantrums), clearly demonstrated the following:

> Our "thinking" chimp started making incoherent ungodly noises without apparent provocation, until a plane flying overhead was belatedly seen by his audience with inferior hearing. He tried harder to drown its noise, rattling the bars of his cage, increasing the decibel of his protests. Almost Godlike, such mock display against intruders produced the desired results: the plane left our chimp's territory.
>
> After the plane's noise faded, the chimp started posturing, strutting around, thrusting out its chest and beating it with both hands, like Tarzan, "King of the Apes," our sanitized version of an alpha male. *(i/7)*
>
> (Such self-assigned credit-taking machismo among primates must have become part of some formal animistic rituals early in man's history. It is not unknown even among contemporary leaders and Nobel Peace Prize winners.)

WHAT MAKES US VERY EASY TO DOMESTICATE?

We are taught—in varying ratios and with varying success—that the church (**F**) is the soul of the body politic (our psyche has its own soul), the state (**G**) the sword or shield, business (**H**) the gold, psychology (**I**) the mind, society (**J**) the child, technology (**K**) the hand, humanism (**L**) the aim, ecology (**M**) the truth, ethology (**N**) the test, and electronics (**O**) the intelligence.

With most fathers becoming more like absentee landlords, often away from the premises of the human factory whose main product is children, are we more likely to expect God to adopt us if we behaved? *(i/8)*

Only *Homo domestici* would permit a silent God or a dumb animal the opportunity to take over their private lives.

(Only an undomesticated phantom or favorite pet would intrude without hesitation in anyone's privacy.)

Believing: We "believe to belong" to a group more powerful or to bellyache or blame.

(Beliefs serve emotional needs, even with juries and their critics—who have no standing in rendering verdicts, e.g., about O.J. Simpson's culpability—but do not know it.)

The first stage of (ii) believing that matters is attempting (F) to please Santa Claus, then progressively preferring what is (G) effective, (H) efficient, (I) self-elected (*sic*), (J) mutual, (K) productive, (L) humane, (M) conservative, (N) convivial, and lately what is (O) rapidly communicable.

Motherless and fatherless in the nursery, *Homo metropolis* must find both (1) father and/or (2) mother outside the family:

1. An absentee Godhead (F) or a "bestial" (V, m) sugar daddy to keep a child-wife as a pet (as in petting or foreplay without fertilization) and to stroke (groom with words)
2. A motherly (A) wife to monopolize during delayed childhood (psychological neoteny) by coercive contraception, including abortion (V, f).

Because society is not, like geography, a series of Chinese boxes, one nesting inside another, we must all depend on sensuality and sexuality if we are not going to be crybabies.

9.00 i/EQUALITY

i/Chapter Notes

[i/1] Ideology includes conversion of recent discoveries to old uses, e.g., TV for evangelism. Electronic wizardry among evangelists only makes them more vociferous.

[i/2] Our sexual development as a WoMan for breeding or not is unique unto itself and separate for each gender. Only medicine heretofore has discriminated between both in gynecology and urology. Even sociology in studying industry studied male behavior. Ethopsychiatrists will not make the same mistake of ignoring "la difference."

In some species, the alpha female is supreme for its reproductive talent; in the human species the female does not aspire to supremacy by simply reproducing.

Our autonomic nervous system mediates (1) sympathetic fighting or fleeing that allows us to live, if only to fight when we are more fit, and (2) parasympathetic feeding and fornicating, which allows the species to survive. This is simple biology. It becomes cosmology if survival means the fittest must pollute with technology.

[i/3] Progress is not progressively uniform.

Acceleration and deceleration, which must not be confused with average rate of speed, is determined by talent and energy.

Reader: It is stasis that sickens.

Editor: "Regression" is only regrettable for being inevitable.

1.   Judgments (**D**) about psychological (**I**) or social (**J**) "maturity" or (**BB**) moral righteousness and (**AA'**) emotional "regression" or

(**BB'**) territorial indignation will reveal either/both theo-secular (**F** + **L**) and/or parochial (**C'**) preoccupations or/and incomplete understanding of human ontology (empty metaphysics).

2. There are separable (**i**) sensual, (**ii**) con-sensual or cultural, and (**iii**) sexual issues at every stage of development, some conflicts qualifying as crises or moments of (**C**) truth, (**B**) decision, or (**D**) ruthless objectivity.

In the technostructure of business and society, scientific breakthroughs occur in several fronts simultaneously, but their institutionalization takes time.

The first to be institutionalized is industrial (**K**) technology (which is labor- and space-saving).

Medical technology (which is lifesaving) is still awaiting institutional sanctions.

At the same time that we have prolonged human life, we have forced plants and animals to mature sooner to full size or larger for our uses and in so doing created hazards (**M'** -> **N'**), from hormone and pesticide use, for both plant and animal life, including ourselves.

Mechanical advances in industrial and medical technology, as well as biochemical discoveries (in botany and zoology), will be helped and might be overtaken by advances in electronic (**O**) technology, which probably saves more time than labor- or lifesaving technologies.

In the end, it comes to whether the domesticated or untamed person was empty or emptied of talent and energy and whether/if both are handed over to one's masters or down to one's heirs respectively.

What do we ask ourselves, now that (1) the third world is no longer just a reservoir for resources to be impounded or a breeding ground for slaves to be shanghaied, and (2) automated postindustrial economies must compete with indigenous workers in indigent countries that are becoming industrialized?

[i/4] If religious fanatics (Khomeini et al.) can capture political power, can political demagogues (McCarthy et al.) hold economic power hostage (the ransom was unmasking and blacklisting "pinkos") or feudalize with five-year plans (Soviet) for serfs (proletariats)?

Must we not only separate Church from State but State from Commerce? (In oil-rich Iran, all three together, **F** + **G** + **H**, are run by a theocracy, **F/G**. Without oil to burn, can Allah accept an unending exodus of martyrs and dissenters? Communist Russia, **G** = **F** and **J** > **I**, lasted long enough, and the conservative Moral Majority, **H** = **F** + **G** and **I** > **H** is gaining ground. Can we improve on all three combinations and match General MacArthur's Japan? Can Japan overtake General Marshall's United Europe?)

Occupied Japan in the throes of inflation (**H'**) was saved by a "czar" under (**G**) MacArthur who imposed austerity by balancing the budget with attendant unemployment, relieved by the Korean War. Its spectacular economic recovery was the result of combined (**G**) state and (**H**) corporate cooperation to compete globally.

[i/5] Human Rights, Equal Justice and Rewards

> Chimpanzee group life is like a market in power, sex, affection, support, intolerance and hostility. The two basic rules are "one good turn deserves another," and "an eye for an eye, a tooth for a tooth."
> —Waal, "Chimpanzee Politics," London, 1982

Primates share a common political background with our preliterate development.

The past is always with us as natural law, whether codified or not. Do we truly want to be judged by an unwritten code? Is it to affirm or deny the unchosen past that we personify justice as a balancing act by a young and unsighted maiden whose blindfold must always remain in place?

Are our icons also our confessions? Is justice blind or blinded and the sword supposed to strike blindly only what it can reach? Does her undeniable blindness accept diminished responsibility as well as show her "atonement" with us? Rights are the elbow room that we are granted by consensus, the deprivation of which makes us feel underprivileged.

Restitution may be delayed, sometimes for generations. ("Vengeance is mine," saith the lord to His long-suffering victims.)

Even for the untamed, life is not at all like a journey a poet once described as a series of irrevocable disappearances.

1. There are many different "mytheologies" (*sic*) (**F** -> **J**, **L** and **M**) and more uniform (**N**) ethology and technology (**K** and **O**) although there is still traditional and modern medicine, which are both an art and a science.

Cultural relativism and humanism conspire with a historical anthropology or "mytheology" to make empathy (objective ruthlessness) and sympathy (subjective kinship) mutually exclusive. Neither moral nor immoral, ethopsychiatry shows that they are more reciprocal. But for reductionists, polar opposites are just dichotomies.

Cultural relativism entitles each tribe to its own claims to dignity and morality. Humanism self-consciously grants the "individual" the equivalent of the same tribal courtesy.

2. Instead of an Old World, a New World, and a Third World, it is useful to think of underdeveloped, developed, and overdeveloped societies (with its new poor and precocious pubescents producing different social epidemics).

3. It is more practical to think of civilization even before the dawn of history as starting with ideas that become art or ritual or theories that develop into science and cults or "-isms."

True art is a matter of acquired personal taste (**A**), raw energy (**B**), inherited talent, (**E**) and learned skill (**B** x **E**) to express it, with total indifference toward any attempts at (**C**) analysis and (**D**) criticism of the artist by the self-expressive (**I**) who is less gifted.

The tension, even for this writer betwixt creative thinking and scientific discipline, is not from the postulated conflict between their practitioners and their theoretically disadvantaged victims among noble yet savage beasts, but the steps from idea to testing to results.

Art is not amenable to scientific analysis. Ideology, however, can be artfully or artlessly analyzed. We shall therefore deal with ideology scientifically (comparatively), artlessly or not.

It is more practical to systematize our cultural evolution by separable steps from (**C**) God-ape to (**F**) God to (**O**) AniMachine as another trinity, proceeding from answers (dogma) to art (icon) to science (data), or from ideals (universally human) to ideology (consensual) to biocosmology (material).

[i/6] Ideologies Seek Ever More Equality

Ideology from God to deus ex machina need (**A**) feelings (appreciative), (**B**) muscles or other energy sources (opportunistic), and (**C**) the mind (dogmatic) to evangelize even robotic-minded groups. But technocratic oligarchies have been perverted in the service of autocracy.

Are "elected" dictators virtual kings by divine right because the electors are God's surrogates? Jesus was less confused about separating church and state: "Give unto Caesar what is his, and to God what is Ours." Communists combine politics and economics. Capitalists separate politics from business conducted by multinational conglomerates, unless threatened by their own competitors/workers/consumers.

[i/7] We must now leapfrog without prejudice to antecedent historical stages of cultural development:

Progress decelerates proportionately with the revival of older ideologies, just as delusions become progressively more intractable the more archetypal they are.

We will later "mop up" where we have leapfrogged. (MacArthur was a master of this military maneuver, which bypasses areas under contention.) If we speed up too fast for you to catch every nuance, rest assured that you're not alone, albeit in a much smaller group than those whom Einstein's theory of relativity "bypassed" without intending to.

We must also compare, in contrast to partnerships for power and profit, classic confrontations that emphasize the alleged differences but not the themes behind the usual pyrotechnics, real or verbal:

President Clinton got good marks in (i) (A) caring and (B) trying but has been accused of (C') lying. He also got high marks for (ii) loving (F), God (H), reducing the deficit, and steadfastly supporting (J), (K), (M) and (O) or, respectively, community, technological, environmental, and electronic endeavors. He is faulted for (G') dodging the draft and (iii) (X, m) adulterous conduct.

Have you ever been bullied? That's what we do to those that can't fight back, including the environment that mothered us. We pollute it to get ahead of those who need it more than us.

Must history recycle? Need we be in awe (F) of electronics (O)? Why are wars (G) popular, even if deadly? Why does not success in conspicuous consumption (H) bring happiness to individualists (I)? Or goodness (A) not guarantee success? Nor being right (B) or being in the right (C) produce superpowers (G x H)?

In our survey of how culture evolved, we are bound to find many different directions of development (daring or myopic in each generation) at every stage, which gets less crowded as we progress. [The Bible approves of filicide; psychoanalysts fear patricide. "True faith" (an oxymoron) demands belief in a God who could drown all kids and then "choose" to sacrifice His Kid to save those who survived His deluge. Conservatives can comfortably stagnate without any malice or second thoughts: William Buckley Jr. believes "that the duel between Christianity and atheism is the most important in the world . . . that the struggle between individualism (**I**) and collectivism (**J**) is the same struggle reproduced on another level" (from his first book, *God and Man at Yale*).

[Whitaker Chambers, the "Witness" (also his book's title), whom (1) Nixon believed, (2) Solzhenitsyn echoes, and (3) Reagan quotes, claims that "economics (**H**) is not the central problem of this century . . . Faith (**F**) is the central problem of this age. The Western world does not know it, but it already possesses the answer to this problem . . . provided that its faith in God and the freedom He enjoins is as great as Communism's faith in (**L**) Man." (He extorts to protect.)]

[i/8] We repeatedly recycle to pan-animist (souls are everywhere) from animist (even stones have souls) to deist (the spirit lives in the soul) to theist (the spirit nourishes the soul) to geist (the soul nourishes the mind) to pan-theist (there is only one soul).

Religion started as animism (concrete and emotional displacement even among fearful animals) and totemism (naturalistic religious rituals among "savages"), then developed into deism (artificial and emotional totemism), which later became monotheism (abstract and rational deism, recruiting believers who are "soulful") and is not evolving into pantheism (abstract and absolute but emotional animism): "All are one." (Not "nothing stands by itself"; there is no "self" in clinical rationalysis.)

Such absolutism undermines monotheism (which needs individual soulfulness) has now changed to "absolute relativity": there are in fact three selves or three subcycles in every life for each of the three subspecies, one of which disclaims centrality to its soul.

(Table 16) What I now call the subspecies *Homo sapiens* was described (as Semitic nomads) firsthand by the first *Homo domesticus* (Sumerian settlers) in Thomas Cahill's *Gifts of the Jews* (1998), as follows:

"A tent dweller, buffeted by wind and rain, he knows not prayers . . . has no house in his lifetime . . . is not brought to burial when he dies."

Dichotomy-driven (but insightfully, irreverently or ironically), he adds, "This is almost a description of an animal: without manners or courtesy—even toward the dead—without religion . . . Behind the description we can detect the prejudice of imperialists throughout history, who blithely assume superiority, moral as well as technical, over those whom they have marginalized and therefore their divine right to whatever is valuable, especially the land."

Homo domesticus can be as primitive as jungle tribes who perform ritual sacrifices or as modern as Jim Jones's suicidal cult of expatriates or Internet Web designers of San Diego's "Heaven's Gate."

10.00 j/Carnality: SEPARATE ODYSSEYS of HUMAN ANDROGYNES (Scene iii)

(An "androgyne" is anyone whose nipples, with or without breasts, enrich one's life when erect, whether there's a suckling or not. Procreation is con-vivial, erotic recreation less verboten for *Homo sapiens* than for *H. domesticus*, and more welcome by *H. metropolis*.)

Males and females start out as females (except among birds) and then develop separately, physically and temperamentally.

In the Philippines, a pubescent male is called "binatillo" on the way to becoming "binata" (or bachelor) and an adolescent female is called "dalagita" when she starts menstruating on her way to maidenhood (as a "dalaga").

Binatillos get circumcised once the prepuce fails to cover the penis as the glans (bulbous head) enlarges and gets too tight around it during erections. And it is not trimmed but merely slit and retracted, without loss of tissue (thus "saving one's skin," so to speak).

In America, I was surprised to find that adolescent sex hormones scare families but teenagers (once they stop being boys or girls) are lumped together and then not chaperoned just when their hormones start differentiating their genders. This sexual dedifferentiation is also reflected in the theoretical psychosexology that greeted me as a postgraduate trainee in psychiatry. *(j/1)*

SEXUAL EVOLUTION AND MATURATION

What is "sexual" is whatever is privately erotic or genitally mediated and differs according to gender or age, within twelve weeks after conception, when the sexual organs of the fetus differentiate, depending on which sexual chromosome it received from its father. Before then, it is Mama's clone, internally and externally.

(In birds, the basic plan is male, and the female is the result of the action of female hormones (cf. *Science*, 190 (1975), pp. 1307–8, Martinez-Vargas et al., on sexual differentiation in birds.) Bird or beast, meiosis doubles the gene pool and therefore the chances for enduring adaptation while asexual reproduction (miosis) merely produces clones.

Reproduction may or may not be sexual (with splitting of chromosomes). Sex in biology is the combining of split plant chromosomes before mating evolved among animals. (Sex is not involved in human rivalry with the opposite sex. Same-sex violence is against rivals in the same species.)

Earlier in their evolution, asexual multiplication, or apomixis in plants and parthenogenesis in animals, alternated with newly evolved sexual reproduction in the same species (pollination or penile penetration). The later development soon proved its reliability, e.g., in unfailingly and cost-effectively reproducing hens from chickens from eggs, etc. (which is why baby roosters are given away free in chicken farms of commercial size).

For their first eggs, hens may be assisted by a gloved finger, but the young is defended by the eggshell from injury attendant to being squeezed against hard surfaces (the bony pelvis). Hatchlings also escape maternal maladies.

Experimental laboratories can now reproduce animals asexually direct from the egg without using spermatozoa. Human sperm banks make reproduction without penetration possible, and therefore rape of the ambivalent to preserve the species has become obsolete for our species, oestrus or no oestrus. (Animals not "in heat" are not forcefully importuned by past or future sexual partners.)

Domesticated males are truly an endangered "species" in competition with (1)(a) plant fossils from solar and (b) other equally natural sources of energy (hydroelectric, geothermal, and nuclear, etc.), and (2) metallurgy to replace muscles with machines, and (3) electronics to program robots.

(The hydrolunar energy of waves can help coastal settlements regain revenues lost to airports.)

Homo metropolis admits less often that one is "in love" and oftener that one is "involved." If social relationship decides sexual relations, love for *Homo domesticus* may be the end and a sex object the means.

Why have we separated love from sex? In order to plot their separate progress in personal adversity (e.g., during smothering) and their historical perversion (e.g., as love of a Father Almighty or motherland, money, self, others, machines, mankind, things, etc.)

The man's role is to insist on the unobtainable in romantic courtship, not in animal rituals, where it is to demonstrate fitness for what is accessible. Love is a game that Mother Nature has invented and sold to unsuspecting writers of fiction for the masses, who have become her best propagandists to suggestible readers. *(j/3)* Romance keeps the poor satisfied with monogamy.

[The author as a family therapist thinks (like Jesus) that the young should have unconditional love and (like lions) that *Homo sapiens* ought to be able to enjoy (1) unconditional sex, (2) the freedom to be disloyal, not open to *Homo domesticus*, as well as (3) the right to fail, not recognized by *Homo metropolis*.]

TO REPRODUCE

Our thumb is our first love,
Second, our mother's smell,
Third, the very sight of her,
Fourth, her approving looks,
Fifth, romping with our peers,
Sixth, petting our pals,
Seventh, humping our pets,
Eighth, practicing with girls,
Ninth, marrying a "dream,"
And sharing ours with kids.

Or, making up for lost time,
During idle intermissions,
Never sublimating sex
By dreaming up utopias.

How come I know?
I was right there:
Running around bottomless,
Letting everything hang out,
And, curious about applause,
Trying to return the compliment;

Playing house doctor,
Then herding animals,
Later, loving buddies,
Raping and/or seducing;

Serially monogamous,
Without wasting time
On silly small talk,
Clever or rhetorical.

MALE and FEMALE EROTOSEXUAL EVOLUTION

Stages **P** to **Z** come from large multitudes with past experience in/of **(P)** autoeroticism or narcissism, **(Q)** pack rats or tomboys, **(R)** peepers or lesbians, **(S)** flashers or "strippers," **(T)** child molesters or flirts, **(U)** gays or babysitters, **(V)** "animal or "baby lovers," **(W)** lover boys or "baby losers," **(Y)** heir seekers or youth fanciers, and **(Z)** grandparents.

Male or masculine—gentlemanly or not—men separately and serially evolve biosexually (after sex change from a female as an embryo at 6 to 12 weeks by Chinese chronology), in transcultural and transtemporal stages from **P, m** to **Y, m**.

- **P:** thumb-sucking → autoeroticism without narcissism, the thumb substituting for the penis as a "pet thing"
- **Q:** security blanket "rat-packing" → fetishism without commercialism, from first smelling Mom's laundry, and/or licking Mom's footwear, to collecting stamps and precious artifacts
- **R:** peeping → voyeurism or sexual "window-shopping"

S: "flashing" → exhibitionism, or sexual "hard sell"

T: juvenile pedophilia ("playing house" with children that concentrates on secondary sexual organs) → another "pet" "thing" ("playing doctor" with curious tots)

U: own pet "thing" shared with peers of the same sex (prurient homosexuality)

V: pet "thing" now shared with "pets" (bestiality and/or heavy "petting")

W: pubescent rape (with or without dating or petting), "kiss and run" rapaciousness or active child begetting without foreplay.

X: leisurely postpubescent heterosexuality ("going all the way" with the opposite sex), sensuous coitus (as among kings of the jungle like lions and elephants)

Y: fatherhood (responsible protector and/or second mother-provider) or midlife metapause (second adolescent crisis of infatuation with "infantile" partners, fast cars and fashionable clothes)

[**Y, m** is mankind's invention, like (**R**) voyeurism, (**U**) homosexuality, (**YY'**) group-grope, (**WW'**) gang bang, or desperate improvisations during political rivalry for sexual favors (office "incest" or nepotism—not child abuse or (**T**) pedophilia—or "sexual harassment" of elusive subordinate by a superior). **S, T** and **V** are practiced by "other" animals.]

In polite society, **T'** → **Q'** is called metapause (sexual, not existential, middle-age crisis though both are characterized by genital hypochondriasis or mental rumination).

Q → **Q'** cycle traces evolution of the pack-rat to fetishism from prepubescent "territoriality" without tantrums to senescent irritability on losing one's "marbles."

Overrepresentation of males in history is presumably a function of man's need to substitute external stimulation for early internal emptiness with his first trimester loss of reproductive ability beyond triggering cell division after puberty. (Over half of embryonic "vessels" become literally impregnable "vassals" who eventually penetrated space itself with prosthetic phalluses.)

Female or feminine, ladylike or not, a woman serially evolves biosexually in transcultural and transtemporal—i.e., con-familiar—stages from **P, f** to **Y, f**.

(Spared from having to change primary or secondary genitalia, she must produce a fixed quota of eggs.)

P: narcissism → "art appreciation" (face painting, standing tall in Mom's high heels, dressed in her clothes, and prettied up with fingernails polished)

Q: tomboyishness → assertiveness with or without grace as a tomboy before she starts preferring more gentle companionship, replayed in future feminists who, outgrowing P and disdaining makeup, evolve from sexual equality to precious sisterhood

R: homosexuality (kissing → necking → petting during pajama parties) or innocent homoeroticism (which becomes lesbianism among consenting adults in later life)

S: "playing house" includes getting "pregnant" sometimes out of plain heterosexual curiosity (beyond voyeurism in boys) without having and keeping child or house

T: spouse shopping, flirting, or exhibitionism (with décolletage and mini or slit skirts, rejected as sexism by bralessness and pants suits)

U: childbearing in or out of marriage or test tubes, or babysitting with clingers or clients, or child swapping as a stepparent.

V: child losing, from "choice" or by "child" leaving nest, or childbearing and losing from emptied womb or "empty nest"

W: child swapping with or without serial monogamy or child (and/or client) saving or adopting and raising or rescuing

X: adult switching (with increased longevity; second careers in carnal research will follow, as among metapausal men) with male or same-sex partners

Y: menopause (may be surgical, can be ameliorated medically) (menarche must be explored in all women as well as how they felt about their breasts at the time)

Y, f May–Decemberhood partner (as mentor, sexual or otherwise, for the young) is uniquely human and a more elegant version of the male cradle robber or child molester or dirty old lecher. [Were Adam's Lilith and Eve (with Cain to beget Enoch) and both of Noah's wives "incestuous" by simple proximity? Today, oedipal "incest" is severely punished (probably to prevent mental retardation): a teacher lost custody of her child and was arrested for parole violation and sentenced to serve seven years for seeing her boyfriend of thirteen a year later the first night she was out on parole.]

W, f above is the "child-swapping" aspect of mothering, where the "child" may be an adult, even a "litter" of needful "clients." It can include managing groups and leading followers in
   a.   nursery sibshiphoods of human "litter" from many mothers or
   b.   "therapeutic (learning/teaching) communities" for conscious conflict-free problem solving by patient with peers in or out of hospital.

Professional parent surrogates are needed to resolve our conflicts since only our own parents can be blamed for them (just as professional grandparents can help with family problems beyond parental competence).

Our unconflicted problem-solving successes from inherited energy and intelligence must be credited to our parents' parents.

To be professionally "maternal," not feminine, is to invest in the child's health rather than for the sake of loving alone:
   1.   Psychiatrists, who invest more time per capita than other specialists, must be more maternal than surgeons or internists.
   2.   Psychiatrists who are not maternal enough behave more like their medical colleagues, leaving the management of their patients' external environment to assistants without specific prescription for titrated interpersonal transactions (milieu therapy). *(j/2)*

Z: Virtual Androgyny

Both sexes eventually converge closer to each other in the twilight of their lives.

In this last stage or (**Z**)enith of our development, which is more sensual than social, there is no sexual division of labor anymore by grandparents, who have bridged the gender gap that androgens, or male sex hormones, created in the first trimester of life as an embryo (primarily for future spermatogenesis).

DOMESTICATION OR SURVIVAL (BREEDING)

1. Reproduction does not have to be sexual. Sexuality originally evolved as a simple but unequal division of labor to supplement simple and equal cell division. (Among seahorses, the male is the "homebody" who supplies the sperm but accepts the eggs, gets pregnant, and delivers the offspring.) Sexual differentiation was thus intended from the beginning to serve reproductive ends.

Since premarital rituals have changed in one generation from women generally saying yes to everything except sex to saying no to everything except sex, sexual maturation in different subcultures must be separable from moral or personal and ethical or social development. Is such separation universally uniform?

2. Outside farming communities, a couple's reproductive "choices" can be reduced to "Our money or our child?" (It is not that our children should be wanted, but that they are, in fact, needed— preferably not by their parents for household help or to love at their leisure—but as insurance by the species as a whole.)

In industrialized countries, labor unions were the first to lobby for universal compulsory education and minimum wage legislation to minimize competition from their young. Lately, working mothers have lobbied for child-care centers as if children are formidable rivals in a tight money market where more dedication from them is demanded.

Biological restitution by multiplication continues to be our only bilateral freedom and obligation (to exercise the right and discharge the equal responsibility to reproduce). The other rights, e.g., to vote, do not impose the duty of mutuality.

For us to be free does not mean that no one should be enslaved, unless we also accept without reservations the obligation to extend equal opportunity to all.)

3. a. Providentially, our sexuality is more autonomous by nature. It is independent of (i) the free development of our programmable virtues or inherited virtuosities, (ii) equal distribution of civilized values and valued skills, or (iii') our blossoming—arrested or perverted, but never "preferred"— sexual compulsion. (True parenting may be sought by and cannot be arbitrarily denied to gays or lesbians.)

    Between maximum receptivity and minimum consent, the paired preservation if not the "civilized" perpetuation of *Homo sapiens* seems to be in no immediate danger.

    b. More of both sexes can now evolve into grandparenthood and even become either grand matron or grand patron. Medical science has helped us prolong life by heroic efforts even after we are bedridden.

But as more *Homo domestici* become the most domesticated (direction dependent) of all animals, the new scientificized fountain of youth further aggravates sexual conflicts for *Homo metropoli*. While children and other species eat with zest and gusto and move with verve and vigor, they struggle hyperkinetically to look physically healthy if infertile from heroic self-improvement, self-absorption, self-criticism, self-flagellation, self-hatred, and/or self-denial, all unwittingly expressed in highly regimented dieting ("downsizing" to another dress size) and exercising as their tribe keeps on increasing.

    It is not our sexuality that stands to suffer but humankind itself, as the more productive among us deny their seed to future generations for the sake of personal convenience and social expediency. We get richer without reproducing our inborn creativity while the poor procreate and grow poorer, unless we export our sperm and ovum during war, by cultural exchange, or in test tubes.

    c. Morality and sexuality were once separated, and then merged, and has again diverged, probably only to converge once again as the pendulum swings in the opposite direction.

        Catholic schools were the first to educate women so as to win the unsuspecting children of mixed marriages, just as the rich marry beauty for their kids to marry the powerful in the next matrimonial lottery. *Homo domestici* tend to spawn children rather than raise them to maturity (adulthood) and often leave their education, except about religion, to total strangers. When it comes to sex (stages **P-Y**), they tend to let them learn on their own, provided they are not too precocious.

Females are merely warned early in life against VD and pregnancy (getting into trouble), and males about VD and fertility (getting someone in trouble).

Among puritan adults, "virtue," when applied to married couples, implies "chastity," and to unmarried women only, "virginity." (Arab wedding parties patiently wait for bloodstained conjugal sheets.)

    [Outside sex, "virtue" (**A**, **B**, **C**, unitalicized unlike in *ABC*'s of science) means whatever our parents deem to be senso-morally good, right, and truthful.

    [Scientifically, "value" is what we ourselves assign to a variable (**D**).

    [Social value (ethical) is what we learned from seers/peers (**F** to **O**) outside our home that often differs from those of our parents or their generation's.]

    4. Before the sexual revolution, sex was thought to be dirty, and to be sexy is simply to be inexplicit. A mate may not be a roommate, and a roommate not a mate.

"Feeling very close" used to mean "very close to orgasm," not to the partner. Does "sexual revolution" for *Homo metropolis* mean spinning in the same orbit of erotic, not genital, hypochondriasis about social relationships?

5. Once upon a time, when virtue and virginity were mandated by the institutionalization of private property for *Homo domesticus*, monoandry and primogeniture both remained stable expectations until the Age of the Pill. (Ultimogeniture was the first step toward granting equality among rival siblings.)

For males, sex is pleasurable, not reproductive, but even premature ejaculation can have survival value (as a "kiss and run" habit).

For females, sex is procreation, or else there would be no oestrus. (Philanderers who must reproduce their pleasure in their partner delay consummation and increase the risk of being caught with their pants down.

6. The male protects the female protecting the children. If the mother of *Homo domesticus* is overprotective, the father is lost to the children. If the mother and child are underprotected, everybody suffers in the next generation.

All *Homo sapiens* needs to be is warm, fed, and fertile—instead of healthy, wealthy, and wise—and to be strong even if paraplegic, rich in relations, and confident even if naive.

HUMAN FAMILY HUSBANDRY

To breed or not to breed, before or after courtship or marriage, is our unpopular (controversial) population dilemma.

Animals and *Homo sapiens* don't plan (want) or reject (as bastards) what they procreate.

Industrial age boys used to dream of cars and girls of home and family. Now if you ask either to choose between a child and a car, they'd agree.

Homo domesticus would rather be spouses or divorcees than parents and/or raise kids to be good kids rather than be good parents who would not domesticate their kids.

"Prudent" *Homo metropoli* plan "anal" parenthood as a budget movement with annual rationing, like going abroad, touring with a new car, and shipping it home.

For both subspecies, investing in a boat or a second domicile or in income housing sometimes precedes planning for a nursery.

We are the only animals who build nests (but not exclusively for our young) and lay up a nest egg for adults.

(This is how the author happened to include "environmental design" in his family therapy strategy, diverting the traffic between generations at home so that the decreasing social gap is not as highly visible [and therefore more deniable], especially during the more troublesome adolescent years of covert rivalry or invidious comparisons.)

The evolution of all the different levels of human development follows comparable patterns during our life cycle because humankind, like all other species, can interbreed. This is why *Homo sapiens* will endure alongside *H. domesticus* and *H. metropolis*.

Begetting: Born of a man and a woman, we . . . beget before dying.

(Every WoMan's life cycle seems near completion with strident narcissism or defensive autoeroticism [**P**] in the aftermath of the vaunted sexual revolution against man's own double standard at home, once his divine right to rule others in the name of his Father Almighty was no longer self-evident.)

With senescence, premature or not, our behavior ceases to evolve and instead involutes to a second adolescence (menopause or the middle-age crises of metapause) or a second childhood, reborn to God for fear of hell or to Mammon in miserliness.

Aging in institutions or people also accelerates bureaucratic tendencies, especially among the menopausal who are not adventurous.

Metapause seems to make the uptight more venturesome in a last-ditch effort to find meaning in their empty lives.

10.00 j/CARNALITY

j/Chapter Notes

[j/1] Have those who feel they can never satisfy a woman ever satisfied their mother?

Reader: Is that why Freud asked, "What do women want?"
Editor: He started writing about female sexuality in 1925 at age sixty-nine.
Author: Passivity provokes thoughts in the wakeful and therefore a theory to justify nonintervention.
Editor: Freud saw only a handful of patients, Erikson even fewer, and Piaget none.
Author: I had more, taught trainees, directed other doctors, and supervised staff-patient transactions.

[As expectable, author excludes from training even brilliant believers and unbelievers, who are both more free not to think, and accepts only very promising disbelievers. (He has often said that few besides him would have welcomed the young Freud, who never received specialty training.)]

[j/2] The Etho-Ontology of True Love
True lovers are nonnarcissistic and heretics where their beloved is involved. Only the half domesticated can be heretical.

Among *Homo sapiens*, mothers will desert their God or country for their children. Fully domesticated "smotherers" of both sexes won't. Even after they become ethologically redundant to the young: *H. domesticus* want to be needed. They love to be loved to stay alive, not live to love (as a lover, lr), beloved (bl) or not.

Would you rather give than receive, be loving (e.g., a pet lover) or lovable (i.e., a pet)?

Mother Love:	bl:	I need you.
	lr:	I am yours.
Puppy Love:	bl:	I want you.
	lr:	I like you.
First Love:	lr:	I love you in me.
	bl:	I love me in you.
First Leap:	lr:	I love you more than anybody.
	bl:	I love you more than anyone.
Last Leap:	bl:	I need you, love me more.
	lr:	You need me, I am yours.

Limited elbow room exacerbates civil (ideo-cultural) conflicts for *Homo metropolis* in crowded cities. All can therefore retreat inside the place where we all started (with parental cohabitation) but also to relax, perchance to sleep.

[j/3] Fiction writers owe much of their eloquence to their mother's conditional love or to longing for their father's possessions.

Dual parenting (pair bonding) is more common among birds than mammals: most birds, a few foxes, coyotes, marmosets, and gibbons. (Marmosets are South American monkeys; gibbons are lesser apes.)

Is it coincidence that courting males call their British sex objects "birds"?

(And that Americans call the object of their admiration a "chick" or "foxy lady"? Or that COYOTE is the name prostitutes "chose" to call their organization for equal legal standing in the community?]

If we cannot exhume the equivalent of gibbons and marmosets in the vocabulary of lust, can we assume that our colloquial terms come from a collective unconscious, lost among the great apes including ourselves but foreshadowed in the avian and mammalian forebrain, including the canine (whose domesticated members qualify as man's best friend)?

Adult male involvement in human families evolved for economic rather than "masculine" or sentimental reasons:

a. Among other primates, because marmosets tend to deliver twins, the father assists in raising the offspring.

b. A few families in some other species are more monogamous partners rather than parents.

c. In the affluent among *Homo domesticus*, monogamy allows property to remain in the same family, except for the dowry. Daughters without dowry may be sold as white slaves: black slave trade in males was never a family enterprise.

    The wifely duty is to provide male heirs. Daughters are raised as drones for other families in need of her dowry. Poor daughters married poor, if not poorly.

d. Romantic love, on the other hand, is the common man's compromise with poverty that precluded having both a wife and a mistress.

    It is better, of course, if your mistress is a great beauty or celebrity. The extra rich and more "depraved" also boasts of lovers of the same sex and various ages.

e. With romantic love, extramarital affairs became suspect, and soon after, the enduring profession of prostitution became an enemy of the nuclear family as an institution. Males arrested for loitering are either their customers or transvestites, even with the trend towards unisex in dress fashions.

f. Eventually, romantic love was legislated, and male control by pimps of small stables of street prostitutes replaced female control by madams of lavish brothels, even if the first pensions for those who played now to pay later, called alimonies, were awarded only, until just recently, to women who have loved and lost board (alimentary) privileges.

g. Marriage for males is thus for procreation or economic recreation.

OF our "BIRDS" and BEES, if you PLEASE

1. a. For show-offs, like peacock and deer, courtship is a contest.
    b. Only in parental partnerships are the sexes difficult to tell apart by size or color, except in the human species (hair around the clitoris or penis and other erectile tissue distribution and secondary genitalia: in the nipple on a flat chest or soft breast). "Menopausal" males develop breasts (gynecomastia).
    c. Ringdove males also produce "crop milk" to regurgitate from the gullet and feed the newborn (hatched and fed by both partners). Prechewed solid food from mothers is now marketed as "baby food" for infants.
    d. Passerine (or perching) birds are also as territorial as jealous husbands. Vasectomy, the unkindest cut and second sexual assault that all undomesticated males escape, reassures the territorially cautious or jealous. The spouses can still mate and/or "get laid" in conjugal or forbidden bliss but cannot fertilize eggs in their nest or nidus in the uterus. (Ligating the fallopian tubes is not unkind but convenient to forbidden extramarital affairs.)

2. a. Bees were among the first species to leave the swamp, and no insect family has become extinct to date. Will zero population growth extinguish ours?
    b. Adults in the beehive of a queen bee must gather honey regardless of sex. Gender alone does not assign their social roles or decide economic success.
    c. Queen bees first clone daughters to become workers and then fertilize later eggs with previously withheld sperm from drones to found new colonies with their nieces. (Has nature discarded its bimodal reproductive strategy only for sexual

"democracy" to be defeated by social, especially economic, pressures for androgyny before senescence?)

[Because people do not want their children to die, those who had better brains discovered the healing power of plants, and now the value of transplantable organs of animals. But human brains have also endangered our planet, which would have been better off without *Homo domesticus* males and now without *Homo metropolis*.

[Yet doctors will continue to prolong life with their science like lawyers prolong litigation with lies (edited untruths) as artistic or crafty ghostwriters of "faction" (in the form of depositions). The judicial system, however, helps lawyers more than litigants, and the legislative helps its Democrats to reform everything but the judicial system while Republicans try harder to be accountants.]

3. a. Before 1984, twelve countries, all in Europe, have established a stable equilibrium between their birth and death rates while at the same time, the import of arms has surpassed that of grain for the Third World.

    Reader: Even Communists do not live by bread alone.

    Editor: Lenin once conceded that Communism progresses by making one step forward and two steps backward in history.

    Author: Yeltsin, more than Gorbachev, acknowledges that history is not a record of progress. Nor, for me, any guide at all.

    b. Usually male, (the common man), as "cannon fodder", they are expediently expendable, for raising the young among the newly rich or "new poor" (skilled but unemployed) wherever sperm banks are accessible.

    c. In this age of technology, man does not even have to be potent to ejaculate to make deposits in sperm banks to procreate, any more than females have to reach a sexual climax during "oestrus" to reproduce even before we left our caves for outer space.

11.00 k/Violence: All Levels of Violence, OLD and NEW CENTURY DILEMMAS

[A treatise on pathological violence during life and self-prescribed physician-assisted dying combined with a new look at abortion, battered wives, child abuse, death rows, euthanasia, fear of failure, geopolitics, etc.]

HUMAN AND DOMESTIC VIOLENCE (Physics, Biology, Neurology, etc.)

It is artificial and arbitrary to select certain sexual or violent trends and focus entirely on them without tracing their origins as far back as we can and tracking their ramifications that are responsible for shaping other human dilemmas. (We cannot afford to judge behavior by human standards without justifying genocide as an excuse to ensure social survival of *Homo domesticus* by "ethnic cleansing.")

Small-scale violence is on the rise But the perennial spread of all kinds of mass murder (genocide in intertribal wars and filicide in civil wars) are (1) rooted in the same soil as long-standing dilemmas among people, families, and societies; (2) seeded by alienation and *ennui*; and (3) fertilized by conflicting ideologies.

Today, we can look at violence from widely different perspectives, answer different questions, and offer new avenues for testing novel solutions. *(k/2)*

In ways philosophers never dreamed of, scientists now know more about killing and dying and the abuses in-between and the vicissitudes of large- or small-scale external and internal or mental violence and their incidence and prevalence as strictly human, self-destructive or deadly, dilemmas from, respectively, unsorted or distorted impulses.

Violence beyond human understanding and imagination gave birth to our universe. Its power and explosive might have given it gender, and as Father Almighty, it is now sometimes known as Jehovah, Allah, etc. Among His children is our star, which we used to call the sun god, Ra. It is really (**Z, f**) the grandmother of life on our Mother Earth.

In the material and animal world, violence remains routine except in incidence among humans, where it partakes of the variety found in solitary or shared sexual practices (**P–Y**). Only in our species are family members hurt by close "loving" relatives. *(k/1)*

> (Incest is strictly a natural family affair between mother and son or father and daughter. Also provoked by proximity, like bestiality, sexual abuse of the same or opposite sex may be pedophilia in step or surrogate families. Sexual harassment, unlike philandering, may just be attempted nepotism between unlikely pairs.)

We started a cycle of decay with the big bang, interrupted at intervals by reunion of unlike particles. So does our vegetative nervous system recycle between violence and sex, by division of labor between its sympathetic and parasympathetic halves. *(k/20)* This is basic cosmology and simple neurology.

We carry around with us natural residues of primeval violence that still produces our water, acids, bases, and salts. We grow cells, tissues, and organs from them in the same way that animals do. All our brains, animal or human, are connected to our bodies to produce behavior that evolved in a shared environment. *(k/3)* This is nuclear physics and elementary biology.

Yet we behave like tourists who know very little of the history of the place we happen to be visiting: We look down on its indigenous population and do not care too much about the cost of what we want or how it affects the native ecosystems. And often end up feeling "out of sorts" without knowing why!

> Nature, including animals and people, struggles to sustain itself, just as toddlers try to keep their footing. (In cosmic terms, we are toddlers in this universe.)

We work while seething or trying to reconcile ourselves to dying, abdicating, staying together, or killing each other. As with all afflictions, early diagnosis can be lifesaving.

Are prudence, pride, and prejudice the modern-day substitutes for aeons of preprogramming in ancestral animals who have survived longer than *Homo sapiens*? (Violence gets things done for them.)

Can we more critically examine (**i**) personal, (**ii**) social, and (**iii'**) "sexual" violence, which end with killing and dying?

Only men who have been bullied in the past are cruel. Abuse begets abuse, and abuse among human beings starts early. Sexual abuse in the form of genital mutilation as circumcision or clitoridectomy without consent is traditional in some cultures.

HUMAN FAMILY VIOLENCE

Are families, fetuses, and the elderly today's designated sacrificial victims? If abused children become violent criminals, does bruising our brain during natural childbirth make us violence-prone? Does infantile circumcision produce more bloodbaths among victims? Psychiatry can decriminalize or "exorcise" without "purifying" or domesticating.

Why are our teenagers more tempted by drugs, cults, and gangs? *(k/4)* Are their parents less able to help them after fighting with their own enemies, real or imaginary, dangerous or implacable? Is there ever violence, lethal or mental, without opposing forces, mismatched or balanced in pairing or grouping? For some age-old problems, we can now propose a few partial solutions as well as better questions to answer *(k/7-12)*, from a quarter century of animal and clinical study and observations.

Homo domesticus impulses, if unsorted about (1) life, (2) work, and (3) time and place in the universe (resulting in alienation), can produce self-destructive dilemmas and eventually result in violence against ourselves and others.

Those distorted by borrowed beliefs of *H. metropolis* are deadly. They thereby invite unwarranted socio-ethical (legal) "remedies" that are worse than the "disease." These can be analyzed behaviorally and scientifically. *(k/5)*

(one) SILENT, SELF-DESTRUCTIVE, and DESPERATE DILEMMAS

These less deadly dilemmas for *Homo domesticus* are specifically human. We suffer and torment ourselves or defend our bias by academic (impractical) arguments.

(1) LIFE (An Idler's Dilemma)

If (a) the human condition is to be explained by "original sin" and (b) blaming Eve has only enriched our churches, might the answer lie elsewhere?

Homo domestici believers in "original sin" are permitted or expected to exercise control over their impulses. Animals do not have such permission to resist, or expectation to live up to, in order to achieve delayed but eternal gratification. Their lives are therefore safe in their own keeping. They would only die for their young and fight to eat or mate, but never for strangers or absent masters.

For *Homo domestici*, life as they see it is central to their philosophy, e.g., a game or a gamble, a good or hard bargain, a loan subject to foreclosure without warning, a pimp to make us happy or a parent to take care of us, a trial by ordeal or a curriculum for obtaining credentials, etc. *(k/7)*

(2) WORKAHOLISM (A Puritan Dilemma)

There is work that for *Homo sapiens* is fun during the doing, and there are *Homo domesticus* workhorses who are driven to keep going. There is ease and disease, stress and distress.

1. Some overdomesticated or overcommitted candidates for future alienation (postinfantile to presenescent) as *Homo metropoli* may be overachievers, rich or successful, but still striving to get out from under smotherers and social matriarchs (mothers and their surrogates or **A'A**), or betters and superiors (or **F, G,** or **H** bureaucrats and powercrats) in later life. *(k/6)*
2. These candidates for nearly inevitable midlife alienation can also ripen prematurely into "type A" personalities, male or female,

successful or not, who are prone to heart attacks. (Or stomach ulcers from gut reactions to hidden "constricting" regrets.)

3. Some alcoholics now see workaholics as "humanolics" who are driven (**AB**) to work (suck) their thumbs (which, with sweat and tears, differentiate them from *Homo sapiens* and from playful dolphins with bigger brains per pound).

4. For workaholics, work is an opiate or security blanket, a penance or prison, etc. *(k/8)*

Sex for its own sake, like work itself, can anchor *Homo sapiens* to "reality" certainly better than ideas (fantasies) or even love (or romantic insanity) outside mothering. (Like *Homo domesticus* alcoholics who must replace their addiction with another less lethal, *Homo metropolis* intellectuals must also replace myths with facts that soothe or suit.)

Both sex and maternal love (whose abdication is legitimized in legalized abortion) are of course also truly territorial, like all works and ideas that can be copyrighted; but work products and even playfulness, if supervised, depend on social judgments to be real enough for the domesticated workhorse or alienated intellectual.

(3) ALIENATION (A Subjective Time Dilemma)

There is

a. self-exile (active dropping out for "hip" *Homo sapiens*) *(k/11)*;

b. the socially alienated (passive and lonesome *H. domesticus*) *(k/10)*; and

c. self-alienation (internal doubting, without being a schizoid loner nor solitude lover) for *H. metropolis (k/9)*.

All three groups feel out of step, but the self-alienated is (c) out of step even with hirself *(sic)*. Not to be in tune with yourself is different from (b) being tuned out by others or (a) tuning others out to tune in on oneself by dropping out.

Time makes the alienated pause. Animals do not get bored; they go to sleep instead. People without imagination (theirs or on loan from fiction mongers) suffer ennui with insomnia and/or distort their time perception—the self-alienated worry about time being absolute, short, dragging on, precious according to purpose, etc.

The only antidote for alienation is ancestor worship (illusory in myth-based theology) or personal deeds (not good works for social reward, now or later). The better leaders (gurus) are more mammalian (nurturing) than anthropocentric (driven to prove something).

Homo metropoli feel alienated once they suspect that the world was not created for them. They cannot accept that clean air or water is ours to share with all, like our other unearned gifts, including inherited talent.

Unlike *Homo domesticus*'s sheepish endorsement of society's biases, *Homo metropolis* consumers of cosmetic surgery, padded brassieres and shoulders, high heels and elevator shoes deny the imperfect source of their chromosomes at great cost and inconvenience.

(two) DRAMATIC and DEADLIER DILEMMAS

[Below are personal, educational, neurosocial, medicolegal, and global extensions and solutions of life and death problems that require our sorting out new, different, and/or ignored data if we are to handle them better. They need extended attention because of the mounting (**F–O**) ideological baggage that makes us animals of burden for (**ii**) venerated believers among our leaders. (We shall not dwell at length or repeat the tired old arguments of their advocates and adversaries.)]

For *Homo sapiens*, what is moral is strictly personal, what is ethical is purely cultural. The potential conflict is between (**i**) family virtues and (**ii**) social values.

Other species have problems and solve them. Only the dominant can be loud. Rivals vie in who can make louder noises.

Though there is no interest in the topic, increasing our staying power as animals and contrasting their behavior with our troublesomeness as *Homo domestici* and *Homo metropoli* may not yet be too late.

(1) TERRITORIAL VICTIMS (A Geopolitical Dilemma)

Politics, as pecking order, was intended to cope with disorder. It has, instead, increased mortality rates. (War killed 170 million in the "enlightened" twentieth century.) Only *Homo domesticus* and *Homo metropolis* would "choose" (**G**) national and (**H**) economic security over life itself.

Unlike the church (**F**), the nation-state (**G**), like street gangs, started playfully with urchins as warriors, juveniles as athletes, and adolescents as lovers: "Youth preoccupied with women and resolved to fight" (Ortega y Gasset's "The Sportive Origin of the State" in *Toward a Philosophy of History*, N.Y., 1941).

Only much later did government become a gray-bearded senile senate "constitutionally" (*sic*) incapable of rape and pillage by virtue of age, not virtue. (It takes alienation from collective membership in their universe for boys to kill brothers in other lands who bought another God or slogan from their social propaganda machine.)

Territoriality for plants and animals is purely defensive. It is exercised by our own tissues against what seems to be foreign bodies, including our own sperm cells with only half their normal complement of chromosomes. (Is this why they want to get away at any cost? Spermatozoa have to be "nursed" to maturity by "sister cells." Do they feel unwelcome in their testicular sac?)

Imperialism, on the other hand, is offensive. Old World piracy of ships carrying spices from the Orient precipitated war over trade routes.

For either (**A**) emotional or (**B**) willful "reasons" (**C'**), we are willing to let others, usually younger rivals, die during the recent Gulf War to keep cheap oil flowing from the Mid East to the more industrially developed West or Far East.

Politically (**G**), economically (**H**), and ethologically (**N**), as well as environmentally (**M**), this makes sense: Oil is not a renewable resource, but donors for blood banks and bloodbaths are virtually inexhaustible. (Heterosexual AIDS epidemics and homosexuality are, in fact, more ethologically ominous.)

If only we must eat whatever we kill or get killed! Officers must then have an attack of bulimia to engage in "search and destroy" missions in our gas-guzzling conventional wars.

In nuclear wars, their commanders-in-chief would be too nauseous to indulge in gluttony after enough radioactivity reaches their underground sanctuary.

(Hunters enjoy eating the animals that they kill when they represent a transfer of strength from the admired animal to their killer. When we kill out of hate, we do not want to partake of what we have hated.)

To internationalize capital punishment for wanton slaughter in Bosnia, etc., needs another better Nuremberg (ad hoc adjudication is technically post hoc and therefore legally flawed).

Bloodthirsty "bounty hunters" of future war criminals will just have to await another Marshall Plan to rehabilitate their surviving victims before they can be the talionic God of the Old Testament who would rather see the families of serial murderers also suffer from what they have already made other families go through. (The nemesis of Nazi deserters had to be strong enough geopolitically to pursue their predators to the ends of the earth as preys more unworthy of life for the rest of their days than their unsuspecting war victims.)

(a) THE RIGHT TO KILL AND THE PRIVILEGE TO LIVE

(Oriana Fallaci, Italian writer and dying of cancer, when asked if she knew beforehand that she would die in a concentration camp, confidently affirmed that she would still want to have been born.)

There is a right but no duty to kill or die, only (i) the freedom to feel fulfilled, (ii) the right to believe and fail, and/or (iii) the need/opportunity to multiply.

"Infanticide" in the first recorded genocidal holocaust is reported in the Bible (Numbers 31). It is also committed by male animals other than a nursling's father so that the nursing mother can go into "oestrous" sooner. Females other than a mother can do it to safeguard the ascendancy of an offspring in the pecking order. (Divorcees, like Susan Smith of South Carolina, may kill their boys to have more daughters by another man.) Only fathers, human or divine, also expect their sons to kill or die for what they believe.

Physicians are now being asked to be more like veterinarians who can actively help paying customers put their loved but now useless pets "to sleep" before they die from natural causes. (Why is "sleep" used when we mean killing or sex?) Mercy killers of animals do not consult their "beneficiaries" as to their wishes or request their permission to end it all. *Homo domesticus* "benefactors" are more compassionate toward their own oversensitive ears or eyes.

As an emotional crossroad, abortion is also increasingly sold as euthanasia by *Homo metropoli* for a child who is not wanted ("emotional eugenics"). In fact, wanting children is not unselfish but an additional burden for the child of total strangers with old expectations that are rooted in the past but increases in weight with each child of every generation.

The right to die during acute distress is not legally sound. (Or biologically defensible because there is no pain that is truly unbearable: we start falling unconscious to the ground to rush more blood to our brain as soon as its own supply of endorphin opiates proves to be inadequate.) In legitimized mercy killing of *Homo metropoli*, their declaration of consent must also be signed while their imagination is sick with what still sickens them about memories of the sick in their past. Are they to be adjudged sound of mind and body when they sign their name so as not to be as sick as those?

> With "no pain, no gain" autohypnotic suggestion, brain endorphins enable long-distance runners to "hit the wall" without stopping and to feel euphoria on reaching and breaching their wall in a test of endurance.

(2) BETWEEN THE RIGHT TO LIFE and THE WISH TO DIE WITH DIGNITY (A Professional Dilemma)

Premeditation makes killing with abandon, without eating the victim, truly malicious murder, even for vengeance.

> If ritual use of intoxicants is not criminal, cannibalism for religious or other reasons is not malicious. But vengeance by proxies (using contract killers or legally hired uniformed "hit men") is premeditated murder, in contrast to killing in the heat of battle or passion.

During periods of affluence, *Homo metropolis* dogfights become more vicious over the unborn and the dying who are prime candidates to be sociopolitical victims of technotronic progress in obstetrics and geriatrics. Except as precious passengers or patients with a family, they are either "unpersons" or second-class denizens of urban "civilization."

Resolving this modern professional dilemma requires our knowing moral or ethical principles and legal or cultural standards:

Constitutional law for *Homo domesticus* is based on moral standards of what constitutes wrongdoing against person and property, which was unwritten among *Homo sapiens* and today's birds and beasts. Yet in more and more cities, local laws are passed to codify what has recently been conceded by *Homo metropolis* as either illegal, unethical, or uncivilized, e.g., smoking in public places if only to protect the health of bystanders and not just their acquired tastes/distastes. Amoral in themselves, such laws are also unconstitutional, unless health is property. (In medicine, by definition, our body is our "constitution.")

We have to separate moral virtues from social values and universal norms from the new "facts" of legal fiction, e.g., "Smoke from cigarettes is like firing a concealed weapon, but smog from commercial burning of cheap oil is a sure sign of urban progress." What is ethical involves social value, not questions of personal judgment about what is (**A**) good or bad, (**B**) right or wrong, or (**C**) true or false.

The morally upright but not socially righteous *Homo sapiens* will not be in personal conflict, but may be collegially disapproved of. Hir *(sic)* self-esteem will not suffer, but group estimate of hir will change. Professional evaluation of hir guild membership depends on collegial standards. Hir family's estimate of hir will not change if its standards are separate from those of hir peers. Social indignation affects only our personal identity (derived from identification figures), not inherent human or animal dignity or earned self-respect. *(k/12)*

With aging, is dignity lost through (**A'**) emotional instability, (**B'**) involuntary incontinence *(k/13)*, or (**C'**) unintelligible irrationality? Or through loss of dignified memories that the departed can leave behind to be cherished in authentic (**iii**) or proxy (**F**) ancestor worship before age and/or disability changed them and the family? Who dignifies what or whom, the doer or the observer?

We can comprehend more of what we take for granted only if we assign to them separate consequences *(sic)*:

1. The elderly used to be revered because they were rare. Geriatric ghettos have not attracted behavioral scientists in proportional numbers and leisure.
2. Aging ghetto dwellers are forgetful as well as forgotten, a fate that they share with other old mammals, including old rats in their rat holes. (Of lab mice and wild chimps, this is also true.)
3. There would be for others more and more consequences as our elderly increase in numbers exponentially, in sickness and in health and (**H**) wealth and (**G**) political clout to replace democracy with gerontocracy.

Adolescents used to have neither money nor political opinion. When senior citizens become the majority (gerontocracy), they will threaten adults more than long-haired teenagers from the "baby boom" generation among Elvis Presley fans.

(3) EUTHANASIA: From Fear of Dying Alone to Dying on Cue (A Neurolegal Dilemma)

(Please fasten your professional seat belts while we go at a fast clip over some points about life and death that are often ignored while we spend more and more time—as in political rallies—or reassuring each other about what we already share.) *(k/14)*

All that most people know of living is the life that they lead. That range of experience is too narrow for professional consensus about dying itself. *(k/15, 19)* (Brain death does not stop our hair and nails from growing after we are six feet underground.)

Homo domesticus and *H. metropolis* hurt those whom they love, kill them or themselves, or ask to die.

Except for self-defense and for the very same reason, they have delegated the right to kill to the government so that it can (1) kill convicted killers in peacetime or (2) order their sons to kill enemy soldiers and civilians in wartime. (Occupying and retreating forces behave differently.) No animal would kill (except to eat or escape) or be heroic and die (rather than retreat) unless trapped.

Both subspecies, *H. domesticus* and *H. metropolis*, are now trying to reserve for themselves the "right" to die (with dignity) and have started asking the government to legitimize assisted suicide by delegating it to those willing to kill them. No animal or *Homo sapiens* would dream of asking for such assistance.

> I know of no animal outside of these two subspecies who would delegate either the decision to kill or to die to another, nor exercise the second or feel guilty over the first. Instead, unlike them, it would, just proceed to feed on what it kills. [If that were the only reason for killing, there would be fewer wars. Only "advanced" primates, like chimps and people, have decimated each other's herds out of greed, not hunger.

In cases of physician-assisted suicide, we must talk of professional ethics, not personal morality. Should the physician who assists suicide charge for the exercise of his bias or his expertise?

> What is ethical may not be moral, just as what is socially legal may be privately perverted. Thus, euthanasia in our medical practice becomes an ethical, not a personal or private decision.

If we substitute what is personal or moral for what is professional or ethical, then we are practicing medicine under false pretenses. We cannot charge for what we learned for ourselves about (**A**) good or bad, (**B**) right or wrong, or (**C**) true or false before we went to medical school.

Professional ethics is not about family virtues but about a scale of social values that are arrived at by cultural consensus. Society may not agree on what is good, right, or true, but medical licensing agencies can punish those of us who violate accepted professional procedures.

Is it ethical to assist the suicidal for whatever reason? There is morality, ethics, and eroticism; but for the biologist, there is only sensuality, social sanctions, and sex.

> For the erect penis or turgid clitoris, there is no morality or ethics. The sexually potent do not seek the power that those who are weak seek as a substitute. Those who are erotically aroused only

seek relief of tumescence. The sexually excited male or female has no time for values or virtues until much later.

Some professional practices may be more or less ethical than others, according to peer reviews. That is why we can have a panel about the medical ethics that apply to assisting patients to die after they prescribe for themselves how they should be treated in order for their death to be painless and dignified.

Soiling itself is usually the last act of a dying animal. But *Homo domesticus* and *H. metropolis* do not want to be identified with the very ancestors whose evolution gave them their lives. They're like second-generation immigrants who are ashamed of their biological parents, their native accents and traditional customs.

For the dying not to want to suffer pain or be embarrassed by soiling their deathbed on their last day of life can be understood best by psychiatrists. We are the only animals who are born crying out in pain with our first breath. The pain comes from a headache that is worse than the worst hangover we can have after trying to drown our life's sorrows with alcohol. The headache comes from our head being too big for our mothers' breeches, so that even the lips of her vulvae are torn or have to be cut to accommodate our head as it emerges.

And if to bruising our brain we add circumcision without consent, the fear of future pain can be paralyzing, even after prisoners of war and professional athletes have proven that no pain is unbearable: that we fall unconscious to bring more blood to our brain to produce more endorphins when available levels cannot cope with the agony that torture or injury brings to either high-risk group.

Myself, I have always refused anesthesia against my dentist's advice because I can survive pain but not toxic side effects from painkillers. My dentist seems to suffer more from watching me "grit my teeth." Nor did I need anesthesia when I was circumcised at puberty with my cousins by our maternal uncle.

Except in the Netherlands, when we talk of euthanasia, we're only talking about killing animals or adults. Is it because neither animals nor adults are needed for our survival, but only the young are needed to replace the dead? (Plants just need that seeds be scattered to germinate in order for them to propagate.)

But the unborn can be killed, and then it is called eugenics or involuntary feticide or voluntary abortion. If eugenics is practiced on potential parents of the unborn, it is then called genocide.

In eugenics or euthanasia, we kill those whom we do not want. This is different from "triage" as practiced when war or disaster strikes. Then we look after those whom we can immediately help ahead of others, whether or not they are more deserving of living longer. *(k/16)*

Euthanasia was once called "mercy killing" for animals and is now called "assisted suicide" for adults. Animals are not consulted as to their wishes; adults leave instructions as to who will decide on when they should die if they can no longer speak, along with details for the disposition of their savings after paying off all hospital bills.

Who were the first practitioners of euthanasia? So-called "animal lovers." Did they tell their pets that if they cannot have the good life, they might as well be dead? And did they hear their pets agree, "If I cannot have the good life, you might as well kill me now"?

> Thusly did the American cowboy, with a tear in each eye, bring himself to shoot his horse after it breaks its leg from stumbling and throwing him off its saddle. The Hemlock Society is the human version of SPCA.

Both groups who kill their pets or wish to die are operating on the strength of past memories of distress and anguish that they do not want to relive. When one writes instructions for assisted suicide, that death seeker is reliving hard times of sickness and pain and cannot be said to be of sound mind capable of sound judgment.

Thus, the issue of legal competence to demand assisted suicide cannot be taken for granted. Those who do not want to be a burden to their families are the same people who found it burdensome to look after relatives and feel that it is better to relieve their relatives of that burden long before they also find it too burdensome.

Is euthanasia (1) a sin, (2) a crime, or (3) a face- or money -saver? Is it (4) an escape from indignity, and in whose presence?, Or is it (5) a boon to a society eager to supply its products and services for killing the dying?

[Dignity/sphincters = "face," not honor (reputation/cowardice)]

Or is euthanasia (6) a declaration of independence based on a self-serving idea that we are better than animals? Unlike us, other animals are all doomed to live until they die unless they have been domesticated by us, their merciful killers.

Or is euthanasia (7) an expedient experiment in faster recycling to save the environment, and/or is it (8) a repudiation of electronic progress in automating the vital functions of our heart and lungs? The only wealth is life, but time is all we have to spend living. *(k/17)*

Animals who are not pets of the rich and fastidious do not have to risk dying before their time. Is it because veterinarians are not as good as physicians in prolonging life? Are we or our patients to be penalized for being/having better doctors? Or are our patients being asked to choose, "Your money or your life?"

This "mugger mentality" first appeared to compel surgical contraception for parents likely to have retarded children. Are the retarded less intelligent than animals? Or do *Homo domesticus* and *H. metropolis* just not want to see living fossils of their ancestors in their living and dining rooms, even if they keep pets in the house?

What I call a "reverse mugger mentality" reigns when bioethics committee members with a conflict of interest ask to be relieved of the economic burden of sustaining the indigent on expensive life-support systems. *(k/18)*

Instead of "Your money or your life?" the question then becomes "Our money or our soul?" *(k/19)* and money always wins, hands down. What is particularly pernicious about this "lip service" to ethics is that even triage decisions are taken out of the hands of doctors to be decided unethically by "concerned" *H. domesticus* and *H. metropolis* members of bioethics committees.

How much of this problem of arranged suicide arises exclusively with loosely knit families? My father had a series of strokes, each more severe than the last, for a period of seven years. At no time was he neglected, even when he had to be carried and cared for like a child.

If you examine in depth the relationships around patients who are asking to die, those closest to them are more likely to be spouses or siblings than parents or children. If their parents were alive, who of the two will volunteer to assist their dying? Probably not full-time mothers.

Are those who ask for help to die also the ones who claim that it does not make a difference wherever or whomever one comes from (by which they do not mean geography, social class, or race)? *(k/13)* Disowning makes leaving the disowned easier.

In every situation where euthanasia is the "final solution," the survivors might also need a psychiatrist. For survivors, euthanasia raises questions not only about what they agreed to do but also about who had really needed something done, the deceased or the relative who now regrets and grieves for having agreed.

Would their mother have done it for them if they were the ones dying? Only if all throughout their childhood they felt that they were loved only under certain conditions. Once they failed to meet those conditions, did anyone wish that their mother had never carried her pregnancy to term?

> Who is less ethical, he who sires bastards or she who terminates pregnancies? Is the abortus terminally ill or conceived conditionally, or the egg fertilized without its consent? Is abortion involuntary euthanasia?

It still surprises me to meet people who can only accept life conditionally. They must have been loved conditionally as children. And like their parents, they have set conditions under which they will continue living. Absent those conditions, they would rather cease to exist. *(k/21)*

For a doctor to assist self-prescribed suicide in the demented, incontinent, impotent, vegetating, or apathetic is to be even less like the veterinarian who himself decides when the animal must go and gets agreement from its owner for what he has recommended. The issue is not one of consent. Consent is short for consensus and therefore a confession that the attending professional is not coerced to comply with the mugger's demand for money or a life, even another's pet's life in the case of the veterinarian.

Should your role in active euthanasia be judged on the basis of what you know or what your parents believe? It is easy to find out if what you do as a doctor is based on belief or knowledge. All you need to ask—if your parents are not doctors—is whether they would not agree with you. If they would, then your fees are charged by their daughters and sons, not by a doctor.

When you agree to assist a patient to die, did you, deliberately or not, mentally consult your parents, or will they applaud your medical judgment? Is their consent or applause needed? If so, then your action is not dictated by what you learned after entering medical school, and you should not get paid as a professional for your services as an agreeable or scared amateur.

Your fees should not be dictated by your parents, or by prior fear of the unknown or of bullies or of going hungry. Even preliteral societies had gods, leaders, and tokens for barter. None of these have anything to do with the practice of modern medicine. Are you willing to kill or die for your God, your country, or for money? Doctor or not, if a mugger threatens, "Your money or your life?" would you happily part with your wallet?

Nor should your services be influenced by loyalty to your alma mater or your profession. You cannot subscribe to all that you were taught or do all that is expected by your peers. The medical decision is yours alone and so is the professional responsibility.

The right to live also means the privilege to live. The right to fail does not mean a duty to die. *(k/22)*

Those who neither accept failure nor blame others tend to accuse and punish themselves. Those who believe in God as Father or blame Big Somebody for Little Me keep themselves studiously ignorant of another way of looking at everything that happens, even around dying: Are they not just events trailing after others, not in any linear "cause-effect" progression but in a vector-convergence process? Failure may be foreordained, but is sought to be postponed if not repudiated by delusions to deny irreversible inevitability.

(b) THE RIGHT TO FAIL (An Educational Dilemma)

We want our alumni to be competent, but we also want them to be professionals. We measure competence by success. But that is a social standard. Training for competence in order to be licensed and educating for professional practice presents a curious dilemma.

Professionals need to do their personal best, whether they personally like it or not, whether they fail or not. Only the socially negligent or reckless physician can be convicted of medical malpractice as a licensee. Personal failure must not be punished or the profession stagnates.

When amateurs succeed in what they want to do, that only tells us that their inherited talent matches their ambition. When they triumph, we should congratulate their grandparents. Only when one fails is credit personally earned for trying to reach way beyond one's grasp.

In our psychiatric residency training program, where as director I also hold the title of chief of professional education, to fail is not penalized. If to live is to test limits—because/while indoctrination encourages cowardice so that one plays it safe within the rules—then not to test limits is tantamount to dying before one's time.

(c) OPPORTUNITY/NEED TO MULTIPLY (A Socio-Sexual Dilemma)

[To start with the cell and end with the cell is scientific (transcultural) medicine. To start with the soul and end with the soul is voodoo (tribal) medicine.]

When "life" begins is a rhetorical question if the inquirer is an "ideologue" selling his opinion. If the query is prompted by personal circumstances, the answer maybe "As soon as the children (1) leave home, (2) graduate from college, (3) find a job, (4) get married," etc.

The easiest part is getting pregnant, which the body human or not, carries to a successful conclusion, even at the cost of the mother's own life. The next hardest is the next eighteen years of child rearing.

Some welcome children—saint, sinner, student, etc.—of all ages. The unwelcome are left with fewer options but often become, as novice *Homo metropolis*, the most vociferous about freedom of choice. As if they had one that counts. What counts nature takes care of. In our case, by our autonomic (*sic*) nervous system outside the spine or, at its end, the reptilian brain. Even Supreme Court members think they can choose, but they are as dogmatic as kids in kindergarten.

In science, the first question that we must answer in studying human life must be "Is the fertilized egg, or zygote, alive?" The second has to be "Is the fetus viable?" Viability of the fetus depends on a more special relationship than for hatchlings and, like our own lives, depend on what generally surround them and us even as adults in crowded cities.

The fetus, in fact, gets practice in not rejecting the mother, and the infant accepts transplants easier than grown-ups. Voluntary abortion, of course, is not tissue rejection. In fact, fetal tissues are better risks for replacing older organs.

Can we bank fetal tissue, like we do sperm, so that we can transplant them to relieve symptoms of Parkinsonism, etc.? (Birds and amphibians can regenerate their neurons and never risk Alzheimer's disease.)

Can a fetus outlive its brain-dead mother? Technology now allows it.

Involuntary abortion among animals depends on their external circumstances. When resources abound for species survival, even tuberculous mothers give up calcium to the fetus at the risk of dying from "galloping consumption" as tubercle bacilli are released from decalcified cavities in their lungs into the bloodstream. (Some larvae eat their mother fly from the inside.)

For egg-laying animals, both queries above can be combined into "Will it hatch?" The two questions cannot be combined for those who emerge alive and kicking:

In womb users, a series of questions about nursling and nursing must be asked: We need to know if nurslings are disadvantaged for being small. For humans, especially, we have to ask because their sire may be hanging around, unlike most fathers of other animals, whether his size tilts the balance against their usurping their mother, if he feels like their rival: "How many others share its mother, and is one of them its father and bigger than its other rivals for the mother? Will the newborn be the runt in a nuclear household (or human family litter)?"

The answer will decide whether it is more or less (ii) indentured or (i) free:

Domestication/Liberty = ii/i
Disloyalty/Equality = i/ii
Liberty/Equality = Disloyalty/Domestication
Stagnation = Fear of failure/Need to be loyal
Progress = Freedom to be disloyal/Right to fail

We must ask if the unborn will, sooner or later, be asked to give up its mother as well as its mother tongue as a price for survival. We are the only animals who insist on teaching our young another vocabulary to replace their vocalizations.

The next question that is quite peculiar to our species has to be "Is it human?" And this cannot be answered before birth but only after its tongue and thumb have gone to school. (Einstein was a slow learner.) For training to succeed, it needs a human brain, not the largest, proportionately (which porpoises can claim).

The next question must be "Is it a mutant?" Einstein and Edison were dyslexic, which means their brain architecture is different. Dyslexics have a different notion of time.

[Edison would not give up trying no matter how many times his experiments failed. Einstein, mutant or not, turned our notion of time upside down and said it depended on speed and is not absolute. He claims that a long childhood also prolonged his curiosity.]

The most important question about our progeny has to be "Is it a 'monster'?" To answer this purely biological query in the negative, it needs to reproduce itself.

Scientist or not, after answering all questions about life from its beginning with all the reasons we may advance in support of our stand, is it not enough to be born and loved, to feed and drink, cavort and breed? Is it fatal or simply expectable to fail in the end? Can we die naturally? Should we schedule dying or killing by our hands or by appointed proxies or total strangers?

(4) VOLUNTARY ABORTION (A Global Dilemma)

Options are silent hallucinations until we assign priorities to our choices. For boy or girl, man or woman, truly (**B**) voluntary "choice" of toys to play with, time to share, or dates to wait for is seldom open-ended. Options are closed off by contingencies beyond our control. Even (**B'**) righteous (**A**) anger under these circumstances is not freely (**C**) expressed. "Correct speech" and "choice" are neither free for anyone nor equal for everybody if, or especially when, they are really consequential!

As soon as we assign some importance to their consequences, we act to ensure that we do not miss out. So we tend not to wait to decide until enough data can be gathered to guide our actions. We act out of inclination. Choices and beliefs are just bets.

Abortionists by "choice" generally not only do not but also cannot believe in either or both motherhood or/and childhood. Can those who cannot be mothers accept adoptive parents for their children? Can those who enjoy children accept surrogate mothers who are receptive to their husband's seed?

Those who, because of their past for which they must not be held responsible, can neither adopt nor accept rivals may but just barely help themselves by sharing secrets with each other so that what they feel badly about is no longer too private to hide. (Only in this sense can "truth set us free" to let something go.)

We are not born equal, all organisms are born with variations from each other, which allow the survival of whoever is fitter (even among organisms attacked by antibiotics and pesticides) to adapt (as new "creatures") to the environment surrounding them.

A sheltered life literally produces fat cats who die early but happy. The lean and sinewy beget more progeny from longevity. Adequate sex hormone levels can, with clever electioneering more peaceful than "sit-down strikes, overcome political oppression in big cities with large fertile ghettoes.)

The ideology of social equality among *Homo metropolis* is more advanced than the philosophy of potential perfectibility among *Homo domestici*, who have bought into a "Goferobot" Who invites all to share His perfection simply by dedicating their lives to Him. Both ideas beguile those who feel unequal and jealous and invigorate those who are zealously treated as inferior.

Ideologies promise to make them "equal" before (**F**) God, (**G**) the law, (**H**) in the workplace, as (**I**) individuals or (**J**) groups, with (**K**) producers, as (**L**) people and (**M**) passive (vegetating), (**N**) active (moving), or (**O**) intelligent machines. Such socialized values both accuse and say "I am OK" to serve better as crutches.

Almost all ideologies meet head-on in understated (subconscious?) arguments about abortion in the best of democracies. They are silent marching orders under the Stars and Stripes against abortion surgeons or for their clients. But believing they can choose, even tenured bureaucrats including sitting justices of the Supreme Court, most are more opinionated than knowledgeable.

There are not just two sets of beliefs for or against the right to life (besides one's own) or the right to choose, among those who denounce or applaud abortion, dividing even critics of U.S. Supreme Court nominees into two camps.

Both camps as well as the justices themselves are prisoners of their past and cannot but compulsively "choose" the most congenial set of parroted slogans: therefore the total social toll for the species will keep on rising as natural selection is abandoned for borrowed beliefs that are listed below that polarize potential parents.

In the following list, the initials refer to faith, government, hoarding, individualism, etc., and competing assumptions about (**F**) the Great White Father, (**G**) Big Brother, (**H**) Big Business, (I) Little Me, (**J**) Big Sister, etc.

(**O**)verintelligent computers have been least used/blamed by either "pro-choice" or "pro-life" camps. In this most biological issue, it is the least abused.

(They threaten only the socially preprogrammed or sedentary who are redundant or repetitious. If their hardwiring is as good as that of animals, they will make fewer errors than unskilled help. To err is human, robots err less, pets least at less cost than kids.)

Which social excuse or accusation appeals most to those "pro-life" or "pro-choice" ideologues whom you know enough about?

F: The Bible demands that we "go forth and multiply." (Even now, multiplication is seldom the reason for fornication. This order could only be obeyed after the invention of the calendar in the Bronze Age.) Can one will only the will of God?

G: What is legal is not criminal. ("My country, right or wrong.") What is private depends on the public. Privacy includes private parts as property. (Only the soul is jointly owned.)

H: We must provide for what we bring forth. There is no "free lunch." (Only the offspring of mammals drink gratis. The Gulf War for finite fossils was won by recyclable red blood cells of expendable volunteers.)

I: Everyone is entitled to hir (*sic*) place under the sun. (If tall trees stunt saplings, should adolescents on minimum wage have equal rights? Animals also cross-pollinate stunted vegetation, birds where winds don't help, humans just by sneezing!)

J: We do not take food from anyone already hungry. Those whom we cannot love must not starve. (Even if "charity begins at home," kindred suffering is mostly emotional [affective], only pain is neurological [and produces unconsciousness whenever unbearable].)

K (industrialism): We can produce surplus food and feed the needy. Only the greedy grab what they can.

L (anthropocentrism): *Homo domestici* are entitled to more than creature comforts. *Homo metropolis* deserve more.

M (environmentalism): *Homo sapiens* cannot hog the planet's resources, even if or precisely because *H. domesticus* and *metropolis* claim to be its custodians.

N (animalism): If animals can take care of their own, so can *Homo sapiens* who are more intelligent.

O (cyberneticism): Computers can reduce redundant employment. (Like animals, they are not as erratic as bureaucracies that institutionalize the errors they seek to reduce. Bureaucratation by criminalization of domestic violence by *Homo metropolis* is a sign of failure to recognize that only *Homo domesticus* abuse their relatives. Education helps *H. sapi*ens more than either subspecies. Precocious senility handicaps desperate *H. domesticus*; premature menopause dooms bitter *H. metropolis*.)

Your selected answer for any social units from any subculture, affluent or starving, self-indulgent or spartan, shows where ideological development has taken them to date, which also opens up vistas still ahead in life.

[All ideologies, like theories, are true in part, as well as necessary for a while, like all religions. The Bible expected multiplication before it talked of marriage. As thoughts, ideas are the music of the mind, without (**B**) force—except what may be evoked in those enamored of its beauty (**A**), not its truth (**C**)—unless ideological intoxication interrupts and listening to other composers is postponed.]

(d) AGGRESSION AND HOSTILITY

Are not abortions sexual or marital civil wars, with casualties and scars that militant ideology hides? Is "freedom to choose" a clever slogan of the equal right to escape from sexual oppression but the oppressor is not the casualty? Is the fetus a tubercle bacillus on the loose or an early cancer ("crab") that will claw its way into the rest of its mother's life?

Or will self-pitying guilt (for their own suspected automutilation surge) drive bereaved (*H. domesticus*) or relieved (*H. metropolis*) mothers-to-be to join special-interest groups of coconspirators, self-flagellants (*H. domesticus*), or sisters-in-denial (*H. metropolis*)? Both groups need sanctuaries to hide in, beyond the support such groups offer with varying effectiveness.

ANGER and CRUELTY

When violence becomes a household event, there are (1) ethological considerations that apply to males and females (husbands are the only "henpecked" males in the animal kingdom) and (2) cultural sanctions that operate between adults and children. What is "etho-cultural" is also neurological and involves newly evolved cortical speech centers.

1. Lions and lionesses play by different rules, but the rules are clear. So also are they among aristocrats and the poor, more than among the middle classes who like to change the rules. That makes boundary conflicts erupt into violence, as it does among adolescents testing their strengths against each other or among developing nations pitted against superior forces (colonial or global superpowers).

The ambitious middle-class mentality of *Homo metropolis* is the opposite of the colonial mentality that survives among *Homo domesticus*, the poor and the powerless. Adolescents who have tasted power and middle classes who do not feel powerless seek parity. Equality is not a priority among *Homo sapiens*, the wealthy or the elite who do not feel guilty.

2. Children at risk are those in "no-man's-land," unprotected by a physically or emotionally absent father and unsocialized by father substitutes or stepfathers. The risk is greater for stepsons who present a social challenge to a strange adult who is more likely to respond to sexual attraction from his mother or sister.

   Grandparents are better for the sensual than social or sexual development of grandchildren.

Differential diagnosis must be done early:
1. Men who are cruel do not allow their outraged women to pummel them at any time without returning their blows.
2. Parents who are cruel do not hesitate to bruise or disfigure their unruly children.

Both distinctions hold for other cultures and animals, *mutatis mutandis*: Dominance by the strong is not cruel. Disapproval is not denunciation. It does not reject the weak. Surrender may be unconditional, but without reparations or annihilation. *(k/23)*

HIGH-RISK FAMILIES

   The first latchkey children came home from school before farming families quit working for the day. Their household life did not invite violence.

   The highest risks are in mobile families who change jobs and kids. Drugs and alcohol for both parents, and during pregnancy for the mother, substantially increase for all the risk of brain damage and violence proneness.

   Hazardous drugs (including tar with nicotine) and violent crime sequentially and directly victimize present and future generations.

   Women and children, when brought to emergency rooms, are now being evaluated as possible victims of assault by nonstrangers. But the only innovation in their management is limited to counseling against recurrence of, or providing shelter away from, further harm until now. With new findings and discerning questioning, we offer more before and after physical and emotional injury.

(5) Why are KIDS ABUSED and WOMEN BATTERED? (A Neurosocial Dilemma)

(Any dissertation on this subject must touch on beast vs. brute, altruism and dimorphism, neurology vs. sociology, clinical vs. legal intervention, noise and appeasement gestures, violence-bashing and nonviolent biases.)

The question could well imply that women and children should not be beaten. Such an implication quickly ensures that the very dilemma that the query seeks to resolve will endure from blind ignorance. We cannot grasp the horns of this dilemma if we immediately answer with "women and children need not be brutalized at all" because they are, in fact, often brutalized. "Just don't do it!" won't stop *Homo domesticus*. "Violence-bashing" by *Homo metropolis* is humanistic, but not scientific. To socialize aggression is an asexual perversion of nature.

Perhaps the query should be framed more simply to read, "Why are the weak brutalized?" Asked like this, other answers can be discovered, heard, and explored. *(k/24)*

It is even better if the question is more specific and reframed to read, "Why are women and children manhandled?" (Or as specifically in parallel cases, "Why are disturbed patients mistreated by those they disturb?" who is disturbing whom?)

The right question can discover connections that are not necessarily obvious. *(k/25)* To reply that we cannot help being beastly some of the time gets us nowhere. A better answer may be that being human, we cannot help but act like human beings.

Having to be human in order to produce a victim of cruelty, of course, needs volumes to elucidate with accuracy. But with little time and space, we have to start somewhere and be as brief as possible and curt when we cannot be courtly:

1. Violence between species guarantees their joint survival in the food cycle.
2. There are no winners in human family violence.

What does being human mean in this particular context? It means not being a beast and yet being a brute. Beasts are ruthless or single-minded, not brutal or heavy-handed. When they are not hungry, they let the weak escape their clutches even when their territorial rights have been violated.

Children and women often cannot easily escape predators (relative strangers) or angry providers (relatives) and protectors, and so a shelter for abused children and battered women is the first step toward saving the victims of domestic battles from irreparable injury.

And it works! But to stop there is to fail and risk ending up criminalizing the villain.

Hot pursuit of the "refugees" by the "predatory" male relative—far from being a sign that he had been deprived of his "prey" or that he is acting more like a paid security guard who must prevent shoplifters from getting away—is only a symptom (subjective) and a sign (objective) that his family is an extension of his territory (protectorate) that cannot be taken away from him without a fight.

Shelter keepers must then avoid hot pursuit by him because they are not shoplifters. But for protection to go beyond engineering an escape and vociferously claim afterward that a "refugee" has the right to insist on freedom from harm is to be a self-deputized sheriff who must protect civilian rights to equal treatment but cannot truly guarantee personal freedom.

(While the court may punish those who deprive others of their freedom by illegal means, it cannot guarantee to the deprived that they will thereafter be free or alive.)

1. For women to be human means that they are less skilled at appeasement gestures than animals and, in fact, as *Homo domesticus*, are traditionally taught that words are better than silence, without bothering to compare results with the less verbose. So women are battered in the process of protesting their right to retaliate by exercising freedom of speech, which is fortunately denied other more serene (silently expressive) species. *(k/26)* Psychobabble is our modern Babel. Broca's and Wernicke's areas enable us to use consonants, but only at our own risk.

2. For children to be human means that they are unable to escape injury by standing on their own two feet and taking flight. (Even as adults, we are dependent on superior force to protect us longer than other animals: and must seek court injunctions against potential assailants.) Abused children are usually those who cannot flee and must cry for help from their abusive relative who then uses more force in trying to silence them. *(k/27)*

Abused children (vocal) and wives (verbal) are more noisy than the needy (oral) or ready (agreeable). All animals make sounds; human beings use speech centers.

To be humane to women and children then means that either (1) we must take them away from brutal relatives or (2) teach them (a) to be silent in the face of attack or (b) to make appeasement gestures before the attack begins. *(k/28)*

Unless, of course, *Homo metropolis* seeks to be voluble but misguided agents of social change—or self-taught "experts" on the Bill of Rights who confuse it with civil liberties—instead of dispassionate clinicians who are acting with scientific knowledge of comparative ethology and evolved neurology.

1. In ethology, altruism is the norm only in those species characterized by dimorphism or imbalance in muscle mass between adult males and females. Is it altruistic to equalize might in the battle between the sexes? *(k/29)*
2. As for domestic violence against captive children, we have to deal with a strictly human invention. Among nonhuman primates, the young who are not yet neurologically mature do not have to please/obey two parents. *(k/30)*

So what else can we do besides wish that we had regular annual budget movements—which anal hoarders resist—to subsidize another series of community asylums in suburban America for the world's weak and oppressed?

It is also easy to see the abused and battered victim as a dog whose "master" kicks it after a hard day at the office. But mistake neither for "scapegoats," which are necessarily stronger or they have to be frequently replaced. The best scapegoats, like Satan, are beyond harm.

Dogs and children and women are hurt because they tend to forgive like Jesus and to forget, unlike His Father.

I know as a doctor and ethologist that our nervous system is geared to fight or flee and that we cannot even procreate if we are still engaged in battle or retreating from it, but only afterward as well as immediately to ensure survival of the species. (Which is why "wakes" can end up as orgies, teenagers go to horror movies, and power becomes an aphrodisiac.)

Which also explains why a woman rushes back to her husband after a brief respite in a battle that she lost, often against the advice of the managers of shelters for battered wives.

(Besides which, as *Homo domesticus*—like abused children and believers in a vengeful almighty father in heaven—she feels both guilty and forgiving.)

And the husband, not just from guilt but out of the workings of his own autonomic nervous system, welcomes her arrival with offers of food (which relaxes even "blind dates") and profuse foreplay, grooming her for sexual congress.

You see, once the "sympathetic" nervous system is exhausted by fighting or fleeing, its mate in the autonomic regulation of animal behavior—namely, the parasympathetic nervous system—takes over and can expeditiously proceed to digest food that it has ingested and to preserve the species by procreation. *(k/31)*

Some may protest that we cannot treat our men, women, and children as just members of the animal species. We can only reply that as philosophers we cannot, nor are we claiming to be philosophizing. (Yeats wrote that fantasies make hearts brutal.) *(k/32)*

To answer our original query nonrhetorically, women and children are not brutalized by the beastly, but are traumatized on the field of battle that they cannot leave without protest. (All battles, animal or human, are intended to resolve conflicting claims.)

My daughter once told her son to let his cousin go because she did not like being pinned down. I said he would if she stopped struggling. I was wryly reminded that my grandson had not read my work on ethology. But he let her get up as soon as she stopped fighting fire with fire.

For sound clinical practice, to be "client-centered" for whoever needs a leaning post is not enough, nor just simply to be "'system'-conscious" *(k/15)*. We need to be species-oriented at the risk of sounding socially or legally naive. We cannot solve domestic violence by deputizing the police—a new Goferobot—to enforce order by keeping the protagonists apart.

An abused child has, like all of us, an already evolved nervous system that is equipped to cry for succor if threatened and unable to fight or flee. And every woman, like all men, is socially equipped with an alternative vocabulary to protest wordlessly without recriminations.

(Gandhi discovered that cavalry horses, with instinctive "sportsmanship," would not trample prostrate demonstrators despite urgings to do so by their riders. He did not need to make speeches to the British. Martin Luther King, who enjoyed preaching, was much less successful!)

We must also not just think in social terms or the system of values that accrue from domesticity while ignoring established ethological norms and a universally evolved nervous system. To do so may make us better social advocates, but not better professionals in socially "hot" clinical issues:

Wife-beating and conflicted divorces rose after women started working and swearing like sailors. Even in the soft social sciences (humanities), we cannot be human racists (anthropocentrists). We must insist on a clinical, nonlegal, non-client-centered intervention.

All behavior, including body language, is communication, seldom misunderstood unless noise interferes with direct transmission.

Words can cut deeper, and the invisible scars can remind us of the battle longer than external bruises from flying fists or flailing arms.

My violent female patients and I have fond memories of each other and learned from our fighting more than we could have from talking. (Nonviolent people should not presume to look after the violent.)

We certainly must not increase the volume of hot air in an already overheated habitat. Which we tend to do by disinformation (language abuse and misuse) in this Age of Rhetoric. *(k/33)*

Unlike politicians, we cannot favor incisive speech over blunt instruments when engaged in resolving conflicting claims. Only professional surgeons must be licensed to wield the scalpel if the incision is not to damage wantonly.

What disturbs the brute is not force but noise. Violent relatives are puritans against noise pollution at home. Noise annoys them more than loud sounds.

What the victims need to escape unhurt is a sure way of sidetracking a rushing bull. Just as it is a serious mistake to stop a tank with platitudes—"people power" in the Philippines succeeded with flowers and food from nuns and young girls for soldiers in their tanks, not offered by confrontational males in Beijing—so also is it prudent to flee noiselessly from a raging bull and then from a distance sort out what enraged him. (Whether the field is greener on the other side of the fence is a separable issue.)

One may cow the "bull" of a brute with a big stick or loud threats of imprisonment, but one must know more precisely why whatever works does, not why it should because the batterer or abuser is as human as you and I, or a clone from Adam's rib (an indefensible ideological ambush for lingual lashing of the animal under our thumb).

After we hit our thumb with a hammer and there is bleeding under the fingernail, the pain can quickly be relieved by drilling through the nail to let the blood trapped under it escape. So also must we provide ventilation for accumulated poison in the air.

How do we replace the hot air of embattled households with fresh air? We only increase the tolerance of the occupants for polluted air by desensitization to verbal red-flag waving. It is better to combine the following to keep the doctor/police/lawyers away:

1. Battered wives are usually counseled separately from husbands by nonviolent "talkative therapists" who are uncomfortable with violence. (Practitioners cannot have narrower comfort zones than patients.) Husbands are similarly seen together as a group, as they are now in the new "Men's Movement" against failed fathers of impotent sons. (Would Viagra reduce their need for support groups?) Both these approaches are outgrowths of identifying the needy separately from the needed.

    Unsatisfactory results invite defensive stigmatization. It is better to see both partners, preferably at home, as we now do in family and sex therapy, where the whole family and total bedroom behaviors are more accessible for intervention beyond rehashing the past.

    (When I find the porch-light unlit, the scheduled family therapy session at home proves to be of lower priority than when the house is ablaze with lights.)

2. Try holding your spouse by the sleeve or little finger (if you have marveled at how perfect it is in an infant: silence in the presence of beauty is an invitation to be at our best), with your head bowed (examining the digit, to distract him) against his upper arm (to keep him close without clinging to him) while speaking from your heart about your present hurts and future hopes, never of past disillusionments and disappointments. And speak softly so that your spouse has to listen hard to hear you instead of rehearsing a rebuttal or refutation, which would be out of place since you are only talking about now and yourself alone.

3. Film strips of appeasement gestures by Meryl Streep (she did strip for *Silkwood* where, however, she displayed fewer appeasement mannerisms) that are the best available for highly articulate women can be very instructive, notwithstanding what so-called "cognitive psychology" (brain stuffing of adults) recommends. *(k/34)*

But role-playing or mirroring successful or imaginary models may be too late for those already brainwashed as children to talk back. "Choice" of other legendary or celebrated images may also be already biased/colored/doomed for "losers" by prior failures to change deep-seated unsuccessful coping behavior.

Encore performances are guaranteed by the same cast of characters with different script names. (Typecasting and sequels succeed among those afraid of novelty.)

4.   Social exclusion soon leads to criminal prosecution. As a last resort, the court on my uncontested recommendation deported an Asian mother who killed her baby to shut it up. Once home, she would have help from her extended family with her other children whom she had been able to cope with before her American husband brought them here.

Otherwise, she would have to be locked up and their children farmed out to foster homes that taxpayers subsidize. This is also closing the barn door after the horse turns up missing.

It is scientific malpractice, compounded by human arrogance, to expect a family to disown their animal heritage and it's "fine-tuning" to fit, from childhood on, the size of a modern Procrustean bed that it did not design. To ensure peace by the absence of challenge is to retreat from struggling to adapt better to life, which changes with age.

(6) To KILL or NOT To KILL or LET BE KILLED (An Educational Dilemma)

When a battered wife chooses silence, fights back like a man, and becomes lethal, the courts can accord her the right to self-defense and acquit her on grounds of justifiable homicide. (Homicide requires tools that dangerous animals do without.)

Otherwise, unlike justifiable homicide and active euthanasia, absent sufficient social consensus about what bugs us—which is not easy to explain to kids or their elders—killing becomes murder:

It is but a short journey from killing bugs to hounding "buggers" who must not be allowed, as convicted murderers, to live out their natural life span.

Early indoctrination also sanctions mass murder by *Homo domesticus* and *H. metropolis* in the name of God, country, etc. And not letting one get killed is then and there overcome by fear of loss of solidarity with fellow travelers.

Animals defend themselves, tooth and claw, but do not regard battles as crusades. Vengeance is properly not our business, unless acting as agents of prophesied or popularly elected superiors.

Contract killers are the only murderers who are truly "rational" (calculating on the basis of cost/benefit ratios) and therefore subject to the legal quasi-mathematical operation of the talionic principle of "a tooth (or claw) for a tooth (or claw)."

(This is, of course, simplistic and arbitrary, like arithmetic and geometry. [Algebra and physics are better computational models for behavioral investigation.])

(7) CAPITAL PUNISHMENT (A Medicolegal Dilemma)

In capital cases, the questions sometimes posed are as follows:

1. a. Should a surgeon operate on an acute appendicitis just before a scheduled execution?

   b. Would a doctor rather have the convict die of natural causes?

2. Is there shared guilt in electrocuting or suffocating a successfully treated patient on "death row"?

3. a. Should a psychiatrist certify that a convict is competent to understand capital punishment, or

   b. treat a patient—who is found contractually incompetent to accept his sentence—in order for him to begin serving it?

Where the politics of penology touched the prisoner but not the physician, no guilt needs to be shared except by appointed jurors and elected legislators, judges, or prosecutors. If they are not cannibals, they have no business as animals in killing another. If they kill legally, they probably could not help what they had been taught, just as the criminal couldn't help himself enough.

Only the chief executive cannot legally deny clemency unless prudence compels him to be cowardly and grateful toward his own employer, the political majority, which is also not entirely his fault.

No one (except some honest jurors) would easily acknowledge their hidden cowardice because regret or rejoicing (especially among avaricious expert witnesses who want to remain anonymous in order to practice their craftiness with a professional mantle of credibility) is easier, respectively, to accept or deny. (Wars waged by men are also fueled by fear of betraying crawling cowardice and/ or creeping ingratitude to their comrades at arms. To lose one's life in order to preserve "solidarity" with others conscripted by total strangers is sheer folly. "Conscientious objection" is no solution for Homo sapiens.)

There are prestigious consultants who, on the record, have recommended that physicians—instead of ministering to the sick patient, who happens to be a prisoner—flatly deny treatment to the person who is sick on death row. As Homo metropolis, they must know more, if only from the sidelines, about persons (including themselves), prisons, and death rows. But from whom and exactly what (besides their bias) must remain a secret (for each to continue masquerading as a humanistic, but not humane, healer).

Obviously, one who is without divided institutional loyalties treats all hospitalized patients, even incarcerated prisoners. If the prisoner dies for what he was convicted of, it is not the doctor who executed him. (If medical treatment or psychiatric certification was intended to kill the convict, the doctor must partake of the remains instead of simply mourning the social side effects of his professional calling.)

Cancer and crime can be traced, sometimes, to learned lifestyles in which the victim and villain are bystanders from the beginning.

CONCLUSIONS, IMPLICATIONS, SPECULATIONS

Ivan Pavlov was awarded the Nobel Prize right away for training dogs to salivate over "meaning" attributed to preprogrammed co-incidences (*sic*).

We can look again into each chain of con-sequences (*sic*) instead of purposes or causes—dying is just the end of living—but only after understanding the circumstances that preceded, without necessarily prompting, their emergence.

Then we need to be concerned with effects rather than motives (excuses) or ends and begin to compare what are more originally homologous in derivation than logically analogous by analysis: Analogy is a poet's precious gift, homology a scientist's "open sesame." Do you identify with aggressors (bullfighters, a jealous Jehovah who evicts the tempted but helpless anal Republican accountants or with victims (bulls, Jesus, or oral Democrats who wish to feed the hungry)?

Violence and destruction, cosmically and terrestrially—as far back in time as we can go—precede creation and renewal or rebirth. Our own lives started with domestic violence when we were evicted forcefully from the womb. Our head and brain were squeezed and even our genitals abused when some of us were immediately circumcised. (Circumcision is the only operation more frequently performed than abortion.)

> More crowded and less circumcised, Hong Kong and Amsterdam are less violent than less-crowded American cities with no fewer churches, where human racists (NRA) and white racists (KKK) are defended by biblical and constitutional fundamentalists (animals are inferior to man and Negros are only three-quarters human). Both kinds of learned racism, white and human, are abominations of nature. And not just simply rewarded geographically [as claimed by Jared Diamond, the author of *The Third Chimpanzee* (or *Homo sapiens*).
>
> (Time [timing], more than space [crowding], accounts for the covert battle between the sexes because the penis and nipples [in androgynes] will erect without embarrassment according to their own agendas.)

Whatever one does in the name of ideology dooms even disbelievers if we are biologically one family. Human dilemmas arise from our cerebral cortex, not the vegetative nervous system.

> Sex and violence are separately mediated outside the brain and cannot be fused, even with the plunging necklines of black leather dresses. Neurologically, no one can stay erect while cowering in fear, physically or sexually. Among animals, male rivals compete

before the victor mates with the female of smaller size. In nature, there is liberty, there is carnality, there is no equality. Only after equality became standard ideology was the battle of the sexes added to human activity.

Domestication by criminalization of aggression is as perverse as sublimation of senso-sexual "self-abuse" by psychosocial introspection about why we are here. (Other animals masturbate without suspecting that idleness is the devil's workshop.)

My father used to joke about man being created on a Friday when God was exhausted and not as careful and that the Great Deluge was a middle-age tantrum (alternatively, oxymoronic political science claims that absolute power corrupts absolutely when, in fact, power corrupts only the corruptible) and siring Jesus a grandfatherly gesture! Wholesale drowning and suffocation by crucifixion (diaphragm immobilized, as in lynching) end up "washing away all sins" by irreversible decortication.)

Biologically, there is the right to kill in order to live, but not the right to die for *Homo sapiens*. For *H. domesticus* and *H. metropolis*, there is fear of death and fear of failure. Life for each then becomes a curriculum or test that one must pass to get promoted even unto heaven, after applying for admission with the right credentials.

Animals and *Homo sapiens* take calculated risks and fail, but the calculation is not from fear of dying, but in order to live and multiply. There is thus (**i**) the freedom to live, (**ii**) the right to fail, and (**iii**) the need to multiply. *H. domesticus* who must not fail live lives of quiet desperation, which is hell on earth for ambitious *H. metropolis*. If their scapegoats are sturdy (God, Satan, heroic black icons like O. J. Simpson), they may rest comfortably but never peacefully.

All modern social progress seems to have been achieved at the expense of children—laps now hold computers instead—in order for their parents to be able to compete better with adults. Duties to children remain unchanged and should not be confused with rights against or responsibilities for partners.

11.00 k/VIOLENCE

k/Chapter Notes

[k/1] In the most violent country in the world, Americans killed 4,000 women and 5,000 children out of 10,000 domestic deaths in the first year of the last decade of the twentieth century.

[k/2] The world was surprised when civilized Aryans used technology to kill millions of Jews and again when Manila, Managua, and Moscow suddenly changed direction, but Beijing and Bucharest did not immediately follow, even after the Berlin Wall fell sooner than anyone anticipated.

George Santayana (1863–1952) was wrong in predicting that those who are ignorant of history are bound to repeat the same errors. Our era has spawned more historians than all of history has ever known. Yet no one foresaw what eventually happened to old enemies (Japan, Germany, and Russia).

[k/3] There are three different kinds of intelligent coping behavior, namely, aerial, aquatic, and terrestrial. Our kind is different from that of dolphins because of the environment (not geography) around us.

Pound for pound, we have larger secondary genital organs than they have, but they have bigger brains. We also have opposable thumbs, like dinosaurs who, as winged amphibians, shared aerial, aquatic, and terrestrial habitats with all. (They survived longer than we have so far.)

We must breathe in and out (inspire and expire) or we hyperventilate. We have to drink (hydrophobia is fatal). We must sweat (hyper or hypothermia may be irreversible). We need to eat (anorexia beyond forty days is dangerous). We must replace our progenitors or we become extinct.

Thus, to survive, we require air, water, warmth (clothing and shelter), food, and sexual partners. To live, we can do without the last. These are all that life asks.

Life, in fact, is interesting in itself. Not realizing that to want it to do things for you can only be presumptuous. It already knows what it can do; all you have to do is simply go ahead and live it to the end. To do otherwise is to change it just to suit yourself.

The wiser you are, the less often will your acquired tastes dictate what you need.

All *Homo sapiens* need to do is whatever they can, as long as they can say approximately when they began to assume what is "self-evident." Each such assumption—even if internally consistent and invulnerable to direct attack—may be a subspecies delusion, regardless of the logic of prevailing consensus (e.g., in the old premise of a flat earth).

[k/4] From Groups to Gangs or Cults to Sects (Splinter Groups)

Acceptance of failure is acknowledgment of the limits of our genetic heritage. Cheating among adult social climbers and gang membership for the young and alienated can allay/confirm doubts that their parents are flawed. ("Machismo" for adolescent gangsters comes from shared prestige that attracts the opposite sex.)

"Sense of failure" (chronic need to overcome) may complicate testosterone poverty among noncharismatic cult leaders of nonviolent sitdown strikes against racial discrimination, to reverse which the oppressed must go to the election booth in droves, even in Atlanta, Georgia, of the Deep South.

Groups become gangs if the need for affection (e.g., from the Catholic Church) becomes the need for direction (e.g., in the Cosa Nostra) for *Homo domesticus*. Groupies then become gangsters. Groupies are children of all ages in need of father figures of all ages; gangsters are adolescents of all ages in need of stronger leaders. The difference is that children outgrow their fathers (even if they are rock stars or gurus) and they are called agnostics; gangsters only change leaders (dictators), and they obey orders. When religious leaders get a large enough flock of sheep, they go from heading a cult to that of a sect before being recognized as a church after their militancy (gangsterism) becomes attenuated (doctrinaire).

[k/5] Is euthanasia either or both an ethical and therefore social issue, or a clinical and therefore scientific dilemma, or both? Is the answer a social revolution and/or a scientific analysis of the issues?

There have also been other revolutions in science, and society is only now slowly recognizing the revolutionary scientific discoveries of radicals who unintentionally made liars of their parents, like Copernicus, Galileo, Darwin, Pavlov, Freud, Lorenz, and Goodall.

[k/6] Try to distinguish the "oral" self-indulgent (**A'A**) spender (*Homo metropolis*) from the "anal" overachieving (**BB**) doer and the successful (**CC**) "talking heads" (*Homo domesticus*) as to their primary pathogenic partner (mother, authority [or **F → H**]) or peer.

Subspecies "demons" (goading one to overspend, another to accumulate inconspicuously, and the other to be envied: "If only they can see me now!") are different, but they may share each other's drivenness, depending on whatever dominated their domestication at any stage of their senso-moral (**i**) or socioethical (**ii**), not psychosexual (Freud's) or psychosocial (Erikson's), development.

[k/7] WELTANSCHAUUNG

This is the social (**ii**) equivalent of Lorenz's "umwelt" (subjective or stimulus world) in every person (**i**), developed in other animals by "imprinting" during the early critical stages of their development.

Choose your client's underlying worldview (ideology) and compare or contrapose with your own weltanschauung:

a.   Life is a game, everyone plays games.
b.   Life is a parent; it should take care of me.
c.   Life is a bargain (vs. it is a bonus for those who have survived hard times).
d.   Life is a hard bargain. (To justify euthanasia: Life is a bitch, it won't let go.)
e.   Life is a pimp, it should make me happy. (To practicing hedonists: Life is a beach.)

f. Life is an obstacle course without purpose (vs. life is meaningless but fun).

g. Life is a trial by ordeal that must be won.

h. Life is a curriculum that proffers credentials.

i. Life is change.

j. Life is a conspiracy; trust with utmost caution.

k. Life is fear of failure, escalating into the terror of annihilation, ending in a horror of oblivion.

l. Life is anxiety, always verging on panic over impossible deadlines of uneven but inevitable urgency.

m. Life is unresolved guilt, mounting into agitation, with peace always beyond reach. (Popular with Jews.)

n. Life is work toward retirement or extended vacation from it.

o. Life is the use of daylight to sleep better at night.

p. Life is a chain of joys and dangers, ending in death, not defeat (the good fight goes on). (Author's stance!) (This last explains the author's yielding to weak opposition and putting up a fight only if the risk of losing is great, which puzzles his trainees but encourages them not to retreat against worthy rivals, including him. (To bully the weak is reserved exclusively only for Mama's boy. To threaten wheat-poor Russia with economic sanctions in the form of a grain embargo is pure machismo, unworthy of a reincarnation of Mrs. Roosevelt's liberal compulsions in Mrs. Carter's oldest.)

[k/8] WORKAHOLISM

Compare your/hir (*sic*) "work style" (which may be as revealing as body images and self-estimates or time sense [below] and lifestyles [above]):

a. Work is an opiate.

b. Work is a prison.

c. Work is a window to the world. (Freud thought work anchored adults to reality.)

d. Work is a security blanket.

e. Work is a weatherproof refuge. (Symbolic or not, and less true in the tropics, which may account for local underdevelopment.)

f.   Work is a screen against intrusion by the "petty," e.g., welfare eligibility examiners. In turn, working is unsuccessful as a screen for those critical of obese welfare recipients: "Equal calories = equal work" is good physics and metabolic medicine but poor social science ($J + K$).

g.   Work, for *Homo domesticus* is an insulation against cold reality. (Loyal bachelors and spinsters may be against union activity, like picketing, slowing down, or striking.)

h.   Work for *Homo metropolis* is an island away from intimacy: unilateral "ass-kissing" is expected and only mutual "back-scratching" is allowed by reciprocity in superior-subordinate hierarchy. (Neither party as partners is able to relax at office parties and becomes virtually a divorcee even if married, commuting to work from a single-family day care center run by the spouse.)

i.   Work for *Homo sapiens* is the wife, the wife the mistress. (This describes my work style.)

[k/9] STATES OF SELF-ALIENATION

See if your sense of body rhythms is congruent with your sense of time:

1.   Time is everything. (Those with spatially oriented right brain would disagree and claim that position or topology, as distinguished from geography, is everything. Author finds deadlines too artificial [arbitrary].)

2.   Time is money. (The parsimonious would disagree with the punctual and claim that money is everything.)

3.   Time waits for no one. (The ambitious feels that life is too short.)

4.   Time is absolute.

5.   Time can be wasted.

6.   Time can be borrowed.

7.   Time can be loaned. (The religious would claim only God, as prime lender, can check our credit ratings.)

8.   Time can be shared. (These are the sort who would classify time as quality time or fun time.)

9.   Time can be bought. (These people will travel by supersonic jets on their vacation.)

10. There is a time and place for everything.

11. Time heals.

12. Time decides the end. (These are the debtors waiting to be foreclosed by the Grim Reaper.)
13. Time is a deadline. (Crisis-ridden, everything at the moment seems to be almost a matter of life and death.)
14. Time drags on and on. (These feel left behind, but know no way of catching up and feel betrayed by their biological clocks.)
15. Time flies too fast. (There is some regret that they were distracted even if enormously enjoying them.
16. Time crawls along. (Not much is happening or about to happen.)
17. Time races by. (Barely able to stay on top or up to date.)
18. Time is becoming.
19. Time is the beginning.
20. Time is what the clock says it is. (No inferences or blame should be placed on mere intervals.)
21. Time is elastic. (This is absolute relativity even within Newtonian parameters, unrelated to Einstein's theory.)
22. Time is a taskmaster.
23. Time is a whipping boy.
24. Time spins up, in and out.
25. Time and motion studies are a waste of time.

[k/10] LEVELS OF PASSIVE ALIENATION
1. "Minority mindedness" means being better at accepting different forms of loving (or the need to complain for *Homo metropolis*) than different levels of alienation (or the demand to explain by *Homo domesticus*), both of which are historically determined but, nevertheless, personalized.
2. Alienists must also distinguish between minority victims (powerless), dropouts (abdicators), and alienation (among ambitious social ladder climbers or workaholics).
3. Those who have not dropped out may (a) accuse as minority victims, or (b) be alienated minorities demanding equal opportunity to be loved, or (c) themselves be charged with "sexual harassment" of members of a minority.
4. The sequence listed below imply progressive desperation among those who are alienated present company (not a social butterfly for whom this book would have been distasteful to read) excepted as follows:

a. Dismay that others are more upwardly mobile, self-congratulation for hard-earned mobility (taken for granted among animals) and a reactive search (**A** x **F**) for roots (trees also topple if too tall from reaching out for their place in the sun).

b. Denial of animal origins (**N**), invention of superpowers (**F** or **G**) as "parents," patricide when disillusioned (God is dead), population control to preserve prosperity for posterity: "Abort (**V, f**) the bastards, we love (**A**) children!"

c. Although unlike dropouts who in deed denigrate unearned blessings (inherited power or **G**, wealth or **H**, and health), the alienated nevertheless search for instantaneous sensations, even out of brain pollution to amplify dreams and also use meditation to still agitation (**B'**), medication to sedate by reducing mental irritability (**C'**) or stimulants to increase "spontaneity" (**A**) by disinhibition of "superego" (**F**).

d. Nostalgia for the extended family destroyed by piecework in factory towns (**K**), "me too" (**I**) approach to "nuclear" parenting (impermissive or not), unionization with littermates to participate in family or corporate decisions (**H** x **J**), decapitation of (**G**) heads of state by assassination or electioneering.

e. Search for meaning (**C**) in martyrdom (**F**) or heroism (**G**), including manliness or gentleness for both sexes; exclusion of fashionable untouchables, including chauvinists, etc.: **GG** or "jingoist" if patriotic, or "sexist" if (**B'**) unfair, (**W, m**) rapists, (**H'**) vagrants, etc.

f. Indecisive relationships with (**F**) God, (**iii**) partners, (**ii**) peers, and/or (**i**) offspring.

g. Fanaticism for excellence in sports (**B**) and techniques (**K**) that surpass animals with the help of mechanical prostheses: playful professionals (*Homo sapiens*) burn out later than workaholics (of both other subspecies).

h. Rituals of worship of the (**iii**) flesh or its "opposite," (**F**) the spirit.

i. Conspicuous consumption (**L**) or "secret vices" (**iii'**).

    j. Resentment over any further delay in recognition (**C**), appreciation (**D**), affection (**A**), union (**iii**, unisexual mutuality, or androgyny), etc.

    k. Despair over irregular rewards (**D**) or implied promises (**F**) without deadlines.

    l. Self-realization of need for inaccessible or undependable (**F** -> **H**) "allies" or fear of (**I**) independent failure.

    m. Indignation with strangers (**G**) competing (**B**) in areas where the estranged cannot excel.

    n. Outrage at friends and relatives (passive, not active, dropouts) who die or withdraw from the alienated.

5. Only the last two (m, n) spell actual isolation. All other forms of alienation can be ameliorated, if not eradicated.

6. "Dropping back in" to adult "nurseries" (**A'**) and "kindergartens" (**B'**) on weekends under cult gurus can be mentally addictive (**C'**) for the alienated.

7. Acidheads who drop out would rather depend on internal titillation with drugs than by kindred spirits.

    With toxic tuning out, time has been transcended as the central preoccupation by getting the central nervous system intoxicated with its own immediate perceptions while ignoring what is happening nearby.

[k/11]   NEUROTICISSIMUS EXISTENTIALIS

Affluent rebel, / Living on raisins,
A rolling stone / From the desert plains,
Searching, yearning / For the mountaintop,
But refusing to rise / From the ranks /
In ritual irrelevance
Opting instead / To grow grass on the farm, /
Or drop acid in the slums,
To escape / The emptiness /
Of the Establishment,
"Because all common sense. /
"Becomes an ego trip in the end."

But getting busted instead /
From battling boredom with dope,
Or drinking to deny nagging doubts, /
Until his brains give out;
Coping with crisis by cracking up, /
Yet shrinking from shrinks,
Except those who are "stoned" /
From murmuring mantras,
To fill the silence / Of their science,
Once they mixed up / Mood with doom,
And mistook their malaise / For their soul.

(By befriending drugs, "hippies" are lost *Homo domesticus*, who have no ambition to join what we now call "yuppies" or *Homo metropolis*. Those who drop in without brain damage (below)—like the author after decortication from drowning—can be more tolerant *Homo sapiens* who see both subspecies as not more responsible than paranoids for their self-defensive beliefs/ delusions.)

8. Those in transition between alienation and addiction (a) do both "trips" with drugs or other "friends" ("gurus" instead of God for *Homo dome*sticus) or (b) seek success *as H. metropolis* (to be remembered while forgetting past and foregoing present family ties) instead of sex (or memories to enjoy again in the future) among *Homo sapiens* (whom both other subspecies now enviously dismiss as "sex addicts").

PSEUDO-DYSLEXIA TARDA (An Alternative Diagnosis)

1. As in some dyslexic children, poor psychomotor coordination raises doubts about a healthy mind in a healthy body (the brain evolved to manage muscle).
2. a. As in tardy and acute (**iii'**) sexual perversion, undefended as "preference" or "orientation" (both or either necessarily chronic by definition), test patient for early organic disease:
    b. Suspect latent "dyslexia" in abrupt acceptance of the fatherhood of God, instant brotherhood of man and sudden

sisterhood of the species, e.g., among acute vegetarians. (History may suggest subtle brain damage from drug use, abuse, or misuse.)

[k/12] Bioethical Test Question: Name two ethical principles involved in the right to die or the right to live.

Choose your answer and compare what you would do as a democrat or gerontocrat:

First-Level Answer (admissible according to the legal code): It is illegal (1) to commit suicide but not (2) to defend your life even by homicide if it is justified by social consensus after the fact.

Second-Level Answer (satisfactory according to common law): The right to die or the right to live must examine both (1) (a) sanctity or (b) quality of life and (2) the sanctioned (a) autonomy of the patient and (b) changing priorities of society. (This is rationalization.)

Third-Level Answer (ideal according to natural law): There is (a) right to life but no duty to die; there is only (b) the right to fail and (c) the opportunity to multiple.

[k/13] A debating society is too ridiculous for words if it insists on tidiness not only in recall and rhetoric for its ear but also on fresh personal garments to protect its nose and/or on neatness in its private residence to please its eyes.

[k/14] Holland has legalized euthanasia for more people, including the newborn, than any other country in the world. (It has also legalized prostitution and substance abuse.)

Their first neonate who raised doubts about being allowed to live had a split penis, but even after its conversion into a functional vagina, incontinence still persisted. The next was colon obstruction in an infant with Down syndrome, who was allowed to die without surgical intervention. The only handicapped infant that Dr. Molnar, who pioneered neonatal euthanasia, refused to sacrifice despite its parents' wishes was born without arms or legs. (They can live longer, unencumbered, in outer space.)

Thus, the newborn with genital and mental handicaps were not thought to be deserving of a better quality of life than the physically disabled. (Power is sought, impotence feared.) Voluntary purpose and control enhances, but does not define life.

For adults, euthanasiasts feel in control of the way they spend the rest of their lives. Fear of loss of control is a human embarrassment. "Control" thus becomes a question of attitude, not one of conquest, even of incontinence. (Nor is unassisted suicide a victory; physician assistance merely ensures success.)

The need to find purpose in suffering makes euthanasia attractive. (Purposiveness is also a human invention.)

But legalizing euthanasia can easily victimize those who cannot even decide about their lives before they become disabled. That includes many of us, but especially most minority groups who are either disenfranchised or poor or poor and old.

[k/15] All animal behavior was originally regulated by the vegetative nervous system (ignored by "system theory" formulations), which still enjoys autonomic control over violence and sex, no matter how hard our cerebral cortex programs our thinking with dreams of utopia, now or in the hereafter. Neurologically, our cerebral cortex is like an adolescent who is full of ideas but has no experience, yet quickly criticizes its elders for not letting it take over right away.

From animals to people, waiting proceeds to stalking or fleeing, standing to fighting or kneeling, thinking to planning or praying, sorting to mapping or exploring, surprise to inventing or toolmaking. When the urge to multiply overtakes any such less-urgent pursuits, we dress up for dates, dinner, and dancing, mentally or actually undressing each other for debauchery, erotic or carnal, seductive or sexual, sedentary or horizontal, before we die in time or on our own.

One only needs to commit enough energy in order to exist, and the excess energy that is hereditary can be used for something other than getting food and warmth. Why work hard at playing when one can relax instead?

Unlike us, no other animal works more than it absolutely has to, nor ever feels naked when idle. Or would sacrifice its sleep unless surrounded by enemies.

[k/16] When I was in medical school, doing everything to keep a patient alive was called "heroic." In England, I was asked to calculate whether such heroic measures were cost-effective before I ordered them when on emergency call. I refused to let cost cloud my judgment on what is medically indicated, and I was removed from the night-duty roster. I was able to sleep a few more hours, but some patients did not live a few more days.

I did not go to medical school to be an accountant. Now doctors are being asked to make educated guesses about whether a patient will die in six months or sooner so that they can be treated accordingly, including assisting to die.

Personally, I do not want to die as long as I can see my nurses or feel them or their touch. I don't have to move many muscles or talk (my father could not manage his tongue after his stroke) or hear their voice or smell their presence (odors are for tracking prey or predators, or sexual stimulation).

(Expecting to suffer from a stroke like my father, I have surrounded our house with paved walks where I can wheel my wheelchair around and around and have connected our bedroom to the grandchildren's tree house with a suspension bridge. Have also added a ramp.)

[k/17] We used to think that what distinguishes us from animals is that we know that we are going to die but not when. Then we begin to lose our belief in our own immortality soon after our first series of defeats.

We may be different from other animals in being death-conscious. Today, we are emphasizing that distinction from other species by selecting the timing of our dying. We have now "decided" on the terms of our surrender after repeated defeats.

We have even stopped asking to live happily ever after, or hoping for a "happy ending in the hereafter (A') among angels in heaven, and only ask that we die without loss of dignity (unsoiled, **B**) or lucidity (**C**).

[k/18] There is also the "vegetarians' mentality," which would sacrifice "vegetables" in coma because they cannot think. But they are still more tolerant than those who sacrifice fertilized eggs because they are not yet "hatched," which characterize enthanasiasts who are eugeneticists with an "abortionist mentality."

[k/19] Casanova wrote, "If to think is to live, then I have vegetated for eight years!" If we only kill ourselves after sexual satisfaction has proved beyond our reach, does our spirit reside in our gonads?

We have a biologically valid intuition across cultures that only our seeds are immortal. Is that what makes erotic lethargy a sufficiently terminal reason to kill ourselves?

Some insects die right after the act of procreation. Some men half seriously wish to die the same way from a heart attack or from a bullet in the back while escaping from a conjugal bedroom that belongs to another.

A clear memory without self-deception is mental health. In New Guinea, where farming started ahead of Adam's biblical family only 10,000 years ago, once the power of speech is gone, the sick is buried alive because they believe that the soul resides in their throat. In England, one who is not a criminal can be killed if no longer lucid, perhaps in the unspoken understanding that the spirit resides in the mind. In America, the patient who becomes incontinent or comatose can be allowed to die, probably from an unstated suspicion that the spirit resides in the sphincters or other muscle groups. Must we offer euthanasia to the bedridden who cannot move like animals and can only vegetate like plants?

An arthritic mother of one of my trainees committed suicide even if she was not terminally ill. Was her loss of mobility the underlying reason? She used to enjoy dancing the Charleston in her youth. Did she mourn the loss of sensuality that plants cannot experience, namely, proprioception, especially during copulation? Did her eggs or soul live in her joints? (A sense of animal well-being comes to us from our joints, which distinguishes us from vegetation).

Must doctors take responsibility for having prolonged life beyond reasonable costs to keep us going? And therefore should agree to assist the suicidal, for whatever reasons that they care to cite to justify their dying with our help? Not unless we have prolonged life only to keep on getting paid for the care of the living. If we were that greedy, more of us would be specializing in geriatrics.

All terminal cases, of course, see our muscles as separating us from plants that can only vegetate where their seeds have taken root. It is therefore not at all surprising that when we can no longer move like an animal and can only vegetate like plants, we could accept being killed. Just because our muscles cannot be idle and should be used, must we produce until we drop? The idle only stagnates and cannot produce while plants continue producing while they vegetate. Or is it our idle mind that we want to stop from fantasizing?

Don't plants also have souls? Both animals and vegetables are supposed to have them, but we seem to reserve the hereafter only for human souls. Plants and animals, like us, of course, take on another life after death as we all continue in our planetary carbon dioxide cycle. Are we reconstituted in body but not in spirit when we are recycled?

I have used spirit and soul interchangeably because the Greeks believed in spirits until Aristotle combined them all in the psyche. Not until after St. Thomas Aquinas mistranslated psyche to soul and then made the soul immortal can psychologists begin to specialize in whatever was left of the ancient psyche in succeeding generations.

Throughout medical school in the University of Santo Tomas, we only heard of the soul in rational psychology courses. We dissected dead cats and the cadavers of paupers to learn about what lies under our own skin. In my own specialty of psychiatry, I have also used mammals and other animals to learn about basic behavior, including violence and dying, love and altruism.

(k/20) From Stark REALITIES to Conceptual FANTASIES

"STAINED GLASS WINDOW" between the DARK AGES and the AGE of SCIENCE

(Ancient cathedrals use sunlight, like old moviemaking, to highlight powerful biblical scenes for the illiterate.)

SEX and VIOLENCE: NEUROLOGY and PSYCHO-SOCIOLOGY of STRESS and STRAIN

Structure derives from functions, symbols develop from sharing, centralization institutionalizes systemic abuses.

The vegetative nervous system is autonomous or able to make us breathe or not, etc., whether we like it or not. What is autonomous may be orderly but does not imply control. DNA may be split, but only the combinations will change. Mutant combinations can be biological monsters only if they cannot multiply.

The autonomics is Dionysian and instinctively biosocial, the cortex Apollonian and ideologically humanistic, a public relations amateur that disinforms us about our Dionysian autonomic nervous system, substituting intellectual hypochondriasis of abstract thinking for a more visceral lust for living. Because fighting and fleeing are complementary in the autonomics, I can't further polarize cowardice and heroism except as prudence and recklessness. Neither is bad, but cowardice and heroism, prudence and recklessness are all name-calling by the cortex.

[k/21] Proudly offered by *Homo metropolis* is the afterthought that self-scheduled dying is, after all, only an exercise of their divinely imposed freedom of choice. Being free is not the freedom to choose under what conditions one will stay or die. To be free is to be unchained by choices, including choosing between exercising or abdicating the right not to choose what others can withdraw. Such precious "freedom of choice" is no more than the "right to reject," and those who exult in choosing may well be gloating in rejecting. But they can only reject the vulnerable and accessible. Their exclusion may add to a bully's self-congratulation. Bullying either an adoring suitor or an unwanted child is simple exploitation, not an occasion for celebration or exultation.

Freedom to choose one's parents is as important as the first move in chess. Thereafter, the range of options progressively shrink until a stalemate (coma) or checkmate (death) is reached. Yet chess does not cease to be enjoyable. Why not enjoy life as much and for as long as the game goes on and decide from data, not desire or dismay, even when we are losing? (Original sin has been sold as the first chess move in the game of life. What keeps the game going must then be the equality of skills between God and Satan, His designated deputy/temptor.)

[k/22] In animal life and before there were farming communities, the mother or family were there to serve the offspring, not the father or society nor herself. A mother cat, GG, is a maternal model of altruism. Another, R., is a social model of altruism. GG flees from sister R., who is the matriarch of their group and dislikes GG for her affectionate nature, which earns her special treats from generous housewives. My wife suspected R. of trying to weed out the weak from her litter so that she ended only with one, whom she barely pays attention to.

[k/23] "Strong" means "staying power": (Germany in the first and Japan in the Second World War were overwhelming for more than the first half of the conflict but could not maintain superiority.) Reparations against the German kaiser helped Hitler. American demand for Japanese disavowal of militarism is more like parental "grounding" of an errant adolescent. Today, when staying home does not isolate, phone privileges may have to be curtailed and computer games probably denied. (As denial of liberty of movement or association, none of these is recommended at all but that they are imposed cannot be ignored.)

In domestic conflict, taking the victims from the villain is tantamount to separating the toddler from a precious toy until he learns how to play with it. (This is how knowing developmental stages help, by homology, as it has in linking the evolution of arms and wings with freeing the forelegs of bipeds for other uses than walking.)

[k/24] Perhaps domestic violence could be probed in more general terms and we should wonder, "Why are the weak victimized?" Asked like this, the answers can be heard more easily, provided they are not accusatory.

If the question implies that the weak ought not to be victimized, the implication aborts the quest for, if not the queries about, all the different reasons why they are. The reason for not going ahead is because it is obviously (C') unreasonable that women and children should be victimized. (Questions only confuse the complacent.)

Nor are we any closer to the solution by asking what makes them accept the role of victim in a counterphobic attempt to avoid assigning all blame to the villain. The fashionable answers are that victims are hungry for their presence to be acknowledged, even if cruelly, or that they are dependent on their tormentor. Yet their dependence is now becoming more obsolete with equal employment opportunities for both sexes close to well-endowed and better-staffed child-care centers. (Details are ignored by the smug.)

It is worse if words are strung together more rhetorically: "Why are the weak victimized by the villainous (or by the virtuous in righteous retaliation against victorless crimes that [1] offend our hypersensitive sensibilities [when the world's oldest legally or illegally bedded professionals still tempt us] or [2] overload our oversensitive senses [as when infants cry continuously])?"

Even those who would license prostitution as a profession shy away from relatives who become certified practitioners, thus acknowledging that they see legalized whoring as a business rather than a professional service, a form of supportive psychotherapy for the inept and lonely, even if it also provides prophylactic venereology with medical supervision of the prostitute as another larger condom, the distaff version of the uncuckolded husband of a traveling saleswoman.

[k/25] Adam himself was "bestial" before Eve arrived, along with Lilith in old translations of the Bible.

[k/26] And absent in "dumb" adult "marital aids." An estimated four million American women are battered annually, 30 percent of female homicidal victims are killed by their husband or lover, 6 percent of male homicidal victims are killed by their wife or partner.

Women used to gossip more, now they argue better. The difference between gossip, arguments, and facts is that the latter is impersonal, the others less so. (Is there a correlation between the status of women and the popularity of certain dances?)

[k/27] At this writing, only four out of fifty states report decline of child abuse incidents.

[k/28] The best role model for human appeasement gestures is a consummate actress whose very name, Meryl Streep, is itself probably an unconscious concession. (The first black male to get away with self-assertiveness did it by having, as world champion Muhammad Ali, faster fists than his critics.)

Gandhi learned nonviolence during civil disobedience demonstrations in South Africa when cavalry horses, urged by their riders, adamantly refused to stomp on the prostrate. Dogs, as Man's best friends, are easier to sic (*sic*) on their master's enemies.

[k/29] Are we (**B**) right or (**B'**) righteous in cases of terrorism at home or abroad as a matter of "principle" taught during kindergarten? We do not increase altruism by insisting on parity between the terrorist (who may be voluntary martyrs) and the terrified (who may be involuntarily sacrificed by equally patriotic rescuers) unless it is future victims whom we are trying to save by present sacrificial offerings, as declared international policy.

The alpha male represents the "superpower" when there is dimorphism. Where dimorphism is not a significant aspect of tribal life, as in humans and Costa Rican rhesus monkeys, the dominant male is more apt to keep the female away from his rival rather than wrestle with her suitor.

[k/30] Our two-headed aberration of a nuclear family was born only recently as a social mutation when the head of the household decided to hand down to his heirs what he has hoarded in worldly goods instead of just regretting that he cannot take them with him beyond the grave. Families are economic, not sexual, bureaucracies.

Now that more and more parents derive their income as earned salary rather than as dividends from property cultivation and development, we still keep our kids under our thumb only by discriminating against the young through adult-aggrandizing compulsory education, child labor laws, and minimum wages for teenagers. Ideological reductionists, *Homo domestici* or *H. metropoli*, tend unwittingly to accept social legislation literally by the "buzzwords" in their highfalutin titles.

[k/31] The sexual revolution that multiplied H. metropolis was fueled by sympathetic contagion (as in stampeding lemmings) among rioting college students, which became parasympathetically orgiastic after prudent retreat from security forces mobilized by the Establishment For Free Thought in Culturally Correct Words who felt threatened by "freewheeling speech." (A swing in the opposite direction explains the surprising strength of rescuers of strangers who needed succor right away. Women have lifted cars off children's bodies.)

[k/32] Philosophers specialize in analogies that make the unfamiliar familiar and sterile. Homology renders the very familiar more unfamiliar and promising.

Does philosophy come from inclination or gullibility? Is the inclination motivated by human nature or is the gullibility prompted by the fear that we are vulnerable without philosophy to justify chivalry?

If philosophy, like theology, is self-serving, should it neutralize what science contends? To make science equally self-serving is anthropocentric. The Age of Rhetoric then becomes a Renaissance of the Age of Ptolemy, when astronomy (1) was used to serve both philosophy and theology, which (2) insisted that "science" and problem solving must remain geocentric.

[k/33] I once lost my "cool" and spanked a teenager during a hand-to-hand struggle in an isolated padded cell—it was not a seclusion room because she could receive patients and staff who wish to visit her—and she explained her increased "self-control" afterward by claiming that I would spank her again if she misbehaved, but no one would believe her and so she had to prove it by sustaining good behavior (which changed the social climate around her). In fact, she no longer associated intimacy with annihilation. (Even if I did not know all of the above at the time as a psychiatrist, I instinctively knew that words had not helped violent people and that they must be free to fight if we are going to keep them in a mental hospital without locking them up.)

For my "disturbed" female patients, I insisted that they could only attack me with closed fists (and pull my hair since my scalp seems to be highly insensitive), but never slap or kick me.

(They are actually only "disturbed" enough to be under maximum security elsewhere when they are disturbing to staff [cf. Ortega, MENTAL HYGIENE, Vol. 46, No. 1, Jan. 1962]).

My violent male patients, in turn, were also expected to hit me with an open hand and always managed to miss me when they threw a clenched fist. (You can hit those whom you like without having to make amends, but not those who like you who may change their minds. It is therefore safer and better to like your patients, whether they like you or not.)

Is it necessary for me to carry insurance against lawsuits in dealing with stepfamilies in my private practice when they soon trust me with their secrets? (In solo practice, I am even expected to make house calls to prevent fisticuffs!)

For the so-called "talking therapies," it is often claimed without smiling that healing can be hastened by "catharsis" and "ventilation." In medicine, "cathartics" is another name for "laxatives." "Ventilation by catharsis" is therefore "verbal farting in public." We can empty ourselves of noxious gas but will also be spraying others nearby.

(If my use of words is too explicit, it is to drive the point home: to expect ventilation by encouraging catharsis is to create more pollution with what is purged by the cathartic.)

Women today, like adolescents and lawyers always are, seem to be more and more argumentative. Is stridency an early sign of adolescence (first or second: a menopausal "What if?" or Chicken Little ["Sky will fall"] mentality)? (Both buy the "domino theory" unquestioningly.)

Another misused term is "catalyst," which, in chemistry, remains unchanged, but "change agents" claim "growth" for themselves during social intervention. People may change for the better or not after crisis, but "growth" is strictly DNA mediated.

[k/34] A less well-known appeaser is Mary Steenburgen, who crinkles her nose to soften her words when she is uncharacteristically outspoken. (Men also make anticipatory appeasement gestures: Latin Julio Iglesias, who describes himself as "humble," clasps his hands in front of him. Afro-American Arsenio Hall begins his TV talk show by clasping them in front of his crotch and slaps his own wrist when he has been overcritical. Passive psychologists also tend to nod their heads more than active social workers.)

Is apt role-model aping a successful but unthinking attempt at imitation by "copycats" or a selective and thoughtful rehearsal? Or is it a return of adolescent vulnerability to a form of more distant peer pressure?

(The *Wheel of Fortune* is copied worldwide on TV with the same pairing of vocal host and silent hostess who only smiles graciously and moves gracefully to display letters of the alphabet in obedience to verbal cues.)

12.00 1/Addendum:
CONTINUING EDUCATION in the
BEHAVIORAL SCIENCES

(This section for students and scholars can double as a seminar on clinical rationalysis and the theory of absolute relativity. These topics can stand alone, as needed. They begin by concentrating on Believing more than on Becoming or Begetting, then next on Becoming. What can disbelievers do to help those blinded by faith?)

A. CREATIVITY, IDEOLOGY, AND MADNESS

Because we have a shorter history than other animals, we have not learned our history lessons well, and many of our teachers have let us down. One of the often-quoted history teachers in our classrooms is a philosopher. His name is George Santayana.

Like most philosophers, he is often wrong *(l/1)* though he has traveled more: He told us that if we knew our history, we would not make the same mistakes. This justifies gossiping about the dead in the halls of academia.

But we all own one of the best-researched history books. The Bible has been a best seller since the printing press was invented.

If we compare the genocide recorded in chapter 31 of the book of Numbers and those reported in today's newspapers, we see immediately that only the words have changed.

What the Bible calls "ritual purification"—after "screening" for virgins among the heathens—is now called "ethnic cleansing" (after gang bangs in lieu of pelvic exams) in the Balkans. *(l/2)* Is it humane to keep killing each other in numbers unmatched by other animals? Is it because human beings are capable of idolatry of dead idols and disembodied ideas? It is idolatry of ideas that makes ideology a form of insanity.

Can you identify and differentiate two great ideologues from continents on each side of the Atlantic? Both were failed artists. One dropped out of school but authored a book. The other graduated from a second-rate university and on assuming public office fired the head of the biggest university in the world. One joined the armed services and was honored for bravery. The other publicized the war effort and fought for his country only with words. One married quite late, and his wife died in his arms. The other divorced a better artist than himself. Both were popular and won elections with wide margins, but only one succeeded in securing emergency powers from his legislature. The other bypassed his to invade a small country without warning. Both tried to prove themselves worthy of command, but only one stood fast before three worthy adversaries. Both appealed to God against their enemies and lied about them as "germ carriers of spiritual pestilence worse than the black plague" or as "leaders of an evil empire" *(1/3)*. One was jailed as a revolutionary; the other was a famous reactionary. Both were great communicators, repeating what their followers applauded.

One was, of course, Adolf Hitler and the other Ronald Reagan, who became evangelical after his attempted assassination. What they shared was a passionate hate for what they believed was the cupidity of the enemy of their people, and for this they remained popular to the end. The difference was in longevity of power. Hitler's American adversary, Franklin Roosevelt, died in office, and Reagan was constitutionally prevented from following FDR's example and even from trying to get reelected a third time. But constitutional term limitations do not prevent ideological madness that is shared by the always-mediocre majority.

What makes any ideology more dangerous is the microphone that amplifies the voice. Would we have had a Second World War if the microphone had not been available for mass rallies?

The microphone separates the ideologue from the creative. *(1/4)* Socrates, Plato, and Aristotle did not have microphones to win crowds to their errors. (Socrates chose to die after a thorough self-examination, Plato failed in ruling Sicily, Aristotle deserted his own school.)

The Golden Age of Greece produced all three of them in one lifetime. Can you think of another country that produced three giants in just half a lifetime? The country is Germany, and the triad of giants are Karl Marx ("labor is capital"), Sigmund Freud ("memory selects to suit"), and Albert Einstein ("neither time nor space is absolute: $E = mc^2$").

All lived under German ideology but were creative despite it. All three were Jews, but did not practice their religion. The ability to create and be original is more limited by the right to believe than by the climate of the times.

Words and numbers on paper can change the world. But when what has been written gets proclaimed loudly and long, it gets heard by the gullible, who believes the message, erroneous or not, that is loudmouthed.

So far, we have assigned madness to all idolatry by the lonely and the ideology of the loudmouth. Both aspire to equality with their superiors. What can we do to save ourselves from idolatry and ideologues?

Ideologues, who also believe out of a need to belong, respond to overtures that increase their stature. Four world leaders made other "wannabes" believe that they belonged and thus saved the world from universal and religious genocide.

How did they do it? The obvious answer—missed by reporters, who risk their lives for the right of the public to know the score—is simply by visiting one another.

Richard Nixon visited Mao Tse Tung and made him less dependent on Leonid Brezhnev. Anwar Sadat visited Menachem Begin and made a statesman of an ex-terrorist. Margaret Thatcher welcomed Michael Gorbachev (in sharp contrast to Khrushchev's tour of the United States, when he was dwarfed by towering Secret Service men), and the Berlin Wall started to fall. Bill Clinton welcomed IRA's Gerry Adams who ordered a cease-fire in the protracted Irish civil war.

Can ordinary people prevent civil wars? Journalists call it "people power." In the Philippines they did just exactly that and prevented a war between brothers by sisters visiting the warriors in their war machines with flowers and food in hand. People call it "people power." We should call it "sister power."

In Moscow, people tried to prevent the shelling of their parliament, which was occupied by members defying President Boris Yeltsin. A shell that shattered its walls dispersed the occupants.

Men who would rather fight than visit end up with wars and riots.

In Beijing, a male student stood proudly in front of a tank, daring it to run over him. He ended up in prison.

Against Vietnam, American students chanted, "Make love, not war." That is precisely the wrong slogan. Their elders always send young men to battle to reduce competition for the women whom they must leave behind. (More women go to battle when the front is not too far from home, which must be defended, as in Israel.)

When men kill instead of hunt, they lose their ability to look out for their own families. When women act for women, it defeats their effectiveness to deal with mothers or sex.

To immunize against ideology, we should be careful to separate matters of fact from matters of faith in teaching our children, just as we do with patients, because they cannot check things out for themselves. What adults proudly call "principles" are kindergarten-conditioned moral reflexes ingrained in children before they could think for themselves.

Emerson once said, "Whoso would be a man must be a non-conformist." The freedom to be a radical is limited by the right to believe. The right to believe must be granted to those who need to belong. Is to belong to be owned and traded, like slaves by their owners? The willingness to share allows believers to be less militant.

In the Philippines, we do not have social welfare recipients. The poor visit the rich around mealtime, and they get fed without fuss. They do not have to call ahead to say they are coming. They have no telephones to announce their visit from a distance. As we become more affluent, we visit not each other but our children and stay with them less and less. Visiting is for strangers, staying together is for families. *(l/5)*

I want to sum up by listing three things that we can all be doing to prevent creativity from becoming ideology and sowing the seeds of genocide.

1. Admire but do not worship ideas, especially those that depend on abstractions (monocentric), like "mind." "Minding," like other gerunds (process-oriented), will not deceive the unwary. Abstractions are neocortical and Apollonian (intellectual hypochondriasis); lusting for life is visceral and Dionysian, not devilish.

2. Doubt the premises and promises of ideologues. Believing is gambling for gold at the end of a rainbow.

3. To be trusted and believed is to be idolized by the timid who need to belong. Resist the idolatry of closure-prone believers that ideologues inspire with just nouns, the root of all evil.

On the headstone marking the grave of the author of *Zorba the Greek* was inscribed, "I fear nothing, I believe nothing, I am free!"

I shall try to (1) differentiate divisive and dangerous ideologies that attend and distort the evolution of humanimal social institutions.

Can creativity (2a) uniquely link random but repeatedly reported events to (b) show us a way out of the madness of institutionalized killing that is (c) rooted in ancient thinking about the world? Creativity is the inspired blending of what had not been combined before.

Animals kill what is not theirs. Can (3) we choose to kill others like us, or die fighting them just to please jealous and zealous ideologues?

If we are the only animals who talk and kill our kind, (4a) are we prisoners of our words, and (b) are some words more lethal than swords?

If we are not all imprisoned by old thoughts, (5a) can we invent new words? And (b) not understand more?

Did the Berlin Wall start to crumble after Great Britain's Margaret Thatcher first made Soviet Union's Michael Gorbachev feel accepted as a world leader without threatening his leadership?

Was inviting Russian president Boris Yeltsin as a nonvoting guest to the Economic Summit enough? Or Bill Clinton giving his first state dinner to welcome Japan's Emperor Hirohito useful? For how long?

Athens used to be the meeting place for Eastern and Western thought, like San Francisco is today. As the site of Aristotle's school of philosophy, a different type of intellectual traffic crossed Athens at the time. (His school was closed when its founder was accused of conspiring in the death of Alexander the Great.) Did Alexander's soldiers bring Aristotle a truncated version of Buddhist philosophy? (Left out were initial proposition and data that induced or generated it.) Going directly to premise and application resulted in arriving at a conclusion only by deduction. *(1/6)*

If I were speaking of what used to be the Golden West that is now called the Pacific Rim of the United States, I would not limit myself to creativity and madness in Western philosophy and ideology, respectively. Since Greece gave birth to Western civilization, I will speak of its counterparts elsewhere only in passing.

Creativity is originality that endures. Like all things that are new, what is original may scare the mediocre and be scorned by traditionalists in the new tyranny of an uncreative majority.

Originality as novelty briefly carries and then loses its own momentum to be just a fad. If novelty endures to become fashionable, it develops enough class to be what is classically called creative. What does not last may be self-expressive, novel enough, but wearing thin. Self-expression dies quickly; creativity survives the test of time or is perverted into ideology by the charismatic and/or opportunistic.

Words like "perfectibility" embody creative concepts and ideas (potentiality + Plato's perfect forms) that can become transformed into valued ideologies or institutionalized belief systems that have concealed the social insanity of organized, mass, or serial murders by American KKK, Arabian Hamas, etc.

Some ideas can be old and pre-Copernican, reasoned or pre-Cartesian, and biased or pre-Darwinian. To be scientific, we must doubt them. As doctors, we cannot separate body and soul or be pre-Hippocratic. A psychiatrist cannot separate mind and body or be pre-Pavlovian. [*1/7 (sic)*]

Among doctors, Hippocrates was the first to deny that epilepsy was a sign of divine displeasure. In Greece as well as in the East, epilepsy was seen as a sign of divine intervention with the epileptic as an intermediary. Some epileptics themselves seek explanations for their "spells." (Others, like St. Paul, who also had "fits," devise rules and rituals and expect compliance to maintain control.)

Deism (Providence cares!) may be universal. Theism (A jealous God watches!) is more occidental. We do not need to believe St. Paul's Bible for people to have faith in order to forgive. A stronger faith is needed the greater the suffering. Worse off are those whose suffering is deserved rather than imposed by others whom they must try to forgive.

Belief in God or a spirit or soul is for people (*Homo domestici*) who must depend on someone besides themselves (including farmers whose adjoining land may be flooded by heavy rains) and so have learned to trust in utter dependency. Blind trust (e.g., in an absent, silent God) is a one-way street that needs no traffic signs to direct heathens who are ready to be led to a better future. (Whom did Jehovah or Jesus trust? Noah and Peter?)

"Ideagogues" with ideas to share are often reinterpreted by ideologues who mislead those who are not free to compare different ideas in pursuing their right to believe someone. The most dangerous of beliefs claim that what is old (e.g., the Koran), once it is written down, applies to all who read it. But ancient texts were written for those who can read them, mostly men. And to this day, some men still attribute only to their gender what those same-sex writers recorded.

> Religious, political, and economic dogmatisms are the most dangerous forms of socially correct madness among terrorists and antiterrorists in the world. *(1/8)*

All ideology is based on ideas that were original but eventually coopted to become systems of belief without a basis in reality. For instance, the idea that man is imperfect has given rise to the idea that therefore there must be perfection. Nothing is perfect in nature, no straight lines or circles, and therefore what is perfect must be supernatural. If it is unnatural, it must be spiritual. And there cannot be spirits that are all perfect; only one spirit can be perfect, and so polytheism in Greece gave way to monotheism from across the Mediterranean.

Modern pluralism has then again given way to recent "ethnic cleansing": "Ritual purification" after massacres as symbolic undoing was ordered in Numbers 31 by Moses: "Kill every male . . . and every woman who has known man by lying with him . . . Purify yourselves . . . on the 3rd day."

> Beliefs (e.g., in a flat earth) can come from purely logical reasoning rather than reality testing, and without reality testing, what is believed can be inane or insane or dangerous. We cannot proceed to test reality without first doubting what we must test.

It was Galileo who first doubted that anything can be decided by logical thinking. He dropped objects of different weights from a convenient height to show that a heavier one does not travel faster when they all fall freely. A contemporary, René Descartes, clinched the argument against thinking being decisive and substituted doubting for it when he wrote "Cogito, ergo sum." What he meant literally was "I cogitate (or 'doubt' rather than 'think'), therefore I exist." Thusly was existential psychiatry born, which Jean-Paul Sartre rescued from essentially Western logical deductive thinking. Eastern philosophy is basically more inductive ("Yes, but . . .") and less Aristotelian ("Perfect is not not perfect").

If ideology is the use of ideas to distort social reality and madness is a break with reality, then abuse of ideology is social insanity (mad but not bad) that is more mad than common psychoses, i.e., schizophrenic, paranoid, and manic-depressive psychoses.

Is believing more mad than just highly addictive gambling for the big win?

1. Manic-depressives are optimistic about the future and pessimistic about an unforgiven past. The sequence of mood changes mirrors the foreboding that pervades the Lenten season after the uninhibited celebration of Mardi Gras. The range of moods reflects what is prescribed by religious ideology about sin and salvation by resurrection of knights or knaves who believe their Bible. (Resurrection has little in common with reincarnation into another species or social group.)

2. Schizophrenics are characterized by constant preoccupation with the self among those who are very sensitive about what intrudes into their personal space. Those who treat them need to keep their distance, as if their patients are defensive porcupines who suffer from chronic isolation but fear instant intimacy. This territorial imperative or suspiciousness is not envy but more like preoccupation with national security that gives leaders legitimacy to defend their domain against any enemy. What is legitimized is thereafter beyond appeal and must be respected by all.

3. Paranoiacs are convinced by formal logic that dictates what can be assumed as proved, once their premises are granted. Delusion = deduction/data. This is true of all deductive reasoning, even when it leads to unacceptable conclusions or social delusions. Logic once made all but a few accept that their world must be flat. Thus, the ideological equivalent of clinical paranoia is all prescientific Western philosophy. (Philosophy is here defined as a critical study of fundamental beliefs and the intellectual grounds for holding such beliefs. Is believing habitual lying in the face of new relevant data, e.g., shared DNA among primates?)

Expectably, the most enduring ancient ideology in the West is pre-Copernican theology that is based on pre-Christian Aristotelian syllogism. In its intermediate form, it tries to reconcile itself with pre-Cartesian philosophy by claiming that reasoning leads to knowledge. All that reason does is help us understand what is already known. Its most recent attempt at reconciliation with science is to espouse pre-Darwinian anthropocentrism, which limits scientists to what can be understood.

Pre-Copernican ideology, simply stated, is "I believe I was created in the image of God, therefore there is a God." Egocentricity eventually led to geocentricity: "The earth is the center of the universe because God's chosen image deserves the best habitat." His only Son came in the flesh to us to be sacrificed on the cross to save all who had displeased their Creator. (His resurrection makes Eastern reincarnation a slow boat to another heaven [Nirvana]. For the Incarnate not to die in vain, cross and sword crossed oceans to foreign lands. Today, religious correctness sponsors revivals.)

Descartes tried to get away from matters of belief and replaced it with incertitude: "Cogito, ergo sum." But "I doubt, therefore I am" was too unsettling for closure-prone, opinion-driven intellectuals who mistranslated it to "I think, therefore I am." Thusly modified by philosophers trained in sophistry and tautology, modern "critical thinkers" can try to survive intellectually in a new world of science that, like Descartes, starts out with doubts rather than certitude.

In fact, by claiming that even if God created a clockwork universe, only by cogitating or doubting can we be sure that we ourselves really exist, Descartes avoided religious persecution as a heretic like Galileo.

Only after I introduced postlogical thinking as the essence of Western science *(l/9)* was the old Cartesian dictum "Cogito, ergo sum" correctly entertained to mean "I doubt, therefore I am." Can we doubt that we doubt if we doubt?

Science is the only discipline that makes a virtue of uncertainty.

In (**A-E**) becoming, (**F-O**) believing, and (**P-Z**) begetting, all adults lead at least three lives—sensual, social, and sexual. They have coevolved in human beings from prehistoric illiteracy to postindustrial electronic technology.

Those educated in the West live in at least two other eras, ancient and premodern, before science replaced taste with tests and falsehood with facts. Western prescientific civilization was dominated by pre-Copernican creationism, pre-Cartesian syllogism, and pre-Darwinian humanism. We were geocentric, logicentric (closure-prone), and anthropocentric (biased).

In order not to join the ranks of the socially insane or acceptably mad, you have to be post-Cartesian, post-Copernican, and post-Darwinian. That means that you have to be (1) postlogical (paranoids are extremely logical), (2) noncreationist (to be spiritual, you have to believe you are created in God's image: even Zeus looks Greek), and (3) nonanthropocentric (not like humanists who want to create God in their image: imperfect, absent-minded, shortsighted, deaf, or dying).

The evolution of ideas, personal ideals, and social ideologies can now be studied:

Ideas are opinions.

Creative ideas come from curiosity in children and from suspicions in adults, provided both are gifted.

For the uncorrupted but corruptible, ideas lead to idealism.

Idealists create ideals, ideologues idolize images.

Ideologies are social inventions that turn ideas into ideals, which are converted into "cloning mechanisms."

When a body of opinions becomes believable, it becomes an ideology.

Believing is singing other people's songs; creativity is composing your own.

The deluded are only mistaken in their beliefs. The fanatic is consumed by belief. Both are blameless.

Promises give hope to the helpless.

Rivalry enriches or destroys rivals.

(S)He who believes and stands up for hir beliefs becomes front-line cannon fodder against rival "creeds."

Tradition is the enemy of creativity. Traditionalists do not seek to change what is traditional because they cannot return to it once they change since change by itself unmasks tradition for what it is.

Words can be the enemy of thought, just as logic is of science. This is the difference between creative and critical thinking. Logic produces critical thinking, creative thinking starts out by being unreasonable.

For people to be more creative, they have to change their minds. Little minds cannot change much. This change, once under way, can change direction or momentum. Both unpredictable direction and expectable momentum scare those who fear change.

Old creative or new crazy ideas can become maddening cultist beliefs for the lonesome. Personal idiosyncrasies or suspicions that are often misdiagnosed as insanity can never be as dangerous as ideologies that make dissenters targets of social sanctions, including death by extermination.

(Did the German holocaust kill Jews also to deny their claim to being the chosen people after Hitler picked the Aryan race as being more special and deserving? *(l/11)* Did defeating Aryans make us confident that supermen are made, not born?)

Homo domesticus or *metropolis*, timid or weak and used to yielding or blaming, do not want to investigate or explore our world, especially at the risk of blowing up parts of it and themselves, partly because it will not stand still for us.

STAGES of DEVELOPMENT of CREATIVE TALENT

Art uses ideas, scientists call theirs theories, ideologues do not distinguish between them. A balanced education in arts, letters, and science requires that we know about the *ABC*s of nature and culture or enough *a*nthropology, *b*iology and *c*osmology to ensure that we see everything as interconnected. *(1/10)* Such absolute relativity is the theory behind the new art and science of clinical rationalysis.

(C. P. Snow spoke of only the two cultures of art and science. There are now three, creative theory linking both art and science.)

Our sensual evolution proceeds from the purely subjective to the more objective, starting developmentally from the passive or (**A**) emotional, to the active or (**B**) volitional, to the defensive (rhetorical) or (**C**) reactive (reflective), to the unmoved or (**D**) comparative, and the proactive or (**E**) creative. Our social evolution (**F** to **O**) traces our progress in history; our sexual development (**P** to **Y**) culminates in (**Z**) grandparenthood. Broad database from Freud, Erikson, Piaget, and Maslow all agree. *(Tables 4D-15)*

Creative innovations can be exploited socially and lead to schisms in (**F**) religion as in Bosnia, (**G**) politics as in the Falklands, and (**H**) economics as in the Gulf War. Newer and less dangerous but divisive "-isms" are (**I-O**) individualism, ethnicism, industrialism, humanism, environmentalism, animalism, and unionized robotism (in Japan!)

I once spoke of a thinking and talking brain instead of a right and left brain. Now, I want to include a dreaming and sorting brain with the thinking brain and a believing and writing brain with the talking brain. We cannot believe without words. We can understand without words, but we cannot be fanatical about what words did not help us understand.

The thinking brain starts with verbs that become gerunds before the talking brain makes them nouns.

For instance, the thinking brain begins by minding its surroundings, but by the time its thinking gets to the talking brain, thinking has become "thoughts" and minding becomes "mind."

(Robin Dunbar in *Grooming, Gossip and the Evolution of Language* thinks words were assigned to the left brain because the right brain was already fully occupied.)

Now, we'll talk about brains, not minds. Animals are creative because they have brains. The talking brain is separate from the writing brain. The writing brain is connected to both the talking and the thinking brains. The talking brain is only required to use the tongue and so it can talk to children. Since children do not have to write early, the writing brain talks mostly to adults.

Children cannot distinguish what is based on science or on belief when you answer their questions. You should separate them and tell the children where you are coming from. Fantasies have to be expressed in words children can understand unless we use animation. With TV, words are less necessary. Soon, it seems ours is going to be a different world before we get too old to appreciate it.

SUMMARY and IMPLICATIONS

Ideologies were strange or creative concepts that became opinions but are not seen as opinions by those who believe in order to belong, blame, bellyache, or avail themselves of an excuse. Because opinions are not always rooted in reality, when they become shared beliefs as values that are culturally valuable, they assume a form of tolerable social insanity. Values accuse as well as say, "I am OK" or serve as crutches for the infirm. This social infirmity is different from simple insanity (marching to a silent drumbeat), which is more frowned upon.

Those intolerant of personal idiosyncrasies may be doubly mad. Ideology (marching to the same drummer) can be madness and become dangerous, like McCarthyism, if intolerant. All "-isms" are ideological. Weapons in the hands of jealous zealots make many dangerous ideologies genocidal. Envy enhances competition; jealousy makes it fierce.

When does zeal and insanity begin? It is too late to ask Hitler and Stalin this question, but do other authorities have the answer?

Hitler appealed to those who worshipped God and capitalism, Stalin scared those who believed in both.

We use old ideas for our own purposes, and the more we try to look for meaning in life, the more our perceptions are colored by our dreams. Mental somersaults are incontestable as natural, but not in the sense that they are based on the reality around us. The distortion may not be apparent nor psychotic, but when the bias is inapparent, well-reasoned ideology becomes more dangerous in the hands of insanely jealous zealots. Zeal can be formulated as Facts/Assumptions = 1/Passion, or as Passion = Assumptions/Facts.

With a gifted leader, dreams of social cohesion by arms or indoctrination dominate or domesticate followers. Jealous leaders decapitate doubtful subordinates.

Ideology thus serves to enslave, which is why the right to fight to be equal is inversely proportional to the freedom to create. Initiative does not imply innovation, but the reverse holds.

Inspired creativity, as distinguished from resourceful ingenuity *(1/15)* to cope expediently with necessity, which raccoons exemplify, should bow to no master in discovering what others may have overlooked, whether useful to anyone, including the creative, in tangible rewards or not.

> Creativity, like beauty, has no utilitarian value and appeals with a newly revealed esthetics and elegance. Necessity among the free is the mother of invention by the talented who are also ingenious in their resourcefulness.

> Uninspired ingenuity must be useful to be appreciated. The value to doers of ingenuity is based on facts. Ideology is valued on the basis of the fantasy that it inspires among believers. The unimaginative need leaders. Facts and fantasies have different uses for doers and dreamers.

Language to some extent falsifies memory, which makes it less candid than faded pictures. We can also edit, without conscious intent, what we record and remember even while we are recalling it. (Reasoning is for the lazy who can't be bothered to look. It is easier to process words than facts. To examine facts, you need knowledge. To play with words, you only need rhetoric.)

> Unlike new words and ideas that take getting used to, old words and beliefs are comfortable like old clothes and shoes.

Scientific study is more sensual than social or zealous, ideology more jealous and dangerous. The more in awe we are of the world, the more we tend to think about recent developments in familiar, reasoned, and human racist ways and to reorganize them without wondering at all about the timing of their emergence.

Old words give us a Rip van Winkle outlook. Language organizes our thoughts. Abstractions, like psychobabble, hide important particulars.

Today, we can trace our behavior to their source, whether visceral or instinctual, process-centered or mindful, and iconic or symbolic. If you are not a prisoner of culture, have you invented a new word lately?

Words are powerful only in a relationship of trust, as in hypnosis. The hypnotist is trusted.

Those who believe but are not ignorant or inhibited may become trusted leaders. Leaders who are accepted and derided as leaders remain loyal to their followers (like Nikita Khrushchev who was refused admission to Disneyland by Walt Disney of the American right) if not to their comrades (like Mao Tse Tung who drifted away from Russia after Richard Nixon came to China to divide the communists).

It is only when you cannot think for yourself (out of ignorance or inhibition) that you have to believe (in order to belong) in promises (of equality).

After Margaret Thatcher accepted Michael Gorbachev and Ronald Reagan talked to him as one grandfather to another, communism gave way to camaraderie. The need to believe in order to belong then gives way to belonging to an elite instead of struggling for equality. (They may keep their beliefs, not in order to belong as much as to be able to blame.)

Even if or when we are unequally free or creative and lustful or procreative, old schools of thought are bad for our continuing education to be the best students of all that is accessible in this world and beyond. In our human odyssey, we have gone from the sacred to the secular in confronting

1.   the void in our lives that would be better filled by shared feelings with those around us than by borrowed meanings from total strangers and

2. the chaos of the universe that is more disturbing for the ritualistic (*Homo domesticus*) and uptight (*H. metropolis*) who dread deadlines than to the realistic and playful (*Homo sapiens*) who do not need to make a difference. Search for meaning and symbolic rituals are safer than feelings or success among those whose mothering ended prematurely and who are afraid to fail again in more personal relationships with surrogate ("meaningful") others.

Incomplete mothering makes the search for meaning necessary for those who long to belong. (Will the mother staying with the newborn and not going back to its father at night make it feel less exiled at birth or alienated in life? Does society advance by abandoning the helpless of all ages part- or full-time in nursery cribs, day care centers, boarding schools, and nursing homes and hospices? Is euthanasia born of the fear of dying alone?)

Longing is met fraudulently by belonging, even to a family. Our mothers belong to us, not the other way around. They'd die for us before, during, and after our birth.

If you trusted your father, you don't have to trust God. If your father loved you, God will also.

Those who are closure-prone must resort to myths to enjoy peace. Even the almighty dollar cannot resolve uncertainty. Hope can bankrupt the helpless who believe emotionally or passionately but passively. Believers have a borrower's mentality.

There is only one self-evident truth: "I doubt, therefore I exist. How can I doubt that I doubt if I doubt?" All other matters that cannot be disproved are matters of faith and belief. Science is the only discipline that makes a virtue of uncertainty.

RESERVATIONS and CONCLUSIONS

All excerpts (below) start with answers to unstated questions. Can you find the questions that resulted in the following excerpts?

Optimists ask questions and look for answers; pessimists find answers that disappoint them.

Oscar Wilde claims that when (students are) given a choice to go to heaven or attend a lecture about heaven, there would be more going to a lecture hall.

Postgraduate education is like a secular purgatory, where one can purge what is not essential. But that is not easy to do.

The object of continuing education is not so much to answer old questions as to raise new ones. *(l/13)*

Even if they do not raise fresh doubts, summaries suggest new questions to all who are not "mentanorexic." They serve as magnifying glasses that highlight oversights.

It seems to me that the creative are those who give up on old ideology. Karl Marx, Albert Einstein, and Sigmund Freud were all nonpracticing Jews. Copernicus was a lukewarm Christian, as was Descartes. Darwin went to a different island from the British Isles and saw animals coexisting more peacefully than his proud forebears.

All ideologies are based on promises, as are all propaganda. The only antidote to matters of belief is the injection of nontoxic doses of doubt in those confident enough to question old assumptions. We cannot disempower the believer by making his targets more heroic. We can only make what he believes less lethal to those who do not believe. We also must not take the believer's crutches away all at once but wait very patiently until he can stand alone.

Chairman Mao Tse Tung leaned less on Moscow after President Nixon went to China to meet him as a world leader. Likewise, Egypt's Anwar Sadat's visit to Israeli's Menachem Begin makes an ex-terrorist more of a statesman in order to stand as tall as his visitor.

Can Syria's President Assad stay in the shadow cast by PLO's Chairman Arafat and Jordan's King Hussein, or will he overshadow them by stealing the spotlight from peace talks with their common enemy? Could these talks have survived media coverage of posturing by negotiators? Is historic news just gossip or information?

Ideology capitalizes on the right to believe in equality of the unfree among those who need to belong. The right to believe will limit our freedom to create. Rationalysis, which emphasizes ratios or relationships instead of reason or rationale, can formulate this relative reciprocity as follows: Freedom to create = 1/Right to fight for equality.

Rivalry enriches or destroys rivals.

If delusions are defensive and ideologies defend convictions, we should not seek to unconvince the deluded but instead try to offer what their convictions cannot supply.

The need to belong can be met by others who have the urge to share without competing for the opportunity to lead.

Granting a visa for the IRA leader to visit America changed his mind about the prospects for peace.

Rivals irk the powerful.

When "sister power" offered soldiers food and flowers from young women, it succeeded in Manila. "People power" failed in Moscow, Bucharest, and Beijing—where a young male student stood proudly confronting a tank during Michael Gorbachev's state visit. People power is less manpower, but more gentle women prevailed upon warriors to change direction.

Creativity can change our lives, ideologies and enemies supervise our efforts to survive the changes. Friends and families are not enough if they were not enough when we were too young to enjoy them. Those who did not enjoy them then are likely to use them as targets of their frustrations.

PRESCRIPTIONS

The right to believe to meet the need to belong makes us vulnerable and gullible. The right to believe cannot be denied.

To reduce the risk of dangerous beliefs, believers should not be asked to defend their beliefs, but must be accepted for other things than their ideology.

Only those with the urge to share what they have with rivals can distract their competitors. What they have that they can offer those who are isolated by their ideological commitments may be membership in an exclusive club of world leaders. Or simple food and flowers to those manning the weapons of war that isolated leaders deploy to defend their claims.

Freedom to create + urge to share = 1/(right to believe + need to belong)

Steps to freedom from ideology (which starts with ideas as premises and ends with promises of utopia):
1. Secularization of science (this is slowly gaining ground)
2. Demystification of thinking (this dismays advocates of "critical thinking")
3. Dethroning of language (TV and "virtual reality" may help)

Without words, there cannot be a God. If the only evil are abstractions, we should try to replace common nouns (which deindividualize experience) with gerunds.

When thinking becomes a fetish, language an amulet, and words a charm bracelet, we have become mad.

If you think this is unreal, you'll find the following quite surreal or very odd. *(1/12)*

There is no deity but deification, there is no thinking but brain work, there is no magic in clever metaphors. (With their brains, animals can paint, invent tools, and exploit gravity.)

What you should say to yourself is, "I do not believe that there is no deity but deification, I do not believe that there is no thinking but brain work, I do not believe that there is no magic in clever metaphors."

To disbelieve leaves room for exploration, discovery, and disproof.

We have the freedom to create only if we do not have to believe in order to belong.

B. Creativity: How Talent Develops

We can go from passion to reason to reality, from
emotion to essence to existence, from danger signals to
abstract symbols to tell-tale signs, and beyond
to creativity in art and science.

—Ortega

I'll try to define creativity, identify its sources, trace its evolution, follow its unfolding, cite illustrious examples, and then redefine it and tell you what helps and hinders its expression.

There are eight subtopics that can be covered briefly only at the cost of clarity.

What is creative must be original to begin with and then survive the test of time. It is fed by curiosity in the gifted of either sex with any intelligence or imagination among us and other animals. It evolves like everything else in order to adapt to a changing environment. It unfolds by stages, which also reflect how it unfolded through the ages.

This unfolding proceeded without words and movement, as in music, then with motion without description as in dance and design, then in spoken or written language, then as the result of study rather than fantasy, and lastly by putting together what had not been combined before.

What is the biggest but most inarticulate animal you can think of? Kids (who move their lips when they read) say elephants do not forget because they cannot write. Domesticated, they also stay put when tethered to a tree much smaller than what they can already uproot.

An elephant who paints with its prehensile trunk got me wondering about how such talent might develop among animals, including us.

It works out like this:
1. Eye + trunk or thumb = ingenuity
2. Thumb + training = craftsmanship
3. Tongue + ear(s) = ideology
4. Talent + observation = originality
5. Talent + inspiration = creativity
6. Talent + skill = virtuosity
7. Talent + intelligence = genius
8. Talent + savvy = wisdom

(We were once untalented but ingenious *Homo sapiens*; some became *Homo domestici* in needing to belong, then *Homo metropoli* who now need crowds who think just like them.)

Creativity can be (**A**) "e-motional," (**B**) athletic, (**C**) clever, (**D**) studious, or (**E**) inspired. *(l/14)*

We can remember each stage better if we give it a letter of our alphabet from A (passion without motion) to E (or creation) for what was original and now is classical.

An example of **AxE** or creative expression without words or movement is music and painting like Da Vinci's *Mona Lisa*. An example of **BxE** or creative expression in dance or design is Olympian ice-skater Torvill and choreographer Dean's presentation of Ravel's "Bolero." An example of **CxE** in spoken or written language is Shakespearean drama. An example of **DxE** is intensive and cumulative study that allowed Copernicus to move the earth from the center of the known universe. An example of **ExE** is Einstein's novel combining of space and time so that they are no longer separate as absolute categories. Unexpected, this is now accepted.

STEPS in the DEVELOPMENT of TALENT (xE)

	Inept ->	Talented ->	Gifted ->	Great ->	Exemplary
A	Cry-baby	lullabies	"blues"	jazz	L. Armstrong
B	Clumsy	Dexterous	Athletic	Olympian	M. Jordan
C	Dim-witted	Clever	Smart	Wise	B. Russell
D	Dogmatic	Eclectic	Ecumenical	Visionary	C. Darwin
E	Copycat	Precocious	Virtuoso	Genius	A. Einstein

We have now redefined "creativity" as the evolving relationship of the likes of Da Vinci, Dean, Shakespeare, Copernicus, and Einstein with (**i'**) unoriginal copycats and (**ii**) receptive beneficiaries.

The two worlds of art and science can be crisscrossed by talented activity or inspired theory, pre-Hippocratic or neo-modernistic.

Even skill in counting (measuring) is influenced by personal growth and development:

A. Arithmetic is digital (roman numbers became obsolete with the invention of zero).

B. Geometry facilitates manipulation (even if there are no straight lines in nature); the ungifted doodles.

C. Mathematics is consistent (exact); the literate writes to get around factual constraints.

D. Algebra and calculus are relational; the talented draws or drafts plans to scale.

E. Physics is probabilistic.

Precocity is tested by music recitals and science fairs. (There are *idiot savants* in music and mathematics.) There is no such testing ground for mathematical or intellectual *idiot savants*. Mathematics and philosophy are trivial to the extent that they are tautological. Music and physics are exact enough for their replication to be profitable and practical.

We can innovate in art or science or conform to tradition and, with virtuosity, be skilled craftspersons or technicians. Absent precocity, handicaps force the talented to be resourceful.

It is easier to be precocious virtuosos in music and mathematics because they require the manipulation of fewer symbols as notes and numbers than the alphabet. (With words or numbers or neither, inspired artists and scientists live to create while footloose sensualists love life itself more.)

It is harder to be precocious in biology because the variables are many. And it is harder to be precocious in human affairs where permutations approach the infinite and only eternity can produce sagacity equal to God or His creator. (His shepherds are parrots, their followers sheep.)

(Some claim that God is a mathematician and that mathematics supports Plato's abstractions. Plato's abstruse philosophy is creative, but just like Buddha, he is not as precocious as Jesus. [Our creative use of unicorns and centaurs from the past do not make us a creator.])

We can trace the evolution of language from verbs to gerunds to nouns, from monosyllables to pidgin to paragraphs. We go from uttering buzzwords and repeating sound bites to comparing data.

What all this implies is that the development of speech (naming and describing) is itself also stage-bound.

Mothers and nursemaids speak simple "motherese" (**A**) to kids, which chimps can duplicate from representations displayed on a computer screen. Both kids and chimps have memories that will not tax the storage capacity of slow computers with soft floppy discs.

"Pidgin" dialect (**B**) serve subcultures and "journalese" (**C**) nonminority, nonscientific institutions. A better nomenclature (**D**) for serious writers and scientists must go beyond "newspeak" or "psychobabble." Adult human brains develop enough long-term memories to fill hard disks.

(Koko, the gorilla who uses sign language, can create simple sentences without clauses. Computers need more memory than Koko's to process complicated sentences.)

What helps creativity is a good set of talented grandparents. (They inherited rare genes that had accidentally mutated and proved to be adaptive.) What hinders free creative expression are parents who mix up good with right and true, or bad with wrong and false. These categories are minimum-security prisons that artists and scientists enter at great risk to their talent. Good and bad, right and wrong, or true and false have nothing to do with art or science for their own sake.

Artists, like scientists—whether or not they find meaning in (**A**) feeling "good," (**B**) doing "right," or (**C**) reaching for the "truth"—develop by stages. Science advances by trying to disprove what is taken to be true without (**D**) testing to find what has wider applicability.

As long as we are awed by anything, we can be cowed into slavery by whomever we believed is awesome, including God. The only antidote to being awed is to demystify the mysterious, including creativity.

There are also stages in the evolution of ideology (social), as there are in the development of creativity (sensual) and sexuality (erotic). There is an inevitability in the universality of experience because as animals, we are all made in the same way out of the same materials. But there are different ratios in the way we experience our world sensually or each other socially and sexually.

Those who are sexually and sensually excited forget themselves. Those who are creative get lost longer in a world not entirely their own. They seem to be driven, maybe from inside or by a Muse outside to do what they then must finish to their own satisfaction.

Without pictures and because creativity is sensual, we can talk more about sensuality than society or sex. Sex is unsuitable for talking except during foreplay. Social events are not of our own making, so talking about them is secondhand reporting, just like backyard gossip.

There's procreation (when we supposedly are God's proxies), recreation (which we do for our own pleasure and includes artistic self-expression), and creativity (which is feverish and not entirely comfortable, but all-consuming in the short-term and more satisfying in the long run).

(The creative is driven to achieve, the obsessed is a wound-up toy that burns out, tolerated or not. The creative can destroy to build, the obsessed only tries to undo the past, usually by ritual activity.)

There has been no sustained attempt to understand (**E**) exceptional creativity according to stages of sensual development from **A** to **E**. For Piaget, the peak of achievement is formal abstraction; for Maslow, self-actualization; for Freud, genitality; and for Erikson, generativity. No one allows for precocity. To bring new talent to mature virtuosity depends on the stage of development when the gift first shows itself.

Touch is the first of our senses to be stimulated on being born. When we feel ourselves touching something and a pleasing sound— purring or musical—follows, we are rewarded. If gifted in hearing, we make music as soon as we can. (Drumming, however, waits for more proprioceptive than tactile control, as in walking. And if gifted in moving, the toddler drums or dances or leads by conducting those more gifted in playing than coordinating.)

All of Piaget's, Maslow's, Freud's, and Erikson's stages of development can be seen as proceeding from the subjective to the objective, from the emotional (**A**) to the intuitive (**B**) to the cognitive (**C**) to the comparative (**D**).

(This analysis itself is an example of comparative creativity, which, like Darwin's, does not invite consensus. During formal or informal argument, nothing is said that is quite true or fair.)

The essence of (AxE) emotional creativity is the facility to elicit a wider range of feelings than usual, without using words. The essence of (BxE) motor creativity is the increase in the facility of motion and locomotion by inventions, whether prosthetic or choreographic. The essence of (CxE) cognitive creativity is the ability to ask different questions of the same assumptions. The essence of (DxE) comparative creativity is the greater use of homology (structural, cladistic) than analogy (functional, syllogistic), and of simile (tangible) more than metaphor (abstract) for research and exploration. (Analogy and metaphor, wistful or wishful, beguile and mislead the literate. Simile [verifiable] and homology [genealogy] are based on reality and more reliable.) The essence of (ExE) excellent creativity searches for something different or discovers the unfamiliar.

There are risks in staying at any stage, no matter how creative as Mozart and Jesus demonstrate.

Einstein himself could not progress beyond the logical duality of an alternately expanding and shrinking universe. Precocity thus poses hazards for the gifted. "Late bloomers" like Buddha and Jefferson can have it all.

Late bloomers or not, none of us can be well-rounded, creative people because our senses are flawed or limited. We are not as generously endowed sensually compared to other animals whose brains are smaller.

Talent is inherited by our brain, opportunity is provided by our skills. Proofs are Buckminster Fuller and Helen Keller.

Echoes or images of emotional and intuitive creativity that resonate with their consumers are not as original as those that must be incubated to hatch in their own good time before gaining universal acceptance or achieving commercial success. Incubation periods are shorter for the gifted.

C. EFFECTS OF STAGING IN THE DEVELOPMENT OF TALENT

Between being born and getting old, we become (**A**) emotional and passionate while passive or immobilized, (**B**) mobile and active or intuitive and decisive, (**C**) reactively reflective (mirrorlike) or deliberative, then more objective or (**D**) comparative, and—at any stage, if free and talented—(**E**) inventive or innovative and proactive.

During the emotional stage, sensual innovations in music and painting, like rock and roll and cubism, can be divisive but not very dangerous because their religious or politicized practitioners are passionate but passive, instead of active or reactive, even at Woodstock concerts.

In the more active stage of sensual development, divisive trends are dangerous: Moving leads to marching and marches become battles for dominance by political or economic imperialists who use war dances, martial music, and flying colors to rally and galvanize their idealistic or mercenary followers. (Social imitation of others slows down sensual stages of becoming or individuation of the self.)

In the more reflective stage of sensual development, we use fighting words and our brain more than our muscles to defend our actions. We can reactivate or mobilize those who need leaders and proselytize or evangelize those who need causes to die or kill for.

After passing these passive or active and reactive or reflective stages, we can compare and contrapose all the risks that creative ideas hide and reject the easy or costly defense of the ideologies that they produce, which have excused jealous genocide since biblical times.

In stark contrast, the purely creative stage of sensual development produces art with/without words only for art's sake and science with/without technology only for the sake of knowledge, not genocide. Humanity faces extinction when what artists and scientists produce are misused—e.g., stirring music as a summons to arms or orbiting satellites for star wars—by "socialized", active/reactive sensualists like those who think that *Lord of the Flies* is about power-hungry kids.

Fiction (verbs) and philosophy (nouns) have their roots in the same soil that feeds ideagogue and idealist fantasizers and fanatics. Their varying senso-socio-sexual ratios—based on the absolute relativity of WoMan's nature, culture, and nurture—unify whatever matters in the universe or at home we do mind.

Science with a capital *S* can itself be an ideology. If viruses are virtually immortal and other cells, lonesome after cell division, begin as souls, scientistic pantheism can even become more benign than Buddhism. Only in heated debate does Science become strident, especially when It (*sic*) is contrasted with Art with a capital *A*. (True artists/scientists let their works speak for themselves.)

Newer ideologies, even those with the Unconscious as centerpiece, tend to be capitalized when written about. But Science and the Unconscious by themselves are never lethal weapons though their advocates can promise copycat utopias like any uncompromising evangelist.

My new synthesis that simultaneously embraces and transcends Piaget at his most experimental and Jung at his most mystical is that "(1) the brain is (a) preprogrammed by 'instincts,' which it processes as (b) internal 'sensations' to which it may then (2a) 'intuitively' respond unfeelingly or, (2b) by 'reflex,' react 'unthinkingly.'"

> Animals, like many of us, can (**A**) feel good or bad, (**B**) do right or wrong, and (**C**) be curious enough to think straight or not. But we must not confuse (**A**) e-motion with (**B**) action or (**C**) answers with (**D**) correlations.
>
> (This notion sweeps away old theories of emotion from Angyal, de Rivera, Freud, Hillman, James, Jung, Lange, McDougall, Paulhan, Pribram, Sartre, and Wundt. It simplifies those of Basch, Darwin, Demos, Nathanson and Tompkins. (*Psychiatric Annals*, Oct., 1993)

Behavior is humanimal; human behavior is people. To understand both, we need to compare as many of each as we can and, mindful that they are seeded by our past, not forget that they are more than just fruits.

We cannot compare from just one point of view. We have to have different representatives speaking their lines. They can assist us in discovering other facets of human behavior that we have not fully understood and cannot explore—because we take them for granted in members of our own family or because they come from different neighborhoods populated by strangers we have not met.

To compare various combinations is not easy for many (for whom heretics must go slow) and they usually remain dogmatic (uncognizant) who depend only on reasoning by (**C**) analogy (using Piaget's abstractions).

Creative thinkers like Einstein and Freud theorized beyond logic without testing.

Galileo doubted logic was conclusive and experimented.

Stages in the development of talent depend on the freedom to (A) feel, (B) act, (C) think, (D) correlate, and (E') destroy. (To believe in one's art or science or self is to narrow one's creativity.)

Creativity begins with originality. By definition, originality is new to the audience, and it may tease their fancy or insult their intelligence. Thus, its reception goes from ridicule to rejection to dismissal as nothing new.

To be creative, the pioneer therefore risks being ignored, unless hir (*sic*) originality appeals to enough people long enough to become contemporary art or passes enough tests to become part of modern science.

To succeed, art and science must loom larger than the artist or scientist, the potter becoming the pot. Life is short but wide, though narrowly creative people can "live" longer than most, even beyond their grave as legends.

But when art or science is used to advance old "truths," then we have a noncreative perversion of talent.

CREATIVITY EVOLVED GENETICALLY and CORTICALLY

To both mind and soul, the brain is central, but it is not in life. Our lives are governed by older nervous systems that evolved before we acquired brains for thinking and talking.

Our reptilian brain (archipallium) programs vital functions and survival instincts below our level of awareness. Primates achieve self-consciousness before the mirror (a woman is therefore more evolved than kids or men: her genitalia has evolved beyond the male "cloaca" for both semen and urine).

Did Socrates at the very end ask self-consciously, "I drank what?" Or did he decide after examining his life that it is not worth living? And in not coming back from the dead ever since, was he right? Or as he hoped, is he in better company?

Aristotle and other ancient philosophers counted on us being rational, and Freud and modern metaphysicians found us irrationally inhibited in (**B**) action. In fact, computers are more (**C**) logical and less (**A**) emotional than all animals, including humanimachines. (Sensually, other primates can also (**D**) compare effects and (**E**) innovate, even if they do not dwell on it.)

EXCERPTS FROM EXTENDED EXTEMPORANEOUS ELABORATION

1. Good people are more maternal and think less in terms of right or wrong or true or false. If what I say confuses, it is because some words now used to describe what is neural as well as moral (e.g., good) are more factual than familiar (e.g., to communicate is very simply to be repetitious.

2. To inform is to break new ground (which can make each paragraph a megadose of strange food for thought), to communicate is to find common ground. Homology in science makes what is obviously different more alike, such as arms and wings being forelimbs among bipeds. Analogy in literature makes what is difficult to comprehend understandable—e.g., ideology is like bureaucracies, good intentions gone bad once institutionalized—by showing how they are similar to others from which the word "simile" is derived. Metaphors—e.g., marching silently to a different drumbeat—provide more color or drama, but add little to our fund of knowledge.

3. Art resonates to communicate with kindred spirits, even if James Joyce's words may be Greek to many. Science informs about what is old that is disproved and what is new that needs testing, whether or not it is understandable, like the unique fusion of previously absolute categories of time and space in Einstein's theory of relativity. (Humanists, who love to be their brothers' keeper, like to be consulted about new research studies by nonanthropologists who work in any basic science.)

4. Schizophrenics do not talk like us, which is why we burn them at the stake, incarcerate them, or abuse them with surgery or drugs. Nor can we use words like James Joyce does. Few of us can understand him or Einstein.

5. Some thoughts can be expressed in words. What distinguishes us from other animals except parrots is our ability to pronounce consonants in combination with vowels—e.g., "whatchamacallit?" "thingamajig," and "gizmo." Many words are unspeakable because they have too many consonants. We call them polysyllables. Scientists like them. (And stated simply with silent hands and shoulders and face, Marshall McLuhan thinks that spoken thoughts lose a lot [in transit to Broca's speech center.])

6. If words were decisive, art and science would be poorer. There are inarticulate artists (elephants and chimps who paint collectible works with their prehensile trunk and opposable thumb, respectively) and scientists (monkeys who, without any lessons from Newton, separate grain from sand by dumping the mixture in seawater). The animal constitution we all share equip us for creativity.

7. We had a cat who pulled a doormat out to open a door wider. In thus discovering the principle of the wedge, the plow was reinvented and the fulcrum of Archimedes and surpassed those who designed the Parthenon before keystones were used to keep arches from collapsing.

8. We are different from animals in being able to use numbers. Data processing produced science even when they were roman numerals. But not many of us can use numbers like Newton did. Of course, Einstein made some of Newton's thinking obsolete.

9. Without a tail, I was able to build a tree house with the help of my thumbs. Only once did I feel like using my tongue to ask for help. Then it dawned on me that if in the beginning was the Word and the word was "Help," it would not breed fanatics. Who could be fanatical about helping? *(l/15)*

10. I did not build a tree house to learn about the idiocy of turning nouns ("And the word was God") into icons. But the tree house became a Tree of Knowledge, which taught me not about good or evil but about the virtue of verbs.

D. Our Life through Time; How Behavior CHANGES with AGE

Human parents expect more from their offspring than other species from theirs. Wanted children are therefore burdened with all the dreams their parents have for them while all along being weaker than other animals at birth.

Both liabilities make them more dependent on, and beholden to, their parents longer than other animals have to be.

Throughout our lives, we are therefore handicapped by inferior preparation for independent living and by external expectations from those on whom we depend. If what we inherited from our grandparents cannot carry this double burden, we get sick before we need to wear out.

First: Cautionary CONSIDERATIONS

As long as we rely entirely on what is (**C**) logical, reasonable, and justifiable in the calculus of (**A, B**) emotion and motivation, we end up with self-deception or lives of quiet desperation. *(1/19)*

> Philosophers, who embalm their ideas—once their fictional premises are granted—are weak (and self-protective) or suffer from intellectual inertia (momentum of memories) and become (**D'**) the least self-critical of (**C**) "critical thinkers." Theologians and politicians are better at recollection (nostalgia without agitation) than reflection (cognition after cogitation) about what they remember and recognize by virtue of redundant familiarity typical of bedtime stories. *(1/18)*

Second: WHAT DOES LIFELONG EDUCATION YIELD?

Health and education are clearly linked, like population and environment, in changing the human condition. But health care must be independent of social fads, and education cannot concentrate on literacy in literature, sacred or profane.

The *literati* can be depended on to expand their own bureaucracy by reformulating the same old questions and redundantly repeating the same tired answers. Scientific and computer literacy is growing in importance as the world shrinks to the size of a village in the tightening grip of technology.

A new emphasis, based on extended studies, by this writer and heretofore ignored predecessors, embraces all behaviors that are "transcultural." This implies that they are likely to be found in other animals, in the same sense that stereoscopic vision also evolved among natural predators who/which must surprise the unsuspecting that may be camouflaged or/and moving out of cover. *(l/16)* (They should also have DNA segments in common.)

"Cross-species" behaviors include toolmaking, using and abusing, parenting and caring, growth and change, "willing" and complying, curiosity and ingenuity, wanting and helping, incest and pedophilia, programming and learning, liberty and survival, power plays and ploys, sex and violence, etc.

We will therefore trace behavior that we share with other species as far back as we can and note the variations ("perversions") that make us different, now that we have our own versions of man-made "saber-toothed paper tigers" to pit our wits against. *(l/17)*

> Did Aristotle solve any problems or clear up any issues in ancient Greece? If so, what? Or except for some problems that postlogical approaches have preempted, do those issues still plague the world today?
>
> (If Athens had not wrested intellectual preeminence from Ionia, we would now be probing the stars instead of gazing at the light that left them before our time.)

1. a. According to the Jesuits, we are a bunch of seven-year-olds running around trying to reconcile present brain-stuffing by our teachers with past brainwashing by our parents and theirs. (The result is a consistent effort to be consistent in rejecting "stuff" that we had been brainwashed against.)
    b. In my case, my brain had been literally washed by near drowning before I was nine, leaving it more childlike than yours at that age. I was glad ever since just to be "alive" rather than desperate to "survive" then or, later, to "achieve" in order to outlive an unlived life.
2. a. Before medical school, we learned that dinosaurs were masters of our planet almost a quarter of a billion years before we arrived. Sharks, the first mammals, outlasted them and still rule our

oceans. Birds have succeeded dinosaurs as masters of the sky. The later evolution of our feathered friends did not create new problems like ours still does. Moreover, unlike our brain, their "bird brains" are able to regenerate during their lifetime.

b. We also accepted without hesitation that we are not human unless we have a mind, a body, and a spirit. Other words for them were, respectively, "psyche," "flesh," and "soul." But during pubescence, we were more curious about biology. *(l/20)*

3. In medical school, we paid very little attention to psychiatry and soul-searching and concentrated on patients who are diagnosed as "sick" from demonstrable "weaknesses of the flesh."

4. After medical school and lifelong continuing education, can we today deliberately replace spirit, mind, and body respectively with "ideology" (or bias plus opinion) for *Homo domesticus* and *metropolis,* and "sagacity" (or knowledge plus experience), and "carnality" (inherited "flesh") for *Homo sapiens*? *(l/21)*

Third: HOW SPECIAL ARE WE?

All living things on our planet live the carbon dioxide cycle. We additionally have a pyramid to ascend and descend erratically after we are born.

1. What distinguishes us from other species is not our achievements. They are not more beneficial than theirs. We cannot even synthesize feathers to match those of birds. It is rather that our successes will get buried like those of other dead civilizations. Some of their ghost towns are exotic enough to be tourist attractions today.

2. What distinguishes ours even from those of prior civilizations is the speed with which we change "direction." But our "goals" have always been dictated by accidents of science and technology.

a. Among these unexpected and erratic developments are those of the printing press and wireless broadcasting, the steam engine and internal combustion, jet propulsion and space travel, radar tracking and computer simulation, nuclear physics and molecular biology. And now electronic monitoring of lifesaving devices.

b. Some of them will eventually become obsolete. Many "social mutations" fail to make it, just as other mutants fail to find a niche like ours. (Our niche appeared by accident after the unexpected demise of dinosaurs.)

Fourth: WHAT HAVE WE WROUGHT?

1. We have come a long way in a short time. In the time we have left, it will cost us more and more to travel in this fast lane. But to be able to change lanes, we have to get reoriented. To do this, we must first slow down and take our bearings:

a. The printing press gave the Protestant Reformation a pulpit from which Martin Luther can preach to distant multitudes who will listen to those who can read. *(l/22)*

b. The steam engine helped us produce more goods than our neighbors can use and then haul the surplus wherever advertisements in transistorized media can create demands for them.

c. Radar tracking allowed us to shoot better than cowboys and the internal combustion engine to reach places our horses cannot.

d. Jet propulsion got us to the moon and nuclear science the ability to study the sun.

e. Molecular biology can now let us compare ourselves with other animals better.

2. It is increasingly clear that without building a better world for our children, we have merely advanced in toolmaking.

a. We still misuse the printed word and wireless broadcasts for propaganda.

b. We have exploited the steam engine and jet propulsion for transporting death.

c. We now abuse internal combustion and nuclear physics to pollute the air.

d. Yet we stop short of finding out just how bats navigate by radar.

e. We still do not know how far computers can go beyond doing our bidding. (Can they develop consciousness like primates eventually did?)

f. Nor how molecular biology can help discover laws of animal motion and evolution.

g. And some object to living on and on. (A 120-year-old recently asked if God had forgotten her.)

Fifth: WHAT is it that DRIVES US?

1. a. Life for animals is a struggle to survive. But for most of us, it also began with pain from acute brain trauma, compounded for some by early circumcision, which begets chronic circumspection. The first part of our carbon dioxide cycle is spent learning to escape pain before we can discover who inflicts it.

   b. Until we learned to lie without being found out, we thought pain did not come from without. But by then, enough pain has been stored in our memories that we cannot escape it all by getting away with lying skillfully to others. We end up lying to ourselves without knowing it.

   c. Only if those memories can somehow be erased can we identify the present sources of pain in our lives. Otherwise, we will blame ourselves for what our parents blamed us, and what their surrogates among our superiors now blame us. Thus we never escape the pain that resembles what we suffered when we had no easy way of fighting against those who inflicted it. Can such suffering be honorable? And to accept it, are we now prepared to support drug peddlers or to assist in the suicide of those in chronic pain, especially when the sick is dear to us? *(1/23)*

2. Contrast our childhood with what life has to offer young penguins.

   a. Their parents alternate sitting on their eggs until they hatch. They are fed until they can feed themselves. They have first priority over adults for choice morsels of food. They are protected from predators while they are weak, at great risk to their elders.

    b. Because their aging brain cells regenerate themselves, they never have to be as helpless as hatchlings again. They therefore need not test how they will be looked after by relatives when they need looking after.

3.   a. Some of our children, in their first or second childhood, do not even sleep with their parents. They are left to sleep alone from the time they are born. They are fed at the convenience of adults or babysitters. They are programmed to limit their demands on their custodians. Or just promised better future rewards. They are told not to complain under threat of punishment or sedation or internal exile to their bedrooms without dinner. *(l/24)*

    b. No wonder that in their first or second adolescence, when metabolic changes should have had enough time to achieve internal equilibrium without additional help or expatriation, *Homo domesticus* and *metropolis* become anorexic or bulimic, and/or insomniac or addicted to drugs or fantasies or social clichés (sacred or secular).

    c. If not a biological norm, what can we do now to divert this retreat to past fixations in childhood and adolescence? Is this expectable only for our species, but not natural among other animals or mammals?

Sixth: HOW DO WE CHANGE?

1.   a. *Homo sapiens* used to work to have something to eat to give them energy to do more than eat. Now *Homo domestici* tend to eat more when they are idle. Then in their second adolescence, *Homo metropoli* work harder at eating less in order to lose weight.

    b. Work used to keep *Homo sapiens* fit for work. Now *Homo metropoli* works at staying fit in order to look young and healthy.

    c. *Homo sapiens* used to build houses for shelter. Now *Homo domestici* have them built as furniture showrooms by architects whom they can afford to hire and who build them to be nest eggs for their adult clients to profit from as investments. Animals build nests to suit the needs of the young, not their taste.

d. *Homo sapiens* used to work to support their kids through college. Now *Homo metropolis* works to support their estranged mothers who were liberated from housework by time-saving appliances. They can now afford better day care facilities for their kids while they resume studies or careers interrupted by childbearing. (Parkinson's law to fill time works only with human beings.)

2. Intelligence is not like the sun and therefore not a matter of geography, shining brighter in some places more than others. It is more like a spotlight, focused on what it shines upon. To search is to use a searchlight. Research is more like looking for something where there is already enough light. Keeping all these considerations in mind may make the monitoring of otherwise strange discoveries worth doing.

3. If what is cultural is traditional in a society and by "transcultural" we mean behaviors that transcend culture—like religion as animism, politics as pecking order, and trade as barter—and if behaviors that we find in all human cultures imply that they may not be uniquely human, we can then go on to "cross-cultural" studies of any behavior that is peculiar to several species.

Seventh: WHAT HOLDS US BACK?

1. With unskilled labor, we can produce energy-efficient, if inaccurate, "computers" inside the skulls of our children. As untrained programmers, it takes us longer to program our children's brains to meet all our stock expectations. Are our own expectations also unskillfully programmed in us by our parents or their surrogates?

a. But instead of studying ethology and history, *Homo domesticus* concentrates on theology and current events: we grant research subsidies for computer techniques that only allow Americans to compete better with groups of our own species who are catching up with us while molecular biology reveals how evolution has not even fully prepared us for a niche to occupy longer than other species whom we still believe to be inferior to us.

("Acts of God" and man-made disasters are not a test of our faith in a benevolent despot, but Mother Nature's way by trial and error to cope with still unresolved problems in her evolution.)

   b. Knowing that birds and "lower animals" regenerate brain cells effortlessly, can "microelectronics" and "microbiology" combine to produce "biochips" that will give us additional "self-starting" brain power before we exhaust our finite fossilized energy reserves? If other animals face scarcity fearlessly, might self-starting artificial intelligence free us from inhibiting fear of what's ahead? Is this what we need today to live unfettered by our past that cannot ever be undone?

2. Even after enjoying health, wealth, and wisdom, we tend to recycle to past developmental milestones in our minds, bodies, and ideologies. Just like us, primates and "lower" animals also (**F**) practice animistic thinking, (**G**) form pecking orders, and (**H**) use barter trading. Their "ideologies" are as self-centered as ours to maximize power and profit, but usually just for procreation, not to rescue the weak or aging.

(Healthier at birth and less dependent soon after, animals do not need our "rescue fantasies" from a lost paradise by a powerful "Parent" Who has only temporarily abandoned us to be the orphaned "foster children" of our "adopted" human family.)
(1/25)

   a. As they age, *Homo domestici* may shun newer social slogans promising paradise on earth and hope to return their soul to God in His heaven to rest in peace.

   b. All being to retrace their steps, carnally and mentally, through a second childhood and a second adolescence, in reverse chronological order.

Eighth: DOMESTICATE OR BREED?

1. Unlike our pets, we are bred to be domesticated by brainwashing from our parents and by brain-stuffing from our teachers to prepare us for sale as a commodity in the urban labor market—like animals in the farm—to produce profit until we can be dumped in the trashcan of culture as waste, once any residual

human dignity is defiled by incontinence, from disease, or senescence.

a. Can the trauma of natural birth and early genital mutilation (circumcision or clitoridectomy) be avoided and each child helped rather than trained like pets? To be given the run of the house like a cat, but not declawed as an internal risk, is better than being raised like a dog to be loyal. (The acid test of true loyalty or blind faith comes once they are seriously questioned.)

b. Even sexual relations become social relationships for *Homo domesticus* when procreation becomes recreation. If both partners accept responsibility for each other's orgasm, premature ejaculation can appear like conjugal rape without consent especially when it results in fertilization.

2. a. For other animals, sex without procreation is playful and is not restricted according to age or sex. In this age of technology, even recreational sex becomes a serious pursuit for *Homo metropolis*, with organized institutions like singles' bars, computer dating, sex therapy, etc., to assist the inept.

Now that technology does not demand more human horsepower, reproduction is replaced by contraception or, worse, by intrauterine homicide. Even animals raised as pets but not castrated are separated from their litters, which are sold or given away to be sterilized.

b. Among other mammals, spontaneous abortions, stillbirths, and infanticide are dictated by droughts and protein deficiency, not by competitors for status or, if unsuccessful, for status symbols whose cost enslaves social climbers most of their lives. It is therefore understandable that the animal fetus is reassimilated in the maternal metabolism, the stillborn and all afterbirths are eaten, and the dead cannibalized. Among us, the aborted fetus, the stillborn, and all placentas are treated as garbage or buried, to benefit scavengers out of our sight and notice or underground.

Ninth: What do we need? A BOLD, CLEAR, DEFINING EXPERIMENT

1. If all of us use tools and worship totems, then ingenuity with dexterity and imagination with animism can be expected among our cousins whose DNA are similar to ours. If only some religions believe in "original sin," then it must explain something peculiar to their collective past. (Infidels serve their killers in an Islamic paradise populated by not angels, but virgins that widow-marrying Mohammad missed.) Did excruciating headaches from natural birth and traditional genital abuse by early circumcision jointly prompt male biblical writers and believers to imagine that they are being punished for the sins of their forebears? Can we find out?

   a. Any behavioral research must start at the very beginning of life, or it is already flawed by overlooked experiences, which the subjects cannot remember due to traumatic shock to body and brain of the newborn and from abusing the child by forcing it to give up its vocalizations to talk with us. Like abused children, who are battered when they keep on crying and then ask for forgiveness afterward, silent newborns' brain and/or genitalia are traumatized but then *Homo domestici* have to pray to be rescued by a tooth fairy's alter ego to soar with Him to paradise. (Fertilized by natural sperm donors, are natural mothers like our milk teeth that must give way to a fairy tale Father to replace them more permanently than dentures?)

   b. Except for some birds and mammals, most mothers stay with their litters instead of their mates. Successful single-parent "nuclear" families of birds and other mammals can teach our still-evolving and equally mobile postindustrial households how they might revise their life cycle (which starts going on reverse in midlife and old age).

2. a. It is not easy to test the effects of socialization against breeding or of sexual recreation against simple procreation. To compare the results of biological or social childbearing and rearing, a suitable male sponsor can artificially or naturally impregnate identical twins born by elective Caesarian section so that neither is initially handicapped by acute brain trauma, even if their heads

are slightly larger than those of triplets. After elective Caesarian birth, uncircumcised in infancy and not "house-broken" as a toddler, their offspring can then be more simply raised either as children or as social conduits.

(In other species and some subcultures, the offspring need only wait for puberty [or circumcision—if it is a rite of passage during puberty and not ritual abuse of infantile genitalia)—in order to reproduce.)

    b.   Testing will take longer without identical twins. It may take at least two generations when two sets of (uncircumcised) dependents, born by elective Caesarean section, can be raised separately. With guaranteed annual income from sponsors or public subsidies to help raise the children differently, the relative success of both pairs of research subjects can be measured periodically.

Tenth: Are We Our BEST FRIEND?

1.   Can one of each research pairing or an identical twin not have to please a second adult to maintain a favored position in their household?

    a.   This will give that one a sense of being "Number One" right away, instead of waiting until adulthood to be "Number One" by marriage.

    b.   It will also not pray for a better father, if it must have one, and can easily stop living up to the expectations of an absentee godhead as soon as it can sort things out without trying to please its master like a "lapdog" must.

    c.   It will also not have to be an "attack dog" protecting its master, but can remain its own master, protecting its dependents by leading them away from danger or defending them when cornered.

    d.   It will not have to be a "sheepdog" herding the sheepish for a shepherd, but keeping its dependents safe together or separately, even if it must risk danger in order to distract their predators.

e.   It will not also have to be a "watchdog" for its paymasters and
need only be vigilant against those of its own enemies within
striking distance.

2.   Brainwashing and brain-stuffing make *Homo dome*sticus lap
up social slogans about Paradise Lost, Evil Empires, Worker's
Paradise, and Peace by War-mongering from Cold War warriors.
These slogans recruit slaves to serve disembodied masters like
God, the State, the Stock Exchange or, among *Homo metropoli*,
the Fourth Estate (a free press to keep the first three from
recruiting greater numbers to faith, loyalty, and gluttony
respectively).

Eleventh: CAN we UNLEARN the PAST?

1.   a. Human "lapdogs," "attack dogs," "sheepdogs," and "watchdogs"
are social perversions of our animalhood and personhood by
domestication.

b.   Only "hunting dogs," "seeing-eye dogs," or "hearing-ear
dogs" among *Homo sapiens* use their senses to monitor and
master their surroundings for their dependents until they,
in turn, are themselves ready to reproduce and dependable
enough for parenthood in their sensual, social, and sexual
development.

2.   a. Until then, intelligent beings from other worlds are bound
to be puzzled by how skillfully we fail to use our intelligence
except for toolmaking as they observe *Homo domesticus*
behavior throughout our first childhood and adolescence and
Homo metropolis reactions to midlife and old-age crises during
our second adolescence and childhood. (We create civilizations
to which we sacrifice our own children and then abandon our
elders to their mercies.)

b.   They would be puzzled even more at how resourcefully we
use our intellect (memory, not intelligence) to hide these
facts away during an increasingly longer adulthood that our
advancing science and technology have given us.

Finally: WHAT INHIBITS US?

1. a. When an animal grows a new tail, it does not need to learn what the old tail had to learn. But unlike birds, we cannot grow new brain cells. We must therefore get rid of those cells that we have tied up with painful memories before we get too old to replace them with more pleasure-prone interneuronal connections.

   b. Unless, like cats, we do not as children have to please any grown-ups. Only then do we not end up at an early age like old dogs unable to unlearn old tricks.

   Our old "moral scruples" are borrowed principles that we fall back on to avoid indecision. (That is what I mean by "lying to ourselves without knowing it.") "Standing on principles" that we had learned secondhand without testing is "freedom of conscience" or the right to freely parrot platitudes or, worse, to use principles like knee-jerk reflexes.

   c. We ought to be able to go beyond standing on moral grounds on any issue. Only then can we compare the morality of our parents and their allies and adversaries with those who are now ours. To do this, we need to identify our emotional links as links instead of "feelings" and our impulses as intuitions instead of "initiatives."

   d. Once we isolate **(A)** emotion and **(B)** intuition, we can **(C)** reflect to arrive at a position that does not simply justify our feelings or impulses. But that is not enough. We have to do that for our allies and adversaries also and **(D)** compare their respective merits. *(l/26)*

2. Because talent is inherited, **(E)** creativity and virtuosity may be precocious and can develop independently of **(A)**, **(B)**, **(C)** and **(D)**. *(l/26,27)*

3. To see all this, we need to bring evolution to life as ethology and history merging together.

Rights are for the weak, freedom for the strong, and God for the frightened or puzzled, who pray for help from the Omnipotent and Omniscient (a Super-Computer).

Why did God make little apples green and children small? Everything we learned before puberty and selfhood can conspire to make us dependent and childlike. It is no accident that we are seen as sheep to be herded around by a shepherd. (Even drug addicts reach for a state of altered consciousness in which they can do no wrong.)

The sheepish *Homo domesticus* seeking reassurance tends to postpone living to some remote future by mortgaging the present to secure their tomorrows. Wolfish about knowledge, *Homo sapiens* risk danger lurking in the unknown to add to or subtract from what is known.

We reward fiction writers who can lie artfully if we agree with their characters. (Those who would rather talk of relationships remember relatives who failed them.) We treasure our mind because we think we can control what it thinks more than what it minds. We are wrong.

E. The "PSYCHE" AND Today's SCIENCE

The old concept of "psyche" as spirit is unchanged, but as "mind," it changed after "logos" as "intelligence" or information produced such absolutes as "truth" and "beauty" with the predictable tautology or circularity contributed by "logic," also known as "methodos." "Mind" as "consciousness" was separated from matter by the Greeks, from the body by theologians, from spirit by Descartes, from "reason" by Freud, and then from logic by Piaget.

Piaget lists (**A**) sensorimotor development in infants, (**B**) preoperational or preconceptual intuition and concretistic trial-and-error search for solutions among children, and ends his theory with (**C**) "rational" thought or formal abstractions and logical reductionism.

All sentient animals perceive; some have better memories, and others are more able to combine bits of memory in a process called "recognition" (which is largely inherited and "conflict-free," unlike "remembering," which may be spotty).

Though our brain is tightly squeezed during delivery, we start (**A**) "feeling" again and, as we move, regain (**B**) "reptilian intuition" with leaps of insight or visceral knowledge without intellectualization. Some doubts induce Cartesian "cogitation," which get recognition as (**C**) "thoughts" or "theories" or "reasons" to (**D**) probe, test or disprove, or let us (**E**) reconnect, invent, or create.

Our doubts can take us beyond Piagetian cognitive psychology and Freudian introspective psychoanalysis and away from their limited goals of liberating or leading the mind from or out of irrational (ratio-unconscious), if not illogical (logic-blind), oppression of, or arrested growth in, senso-socio-sexual perspective.

Deliberate (a) development of (**D**) comparative rationalysis to sort out ratios in critically exploring behavioral correlations and (b) encouragement of (**E**) creativity in discovering nonrandom connections can (1) restore (*sic*) "spirit" to mythology and mysticism, (2) reunite the "mind" with the body, and the brain with behavior as matter in motion, and (3) get us past syllogism or analogy to reexamine history and evolution (4) in order to test reasoning as logic against ethology and homology for (5) a new postlogical, postindustrial, transcultural psychiatry.

1. A NEW GLOBAL PERSPECTIVE: MIND AND MATTER, BODY AND BEHAVIOR

The greatest difficulty encountered by animals with our language is its pronunciation. Their difficulty is unrelated to intelligence. Have you noticed that commercial advertising uses fewer words and more nonverbal messages and body language to sell more products? *(1/28)*

We have, in California, a Nobel laureate who thinks professors are instructors in forgetting. Each postlogical advance in modern science costs immediate loss of intelligibility. Such losses were avoided in the Dark Ages, when tautology decided issues to preserve sanity at the expense of progress. Today, we have to face the fact that "matter, mind and spirit have been superseded by an expanding universe of curved multi-dimensional empty space" (Koestler).

a. BEFORE AND BEYOND MIND AND BODY or MATTER AND SPIRIT

I am going to talk about the "psyche" as a common noun and briefly as a proper noun. As a common noun, the "psyche" has had a long and checkered history, not all of it legitimate and some of it downright harmful to its users. As a proper noun, it had a fairly uneventful history until the relationship between Cupid, who is divine, and Psyche, who was not, was satirized first on British TV. Exported as a "sitcom" (or situation comedy), *All in the Family* portrayed Archie Bunker as a bigot and his wife Edith, who, like Psyche, did not mind being bullied, as a "dingbat."

But in the beginning of time, before there were Greek gods and TV sitcoms to satirize sacred cows, God created hydrogen but did not give it a name. Long afterward, the Greeks gave the name "psyche" to what was known as the "spirit." We shall try to bridge the elapsed time between both events and share our understanding of history as a morality play and of evolution as biochemistry. Evolution, of course, did not stop with inert objects in the world of matter, or we would not be here today.

As with material forces, there is a terrible inertia in ideas. We have always been taught to suspect our instincts because they tempt us to do what society prohibits. In fact, instincts are older than society and are not as prone to fragmentation over the aeons like all dead civilizations. Those who live by their instincts outnumber those who are too inhibited to be tempted.

Our brain evolved from our skin in order to centralize our sense of our surroundings. But like an officious Colonel Blimp, it did not stop at monitoring our senses. It also tried to make sense of what little it could apprehend with only five senses. Incomplete apprehension always leads to ideas, but only human beings accept ideologies. Thus, our senso-social heritage may not be uniquely human, but a few twists in our thinking have evolved beyond reptilian intuition. Most of these twists are self-serving, assigning to us a central role in a vast universe that we cannot even comprehend as a curiosity-ridden tourist in space.

b. From SOCRATES to SARTRE

The ancient Athenians who gave what we have always regarded as the "spirit" its own special name. They called it the "psyche." This was long before the most spiritual of spirits appeared to His chosen people across the Mediterranean from Athens. Only afterward did Greek gods and goddesses also merge into a single deity.

But "psyche" as "spirit" did not change meaning until "logos" or "intelligence" entered intellectual discourse. (We speak today of "psyche" and "logos" as one word or "psychology," when they were originally worlds apart.)

The oracle at Delphi once told Socrates that he was the wisest man in Greece. Socrates could not believe his ears, and he died piously protesting his ignorance. He knew he was more logical (or methodical, from "methodos"), but not better informed than his fellow pedestrians.

"Logos" (or "intelligence" as "information," as in intelligence gathering) soon became mixed up with logic or "methodos," which then became a methodical search for abstractions.

(Greek gods and goddesses were eventually replaced in Western logic by abstract "truth" and "beauty.")

Along came Aristotle who made syllogism seem more methodical as an exercise in logic to his successors. (Modern science is not philosophical but postlogical.) The origin of syllogism can be traced to India. It may have been imported by soldiers of Aristotle's student, Alexander the Great (356–323 BC). On return from their military tour of duty, in their debriefing before demobilization after Alexander's unexpected demise, did their memory fail to recall two of the five elements of Indian syllogism? (l/29) Western logic has had to make do with only three ever since. *(l/30)*

In the older, wiser, nonreductive "methodos" or logic of the original Buddhist syllogism, which was simultaneously inductive and deductive as premodern natural science must be *(l/31)*, there were five elements. *(l/6)*

There is knowledge to be gained from each of the five and additional knowledge when the five are used together:

1. Prediction: "You will die."
2. Reason: "Because you are imperfect."
3. Example: "Since you get sick."
4. Application: "The imperfect get sick."
5. Conclusion: "Therefore, you are mortal."

In Aristotle's truncated version, without (1) proposition (prediction) and (3) example (data), what is left is metaphysics:

(2) reason (logical), followed by (4) application (teleology) and (5) conclusion (essence):

> 2. Logic: "Because you are imperfect."
> 3. Teleology: "And the imperfect get sick."
> 5. Essence: "Therefore, you are mortal."

Buddhist logic (1–5) does not assume a nonempty universe but gives the existential condition explicitly each time as an independent premise. It begins with observations (1: "You will die"), Aristotelian syllogism (2, 4, 5) starts with assumptions (2: "Because you are imperfect"). Buddhist logic continues inductively (3: "Since you get sick") rather than deductively (4: "The imperfect get sick"): because of this difference in premises, theorems true in Aristotelian logic (5: "Therefore, you are mortal") may be false in Buddhist logic and vice versa.

The strength of Indian thinking lies in their human sciences, which have always lagged behind in the West, even after secularism as humanism replaced worship of the spirit. Unlike Western logic, instead of making a general assumption at the very beginning in order to cover all cases, Buddhist logic employed in every individual case an additional premise in order to make the major premise existential.

> To defend this practice, their philosophers demand of Western logicians, "If you want to cover the earth with cowhide simply to protect your feet, why not just wear a pair of shoes?"
>
> (Bertrand Russell, after World War II, said, "If we are to feel at home in the world . . . we shall have to admit Asia to equality in our thoughts, not only politically but culturally. What changes this will bring about I do not know, but I am convinced that they will be profound and of the greatest importance.")

Only recently has the West found its vaunted logic to be metaphysical rather than phenomenological. It took Sartre, a French existentialist, to point out that in our thinking, the only evil are the abstractions that we defend vigorously. Logic is conspicuously absent from the koans (Chan) of the Chinese and the Zen Buddhism of the Japanese.

Western logic today is even more restrictively tolerant in demanding only very simple dualisms: (**A**) good or bad, (**B**) right or wrong, and (**C**) true or false. Even Western science demands only the dualism of (**D**) testable or untestable to separate theory from metaphor (e.g., a tantalizing serpent appeared to recruit occupants for heaven and hell). And artists universally demand only that what is artistic be (**E**) enduring or avant-garde.

These dualisms infected Western psychiatry. "Psyche," now mis-translated and misused as "mind" instead of "spirit," became hyphenated. Freud theorized that our mind develops along psychosexual lines. Erikson, who never knew his own father, denied patricidal impulses as a problem of Oedipal proportions for his clients and tried to change "psycho-sexual" violence to "psycho-social" gentility.

Today, we can take the first step away from dualisms and the psyche by accepting mental subjectivity and correctly spelling "mind" as "mynd" to signify "myths of the mind." Only then can we examine new data or "logos" or intelligence postlogically, separately from armchair logic or "methodos" or critical thinking by internal reflection. We can then (1) change the dualisms of what is restrictively psychosexual or psychosocial to a more universal senso-socio-sexual series of stages in our evolution that can be (2) analyzed after active investigation of all variables by the process of ratiocination and (3) postanalytically expressed as ratios rather than reduced to self-serving rhetoric or rationalizations.

c. A TALE OF THREE CITIES: ATHENS, PARIS, AND GENEVA

We will now take you on a fateful journey that detoured through three cities over several centuries. The cities are Athens, Paris, and Geneva.

Three words took the same detour and changed their meanings over the centuries. The words are "psyche," "logos," and "eudaemonia." Their original meanings were, respectively, "spirit," "intelligence," and "fulfillment."

During this journey through history, the respective meanings of these three words first changed to "soul" (which is more properly "anima"), "logic" (which is more properly "methodos"), and "happiness," which is more emotion (**A**) than action (**B**).

In modern times, "psyche" has stood for "mind," "logic" for "thinking syllogistically," and "happiness" for "purpose," as in the "pursuit of happiness" for the Founding Fathers of the United States. (Would absent mothers agree?)

In our journey, we will stop over briefly to revisit Aristotle (384–322 BC) in Athens, Descartes (1596–1650) in Paris, and Piaget in the twentieth century in Geneva. On returning to these three cities, we will find that Aristotle in Athens thought of "active intellect" as "De Anima" and never talked of immortality of the soul. ("Anima" in Latin is "breath," and to the north of the Roman Empire, including the Nordic and Teutonic tongues, it means "sea" [gill?].)

There may be treachery as well as indeterminacy in any attempted translation. St. Thomas Aquinas, after selective reading of Aristotle, sought and found the dogmatic certitude that he was after: that the soul exists separately from the body. On this dogma, mistakenly attributed to Aristotle in Athens, St. Thomas built his scholastic philosophy and its unshakable faith that ergo, there is also an immortal God (F) who created (E) all mortals with an immortal soul.

(Buddha himself, 200 years before Aristotle, thought that any discussion of the soul only clouds the debate. [Reincarnation is the opposite of sainthood.] With Aristotle as the posthumous darling of Catholic philosophers, the West had always had a special relationship with God. In the Orient, there is no special place for our species in the scheme of things.)

We now depart for Paris where an unpublished rebuttal to St. Aquinas was being written. Descartes wrote, but did not publish until he was resting in peace and beyond harassment for heresy in his grave, that "cogito" or "personal doubts" or cogitation prove only that he exists cognitively, not that God does or does not. "Cogito, ergo sum" did not say "I think, therefore I am." He insisted that cogitation made him aware that he is in doubt and that therefore as a doubter, he exists in his mind. He separated his mental life from all else to escape charges of heretical doubt about the soul.

By delaying tactics and with such sidestepping mental somersaults, Descartes tried to separate the "psyche" as our "mind" from the seat of "logic," which accepts dualisms as divine, only to fail in his intent until now. Instead, the mind was separated ever since, not from the "soul" or spirit, but from our body. (Many "psychologists" today still sound like priests in emphasizing "spirituality.")

Thus, peace of mind and happiness in bed even now requires that *Homo domestici* continue to worship the Supreme Spirit Who saves sinners who try to reproduce themselves. Unhappy *Homo metropoli* cannot comfortably separate the mind from the soul: they would sooner divorce their body.

Descartes encouraged secular doubts or simple cogitation to prove only that we ourselves really exist apart. It is too bad that by delaying publication during his lifetime, Descartes could not himself correct the mistranslation of "cogitation" or doubting to "cognition" or thinking by uncritical philosophers and unsuspecting cognitive psychologists.

(Like his contemporaries, Piaget in Geneva was trained in the philosophy of the times. Like other cognitive psychologists in the West today, he was also never taught to distinguish "cogito" from "cognizance" or "notice," which had a separate Scottish origin in legal terminology.)

The unfortunate result was that "I think, therefore I am" led to other perversions like (1) "I feel (**A**) good, therefore I am good"; or (2) "I feel (**A'**) bad, therefore I am (**B'**) wronged"; or (3) "What feels (**A**) good must be (**B**) right"; or worse, (4) "I want, therefore I should" (**A**, therefore **B**).

In fact, "I doubt, therefore I am" could read, "I hurt, therefore I am" without unduly perverting it. If we do not have mental indigestion from doubting, we would not even be conscious of "conceiving" mentally. Doubt is distressing: "I do suffer, therefore I exist" -> "I am now conscious (of suffering)" -> "I know (that I mind), therefore I am."

Misreading "cogito" as "cognitif" is easy to do for those who are uncomfortable with, instead of challenged by, doubts. Doubting is initially destabilizing and, unexamined, can be chronically incapacitating. We all seek answers before we formulate different questions raised by our doubts. We even worship God (**F**) as the Fountain of Truth—the Bible that He inspired cannot lie—and ignore His decision (**B**) to evict Eve from Eden for testing (**D**) the truth (**C**) about good (**A**) and evil (**F'**) residing inside the fruit of His own creation (**E**), the Tree of Forbidden Knowledge.

Later, in Geneva, both as a philosopher and as a psychologist, Piaget tried to validate Kantian categories: For Kant, time and space were objects of an a priori intuition. Newton proved Kant to be correct in his intuition (reptilian), Piaget's neighbor (Einstein) showed that both were wrong by thought experiment: speed through space can affect time. *(1/32)*

Piaget as a psychologist made the ability to think in the abstract the end point of his schema of cognitive development (though his own daughters barely reached it). As a theorist out to prove that Kant's categories were psychologically valid, he was more epigenetic like Erikson and Jung than a soft pornographer like Freud (who thought good sex resulted from, but was not the aim, of healthy parenting). *(1/33)*

Teleologic search for Aristotle's "final cause" is a dead end, as is Piaget's epigenetic insistence on a sequence toward a predetermined ultimate aim: The old "psyche" is no more than an invisible spirit, like ether. It is not "logos," which means "intelligence," nor "logic," which is "methodos." "Eudamonia" itself is not "happiness" as the ultimate aim or end, but "fulfillment" of need.

> Fulfillment is not just the sense of being filled or (**A**) fed but of involvement in (**B**) deeds that meet our needs and match our resources, whether or not we achieve (**C**) mythical epigenesis or (**F**) mystical aims or not. Nonstoic ("ataraxic") serenity may be (**A**) happiness in a sleeping infant who is dry and satiated or postcoital for courting and consenting adults following a love feast ("agape"). Selfless love allows tired partner to snore on one's shoulder.

d. The LESSONS of EVOLUTION: BIOLOGICAL, GLOBAL, and COSMIC

In embryology, we were taught a long time ago that ontogeny recapitulates—but does not exactly repeat—phylogeny, i.e., that our intrauterine development approximates the evolution of our species. This is why babies can be born underwater before we cut the umbilical cord and we can get the heart pumping again even after we have ceased breathing. Similarly, just as the history of humanity keeps repeating itself, so does our cultural development also retrace the behavior of other social animals.

"Lower" animals have been (**F**) animistic (primates believe in frightening unseen enemies or in magical thinking), (**G**) subservient to a pecking order, and (**H**) enterprising in hoarding.

Bees and ants have no religion, yet they live together harmoniously. (Conflict produces poets who sublimate it and dictators who externalize and control it, not only to survive and thrive, but to prevail. Both groups were "blessed" with dominant mothers. So were the last eight American presidents [Helen Thomas, dean of Washington correspondents].) In groups, we are more suggestible, above and beyond our need for shepherds, because we felt more helpless than most animals after we were born.

It can take a village to raise a child properly.

Our purpose in (**F**) religion is not peace on earth but the multiplication of sinners to be forgiven in heaven. In (**G**) politics, our purpose may be peace (law and order) even without progress; in (**H**) economics, progress in order to prosper; as (**I**) individuals, to be (**A**) happy; in (**J**) society, less inequity (**B'**); in (**K**) technology, to save more time or space, etc.

Whatever our more maladapted species shares with healthy animals is not sick nor human but adaptive. If we are merely different in degree and not unique "in toto," we can establish behavioral science on a footing more solid than metaphysics, mythology, teleology, and epigenesis, whether we are children of God or descended from hydrogen, as we recycle ("procreate") regularly.

> In my culture, there are women I must not marry; but as an infant, I can suckle from the breasts of their mothers. (In America, cows are our wet nurses.) All females are, therefore, mammals before they become sex objects. (Breast augmentation is now sought by those who fear failure as sex objects.) The more universal the basis for any interpretation, the more valid it is.

e. ALL THEORIES HIDE PART of THE TRUTH IN THEIR DATABASE

We must not discard Piaget's data (or his old neighbor Jung's) nor ignore those produced by Maslow, Freud, and Erikson. We can accept all of them as part truths. But beyond tasting without testing their restricted theories, we must discover another that also allows us to see our development as proceeding from hydrogen out of the big bang to a literally mundane existence. *(l/34)*

Like all animals, we tend to swallow what agrees with our taste. Such gullibility easily leads to systems of belief, which psychiatrists suspect of being irrational only among their patients. (As long as beliefs are shared by a majority, they will probably not be diagnosed as paranoid even if they are delusional.)

People who believe may not be sick but are studiously ignorant about the evolution of their social delusions. (It is impossible to learn less, but possible to learn nothing. Invincible ignorance is the chastity belt of true believers. In fact, we all become victims of our own delusions as soon as we believe in order to escape doubt.)

To shake off the tyranny of mediocrity among the majority of believers of social delusions, each member of subspecies *Homo sapiens, domesticus*, and *metropolis*, somewhat Haeckel-like, can try harder to retrace the historical development of their behavior. This is necessary because even behavior, like all of biology, evolves. *(1/35)* Each can expect to appear somewhere in a bell-shaped curve of distribution for our senso-socio-sexual development in its particular population.

i. Our personal sensual development starts with (**A**) the use of our senses during infancy to monitor what is good or bad about our immediate environment. As our brain recovers from acute birth trauma, ancestral memories lodged in our reptilian brain serve as a blueprint for (**B**) reactions to our environment that we call intuition, which we instinctively use to enable us to survive, rightly or wrongly, without reflection.

As we approach adolescence, we begin to reflect idealistically, and our reflections produce (**C**) nonnegotiable answers prompted by mental knee jerks or automatized reflexes that we call moral principles. They are based on whatever mythology we have accepted as history and that we file away as truths when they are just metaphors or even demonstrably false.

Only after we develop the ability, without taking sides, to distinguish what is metaphorical or fanciful from what is factual or demonstrable can we start making (**D**) comparisons as budding scientists.

Only then also can gifted but stifled or unprecocious artists be free (**E**) to create new metaphors. But before then, (**B**) intuitions can lead to insights (ideas and theories) and inventions (techniques and prostheses).

The scientist and the artist do not necessarily follow each other except in the rarest of instances that are prefigured in the bell-shaped curve of sensual growth independent of social progress and sexual maturation. Because of necessary constraints invoking territorial rights, we have only begun to perceive the outlines of the parallel development of the three worlds of art, ideas, and science.

ii. There were deities before Jehovah. We therefore start retracing our social history with the "psyche" as spirit becoming God (**F**) the Watchmaker "creating" (**G**) His chosen governors, and (**H**) their chosen traders for colonizing heathens, down to postindustrial inventors converting (**K**) God in the Machine as Shop Supervisor to (**O**) God the Watchdog in orbiting satellites with computerized sensors. This modern socio-ontogeny is neo-Haeckelian.

iii. Sex and the birds and the bees are older than the human species. Therefore, instead of thinking of sex as creative or compulsive or otherwise oral, anal, or genital, we can return to the biology of largely automated procreation.

It starts with (**P**) narcissistic auto then homoerotic sex and proceeds to experimental sex before parenting and surrogate motherhood, adultery and/or divorce, and then achieves, if we live long enough, (**Z**) grandparenthood.

f. CONCLUSION: The Challenge to Unite our Nature with Nature

Our first paradigm shift was away from Ptolemy's epicycles. It was the Aristotelian, if not Artistotle's view of the world that Copernicus and Galileo unregretfully helped to destroy.

Some scientists still believe that the monk Copernicus did not live long enough to debunk their faith. Even Galileo (1564–1642) could not shake their supernatural superstitions.

The teleologic bias of St. Thomas had successfully perverted Aristotle's ideas to delay this paradigm shift. Only since the Renaissance has scholastic logic chopping lost the power to argue "final causes" even in astronomy and physics.

This major paradigm shift away from dogmatic debate could have taken place sooner with Descartes (1596–1650), but he was too fainthearted to risk prosecution for heresy, which Galileo suffered.

Newton (1642–1727) further postponed the investigation of incertitude by his strict adherence to his faith as a deist. He made our world more like a watchmaker's dream, but did he dare pluck the Tree of Knowledge only after promising a lifetime of celibacy? (With enough data, he hoped to be more like his dream Deity.)

Even Einstein (1879–1955) as a theist could not accept that his God ("The Old One") goes to the cosmic crap table to play or at least throw dice.

(To me, God could be playful enough to take His chances. If He could not veto what is thrown His way, then He at least should be allowed to play. If we cannot bear to see Him lose, we should keep away from the cosmic casinos of natural science.)

(Buckminster Fuller, no less, also insists that God does not fudge and therefore rejects irrational numbers like the value of pi or circumference divided by diameter. [Fuller knows that no straight lines or circles exist in nature but also does not realize that he automatically expects God to count by arabic numbers, just because we have done so ever since we gave up roman numerals.])

The next major paradigm shift won Nobel recognition as the principle of uncertainty proposed by Heisenberg, born at the beginning of this century. Then to the uncertainty of physical measurement, Freud added unwitting selectivity in the observer.

Now I propose that though these delays compound our mistakes, they are tolerable (like the tolerance for expansion and contraction that mechanical engineers allow in their work) and, if allowable, then relatively correctible though not absolutely perfectible.

I have talked about the terrible but natural inertia of frozen concepts. I conclude with the inclusivity among the natural, in philosophy and in science, even of ideas about the supernatural. But to achieve this inclusivity, we need another paradigm shift to "absolute relativity."

(This very comprehensive notion can be more periscopic than a bird's-eye view and only needs for you to catch its drift away from current thinking,—even so-called "critical thinking"—to understand how it works. I may not persuade, nor am I keen on doing so. But then I only hope to inform, not to convert. *(l/38)*

Are we prepared to learn our history and learn from it? Does history have to fit our (**A**) taste, (**B**) predilection, or (**C**) reason, or is it a matter of (**D**) comparing different versions and (**E**) spotting elusive connections among unattended facts that can illuminate the murky darkness around us?

(In order to reconcile facts with ideas, including Maslow's as well as Ortega's, we tried to look for what is hidden but significant in the contemporaneous lives of Aristotle and Alexander, Galileo [who died the year Newton was born] and Descartes, Einstein and Heisenberg, Freud and Erikson, and gentile Jung and epigenetic Piaget. The reconciliation needed a different view of history to reunite human behavior with the evolution of matter wherever, in absolute relativity, both animate and inanimate phenomena can be compared.)

2. Beyond OPEN SYSTEMS Theory to ABSOLUTE RELATIVITY for UNIFYING NATURE and LIFE

(Postscript: This is not just the "science of history" that Jared Diamond recommends in *Guns, Germs and Steel* (1997) to understand "the fates of human societies" from their geographical distribution and the flora and fauna that they can handily domesticate, but also a "history of science" to plot its uneven and spotty progress through time.)

It is unscientific to treat life as a singularity. It is self-serving to explore space for life-forms.

As we keep growing, we learn that the whole cosmos is a closed system, that everything that happens to it, whether of our doing or another's, affects everything else, one way or another, to a greater or lesser extent, largely unpredicted by the doer and lost on the bystander.

Great civilizations, now dead, never accepted this emotionally. In this postindustrial age, what we know to be ecologically true we can now simulate electronically; but whether we know our history or not, are we doomed to repeating its mistakes?

Copernicus changed the "landscape" in cosmology, Darwin in biology, Einstein in physics. I want to build on their discoveries to make psychiatry a modern science.

> My students and patients and their parents and mine and my grandchildren helped. Try to separate what is informative and/or disruptive from the comfortably old or acceptable. (Can you all see where you entered our world's history? If bogged down, switch thinking gears to get out of rediscovered mental ruts.)

To study human life, I have singled out our alphabet so that, like Aristotle in his A=A, what one stands for, from A to Z, cannot be confused with what another has been assigned to designate. Mathematics does the same, using numbers (instead of roman numerals) and fractions (ratios) for convenience. (Fractions quantify but do not compare what ratios can.)

> When we pray, it is to ask for (**A**) what we wish or want. When we meditate, it is to listen to (**B**) our inner reptilian unconscious. When we think, it is to (**C**) remember and recognize what we have recently heard or read. When we compare, we (**D**) contrast wishes with wishes, silence with silence, words with words, and deeds with deeds. When we (**E**) create, we juxtapose what is conscious against what is unconscious with or without words or hitherto unrelated events that belong together.

a. PRESCIENTIFIC WESTERN PHILOSOPHY

You can have a mind, human or not, conscious or not, thinking or not, scientific or not.

Philosophy may be moral (Socratic), metaphysical (Platonic), or natural (scientific): "Cogito, ergo sum res cogitans." Only in the twentieth century did we stop consulting our internal images to verify the extent of our undoubted knowledge. (For cultural comparison, read I. M. Bochenski on Indian logic and Janusz Chmielewski on Chinese logic.)

Before Aristotle, the first H., Heraclitus, was more of a natural scientist. Another H., Heisenberg, 1926 Nobel physicist, made the three other H.'s (Hegel, Husserl, and Heidegger) obsolete, which is expectable because only art, not ideas nor science, is ageless. *(l/36)*

Bertrand Russell (1872–1970) tried to limit philosophy to analysis. With the accelerating and independent development of the natural sciences, his student, Wittgenstein, recommended abandoning metaphysics (inquiry into the nature of reality) and expected philosophy to be just a critique of language to clarify thoughts or to achieve logical adequacy in our use of words.

(Wittgenstein's colleagues in the Vienna circle of the 1930s also wanted language to record only actual or possible observations verifiable by the senses.)

John Rawls in 1972 did not simply analyze the word "justice" but asked what a just society would be.

Today, we define "mind," better spelled as "mynd," as the relationship of one brain to its internal and external environment, which may be respectively repressive or oppressive in differing ratios.

There are the senses and sensuality, sensibilities or sense data, and there are images: there is a functional interdependence between them. There is brain or instrumentality of the senses, but there is no grasping of the object, no fetching of its forms nor delivering of it to the Soul.

b. POSTLOGICAL THINKING

Scientific inquiries do not aspire to final answers. Unlike plants and animals that are necessary to each other, we are necessary only to ourselves. We are not their problem solvers. Life, as both subspecies *Homo domesticus* and *Homo metropolis* live, is not meant to be lived by *Homo sapiens sapiensis*. Evolution has solved more problems for birds than for us; many of us still fear flying.

There are domesticated animals, including *Homo domesticus* and *metropolis*, who are taught what to do. The rest, including *Homo sapiens*, are scavengers who will find some use for everything, especially those that the others throw away. To a human scavenger like myself, there are no ideas that are so uninviting but that they must fit somewhere.

We must date the certitudes that we treasure. If they hark back to the time before we can compare them with competing dogma, we must start asking the obvious question: Why are we still sold on them?

A less petty or pitiful interpretation of "original sin" than competing with God for knowledge is that we are driven by our inordinate pride in being a "thinking" human who is more than just aware of merely "being." Only in doubt do we exist. And doubt starts us thinking.

When not in doubt, we are as (**B**) intuitive as our pets, going about our business without self-consciousness.

When "Cogito, ergo sum" (I doubt, therefore I am) is perverted into "Credo, ergo est" (I believe, therefore it is), then *Homo domesticus* and *Homo metropolis* have substituted fancy for fact, rationalizations (excuses) for ratiocination.

All logical thinking needs is another "rational" person; comparative thinking (ratiocination) needs data to convert into ratios. (Specialists cannot compare what they have broken into smaller pieces. They end up with fractions, not ratios. Fractionation is not ratiocination.)

> "Mind" (not as "psyche" or spirit), which could have been translated to "understanding" or "attention" by the ancient Orientals or early Greeks, is a modern abstraction that was disengaged from the soul, not the body, by Descartes, but his posthumous opus was misrepresented as a treatise on thinking, not on doubting. Postlogical thinking is post-Cartesian substantiation.

Sensuality is nonerotic arousal of the senses, including that of our invaginated skin that we call the brain. Eroticism is arousal in the service of sex. Sex is coupling, with or without procreating.

What is sensual is personal, even if consensual. What is social is public. What is sexual is private, even if shared. We therefore have personal growth, civic development, and sexual cycles.

> Whoever has not in early life adequately practiced (**F**) religion and (**P**) autoeroticism will likely find them adequate answers later on in life.

c. BEHAVIORAL SCIENCE

Both reactive, (a) defending psychologically is mostly unconscious, and (b) coping socially a response to conscious challenges.

To be proactive is to be unresponsive to what surrounds you in space or to anticipate what is far enough in the future that you're ahead of your time. It is neither rebellious uprooting ("radicalism") nor worship of conventions ("conservatism"). You just don't care enough to take seriously what others value.

(Persons and generations—like the subspecies to which they belong—distinguish themselves by the things they take for granted or seriously.)

Can we say when we became more
i.   personally and/or covertly (A) emotional, (B) motivated, (C) reflective, (D) comparative, (E) creative, or/and
ii. publicly and/or overtly (F) spiritual, (G) political, (H) materialistic, (I) psychological, (J) sociological, (K) technological, (L) humanistic, (M) ecological, (N) ethological, (O) cybernetic, or/and
iii. privately or in partnership (women and children first), (P) narcissistic or autoerotic, (Q) acquisitive or fetishistic, (R) homoerotic or voyeuristic, (S) flirtatious or exhibitionistic, (T) seductive or pedophilic, (U) pedophilic (*sic*) or homosexual, (V) abortive or bestial, (W) adoptive or rapacious, (X) adulterous or monogamous, (Y) adventurous or paternal, or/and (Z) androgynous as grandparents?

These **ABZ**s in our life cycle encode all that we can live through, from (i) sensual liberty to licentiousness, (ii) social equality to slavery, and (iii) erotic sexuality to sterility. *(l/37, 38)*

Today, the question of when (or even if) the soul enters the body has become a legal issue (reuniting church and state and reversing the course of history which had once claimed and then denied that the state was God's surrogate on earth and our kings His heirs with the divine right to reign).

Only the untamed or scientific *Homo sapiens* tend to be skeptics or disbelievers. *Homo domesticus* tends to believe slogans and *Homo metropolis* to unbelieve only to believe newer slogans. The slogans may be **(F)** "Jesus lives" or **(G)** "The state is sovereign," or **(H)** "Money makes the world go round," or (**I**) "Individuals are indivisible," or (**J**) "Society has priority," or (**K**) "Technology saves," or (**L**) "Humans are custodians," or (**M**) "The Earth is our Mother," or (**N**) "Animals are entitled," or (**O**) "Computers err less than brains."

Does either "mynd" or reason hover like guardian angels to supervise our mundane existence with a brain that was hurt for being squeezed more than that of any other animal's before we were able to see the reflected light of the sun?

There are sensations and there are conceptions (recognition or reasoning), and there is coordination, a kind of harmony, between them. (Disharmony dogs the heels of ideology.) Coordination of the object with its images and the image itself are not two different things; they are the same thing differently viewed: "Beauty is in the eye of the beholder."

> Conception is more often a source of pride than knowledge, and it is also the result of our reasoning or recognition of impressions that we call thinking, and therefore subject to misimpressions.
>
> Creativity is finding connections without relying on reason, discovering them by inspired juxtaposition or by pure accident, a happening, which may be happy or unhappy for those who plumb hidden implications.)

We teach psychiatry differently from the Pythagorean brotherhood or the psychoanalytic fraternity. Both of them require their apprentices to be pure of heart by cleansing their soul.

We require that the heart and mind unite. We dethrone and decentralize the "psyche" or spirit, and what is now understood as mental subjectivity we try to spell differently as "mynd" to help heal minds and wounded self-esteem.

Minds may be hurt and unable to mind. To mend, *Homo domestici* must be able to attend to what is happening. Then they can begin minding, even if *Homo metropoli* still doubt what, if anything, is in it for them. If both need to be superstitious, *Homo sapiens* can live with their magical thinking, as long as it keeps them standing with such crutches.

> Animism is taboo only for our trainees with whom all slogans and their "isms," including scientism (chauvinistic human racism

or anthropocentrism), are residual symptoms of domestication, ignorance, or both.

3. SUMMARY: PSYCHIATRY'S GLOBAL PERSPECTIVE ON HUMAN BEHAVIOR

a. PHILOSOPHY AND PSYCHIATRY

There is a growing "generation gap" between the much-older discipline of philosophy and the much-younger discipline of psychiatry. But they still speak to each other when both can talk about behavior instead of selling metaphors.

In psychiatry, we can use the same language that philosophy uses by dividing our words into proper nouns, common nouns, and transitive and intransitive verbs.

We can reserve proper nouns to personalize our sensual experiences and use common nouns to popularize social slogans. We need intransitive verbs for private erotic experiences and the transitive verbs for shared sexual intimacies. Thusly can we talk or write of our total senso-socio-sexual behavior.

This is how our spoken and written language evolved from the vocal and body language of animals, as our mouth and thumbs began to occupy more of our cortex than the rest of our face and body taken together.

In time, common nouns that we called "abstractions" began to outstrip proper nouns in their ability to attract our attention. With social slogans constructed out of abstractions, proper nouns came to be used only for more intimate relationships. Thus, we have more people marching to the same slogans than are today looking after their own families. We now reduce the size of families in order to keep up with those marching to social slogans. Do we continue to depend more and more on society for personal satisfactions and less and less on our family for our sense of identity and continuity?

b. ETHOLOGY AND PSYCHIATRY

Thinking in the abstract with the help of common nouns is mostly window-dressing. It allows us to hide our nakedness. Naked, we would have to accept that we are just like other animals. All other animals do not think as much as they plan, as predators or rivals.

If we are planning today what to do tomorrow because we do not have to fight or fornicate right away, then what we are doing now is exactly the thing to do. But if we are only exchanging our thoughts to persuade each other to think differently, it would be lamentably pre-Darwinian.

Can you imagine Charles Darwin trying to persuade his peers that they are all primates? All he needed was the evidence that he had collected from his observations—without trying, by argument, to defend them.

Nor did Darwin use analogy or metaphor. He reasoned by homology in comparing our forelimbs, the wings of birds, and the fins of fishes. Any theory of behavior that does not also consider that "ontogeny approximates phylogeny" is not psychiatry but philosophy.

In life, Aristotle was not only a philosopher but also a naturalist. Yet his detailed observations of nature cannot be found in any biology textbook today. (Darwin had made them all obsolete.) Even Aristotle's philosophy is under attack by existentialists, who would rather begin with Rene Descartes, who was both a philosopher and a mathematician. His mathematics was practical, but his philosophy was beset by doubts (and his followers by "angst") and is now under attack by logical positivists.

(Like old soldiers must, philosophy may be fading, but like Gen. Douglas MacArthur, it is not going quietly.)

Jean Piaget is a psychologist who trained in philosophy and admired Immanuel Kant. He tried to verify his hero's separate categories of time and space, but his own daughters as experimental subjects could not validate his dream. Long before they were even born, and not far from where they lived, Albert Einstein had already made the Kantian categories obsolete, with his discovery that speed influences time itself. Any science of behavior cannot afford to ignore any other natural science. (Psychologists also owe it to their clients to study biology.)

How much of animal behavior is governed by the autonomic nervous system outside the brain? And how much of our "common sense" comes from our reptilian brain whose intuitions enabled dinosaurs to survive longer than our species? (Psychiatrists owe it to their patients to know ethology.)

And how much of our wrinkled cortex contributed to the decay of many dead civilizations with equally advanced abstractions and still popular social slogans? (Philosophers owe it to their students to be themselves familiar with very ancient civilizations.)

c. Post-HIPPOCRATIC PSYCHIATRY

An ancient Greek doctor named Hippocrates is the father of Western medicine. It amuses me that some psychiatrists still think of mental disorder in pre-Hippocratic terms: as some form of "sacred disease" like epileptic spells and convulsive seizures. Mental illness, violent or not, is no more a sacred disease than epilepsy, as Hippocrates found centuries ago. We should now be able to enlighten our pre-Hippocratic colleagues even if, for some time to come, they will continue to be pre-Darwinian. Mental illness or health do not have to be signs of supernatural attention or indifference and do not demand spiritual preoccupation or intervention. (Similarly, our laws are not the result of divine revelation to Moses, but a natural evolution of the pecking order of primates, just as banks evolved to exploit what we "squirrel" away for a rainy day.) Divine concern only permits us to believe that we have equal opportunities to reach heaven, no matter what inequities we suffer on earth. It is beguiling to cloak with mystery whatever it is that our few and imperfect sense organs cannot sort out. If the mystery is sold under a social slogan that also promises eternal peace in paradise, then the mystery revealed is sure to be a best seller.

d. Our THREE LIVES as "Individuals"

Can we learn to live with the imperfections of our senses? It depends on the other two of the three lives that we lead simultaneously.

These three separate lives that we lead in varying ratios can be simply identified as "sensual," "social," and "sexual." (The ratios should change unless we stagnate as socially domesticated pets who must please our providers and "burn out" rather than breed and provide for our brood. To be caretakers instead of caregivers as adults is premature senescence for *Homo domesticus* and *Homo metropolis*.)

Succinctly, what is neither sensual nor sexual is "social." What is primarily "sensual" is all that is not also experienced as erotic.

Comparing sense data without genital hypochondriasis is "sensual." Our sense organs include proprioceptors deep in our muscles and tendons, which are stimulated by our movements, which become more sexual than sensual during fornication.

What is "erotic" is all that serves sex without procreation. What is potentially procreative (primarily "sexual") is coupling between any fertile male and female. (Sexologists like Freud who see only negligible differences in the asymmetric development of the sexes are prepubescent!)

"Freedom" is a sensual experience. "Equality" is a social experience. "Erectility" is a sexual experience.

Our sensual life decides how healthy we are, our social life how healthy our leaders are, and our sexual life how healthy our parents were.

e. Personal "GUILT," Social "ACCOUNTABILITY," SEXUAL "GENOCIDE"

By separating epilepsy from the supernatural, Hippocrates removed its stigma and erased the imagined giftedness of the epileptic. Yet some *Homo domestici* and *metropoli*, even now, still tend to deify or to blame the sick. There is really no need to do either.

We are not responsible for our sensual health. As their genetic claim to immortality, only our grandparents can be. (Proprioceptive harmony with music—as in floor gymnastics, dancing solo in discotheques, in pairs in ballrooms, or in group aerobic exercises—is an index of sensual health. Jogging only says we are human since no other species jogs to stay fit. In fact, stretching to stay limber is all they ever do.)

(Some large cats and wild dogs may jog when not in a great hurry. (Wild dogs also feed the sick in their pack.)

Unless we happen to be leaders, we are not responsible for our social health. Only our leaders can be, no matter how misguided their followers are.

We are not responsible for our sexual health. Only the parents, as their parents, of our parents can be. (Did they say no when they could have said yes to our parents?)

Our three different lives are there for us to live, but the critical decisions about them, lucky though we are to call this planet home, have already been decided and our future constrained by the very limited options still open to us. What options we freely choose among them depend more on the alternatives than our exercise of choice. (We may set priorities, but cannot change the "choices." Opportunities are our only options, and we waste many of them whenever we prioritize.) *(l/39)*

Some may be luckier than believers if their options include people who are luckier than themselves (whether these happen to be doctors or not) and whose zest for life can infect nonbelievers who do not wish them misfortune out of envy.

Worse than the envious are those who rejoice that there are others even more unfortunate than themselves. (Like animals guided by reptilian brains, children and clinicians draw closer to those who are hurt, but not in order to gawk.)

Only those who passively console themselves secretly with "There, but for the grace of God, go I" (thusly thanking an absentee father) are better off if they can find public enemies to hate and actively bully. Passivity gets them nowhere; action allows for corrections. But only as long as they do not get to be big enough bullies who can start a war that even they cannot survive. *(l/40)*

Our only hope for these powerful bullies (**BG'**) is that there is enough time for sufficient (**i**) sensual development to reduce their need to believe in (**ii'**) failed social slogans. To go outside one's circle, one has to outgrow the philosophical bias that colors its favorite ideologies (socially distorted ideas) and give up old tautologies to be postlogical instead.

Sexual development can also provide other better, if temporary, satisfactions. (President Eisenhower once pointed out that his vice president's problem is that he is monogamous, little suspecting that he, like him, is also a philanderer but more socially discreet and sexually fulfilled. Nixon's Hong Kong mistress was a long-held secret. More public is his love for his family.) *(l/41)*

But social slogans (like "God is great," "The state is great," "Money is great," etc.) outdo each other in promising more to their followers. The numbers who swallow such promises are increasing faster than our birth rate.

We're different from other animals when we are better for being more creative as Homo sapiens and when as *Homo domestici* or *metropoli* but "homicidal" we are worse for being insane.

There are golden ages of creativity, two of which produce insanities.

The first to be abused is the creativity that produced monotheism for *Homo domestici.* The second is the centralization of power in envious *Homo metropoli.* Both produced believers, and their ideologies produced widespread insanity.

f. **ABZ**s from ABSOLUTE RELATIVITY

From the *ABC*s of science come the **ABZ**s of life (an open system).

A to **E** is the alphabet of creativity in art and science. **F** to **O** is the alphabet of ideology in feticide and genocide, **P** to **Z** the alphabet of eroticism, procreation, and grandparenthood.

The senso-socio-sexual rationalysis of our (**i**–**iii**) three lives as members of the human family is the third (**III**) dimension of our three theories about the absolute relativity of the natural and basic sciences of *A*nthropology (**III**, specific con-familiarity), *B*iology (**II**, general con-viviality), and *C*osmology (**I**, universal con-naturality) *(Table 5).*

> This must not be confused with the three worlds of art, theory, and science, where theory as untestable fantasy or testable hypothesis allows the talented to commute between the two communities of artists and scientists.

If architecture is "mother of the arts" (which it is not because the arch came later than the Parthenon), then absolute relativity is the "baby of the sciences" and clinical rationalysis the baby of the practical arts. As babies, both are free to taste and test without malice.

If absolute relativity is science's baby, is mathematics the mother of science? Plato and Penrose would claim that mathematics is more than numerology even if there are no straight lines in nature to enthrone Euclid.

> There are no constant regularities, there is only contained chaos.
>
> Nor does Penrose seem to have heard of "fuzzy logic" that makes computers think like us. I don't know if he means cortical "thinking" (2, if a, b, and/or c, below) when he speaks of "consciousness."

I think (1) intuitive thinking is reptilian and subcortical, (2a) clear (unbiased, helpful) thinking bicameral but less abstract than both (b) critical (premise-driven, argumentative) thinking (more left-brain, literate, and opinionated), and (c) scientific thinking (postlogical, less self-serving, and sometimes counterintuitive), e.g., as "thought experiments":

Logical thinking (or 2b) based on Platonic perfection or Aristotelian "excluded middle," like old computers, deals compulsively with absolutes (all or none or either 1 or 0). "Fuzzy logic sets" to program "smart" robots is more relativistic. ("When . . ., then . . .") than reductionistic ("if . . ., then . . .")

g. ABOUT KANT'S CAN'T

Kant *(l/7)* had asked how it was that science had achieved so much and philosophy so little: "Since Aristotle, logic has not been able to take a single step ahead."

Immanuel Kant (1724–1804) as a boy was the favorite of his strict, Pietist mother, whom he resembled even as a man. In his preface to *Critique of Pure Reason,* he honored her memory with the promise "to limit knowledge in order to make room for faith." He found that logic organizes but does not contribute to knowledge.

In trying to prove what Kant cannot mean—that our planet is peopled by damaged goods—I once began by saying, "We are not less than angels."

The comment I got was, "But there are no angels." Precisely my point. If there are no angels—"Unding" *(sic)* or not—we cannot be less than nothing.

If you cannot prove that you exist, you have bought Kant's cant. But if you know that you exist only when in doubt, then Descartes is right, even if his translators were wrong in thinking that he was thinking when he was just cogitating or in doubt.

Kant's "can't" *(sic)* had prompted Piaget's search for the earliest sense of space and time in children's mental development. *(l/42)*

12.00 l/ADDENDUM

l/ChapterNotes

[l/1] Santayana thinks that "scepticism (*sic*) is the chastity of the intellect" (or mental naïveté). Chastity procrastinates, promiscuity tastes, but the skeptic need not swallow before more tests.

[l/2] What we learn from history is that we do not learn from history. Gene pools, not cults, gain from mutants among geniuses and bastards born through miscegenation in sperm banks and tribal and foreign wars:
In Numbers 31, the Lord said to Moses, "Avenge the children of Israel" (on the Midianites who caused a plague by the counsel of Balaam) "12,000 armed for war . . . and slew every male. And the people of Israel took captive the women of Midian and their little ones . . . Moses said, 'Have ye saved all the women alive? . . . kill every male among the little ones, and kill every woman that hath known man by lying with him. But all the young girls that have not known man by lying with him, keep alive for yourselves. Encamp outside the camp for seven days, whoever of you has killed any person, and whoever has touched any slain, purify yourselves and your captives on the third day and on the seventh day'" (numerology!).

[l/3] It was failed assassin John Hinckley's bullet that prompted Reagan's quip that he "failed to duck" and got "supply side Reagonomics" passed by an ambivalent Congress. Mother Teresa also visited Reagan and told him his survival was an omen and the bullet a messenger.

[l/4] Creativity contributes original ideas. Ideologues loudmouth them. (The loudspeaker was invented in our town of Napa, California, in

1915. Its reach has now been extended worldwide by television. Its abuse has recently been amplified in "news talk shows.") Their followers' need to belong to feel equal makes them idolize their ideologues. Ideology produces tunnel vision and rose-colored lenses, institutional inertia, and intellectual anorexia. Danger looms when ideology becomes an agenda, like Plato's philosopher-king experiment in Sicily that failed. Social insanity ensues when idols are insecure.

Ideologies are promises based not on actual experience, but on ideas as given premises. And ideology and idolatry make man mad at others who do not have the same beliefs and idols. In a world where ideology is king, nobody gets killed except in the king's name. The name of the game is commitment, and the stake in the game is loss of freedom to be footloose and fancy-free. To hang loose today is to be hung in effigy and be consumed in the fire of hatred of those who feel betrayed. Worship of old dead heroes or new ones from Lenin to Mao is the insanity of necrophilia.

Belief in martyrdom and the reincarnation of martyrs is a great self-esteem-enhancing delusion. This delusion is dangerous when used to coerce conversion of cynics. Cynicism is not the answer to idolatry. Skeptics are less vulnerable to militant conversion. Cynics are defensive and therefore more dangerous to the believer, skeptics are open-minded and so have no beliefs to defend. And the older the ideology and the defenders, the more insane it is. (This is also true of all delusions; the older the reasons, the more intractable and difficult to treat the paranoids become and the longer their convalescence.) Does insanity interfere with creativity?

[1/5] a. Is single parenting as the norm better for animals like us?

b. Being a mammal means nothing if it does not mean that a mother is adapted to be a single parent when the child is most dependent. Maternal care is ensured by the animal subcortical limbic system.

c. We are also the only species, outside bulldogs, who suffer through childbirth. Our children should not have to be born misshapen with a headache worse than any hangover and with the same loss of short-term memory for the most momentous event of their life. Cesarean sections must not be routinely elective only for bulldog owners. Brains, our original sinner, need more tender care than pets' faces. (Contrast ours with kittens' heads in cats' mouths to move them to another location.)

After the child is totally cut off from the mother when the umbilical cord to the placenta is cut, it must attach to something else, preferably nipples of engorged breasts, and feel enveloped by warm arms and soft bosoms. This need for closeness is called "thigmotaxis."

Only recently have infants achieved the same civil rights as blacks to be fed publicly wherever they happen to be. Pets are immunized earlier than children. Except for those who deliver in prison, mothers seldom stay with their newborn from the first day of its life, ostensibly to reduce risk of sudden death, which still happens with the infant alone in its crib. Their mothers also stand by, merely mildly concerned, while the male infant is sexually abused with circumcision more painful than anal penetration by a similarly abused pedophiliac. Startled and hurt, it is made afraid to explore what is exciting or to enjoy discovering what may be disapproved. Curiosity is replaced by circumspection and compliance.

d. In the Philippines, "dorcision" is done only after the prepuce gets too tight for the glans, or bulbous end of the penis, when the boy asks his father for permission to have it slit dorsally by his maternal uncle after an early morning shower to numb it with cold water. It thus becomes an initiation rite that starts him "sowing wild oats" when fully recovered.

e. We also wait for children's sphincters to help us keep them dry (we sleep without mattresses on floors made of bamboo slats for ventilation). Undiapered, our boys are therefore often complimented for their "birds" flying while they are playing "bottomless."

f. I try not to teach my grandchildren a second language in the hope that they can remember their childhood before we took away their native tongue. My youngest taught me thirty-one syllables, which, with hand and facial gestures and body language, covered the whole gamut of his needs. Early language training is another form of inapparent child abuse that is no different from housebreaking pets for the benefit of their masters. (We are also the only species that abuses members of its own family physically and sexually! Why is that?)

[l/6] We can compare Western rhetoric with Buddhist philosophy and its modern version ("fuzzy logic," which uses detailed programs to process sequences) that makes Japanese electronic appliances "smarter" than ours.

Buddhist philosophy is inductive:

Proposition	You are imperfect.
Finding	Because you get sick.
Premise	The imperfect are mortal.
Application	Since you get sick,
Conclusion	Therefore you are mortal.

Aristotelian reasoning is purely deductive:

Premise	Men are mortal.
Application	You are a man.
Conclusion	Therefore you are mortal.

"Fuzzy logic" is realistic. (There is no white even in white snow; there is no black visible in the black hole.)

[1/7] History slowly evolved over five separate eras of opinions and delusions (or covert rationalizations, whose overt premises may be faultless or popular). It left identifiable pockets of resistance against modern postlogical thinking (or ratiocination, always conscious even if inconclusive, and therefore quite unlike rationalization on both counts). The separable eras are pre-Hippocratic, pre-Copernican, pre-Cartesian, pre-Darwinian, pre-Pavlovian.

Pre-Cartesian logic even today substitutes (**CC**) certitude for (**A'B'**) cogitation (the agitation that comes with doubting); philosophy much prefers (**C**) cognition (reflection about what we recognize) to (**D**) ratiocination (comparison of ratios, not logical reasons or rationale), or (**E**) original nonjudgmental postlogical thinking.

Kant had asked how it was that science had achieved so much and philosophy so little.

Logic predictably lets us compete traditionally and academically but redundantly. Postlogical thinking makes us reliably competitive clinically and scientifically.

That is because logic without knowledge is useless. George Bernard Shaw, when informed of the speed of light, thought that it was the most obviously preposterous lie ever told. Thoughtful intellectuals use their ability to understand science as a valid standard for judging what is not clear to them. Ideologies are substitutes for knowledge among complacent "mentanorexics." Dogma, not data, drove pre-Renaissance science. Righteous beliefs judged ideas and deeds in the Age of Reason. Beliefs still end up as slogans or credentials.

Unexamined ideas can lull us into the complacency of both undiscovered ignorance and long-term denial. Data/deduction = 1/delusion. The black death (bubonic plague) was blamed on angry Providence and the Jews. Heretics who expressed treasonous reservations about prevailing dogma were zealously and profitably investigated by medieval inquisitors in the Dark (Middle) Ages of Western Europe.

That is what silent, unquestioned deductive rhetoric (Aristotelian logic systematized into pre-Renaissance scholastic philosophy by St. Thomas Aquinas) did to Christendom for a millennium (sic). It delayed science (inductive) that materialized in Ionia but languished in Athens while it blossomed in Marco Polo's China.

Deductive reasoning is analytic critical thinking. Inductive logic is clear, informed thinking.

The law of contradiction cannot accept light as both wave and particle. Data show it to be both.

Postlogical science goes from quantum probability to nondiscrete continuity of artificial categories.

[1/8] Genocide, e.g., in Bosnia, is once more a demonstrated risk of widespread ideological correctness. Ideologically to be correct is to join a powerful but mad bureaucracy. And one that is also creatively inert for being socially domesticated. Thinking must be free or it is social plagiarism.

To be ideologically incorrect is to be controversial. To do that is to think for yourself.

Philosophy suits those who want to think about what others think.

What distinguishes us from animals is not that we can talk and think but that we believe in dreams of glory. That is what ideology is.

Because talking follows listening and reading follows talking, we do not always think first when we talk but often just repeat what we have heard or read. Only after some words lose novelty can we begin to compare ideas.

To be free in mulling over what others think is limited by the right to believe any one of them.

Man can be measured only by what is unique to him. That does not include creativity. It includes ideology and the institutionalized insanity that it excuses. For this, he cannot be blamed. It is part of his nature to err. Animals do not make many mistakes until they are domesticated.

The need to believe or deceive oneself is not unique to us. But the talent to systematize one's beliefs is man's special gift. And the cost of collective delusions is increasing with each new advance in weapons technology.

Ideology is a system of thought that inspires believers. Dogmas only need a believable authority. Ideology needs a credible leader.

Believers are the workaholics among gamblers for glory. They trust promises more than distrust or suspect patent medicine hawkers. (In medicine, we allow for hope by assuming that 30 percent of improvement is the placebo effect of a new miracle drug or technique.)

Theories cover what must be compared and offer conclusions that can be tested. Ideologies defend what is believed and offer remedies in the form of promises. Mentanorexia is an exercise of mental eugenics that keeps the ignorant undisturbed by facts.

> After World War II, in the UN Security Council, Russia and Poland blocked Barnard Baruch's plan for total disarmament, confirming Albert Einstein's version of "mentanorexia": "The world was changed by the atom bomb, except our way of thinking."

[1/9] I had just told my grandson who was named after me and is three and a half years old that he is a great kid. He wanted to know why. I said because he is Magno's grandson (my other self). Again he said, "Huh?" And I said he would carry our family name (Ortega) after I die. And then he asked, "How come?" I heard myself saying because I'd get old and sick. He stopped asking why. If I had said because we are mortals, he could just have asked again, "How come?" He might then learn the dictionary definition of "mortal" but nothing about life or dying. (Definition depends on the familiar, syllogism simplifies, and old "news" gets communicated effectively by repetition or redundant rhetoric, but only data can add information or new knowledge. Experience weeds out what is irrelevant; sorting the rest brings wisdom.)

[1/10] THE *ABCs* OF SCIENCE: *Anthropology, Biology, Cosmology*

Is science larger but not more interesting than art, and life broader than all of humanity itself?

These are the seminal concepts in absolute relativity:

I. Universal con-naturality or *C*osmology (nature around the universe and inside us)

II. General con-viviality or *B*iology (our life with other species on earth)

III. Specific con-familiarity or *A*nthropology (our species studying its family)

A new paradigm shift to absolute relativity is possible with (1) postlogical sorting (**D**) superseding logic (**C**) and (2) postideological demiurgy (**E**) superseding (**ii**) old idols.

[l/11] How Hitler went from avowed religious tolerance to jealous genocidal mania:

(Mein Kampf, pp. 52–61)

The fact that they (the Jews) had . . . been persecuted . . . (because of their strange religion) turned my distaste at unfavorable remarks about them into horror . . . On grounds of human tolerance, I maintained my rejection of religious attacks in this case as in others. Consequently the tone, particularly that of the Viennese anti-Semitic press, seemed to me unworthy of the cultural tradition of a great nation. I was oppressed by the memory of certain occurrences in the Middle Ages, which I would not have liked to be repeated . . .

As always in such cases, I now began to try to relieve my doubts by books . . . I bought the first anti-Semitic pamphlets of my life. Unfortunately, they all proceeded from the supposition that in principle the reader knew or even understood the Jewish question to a certain degree. Besides, the tone for the most part was such that doubts again arose in me, due in part to the dull and amazingly unscientific arguments favoring the thesis . . .

What had to be reckoned heavily against the Jews in my eyes was when I became acquainted with their activity in the press, art, literature, and the theater . . .

It sufficed to look at a billboard, to study the names of the men behind the horrible trash they advertised, to make you hard [*sic*] for a long time to come. This was pestilence, spiritual pestilence, worse than the Black Death of olden times, and the people was [sic] being infected with it! . . . (F)or one Goethe, Nature can foist on the world ten thousand of these scribblers who poison men's souls like germ-carriers . . . (to) . . . their fellow men . . .

It was terrible, but not to be overlooked, that precisely the Jew, in tremendous number, seemed to be chosen by Nature for this shameful calling . . . Is this why the Jews are called the "chosen people"?

[Chosen by whom? Did Hitler think he could do better?]

I now began to examine carefully the names of all the creators of unclean products in public artistic life . . . Regardless of how my sentiment might resist, my reason was forced to draw its conclusions.

The fact that nine-tenths of all literary filth, artistic trash, and theatrical idiocy can be set to the account of a people, constituting hardly one-hundredth of all the country's inhabitants, could not simply be talked away; it was the plain truth.

[Freedom to think begets the right to believe but not vice versa or Hitler loses.]

One thing had grown clear to me: the party with whose petty representative I had been carrying on the most violent struggle for months was, as to leadership, almost exclusively in the hands of a foreign people; for, to my deep and joyful satisfaction, I had come at last to the conclusion that the Jew was no German.

Only now did I become thoroughly acquainted with the seducer of the people.

[Hitler could not seduce without promising violence. A jealous, opportunistic leader of zealous, loyal followers can cause a holocaust. It took three armies—Churchill's, Stalin's, and FDR's—to beat the war machine of a school dropout and failed painter!]

[l/12] COMMUNICABLE IDEAS (? DISEASES)

> The real question is not whether machines think but
> whether men do.
> —B. F. Skinner

Ideology can be defined as the logic of ideas or a system of illusions about society.

Freedom to think is inversely related to the right to believe.

The less excess baggage from the past that the talented brings to the present, the more creative does (s)he become.

Communism needed the creative interpretation of history by Karl Marx that labor is capital for Lenin to overcome Russian royalty. But to raise Lenin to sainthood meant the slaughter of millions who stood in the way of Stalin.

So we see the transformation of creativity to ideology to madness in the lives of Karl Marx, Lenin, and Stalin.

If idolatry is madness and ideology produces idolatry, can we reverse the course of history with another creative interpretation of history?

To be a follower, you only have to be selectively blind (studiously ignorant). To be a zealot, you need to be ignorant as well as passionate. When you combine zealous followers with jealous leaders, then you have dangerous idolatry that can explain genocides since biblical times. In the Bible, "ethnic cleansing" was called "purification ritual."

We can trace the evolution of society by its insanities. What was the first public record of mass murder? Today, we call it "ethnic cleansing." Ideas like "ethnic cleansing" were once original and then got borrowed and exported (recently to Bosnia). Ideologies are therefore borrowed ideas.

If the people who borrow them find a leader or a leader finds them, then we have a cult.

If the cult leader is a good fund-raiser, like Jim Jones, then the cult becomes a movement and, like the Mormons, finds a new home where it will be left alone by those who do not want them for neighbors.

If the leader is charismatic, the movement takes over a party, like that of the Nazis' or National Socialist German Workers' in Germany. The danger increases the more weapons the party acquires.

Abuse of the right to believe kills creativity. That's why Albert Einstein left Germany before—like Russia did, later on—it repressed nonutilitarian art and science that humanists now frown upon.

Believing is the only way you can unknowingly lie to yourself.

Society is a social network, and the network is made of shared beliefs. It is slightly different from "culture," which is shared kinship and traditions.

Ideology gains converts by promising what is missing, even if it is only equality.

Once bad faith grows between factions, words become swords and icons are publicized by bumper stickers.

When an idea becomes more than just an idea and gets idealized, then all it needs is a sponsor for the idea to become an ideology.

Those who do not do well in the arts (Hitler in painting, Reagan in acting) get unstuck and diversify in their careers.

Like everything else, humanimal social institutions have a history. So do ideologies.

Ideology is hanging on to old ideas that comfort us.

A sense of wonder reveals ideologies that hide behind awe.

We are more like other believers when we believe to belong. We are more unlike them when we do not need to.

The need to belong is the same as the need to be loved among dog lovers. The urge to share is the same as the urge to love among cat lovers. Dog and cat lovers in the same house need both as well as the other who is cast as the beloved or lover.

Wars started as gang bangs.

Zest instead of zeal, facts instead of fantasy, and sensuality instead of sociability would delay the spread of ideology.

Opinions that become institutionalized give us a sense of being special because of race, religion, etc., for example, of being Aryan instead of a Jew -> institutionalization of Nazism.

Americans, like the Nazis, pride themselves in feeling privileged. When ideas are established in our mind, we become believers instead of thinkers. Believing is inimical to thinking. The right to believe is reduced by the freedom to think and vice versa. Ideology is the refuge of the homeless and the sanctuary of the scoundrel.

Ideology is as uncreative as crutches and shares the same purpose. Creativity comes from ideas or images that cannot all be captured by words. When words incorporate dreams, they become icons instead of the embodiment of an idea; and when icons dignify promises, they lead to insanity. When words are used as euphemisms, deception is at work. Today, we even give deception its own euphemisms, such as "slant" or "spin."

There is no freedom in moderation, which is why freedom is feared.

In the computer age, our mind is a kind of Chinese abacus that Japanese transistors have rendered obsolete. Even more backward are those who still use logic when we have microscopes and telescopes to assist our senses.

Our greatest global achievement is longevity for all.

We tend to give people more credit than they deserve for being creative or mad. We forget that creativity is a gift from grandparents and madness a legacy from our parents. We also take undeserved credit for believing what we did not think through before accepting.

If our learning takes place when we are helpless, we cannot learn what is contrary to what we have been taught. That is true of language skills also.

The value of education therefore diminishes the earlier we teach children what, not how, to think.

[1/13] Continuing education for adults can be fun, like sliding downhill with the force of gravity without asking how gravity works. Education can also be exhilarating, like mountain climbing, without wondering if the exhilaration comes from not getting enough oxygen. Education can be both, but also enlightening if we ask the questions that experience raises.

It can be like walking on unpaved roads where you have to watch every step and the going is slow. Or swimming upstream in the Amazon to less polluted waters. (The gradient of purity in the Mississippi River is not worth the effort of going against the current.)

The worst pollution comes from mental or intellectual stagnation. And like air and water pollution, it is not obvious at the beginning, but gets worse and even genocidal at the end. (Can there be a more impure metaphor? Is consistency purely philosophical puritanism?)

Unlike writers of fiction, I try to make sure that those whom I reach do not suspend disbelief. To make sure that for every answer I offer, one or more questions can be raised right away, I tend to exaggerate. Whatever I say then and now needs to be taken with two or more grains of salt.

I think the relationship between creativity, ideology, and madness is the most important issue in the post–cold war era that we can explore expeditiously. Can you think of a more important one that we could spend an hour talking about? I'll top that exaggerated claim by saying that we already know but are not yet conscious of our answer to the scattered trouble spots since the Berlin Wall crumbled. The answers have been tested in the field of fire and found effective in basically identical circumstances, but no systematic review of the reported successes has yet been undertaken. Nor are we all privy to the instances where they could have failed but did not, or succeeded but did not. To bring all this together will help us see how well we have solved some problems, even if we have not yet found the words to explain them.

What I have to say will anger philosophers, theologians, and politicians. Of these, only theologians and politicians can benefit from what they allow themselves to hear. Philosophers are more deaf than both. But the children of all three groups and our own group can benefit, if ideology had not enslaved everyone who reads or listens.

Ideologists are slave traders, trading on ignorance and envy to make their followers jealous for their future and zealous to safeguard it. Ignorance can make zealots of the followers of the jealous.

What problems have we solved? Again, what is the most important problem of the post–cold war era that caught us napping? Old enemies made life understandable. New enemies give a fresh focus to our efforts or make life simpler for those who do not ask "How come?" (Without the Soviet Union [Ronald Reagan's "evil empire"], we can once again rely on Satan to keep us from blaming ourselves for our frustrations.)

Once we make friends of our enemies, we need new ideologies to keep us from seeing ourselves as we are—a speck of dust in a sea of change.

[1/14] Anorexia nervosa lowers fertility; mental anorexia reduces creativity. Groups interested in creativity have more gusto than anorexia, more hedonia than bulimia. *Mentanorexics* who cherish simplicity are either narrow-minded or aging and cannot remember details that the devil thrives on. (This is why honesty is the best policy; lying waylays the unwary once deception is attempted.)

The judgmental are less original. Critics specialize early and find their work more enjoyable than creativity. Only later in our development are judgment and creativity combined.

Personal originality (mutant ideation) may be more determined by brain architecture (hardware) than by cultural programming (software). Creativity can be viewed socially as a relationship among inept, talented, gifted, or great leaders and users of art and science.

It is not necessary to credit user or leader of more than just having been accidentally delivered in their birthplace on their birthday with their accidental combination of genes. Very few can choose their neighbors, parents, or playmates or schoolmates or roommates or associates.

[1/15] What is unique about this study is that it was not planned but was done while observing grandchildren grow up.

Is the loss of our tail and the location of other mutations (e.g., the thumb) what favored us more than creativity, which did not spread throughout the human race?

When I was joyfully building a three-story tree house single-handedly for grandchildren who wanted separate rooms, I thought that we developed ingenuity because we lost our prehensile tail in becoming one of the great apes. And that we developed speech because teamwork is superior to ingenuity. And then I remembered that elephants who had prehensile trunks paint collectible masterpieces with them. Do we talk because we are not dexterous? And sit on our butt whenever others agree to do our bidding?

Words are just like paper money, a medium of exchange that must be honored as worth more than the paper it is printed on and less than first editions. There are a few hundred-dollar words.

Sometimes, words are used like incantations, and the excitable chant them or worship them. This is like treating paper money as sacred objects.

[1/16] We test whether a person can see, when it seems that he cannot, by moving our hands across his field of vision. That is the opposite of "playing possum" to escape being spotted. Our eyes evolved for scanning, not spotting as in reading. (Reading disembodies experience, which, vicariously enjoyed, leaves us with quotable quotes but no other personal memories. Is the macula, where focused vision is clearest, as differenti-ated in eyes that hang out on a stalk?)

[1/17] People speak of "love" as the "final solution." Love of others like ourselves, or the way we want to be loved or were not loved? Should we love everybody as if they were children (can this behest come only from a Child?) who could not hurt us (my wife sometimes tells her friends when I hand over the phone that I call all my women "Baby" to keep from using the wrong name), especially when asleep? (My younger grandson got more tender smiles from Christmas shoppers when his eyes were closed than while he was awake.)

Other animals look after their unplanned offspring without expecting to be honored (did this requirement originate with a Father?) or mobilizing upwardly in case they are not. (We are one of a few species with two parents to please, and ours also must kneel before their masters as they climb the social ladder.)

[1/18] Because the brain is made to manage muscles (in fact, ours is not as good at that as other animals, except when it comes to our thumb), even our major mental illnesses become visible movement disorders (depression, melancholia, catatonia, agitation, etc.), even of our tongue (in unpredictable coprolalia or unexpected expletives or obscenities). Indecisive catatonics can go into panic.

You have heard of people who are called "neurotic." That word came from "nerves," and it means "nervous," on edge, "anxious," or "agitated." Overtly, the anxious (neurotic) drum their fingers impatiently, and the agitated (depressed psychotic) use larger muscles to express their guilt, wringing their hands in remorse or pacing up and down.

The anxious are afraid for themselves, the agitated feel that something is wrong and that they had something to do with it, but keep wringing their hands, wondering what it is that they did or failed to do. The guilt-ridden who is denervated (depressed) is not as active as the worried well or their opposite, the anxious, who are afraid that what they are worried will happen, won't.

This is why it does not help to reassure the anxious that their fears are groundless, in the same way that it does not help the paranoid for us to question whether they have persecutors or fans. (To believe is to deceive ourselves, if only to sleep.)

[1/19] "Cogito" was never "cognition" but "cogitation" (from doubting): "*Traduttore, traditore.*" (Translations are traitorous.) Cogitation distresses. Cognition relieves doubt. Re-cognition is illustrated by TV shows like *Stop the Music* or naming authors of classical quotations. What the musical or intellectual appreciation of any composition or fiction reflects is not reflection, but emotional ties with their source.

Memories are organized according to context or meaning and become the basis of public identity or "persona." This "mask" or image or personality is then protected as personal "integrity" or even as "intellectual honesty" by the unthinking. (Computers are more accountable in storing memories.) And when meaning is separated from context, we have abstractions, like "mind." (Gerunds," like "minding," are better.)

[1/20] If Aristotle's singular sense of "anima" had not superseded the plurality of Greek spirits, we would still have gods and goddesses instead of only One. And if St. Thomas Aquinas had not misinterpreted "anima" as "soul," we would not sacrifice anything for the immortally invisible and claim good reasons for doing so.

[1/21] Simply to translate "psyche" as "mind" today, as in "psychology," simply denies its being more "mynd" since, as a noun instead of a verb, it no longer means "minding" but "myths of my mind."

[1/22] Luther criticized shrines for selling dispensations to ensure a better reception for the buyer in the hereafter. They have now been replaced by stores that sell presents for the neglected to relieve the guilt of the neglectful, especially around Christmas, when it is "more blessed to give" and be forgiven by some Scorekeeper than to receive and barter unwanted gifts the morning after.

[1/23] Previously, Otto Rank and Sigmund Freud had proposed and then professionally parted over the primacy of "birth trauma" or "coitus interruptus," respectively, in predisposing us to anxiety and/or neurosis.

[1/24] A Supreme Court justice sent her rebellious son away from dinner in the presence of guests to his room to discipline him by denying food as a basic entitlement.

[1/25] Our synthesis complements Carl Jung's perceptual "sensing" and "intuiting" and judgmental "thinking" and "feeling" subtypes among both the introverted and extroverted. It also supersedes Edward de Bono's lateral thinking by selection, rejection, combination, and separation in *The Mechanism of the Mind*, as an alternative to vertical or critical reductionism. Vertical is more linear, lateral more contextual in historical dynamics and kinetics.

[1/26] Postlogical creativity (**E**) is missing in Jean Piaget's developmental schema of sensorimotor perception, preoperational and intuitive impressions, and concrete and abstract thinking. The omission of (**E**) also makes Robert Sternberg's triarchic theory of analytic, innovative, and practical "Applied Intelligence" incomplete if not obsolete.

[1/27] "Original sin" can conveniently explain why we are born with a headache. And why only human males or their female heir apparent would divide to rule, even children in "separate but equal" schools or—to kill both their rivals before their prime—willingly sacrifice young blood for buried oil. Blood, of course, can be replaced easier than oil, even if substitutes for both can be found for emergencies. Is it better to parrot priorities rather than probe propensities?

[1/28] One summer, my seven-year-old granddaughter was reading to us in bed. She began with, "This is a fantasy. Wolves don't talk, and they don't wear clothes." My wife asked, "What is a 'fantasy'?" My granddaughter promptly replied, "Red Riding Hood." The next morning, when I was writing this down and double-checking with her, she changed her answer from "Red Riding Hood" to "A fantasy is something that is not real." After my wife told her, "You're weird," and I asked my granddaughter what "weird" means, she replied, "That's me!"

What this tells me is that children are more innocent than their elders in that they deal in particulars first and only afterward with abstractions. This might be why Jesus liked children better than their elders. Children think of Him as their friend, not as their Savior. Like children and Jesus, beautiful women also want to be appreciated for themselves, not for their bodies, unlike rich men who want to be loved for their bodies, not for their wealth.

Would children, unlike Jesus, die for an abstraction? Not on your life.

[1/29] Aristotle (384–322 BC) claimed that his syllogism was entirely his creation. There was no mention at all of Buddhist logic in "Alexander's letter to Aristotle about India." (The only thing in common between it and Aristotle's writings is the recorded habit of night crows to hunt at twilight or dawn.) This was, in itself, startling, unless Alexander the Great (356–323 BC) did not want to wound Aristotle's narrow Hellenism by contrasting it with Buddhism. (Buddha was at least 200 years older than both.) Alexander's letter tried to reassure his teacher that he had not taken up Oriental ways and fully intended to return to Macedonia, but India had, in fact, "conquered" Alexander.

(As an alumnus, Alexander wrote, "My dear preceptor, . . . dear Aristotle, . . . my immortality and my reputation . . . would be perpetual." Aristotle had never seriously discussed immortality. He was to flee from his lyceum after it was widely rumored that he had prepared the poison that killed Alexander the Great in the prime of his life. [Only one of four writers recounting his death leave Aristotle out of the list of suspects.])

(Isn't it ironic that one great Greek philosopher had been suspected of murder and another [Socrates] of suicide?)

[1/30] Three of anything was more than enough for the West. Poseidon mastered both ocean tides and earthquakes, but the larger concept of the divine Trinity of God is still a mystery.

The only accepted application of the concept of a Trinity in modern technology can be found in the patented trademark of Three-in-One oil. (Its owner is better known for marrying Margaret Sanger, abortion advocate.)

[1/31] Any intellectual tradition based on Aristotelian syllogism is bound to be philosophical, not scientific. It may be logical but not intelligent. Intelligence, whether secret or communicated, means information, not argumentation. Argument may produce oral diarrhea or a catharsis of self-expression, or even improve communication, but it does not add to information. Argument only reiterates what the speaker has already accepted. (S)he (*sic*) may be persuasive without being informative.

It is not that some intellectuals are unintelligent, only that they lack intelligence (logos) even if the information is intelligible (logical). Intellectuals are more opinionated than open-minded. That's why we do not think of children as intellectuals: they have not yet lived long enough to edit data or reject them selectively. Children are more open to "logos," even trivial information.

[l/32] With Piaget's own daughters, age can be intuitively confused with height, etc., and "before" and "behind" and "left" and "right" only later coordinated.

For Gestalt psychologists, perceptual contours belong to objects, not to observer's age and his trial-and-error activities. Locke's sensationalism saw empirical facts as passive perceptions. In fact, reality may be interactive, but Buddhists only assume functional interdependence.

Both of Piaget's daughters progressed on schedule from early sensorimotor development to nonintellectual intuition and concrete operations but dashed his hopes of their ever-developing abstract thinking to his satisfaction.

In this, they were like other subcultures: The Hopi subculture among the Pueblo Indians of Arizona do not automatically separate spatial and temporal categories. For the Hopi Indians, Einstein's theory of relativity, which startled Westerners, would be easier to assimilate. (For our New Psychiatry, relativity is totally absolute in that we find "means and ends are problems which we must always remain a part of, not apart even from the theory and practice of rationalysis.")

[l/33] Kant (1724–1804) had prompted Piaget's search for the earliest sense of space and time in children's mental development. Lawrence Kohlberg in thinking of natural, role, and ego identities as milestones, based his neo-Kantian theory of moral development on Piaget's findings and John Rawls's "*Theory of Justice.*" (Do role models inspire mirror images for "copycats"?)

Jung was another Swiss and the only gentile in Freud's original circle of sycophants. He later favored archetypes more than sex and saw his clientele as unfulfilled ("dis-individuated") sensationalists, emotionalists, intuitionists, or intellectuals. His classification was cross-sectional, Piaget's sequential. How is theory affected by a struggle for preeminence between/among contemporaries?

Can we use all of Freud's and Piaget's and Erikson's and Maslow's findings and compare them with ours to understand ourselves or only our "brothers in gender"? *(Tables 4C-15)*

Otherwise, our subjects do not inhabit the same universe, subject to the same laws. Are we unique in a special universe of our own? Or are cherished differences only self-serving claims to distinguish us from inanimate matter or nonverbal animals?

A behavioral science that is not based on physics and chemistry cannot endure. It must follow the same emerging pattern of evolution that starts with hydrogen fusing together to form helium and then silicone in its turn linking with protoplasm to produce biochips for tomorrow's computers.

In hardheaded theory building, we exclude what strays from the pattern of universal evolution as soft scientism or the pursuit of self-expression in art. If applicable theory is necessary, then the theory must apply, whether it is astrophysics or behavioral science.

[1/34] If astrophysics is a hard science, it is not because its subject matter is harder than that of behavioral science. If behavioral science is a soft science, it is not because its subject matter is softer than that of astrophysics.

It may be that astrophysicists are more hardheaded and skeptical and behavioral scientists more softhearted and gullible.

If the animals studied were domesticated, they can only tell us about us, not about global behavior that all animals, including us, have in common across time and dogma. I originally called this global study a transcultural approach to psychiatry because it transcends all cultures in studying basic behavior that is shared by many mammals, especially by us.

When dogma enters the picture, then we have people misquoting Descartes and Genesis as both were translated or edited for deliberate brainwashing or brain-stuffing.

Descartes did not say, "I think therefore I exist." Correctly translated, he said, "I doubt, therefore I am." "Cogito" comes from cogitation, not cognition. Cogitation comes from agitated doubting.

The missing letter *n* from "cogito" did not deter philosophers and psychologists from separating mind from body (of which, of course, they knew very little) when Descartes only wanted to separate human doubt from immortal soul in order to escape persecution during the Inquisition as a troublesome thinker, which a famous contemporary (Galileo) could not avoid.

As misleading as mistranslation is religious censorship. Paradise had Adam, Eve, and Lilith in old manuscripts, but only Adam and Eve were evicted in the King James Version of Genesis. Evangelists make campaign speeches every Sunday that gain them contributions as they drive their message home that asks, "What doth it profit a man to gain the whole world and then lose his soul?" (Who'd rather live in heaven than on earth? Not very many want to move.) No Madison Avenue advertising agency would dare concoct such a slogan. That it is still working after all this time validates Joseph Goebbels's claim that if the lie is big enough and repeated loudly and long enough, it will be believed. His success in countering even more outrageous lies with bigger ones got his audience believing that it is the Aryans, not the Jews, who are the chosen people.

For surgeons and psychiatrists, to dwell on the life of the soul may be useless rumination. To exclude it challenges the complacent mind to face facts. To wish to serve or preserve it on the basis of past promises may be foolish, not to foreswear hope on the basis of well-known facts can be helpful yet still not enough for true believers. At any rate, to believe is to gamble.

[1/35] Both as animals and by ourselves, we go from sensation to intuition to cognition to comparison to creativity (sooner for the gifted in music, movement, and mathematics). Animal "intuition" is visceral "knowing" (as in "carnal knowledge"), "cogitation" the kind of agitation that our guts suffer from not knowing; only "conception" is totally cerebral.

"Making up one's 'mind'" is forming an "opinion" before acting on one's options. Such options, of course, get fewer with age as we resist change while change within or without is itself not a matter of choice. Even among monkeys, it is the young who break new ground, for example, plunging into the sea for peanuts.

[l/36] In the West, somewhat like the three Bs in classical music, there are three Hs in modern philosophy: Hegel (1770–1831), in the first half of the nineteenth century, believed that everything is "mind" (not mind and matter as Descartes and Locke believed or a collection of minds as Berkeley believed), and philosophy is logic, but also evolving toward an end point of total rationality. Husserl (1859–1938) believed that philosophy is phenomenological (existential). Heidegger, born at the end of the nineteenth century, modified Aristotle's "rational being" to the "being that speaks" (in vowels and consonants).

[l/37] For Janis Joplin, an American rock and roll star who ended her young life, "freedom" was just another word for "nothing left to lose." You'd be a social failure if you have to work at what you have been trained to do skillfully to eke out a living after fifty-five: there is learning to make a living, earning a living, and learning by living. (We must not substitute living to learn for plain living.)

[l/38] Our database consists of a kaleidoscope of "periscope sightings" from the past and present by my personal and professional family, looking back to animals, sideways at us, and ahead with computers. Unlike Marx, who wants, not to understand "reality," but only to change it, I do not think much of it is up to us. I have no vested interest in my synthesis (more comprehensive than eclectic), though I can defend it. It is not even mine (though the words are), it is "nature's behavior" that triggered it.

The basis for this compendium is largely empirical (inductive and heuristic), not inferential (deductive or epistemological); the process itself is less (C) conceptual (or metaphorical) or analytical (dependent on logic), more simile than analogy, and more (D) postlogical (historical and evolutionary), using homology (genealogy) rather than ontology.

Only when professionals rely on (C) deductive logic (untestable certitudes) instead of (D) comparative study do they reenter the Dark Ages of Aristotle and St. Thomas Aquinas and cease to be post-Renaissance scientists.

Who among us are still pre-Hippocratic, pre-Copernican, pre-Cartesian, pre-Darwinian, and/or pre-Pavlovian?

We can forever chip away at tradition as mental ramparts defending against intellectual onslaught. Instead, I have used it as a natural catapult to leap to higher ground for a wider panoramic view of more distant scientific horizons.

[1/39] We are lucky if our first choice is among our options (like a window seat in an airplane). Those who are not so lucky can still believe that they have chosen well (e.g., an aisle seat). Of course, those who need to believe are apt to deceive only themselves. (An aisle seat allows easier access to the plane's toilets, but inconveniences its occupant when others in his row have to use them.)

[1/40] Notwithstanding the continuing increase of patriotic terrorists and urban guerrilleros, the looming threat of "overkill" by better armed bullies extended the uneasy global "peace" of the old cold war after a worldwide "cease-fire."

[1/41] President Nixon did not die of phlebitis from stress and has since become less a disgraced politician who mistook state sovereignty for official immunity and more of a respected statesman sought after as a consultant by world leaders for his ability to observe and (**D**) compare emerging trends in international affairs.

[1/42] COMMENTS and DISCUSSION

      C - Correspondent (a rabbi)
      D - Discussant

   C: Your approach leads to some extremely radical comments that appear to be self-defeating. Somehow you do not consider the "arbitrariness" of nature, quantum physics, intermediary principle, etc., that allows for interpretations that contradict Darwin's ideas, separating the "thing in itself" from our perception of phenomena. They are not made obsolete by Einstein's theories that, according to Kant, could be applied only to the phenomenal world.

D: The theory of absolute relativity (as distinguished from general or special relativity) and our clinical senso-socio-sexual rationalysis (beyond cultural relativity) see a "thing in itself" as an "Unding," an absurdity. No man is an island, nor is his God. Did God or man create each other out of sheer vanity?

C: Aristotle's philosophy became obsolete as he failed to separate physics and biology and saw no duality between mechanism and organism. Can one not see mind and body as belonging to two different categories that interact? The assumption that mind and life be limited to organic matter is, in the light of the way nature behaves, not compelling.

D: True, if God created hydrogen with a big bang and then kept water-laden amino acids orbiting in space until they could create life in our barren planet. (Kant hoped that species evolved out of life.)

Do we now need to create God anew to fill the void left behind by the big bang? Did an infinitely intelligent being also evolve out of amino acids? Only if even subhuman primates can and do deceive themselves with their creative imagination. (And they have and will!)

Where there are no grandparents, God and His saints can replace perpetual reward with the promise of eternity and offer an infinity of space for the landless and as a reward to the faithful for taking the lives of infidels.

The carbon dioxide cycle is the only wager at stake that scientists and vegetarians stand to lose. (Because animals eat what they kill, they cannot lose even when they believe in magic, like lab primates beset by unidentifiable stimuli that they struggle to get a handle on.)

C: The idea of a directing mind pervading the cosmos to achieve some specific purpose cannot be rejected.

D: Kant revived the dying dichotomy between mind and body and gave mind a new name that he called "duty" to replace "original sin."

Does "duty" give birth to guilt? Or only when conception is conceived of as a failure of contraception?

Duty and guilt require cause-and-effect relationships that ignore contextual richness and the ratios of impinging forces.

Does denying linear causal progression result in "circumstantial ethics"?

Not necessarily, just more science and less superstition, sold as the mystery of miracles. (Can a male be produced parthenogenetically? Or with hair described like "lamb's wool," was Jesus a mulatto?)

C: Nature becomes an organism that observes and organizes itself; our own minds are individualized parts of it. This would be a more holistic approach.

D: It would be wholistic but irreverent to view entropy as simply demolition to create new worlds, but metabolism can reorganize only if life is renewed. For God to live, He has to multiply or He will simply die, as did His Son. Is He still MIA (missing in action)?

We can fool seeds into germinating in the middle of winter by supplying artificial light and warmth, just as computer hackers can confuse the early warning system by raising the alarm to arm with a simulated preemptive nuclear attack. Is the cosmic mind modeled after both, either, or neither?

C: Religion, however systematized, is basically a call to social justice, and heavenly rewards an incentive for those who need compensation for acting ethically.

D: To the extent religion succeeds, Kant has erred in thinking "duty" needs no salesmanship. (It would not be his first. He was also convinced that all planets are inhabited and that the moral qualities of inhabitants increase in proportion to their distance from the sun.)

To Kant, all secondary gains from dutiful obedience is self-serving servitude. Man can only do his duty if he is free.

For Kant, to be free requires that life lasts into infinity. Thus, man is assured of immortality. It is God who sees to it that man is distracted by promises. (Kant here outdid Plato's reductionism, which argues that if we are imperfect, somewhere Someone exists who must be perfect, or the very word is its own contradiction. Why idolize a mere word or spend a lifetime of study trying to perfect it?)

Therefore, for man to be immortal, God must exist. For this unorthodoxy, as a state employee, Kant was threatened with dismissal, and he stopped dead on his tracks. He was able to keep his job. (Descartes, on the other hand, never held a job for pay in order, he claims, to protect his freedom. That he refused to defend his "cogitation" and burned his manuscript of *The World* after hearing of Galileo's inquisition raised doubts about the courage of his convictions, but none that he was deluded [convinced]).

Never afterward did Kant try again to restore man to the center of creation from which a neighbor he never met, Copernicus, had expelled Adam's descendants: The central cosmological principle is that the cosmos has no center, no hell, no height, no altar.

Kant was, not only pre-Copernican, but he was pre-Galilean as well as pre-Darwinian in thinking that the nature of nature and of man, respectively, is arguable from an armchair, and pre-Hippocratic in thinking that the unfree (religious slave aspiring to be his brother's keeper) is responsible for his imperfection but proves thereby that there is One free to distract him. This is pre-Cartesian, harking back to Aristotle at his most deductive (in his truncated version of Buddhist logic, which inductively starts with man getting sick—where man dies because he is mortal).

Does a slave require a master? The fact is that throughout life, depending on the stage that they have reached in their development, believers edit out what does not help them stagnate in that stage; all believers are borrowers, and to die for one's beliefs is to die for their transmitters, unless their experiences open them up to the rest of life with a different set of questions.

What is radical about absolute relativity that is different from Kant's "duty" is that from the start, it had nothing to do with contemporary philosophy, but substitutes rationalysis for reason. Rationalysis sees reason as programmed rationalization or excuses after the fact, whereas ratiocination uses ratios to explain our senso-socio-sexual behavior.

We err not because we are human, but because the universe that we all inhabit cannot be comprehended by just our five senses. Thus, we do not need to be forgiven for neglecting our "duty" because of our natural handicaps. What may be needed to avert feuds that feed on each other is amused tolerance for blind beliefs about our pivotal role in cosmic metabolism.

There is no content without context. There are no tall hills without deep valleys even if meadows separate them. If the cosmos were a string instrument, the music becomes discordant with just one loose string. (A pilot would rather feather one failing engine than have the plane vibrate to pieces.)

Anything can distort everything else, even matter in expanding space, and vice versa. Kant believed that the mind imposes on the raw material of the senses the "forms" of space and time. His devotee, Piaget, tried to prove it by research on cognitive development and found that they, in fact, also evolved from experience.

Kant relies on a noumenal world to destroy the world that exists, just as religionists invoke original sin to evoke universal guilt. But like Plato at his most formal and Picasso at his most surreal, Kant and his followers make "phenomena" inferior to "noumena" even after the Industrial Revolution.

C: If I understand you correctly, a man is born when hereditary and environmental "forces" converge accidentally through evolution that just "happened."

D: Just so, a random combination of mutations that have survived the test of time.

C: Man develops consciousness and imagines somehow that he can make choices, so he did. But actually the individual choices revolve around whether he can or cannot do something: If he can, he did, especially by using his hands, which makes him "man."

D: "Choices" can be made intuitively, without deliberating or imagining what options are available.

C: Once man made a choice, the outcome of that choice is dependent on "luck" (favorable or not).

D: The variables that influence the "end result" are beyond imagining.

C: As we age, we have chosen and made decisions that in turn narrow both our choices and further limit our options (we can never go back and undo past actions and decisions).

D: "Decisions" are required only in situations where information is insufficient and arbitrary judgment is substituted for missing data.

C: Senility or death confirms that man had no choice: life is meaningless, he is meaningless, his actions have no effect whatever on other biological beings or his social environment, and he therefore cannot assume responsibility.

D: Man subjectively assigns meaning to his life, he objectively affects his family and is responsible for what he bequeaths to them; but of his bequeaths, none has lasting value except his genes, which do not die until his family ceases to multiply. Everyone who feels responsible is in a hell of one's own imagination. Anyone who ascribes responsibility to anybody else wishes to consign them to a hell of their imagining.

C: The sole criterion for doing something (deciding) is whether man can or cannot, but even if he can and does something, it is pointless: random and purposeless acts are the same, i.e., pointless.

D: But not to do what one can also add to the variables that cannot be counted, the end result of which may be tangible and not pointless, but only to those who find meaning in them.

C: Man's "accidental" birth, subsequent development, and eventual decay merely served to multiply the numbers of consumers who eat and play.

D: Reproduction multiplies feeders and players. Population control is aimed only at feeders.

C: If man does not come to grips with the above "biological fact" or denies it by using metaphors and "explanations," then he has gambled on "beliefs" which have produced all that is "evil" and horrible that we see around us, in that they lead to terrible acts (like the Inquisition) which are, nevertheless, not anyone's responsibility (though it was St. Thomas Aquinas's logic, which had made it justifiable).

D: Because all beliefs are self-serving, defending them can produce love sonnets to kindred spirits and bitter, hateful persecution of unbelievers. Disbelievers are not a serious threat since they present no counterclaims.

Evangelists (spiritual, political, economic, etc.) are responsible but not accountable for those they reach, fathers (God, etc.) only for those they raise. (You can sue for breach of promise but not get reimbursed for your gambling losses.)

C: The gist of it is that something is happening (bad, some kind of "judgment," in poor taste, unlucky or untestable, etc.). The explanation (reason) is some belief system (justification) that is there to persuade (deceive, etc.) someone who, in turn, tries to make something happen. Did his biological makeup, upbringing, environment, etc., give him the propensity to be so susceptible?

D: Man remains dependent longer than any other species and, more than pygmies, learns to con his keepers and himself while captive. (Cats are pubescent before their first birthday.)

People who smoke believe in a second chance in an afterlife or that life must be tolerable to be acceptable. (It is interesting that I quit smoking after I nearly drowned at the age of nine. Did I lose the capacity for self-pity that compels mystical orphans and mythical bastards to think that they are sired by absent nobility who will come for them sooner or later to share a better life elsewhere?

(What the river failed to erase from my memory was the cadence of martial rhythms, as in the musical *Les Miserables*, that can make my heart beat faster even if the lyrics sound trite. Can music soothe as well as stir the beast in us?)

C: So therefore, if we destroy all belief systems (Can we? How? Expose them?), man would soon revert back to being just another animal, and everything will be "wonderful," "great":

"All animals merely reproduce, eat and play, thus satisfying their biological urges, instincts, etc. And when every woman, man and child can do the same, we will have peace, utopia, the ideal state or goal."

D: No psychiatrist who knows what he is doing will ever try to persuade a paranoid that he is working from the wrong premises, whether or not they are shared by others. All paranoids (those whose beliefs are unshakable) need to believe what they preach.

What an able psychiatrist can do, when he happens to be around and able, is make the believer's need to use those crutches less urgent, but not by throwing both out of reach at the same time. The doctor allows each patient to lean on someone stronger until he can throw one crutch away and then the other.

Beliefs make one withstand adversity better. That the crutches, which are tangible signs of weakness, come off is not the "purpose" of the transaction. Otherwise, our intervention merely results in pure and simple "symptom reduction" as a side effect of the patient relying on others or himself instead of betting on his mind, which is the newest- and poorest-tested toy to evolve from his gray neocortex.

Nor is the "can-do" effort aimed at greater peace or deeper happiness: Those goals are what make man a more dangerous mutation than his playing around with DNA itself. Whether the patient gets stronger and better with or without reliable help should not depend on whether he will be better off: that judgment is not ours to make.

Can we endure the knowledge that nothing endures? Only then does knowledge become wisdom.

Without wisdom, we remain as children attending to bedtime stories that adults read out of books to lull them to sleep until Santa Claus comes or Mr. Right rides by or the Messiah arrives.

Simple facts, not revelation, will set you free, but only from social pretensions and endless procrastination that old prophecies and promises encourage in *Homo domesticus* and *Homo metropolis*.

Data can clarify ambiguities; the search for eternal truths always enslaves the seeker.

Do we try to recreate our birth with a headache by greeting the New Year with a hangover but with renewed resolutions to overcome the irresponsibility we enjoyed longer than other animals born without their smaller brains being hurt, if only because their mothers had enough nipples for sextuplets? Why do we have hospital beds and nursery cribs for our young?

Why do we believe others more and model ourselves after legendary strangers? Only our sexual endowments survive to withstand sensual and social distance between us and our partners from different backgrounds. In fact, no more than one other needs to understand and put up with us, unless we need to be appreciated or assisted in bed or to be bottle-fed.

C: The bottom line, then, is eventual extinction?

D: In cosmology, it is called "entrophy" produced by what physics calls "inertia." In clinical neurology, inertia is propulsive in cases of Parkinson's disease (agitated paralysis), where the Parkinsonian loses control of his momentum. In history, ideas endure out of inertia when an ideologue's cortex ages faster than the rate of depigmentation of a Parkinsonian's *substantia nigra*.

13.00 m/OVERTURE

PRELUDE

> I imbibed as a kid what I still believe without doubting,
> but what I do know I have tested or learned by doing, and
> compared with what was known before, which leads to
> other questions as we explore patterns and part-answers,
> even among changing ideologies of near total self-deception
> or auto-intoxication.
>
> —Scientist's Manifesto

(Logic may rationalize or excuse with understandable reasons; science ratiocinates [deals with ratios, not with understandable reasons].)

If the world is our stage, the three-act play to see today stars Nature in the first act, animals in the second, and people in the third.

If our audience misses the first two acts, it can easily misread the action in the third. Its vocabulary is radically different from what divides people. It sees each person or group as a combination of what is true of all nature, and can identify them and their problems by the ratios of those combinations in *Homo sapiens*, *domesticus* or *metropolus* rather than by their membership in any race or class.

SYNOPSIS of a THREE-ACT PLAY on the WORLD STAGE

(The cast of characters takes part in a dialogue that ends with a critique of global behavior as it has evolved through time.)

To learn all about us, we have to explore without old presumptions the bonds between mind and matter, nature and human nature, ideas and history, child and family, citizen and society, and gender and species. What is (**I**) natural links us with the world of matter, as we obey the laws of nature, whether we are sick or well. Whatever is (**II**) biological we all share with other living things, vocal or silent, whether we are strong or weak. (To beg from the strong, including God, is the prerogative of the weak or sick or dying.) What is (**III**) human makes mankind one family, including children before they can read and their elders, whether irrational or forgetful, reasonable or logical, sensible or postlogical (scientific or creative). Thus, what is con-familial is also con-vivial and con-natural in the *ABCs* of *A*nthropology, *B*iology, and *C*osmology. Our species differs a little from others in its sensual, social, and sexual **ABZs** of life. Its subspecies of *Homo sapiens*, *domesticus*, and *metropolus* differ more from each other also *(Table 16)*, just as persons are quite distinguishable from others.

Act I. All forms of matter, "dead" or alive, share a Universal "Con-Naturality." Plato (427–347 BC) thought that geometric figures were memory traces of perfect heavenly forms. (Euclidean geometry did not count on gravity bending rays of light so that nowhere can a straight line be found in nature.) Ptolemy (second century, BC [AD 90–168]) invented epicycles to maintain the illusion that the orbits of heavenly bodies around the earth are symmetrical.

It took more than a millennium before Copernicus (1473–1543) could displace the earth from the center of the universe and for Kepler (1571–1630) to show why orbits are elliptical. G. Galilei (1564–1642) questioned what had been taken for granted by philosophers like Aristotle and tested whether objects fell according to weight or distance of fall, etc. I. Newton (1642–1727) explained what influenced motion and acceleration anywhere, and A. Einstein (1879–1955) the interchangeability of matter in motion with energy (which also empowers our own sun to keep us alive for as long as it shines).

(What Copernicus had done to the Dark Ages, relativity theory did to reason and, now, "virtual reality" of special effects can begin to liberate us—by simulating reality—from all too common nouns (proudly, if not pompously, called "abstractions.")

The universe exploded, and particles of matter were set free to unite in heat and achieve equality of force fields in keeping with quantum theory (M. Planck, 1858–1947, as applied by N. Bohr, (1885–1962). These fusions fissured further into independent units to reunite in different imprecisely predictable combinations according to W. Heisenberg (1901–1976).

Act II. All living forms enjoy a General "Con-Viviality": G. Mendel (1822–1884) found that more random recombinations are facilitated by sexual differentiation with statistically determinable probability under controlled conditions. Rooted plants reach out for equal shares of the sun to survive and of the wind for freedom to spread their seeds. L. Pasteur (1822–1895) proved that we are surrounded by duplicating and dying things too small to see, including viruses, which are mostly nucleic acids. Inside us we harbor more life-forms than there are people on earth. "Con-viviality" is the rule, rather than the exception.

In 1859, A. Wallace and C. Darwin (1) confirmed the doctrinal origins, (2) demonstrated the unflattering improbability, and (3) established the scientific superfluity of special creation for each species. *(m/1)* K. Lorenz, 1935 Nobel laureate in medicine and physiology, showed that nestlings needed mothers and adopted even men like him for their own. In 1953, F. Crick and J. D. Watson showed a double helix of nucleic acids to be the instructions that organisms obeyed to replicate themselves. In 1954, S. Miller found amino acids in a test tube of suspended chemicals that he had exposed to simulated electrical storms. By freezing same, L. Orgel found adenine, a subunit of DNA or deoxyribonucleic acid. (If lunar lightning and rocks are like ours, did our Ice Ages make Earth our mother while her sister planets remained barren?)

Goodall later observed that chimpanzees led almost the same lives that we lead in close quarters, including use of tools and waging wars. Their DNA set of instructions is nearly identical to ours. We are now retracing evolution by duplication of DNA instead of relying entirely on fossils to discover other still-missing links to the living who were born of fertile mutants but whose remains were not easily preserved for posterity by accidental "acts of God." (This takes our genealogy beyond the human family tree. Cats also have their "matriarchs" and mates who are "dead-beats.")

Act III. All members of the human family are party to a Specific "Con-Familiarity": I. Pavlov (1849–1936) proved conclusively that living organs can be trained to respond to artificial stimuli associated with biological needs after initial deprivation. S. Freud (1856–1939) discovered that when social superiors, including our parents (who share the same prejudices as virtues or values), frown on our natural sensual or sexual expressions, we bury our primal impulses below consciousness, only to have them distorted in recurring dreams or slips of the tongue or errors of judgment about the same kind of people. But like Ptolemy, who thought of the universe as a cosmic onion, Freud saw us as defending our peace of mind during psychoanalysis by concentric barricades against unwanted memories. A Graecophile, Freud barely got away from linear cause-effect theorizing to espouse curvilinear "overdeterminism." *(m/2)*

(During psychiatric training, one question often asked us was not "Are you in analysis?" but "Is it your first?")

Instead of "epicycles," Ortega visualizes steps in a truncated pyramid from the New World *(Tables 2, 3A, 5, 6, 7)* to locate our present itineraries of personal or (**i**) sensual and private or (**iii**) sexual journeys of discovery and the recurrences in it of the same (**ii**) social errors throughout recorded history—religious killings, tribal feuds, hit-and-hide piracies, etc., that are nearly as predictable as stages in our biological evolution in utero. (Our past and present is a mix of material, biological, and anthropological phenomena.) Each future senso-socio-sexual step up or down the pyramid can be plotted from what we are leaving behind and what is therefore within our reach.

> The crucial difference beyond the shape of the models which we have selected is that Freud's concentric barricades defend a core conflict, whereas my pyramid invites everyone to climb at self-determined speeds from the comfort and safety afforded by the lower rungs. More are now reaching the higher less-crowded steps.

The data for each face of the pyramid are (**i**) sensual, "I see us as (our family)"; (**ii**) social, "You see us (as my family)"; and (**iii**) sexual, "We see us (as partners)" (on opposite sides of the pyramid). Conformity hides dependency.

Single-issue writers and consumers are slow learners. With overactive wrists when speaking, they try to gloss over what separates (**A**) good (tasteful) from what is (**B**) right (equitable) or (**C**) reasonable (excusable).

Separable stages in development for EveryWoMan clarify what makes one more of a dreamer (**A**) than a doer (**B**), more reductionist (**C**) than heuristic (**E**). What decides whether we depend more on (**A**) taste or (**B**) limit testing or (**C**) analogy or (**D**) homology? What makes us fall back on (**C**) rationalization rather than relying on (**D**) ratiocination? If **F** stands for Faith, can we separate a deist (**A+F**) from a theist (**C+F**), and atheist (**AxF'**) from agnostic (**D/F**)? Saints and shamans can reach more gullible people than scientists ever will during our life cycle from **A** to **Z** to **A'**. We need to date and cross-examine acquisition of notions that became convictions.

(**A** to **Z** to **A'** are stages in our life cycle: "The wish [**A**] is father to the thought [**C**]"; "Corruption [**B'**] always starts with a cigar [**A**].")

Myths, like original sin, are stories that are never (**D**) testable but will always be (**C**) true for those who (**A**) need them to be. On them rests what is then called the true faith (**F**). (Was this the first oxymoron?)

But there is no need to assume that greater genius resides in (**F**) God or (**G**) the voters or (**H**) the market. "Why not" for (**B**) the toddler becomes (**C'**) "what if" during midlife crisis.

Those who pray to (**F**) Father Almighty or quote (**G**) "our Founding Fathers" are not nostalgic for their own fathers. Both seek to establish a fraternity or sorority with others than their own siblings and can switch back and forth between Big Sister for support and Big Brother for protection.

The open-minded—who have stopped prejudging other automatons and blaming others—soon develop the ability to comprehend and compare (**D**) data from knowing more than their moral ABCs after going to the university of "hard knocks."

Undergraduate education often means a faculty professing by rote and just echoing what others wrote. Should training for the professions be less intellectual rather than another succession of Rs in Reading, Regurgitating (rote learning), and Researching?

(Pallid "research" should never be equated with bold "experiment." The most modern example of true courage is a Pierre and Marie Curie University scientist (Dr. Daniel Zagury) inoculating himself with a potent but potential AIDS vaccine.)

Whether sybaritic (sensual) or rapacious (forced feeding), teaching cannot be "hands off" or uninvolved, as long as each experience can be examined or remembered even without words, as in surgery.

Are even our postgraduate ideas about different forms of (i) sensual expression, (ii) social preferences, and (iii) sexual practices a statement about arrested development in our personal, public, and erotic climb up the ladder of liberty, equality, and sexuality, respectively?

(Our personal and professional evolution both become our manifesto that we can only know our past and that it is only as rich as our unconsciously edited memories.)

In psychiatry, those who judge a patient's behavior according to what was appropriate in the eyes of their parents or friends have their parents or friends as unpaid psychiatric consultants for their patients, and their fees are therefore unearned.

(The clinical implication is that all patients exiled to mental hospitals elicit psychological reflexes from staff, who must discard their first impressions, which reveal more about them than about their patients. In fact, whenever in doubt, we should do the opposite of what we felt like doing with each new admission and then tailor (or "titrate") our interventions according to their tangible effects.)

Historical FORERUNNERS in this Global View of Behavior

Late in the fifties, C. P. Snow divided the world into the two cultures of art and science of different words and goals. Joseph Campbell thought myth married art and science in his hero of a thousand faces. But he uses *Star Wars* to replace King Arthur and the Knights of the Round Table and gives Luke the Skywalker a mentor who tells him to listen to his instincts, which he defines as the wisdom of the heart, probably his organ of courage. For me, our instincts are preprogrammed in the autonomics to be an intelligent life-support system that does not depend on the brain.

There is an "autonomics of values," which the heart monitors ("save your children") and a "bureaucracy of values" ("save your soul, country, money, etc.") which the brain regulates.

(Ortega's original *ABCs* of Science and **ABZs** of Life is a theory in the practice of transcultural psychiatry that connects life with art and science in absolute.)

There have been at least six comprehensive surveys of distinct stages of historical progression. (Computers can now improve on earlier attempts.)

This is the first compendium of behavior to include (**i**) sensual, (**ii**) social, and (**iii**) sexual stages in human evolution from its material and animal origins by a clinical rationalysis of becoming, believing, and begetting. (James Joyce and Kurt Vonnegut Jr. tried to clear their adult minds of what they were taught by *Homo domesticus* before they could think; floodwaters did the same quickly and directly upon my brain when I was nine.)

1. An eighteenth-century Scottish professor of history (Alexander Tyler) studied the rise and fall of great civilizations (average age two hundred years). They were all consumed with (**F**) "spiritual faith," (**G**) national "courage," (**H**) economic "abundance," (**I**) individual "liberty" and "selfishness," (**J**) collective "complacency" and "apathy," and (**L**) communal "dependency" and "bondage." (Developmental stages inside parentheses added.) Since then, (**K**) industrial technology has created other human hazards that (**M**) ecology, (**N**) ethology, and (**O**) high technology might conjointly overcome altogether.

2. H. G. Wells (1866–1946) dealt only with (**ii**) social developments. On a more limited scale, he tried to link biology and sociology before—in his own version of "human ecology" (to guide world planning and shape the future)—by weighing and working out a general resultant for biological, intellectual, and economic forces in wide-ranging social changes (cf. H. G. Wells, *Experiment in Autobiography*, J. B. Lippincott, 1967, p. 553).

3. A modern oracular "do-gooder," literature professor Duncan Williams, parroting what he has read but not researched, declares didactically as (a) social arbiter and (b) teleologician:

    a. "Men are qualified for civil liberty in exact proportion to their disposition to put moral chains upon their own appetites ... Society cannot exist unless a controlling power upon will and appetite be placed somewhere, and the less of it there is within, the more there is without.

    b. "It is ordained in the eternal constitution of things that men of intemperate minds cannot be free. Their passions forge their fetters." (Did lust leave him?)

4. A poet, Ezra Pound (1885–1972) in his "Cantos," tried to include (iii) erotic events, but could not complete it before he died.

5. Sociobiologist E. O. Wilson, in his 1998 monograph *Back from Chaos*, dreams of "consilience" would like biology, social science, ethics and environmental policy to unify all new knowledge of the human condition.

6. Ortega's unifying version of bio-socio-cosmology—based on the evolution of animal behavior (neo-Haeckelian socio-ontogeny) in a postmodern, postlogical world of universally absolute relativity—tries also to facilitate better macrocosmic understanding of our present predicament.

Further studies can be pursued under multinational or private grants.

The following can be read and repeated, thought and talked about, but must also be tested to its limits if it is to add to our knowledge of (i) people, (ii) populations, and (iii) potential procreators.

As in learning a new language, we don't have to know every word in a sentence as long as we can follow the trend or pattern of thought within paragraphs. (Actually, almost any sentence in this book can begin a paragraph, each paragraph a chapter, and each chapter a volume so that this enlarged edition is virtually an unalphabetized encyclopedia but well-indexed compendium of behavior with detailed tabulations.

What we propose to do is peek into a modern Pandora's box, and just like particle physicists are presently doing, (1) call into question what we blissfully take for granted as common sense and (2) offer answers that work but must be tested on a global scale.

(Human predilections as yet unsorted may already be distorted by valued beliefs. Are all "-isms" self-serving? *[m/3])*

MIND OR BODY, BRAIN OR NERVOUS SYSTEM

Psychiatry has changed a lot from what was taught in any medical school, before there were tranquilizers, to what is practiced today. In the process, psychiatrists even dallied with Eastern relaxation techniques of transcendental meditation in a semireligious retreat to silence (in order to quiet down a chronically stressed vegetative nervous system outside the brain of human vertebrates).

In transient trances, we try to be less like ourselves and more like plants, barely breathing out what they cannot use, just as we did when animals first evolved after plants have laced the air with enough oxygen. We sit as still as possible, rooted to the spot like plants that we now bring indoors, doing nothing else but concentrating on exchanging oxygen and carbon dioxide with them in what we call in biology (botany and zoology) the "carbon dioxide cycle" of life. (We even say that others simply "vegetate" when they are comatose and, depending on the depth of coma, respond only to what their vegetative or autonomic nervous systems can and ours still do for their owners, without interference from their brains.)

Scientific study is more sensual than social or zealous, ideology more jealous and dangerous.

1. a. Are you a top dog or an underdog? Do you understand how you got that way?
   b. And/or do you have a lapdog mentality? Or that of an attack dog or a sheepdog or watchdog? Or a seeing-eye or hunting dog? Do you know how you acquired that role?

(Even specially trained dogs, however, lose sight of their excuse for a privileged niche—e.g., to sniff out contraband—when smugglers lure them from their appointed rounds with the scent of a bitch in heat. In that they may be wiser than some world leaders, whose artificial priorities are more futuristic while driven by current frustrations.)

2. Can we be (i) free, yet agitate to be (ii) equal only where we work? Does good/bad, right/wrong, and/or true/false stand for We/ They? Is moral virtue just in the eye of the censorious and social value only in the bias of the accuser?

About This Book

The proper study of (a) humankind is not man but child and male and female of all ages, tempered by what we learn about crawlers, mammals, and primates; (b) "mynd" (or myths of my mind) is history repeating itself as serial delusions of adequacy; (c) sex is direct experience, not purple fiction or vicarious fantasy or selective observation; (d) a person is hirself (*sic*) as hir own control.

Studies of (a), (b), and (c) but not (d) can begin with "The **ABZ**'s of Life, Liberty, Parity, and Carnality": It deals with Sensuality, Society, and Sex in Becoming, Believing, and Begetting *(cf.tables)*. This will help us understand the differences among *Homo sapiens*, *H. domesticus*, and *H. metropolus. (Table 16)*

We can study the stars in heaven and their dust here on earth, and from their behavior we can infer their evolution. But words unexamined in their origins or uses, like "mind" or "reason," can mislead. When the stories we tell about heaven, including the Bible, and about our mind, including successful fiction, become the basis for assessing ourselves, we repeat the reasoned errors of our ancestors who could not study the stars separately from what they thought our place in the heavens should be. Our old favorite places and people should be compared with the new to see how far we have come. This does not mean that we cannot cherish them for ourselves or avoid longing for them when the world seems too big for us to comprehend. (We can also wonder without being awed.) To stardust, sooner or later, we must return, after we turn to ash.

Roughly 15 percent of (**P** -> **Y**) our sexual behavior (animal energy) and 60 percent of (**A** -> **E**) our personal programming is biological (intelligence and talent are inherited from **Z**, our grandparents). The rest is parental or (**F** -> **O**) tribal (learned by rote or repetition).

To achieve the natural plateau of life's truncated pyramid (which has plenty of room at the top), we must climb with the freedom to (**A**) feel, (**B**) try, (**C**) think, (**D**) sort ideas from (**F** to **O**) ideologies, and (**E**) invent ways to rise above **F**–**0** and both **P, Q** (isolation) and **R**–**Y** (the battle of the sexes) to the (**Z**)enith of our life cycle. Each step gives us a different perspective of freedom, equality, and eroticism that are respectively senso-moral, socio-ethical, and eroto-sexual.

A nuclear winter will alter for better or worse the ratios of *Homo sapiens*/*Homo domesticus* + *metropolus* or (freedom + instinct)/ (tradition + ambition).

1. E-motions (**A**) and sensations arrived with curiosity and our senses, will (**B**) and imitation with our muscles and neighbors, thought (**C**) and reflection with uncertainty and our cortex.

When we "e-mote" instead of taking action, it is because the "priorities" are not clear (data base is not solid enough to show which option to "choose"). Decisions are prompted by obstacles in the foreground as defined by its background and by the profile of its contour as highlighted by its surroundings.

("Crybabies" (*Homo domesticus*) went into the closet among ambitious men who felt trapped and now among assertive women who still feel immobilized [or "e-motional," passionate from passivity, like poets writing sonnets to absent paramours]. In self-pitying stridency, they gave birth to *Homo metropolus*.)

Decisiveness (**B**) without passion (**A**) is shaped by data (events) that *Homo sapiens* have sensed clearly, peripherally, or even outside conscious awareness—whereupon (a) they become resourceful to survive (as a

"WoMAniMachine")—rather than by (**C**) reason itself consciously "informing" (shaping) outcome, especially when desire (**A**) is the significant datum.

Others (b) do not calculate the risks as much as decide to pick up the pieces, if any, afterward. They are not free agents, only agents at risk. They can be reckless or heroic, but not free, even as to picking up which pieces.

(Philosophers who debate whether or not there is "free will" even as they smoke still live in a pre-Elizabethan England, before Sir Walter Raleigh introduced tobacco to Europeans.)

Will-ing (*sic*) (**B**) is no more complicated than observing ourselves thinking (**C**, intellectual hypochondriasis), not choosing but rationalizing. We process data and (**B**) act on our options, but not because we choose or even (**C**) reason on the basis of the rest of the data that we parade in review for editing with care. *(m/4)*

2. Comparison (**D**) or postlogical correlation came after reflection or reason failed. Artistry—tasteful (**A**) or constructive (**B**) or creativity (**E**) as virtuosity—with or without formal training, arrived, like gender and (**iii**) sexuality, as gifts with our genes. *(m/5)*

Habits are brain-body conspiracies, healthy or not. "Is the brain the prototypic bureaucrat which cannot give up old habits of looking at problems but finds new ways to dress up institutionalized redundancies?"

We tend to forget that our eyes and ears evolved to monitor the environment, not to feed the brain with abstractions that gave us our first addled bureaucrat or idle parrot. (Concentration camp inmates who are herded to hear Hitler's speeches to the masses had to fight to keep their hands from going up in a "Sig Heil" salute; such is the power of his words to intoxicate his audience.)

The brain, originally decentralized as "ganglia" in snails, was meant to manage muscle. Action and reaction both stimulate it cybernetically, but self-stimulation or new formulations, including this new premise of absolute relativity and its application as rationalysis, cannot be its mission.

True, without the thumb, the brain (even of dolphins) is like a wheel without an axle and is inferior to the horse when there are no roads. *(m/6)*

And without words, a new alphabet of nongenetic transmission of information is at hand in our postindustrial world to complement Mendeleev's discovery of a periodic table of elements in chemistry during the Industrial Revolution.

WHAT ELSE IS THERE TO KNOW ABOUT US?

In domesticated herds so aptly called families, whether biological, clannish, or "clique-ish," familiarity tempts us to take things for granted. Thus we tend to be blind or go around blindfolded.

Had I not lived in a feudal village under my father's patriarchy, would I have been amused by both proletarian pretensions and middle-class values? Or even suspect that landed aristocracies (rural) have lost their nerve, like the bourgeoisie (urban) who now aspire to be healthy, wealthy, and safe in reverse order of priority?

For them, "happiness" may be odorless platinum credit cards or filthy lucre that are hoarded as substitutes for what they could not years before withhold from their parents and had to deposit with regularity as toddlers during toilet training.

With virtual isolation in our landed estate, we made and lived by our own laws, using both traditional and ad hoc reasons to defend their lawfulness, much as all the peoples of the earth still do in the only known habitable planet.

Even under our own roof, the validating reasons given were always compatible with various beliefs espoused by elders, who are the Establishment in the world outside our home. Like them, when in doubt, its defendants just repeated themselves.

Had I not been "reborn" (baptized by immersion and almost drowned) and if my elders had not disagreed among themselves, would I have suspected their oft-repeated excuses for what they defend? (My father was a freethinker, my mother a devout Catholic, my aunt a spiritualist who holds séances to communicate with the dead.)

From animism to legalism: Animism is agrarian, deism is feudal, and scientism is industrial. In the postindustrial metropolis, do legalisms wait in the wings to follow it?

DOUBLE MOTIVATION FOR THIS VOLUME FOR PROFESSIONALS

The initial impulse to write a compendium on (**i, A–E**) morality and sensual liberty (**ii, F–0**), ethics and social equality, and (**iii, P-Z**) sex and asymmetric eroticism came from trying to explain to my grandchildren that Easter egg hunters-gatherers may be wishing that the crucified Christ who was abused as an adult be reborn in their time as a second infant Jesus. An Easter egg hunt is a search for another friend.

Life started as an egg before we had roosters. When you are delighted to find one, it may be because it may contain another friend, to your taste, who you would like to share the future with.

WE ARE WHAT WE ARE GIVEN TO LEARN WITH

DNA from our grandparents shapes our constitution, whether weak or strong, for breeding. Parenting decides, consciously or not, our children's moral upbringing. Past history influences our personal or cultural gullibility or nausea towards leaders/pretenders.

1. As an etho-ethnographer, I see us as animals with natural social signals and artful cultural symbols. Signals, verbal or guttural, musical or behavioral, inform and educate. Symbols, lithographic or mathematical, communicate and exhortate, comfort and manipulate.

2. As a scientist, I find that to the extent that life is regulated by symbols (tokens), to that extent is it inanimate (robotic, like a workaholic). We are all, of course, partly inert, as air fills or leaves our lungs and our nails continue to grow even after we are entombed.

When symbol users and active producers are overspecialized, only those dependent on the producers will need to be helped (like the muscles stimulated by the paramedic in case of heart attacks).

In cardiac arrest, the heart becomes just like a muscle in an isolated muscle-nerve preparation, where electric stimulation suffices to make the muscle twitch and act as it is programmed to.

The ability to continue work is in the tissue, and the instructions merely flow through the connecting relays, which seem to be interrupted in the muscles involved.

Neither the heart nor its regulators are aware that they must be connected, and the connections need not let them know that they inhabit the same body.

Such a trilogy of hearts, minds, and hands also works in unison as art, theory, and science in our "New Psychiatry."

(This theory is for those who have forgotten the body, not for the devotees of the left or right brain but for those who must connect them. It will not produce a third brain, but will remind the brainy of the equivalent of paramedics in the *massa intermedia* of the corpus callosum between the "two brains": growth demands oscillation or traffic between halves and someday may be measurable by the thickness of the tissues [massa intermedia] joining the left and right brains.)

13.00 m/OVERTURE

m/Chapter Notes

[m/1] In evolution, cell division produced clones until sexual reproduction produced "sons" and "daughters." In the doctrine of creation, Adam was born fully grown and his first sons farmed and herded. Cain founded the first city in history, which he named after his son Enoch who, like Noah, "walked with God." (Cain's fratricide must not have been one of the sins visited on the sons.)

If Adam lived nine hundred years hunting, fishing, and food gathering in the Paleolithic and/or Mesolithic periods, how old did Cain live (1) to cross the Neolithic period (earliest relics from between 8000 to 6000 BC were found in Asia) and (2) build a city in the Bronze Age by, at least, 3500 BC?

[m/2] Thinking in straight lines is good enough for preachers ("What is sin by definition?") and lawyers ("What is legal, whether right or wrong?"); economists focus on their "bottom line" (whether earnings or profits from profiteering). (Obeying laws is like taking tests, knowing what is allowed more than what is wrong.)

[m/3] What can be said in words or gestured in signs can be expressed in ratios, using our thirty-two markers. (Esperanto failed from its reliance on a derivative rather than a new language. Familiarity only facilitates communication. Uncertainty allows deliberate thinking, spoon-feeding of unambiguous material is satisfying but not enlightening.)

[m/4] Freedom to choose means nothing if not from a choice series of choices. To have to choose a lesser or worse evil is to be enslaved by the purveyors of those choices.

During the "terrible twos," children become not free, but more independent. (Individualists claim this is the beginning of "individuation.")

(*Homo domestici* who still (**C**) think "I think, therefore I am" may be those who cannot say "I am I." *Homo metropoli* often (**A**) wish they weren't themselves at all.

(The wisest *Homo sapiens*—who have no need to (**A**) trust and hope—are those who know "I am not I but am." They can then forego (**F**) faith and learn that "What 'is' is not 'what' but 'is.'")

[m/5] A Filipina delegate from California to a National Education Association convention once stepped up to the microphone and told nearly one thousand delegates that she is interested in (not concerned about) a "meaningless relationship with an 'insignificant other'"!

[m/6] Freud's UCS or the Unconscious is not the VNS or vegetative nervous system, but may be a compromise between the VNS and the conscious cortex of the CNS or central nervous system.

14.00 n/Absolute Relativity: A SCIENTIFIC THEORY and PRACTICAL GUIDE

Any new, if long overdue, theory should

1. make (**ii**) historical events more understandable and reconcile it with all associated behavior, (**i**) personal, and/or sexual (**i** and/or **iii**), factual or fanciful, including theory construction, under one huge umbrella;
2. illuminate the corners still in dark shadows in both animal and human behavior, even if it makes present "true" believers redundant or obsolete: not wrong but wanting, nor delusional but dogmatic for covert but sufficient reasons;
3. test well with a wide variety of patients in different settings over an extended period;
4. discard prevailing practices that harm or do not help or are impractical to continue; and
5. contain in its name the core of what makes it different. (Psychoanalysis implies psychological introspection.)

We tentatively called our clinical approach "SociEthRy," an acronym derived from the insights of SOCIology and the science of ETHology as applied to psychiatRY (which embraces the clinical diagnosis and treatment of disturbances of human behavior).

(A reader suggested calling it simply The New Psychiatry (Beyond the Mind and Beliefs that Blind).]

Whatever it may be called eventually, it has already been repeatedly validated in the crucible of changing emotional and behavioral reactions among those whom traditional approaches have failed to help on both sides of the Atlantic.

(We just surrounded our patients and staff with perceptible if invisible attitudes [not value systems] that were different from theirs, and thereby offered another social climate [subculture], that evoked different but overt emotional and personal, social and public, as well as secret or sexual responses, from both patients and practitioners, virtuous and virtuosos, alike.

(What is professionally ethical [indicated] is then prescribed and titrated [tailored to their response to personalized treatment] to nudge them toward demonstrable health [flexibility in the face of challenge], not morality [rigidity of fixed principles]. What is ethical thereby transcends cultural relativism and becomes truly transcultural.

(As participants change colors [spots] as seen in many different lights, they become more prismatic and controversial, depending on every observer's relative position to the subject. [No patient is ever discharged without being disagreed about by "diagnosticians".])

"Absolute Relativity" (nothing stands by itself) is based on clinical insights that
1. I am my changing network of emerging relationships with nature, life, and people and
2. causation is a superfluous notion.

(Etiology is of limited value even in infectious diseases "caused" by insensitive strains of resistant bacteria that were bred by indiscriminate antibiotic intervention to prevent postsurgical complications in unsterile surroundings.)

An uncaused Cause has "caused" more false certitude that is addictive for being thought to be blessed: once you believe in images, graven or unseen, you can believe anything!

The trusting child is the father to the logic-indoctrinated adolescent. *(n/2)*

As Meta-Psychiatry (Beyond Beliefs), the thrust of my alternative approach is that trusting is what one's sense of taste for solitary testing allows the needy to do, in trial-and-error learning, before swallowing whatever is handy, if it meets its test of taste.

Whoever also deceives one's self by believing in one's talents does not want to be undeceived by testing it against others and tries to substitute thinking for testing. To test is to compare.

The sequence then is tasting (trusting), trying, thinking, testing. If one is talented, creating can happen anytime in between precociously or after testing. (Picasso's hands tell him what he is thinking.)

The stages of development are not, in fact, uniquely human but "con-vivial." It is our life that drives our development, not our minds. Life cycles preceded the brain's evolution and that of *Homo sapiens*. (Lifestyles followed it.) But like any juvenile, the brain tries to take over even what it cannot yet understand. And frustrated at every turn, *Homo domesticus* and *metropolus* substitute lyrics in sonnets and words in fiction for actual experience.

MY BIO-SOCIO-COSMIC HYPOTHESIS

All behavior can be identified by capitalized letters and numerals to encode their origins. We have chosen **I** (*Cosmology*), **II** (*Biology*), and **III** (*Anthropology*) to encode nature, life, and humanity, respectively, as the *ABCs* of Science. Did water taste differently after we learned what it is made of? Our bodies are nearly all water ($H^+ + O + H^+$) with a little salt ($Na^+ + Cl^-$) from the ancient seas to keep us from drowning. (We add salt to what we drink when we are dehydrated or to intravenous fluids if we cannot drink.)

The **ABZs** of Life is an Alphabet of Behavior—or of irritability, as "life" is defined by biologists. Encoding makes social changes less of a "culture shock," given our propensities, though it would not save the world from "ugly American tourists" who look down their noses on unfamiliar cultural icons.

Any WoMan can be best comprehended as responding to socio-moral sanctions as well as sexual imperatives.

1. To reduce each of us to a psychosexual or psychosocial unit is an attempt to abstract, not to systematize.

2. To use abstraction in the service of reductionism is to add insult to injury.
3. Simply to criticize the reductive process is pure polemics.
4. Synergistically to digest the data is better.

We can now silently ask whether to SPAWN or be children of the (S)un, which fuels photosynthesis in (P)lants, thus allowing (A)nimals, including (W)oMan to survive naturally by reproduction or prevail as a radioactive (N)euter, should the sun start resting on Sundays.

Editor: For Freud, (S)uperego influences our (P)reconscious use of (A)nimal energy or id, which is intended by (W)isdom to get us (N)owhere, which is the literal meaning of "utopia."

Reader: For Marx, S = society, P = product, A = avarice, W = war, N = nobody aspiring to be anybody in a classless, colorless community.

Piaget, the famous Swiss psychologist who used his daughters as experimental subjects to validate the separateness of Kantian categories of time and space (which Einstein found to be related rather than absolute), demands that any theory of development guarantee orderly succession and progressive learning. He accused Freud of arbitrary segmentation rather than succession.

In cosmogony, e.g., of the solar system, any new theory must

1. take into account all the laws of nature,
2. be based on verifiable data, and
3. never pretend that the object of study is unique unto itself.

We have so structured this new synthesis.

HARD AND SOFT DATA

There's (**A**) sensation (sensed data), then (**B**) intuition (suspicion), then (**C**) conception (comprehension), then (**D**) comparison (correlation), and then (**E**) invention (integration).

Thinking (speculation) is controlled imagining, dreaming is uncontrolled imagining, and fantasy is associated imagining.

Theory building demands only con-sequential (nonaxial) thinking.

(Teleological thinking also insists on justification of consequences.)

"Hard" scientists and "soft" humanists first split apart with the invention of the telescope and the microscope, but they can now be allies again with the development of the cyclotron and the computer.

In science, what cannot be seen is transparent, not transcendent (hidden behind opacities or obfuscations).

What is intelligible may be plausible but not sensible, what is logical may merely be reasonable, only what is sensible is testable. (You can taste your tongue and read your mind, but cannot grasp your hand without the other.)

Orientals use riddles ("koans" among Buddhists) to liberate slaves of language and free us from conceptual thinking. (Those who are very literal are either angry or litigious, evangelistic or legalistic as fundamentalists shackled by the Word or the letter of the law.)

Our synthesis is also the ultimate thesis: Under the umbrella of the theory is its own antithesis. Reductionists pay lip service to it by comparing it with "Cultural Relativity," which already implies that it cannot assimilate what it tries to integrate, nor digest what it cannot swallow, and thus again ends up becoming tolerant or, worse, condescending to the unassimilable and unpalatable.

There are two levels of comparisons:
1. Logical by analogy between observable characteristics, and
2. Postlogical by homology (inaccessible by casual observation, conceivable only after close study).

Analogy is analytic; homology is wholistic. ("Holistic" is for believers in what is "holy," not for disbelievers.) Logic is (C) analogy for filing away; science through (D) homology facilitates further understanding by sorting or taxonomy and locating or topology. (For example, we group the "upper" arms in the "higher" primates, which are less suited for locomotion, with all forelimbs that have the same number of similar bones, whether they are arms, wings, or fins.)

In one, apples and oranges are classified as fruits, in the other as seeds. Comparing apples and oranges is futile for those who only see that they are not of the same color, but promising for those who see them as seeds from the past, that we have domesticated for present purposes, like *Homo domesticus* or *metropolus*, without changing their essential nature as fruits:

> It is not that birds of a feather always flock together but that for *Homo sapiens sapiens*, the weak must stick together to lick the strong, by (1) turning the other cheek (nonviolent), or (2) being cheeky (a, obscene) or physical (b, mounting mass assault), or legalistic (c, bringing class action suits).

Comparing homologous origins and functions postlogically (**D**), rather than simply selecting shared characteristics syllogistically (**C**), is beyond the majority of primates, naked or not, though some monkeys have used the different specific gravities of sand and grain to float the latter in water and separate them. (Can they pan for gold if bright metal attracts them?)

We see the brain as specialized skin since both originate from the same source. Developmentally, (**A**) feeling is also older than (**B**) trying because muscles came later than skin, and "gut feeling" or "intuition" is older than just (**C**) thinking without "knowing" since we had guts before we developed brains. (Carnal knowledge is for the unthinking, unsophisticated, or unpretentious.)

To go beyond **A** -> **D** (good stuff -> right stuff -> true stuff -> just stuff) is often reserved only for near mutants like Einstein, unless/even if we realize that our personal and social programming started with/without and goes on way beyond our parents' wishes/permission.

To find (**E**) other connections (any connexus) between "core-related" bits of knowledge one has compared is rare indeed and open to misunderstanding as simple nonconformity ("just a maverick") or self-assertion ("just stubborn") or self-expression ("just full of it") rather than creativity ("now that is different"). Social conformity (e.g., to fashions), which feeds vanity, is driven by hidden dependency.

We find more about (**A**) by asking how one feels, about (**B**) by how one decides, and about (**C**) by how one learns. We learn about (**D**) and (ii, F -> O) by asking how one unlearns and about (E) and (iii, P -> Z) by how one relearns. *(n/3)*

Without (A) emotional or (C) intellectual bias, it is easy to see that both (1) those who depend on logic do not know what to do when it deserts them in their sleep and (2) those who need truth to justify what happens feel less *(sic)* at a loss to account for facts than if fact-finding were their job. *(n/4)*

Any new orientation, Orwellian or optimistic, demands some dislocations in the status quo, scientific as well as EveryWoMan's.

EIGHT TENETS

These tentative tenets have proved helpful:

1. Biology is the study of all living things. This includes plants, even vegetables, which many children hate and most adults do not want to emulate. Life, however, can simply be defined as "irritability" or ability to respond to tickling (which some plants visibly do), etc.
2. Bioanthropology is the study of all things that once moved without a mover, and they are called "animals," living or dead.
3. Biosocial psychiatry is the study of, and assistance to, all social animals whose mobility, lateral or vertical, is impaired.
4. Animals and children are preliterate like prehistoric societies that (F) worship whatever moves (animistically), or (G) lead and follow (politically), or (H) trade (economically). *(n/5)*

    (First there was the shaman, then the witch doctor, then the headsman, then the trader, then the headshrinker, then the do-gooder, then the thinking counter, then the craftsman, and then the counting thinker.)

5. Literate humans are guided by the prosaic but inaccessible, including history and fiction.
6. Thinking animals (better than reading humans) tend to rely more on "< or >" or numbers. (Double blind studies are for those interested in marketing their product as superior to others.)
7. Sorting humans use dead languages and digital computers to separate fiction from fact.

Just as (**F**) the unarmed man of the cloth was preempted by (**G**) the man with the sword, the warrior's coat of armor was replaced by (**H**) the three-piece business suit. The economic man himself was soon displaced by (**I**) the psychological man without a tie whose casual shoes were turned in for (**J**) the heavy boots of disobedient civil demonstrators against (**F'**, **G'**, **H'**) rednecks and (**K**) hardhats. Now we have (**L**) consumers critical of consumerism, avid (**M**) bird-watchers, sworn animal lovers, (**N**) and the indoor type who offers the computer (**O**) as the latest solution.

(Contrast powerful technocrats ("powercrats" who can hold their own against machines) with petty copycat bureaucrats ("petticrats" who are compuphobic because they already feel redundant).

(Deservedly mistaken for more "careful" (power-hungry) "caretakers" than caring "caregivers" are administrative petticrats (*Homo domestici*) who prod with and push ballpoint pens because they can only plod through red tape as terrified computer illiterates.)

8. Simulating humanimals use analog computers to predict trends according to different scenarios.

(Will automation, which allows airline pilots to sleep when flying high above still waters, kill Prometheus, wake up Orpheus, liberate Narcissus, and resurrect Dionysius?)

THREE THEORIES (I–III) OF ABSOLUTE RELATIVITY

Our original thesis of absolute relativity in nature, animal behavior, and human experience has become overlapping theories that emerged separately and slowly over a quarter century of correlation and verification: It began by asking disturbing "transcultural" (amoral) questions before reconciling unsettling DNA discoveries into a simple triadic synthesis.

Separable into three levels, this theory constitutes a wholistic view of cosmic and mundane events as (1) universal (con-natural), (2) general (con-vivial), and (3) specific (con-familiar).

NATURE <—> REALITY

Inanimate or organic, Nature is a machine and reality a process (sequential or consequential):

> Human reason and natural rights -> civil liberty and civil rights -> personal freedom and equal opportunity -> natural law (con-natural, for species survival) and social responsibility (con-sensual for the commonwealth).

SCHEMA AND SYSTEM

Contingent sequences from electron to electronics:
1. Pent-up energy eventually results in violence (sudden and explosive), which generates space-time dimensions of varying magnitude ("absolute relativity" in minding and surroundings accommodates finitude for the speed of light) ->
2. Fragmented, and therefore imperfect, matter (if minute, rate of decay is measured in units of half-a-lifetime) ->
3. Life (full or empty) -> mind -> God ->
4. Machine -> artificial intelligence (*deus ex machina*).

In this schema, God is created rather than Creator.

Is neither God nor man an island? Are "the" creator and his creatures interdependent? You can't have one without the other except as abstractions: Eggs must produce chickens to lay eggs for the species to survive.

> How do you spell GOD?
> > G - U - A - R - D?
> > G - U - I - D - E?
> > G - U - R - U? or
> > G - O - F - E - R

All we pray for?
Or G - U - V - N' - R
With discretionary power
Of executive clemency
Just like G-R-A-N-D-P-A?

Where did all the sparrows fall
After God was dethroned?
What is there left to rescue
Except all that is new?

Which "symbiotic"/conflicted relationships below can you and yours give up?

God and the faithful
King and subject

Property (invested) and tenants (indebted) (Is ownership burdensome? Does it hold life hostage?)

Self and independence
Group and interdependence
Technocracy and consumers
Humanism and beneficiaries (Do you have to be human to exercise custody?)
Ecology and "custodians"
Ethology and endangered species
Electronics and redundant workers (Does responsibility for children make them rivals?)

Primates have been known to (**F**) worship (animistically as we once did), (**G**) play politics, and (**H**) obtain special (sexual) favors with tokens (earned for lab performance), but not from (**AA'**) overprotective mothers.

I have yet to see a "smotherer" (**AA'**) who was an adulteress (**Y, f**).

Nor do hairier primates hurt their own mates or offspring, neither of whom talk back.

Physical abuse victims are also different from those who have been sexually molested (needed).

If God is energy, we need not alter anything in this new schema to accommodate the idea of the Word as God or His alias. If the energy is human, the schema still holds for what we produce and reproduce, destroy and recycle.

Thus man and God—as energy, metabolism, or system metabolites—are united, not mystically but schematically.

(We are speaking of "reality" as process [software], not "nature" as machinery [hardware].)

A NEW VOCABULARY FOR ABSOLUTE RELATIVITY

(Inconsistency, even among themselves, drives children crazy. Readers, too. None of what you are about to read is inconsistent though seemingly contradictory [i.e., paradoxical, since all neurons lead to "Rome"]. If unclear, it's our fault.)

"Con-natural"

means whatever is essential in the briefly alive and the always "dead" (mineral substances).

(It also means nothing is unnatural, even what we naturally diagnose as supernatural or abnormal, both of which must be proved such beyond doubt.)

(Scientists can only establish abnormality, even the existence of phantom limbs, but not yet our "spiritual essence." In crisis, ex-converts pray to the phantom God of early years.)

"Essential"

means what is substantive in minerals, vegetables, and animals.

"Con-substantial"

means what is essential (material) in nature (con-natural).

("Con-substantial" is not derived from ritual "transsubstantiation.")

"Con-vivial"   means what is still alive (vegetable or animal) or biological (botanical and zoological).

"Biological" means what is botanical (vegetable) or zoological (animal or humanimal, prehistoric or not).

"Human"   means what is racial or tribal, social or not.

"Con-familiar"   means what is specific to the human family, which consists of a single living species, *Homo sapiens sapiensis*, now divisible into three subspecies, *H. sapiens*, *H. domesticus*, and *H. metropolus*.

("Con-specific" is too pompous.)

"Con-sensual"   means what is essential to all animals (sensation and decision in the form of signals or action).

The "sensualist" (moral or not) does not require ethical consensus which the "social" (socialist or not) seeks.

The immoral sensualist will take liberties and become licentious, unlike amoral animals.

The "erotic" does not necessarily seek partners, the "sexual" (sexist or not) needs them when they blossom into flowers or pubescence.

"Bio-anthropology"   studies behavior that is both animal and human.

(Table manners, toilet training, and dressing for modesty and warmth separate naked apes from other animals.)

(The author offers another alternative for those who ape their gurus, dead or alive: they can model their lifestyle after uninhibited animals. They thrive without the Ten Commandments.)

"Humanoid"	means what is shared with other humans, civilized or not.
"Humane"	encompasses our kindness to our kin or to kindred spirits.
"Domination submission"	is reciprocal, not relative, unlike "reciprocity," which is mutuality and more like "complementarity," which is not equality.
"Domestication"	is taming what is bred.
"Breeding"	is reproduction with or without parenting.
"Parenting"	is brainwashing, or the laundering of "original sin", that parents inflict on their children to persuade them to subscribe to their standards of behavior.

(Outside the home, the process of domestication continues as "brain stuffing" with ideologies that echo the ideals of the clan for *Homo domesticus*, the clique for *Homo metropolus*.)

(Unlike psychiatrists, the best of *Homo domesticus* attempts not rehabilitation, but transformation of outcasts so that they can rise above their debilitated state and surroundings, along with others like them, to join Jesus.)

"Ethology"   is the study of biosocially based behavior.

"Ethopsychiatry"   is biosocial psychiatry.

"Bio-sexuality"   is reproductive compatibility and procreative ability.

From DNA to Unplanned VARIATIONS (vs. ANTHROPIC TELEOLOGY)

All living things are reducible to DNA.
(An alternative universe is basic to animistic anthropic teleology.)

AXIOM: In absolute relativity, DNA is the code, codon the medium, and meaninglessness the message.

"Mutation," the engine of evolution, is simply an accidental misreading of the message (understandable, not nonsensical.)

(They are read in frames of three "symbols" called "codons" in the DNA coda of four (which are 3-nucleotide sequences from the four available that change the instruction inherited in DNA templates for replication) to inform the cells as they divide and grow.)

    a.   The equivalent of "now" becomes "not" purely by chance, not "choice."

(For the *cognoscenti*, "now" is, in fact, TAG but may be TGA or TAA or thymine, guanine, and adenine, which with cytosine produce the four-letter alphabet of DNA.

(From them are formed proteins [combinations of carbon, hydrogen, oxygen, phosphorus, and nitrogen] just as words are— from letters (C-C-C-C, H, O-O, P and N).)

    b.   Something can go awry during the typesetting.

    c.   The environment as proofreader in the process of natural selection may not catch the typographical error (typesetter's ink is indelible).

    d.   The mutant survives and reproduces if a suitable partner is available.

For us, the sex chromosomes instruct the embryo differently during the first trimester, NOW for male and NOT for female to become male but instead to remain female.

(True for mammals, the opposite happens in birds which start out as males [*Science*, 190, 1975, pp. 1307–8.].)

    e.   1. Mammalian Mullerian tubes in the female are changed to Wolffian structures in the male.
           2. The abortus in the "safe" trimester is always or still a female. There is thus a time-table for development. In some species which outgrow their skin or body armor, moulting or metamorphosis takes place when the replicated instructions change from NOT to NOW.

    f.   Those who seek to find "meaning" in the message "NOT" (arguably responsible for general or special relativity), rather than consider the role of mutation (error in typesetting), want to deny the "message" (absolute relativity or meaninglessness of "meaning") in the medium (codon).

g. 1. It is the absence or short supply of "nonsensical" probabilities that allow mutants to survive the chaos of entropy.

2. Natural selection also implies that one man's "noise" (repetitive nonsense) may be music (nonredundant) to another man's ears (e.g., Einstein's).

h. Backbones were the first momentous "NOT" instead of "NOW" in the course of evolution.

1. Instead of bony armor (originally scales) outside the body, bony segmentation (vertebrae) inside some species produced a spinal column to in-form (*sic*) its shape.

2. Only the brain remained inside the bony skin (chitin originally) when the DNA instruction stopped our mutation with "NOW."

3. Because of its segmentation, the backbone also produced greater flexibility of movement beyond a straight linear mode of progression (upward in trees, serpentine horizontally).

(Was that why the ideal tempter in Eden had to be a snake in the grass (**A**) emotionally to induce (**B**) willful disobedience of time-honored (**C**) dogma against (**D**) testing (**F**) God's (**G**) power? [Eve was the first vegetarian poacher of forbidden fruits. Her children farmed or herded in the Bronze Age.])

(All questions should be considered literary criticism if they concern literature, like the Bible, which must submit to the standard of plausible truth-telling that fiction must pass.)

Flexibility increased the need for a bigger vault to accept larger deposits in our memory bank. And the more memory there is as currency, current or not, that we have to play with, the more imagination we can generate to get around obstacles.

("Play" is defined as the longest way to reach one's goal, e.g., batting the baseball around and away from one's opponents in order to return to home plate before it does, instead of taking it all the way home, like work, which a workaholic does.)

  i. As the brain expanded, with more stimulation from increased versatility of vertebrates, it folded back on itself in its surface (cortex) where most connections with the enriched environment eventually terminate.

  j. There is an earlier NOT in our development that keeps us from bending over as early as apes must. Man remains the baby of the great ape family longer than his closest relatives in the animal kingdom.

Apes are bent with age and brain weight unsupported by the shoulders, before we lose our ability to remain erect, standing tall, with our brain directly over our spine.

(Is this also why physical mediocrity among the overwhelming majority of our species "chooses" a quadruped to be man's best friend, from lapdog [trusting] to hunting dog [tenacious], as a model of cultural development, rather than more intelligent monkeys?]

To the extent that social (traditional) reinforcement does not respect man's biological (instinctive) endowment, to that extent is our species endangered.

We did not believe our biology can withstand motorized or space travel, and so our first astronaut (rocket jockey) was a chimp. He is about the right size: Ideally, to support better life on earth and for cost-effective life support systems in space, man should not exceed three feet in height. (Astronauts can be amputees or paraplegics.)

Unfortunately, later social inventions (after "original sin" started us paradoxically believing in "free will") and modern prostheses after the plow are more abusive of our animal heritage:

We enslave strangers whereas bees raise only their daughters for such a caste-conscious assignment.

When our hierarchy of heavy (**K**) and/or high (**O**) technology ceases to be playful (**B**), under political (**G**) enemy pressure, then our biological fist and throwing arm technocratically become both the catapult and firepower of strategic bombers and missile launchers for thermonuclear warheads.

(This godforsaken trinity of technocracy (uniquely human union of heavy industry and high technology) is the most awful— but not awesome, if understood as **GxKxO**—in our alphabet of the apocalypse. (Morality is powerless before a bomb that can vaporize both protagonists and antagonists.)

(Understanding an earlier trinity of material [universal), biological [general] and human [specific] interdependence as con-naturality, con-viviality, and con-familiarity [in absolute relativity] could [but not necessarily would] produce different con-sequences, if causality as an extension of original sin is captured by and a captive of con-comitant contingencies.)

(Apostasy or not, absolute relativity without causality is the only comprehensive abstraction that makes sense. All others are apologetic reiterations from ancient scripts. So for the "cognoscente," it is more fruitful to talk of the new talking and thinking brains instead of the old left and right brain; with the literati, it is necessary to bridge with new theory the old "two cultures" of science and art.

HERESY: THE MEANINGLESSNESS OF MEANING

(so-called "cause," not origin, or "purpose", not ending)

Is mankind man-made but not by deliberate design? Or man only a self-made man, opportunistic under the circumstances in which he found himself? Is *Homo sapiens* naturally nurturing or *Homo metropolus* unnaturally destructive, or *Homo domesticus* just more defensive than protective?

Man has evolved out of the erratic typesetting of his genes that outlived those from whom he was sufficiently different to stand alone as a separable mutant.

He is not his own or Another's composition, especially when he is most creative. But as a creator, he is less a typesetter and more a composer or editor.

Life in all animals is not a pilgrimage but a carbon dioxide cycle. (We exhale carbon dioxide that plants recycle to give off oxygen that we inhale and return to the air as carbon dioxide that they can reuse.)

If God is Ra and not Jehovah, life itself cannot be unfair. (Ra, as Sol, would not discriminate against Cain as a farmer to favor Abel as a sheepherder.)

SOCIAL LEGACY

Skepticism, for which I cannot take personal credit, naturally came with my being raised by a triumvirate of adults who had diametrically different but strongly held ideas about life itself: they cannot help but think the way they do and therefore cannot take pride in it.

SENSO-SEXUAL LEGACIES

Heuristically, it may be of some significance that during psychiatric training, I met the third ideal girl of my life. (Her family suffered from "acroasphyxia," which would make her extremities cold to touch with age. Eventually got married to one with the warmest hands I have ever held.)

I met the first two girls of my dreams almost simultaneously as an adolescent who is younger than either.

One was an aggressive chess player, unlike any female I ever played with. The other was a Caucasian, more athletic and curvaceous than her peers, who felt different as a member of a minority in our society and as a woman, and was too tall for most of my peers: Not in my wildest dreams did I envision her choosing me at my age.

There were no interracial liaisons in the life of earlier theoreticians. [Obviously, students of behavior must transcend tribal bias to be scientific. If Mendeleev had gold fever, would he have relocated "Au" elsewhere in his periodic table of chemical elements?] Thus their theories are products and captives of their culture. But are kinships and traditions what were crucial rather than the timing of these liaisons?

I came to America because it is different (the Philippines was poor except for closer family ties, but more carefree) and for women, like my second dream-girl, who are "freewheeling."

On reviewing my past, I discovered to my consternation that my notions of what is ideal were purely personal, usually decided by fantasies rather than facts.

This prompted my suspicion that meaning may be meaningless if assigned.

Senso-Socio-Sexual SYNTHESIS

Once examined, "meaninglessness" as an amoral judgment made "good or bad" different from "right or wrong" and "true or false."

But for me at the time, it merely separated morality from sex in a sequence of development different from Freud's.

(Feminists fault Freud for his honesty in asking, when he was past sixty, "What do women want?" [Would Viagra have tendered him an answer?] He never became a grandfather by his favorite daughter Anna. He was much more passionate as a suitor in his letters than as a married man. His separate vacations from his wife with her sister are not used or reflected in his thinking or writings.

(Most theoreticians lead sheltered lives. Exceptions seldom survive the consequences of straying from the fold. [Don Jackson, a family therapist who gave us the "double-bind" theory—"You're damned if you do or don't"—committed suicide without having remarried after his divorce.] Philanderers from psychologist Watson to gynecologist Masters bring a new perspective in thinking about behavior. Clinton makes all puritans strident.)

Eventually, I could concisely summarize what I learned, slowly but not tediously, as follows:

> Brain + body = behavior (visible)
> Brain - body = thinking (secret)
> Body - brain = minding (gut reactions)

The brain is hologramatic. Information is stored everywhere at once and retrieved from various terminals, e.g., our occipital visual center is like a microfilm file in a newspaper morgue.

(The brain is a "chemical analog computer" where kindred substances compete, and whatever our brain records is often a combination of expectation [subjective] and event [objective],— just as in holograms where the light is split in two—to create interference patterns that are distributed uniformly and can be retrieved to reproduce what it had recorded wherever stored. Whatever is subjective if it remains unchanged, then distorts all events in the same way.)

As we grow older, we tend to see overlapping edges rather than clear-cut demarcations.

(Or is it only because our "vision" dims? How are Santa Claus and Prince Charming, ugly Americans, and psycho-analysands similar?)

Age changes expectation (Santa Claus becomes a loving Father Almighty or a solicitous sugar daddy, or a younger Prince Charming as Mr. Right, etc.), but unless our subjective life is altered, the patterns we perceive will not be radically different. This is why tourism produces Ugly Americans and why paying to talk does not produce enduring change. Travel also broadens bias, looking and listening are not enough, only by trying and doing can our lives change.)

The human brain is divided into asymmetrical halves for better division of labor, like all evolved organs. (Have males not evolved beyond the equivalent of a cloaca because they are dispensable for procreation? With sperm banks and cloning, few are needed for species survival.)

The literate left half processes linear, symbolic data (words and numbers), demanding specificity and closure like a computer and tightly guarding against openness, which the more creative, graphic right half specializes in.

Thus, in the beginning was not the Word or even an Idea, but matter and energy, which later combined to produce (1) life, (2) partners, then (3) brains.

(Preoccupation with death, sex, or creativity reveal lingering handicaps in *Homo domesticus*, *H. metropolus*, and *H. sapiens*, respectively.

(If paired and present by proxy in every decision, priority between pairs is temporal without earning seniority by emerging first chronologically (e.g., as love of offspring by *Homo sapiens* or of God by *Homo domesticus*).

(No event is more important or more inevitable, whether it is blissful, ecstatic, orgasmic, euphoric, dysphoric, or serene.)

In bureaucratic terms, the left brain tends to display an arbitrary table of organization and the right brain to hide the informal organization or Old Boys silent network (the art of the crafty) that all animals recognize as hierarchical.

NEW PSYCHIATRYs' "TABLE OF ORGANIZATION"

My left literate (talking and writing) brain would prefer to leave it as follows:

THREE THEORIES OF ABSOLUTE RELATIVITY

I.	UNIVERSAL	(cosmic)	Con-naturality
II.	GENERAL	(alive)	Con-viviality
III.	SPECIFIC	(human)	Con-familiarity

My right brain would dream a graphic of it but playfully reverse the relative size of cosmic con-naturality compared to human con-familiarity:

The PYRAMID of SENSO-SOCIO-SEXUAL LIFE

I. UNIVERSAL
Con-naturality
I–II. Bio-physics

II. GENERAL
Con-viviality
II–III. Etho-biology

III. SPECIFIC:
Con-familiarity
III (i–iii). Socio-ethology
i. senso-moral virtues, virtuosities
ii. socio-ethical values or ideologies
iii. eroto-sexual practices or perversions

In (i) our sensual development we go from the purely subjective (A or emotional) to environment-triggered intuitive responsiveness (B or volitional), to the more reflective (C or "rational"), to the more impersonal (D or comparative), etc., to gene-mediated (E) creativity.

In (ii) our social evolution from (F) religious to (H) economic to (O) electronic), we repeat the same process of being subjective to becoming more "objective."

In (iii) our sexual maturation from (Pm, f) autoerotic narcissism to (Rf, Um) homosexuality to (Vf, Wm) genital promiscuity, males and females repeat the same journey toward "object relations."

Life itself is a "dance contest for electrons" (more than just a game) to music other electrons produce. (n/1)

We can all, of course, be transformed from particles of matter to units of energy. But before our "spirit" takes leave of our bodies, we can be centers of force around which our families and patients can orbit. (This axiom of interaction is central to the practice of biosocial, truly transcultural, psychiatry.)

Whatever we do can, in some measure, influence the behavior of others, for the better for them if we are not looking out (1) for ourselves (in self-defense, e.g., by practicing defensive psychiatry like defensive driving), or (2) for our values (i.e., ideology: values accuse or say "I'm OK."). Fear of malpractice suits among doctors by envious lawyers who could not get into medical school makes insurance companies rich. For psychiatrists, malpractice insurance is professionally anachronistic. Does a member of the family sue another?

Wholistic (Absolute) Relativity

Absolute relativity of all ratios ultimately boils down to a net of zero, which was presumably how everything began and where we are headed. It does not demand symmetry, mutuality, equality, or bilaterality but a plurality without hierarchy between phenomena (Wo-Man) and nuomena (God, Ra, etc.).

Thus, there is no constant in our lives, only an absolute ratio between (i) liberty and restraint in the sensualist, (ii) equality and ascendancy in the cultist, and (iii) procreation and recreation for the sexist. There is no cultural relativity but an absolutely personal one that for *Homo domesticus* and *metropolus* is the ratio between what is (i) sensual and what is (ii) social, which we priggishly call "integrity."

Just as no one acknowledges premeditated malice, so will "integrity" be self-defined.

When (ii/i) domestication interferes with (iii) breeding, it is because "integrity" influences eroticism and even sexuality for both male and female, and body and mind are ruled by ideologies, which are mere mental epiphenomena.

(A consultant egghead drew from above the simplistic simile of putting the cart before the horse. A more curious ethologist wondered if ideology accuses the promiscuous or excuses chronic attacks of sexlessness.)

Like life itself, "humanimals" can never be inauthentic, even in one's thoughts.

The freedom to think is, itself, limited to the freedom to think differently from others, not from oneself (with respect to "good" or "bad" mother or father, "right" or "wrong" country or investments in mutuals or multinationals, "true" or "false" science, "disprovable or untestable" doctrine, or "new" or "old" technology, etc.)

There is a dialectic of opposites but only during transitions between adjacent stages in our development. After each transition, we arrive at a synthesis between thesis and antithesis that is not "synthetic" or inauthentic, e.g., God replaces Santa Claus among many adults, paranoid or not.

(Because our different selves cannot be in two places at the same time, [as our transient "self" that succeeds or precedes other "selves" in our life cycle)] for a time we all stay in some stage of development at any time.)

Toddlers who expectantly sat on the lap of Santa Claus can be domesticated to be lapdogs for their gods; urchins who were stirred by the oath of allegiance will willingly go to war as cannon fodders, and those who hawked newspapers growing up will fight for free enterprise as long as it is profitable.

(Some corporate lawyers sold on capitalist cults' hope that private vices, like gluttony, can contribute to public good.)

We can even be "born again" during deathbed conversions to the forgotten faith of our fathers (as did my free-thinking father at the earnest plea of my devout mother).

DICHOTOMIES ARE RHETORICAL (nagging), ARTIFICIAL, AND OBSOLETE

Forced to choose between black and white, few can compare what cannot be so classified or dichotomized. Their mind/brain will instantly freeze in perplexity akin to catatonic indecision in the Alaska or Siberia of natural science, with various shades of white outside "Black Holes" (where there is total absence of all colors).

Today we have recycled to black and white by assigning them numbers. If "absence" of all color is O, then 1 is white, and various combinations of 1 and 0 are the binary digits that our computers crunch.

In 1959, fearful of being frozen out in the cold war between scientists and artists, C. P. Snow wrote of *The Two Cultures*, each with divergent values and analogies in different jargons, both competing for separate funding from public agencies (e.g., the National Science Foundation and the National Endowment for the Humanities in Washington, D.C.)

In trying artfully to get artists to understand his fellow scientists, Snow drove a wider wedge between them. Like Descartes who had only wanted to avoid charges of heresy in separating what he thinks from what he has been taught, Snow is often misquoted by treacherous translators/interpreters.

(In the brain, the left explains, the right compares. When an explanation suffices, comparison is not attempted.)

Mystics are more secure (**A**) and scientists more in doubt (**B**) while philosophers capitalize on their own selective doubting and call it thinking (**C**). Those who compare (**D**) existing doubts are explorers in socioanthropology, and those who find clues in animal behavior are etho-psychiatrists (creative, **E**) who learn from each other's shared habits.

But to attract literary criticism (gratuitous and superfluous), even the reconciliation in the New Psychiatry of the intrapersonal and neurophysiological theories of Freud, Piaget, and Pavlov with the interpersonal and ideological formulations of Erikson, Maslow, and Jung still needs the classical fiction of Sophocles (Oedipus Rex), Marquis de Sade (sadism), and Masoch (masochism).

However minimally, our demystification of the evolution of behavior in human development—by separation of (**i**) sensual freedoms (**A** to **E**, and also **Z**) from both (**ii**) social rights (**F** to **O**) and (**iii** without **Z**) sexual opportunities (**P** to **Y**)—reduces the need to fictionalize or philosophize. But being also a uniquely human phenomenon, Zeno-like grandparents require a higher vantage point in our truncated growth pyramid above the battle of the sexes for their judicious but nonjudgmental assessments.

(We are, thus, different from other animals in that we [1] know our grandparents, [2] [a] live with two parents who are [b] still engaged in the battle of the sexes that other species do not have, [3] abuse our spouse and children [88 percent of child murders are done by relatives], and [4] rape the reluctant.

(Divorce or orphanhood can be cushioned for our children by their grandparents who are now the only relics of the extended family in our urban civilization.)

Our THREE WORLDS of CULTURE

We are the only animals who would "choose" beauty over safety. We build roofs out of wood scraps and proudly call attention to its looks as a "shake roof" while accepting it as a prime fire hazard, even when cheaper fire-resistant materials are now available.

One does not have to be an artist (craftsman with taste) to be original (**E**, inspired) or original to be a scientist (skeptic with tests), but creative art and science must go beyond novel combinations of what was previously random (not yet connected).

There are, in fact, three world cultures:

1. Art (e.g., **A** × **F** = icons)
2. ideas (e.g., **C** × **H** = dialectical materialism)
3. science (**B** × **G+K+O** = astronautics (**B**) trying under (**G**) NASA to unite (**K**) technology with (**O**) electronics).

B+D+E x **M+N** is the science of nature (absolute, not general or specific, relativity).

Though art and science are tangible, only ideas and science are questionable, even if not always (**D**) testable.

Fiction, criticism, and theory unite the three cultures of art, ideas, and science.

Art as fiction is subject to (**D**) criticism as (**C**) ideas from which (**E**) theory may be derived for (**B**) trial and error or (**D**) experimental testing. Like eunuchs in a harem are critics or cranks, gurus or quacks, commentators or kibitzers, none of whom are themselves original (**E**) or "creactive" (**B** + **E**), though they may be arty or artful in their self-expression.

Self-expression (sublimation of internal conflict, e.g., between Snow as artist and scientist) does not become art unless it endures. Art alone, not animism (religion) or opinion (philosophy), is ageless.

Art (**A** + **E**) may (**C**) suggest fields of (1) discovery (e.g., Freud's psychoanalysis out of Sophocles's Oedipus Rex) and (2) exploration (e.g., Erikson's Eight Ages of Man out of Shakespeare's Seven), even in (**K**) heavy or (**O**) high technological (**D**) research and (**B**) development (e.g., entwined serpentine DNA molecules out of the ancient caduceus logo symbolizing the art of medicine).

Questionable science (testable) and ideas, once contested, decay to become ideology (e.g., as technocracy, etc., or theology, sacred or secular, i.e., humanistic).

But science (techniques) and ideas (theories) evolve while opinions (the opiate for fanciful or fearful people) only involute as abstractions of dead civilizations.

ABSOLUTE RELATIVITY and CLINICAL RATIONALYSIS
(Beyond the Mind and Beliefs that Blind)

> To create a concept is to leave reality behind.
> —Ortega y Gasset

> To return to 'reality' by inventing a different terminology is
> to reach a different one, to which a stranger will react even
> more idiosyncratically.
> —Ortega y Jacinto

A concept is, of course, more abstruse than and distinguishable from (1) a model, as are all of these: (2) alleged intention from remembered idea, (3) secret fantasy from reconstructed memory, (4) dreams—our daily break from information overload—from observable reactions, (5) expectation from outcome, (6) goals from options or opportunities (inherited or accessible), (7) purpose from plans, (8) values (dividends) from significance (meaning), (9) direction from resistance (inertia), (10) form from feedback, (11) shape from surround, (12) foreground from background, (13) content from context, (14) cause from co-variant, (15) succession from connection, (16) con-sequences from sub-sequences, (17) implications from complications or (18) dynamics from kinetics.

Sorting them out (research) and searching for better solutions is triggered by both (1) the probable, according to the past (correlative, **D**), and by (2) imagination bank-rolled by memory, no matter how long ago the original deposits were made. Creativity (**E**) is shaped by both (3) revealed options ("inspirations") and (4) hidden connexions (discovered "nexus").

> (There is nothing to sort out unless there are data crying out to be reconciled. Recording them can also be so distorted as to render them unrecognizable. Then we have sacrificed what is there in order not to be confused by facts.)

We can understand the **ABZ**s of life and still fail to comprehend the cosmos. Even our own world is itself more complicated than a person or group, though we think we are a microcosm unto ourselves.

Nor are we necessarily the shining achievement of our planet. We are of this world; the world is not ours alone. This planet is our home, but not ours to exploit or destroy. Our life is ours, but it is only ours to live, not to end out of a sense of duty even to punish or redeem ourselves.

What we now have is an overarching grand synthesis that makes the past and the present more understandable by reconciling all the verifiable facts under one huge umbrella theory that covers its own antithesis. It will not, however, protect our species from radioactive fallout that is feared partly because it might create better mutants than the ancient dinosaurs whom we have replaced with nosy fussbudgets. But we must separate toilet training (sniffing) from our sexual **P**s and **Q**s and disown the moralistic ABC from early brainwashing, which insinuates that what is (**A**) good is (**B**) right or (**C**) true, and try to learn more about our childhood.

Our own conscious/unconscious concerns center or cluster around different interests as we develop (**i**) personally, (**ii**) socially, and (**iii**) sexually. But we need to teach/learn about others in the same boat who are strangers to each other.

Can we find out more about Adam and Freud as son and lovers? One or both of them never satisfied mate or mother. (Adam lost Lilith; Freud went on separate vacations with his sister-in-law.)

Freud never got farther than being a favorite son and distant father: he never gave away his career daughter's hand in marriage, which other men will later find to be as important a stage as losing one's father (as he did), nor as important as having grandsons (as I did).

We go from needing a mother, then a godfather, then a father or grandfather when we are in trouble and/or a mother or grandmother when we are sick.

1. All can be replaced by an absentee Father Almighty if we are desperate in our dependence, provided we trusted our mothers enough when we could not pray. If not, we blame them.
2. All stages and needs are basic, and we can go back home without shame if ours would welcome us back without reservations or having to call first.

Either or both as (a) family therapists standing in for the children's lost grandparents in nuclear or divided households, and (b) as observers of the most extended family we claim the human race to be, we are besieged with questions begging to be answered.

Many questions, if they are not intended to accuse, need to be posed in a way that do not beg other questions. Some contain the answers in the questions themselves.

WHAT MAKES US PROUD (PROTEST TOO MUCH)?

In the animal kingdom, our double-edged freedom to err and learn is almost unique. It also begs the question of why it has not been erased by natural selection. Is to err to learn to adapt to survive?

Our brains wrinkle before we are even born to fill every nook and cranny of our skull that is already too big for unlabored delivery, just as our penises outgrow their skin covering during puberty.

Why is it that psychiatrists become concerned with the brain that is traumatized during forcible expulsion from suspension in the womb? Is this not tantamount to a cardiologist asking his fluttering heart about fibrillation? *(n/6)*

Their psychiatric equivalents are agitation and anxiety, respectively. (Their reversibility is also in that order.) *(n/7)*

Should "normal" be whatever we share with all animals? And "abnormal" what we do not share with lower if better socialized animals? And psychological, and "psychopathological" whatever we do not need in order to compete with their natural qualities to be at least their equal? *(n/8)* What is "asocial," such as loners who are not lonesome for people, or "dyssocial"?

Is it high time for all to acknowledge in private but without mental reservations that (1) our earth is not the center of the cosmos, nor (2) our species a special afterthought, nor (3) our reason a refuge from our ethological heritage of physical mediocrity?

Even as hosts to microbes, we are different from each other in the way they make us smell or metabolize the scents that we buy to hide theirs. We are more like each other when we get sick whenever one of these parasites predominates over others and we cannot satisfy it as our tenant. In this, we're no different from plants and other living things. We are thus (I) one with nature, (II) con-vivial with the living and (III) con-familiar with our kind.

(Is it time to remember that we still sweat even when sitting on our hands in air-conditioned comfort at work? And that God did not evict animals from Eden during the Bronze Age, and that transplanting His own Son into a human body to strengthen the flesh against potential insubordination has failed to reduce the population of the netherworld?)

But is now the time to accept that (4) our essence is not unique but con-natural with all the elements scattered in space, orbiting in ever-larger electromagnetic cycles? And that (5) our behavior has a traceable history in ethology that constitutes con-viviality? And that (6) our historical past as Homo sapiens shares similar features because of the con-familiarity of human nature in any age or culture? And that (7) our family, not ourselves, is the source of precious personal virtues and (8) that older cultural traditions color our cherished (Homo domesticus) or rejected (H. metropolus) social values? And that (9) ideologies, old or new, are beliefs that are treated as if they are facts rather than theories, (10) thus substituting fantasy for reality, usually to forego exchanging the soft comfort of biased opinions that have become social delusions with new and unfamiliar facts and perspectives?

If schooling in the various value systems is to be known as opportunistic brain stuffing, can we call all parenting timely brainwashing, i.e., the laundering of "original sin" that adults inflict on their tender dependents to persuade them to subscribe to family standards of behavior?

Outside the home, the process of domestication supplements or supplants family ideals or personal virtues with cultural ideology or social values that evolve with (or, for the romantic reader, as) the history of civilization.

Throughout life, inherited energy and talent will decide our self-expression, prodigious or pedestrian. Thus, to study behavior, we have to investigate heredity, feelings, activity, beliefs, and prejudices.

Both psychology and sociology explain facets only of current behavior; ethology and anthropology deal with the continuum of events that explain different civilizations.

Psychiatry must be founded on bio-anthropology or it is bound to become psycho-sociological ideology in search of utopia.

As a psychiatrist, I am more interested in correlations of co-variants or spheres of influence of orbiting matter (electrons or people), programmed or mindful or not.

What works with preliterate, thinking and intuitive social animals, might work with us, mutatis mutandis.

One-upsmanship about "maturity" and self-serving euphemisms about "integrity" (senso-socio-sexual consistency) to the contrary not withstanding, we grow or age with time. Even as (**A**) infants, we have a self-image (expressed emotionally), as (**B**) growing children our self-estimate (expressed in action), as (**C**) struggling adolescents a self-identity (idealized and unshared), and as (**D**) aging adults a changing self-concept (comparative and testable).

All animals, including *Homo sapiens* and excepting *Homo domesticus* and *metropolus*, enjoy the blessings of liberty, hierarchy, and sexuality. *H. domesticus* and *metropolus* are the only ones in the world who limit liberty and sexuality in the name of equality.

Archaic and modern ideologies are the equivalent of noise that must be eliminated as static if we can, to unscramble earlier messages from the past that our cryptographers cannot receive and decode without interference.

1. As historians, we are fast becoming experts at what keeps happening if we do not act differently and, as amateurs, even better prepared, if not eager, to accept blame for not trying harder.

2. There is so much more to blame uselessly as our past lengthens its shadow behind us.

The very variable impact of any event on everything else, depending on its initial state, is the basis of our thesis. It is also the Law of Initial Value. Reductionism affirms that, by definition, all "-isms" end up as ideology; in failing, by default, to assimilate what it tries to integrate, or to digest what it tries to swallow, and ends up falling back on its precious tolerance in order to condescend as a pluralist to the unassimilable (e.g., as cultural relativity) and indigestible (i.e., absolute relativity). This, unfortunately, is how logic processes facts so that classification becomes pigeonholing, which leads to stereotyping, selective blindness, bigotry, and stagnation. *(n/9)*

Beliefs make up for feelings of inferiority from sinning without even knowing because of belief in original sin!

Absolute relativity, for now the most revolutionary theory of all time, maintains that what we believe, or why or why not, or wherefore or how, is not as important as when *Homo sapiens* observed or doubted, when *Homo domestici* lied to themselves about God, country, money, etc., or *Homo metropoli* about themselves, their kin, their skills, their species, their planet, other animals, and artificial intelligence.

Belief is a blissful drug that habituates and produces withdrawal symptoms when believers are denied expression. Then they may become paranoid as *Homo metropoli*, then depressed as *Homo domestici*.

14.00 n/ABSOLUTE RELATIVITY

n/Chapter Notes

[n/1] Hubert Reeves "*Origins*": The nuclear (or "strong force," in contrast to the "weak force" that produces radioactive decay) is just intense enough to produce some heavy nuclei (including carbon and oxygen) but not so intense as to completely eliminate hydrogen. The other two constants are the electromagnetic force that causes cohesion of atoms (like oxygen and hydrogen to produce water molecules) and gravity (which organizes orbits).

Without these constants, life would be impossible and so would the birth of three stars every year in the Milky Way.

[n/2] Blind trust of one's parents, Santa Claus, God, leaders, etc., belongs to the early stages of personal and social development. Only when one no longer depends on parents or leaders, natural or supernatural, does trying one's talents then become a toddler's main pursuit. The adolescent who just sits or the adult who prefers to be sedentary can more easily stop trying and substitute thinking or, worse, logic for experimenting. (Jesus was not tutored, and He died without getting beyond ideas His Father refused to let Him test for Himself. Postadolescence, He could only echo what he learned from reading ancient texts. Which is what adolescents usually do: parrot what they heard somewhere, or sing the lyrics others had written for troubadours.)

With computers, simulation demands loads of data.

Only memories can extend our life, not wisdom or success: Is remembering or wanting to be the rememberee not simply the sequel of sweet sex or success? Without loving, can we survive? Without working, can we prevail?

[n/3] We need to decompartmentalize science and the humanities to unite all behavior, absolutely without exception as natural phenomena: In bio-socio-cosmic terms, if "Nature abhors a vacuum" and "No man is an island," is behavior a reaction or transaction between units of nature, whether electromagnetic or gravitational or alive or human? If human, is behavior a vector that is decided by our sense of past reactions, present transactions, and what they portend for our future as a unit of (i) nature or as (ii) child of God (F), or citizen (G), consumer (H), etc., or (iii) sexual partner or loner, man or woman or pervert? (Between couples, lust is enough. In families, even God's, love is a must.)

[n/4] Until Clinton's lying about sex became a felony, I did not suspect that there were other difficulties, beyond belief in the supernatural and reliance on logic, which our theory must confront, until I was faced with the fact that only human beings accepted arbitration, with or without force. It was then that I discovered the latent force behind all arbitration, without which none is binding. What we easily fail to realize or do not pause to doubt is that the hopes of our contemporaries, whether peers or patients, are also ours unless we are bold enough to meet ourselves around the bend in another leg of our journey beyond the oversimplifications about truth in our adult bedtime comic books (literature and philosophy).

Unless trapped by the arbitrarily unmerciful, when they make their last stand, preferring death to default, like Patrick Henry, a Scot, do not animals also "turn the other cheek"? Will our hope for (F) a Messiah finally give way to another wish for a millennium under (O) an electronic Deus ex Machina? Have we evolved to invite a radioactive deluge? Can we prevail now after surviving the last great sweep of a forty-day flood?

The path of (ii) social "progress" is littered with the corpses of those who once believed in (F) a God Almighty or worshipped (G) the legacy left us in our Constitution by our Forefathers or who became slaves of (H) the Almighty Dollar that they hoard in modern piggy banks to exchange for the better things in life that were promised by the Tooth Fairy to all children who hid their milk teeth under their pillows.

(Why assume a better intelligence from God, voters or the market, unless you are a priest, politician, or profiteer? Ah, the absolute relativity of it all!)

Is there a need to posit an absolute truth beyond what the facts suggest, or to arrive at it on the basis of logic? Whenever one uses a more advanced stage of development (**D**, experimental research) to stabilize an earlier one (**C**, classical analogies or clever allegories) rather than as a stepping-stone to the next one of (**E**) creating something different, there is the fear of the new that prompts retreat to the past. In life, most of these stages are necessary to traverse and explore.

Step by step, it is just a question of when the next stage will be comfortably familiar. Until then, the old will be safer and bound to be presented as "the last word" that must not be forgotten. (Have you often heard this particular reminder? From whom?)

[n/5] If, for Aristotle, equal access to the gods was not as important as the good life that politics can promote, for Niccolo Machiavelli and Thomas More, politics became the chief business of the state, and its mission was to survive. (This is what we mean today by "national security is our first priority.") From physical to material survival (which is still a struggle for the Russians) had been the path from politics to political economy. For multinational corporations, economics has superseded politics.

(This is why corporations can dictate our foreign policy toward debtor nations run by dictators and toward oligarchies that discriminate against entire races by color or against groups according to religion or sex.)

[n/6] Is "unnatural" or "antisocial" what "abnormal" means? And "dis-ease" *(sic)* whatever contributes to "unease"?

[n/7] Both (1) the worried (sick or well) and (2) the anxious are also different from (3) the indecisive whose dread of decision, or angst, is glamorized as "existential" since their (**A'**) anguish comes from (**CC**) certitude that (**B'**) not deciding or trying is itself a "decision" that they are making.

1. The agitated use larger muscle bundles than their fingers, pacing with their legs, without fleeing in panic.
2. The anxious use only small muscles (in drumming their fingers) to quiet their nerves and, if they can't, they go into a panic in which their whole body goes into action.

3. The truly terrified can "freeze" instantly (or "play possum") and, in awe, avoid undue attention from the fearsome and awesome while the catatonic proceeds to panic once he concludes that even "hell is falling apart."

[n/8] Can we call all group transgressions—such as war crimes and terrorism, draft dodging and civil disobedience (as defined by political or social ideologues)—simply "dyssocial"?

And can we confine "wrongdoing" against any person or private property only to behavior that other social animals are incapable of?

[n/9] Editor:	Logic is staging a comeback as "critical thinking" that examines opinions as if consensus is more than consent.
Professional:	In information theory, communication is the transmission of redundancies, not novelty.
Specialist:	In communication theory, what the ear hears must be specific so that its redundancy can be confirmed.
Author:	In fact, the best communication is nonverbal. We know our kitten is impatient when it starts twitching its tail.
Editor:	But reductionists like to parrot what pop culture heroes profess: "Communication is the cure-all."
Generalist:	Before that, Jesus freaks chanted, "Love is all you need." Earlier fanatics preached, "Jesus is our only hope," but His inability to unite his own disciples make Him increasingly suspect.
Professional:	Later, politics was the panacea: "Everything comes down to politics."
Specialist:	Where before, "money was the source of all evil", today the broken home is the source of all trouble and, to save the children, the estranged parents can part but must communicate.
Author:	And now, the catchphrase is "Sooner or later, everybody does business with everybody else."

15.00 o/Clinical Rationalysis: THE DEPTH and BREADTH of RATIONALYSIS

Our emotions (affective, **A**) are mobilized by constraints (1) preprogrammed in our DNA, (2) preset by historical precedents, and (3) sanctioned by social and family prejudices. Thus, all of us are a group within and unto ourselves with separable personal, social, and sexual concerns clamoring for expression (not catharsis for the constipated).

Action (**B**) is decided by friction, imagination by memory, and the probable by the past (how benign or thoughtful "God" or Noah have now become, how malign or clever the devil or Noah's two wives must have been).

Without clear choices, we tend to depend on traditional ritual, forgetting that they are not based on formulas that can be analyzed but on concepts that have become institutionalized. In formal Platonic terms, they began as "forms" (celestial design), and in secular science as (**C**) categories or models to play with. Because they are abstractions, their derivative, fact dependent, content is understandable only in context, and the eventual outcome (consequences) of any activity (recent or ritualistic) is "caused" by (or depends on) in-come (concomitants). Which precludes replication.

We grow as persons by (**A**) feeling for animals and others like us, (**B**) choosing sides, often (**C**) entranced by polarities, (**D**) comparing notes, and if we have our grandparents' talents, (**E**) inventing and creating. We decay in reverse order by ceasing to create, compare, think, select, and feel.

We have become "civilized" by becoming (**F**) "holier than thou," (**G**) powerful, (**H**) wealthy, (**I**) self-conscious, (**J**) civic-minded, (**K**) skilled, (L) humanistic, (M) puritan, (N) protective, and (O) artificially intelligent. We domesticate our instincts if breeding (P–Z) is secondary to conforming.

> Reader: Feeling for others is reassuring to the weak, raises their hopes instead of more doubts, and facilitates sharing both.
>
> Author: Yet it is never whether one wins or loses (we all die eventually), it is whether and how to lay the blame on whom.

(The author wonders if we need more than two out of three of the following: success (to be remembered), sex (to remember), or an excuse.)

BIO-SOCIAL BEGINNINGS

> (To) natural instincts . . . may be safely attributed the social
> instincts, which afforded the basis of the moral sense.
> —Darwin, *The Descent of Man* (1871)

Behavior is universal and therefore also its determinants. Only the relative ratios of covert determinants produce puzzling differences in overt behavior.

We must still be judged by what we do, but what we intend would be easier to understand from what is less perceptible than its epiphenomena (e.g., "reason" for the disinherited but timid).

All statements can be assessed as to (A) emotional, (B) intuitive, (C) logical, (D) comparative, and (E) original content. It is having more than two adjacent categories in a paragraph that disorients. Soap operas stay with (A) and (B) or pits (A) and (C) against each other. Better storytellers shift more smoothly over a wider range.

A NEW PSYCHIATRY

The clinical application of our theory systematically tries to rectify and supplement stages in unidimensional cognitive child development (Piaget's) or two-dimensional theories of physiopsychology (Maslow's), psychosexology (Freud's), psychosociology (Erikson's), or neuropsychology (reward and punishment, positive or negative reinforcement, or operant conditioning).

These now obsolescent but still popular theories have misguided past moral, civic and sex education when, in fact, stages of sensual, social, and sexual maturation proceed separately even if they co-evolve together.

Every senso-socio-sexual stage conforms to patterns that universally recur regularly as we grow and age and even as we revert to old habits when we can no longer cope with new challenges. For the sake of brevity, we have called this developmental theory the senso-socio-sexual evolution of behavior.

The moral stages of mental development have to be purely personal, the social stages repeat the history of our civilization, and the sexual are less personal or social but more chronological (puberty is not a personal or social phenomenon, but a biological event for each sex).

This schema is qualitatively pluralistic rather than reductionistically monistic. It is not interested in quantifying separate events but in analyzing their micro or macrocosmic ratios in recurrent patterns of absolute—not cultural—relativity. In the world of matter, we are all animals, sometimes inferior to many. In the world of the mind, we surpass them most of the time. But not always to our advantage.

(The cost is alienation if our biological clock [unconscious] suffers from conscious [artificial] scheduling that is left to nature in animals.

(Role models from "academe" or literature are obsolete for ideal defensive purposes, like the Maginot Line of yore against emerging technology.)

"Stress" can make us adventurous and ruthless, "strain" retreat and escape, or become violent when we cannot. We tend to rehearse, unsteadily under extreme stress, before impulsively striking out under enormous strain.

The only thing that we need in life (irritable continuity) is stimulation. Scrambling for food, sex, power, money (social lubricant and corrosive), ideas (evocative or provocative), etc., provide the necessary stimuli to irritability (including war proneness, before we rest at peace in dreamless sleep).

A NEW PSYCHIATRY for the Next Century

We have nothing to fear / Except fearfulness / In our puniness.
Followers need leaders, / And leaders subordinates, / To conserve energy.
Democracies succeed / Where energy is plentiful / To spend wastefully.
Nature encourages / Competitiveness / By its wantonness.

Thoughts can move mountains / Only if they touch the heart
Of kindred spirits / Able to act
And bridge the abyss / Separating adversaries
To mobilize energies / Unspent by adversity.

NEED AND DATA FOR THE NEW PSYCHIATRY

There is no such thing as an empty room.
—R. Irwin

Nothing happens in isolation. Simultaneity can be missed if witnesses are separated by enough space and/or speed relative to each other to account for recorded order of occurrence.
—M. J. Ortega

There is no such person as a philosopher; no one is detached; the observer, like the observed, is in chains.
—E. M. Forster

We can now, unphilosophically, sort out differences and compare similarities from our own experiences in life, postlogically and more like D. Mendeleev (1834–1907) and L. Meyer (1830–1895).

They separately invented the "periodic table" of elements according to their atomic weights and found that similar characteristics clustered together.

That is what Charles Darwin (1809–1882) and Alfred Wallace (1823–1913) got out of their experience in scattered locations before they independently arrived at their theory of natural selection.

After Hippocrates, divine visitation can no longer explain illnesses; after Pavlov, "will" alone can no longer be counted on to change established habits; and after Freud, voluntary confessions can no longer be depended on for veracity.

Behavior, like ballet, is difficult to reconstruct with symbols, but I shall try. Because words or Arabic numbers can only represent themselves in the abstract, we use a few roman numerals and every letter of the alphabet, as we have done in chemistry, to stand for the more widely shared clusters of characteristics of (**I**) nature, (**II**) life, and (**III**) humanity among (**A–E** or **i**) persons, (**F–O** or **ii**) cultures, and (**P–Z** or **iii**) kinships.

Thus, with only thirty-two markers, we can use computers to keep track and compare stages of evolution and development of self, clan, or kin with others now, before, or later, whether peers, ancestors, or descendants.

Applied SCIENCE or ABSOLUTE (CULTURE-FREE) RELATIVITY

I. Universal	Con-naturality	->	Bio-physics	->
II. General	Con-viviality	->	Etho-biology	->
III. Specific	Con-familiarity	->	Socio-ethology	->

(**i-iii**) Senso-socio-sexual Rationalysis (**A to Z**)

Specific con-familiarity (**III, i–iii, A–Z**), of course, applies to all three subspecies of *Homo sapiens, domesticus,* and *metropolus* that makes up the human family, unlike (**II**) con-viviality and (**I**) con-naturality, which apply to all around and inside us, whether sexual or asexual *(Tables 2A, 5).*

Cultural indoctrination blinds those who do not later examine their bias. Ostriches have been able to adapt even if unable, like us, to fly, but not by burying their heads in the sand like we do. Will they become extinct by their own deeds, or can we stop endangering ourselves and others?

IS A "BRAVE" NEW PSYCHIATRY NECESSARY?

Might a different approach help us understand old self-deceptions and mass delusions and new legal abuses?

There are always constraints on our choice of options. If it is wishy-washy to act as if there are free lunches, it is will-of-the-wisp to wish there is free will or freedom to choose.

That we need certitude is merely reinforced by our habit of seeking it when unsure instead of just accepting that such needing must be in the nature of things.

The problem then becomes, if the need to be sure started with primates with brains to think with, can we give up certitude for science, or must we convert natural science to Omniscience?

Compared to (i) the freedoms (A–D) to feel, try, think, and compare, the freedom (E) to create what is different is the most fearsome of all, until everyone gets used to what is new.

We have been taught to suspect instincts unless we dress them up first in fancy words (e.g., liberty), yet the lingering suspicion of any form of licentiousness was aroused not by biologists, but by theologians.

Thus, what is old is the most comfortable because even animals have grown used to it. (For them, it is called "instincts" inherited from their forebears. For us, it is called "tradition" bequeathed to us by our forefathers.)

> (Was Jesus even highly literate? If biology is living chemistry, were his heredity and/or hormones mannerly about freedom, equality, or lechery?)

OLD TIMOCRACY (Bootlicking Bureaucracy) -> A NEW ARISTOCRACY

A crucial issue today is whether our society (characterized by subcultural compatibility wider than that of totalitarian societies) or our species (defined by cross-cultural reproductive compatibility) can survive (or should). *Homo domesticus* and *metropolus*, paralyzed by (**i**) knee-jerk principles (virtues) or enamored of (**ii**) their subcultural values, would risk endangering (**iii**) our entire species rather than coexist with the disagreeable (sensual) or the dangerous (social). The untamed *Homo sapiens* knows that peace is short-lived following appeasement without coping with conflict, but annihilation is not the answer.

Can our species risk the replacement of our civilization with another, as it has done throughout the history of unnumbered dead civilizations, without till now endangering the goose for the sake of its glittering eggs?

> (In 2000 BC, the Egyptians were dominant and, in another millennium, the Assyrians. In another two millennia, the British, then Americans and Russians, and later the Japanese and Germans, if not the Chinese, once more. Why? Why not? Was Lenin both destructive and constructive and Gorbachev more creative and destructive but less constructive? Gorbachev tried to be a better politician; Deng was a better economist than both.) *(o/3)*

Morality (**i**, personal) is concerned with what we do with what we inherit, ethics (**ii**, professional) only with how we exercise the skills we acquire.

> The author equates orality with general goodness and beauty, anality with puritan principles (righteousness and truthfulness), or classical virtues (courage and veracity), and ethics with parochial prejudices or social values (which accuse or say "I am OK"):
>
> "Those who must heavily disguise **i**) their senso-moral "preferences" to speak (**ii**) their socio-cultural lines must wear a public mask. This is the original meaning of "persona" (as impersonation) and "personare" (to sound through).
>
> "Our secret (**i**) personal self is but (1) an idea of our inculcated (learned) virtues and (2) an untested estimate of our inherited (unearned) virtuosities.
>
> "Both antedated but co-evolved with (**ii**) our social self which is groomed to be an ideally crafted vehicle to display our acquired skills for culturally valued enterprise.
>
> "Both selves may or may not permit their (**iii**) sexual self full partnership privileges, with or without full-time parenthood. How

many other part-selves come from your past, and which are still in the wings waiting for their turn on the stage?"

HOW Sociological (cultural) and Idealistic (logical) "Sororities" SEPARATED

We shall try to separate (1) what is (i) personal (virtues) from what is (ii) social (values), and (2) what is inherited (talent) from (a) what is naturally acquired (virtuosity, even without equal opportunity) and (b) what is artificially provided by training (skills) and technology (might with machines, artificial intelligence with automation), by (3) tracing their evolution separately from (iii) sexual development.

"Values" are socially valuable prejudices, even about salvageable souls. It is convenient for people to inculcate good behavior on pets and kids. But how do they spend the time they thereby save?

Our children are brainwashed more than taught, and they learn fast because brainwashing and teaching are sensual transactions. When we preach and lecture, what we say are echoes from parrots. Our libraries are full of echoes proclaimed and professed by preachy parrots.

We can confuse culture and civilization with literacy, science and/or art, and mix up (i) personal virtues with or without virtuosity or what is (A) good and (B) right and (C) true with (ii) what is socially valued, e.g., (F) God, (G) country, and (H) Almighty dollar. Because we first learn about them together, virtues and values are seldom separated and often reinforce each other.

Such mixtures tend to make love and family suffer from many heated arguments, not from the calories burned in repeating what they learned before they could think, but from the friction of resisting any change of mind. (If your friends are of like minds, you can be ignorantly but blissfully buying peace of mind.

Learning by living more than by reading keeps our experiences alive, rather than disembodied through generalization, by remembering both when and what happened and not why ever but why it happened then.

One of the roles of consciousness is to manufacture continuity from discontinuity. This is reductionistic and common. It demands the blurring of boundaries as mere details.

1. Both metaphysical abstractions and religious art lost their speculative and secular appeal, and artists and scientists parted ways.

2. When philosophers stopped asking unanswerable questions and concentrated on natural science, priests became doctors and talented idealists "matured" into persuasive demagogues.

3. There is a sisterhood that needs ratification of the Equal Rights Amendment to the American Constitution, and matriarchs who feel it will cramp their style.

4. As science gradually replaced syllogism (logic), data suggested predictions and, when natural experiments were few and far between, artificial testing was expected to validate them.

LIBERTY, PARITY and CARNALITY

In our three- not "two-culture" society of art (ageless), ideas (faddish), and science (testable), in this modern Age of Rhetoric, we all begin with at least five, not just four, personal freedoms. They must each be experienced as uncivil liberties since they are asocial by being (i) sensual, not (ii) consensual (as legitimized civil rights) or ethical (confraternal), nor (iii) sexual (amoral and asocial, unless consensus-seeking or sensuously consenting, if/however leisurely).

Constraints of time and space, at all times and in all places, create (i) interpersonal (senso-moral) tensions at home. Outside its walls, limited elbow room exacerbates (ii) civil (ideo cultural) conflicts in crowded communities. Moreover, (iii) biosexually, each gender (m, f) has at least ten niches (P–Y), which are either not identical or do not coevolve together in any family or society.

Thus, time more than shared space accounts for the battle between the sexes, whether (i) personal or (ii') unchivalrous or (iii) neither. It is independent of the stage of domestication (not synonymous with "maturation" or "ripening") in the development of (i) inculcated virtues or developed virtuosities, or (ii) indoctrinated values and valued skills, or even (iii) the inherited biosexual endowment and/or inverted or perverted instincts of the partners (breeders or not, male or female).

Our five freedoms, or "uncivil" liberties, are also stages in (**i**) our personal growth that allow us to be free (**A**) to feel good, bad, or beyond judgment, (**B**) to be right, wrong, or unyielding, (**C**) to think about what is true, false, or unchallenged, (**D**) to compare what is testable, unproven, or illuminating, and (**E**) to produce what is new, old, or refreshing.

Unless we are individually brainwashed, in faddish terms, we are fully free (**i**) personally and sensually to perceive and, (**A**) with feeling, trust our taste (in art or people) or be "e-motional" (passively passionate) or affectionately immobile; or (**B**) "move," be effective or not in trying volitionally and willfully to change sides or choose other options; (**C**) think rationally, reflect cognitively or conceive of abstractions; (**D**) test theories, correlate all findings; and, if possible, compare ours with kindred theories or their data base, as well as (**E**) create and be original/different.

Our ten civil, not constitutional, rights are stages of (**ii**) social development throughout the ages, in our struggle to be equal (**F**) before God or (**G**) governor, (**H**) in the marketplace, (**I**) to anyone, (**J**) with any group, (**K**) in using machines (**L**) to benefit our species, (**M**) preserve our planet, (**N**) protect other animals, and (**0**) develop artificial intelligence.

With (**ii**) brain-stuffing, away from (**i**) our private study or (**iii**) family, (where, if nowhere else but in a mental hospital, it should be safe to be true to ourselves even in our dissembling), we have at least ten options or opportunities to be civilized ("urbane") about our equal rights to salvation (**F**, spiritual), before the law (**G**, political), as a huckster (**H**, economic), as an individual (**I**, psychological) or as groups (**J**, sociological), in education (**K**, technological), as a human being (**L**, humanistic) or creature of nature (**M**, ecological), and as an animal (**N**, ethological) or artificially intelligent machine (**O**, electronic) or even an animachine (biochip energized by recombinant genes).

Asymmetrical in the timing of their gender-specific stages of (**iii**) erotogenital maturation, males and females can each enjoy or not, but never equally, any of ten forms (**P–Y**) of erotic expression between the unisex of conception and the (**Z**)enith of gender-neutral development in the androgyny of grandparenthood.

FACTS:

1. Sensual organs must be stimulated by objects, inside or outside.
2. Sexual organs must be shared with the opposite sex.
3. In fantasy or in Paradise (except for Muslims), neither need not be shared or stimulated.

It has been said that psychiatry is what psychiatrists do, and psychiatrists do what they please. Our New Psychiatry analyzes the senso-socio-sexual ratios of behavior of subject and object both.

Instead of relying on what we think (thoughts are but middlemen, often like pimps), we distinguish between external sensations from the skin and tongue, deeper internal proprioception from the muscles and tendons, and more distant stimulation of our eyes and ears.

"Anthropists" enamored of quantum physics, like L. Dossey (*Space, Time and Medicine*, 1982), claim that the world exists only for the observer, conscious (wide awake) and equipped with sensory organs (preferably 20/20 vision).

Males and females start out as females (except among birds) and then develop separately, physically, and erotically. We eventually also converge in the twilight of our lives, men even becoming, if only vestigially, more "mammarian" (*sic*) with gynecomastia. Arrest at any stage except the last (metabolic and mammalian and therefore con-vivial) is the equivalent of "perversion,"—that is, pathology—for example, even as smothering (uncommon among adulterers).

FOR THE INTERESTED SCHOLAR and/or THE SKEPTICAL PRACTITIONER

(This section is directed more toward students of science than the humanities. The believer who has already invested in a portfolio of convictions can skip it. The skeptic or iconoclast can profit more from what follows, which enlarges on what had already been previewed.)

Psychiatry has gone from (a) relieving guilt by blaming more recent parents (which the dogma about original sin never intended) to (b) supervising how people felt about and saw their world, to (c) controlling what they did afterward.

(The myth of original sin, and therefore of the Resurrection, rests on the notion of "free will," when in fact those who believe in "free will" have no choice but to do so. Drugs and lobotomy, the new Messiahs, can make "divine displeasure" go away! Is AIDS the new scourge?)

Psychiatrists now seem more like surrogate parents interested in how their patients used their senses so that they can be more like what they saw around them, and/or kindergarten supervisors controlling how toddlers behaved. Monitoring how children used their sensory organs and how they used their muscles in the world that they shared with others make psychiatrists secondary parents and teachers when, in fact, their training did not prepare them to be either. Practitioners now call what they do "management of the patient" rather than "treatment" and thus become caretakers for/from the community rather than caregivers to their clients. More "managed care" is a nightmare.

Animals (**A**) love their kind better without (**A'**) caring carelessly.

Morals (**i**, personal virtues) and ethics (**ii**, social values) can be confused when we talk of spiritual values (or beliefs or dogma), not virtues (or principles, not doctrines).

First, we believe in (**F**) God (or Santa Claus), then in (**G**) our country (fatherland or motherland), then in (**H**) money (the Almighty dollar or source of all evil), then in (**I**) ourselves (saint or survivor), then in (**J**) society, then in (**K**) technology, then in (**L**) humanity, then in (**M**) ecology, (**N**) natural intelligence, and last or never, in (**O**) artificial intelligence. Believers are our exemplars, modular components of our personal struggle to understand the world in our terms. (Atheists who believe in planned economies also do not believe in Santa Claus or auctions.) Faith, belief, trust, dependence, etc., are signs of human weakness that animals who are born stronger do not share.

Personal strengths can be a better basis for social interdependence with or without sexual expression.

The sick use nostrums, the sinking echo mantras, seekers accept slogans. We trust God when we're most desperate (e.g., in our deathbed, if only to hedge our bets) and depend on computers when we're least helpless.

Can we separate (**i, A**) emotional from (**ii, I**) psychological reaction, emotional illness from mental illness, and stress from strain? Or only if our recent past has not distorted present dilemmas as unsolvable, once our gullibility has been exposed? Then we would not need an intense dialectic between (**I**) egocentric and (**J**) sociocentric advocates as (**C**) adolescents in an industrialized society or exchange allegiance to the family for alliances with peers (which was absent in farming communities), as (**i**) personal identification with their kin is exchanged for (**ii**) social identity with kindred spirits.

Does exchanging kin for later kindred identification bring more "broken families" to modern civilization, as our socially shaped conscious evolution veers—away from older instinctive bonding with animals among *Homo sapiens*—toward artificial groupings, based on shared beliefs among *H. domesticus* and *metropolus* from the same (**F**) religion, (**G**) nationality, (**H**) economic class, or educational institutions, etc.?

For DOCTORS of all PERSUASIONS

Beyond merely being human, our animality, virtuosity and sexuality enable us to (**i**) enjoy the freedom to (**A**) feel (emotional), (**B**) will (volitional), (**C**) conceive (cognitive), (**D**) compare (correlative) and (**E**) be different (creative), and to savor (**ii**) the historical evolution of equality from our ancient "psyche" (spirit) to the "methodos" of Western logic to modern "logos" (intelligence):

A self-correcting God now competes with an all-seeing eternal satellite surveillance that we can cripple with laser beams as our value (d) systems changed from spiritual to political, economic, psychological, sociologic, technical, humanistic, ecological, ethological, and electronic.

Only love of gods
Or/and obsolete logic
Defend(s) the ignorant,
Breed the complacent
And delude missionaries
Convinced enough
To demand compliance.

To be (ii) "citified" or "civil", we trade liberty for equality before (F) Father Almighty, (G) government authorities, (H) high financiers, (I) individualists or (J) joiners, etc.

Popular demagogues, even in psychiatry, are the historical archetypes and emerging stereotypes of our cult heroes. Their evangelical longevity and serial reincarnations roughly measure the depth of our desperation, as well as our need to trust (clutch) God, our leaders, or the dollar.

But we cannot all be equal, even under our own roof, much less among brain-stuffed strangers trained in social skills as evangelists, politicians, economists, (I) psychologists, (J) sociologists, (K) technologists, (L) humanists, (M) ecologists, (N) ethologists, and (O) computer programmers.

In our first home or on our own, as male or female, we evolve (from P to Y) separately. (The "gender gap" is not due to domesticated virtues [A, B, C] or acquired skills [B × C, D, and E] or values [F to O] for loners or lovers [P to Y].)

1. Medicine started as (B + A) intuitive healing and then became (F) an exorcist of evil influences and (K) germs (that have taken possession of the body) with the help of leeches and antibiotics. More recently, medicine has become technotronic in its dependence on technocracy and (O) electronics ("high tech") for modern chemotherapy as well as radiation treatments and more accurate computer-assisted diagnosis and laser-guided procedures.

2. Psychiatry started as (B + C) intuitive introspection, then became (P–Y) an exorcist of sexual inhibitions. Our New Psychiatry leans more on (N) comparative ethology and (O) electronic data processing to (D) correlate the variables of behavior among mammals (e.g., seals) and primates (e.g., man).

For every theory, must we ask for the evidence on which its formulation is based? For every model, need we ask why, growing up, the theorist chose to play with his? Thus, should we ask why Maslow (diabetic and impotent) toys with both basic physiology and "inauthenticity," Piaget with logic, Erikson with identity, and Freud with sex.

Among earlier theoreticians in psychosexual and psychosocial development, Freud was a mama's boy and contemptuous of his ever-present father as a fraud (for not standing up to Aryans) while he feared for his penis (Oedipus was neither and did not), while Erikson (*sic*) did not get to know either his absentee father or retarded son and became preoccupied with identity.

Does my pyramid from the New World celebrate the discovery of zero that does away with Western creation myths?

When covert "reasons" decide the ratio of selected/discarded data, the theory also becomes an interesting alibiography.

A BRAND NEW PSYCHIATRY

What is clear—but not to those who cherish what they cannot unlearn—is that we are (**I**) Nature's creatures, whether we are normal or abnormal, (**II**) animal, whether we are strong or weak, and (**III**) human, whether we are rational or irrational.

All psychiatry being biosocial (a study of heredity and environment), our New Psychiatry is bio-cosmic. It studies how we view the universe because of our inherent handicaps, as soon as we learn about it when we can see it without colored glasses. What we know now includes how all of us have it to thank for what we enjoy and why we curse it while it stays itself, noncommittal like Mother Earth herself.

We also accept that our own Earth Mother has other "children" who do not look like us but are more like us than we are willing to accept. From these "cousins," as well as from their fossilized ancestors, we learn about our own family. So we trace our ancestry beyond our blood relatives.

Among our kinfolk, we credit our heredity only to our own grandparents and blame the rest of our troubles on our own parents, just as they had done themselves. (Is this only since we began to doubt whether they were good enough to have children in a world gone mad?) For the rest, we take undeserved credit, just as they did.

Our humanity beyond biology is attributable to (**i**) our family, (**ii**) their history, and (**iii**) our need for other than both, usually of the opposite sex. ("Having sex" is one way to reintroduce our half of the double helix of DNA.) These relationships can be expressed in ratios for clinical rationalysis.

Theories bridge the worlds of art and science. To be more than artful, a theory has to be more than a confession or alibi. To be scientific, it must be a breakthrough but also testable.

LIBERTY AND EQUALITY

For animals, liberty is freedom to move that instinctively makes them as "reckless" as Patrick Henry when cornered by the uncharitable of its own species. *(o/1)* If Jefferson had been conversant about "instincts" with which we had been unequally endowed by his Creator, he would have said, "Liberty was an inalienable animal instinct," not at all a "right" requiring concurrent consensus.

Once, long ago, a centipede got caught in the jamb of one of our sliding glass doors. I watched transfixed by its attempt to wriggle free until, just as we both decided it was time to do something more effective, it cut itself loose by sawing across its body with its teeth.

Thusly did it dawn on me, already a certified specialist in psychiatry, that being unfree to flee is not only not an unemotional experience but an alienating one, regardless of store of knowledge or given gender. *(o/2)* (Of adult animals, only women can be forcibly spread-eagled and men gang-raped.)

Trapped animals, including the meek among us, can feel equally at great risk or murderous.

PROOF: A gentle doctor, who took a year's leave of absence to volunteer aboard the hospital ship, *City of Hope*, returned to work somewhat drained and died by the hands of a young paranoid. The patient had a slight limp and was complaining of his leg bothering him. The doctor decided that the complaints were too vague to get excited about, having seen worse cases in the less insistent and clamorous during his leave. He declined to take the patient's worries more seriously and paid with his life. The doctor's sense of reality was fatally irrelevant:

A paranoid's fantasies must not be abetted by uncooperative flesh, doctored or ignored. Paranoids do not just fantasy entrapment without encouragement or act murderously if they can help it. To brush aside lightly any paranoid's concern for his ability to flee is asking for trouble. He already feels his pursuers are inexorable, and to be threatened by loss of mobility is to feel doubly trapped. Limbs make us the animals that we are, just as roots allow plants to vegetate in one spot. (Movement animates mimes who make illusions come alive with body language, without uttering a word!)

Another older paranoid with religious delusions threatened me with bodily harm if I did not let him leave while I leaned seemingly nonchalant against a column around which I could escape. He quickly persuaded himself I was a karate expert and desisted from threatening gestures.

I could matter-of-factly deny his request because the ward was not locked except at night. It was his righteousness as a religious fanatic that prompted the need to ask me for permission first and then to abscond eventually after the doors were locked for the night since he could not bring himself to betray the trust that was implicit in unlocking the wards during waking hours. (Even this experimental totally open hospital in England locked up before we went to bed.)

Contrast his predicament to that of the younger patient with a limp. Both wanted more (**i**) freedom to move around but were turned down by their doctors, yet the older one did not feel trapped. It is being (**A'**) cornered that makes animals (**BB'**) murderous.

HUMANIMAL MORALITY AND LATERAL MOBILITY

Liberty ensures lateral mobility, ethics has more to do with upward mobility, and sex with what we do horizontally.

One summer, a hundred and fifty years after Pinel unchained male inmates in a French asylum, we kept male and female maximum-security patients out of wards locked up after dark by camping in the countryside near Oxford, England (cf. Ortega, M. J. "Open-Ward Management of Disturbed Mental Patients of Both Sexes," *MENTAL HYGIENE*, January, 1962).

(Pinel's earlier success was tried among the affluent in America as "moral treatment in mental illness.") *(o/4)*

Severely disturbed males and females can live together in an open ward (or even under open skies if friendly or rainless) when the racially heterogeneous staff are collectively fearless since they are expected to be consensus-free. Patients are more disturbing when staff fantasies coincide.

The only true freedom is in moving,
The freedom to play without apologizing,
The freedom to try without flinching,
And the right to fail without regretting,
Before saying good-bye
With tears in our eyes.

We may be moved, even to poetic heights, by something that does not overtly move, like a rose in a vase; but the changes thus wrought are all inside. Only if we are moved to move something already moving—like stopping the lady of the house on her way to the kitchen to hug her—is an event set in motion.

Even gases must already be on the move to explode: their controlled explosions drive our cars.

For the cognoscenti, just as in physics, so it is in psychiatry: the last frontier is understanding and managing turbulence. Events can only be defined by new interactions. Without them, there are no changes to overcome inertia, and objects continue spinning in the same orbit. (0/5)

Freedom of choice is either a mental decision or delusion. To test it, we need our muscles.

When we can only soar in our imagination, we ask ourselves the meaning of life. When we use our organs instead, we can change the question to what being alive means and have answers that speak to all.

WHAT DOES IT MEAN TO BE ALIVE?

Life is not a matter of being born,
And struggling for survival, or security, or seniority.
Nor is it a question of accepting
That we gradually decay and inevitably die.
Life is ours / To live out / With love
And to leave, / Like we must
Without remorse / All that we hate.

In this imperfect world with imperfectible WoMen halves, there are some rare moments of silent but absolute perfection. Of course, such immoderate happiness cannot be planned or scheduled: they are "happenings."

Professional: You have to be lucky if you are lazy and unlucky if you are industrious to come out even.

Such happenings, fortunate or not, because they are fortuitous, also seem to happen to the undeserving. When they happen to the deserving, the fortunate and the world are one, as if they are indivisible.

Generalist: Are they "oceanic" feelings because of our aqueous origins?

WHAT DO WE ASK IN OUR "NEW PSYCHIATRY"?

Questions can reshape the answers / To mislead whoever replies
     Without trying to understand / What is really going on.

"How so?" tests only the logical / In that what is / Cannot be another.

"Why for?" is teleological, / And asks the ignorant / To test his imagination.

"Why not?" is speculative / To open closed minds / To uncertain possibilities

Why now?" is contextual, / Allowing the open-minded / To share limited options.

"How?" is technical, / Enabling the technician / To sort out solutions.

"Where?" and "When?" / Elucidate logistics, / Not alternatives.
Ask not "Why? / Except to blame
Nor "Where?" or "When?" / Except in hope.
Who asks not "Why now?" / Nor "Why not what how?
Asks to be handcuffed / To a formidable handicap.

(We tend to pose the same questions that we had serially asked growing up. Which ones were yours?)

Fritz Perls exhumed (**A**) emotion from the tombs of repression and Adler resurrected (**B**) will from Freud's unconscious motivations, after

Descartes introduced dualism between thought and reality and unwary philosophers unified doubt with (**C**) certitude, which made fantasy and astrology respectable as input. Can we instead reunite fantasies with motivation, desires with ambition, wishes with dreams, and (**D**) compare each pair as data with data from similar sources instead of pairing them with facts and acts, mindful that Newton had (**E**) discovered new linkages where none had existed before and in the process managed to separate physics from metaphysics? Can we likewise rid psychiatry of metapsychology? *(o/6)*

ON THE SOFT SHOULDERS OF MENTAL GIANTS

(The author thinks Darwin's and Lorenz's shoulders are broader and firmer.)

It is regurgitation (research) to compare mental giants with each other. It is testing to validate their consistency with something new or older. If apparent contradictions (paradoxes) are reconciled, an umbrella synthesis can be created. It survives only if it is scientific, beyond the fascination that novelty invites or ideology impels.

For comparison with older theories, we have collapsed clusters of categories and added what is grossly missing from Maslow's, Piaget's, and Freud's. (Erikson's covers more age groups poorly.)

But just to keep adding what is missing becomes tedious. (To Shakespeare's Seven Ages of Man, Erikson in his life cycle had to add an eighth stage). Trying to start from scratch is more rewarding, even if it requires erecting a new edifice *(Tables2A-15)*:

1a.   OUR SENSO-SOCIO-SEXUAL DEVELOPMENT (Table 2A)

1b.   OUR SEPARATE EROTO-SEXUAL ODYSSEYS (Table 8A)
          According to M. ORTEGA and S. FREUD

1c.   COMPARING SOCIO-SEXUAL DEVELOPMENT (Table 9A)

2a.   COMPARING SENSO-SOCIAL DEVELOPMENT (Table 10)

2b.   COMPARING PHYSIO-SENSUAL DEVELOPMENT (Table 11)
          According to A. Maslow and M. Ortega

2c.   COMPARING PHYSIO-MENTAL DEVELOPMENT (Table 12)

3.   COMPARING OUR SENSUAL EVOLUTION (Table 13)
           According to M. ORTEGA and J. PIAGET
4.   PERSONAL LIBERTY and SOCIAL EQUALITY (Table 14)
5.   PSYCHO-SOCIAL EVOLUTION OF EQUALITY (Table 15)
           According to M. ORTEGA and E. ERIKSON

With any of above nine tabulations for comparison, try covering any column to see if it hides or adds to what you already know but do not find in what remains (+signs precede what I have added, e.g., interior proprioception that governs the amplitude of any movement to flee, fight, feed, or fornicate, to Maslow's columns.)

Do these nine tabulations make the tenth *(Table 16)* about our three subspecies (*H. sapiens, domesticus,* and *metropolus*) understandable?

Do the id and superego decide personal morality (virtues) and knee-jerk principles, and the ego and ego ideal our social identity and values (ethics)?

(Freud claims that we naturally tolerate the smell only of what we ourselves excrete. Yet my grandson toddler would wake up, leave our bed to rejoin my wife in the bathroom, and snooze while she sits.)

(Are the permutations in the nine tables above unique but still comprehensible rather than bizarre?)

FREEDOM, EQUAL ACCESS, and SEXUALITY

We have different tests that one could take or give to one's patients, peers, or partners. *(0/7)*

We can learn to distinguish between freedom and equality and how libertarians and egalitarians work reciprocally instead of leading us down the primrose path to paradise.

(Bees were among the first species to leave the swamp. Has any insect family become extinct to date? Will zero population growth spell slow genocide for ours?)

Would history continue repeating itself at greater and greater cost because the domesticated and reactive captives of history (*Homo domesticus* and *H. metropolus*, respectively) are rapidly coevolving with more and more ingenious *Homo sapiens*?

As we get older, fewer still of all three subspecies will keep going beyond each succeeding stage in the **ABZ**s of life.

The generous "sugar daddy" (**F, H, X**) who is married, like Santa Claus, to someone else, is the erotized magnet for senso-socio-sexually confused females (less "liberated" than libertine) who were slow to learn the **ABC** of morality and (**F, G, H**) the preliterate ideologies of history.

Unerotized, a more grandfatherly role (**Z**s) is ideal for family therapists, especially when sexuality and mysticism tend to make troubled adolescents disregard their parents.

> Freud thought that his father's death is the most important event in a man's life. His favorite daughter never made the equally important departure from her father's to her own home, husband, and children.
>
> I thought giving away one's daughter was more eventful than losing my father until she presented me with her son.

(Because rationalysis is new, the careful elaboration of its specific applications, even for professional recruits, will take more time to digest.)

15.00 o/CLINICAL RATIONALYSIS

o/Chapter Notes

[o/1] Do patients asking to die feel trapped like a paranoid? Do they have the right to die even if the paranoid does not have the right to kill? He is free to kill as we saw, but the dying is not free to die. That is the crucial difference between them, the freedom to kill and the right to fail or die unassisted.

[o/2] As animals, we are all brothers, whether we are descended from Adam or Eve. (Might this also be why Carl Sagan calls (**A**) emotion and (**B**) will the Dragons of Eden?

When we are less than animals and we do not see the body politic, like the centipede does as divisible, terrorists can divide us.

Antiterrorists cannot sacrifice the hostages as the centipede some of its appendages, and the entire citizenry is paralyzed.

[o/3] When the Son of God pleaded with His Father to spare His life, the reply He got was that He was a hostage to humanity's fortunes and must die. Was God a terrorist who is coercing His Son's constituency or the Establishment protecting His own?

When Abraham agreed to sacrifice his son, his courage to face the consequences was repaid by his son's life being spared.

(For the Romans, if not for the Greeks, (**B**) courage is not the only virtue; but without it, all other "virtues" are meaningless.)

Terrorism is territoriality inspired by ideology, whether theology, politics, or economics. Territoriality with terrorism failed the communists when they took over Shanghai from the Japanese and its capital assets fled to Hong Kong. Deng used Taiwan as a model for his

Special Economic Zones (SEZ) near Hong Kong, and both Shanghai and Taiwan capital were lured back to the mainland. Hong Kong was eventually taken back (handed over by the British) and is now the model as the second Singapore and first Taiwan for the next handover of the old Taiwan by America and Japan.

(Yeltsin failed to make Moscow his successful SEZ [Special Economic Zone] like his contemporary Deng did, by failing to curb greed and corruption from taking over as "laissez-faire" capitalist ideology.)

[o/4] In his correspondence as an ex-president with his predecessor (John Adams), Jefferson reiterated his belief in an "aristocracy of talents" (inherited) "and virtues" (read "virtuosities").

[o/5] (We can alter trajectories and destinations by moving against clinical problems according to the biodynamic law of initial value [or with it if paradoxical results are intended], followed by successive "burns" [or titration by prescription] according to the principle of equifinality [of all open systems].)

[o/6] I have found sensory deprivation psychosis vs. Kohut's concept of "self" (and his acceptance of the patient as basic rapport, no less) rooted in the early development of affect in the infant, both e-motional (in the literal sense) and somesthetic. (I have also found that nodding my head invariably signals empathetic understanding, which I have, to the schizophrenic who was incomprehensible to others who seek coherence.) Our New Psychiatry has been revised to include as "Kohut's constant" his keeping in touch with the subclinically yet desperately needy.

[o/7] Not what is accurate so much as what is not uncommon (absolute relativity) or wrong that is the test of validity—what is circular is not science, what is recycled cannot be researched in "real time" but must await reappearance.

Occult theories about invisible spirits in heaven or visitors from outer space, power of the pyramid, and healing with crystals may be reconcilable but not testable. Idealism only explains failure, without guiding corrective action.

Test any hypothesis twice and cross-check if tenets are different and promising.

After completing, enter self-assessed ranking before (for you) and after (for your partner) each letter from **A** to **Z** and multiply by the number following or preceding the letter:

From 2 to 10: Are you (your partner) getting more or less ("free to . . .)

A   1) emotional?   (... feel good or bad, with or without passion, guilt, regret or remorse")

B   2) willful?   (... be passive or active, territorial or temperamental, fight or surrender")

C   3) reasonable?   (... agree or think differently")

D   4) critical?   (... explore, test and compare without compromise")

E   5) inventive?   (... destroy, create or discover different issues, connections and solutions")

From 1 to 10: Do you (your partner) now believe more or less in ("equal access to . . .)

F   1) God?   (... salvation or damnation")

G   2) country?   (... the law, the righteous or the mighty")

H   3) property?   (... patrimony or profit")

I   4) yourself?   (... parents or surrogates, self-serving or not")

J   5) your group?   (... superiors or subordinates, self-sacrificing or not")

K   6) machines?   (... time- or labor-saving appliances, devices, techniques or prostheses")

L   7) mankind?   (... human giftedness or talents, productive or decorative")

M   8) nature?   (... renewable or scarce resources for consumption or sustenance")

N   9) animal instincts?   (... superior or inferior creatures")

O   10) artificial intelligence? (... computers or robots")

If male: Are you or yours becoming more or less licentious or

P	1) autoerotic?	(... "Masturbation is a private perversion.")
Q	2) fetishistic?	(... "Fetishism is erotic stamp collecting.")
R	3) voyeuristic?	(... "Voyeurism is a victimless crime.")
S	4) exhibitionistic?	(... "Exhibitionism threatens the envious.")
T	5) pedophilic?	(... "Pedophilia keeps one young at heart.")
U	6) homoerotic?	(... "Homosexuality is safe contraception.")
V	7) bestial?	(... "What you get is what you want most.")
W	8) rapacious?	(... "Rape can be a kindly close encounter.")
X	9) monogamous?	(... "Divorce is easier than coping harder.")
Y	10) fatherly?	(... "Man needs mates, has to want heirs.")

If female: Are you or yours more or less "liberated" or libertine or

P	1) narcissistic?	(... "Narcissism is a form of fidelity.")
Q	2) self-assertive?	(... "Assertiveness is territoriality.")
R	3) homo-erotic?	(... "Aesthetics is better than sex.")
S	4) flirtatious?	(... "Teasing safely tests one's skills.")
T	5) seductive?	(... "Coquetry opens doors of opportunity.")
U	6) maternal?	(... "Mamma means mammary.")
V	7) abortive?	(... "Promiscuity is non-discriminatory.")
W	8) adoptive?	(... "Killing the innocent is too convenient.")
X	9) adulterous?	(... "Adultery is word-of-mouth publicity.")
Y	10) adventurous?	(... "Kids have time, the old too little.")

Male or female, from 5 to 20, if you are now (**Z**) grandparents, show under each number below from 1 to 4 how much more than your partner you have changed from biological or adoptive (1) fatherhood or (2) motherhood to (3) grandfatherhood or (4) grandmotherhood: "Kids will be kids."

(1)   (2)   (3)   (4)

Valences for **i** × **ii** are assigned according to the sequential order of historical rehearsals unfolding without our choosing (**F** to **O**) but coevolving with chronological age readiness (**A** to **E**), yet separate from our sexual development (**iii**).

Multiply each ranking with the number of the statement across from it and divide total (**i**) sensual, (**ii**) social, and (**iii**) sexual, male and female, scores by 10 separately.

The domestication (i + ii) score (not a research statistic) multiplied by the breeding (iii) score, according to sex of subject, is uniquely hirs (*sic*), for clinical or other considerations:

The potentially higher average score for all females because "form follows function" reflects their more advanced anatomy: no male "cloacal" compromise.

(Man still uses the same orifice for micturition and reproduction. Structure is stricture, but not vice versa.)

Communication gaps widen proportionately with valued (*sic*) discrepancies between data gatherer and provider. Each surveyor must serve as his own control and be plotted and scored alongside the surveyed.

If a statistician's part score (**i** + **ii**) is similar to his subject (partner or not), the latter's relative position on the domestication graph (**i** × **ii**) below must be compared only with members of the same cult. (Contemporaneous sexual "revolution" may not actually bias breeding (**iii**) for or against as much as demagogues pro and con proclaim.)

Domestication is the ratio **ii/i**, breeding potential is **iii**/domesticity, absent genital or pelvic surgery or disease. Civilization is inversely proportional to breeding potential. Animality is directly proportional to breeding potential.

TRIANGULATIONS TO KEEP TRACK OF RATIOS

To establish the diagnosis of domesticity, development must be plotted as one evolves in (**i**) the family ("morally") and in (**ii**) society (ideologically).

In navigation, we graphically chart our progress by (1) triangulating from at least two known points ([**i**] and [**ii**], below) in direct line of sight with the ship, and then (2) cross-checking with predicted location from the distance traveled over elapsed time at known speed, and (3) tracking our progress accordingly.

SENSO-SOCIAL STAGES

Try triangulating your socio-personal development:

i. Senso-Moral Stages of Development

1	2	3	4	5	6	7	8	9	10	9	8	7	6	5	4	3	2	1

A	2
B	4
C	6
D	8
E	10
D'	8
C'	6
B'	4
A'	2

F G H I J K L M N O N' M' L' K' J' I' H' G' F'

ii. Ideo-Historical Stages of Evolution

STAGES OF EROTOSEXUAL DEVELOPMENT
(sensogenital, not psychosocial)

(Prepubescent and postmenopausal compatibility can depend more on asexual harmony.)

iii. (m × f) Human Sexual Cycles
FROM unisex at conception
TO serene senescence (androgyny)

iii: **f:**

	1	P
	2	Q
	3	R
	4	S
	5	T
	6	U
m: P	Q R S T U V W X Y T' S' R' Q'	
	7	V
	8	W
	9	X
	10	Y
	5	T'
	1	P'
1	2 3 4 5 6 7 8 9 10 4 3 2	

In plotting anybody's development—as a person and world neighbor (**i** × **ii**), then as male or female (**iii**)—it is not probability (linear) but relativity (absolute) that emerges graphically, without stigmatization, no matter how sick (strained) or stressed (challenged) the subject may be.

Your scores establish the baseline for comparison/further evaluation. Regardless of age, the closer their stage of sexual development, the less will moral and social constraints prevent partners from pairing off. Potential partners can therefore plot where they are in their sexual "revolution," using the self-descriptive subcategories listed, and con-sensually assess their sexual, not psychosocial compatibility (for which the socio-moral axes in the previous graph will be more helpful).

More recent cryptographers read themselves in what they hear about their favorite animals (**N** <- **L**), and now we also anthropomorphize our pet machines (**K** -> **L**).

Some ecologists (**M**) are still in love with their automobiles, and lately we hear of (**O**) electronic widows whose husbands prefer the computer screen to the family television set.

We have TV and computers, upstairs and downstairs, my wife being a published author also. Our computer program allows us to index a manuscript automatically, but recently, when indexing a section on the polysyllables above, the test print kept repeating "Hereafter I shall refrain . . ." Only after that phrase began a paragraph of its own (now edited out) did the repetitions stop. Did I do what the machine wanted or what I wanted? Or more important, is its redundancy necessary?

Coevolving together, developmental plotting (triangulation of i and ii) can eventually transcend traditional (classical) and trendy (fashionable) socio-sexual stigmatization of

1. caretakers (clients) who cannot will ("prefer") or
2. their equally committed (brainwashed) caregivers whose unconscious bias (nonclinical values) may have been violated, e.g., compulsive heterosexuals who become homophobic clinicians.

The battle of the sexes is derived from their nonscynchronous growth and development as well as their experiences in different homes that lead to different expectations from their partner and family.

A grandfatherly figure can sort sexual battlelines better than those still in the heat of battle.

16.00 p/Sensuality: SENSO-MORAL BEHAVIOR THROUGHOUT HISTORY

Whatever is "personal" (**A–E**) or (**i**) "sensual" ("psycho-sexual") is less public (**F–O**) or (**ii**) consensual ("psycho-social"), but not necessarily (**P–Y**) private or (**iii**) sexual or (**Z**) genetic. "Person" discounts gender or age (creativity may be precocious) and disregards sundry theories about "self" (unconflicted ego is inherited) and "identity" (secret self-concept) with which small children (especially orphans) are preoccupied but that except during midlife crises, their more confident postpubescent elders, simply ignore.

A secret self-concept assumes independence. But even those who insist on a sense of identity are, in fact, interdependent. This is not the case with those who are truly free. They sense that they can do without what is demanded of them. It is not that they can control what happens to them, but that whatever happens does not make them surrender their freedom, even if they suffer in the hands of the more powerful.

Power is also a symptom that control must be imposed on those likely to be unimpressed. Only those who grew up unhurt by being dependent, and were sustained without pity, can feel free to say, silently if an animal, "Now go your own way," to the young when it is their turn.

OUR SENSE OF OURSELVES

Our personal development proceeds by (**A**) feeling (e-motion), (**B**) striving (motivation), (**C**) re-flexing our mental muscles (recognition or double-take or hindsight), (**D**) com-peering (core-relation), and for a few, (**E**) crea-teasing (invention).

To be sensual, animal or human, is more an inarticulate state, no matter how intellectualized our edited version of our internal or external experiences are. (This makes what follows difficult reading.) What we sense usually bypasses the brain's Broca's area, where they can be coded into language and shared with those whose Wernicke's receptive center can understand the same code.

We begin with our senses, which grow into feel-ings (*sic*) and then become e-motion when we are not allowed to move as freely as we are capable of. E-motion becomes "affect" in psychiatric jargon when it affects others and, in effect, moves them to relax restrictions on the mobility of the e-motionally overcontrolled before they become moody.

We are moved when we cannot move or get what we want with words. It is the nonverbal movement that speaks for us without words, and it is how we are moved that allows us to decode body language if we allow ourselves to use the same body language, as when we imitate animals or autistic children or depressed adults. It is how we are affected by their "affect" that allows us to read between the lines actors utter, as a sixth sense (deep proprioceptive vs. touch) becomes our third ear.

Thusly do we come to know that "it takes one to know one" or make an educated guess about another, subject to validation with additional data that the guessing of itself also demands, but which pure speculation (truly more a hidden conviction) does not.

FOR NEW SPECIALISTS

> Infants learn "No" with help,
> Children "Bad" with pain,
> Urchins "Wrong" with gangs
> Adolescents "False" with certitude,
> And adults "facts" with prejudice.

Good or bad originally depended on (**A**) how we felt, chilled on our extrusion from the warmth of the womb, hungry or not, dry or wet. Then it became a matter of what smells or tastes good. Our parents cultivated our taste in wholesome cereals and good company, and we acquired otherwise logically indefensible tastes in classical or modern music and art.

Control of where it is (**B**) right to be when we smell bad or where it is wrong to go to satisfy our curiosity soon became questions of freedom to test limits and fairness when caught trespassing. Likewise, our freedom to (**C**) think and falsify the truth is limited by what is known or revealed, whether (**D**) rigorously tested or just simply swallowed. But what is (**E**) different is difficult to digest.

Thus what is moral became what is sensually pleasing or personally unpleasant but traditionally accepted as good, right or true by one's parents. The unpleasant are then sugarcoated as virtues.

We fall back on our feelings or e-motions when we cannot be movers and when we try and fail to integrate what we cannot assimilate. We can bully, coax, and cajole kids into believing what we were bullied, coaxed, and cajoled into believing to be a hierarchy of values. (Values can often be sold without first being tested, unlike other crutches.) *(p/1)*

(A Moral Majority of *Homo domesticus* believes in "one man, one wife," private enterprise, and public prayer in public schools.)

The dreamer (**A**: "Whatever I dream is possible") is different from the doer (**B**: "I do what I can"), as action resolves doubts. Both are different from the thinker (**C**: "What I think is so is so for me"), seeking answers while ensconced in an armchair. All differ from both (**D**) the explorer making comparisons on field trips or correlations in experimental laboratories ("What seems so may not be so"), and (**E**) the pioneer discovering virgin territory ("What I find is whatever it turns out to be").

The dreamer and the emotional stage of development have in common the lack of motion (e-motion) that they can rely on to effect a different outcome. The longer we can stay in the emotional stage of development, the longer we can dream without testing reality or our limitations.

People who live in their hearts (dreamers) do not judge themselves by the words that describe their behavior, and people who live by their muscles (doers) have less need for words and more for "objects" upon which they can practice and act.

People who live in their heads (thinkers) live out the words that they habitually use to judge their behavior (e.g., as "communicators entrusted with fulfilling contracts by inviting participation in decision making"). The talker is more immediately influential than the writer who must first influence leaders who are equally or more literate.

(Even economic theorists who win Nobel prizes are at the mercy of advocates of their theory whose comprehension, for personal or political reasons, must compete with and overwhelm others who think along different lines under identical economic conditions.)

A. We are e-motional (*sic*) as infants or whenever we cannot move when we want to. The more we want to, the more passionately we feel about our enforced passivity. (Plants and, of course, other animals have been reported to warn others miles away of what they sense to be impending disasters.)

Slogans aside, we can never be "out of touch with our feelings." Not sharing them may be failure of vocabulary or communication, but emotion, self-expression, and communication are not really synonymous.

"**A**" is also called "affective" because it affects kinship or relationships. It is the animal-like acceptance of the young (akin to Kohut's constant empathetic understanding of his clients) or a caretaker's preverbal plea for loving kindness (Erikson's trustworthy dependability in the caregiver). Rejection early in life, even among a literate theater audience—like a captive infant without lines—can move the e-motionally deprived to squirm and weep over personal memories of kindred experiences that others had scripted.

B. The striving, willful or willing toddler can be impatient with the pace of its progress but increasingly able to overcome more and more obstacles to his freedom of movement.

"**B**" is also called "conative" or "volitional" or voluntary activity with access, not "choice." It uses inborn energy to lead or trail in unoriginal directions (all ventures must cope with emotional friction or other constraints).

C. The juvenile uses logic to fight critics and is less practical when thwarted and as an adolescent more mystical (romantic) when sexually frustrated.

"**C**" is also known as "cognitive." It is exploited in compulsory education. (Even "friendly" computerized training programs may scold if programmers are overeducated.)

D. The adult can explore more of the immediate options instead of simply speculating.

"**D**," or comparative, does not honor logical consensus among colleagues who use analogy instead of homology. To correlate is to discredit data reported without numbers. (Among those who do not depend on logic, ratios are more decisive. They compare facts rather than swallow hallowed truths.)

Of course, both **D** and **C** can be learned conceptually and tested academically. **A**, **B**, and **E** tend to be genetic and unrehearsed and paper-untestable except as (**AB**) applied ingenuity and (**AE**) problem-solving creativity.

E. The child prodigy and the adult virtuoso will search creatively for new approaches to persistent problems, instead of merely imitating their peers. If their innovations prove to be popular or practical, the talented are hailed as artists or scientists, long after they stopped being productive. How long after will depend on how precocious the child was or how far ahead of contemporaries the adult is. (Changes in taste and thinking take more time than energy to happen in the untalented.)

"**E**," or creativity, is openness to and resourcefulness in exploiting heretofore hidden connections, absent any previous correlations, between "random" events.

All that even Rorschach projective testing can examine and struggle vainly to interpret are the tester's original conceptual or apperceptive constructions, deviance from which are often reported as distortions.

What is reported that cannot be observed are just projections by the opinionated, speaking from another developmental stage about what would have happened to another if tester were the actor:

it would not all be fiction only if testee were a clone or identical twin.

There are no valid standards for (**E**) creativity (inspired and uninvited) or (**B** + **E**) "cre-activity" (once **E** is acted on) and (**B** + **D** + **E**) "compreactivity" (when correlated later). If what is new and unsolicited is treated as inspiration, its apparent randomness disappears as soon as further elaboration pays off as performance that pleases the master, once a patron of the arts, now a partner in grantsmanship.

D'->A' is usually omitted in life cycles ending in a peak or plateau: Mental faculties invariably but not uniformly wane with age in all mammals (mice, monkeys, and man). The slide back to antecedent stages may be gradual or steep (if overindulged earlier) in the same person:

Toddlers (**B**) who were well-rehearsed as whiners (**A**) when trapped (unable to move) can be skillful (guilt-eliciting, **F'**) crybabies in their second childhood (**A'**) from disabling degenerative disease, and even succeed in demanding to die as the sickbed becomes a crib again. Euphemists approve of this as "euthanasia."

All the common features of (**A**) to (**E**) (tabulated from a to z) are compared, two stages at a time as well as all at once, in Table 4E.

FOR OLDER PRACTITIONERS

There is good / and there is bad,
It makes a difference / for whom and whose.

There is right / and there is wrong / for us and for them.
There is true / and there is false / about us and them.

There is proof or not / about some of it.
There is one or part / or no solution / for some of us.

i. STAGES of SENSUAL DEVELOPMENT

Prelogical (preadolescent):
A. Emotional, affectionate, passionate
B. Willful, decisive, motivated

Logical (postjuvenile):
C. Philosophical, reflective, abstract

(Psychologists test for abstract thinking by proverb interpretation, sociologists for ideology by response to slogans. [A juror was disqualified from a sexual harassment case for her bumper sticker "I believe Anita" (Hill that she was sexually harassed by Supreme Court nominee Clarence Thomas)]).

Postlogical (presenescent):
D. Testing, comparing, exploring
E. Creating, venturing, discovering

(A, B, C are given different names by [1] Freud *(Table 8A)*, [2] Erikson *(Table 14)*, and [3] Piaget *(Table 13)*:
(A = [1] oral, [2] oral sensory, [3] sensorimotor
(B = [1] anal/oedipal, [2] anal muscular, [3] intuitive/concretistic
(C = [1] latent/genital, [2] locomotor/genital, [3] formal abstractions)

A. EMOTIONAL (Affecting, Affective)

> I feel, therefore I exist.
>
> —G. Casanova

This is quite literally our first experience, when we were immobilized ("e-motional") during forced passage into separate personhood outside our mother's womb. We felt bad before we felt better and now we always want to feel better and we call it the "pursuit of happiness," our common goal once life and liberty are fully guaranteed.

Good and bad thus characterized our first taste of life. Even when both later evolved into our first moral choices, we continued to be guided by our taste, which we acquired from our elders before we can judge what is wholesome or rotten. Morally, it was no longer enough to feel good but every day we had to be better.

If the baby does not control its daily breast (*sic*), it will need to emote or go hungry. If the parent (or surrogate in the day care center) controls the feeding, the child emotes more than its peers—corrected for age—in other species.

(If you're abandoned from birth by your mother deserting the nursery, you need to be adopted. If you don't need to be loved but have enough love, you'll adopt pets, even God. Of your superiors, you need only ask yourself if they are scoundrels, whether philanderers or not, like some politicians.)

The most infants will grant Descartes if they could talk his *lingo* is to agree that "I feel (hungry, wet, etc.), therefore I am. (And now attend to me promptly, even if I have no words to describe how I feel.)"

(Descartes, mistranslated, was wrong: Sometimes we think, sometimes we exist without thinking. In this, we are no different from our computers, which can operate without knowing how it operates.)

At what age can we limit "good," "bad," and "beyond judgment" to acquired bias?

(In English law, the inability to distinguish between "good" and "evil" was the first standard used by William Lombard of Lincoln's Inn in 1582 for acquitting those who cannot legally commit murder.)
[Infancy embraces what was called "sensorimotor" and "preconceptual" by Piaget, "oral/sensory" (trust/mistrust) by Erikson, and "oral" (id/ego) by Freud. Infants quite naturally learn first what is "good", and sometimes what is "bad."]

For the adult, the transition from **A** to **B** is characterized by righteous indignation.

B. VOLITIONAL (Motivational, Conative)

To will what God wills is the only science that gives us rest.
—Longfellow

Vital decisions, like breathing, or heartbeats, are not up to us. (Breathing has the rhythm of ocean breakers, 5–8 seconds between.)

Energy that is animated is called "will," and it is as free as mechanical energy can be under the right auspices (container and trigger). *(p/2)*

The toddler is more territorial than competitive. It only becomes (**A'**) greedy beyond hunger without orality, and imperialistic in adulthood, from learning how to hoard during toilet training.

As we grew in strength and became independently active, we were led to believe that we were exercising initiative. If we did what was right without knowing it, we were rewarded. If we were wrong without knowing it, we were called naughty.

Mischief later becomes wrongdoing, for which the law can hold us responsible. Right and wrong thus started out as moral judgments and became legal issues about what is fair, if we get too emotional to apply what we had already learned to be either right or wrong. (The lawyer must only convince rather than prove.)

As urchins, our outcry against bullies was "It's not fair!" This becomes the battle cry beyond urchinhood for those who still feel (**B'**) bullied. *(p/3)*

We learn we are truly separate (individuated, different) only after lying to our parents and getting away with it. Those who cannot lie ("emancipate themselves from loyal serfdom"), or will not try to get away with it, must hide and/or hurt inside.

> It does not help the child, unless it counts abuse as attention, to hear that the punitive parent hurts as much as the puppet/moppet. Both hurt from culpability for past transgressions. Who does not hurt has fully identified with past aggressors.
>
> (In family therapy, all are forgiven the "hats" they are proud to wear just like those whom they admired once did.)

The toddler may disagree with Descartes: "I want (to go there, play with that), therefore I am (and don't stop me, this is mine)." If we don't agree (identify sufficiently) with our toddlers, all of us are in for a lot of emotional aggravation and physical agitation during their urchinhood.

> (Descartes, correctly translated, was partly right: Only in doubt do we think we even exist, just as we are aware of our guts only

when we have indigestion. When not in doubt, we are as intuitive as our pets, going about our business without self-consciousness.)

At what age can we introduce "right," "wrong," or "unyielding" (whether or not might is right)? (As we age, we exercise less initiative.)

> [By 1724, "Not guilty by reason of insanity" (after McNaughten was acquitted of killing commoner Edward Drummond instead of Sir Robert Peel, prime minister of Great Britain) depended on the inability of accused to distinguish between "right" and "wrong."]
> (Toddlers learn about "right" and "wrong" early and then later judge juveniles by their sense of what is right or wrong, which animals intuit in respecting the territorial priority of another to a place where it had already established "squatter's rights.")

Adults who become articulate in their righteousness end up being shrill demagogues.

> [The juvenile period overlaps Piaget's "intuitive" and "concretistic," Erikson's anal/muscular (autonomy/doubt) and part of locomotor/genital (initiative/guilt), and Freud's anal (superego/id) stages of development.]

The adult in transition between **B** and **C** is soberly judgmental.

C. COGNITIVE ("Rational," Reflective)

> Thoughts are but dreams till their effects be tried.
> —Wm. Shakespeare

The wish is the father to the thought, not the thought the father to the act. The act sometimes fathers hindsight, recall may produce regret and rationalization, or foresight and expectations can decide strategies rather than tactics, which demand data. Means and meaning may also change or goals exchanged.

It is not that ideas change behavior but that goals goad one to action, action produces experience, experience produces scripts that can be rehearsed, mental rehearsals anticipate obstacles, overcoming which, before being overwhelmed by surprise, ensures better coping behavior.

The truth is often that which you'd rather not know. Cognition is thinking, without testing whether it's true or false. Instead, can we now start asking what is "true," "false," or "unchallenged"?

Before we could, it was not enough to know right from wrong, but we were eventually expected to reason out why. The reasons may be based on what has already been accepted as revealed truth, and reasoning becomes a true or false quiz for the uncritical literati or an exercise in logic for the thoughtful. (This is the empty aspiration of "critical thinking.") What is rational is then replaced by what was more reasonable as ratios became rations (negotiated compromise solutions), and rationalizations replace ratiocination.

Adolescents are expected to learn what is "true" or "false." Adults reach out for this stage to pass judgment on their juniors, but otherwise live by an already established double standard on the basis of what is good or bad, or right or wrong, for each other most of their lives, together or not.

> Those who are "hung up" at this stage truly believe that violence is a failure of communication and turn out in droves as amateur cultists who pay tuition to replace their intuition and body language with sincerity and slogans.
>
> (The adversary method of adjudicating claims purports to distil what is "true" or "false" from evidence presented by both sides and their witnesses' demeanor during public hearings. Their demeanor cannot be captured by the written record and so becomes a jury's impression that cannot be reversed on appeal without a new trial. Thus any judgment becomes a matter of believing or opinion, not of fact-finding, by judge or jury!)
>
> [For a judge or prosecutor to claim they are interested only in the truth (in whose eyes?) is the height of immodesty.]

Those who stay mired (**C'**) in this rut become professional pessimists.

[Piaget's "formal abstractions," Erikson's industry/inferiority and identity/loyalty, and Freud's oedipal (superego/ego) and latent (ego ideal/ego) stages of development all take place during (**C**) pubescence.]

The adult arrested in transition between **C** and **D** cannot yet think logistically to test the unfolding reality and becomes a chronic cynic in a world ruled by analogy, syllogism, and logic.

> (For epigenetic Piaget, social logic consists chiefly in being consistent throughout. Humanists call it "intellectual honesty," a form of "tunnel vision" among the single-minded.)

D. COMPARATIVE (Correlate, Critique)

> If we (**B**) rightly (**C**) estimate what we call (**A**) good or (**F**)
> evil, we shall find it lies much in (**D**) comparison.
> —Locke (bracketed letters added)

This stage (as well as the next) is more sensual than moral. It has nothing to do with virtue or moral issues of good or bad, right or wrong, or true or false. (Only the sensually isolated rely on virtue to be vindicated.) It (or **D**) and (**C**) can be learned and tested on paper or orally. (**A**, **B**, and **E** tend to be untestable but observable.)

Of those who do not want to experiment, can they at least agree on what is testable, unproven, or refreshing?

> [Lawyers tend to ignore what cannot be "proven" in court, whether "good" or "right" or "true." Because of this indifference to those who are virtuous, lawyers are denigrated as merely legalistic. In fact, scientists are equally indifferent to virtues but, unlike lawyers, they do not need to persuade in order to win points by creative (selective) rhetoric. They do not need to score points.]

Postlogical fits better as a description for stage **D** in our classification of sensual development.

> [The author also thinks paralogically like his patients, in swirling waves, much like a surfer travels. (As in karate, he seldom reaches his targets by a direct route but often overshoots, to see if the target may be a shield.)]

Adults who have led checkered lives cope better with adolescents who test territorial limits since limit testing is their own way of discovering reality. Testing means more data are needed and such data should not be denied. All taboos, even against violence, can be violated if the risks are calculable, but not when they are off limits for calculation.

Violence (explosive) need not be cruel (wanton, by definition; without the element of surprise, it becomes cruel torture).

(What is incalculable is the risk of radioactive injury to our gonads. The mutant may well be subhuman or superhuman.)

(Postpubescent are Erikson's intimacy/isolation and Freud's genital [ego/superego] stage of development.)

The adult in transition from **D** to **E** because of lack of talent or inspiration to reconstruct hidden homologies between connections (s)he cannot clearly discern and compare relishes being cleverly nihilistic.

E. CREATIVE (Inventive, Pioneering)

> Invention is the talent of youth as judgment is of age.
> —Swift

[Like prodigies, pioneers may be precocious, escape presenile decline, and enjoy delayed senescence (**D'-A'**)].

Innate talent is not age dependent and precocity endures, if coupled with inborn energy. Instead of inherited talent burning out prematurely, virtuosity develops, whether the presenescent is virtuous or not.

Those who think that the new is absurd, rather than the old simply commonplace, are not free.

The talented, even if unschooled, intuits or senses essential (amoral) connections outside accepted contexts or among apparently random events and then formulates different theories and predicts what was previously unpredictable, which must now be researched (reexamined and validated), with or without discovering new data.

(If we really appreciated brains, we'd raise more children instead of patronizing pet shops.)

Discovery itself is not an exact science as much as it is inspired tourism, like Darwin's (exciting travelogue or imaginative theory). Discoveries by definition are often serendipitous experiences or pure accidents or else not what is expected during exploration by experimentation.

Darwin did not go to Galapagos to discover how animals evolved. Nor did I intend to write about evolution until I discovered how behavior evolved. Darwin feared controversy, I was used to it. The evolution of animal behavior and ours can fuel more controversy but will, I hope, also allow further exploration. (Felicity of language, however, attracts more fascination than investigation.)

(If the thesis proves inherently un-testable, the talented is merely original rather than contributive. If the novelty endures, originality becomes creativity.)

(For the senile, burned out, or pedestrian, is it enough to weigh what is new, old, or interesting?)

(Presenescence includes both of Erikson's last stages of early generativity/stagnation and ensuing integrity/despair.)

In recurring abnormal states, two previously traversed stages may be revisited: e.g., (a) (**AAxBB**) mania with hyperactivity; (b) (**B'A'**) agitated depression or (**A'A'**) resigned melancholia; or (c) (**CC'**) delusions of adequacy (*sic*) in the abandoned (**A'**) who have been orphaned in their second childhood and must spend the rest of their days in nursing homes with nursery accommodations.

With self-deception, they must then convince their cherished and concerned but uncaring children that their adult crib/cage is adequate to their needs beyond simple subsistence.

Unlike both precocity and aging, abnormality is premature recycling of learned skills during previous normal transitions. Underendowed with stamina and/or overburdened by responsibility, some "burn out" prematurely in presenile dementia (to be distinguished from middle-age crisis in the unfulfilled). "Burnout" is equivalent to "metal fatigue" from excessive stress chronically draining one's energy and acutely straining one's strength.

Normal aging is more like active nostalgia where the special privileges that the young enjoyed, after escaping from the special restrictions of childhood, are reclaimed. After (**B**) paying their "dues," adults must receive what is (**A**) their due or they might "agree" to be reborn to love (**F**) God as a lapdog. And then, with advancing age, our life cycle literally stops evolving and instead involutes to a second adolescence (middle age crises) or a second childhood (senescence).

Under this formulation, it is no longer enough to be our own person, we must accept our own nature, a gift from our grandparents, gift-wrapped by our parents and our peers in a domesticated society, and returnable without refund to the genetic pool, unless damaged in transit by radioactivity, etc., to keep our species going in a niche of its own making.

DYNAMICS vs. KINETICS, Logic vs. Logistics, Analysis vs. Ratiocination

In psychoanalysis, there is the usual transference dynamics, which in turn produce countertransference kinetics. In drug therapy, there is the pharmacodynamics of different drugs and the side effects of pharmacokinetics, depending on their metabolism in different people.

The ancient myths of Oedipus and Electra and the reverse mysteries of Supideo and Artcele exemplify dynamics and kinetics. Thusly can history's mythology spotlight hidden conflicts. Rationalysis of sensual, social, and sexual endowments and developments cannot just be separated into discrete and separate stages, but transitions in between as they coevolve must also be studied.

NORMAL TRANSITIONS

As the child grows, it learns by how adults around it meet the following developmental challenges in orderly sequence: emotional, decisional, conceptual, comparative, and creactive.

Normal transitions are characterized by progressive learning of conflict-free skills.

1. Conflicts are produced when departure for the next developmental stage is delayed by attachments to the earlier one and/or out of loyalty to its adherents, at loggerheads or in competition with advocates of that which succeeds it, beckoning or urging one to join them.

2. Ideally, creativity in the talented must be fostered by permissiveness from pressure groups, without expecting performance (When?) to justify their interest in the maverick (Why not?).

a. The creative (inspired) who are not precocious may or preferably should be preoccupied (distracted) by their own projects.

b. Freedom to explore and/or discover for the precocious is thus assured by accepted practice.

c. Only derivative discoveries need group cooperation among the gifted (not the promising, who have yet to deliver).

We have only two hands (whether by divine design or not), some of us are not so handy with them, and more and more must be sedentary (unskilled manually because their DNA did not bestow manual virtuosity). *(p/4)*

The neurology of behavior prompts us to act consciously or unconsciously, and often helplessly, before we can think for ourselves what concomitant stimulation or environmental contingency deserves what response, as soon as we can sense its urgency.

Unless our almost automatic response (limited in its automatism only by our autonomous instincts) is extinguished by pure accident, or later by very precise (synchronous) counterconditioning, we continue to be near automatons.

It is fortunate that parental programming does not itself automatically get transmitted to the next generation, whose genes come from both sets of grandparents.

Oftener, it is less what we want as much as what we need, over which we have no control, that decides our reactions. Choosing is more wanting than judging or controlling. (Do those who are afraid of losing control drive their cars with two hands on the wheel even in light traffic?)

The family, extended in every direction, must be able to give, give in, and give up to the young who, in their need in deed must (A) take, (B) try on, or else (C) think through, (D) test out, and (E) tear to pieces what is precious to us (even the explosive atom and the implosive "individual").

TRANSITIONAL DISTURBANCES

In varying ratios, we are all domesticated animals: a few are freer from the outset, some are liberated, most are indentured by ideology.

1. The human domestication process is naturalistic. It recycles the infant's curiosity to that of the wise old man who observes that everything around him is equally interesting even if unimportant in the long run.
2. The transitions in the process need not be dramatic, but may be akin to our dimly remembered switch from the inner tube to the tubeless tire, which does not blow out but simply goes flat without risk to life and limb.

There are always transitional (<—>) disturbances—and therefore "symptoms and signs"—as one advances from stage to stage.
1. If prolonged, disability may be due to deficiency in endowment.
2. Arrest at any stage becomes retardation eventually.
3. Those who are not mentally handicapped but only temporarily arrested in transition (falling between the cracks, so to speak) are characteristically
   a. **A** <-righteously indignant->
   b. **B** <-soberly judgmental->
   c. **C** <-chronically cynical->
   d. **D** <-cleverly nihilistic-> **E**.
4. If articulate, they eventually become, respectively,
   a. shrill demagogues (**BC'**),
   b. amateur cultists (**C'**),
   c. professional pessimists (**D'**), and
   d. iconoclastic antiheroes (**E'**).

Do those who show more promise than gifts quickly "recycle" or mellow with age into (**B'C**) dissident conformists (e.g., investigative reporters), (**C'D**) accredited commentators (crowned by a halo of credibility) or (**CD'**) syndicated devil's advocates (biased docudramatists)? Those frustrated but not bored may fantasy themselves as (**E'**) iconoclastic anti-heroes.

5. With slower entropic processes in our sensual life cycle or increasing senescence, we recycle to earlier stages of development to reemerge as
   a. chronic iconoclasts (**B − E**) who are not critically constructive,
   b. sober cynics (**C + D**), and
   c. righteous cultists (**B + C**).

To this group characterized by slow serial decay belongs the statistically rare but often gifted eccentric who never contributed hir (*sic*) gifts.

Whenever each preceding stage is not fully traversed, the next in the cycle suffers:
1. What is "right" (**B**) is offered as "good" (**A**) according to God.
2. **C** or "fact" (truth in legal fiction) is used to arrive at what is "fair" (just) or **B**.
3. **D** or "testable" (accessible) becomes the criterion for arriving at **C** or "truth" (in research for science, the God of all gods).
4. And taste (**A**, oral) or prudence (**B**, anal parsimony) often becomes the basis for consensus in socio-political grantsmanship even in the basic sciences.

Thusly did God (**F**) become reincarnated in agnostic technology (**K**) as another Trinity: the fountain of collegial comfort (**A**), the arbiter of human rights (**B**), and the source of universal truth (**C**).

And, like the God of old, Scientism, itself likewise capitalized, does not wish to be
1. compared (**D**) with any rival (even to graven images of art and mythology) or
2. denigrated by other inspired "creators" (**E**) of new "insights" (forbidden fruits of the family tree of evolution and history).

When Truth (uncouth) courts union (symbiosis) with Beauty (e.g. in Ptolemy's symmetry), then
1. we have recycled (**D'-> A'**) and returned to (**A**) taste, the "test" we first used to decide what is good or bad while still a baby and
2. science as "Science" thus becomes only a servant of art as Art, which moves us according to our taste (of which there need be no accounting).

(Theories (**C**) strive (**B**) for (**A**) elegance, in envy of art. Those hung up on elegance become digniphrenic.)

Were Truth not uncouth, would fiction and art be needed to appreciate it?

When we leave (**D**) testing to others, we have gone from (**A**) putting everything in our mouth to (**ii**) the mouthings of those we trust. This sets the stage for clinging (clienthood).

(But in psychiatry, one cannot even just stop with being comfortable with all emotional reactions (**A**) from caretakers, but must be able as caregivers to evoke any of them at will. Evoked discomfort, like rebound tenderness, may clarify issues.)

STEPS IN DOMESTICATION (DIRECTION-DEPENDENT LEARNING)

Values are not always visible, and value riddenness may be quite subtle even among the tactful, who do not need to be diplomatic to survive but only to prevail without bloodshed.

1. Covert or (**i**) virtuous reactions lead to overt or behavioral responses to (**ii'**) value conflicts:
   A. Good or bad: guilt -> death
   B. Right or wrong: avenge -> kill
   C. True or false: search -> surrender
   D. Testable? research -> repudiate
   E. Tasteful? create -> compromise

To die, kill, surrender, repudiate, or compromise are less demanding on energy than guilt, revenge, search, research, or unorthodoxy.

2. a. What is expedient may only be urgent, not a sell-out. To accept compromise is to sell out for immediate gain. For the untamed (ungreedy), renunciation of immediate gain is preferred to compromise.
   b. To react in an emergency is not to abdicate (renounce) or surrender (resign). Even triage (emergency allocations of medical resources) demands quality control, strategic or tactical. Quality must be approved or repudiated.
   c. If strategic, quality control can sometimes result in a policy decision, e.g., the Nazi political solution (**G**) to the Jewish question (defined as a problem of sectarian economic

conspiracy, **F** x **H**, against secular anti-semitic political majorities).

To surrender strategic control is resignation (religious or colonial victim mentality), not renunciation (which Buddhists aspire to reach) or utopian commune orientation (which preaches "less is more").

Ideas are to think with (and idealize if fascinated). Idealism, like virtue, is personal. Values are to judge by (and moralize from, if disputed). The evolution of ideas into idealism and its combination with social values produces ideology, which excuse or accuse.

Unshared ideology may be original or delusional (any of the above ideas, if overvalued, may qualify for either) and evolve as follows:

1. Covert (idealistic) dream ->
2. Overt (ideological) response to (**ii**) historical stasis in anyone's social development: overvalued ideas -> militant thoughts ->
3. Obsessive preoccupation ->
4. Compulsive undoing ->
5. Delusional thinking -> psychosis of projection.

We can go from the very rudimentary in *Homo sapiens* to the most sophisticated behavioral somersaults in *H. domesticus* and *metropolus*:

1. From crying (A) to self-pity (I)
2. From religion (F) to philosophy (C)
3. From divine right to rule (G) to divine responsibility to be our brother's keeper (J)
4. From a political (G) democracy (commonwealth) to an industrial (H + K) oligarchy (corporate profits, not community needs, dictate what is invested where)

Freedom produces wealth, and wealth destroys freedom, even in the wealthy tycoon chained to ticker-tape, fax machines or on-line computers reporting stock market fluctuations during ocean cruises.

Those who demand more of themselves thus become, - without virtuosity or talent which is then over-compensated for by "virtue" – guilt-ridden, vengeful, frantic, frenetic, and worn-out, if unsuccessful in protecting their valued investments with their inherited granary of energy (stamina).

They suicide, accuse, disown, or withdraw and retreat when they "burn out."

16.00 p/SENSUALITY

p/Chapter Notes

[p/1] Asked if he wanted to run for office since he is hypercritical, conservative columnist George Will, Jr. replied that he already has the best job in the world: He could work at home and get paid well for reading, thinking, and writing. He must have come across Plato's personal failure directly to change what philosophically an actual political community ought to be.

[p/2] If the roads to happiness are diverse, then there is no right path to follow. The bitch Goddess called Success is the goal of the heel who wheels and deals.

"Progress" increases "choices" and agonizing options; not reasonable (excusable) but rational (post-logical) ones, not sub-culturally acceptable (biased) but universally valid decisions, popular or not, which are therefore not decisions at all, just a matter of information, reception and response, reflex or reflective.

[p/3] [Bullying can go beyond claiming squatter's rights and becomes empire-building, when joined with (**B'**) greed beyond (**A**) hunger to become a combination of (**G**) patriotism and (**H**) profiteering. Without profits, economic colonialists abdicate and multi-national conglomerates retrench (hoard, **B'+H**).

(Among (**J**) consciousness-raising groupies, it is harder to be (**I'**) self-doubting as women, or for men not to suffer from mental or worse indigestion.]

[p/4] Inherited constraints (genetic) can become man-made chains: Common law (not natural law) can make defense of person or property the only defensible grounds for manslaughter and disallow natural fight or flight reactions, which culminate in unfree choice of contingencies or alternative options, which are many but usually illegal.

17.00 q/Society: STAGES of SOCIAL (ASEXUAL OR CULTURAL) DEVELOPMENT

[Freud (who was a doctor but not a psychiatrist) and Erikson (who was neither but a psychoanalyst) both agree on what is psychological but disagree on how much of what is psychosexual (Freud's creation) or psychosocial (Erikson's revision) is sensual, social or sexual.]

There is God / or there is no god, / it makes no difference to Him.
There is equality/ in the City of Man / according to the Man.
There is enough to go around / but not for those with more.
There is ourself / and others who impinge / without consent.
There is engineering / for the imaginative,
Humankind for the lonely, / Nature for the wistful,
Animals for the humble, / and robots for the lazy.

HISTORY'S LEGACY

There is no conflict between science and religion, science and politics, or science and economics. Scientists must be prepared to study all three as behaviors that evolved before we learned to write. Students must discard the tendency towards a single-issue "dim- sum" (one-bite) mentality.

Believers and atheists or un-believers have no stomach for ambiguity or uncertainty and are easier to offend than agnostics. More open-minded disbelievers can examine "conventional wisdom" (current dogma) as well as the absurd and outrageous:

567

We were puzzled that partly eaten kittens were left at our front door in our absence until mothers started carrying live ones in their mouth to us when we are home. Now we suspect that they were able to fight off or distract predators but were not sure they could protect those who survived. Are they expecting us to guarantee their well-being, like we expect higher authorities—God, the police, etc.—to do what they can to help us? (We have a mother cat that stays away until her next litter is due.)

The reason the more we know, the more questions there are, is not unlike finding that the higher we fly, the farther the horizons that beckon.

Society splinters humanity into subspecies, shaped by shared ideology, defined as a formal belief system. Believing is lying to oneself without knowing, in order to erase one's doubts about what one does not know.

F. God is not dead. He is living in exile in nursing homes, making house calls at intensive care units or midnight visits to emergency rooms or hospices. Those who deal with the desperate sense His presence during their clinical rounds.

G. The politician thrives when there is border conflict. With good boundaries (staked out by excretions among animals) we can do without politics.

H. The economist not only thrives in sweatshops but in times of scarce supply. In times of prosperity and plenty, we can do without the economist just as in health we only need to thank God without asking for help and relief.

I. "Individualists" emerge in an age of affluence (which can dispense with economists and other prehistoric specimens), and gradually become irreligious, anarchic and more complacent than competitive.

J. As civic awareness increases, private citizens become selective but militant in advocating special or ethnocentric interests.

K. Civic consciousness palls as technocracy produces general abundance. Constituencies now worry about the long-term cost/benefit ratio of production, not to the worker but to the consumers.

L. Consumerism ("me, too-ism") is called humanism among those unrewarded, whether by God, the government, or the guild.

M. Currently, as recent recruits to modern civilization become less and less anthropocentric, they become more ecologically minded and geocentric.

N. If altruistic commuters are not quite puritan enough about environmental pollution, they worry about the survival of unwashed but endangered animals and become ethocentric.

O. To be sedentary and still survive smog alerts, commuters can look forward to staying home with a personal computer to make money by prudent networking with the help of cybernetic (negative feed-back) gadgets (circu-centric electronics).

Historically, our social evolution as *Homo sapiens*, the self-teaching machine, to *Homo domesticus* and *metropolus*, went step by step, back and forth *(Table 16)*, from **F** to **O**:

- from awe of God the Father (Stage **F**) among the faithful, then of (**G**) the King among his subjects,
- to worship of (**H**) Property and resources, of (**I**) Self and independence, of (**J**) the Group and interdependence, of (**K**) Technology and progress,
- replaced in the affluent with (**L**) Humanism and consumerism, and with (**M**) Ecology and environmentalism,
- followed by concern for (**N**) Ethology and endangered or intelligent animals, and awe of (**O**) *Deus ex machina* (unemotional, artificially intelligent robots less erratic than a jealous Jehovah or His own creations).

Would a God-fearing scientist have discovered ecology, ethology or evolution? The question is rhetorical since we'll never know now. It is unscientific to pull a thread out of a pattern and declare it irrelevant.

FOR NEW SPECIALISTS

What is not personal (sensual) or private (sexual) is public (social). Virtue (moral) and virtuosity (sensual) are personal attributes, eroticism and sexuality (conventional or perverted) are private affairs (even if shared), and value and ethics are social judgments (a group consensus).

[Value (d) judgments based on socially accepted premises used to be called illative ("All men—not the blacks in America or women even in Switzerland—are born equal except for the right to bear arms"), as distinguished from scientific ("Like presidents as lethal targets, all can bear arms for territorial defense"), which are based on facts. Only the puny (e.g., humans) need guns, even as organized outlaws or their organized nemesis as police or patriots.]

There were, (1) early in our cultural development, at least five pre-historical stages (religious, political, economic, psychological, and sociological) which are still metaphorical and more axiom-ridden, not unlike irreligious Western hemisphere humanism (L) than (2) the rest, which are more scientific or theory-tolerant—from technology to ecology, ethology and electronics—and postlogical (except for the last [so far, until "fuzzy logic" with fuzzy borders prevails]).

Preliterate:

F. Theocentric: spiritual
G. Jingocentric: political
H. Econocentric: commercial

Recent:

I. psycho-centric: individualistic
J. ethnocentric: group-minded
K. technocentric: progress-driven
L. anthropocentric: humanistic

Current:

M. geocentric: planet-conscious
N. ethocentric: animalistic
O. circucentric: cybernetic

Ideologues (**ii**) can and do change, after being needed (**A**), expected (**B**), accepted (**C**), or compared (**D**).

1. Derivative mutants which are as maverick as our three theories of absolute relativity in nature, life and human behavior may augur a change.
2. Does it matter whether it is for the better (**A**), or that we will be better off (**H**)?

1. **F** -> **H**: From Cross to Crown to Capital

The economic era of civilization began when the astrologer/exorcist and the tribal elder were overruled if not overcome by those who owned the means of production, the products of labor, and the system of transport and distribution.

1. The leadership passed from priests and politicians, and the divine right to rule became the profane right to oppress the poor and to appropriate the surplus value of labor.
2. The oppressors may be owners or unions (manufacturers or laborers), and the expropriation may be institutionalized (state owned, subsidized, or regulated) as private or public monopolies of services or utilities as the Old Guard yields to the New Left.

2. **F** -> **J**: The REIGN of ABSTRACT LOGIC (half-life of deductive syllogisms)

Humankind evolved beyond Indo-Hellenic syllogism (Buddha's borrowed by Aristotle), symbolic logic, and teleological numerology as statistics (valid only for nullifying assumptions and researching already discovered facts in search of fallacies) to postlogical natural science, including non-anthropocentric zoology (comparative ethology).

Our future development will be uneven depending on Aristotelians, logicians, and statisticians among us who cannot think postlogically.

1. a. "The moon only shines at night because the sun gives enough light in the daytime" is obsolete teleology. There are moonless nights.
    b. "The moon is an aphrodisiac" is equally inferential if alogical (relational if not causal).
2. Premature closure prevented postlogical examination of solid bodies as mostly empty spaces.
    a. It used to be that only logical explanations were acceptable, preferably preserving symmetry.

b. Now, all that is needed is the least artificial explanation, whether it is logical or not.

3. **K** and **O**: Technotronics sans Philosophy or Metaphysics (syllogistic and speculative)

It took Copernicus to wrest away cosmology from astrologers, Darwin to liberate science from prophets, Galileo to demand testing from philosophers, and Freud to free psychology from statisticians.

The most enduring "anthropic" myth of all is that all order in the world is numerical.

1. In the Middle East, figures were recorded in Uruk tablets to document business transactions and land sales more than a millennium before abstract, and therefore unanswerable, questions were ever asked of heaven: thirty-one different kinds of sheep, from long-haired to fat-tailed, were listed.)

    Geometry itself emerged from Egyptian land tenure requirements. So is the computer now used, as a transaction ledger and balance sheet, more than as a word processor of linear thinking.

    (Only words can be processed unless varying weights are assigned, e.g., to letters from **A** to **Z**.)

2. Tokens, invented another two millennia earlier, were used for keeping track of merchandise and livestock, when animal husbandry made hunting unnecessary.

3. Once upon a time, the world lived with the equivalent of our milk teeth called Roman numerals. Then Arabic numbers supplanted them.

    But they also do not digest our food; they only grind ("crunch") what is too big to swallow.

To change metaphors in midstream:

Although our Roman puppy love is now an old flame, we have since fallen in love with better developed Arabian Night figures.

Today, we use them to quantify and compute "reality" as if they were different from rather than merely more handy than Roman numerals. They have recently been replaced by binary digits (1 and 0).

"Crunching" words to twenty-six letters from A to Z, each with separate significance (not meaning) or valence, is an equivalent revolution in modern times.

Thusly have we progressed from barter to tokens, to symbols (celestial), but the institutional forms had lagged historically behind ethological priorities: We still lack security from inanimate and human violence to life more than to livelihood: mismatch between ends or survival and means or life-style is absent in animals.

Thusly, against fantasied or present dangers have we proceeded—by manipulating (**F**) worshippers, then (**G**) followers, then (**H**) tokens, then (**I**) minds, then (**J**) the collective unconscious by archaic symbols or ideograms—to (**K, O**) things, from heavy ores to electrons.

Stages of Evolution of CULTURE

F. THE MANY FACES OF GOD

We begin with what is "bigger than life." Religion evolved from animism to polytheism to monotheism and has recently been flirting with pantheism from Teilhard (1881–1955, the Omega Point) to Tillich (1886–1965, for whom "born-again" means a "new being", not someone saved), to arrive at the best articulated modern mysticism (a tension-reducing adualism demanding no sacrificial virgins except individual significance).

Thusly did spiritual ideology evolve from

1. one world with many gods (ancestors) to
2. a divided world (geo-religious domains: different gods and class-differentiated worshippers, some untouchables at either end, immune or unworthy, until reincarnation), to
3. two worlds (natural or socially conscious with Confucius, and supernatural or righteous/litigious and divided into heaven above and hell below when the earth was flat, with limbo and purgatory added for borderline cases) with one God of many cults subordinate to the state, to
4. the world as God (a word, replacing many gods with narrow assignments to bring rain, end drought, let the sun shine on, etc.) with even more plastic gurus offering elastic unearthly promises to innocent victims of earthly powers and duplicity.

We can now trace cultural changes in the value of other ideological delusions from political solutions onward throughout the history of our civilization.

G: OUR POLITICAL EVOLUTION

Plato's ideals about the rational relationship between the soul and the state and philosopher-kings failed the test in Sicily. He was superseded by amoral Machiavelli (1469–1527) and Ortega y Gasset (1883–1955) who held that the elite must lead the masses out of chaos.

Scotus (810–877) denied the doctrine that the right to rule is divine, and that property ownership, even of some slaves by the likes of Aristotle, is ordained by natural law. Darwin restored the royalty of the fit. *(q/1)* Jefferson made man supreme over women and black domestics.

Machiavelli had arrived at the same conclusion as Aristotle about man as a political animal, but was deliberately misinterpreted as merely encouraging immoral intrigues. Animal politics works.

Quails queue up for grain after our peacocks have taken their turn according to (**G**) their pecking order. We know now that chimpanzees have more unerring political instincts than our best politicians.

Glorified nationalism grew in monstrosity with the French Revolution. Four million died before Napoleon surrendered at Waterloo, twice as many died in the first World War, 40 million died in World War II, 30 million in Eastern Europe alone.

[Our political system is more chaotic than the pecking order among other animals, even among war-like chimps.]

H. ECONOMIC EVOLUTION

Adam Smith (1723–1790) exalted free enterprise (when it could not yet outdo government abuse of the weak), Karl Marx (1818–1883) state monopoly (did he not feel obligated to our Father, his father-in-law, or fatherland?), and Ortega y Jacinto studied the New Poor in an affluent down-sized society.

Marx discovered in 1848 the dominant influence of economics in modern history. Lately, this has been interpreted as territoriality. Marx was right for his time, territoriality was not the right explanation for urban serfs.

The serfs were freed in Russia before the slaves of the Deep South were emancipated (the proclamation excluded the border states which did not secede from the Union).

You can't blame Stalin for Russia since it is not much better after his death. The slavish invites masters, - Mafioso or not, - the terrorized (including the quaking and/or squawking media) invites terrorists, much more than their oppressors imposing new or worse oppression.

Serfs of the past evolved into labor as capital to be the cossacks of communism or the old left of the New World.

The Right (conservative Republicans, who wish to preserve liberty) can be distinguished from the Left (Progressive Democrats who wish to protect equality). Now that the Union is secure, both are equally slavish.

I. EVOLUTION OF INDIVIDUALISM

Unlike God, liberals think virtue is the fruit of knowledge, and vice that of ignorance. (Ultra-liberals believe that to be perfect in this life is to have changed often.)

For the Greeks, the gulf between mind and matter did not exist.

Greek and scholastic theo-philosophy got dichotomous after Descartes and, from his spirit-brain dichotomy, psychologists who are unversed in natural science derived a mind-body duality.

Descartes was the unwitting source of this old mythological dichotomy that Western mystics (called moral philosophers) have been trying to erase ever since.

William James (1842–1910), son of a theologian and brother to a novelist, replaced old philosophical systems with "pragmatism" and separated psychology from philosophy, but brought it closer to ideology with his book essay "The Need to Believe."

Bowlby, Harlow and Spitz found that maternal deprivation produced psychosocial "dwarfs."

Today, among child psychologists, adualism is still thought to be autism when babies fail to mind the world of difference between themselves and their daily breast (*sic*).

Had we not invented the indivisible soul (psyche), would individual salvation have been attractive? Did individuality become irresistible when an individual (Jesus) died to save each of us? Did black self-esteem rise after Martin Luther King's martyrdom? (Our black waiters in Texas became less obsequious than white waiters.)

Is the "individual" a metaphor like the "indivisible atom" of old? Are our lives a series of "e-merging" and "re-turning" selves like the longer soap opera of history, linked by habits and memories and distorted in translation by calculated philosophical and cultural prejudices?

To convert historical claims into social metaphor because of scientific discoveries is to preserve them as myths when we cannot live without our beliefs. Wisdom to unmask different ideologies as popular delusions comes from correlating without editing or yearning. (Religious paranoia is longer lasting than patriotic or economic paranoia.)

Identity, like an individual's social security blanket number, is everybody's secret mythology, a psychological fiction in the face of deep doubts about ancestry, even Erikson's. When sons followed in their fathers' footsteps, they knew exactly how to identify themselves.

One's "persona" (or mask) depends on one's audience. (In Hollywood, type-casting casts suspiciousness on the stars' versatility, without implying similar rigidity in their fans.)

One's personality is disturbed when one cannot step out of his role. (I have succeeded as a teacher when a student can unmask me in another setting, but the student has not if the role he uncovers is that of a teacher.) Inventing roles instead of aping role models can disturb collegiality.

J. EVOLUTION OF ADVOCACY

Old selflessness (private charity) can become the New Left (socialism) or an egalitarian evangelism (Aristotle's question-begging explanation for revolutionary fervor even among the affluent, e.g., the Kennedys' for their black constituency).

Socialists try their best to achieve equality by giving and receiving "To each according to his need, from each according to this ability." (Even the handicapped are unequally handicapped.) Bureaucracies do their worst to "Do the least for the most money" to avoid offering equal opportunity. (Powercrats are less fearful for their security.)

Fromm, an expatriate wrote about alienation and Ortega y Jacinto on Levels of Alienation.

(Alienation is also "minority-mindedness.")

When ancestor worship was our means to reach joyous union with the dead, extended families did not feel like minorities.

Is it overwhelming to an increasing minority of individualists to inhabit a decentralized satellite as a verifiable beast and a veritable robot? Does it make them doubt that they are deserving of all that martyrs like Jesus, Gandhi and Martin Luther King promised but postponed for themselves by dying before their time?

Do they still need reassurance from the grave that they are worthy? Can we prove that they are by living out the unlived lives of those who died for those who believed that their martyrdom would not be in vain? Do they also want to "make a difference" like their heroes?

Do martyrs self-destruct as programmed by phantoms in their past, not just for the alienated?

Can those deserted by them forgive their self-destructiveness? Can orphans stay optimistic?

K. EVOLUTION OF TECHNOLOGY

Thales of Miletus (Ionia), our first Western philosopher, who was a trader of Greek and Near East merchandise, and the first to triangulate distances of ships at sea, was credited by Heredotus with predicting the eclipse of the sun in May 25, 585 BC. Had their pre-eminence endured, we will be deeper in space by now.

Newton (1642–1727) discovered thermodynamics, Watt (1736–1819) invented the steam engine, and Einstein (1879–1955) arrived at the equivalence of mass and energy.

With the self-starter replacing the crank, women can operate cars and man can drive alone. (In 1903, cars had steering wheels that tilted, turbo-chargers were used as early as 1911. Songs included "Fifteen Kisses on a Gallon of Gas.") The "battle of the sexes" began away from home.

L. EVOLUTION OF HUMANISM

Early humanist Goethe's Faust was anti-technology.

Vico (1668–1744) as historiographer dethroned Descartes and debunked Cartesian anti-historicism in his studies of the evolution of religion.

(Vico was the first humanist who was not an atheist. He questioned whether the world and ourselves are one, or is it our creation.)

M: EVOLUTION OF ENVIRONMENTALISM

(Like Thoreau, even our robber barons and our oil tycoons are truly scavengers.)

Haeckel first probed the "household of nature", Thoreau lived as a scavenger, and more anal and hostile *Homo metropoli* became advocates of zero population growth or limited genocide or abortion pegged to the age of the victim.

Minimal scarcity produces cooperation among *Homo domestici* ("Let us"), maximum scarcity provokes competition among *Homo sapiens* ("Let me"), affluence produces indifference among *Homo metropoli* ("Leave us alone").

Bachelor Gov. Brown of California preaches "Less is more" and Vice President Gore does not want more children.

N: EVOLUTION OF ETHOLOGY

Geochronology, well established by 1815, dated fossils as artifacts, not objects of study. Fossils and radioactive dating triangulates the age of life on earth at about 4.5 billion years, not the Biblical six to ten thousand. (When Adam died at age 900+, Egypt had water clocks!

Darwin (1809–1882) had predicted that many transitional links would be discovered after his death to prove his theory. They have not been.

The fact is that missing links depend on an ability to interbreed between transitional forms. Monsters cannot and so are not likely to survive to be immortalized in the fossil records left by "Acts of God."

Darwin worried that his predictions had not materialized and probably that his theory was invalid. But theories do not depend on their discoverers for validation. (Even Einstein did not have a crystal ball.)

Darwin studied Galapagos finches and turtles, Lorenz his clinging geese, Goodall her chimpanzees, and Ortega other animated lives: an amputee centipede (slow crawler), his *alpha*-peacock (calculating flier), and several families of cats (headlong climbers) and schools of fishes (skillful swimmers). *(q/2)*

O: EVOLUTION OF ELECTRONICS

The first automated machines were Egyptian water clocks, as early as 3000 BC.

Alan Turing first constructed his abstract computer, then von Neumann his programming instructions, and then Wiener propounded cybernetics.

Computers are feared by those weaned from science by Mary Shelley's Dr. Frankenstein, who was himself critical of and terrorized by his creation as we are of and by our own created Creator.

In Eisenhower's farewell address after two presidential terms, he warned "public policy (**G**) could itself become the captive of a scientific-technical elite" (**K**).

Electronic gadgets (**O**) detected deception in Alger Hiss and found Nixon (Hiss' nemesis) out in turn. Thus does science reinforce its reputation for in-human if not inhumane impartiality (disrespect for persons or reputations).

Thusly has technological (**K**) and electronic (**O**) progress delivered the K.O. punch to a jealous God by personifying the *Deus ex Machina*, which remains inscrutable to the common man (neither artist nor scientist):

1. Electronic artificial vision need only the six dots that the blind use to read Braille. Dots and dashes are all that is needed for telecommunication with the Morse code.
2. "Man"-ufacturing has even acquired automated speech, man's last hurrah in the oral soapbox of propositions that he accepted as self-evident when comparing himself with robots and animals (who are better endowed except sexually: his penis and

her breasts and their lips and buttocks are bigger and fuller or flabbier, pound for pound than any animal).

3.   a. "Man" liness from manual labor is obsolete in a world over-populated by people and robots.

   b. In its place, sexists and even hedonists prescribe the more obsolete "man"-ual pollution originally meant by masturbation, especially if it is conjugal or paired.

4.   Instead of design by hand for hired hands, CAM (or computer-assisted manufacturing, where not only our hands but our minds are told what to mind), and CAD (or computer-aided drafting in 3-D), and DCC (or direct computer control of machines) will each make man more and more insecure.

   (Half of all jobs will be automated by AD 2000 even if computers, like hand tools, maximize productivity and, instead of reducing producers, make them more productive in both quantity and quality.)

For Older PRACTITIONERS (F -> O)

Beliefs and dreams, just like our values, are neither accidental nor random. This is true of tribal practices and all behavior, verbal or non-verbal. They are real but not mirrors or validation of reality.

What makes all of the above and what follows extraordinary or exotic is our unfamiliarity with the bias that surrounds them as well as our own lives. The only reality that they reflect is absolute relativity. There is no senso-socio-sexual equality except in legal fiction.

Nor is the issue one of Culture vs. Nature. Such a dichotomy is as naive as that between black (the total absence of color) and white (a mixture of all colors), both of which are abstractions that do not exist except in minds trained in formal logic, (now contested by "fuzzy logic").

Ratiocinationists think, not in terms of black or white (which attract reductive rationalists), but in ratios of prismatic hues (different wave lengths) or shades of gray. For them, life and death are thermometer readings: there are always degrees above boiling and below freezing points at sea level.

In neurological science, the digital computer's homologue is the All or None Law of neurons discharging or not firing. Better "fuzzy" programming replicates nerve-muscle units in operation.

In electronic data processing, we use just 1 or 0 together instead of all the Arabic numerals. They can encompass with more precision than mathematics even the concept of matter and anti-matter in physics.

They also recapitulate the history of the science of measurement all the way back to quantifying on the basis of simply more (>) or less (<), even in self-regulating devices like thermostats. Exactitude becomes relative, unlike in arithmetic:

> Early science progressed from numerology to prophecy (astrology) to gambling (for gold in alchemy) to predicting (in astronomy) to experimenting (in chemistry).
>
> The larger the mass or the number of small but uniform units the better the prediction (as of eclipses and atomic chain reactions).
>
> Objective study of medium-sized clusters of units of medium mass with subjective differences belie most prophecies (as in free market economics and urban community psychiatry where neighborhoods are heterogeneous).
>
> In desperation, social science has developed into a movement (scientism) of advocacy or militancy, depending on the missionary zeal (**F**) or political enthusiasm (**G**) of its cohorts.
>
> [Only the unsophisticated scientist sees politics as uniquely ubiquitous. It is as ubiquitous as religion, and economics, even among "lower" (older) primates. All are subjective perspectives to comfort the weak.]

F. RELIGIOUS EQUALITY

(This ideology does not aspire to political equality for all religions or beliefs, but spiritual equality for "true" believers' souls among those with a lap-dog mentality.)

Theology itself may be said to have started with Aristotle, re-interpreted by St. Anselm, then St. Thomas for the Schoolmen, then by John Scotus the Scotsman, then Rene Descartes, Immanuel Kant, Giambattista Vico, August Comte, Teilhard de Chardin, Paul Tillich (ecstatic naturalism), etc. That may explain the soul, but Plato's perfect forms logically demanded one perfect source.

Only later did (a) equal opportunity for salvation get less attention than (b) equality before the law which expanded to include (c) equality of opportunity to vote or not to vote, (d) equal employment opportunity which drops during recessions, and now seeks (e) equal educational facilities for their children, and (f) equality of sexual opportunity (whether unwed or gay).

Religion (**F**) is rooted neither in thinking (**C**) as crude philosophy, nor in action (**B**) as primitive morality, but in feelings (**A**) of absolute dependence.

More ancient alternatives were deism or ancestor-worship which includes goddesses, and theism or worship of the male "spirit."

August Comte (1798–1857), saw religion (**F**) as appropriate to the (early) childhood (**A**) of man, to be replaced first by philosophy (**C**) and then by science (**K, M, N, O**) which advances by making comparisons and testing its suspicions. (In Comte's view, art is AxE or the marriage of taste and creativity.)

Durkheim (1858–1917) claims that religion exists to cramp self-serving impulses of "individuals" and therefore allows society to exist. (*The Elementary Forms of Religious Life, London*, 1915) (For Durkheim, **F / I = J**.)

The tension seems to be between spiritual comfort and material goods, between the individual and the group. And the tension is reduced by mysticism, good works or mass violence by/towards religious fanatics, political mercenaries, economic imperialists, etc.

Not to be committed is to lose faith. Commitments are habitual restraints whose familiarity is reassuring. Only the faithless will suffer the dreaded return of feelings of emptiness with rootlessness.

Partly because even saints do not live according to the Golden Rule, we have modified it into an Iron Rule for New Psychiatrists and their patients and superiors: "Do not do unto others as you would have done unto you, because you are not their clone."

The unforgiving do not think of themselves as special, and so tend to expect and exact the same kind and standards of behavior that they demand of themselves from everyone:

> Those who have a lot to forgive tend to be more spiritual. But one only needs parents who think their child is special for the adult to be forgiving.

1. Those who fail to live up to their own expectations die a thousand deaths in the hell they invented, and if they fail by themselves

(blaming no one, not even their Creator), then they must die, even by their own hands, and the sooner the better for those who deserve better than their company.

2. The depression-prone are moral snobs, but personally humble, which is why they are liked better than the socially paranoid, who over-compensate for suspected inferiority.

3. Was he who discovered that He was a jealous God also inclined to jealousy? Does your God have your personality?

We ought at least to act as if we are God without aspiring towards *machismo*, personal or political. This is not to say that we should live like Christ as Christians. It is no joke what happened to Him and to others whom the Romans fed to hungry lions.

(After watching one of Pavlov's dogs endure hot probes to get more meat, then salivate when the electrodes were applied and the meat withdrawn, physiologist and Nobel Laureate C. S. Sherrington exclaimed: "At last I understand the psychology of the martyrs.")

If we cannot be God Hirself (*sic*), we need only to behave as if there is a God who is like us and likes or liked us. And to die young as late as possible. (Einstein, no gambler himself, insisted that God does not play games of chance or roll the dice. If He does not, it is because He cannot, not because He chooses not to.)

1. If we ourselves can make choices, it is only because we think we can because He said we may. That is not so much autonomy as auto-regulation, neither sovereignty nor freedom from constraints (independence).

2. Not only are we equally God-like in his Image, but we are con-natural with other creatures who believe or not.

3. Not only do believers believe in equality, but the truly religious must demand equality for our spirit and Maker as well, if not for all graven or spoken images of Him in our animism and amulets, magic and mantras, and ritual and sacrificial offerings.

   a. Sacrifice itself is the closest to the next (**G**) stage in our historical development. *(q/3)*

      Some modern demagogues are as dogmatic as those of yesterday who burned the mentally ill at the stake to drive the evil spirits possessing them from their souls, as demanded by their religious indoctrination. (That is called fighting hellfire with fire.)

b. Both spirituality and nationalism are symbolic and at their best unselfish, at the worst the Cross and the Sword of flaming righteousness.

c. Killing does not produce as much guilt as hurting, religious genocide least of all. *(q/4)*

d. Fanatics successfully deny their fears. Negotiation can only begin with shared fears. Sharing with strangers as well as enemies starts with trusting in the good faith of others. Good faith depends on acknowledged interdependence.

Age of the Spirit (Religious Cults)

> He (**F**, God) is (**E**) the poet of the world, with (**A**) tender
> patience (**G**) leading it by his view of (**C**) truth,
> (**A**x**E**) beauty and (**A**) goodness.
> —Alfred North Whitehead
> (mathematician and tautologist) (letters added)

Animism, which animated primates, including man, allows early spiritual development to be sold by its evangelists as the ultimate goal to

1. those who never progressed much beyond animism, which explains the successes of early evangelists of Eastern religion, or of modern missionaries in underdeveloped countries, and

2. others who have been frightened enough to retreat to it, like a bride going home to mother after the honeymoon is over.

Thus, the first question to ask evangelists, high on acid or ideology (religious, political, economic, psychological, social, or scientistic), is how solid is their knowledge of alternative explanations which reconcile contradictions.

It is but a short step from primate or "primitive" animism to man's taking responsibility for his Creator (whose jealousy was fed by rumor-mongers during the Grand Inquisition that justified vengefulness in His name). Ecologists feel a similar custodial responsibility for today's endangered species, in their belief (un-shared by ethologists) that the last, or best, mutations were Adam and Eve.

Did (**F**) religion start with estranged hairless chimps capable of magical thinking and then produced Buddha?

(Are chimps also capable of the graphic and plastic arts? Naked Ape author Desmond Morris says they are. But if they live amidst natural beauty, do they need to bring it indoors, like we do house plants? Will television replace conversation among chimps?)

Orthodox Buddhism is split into the "great vehicle" or "great path" (Mahayana or maximum demand), and the "lesser vehicle/path" (Hinayana, or medium distance morality, non-absolute, not dictated by the "causes" of Aristotle and the "ends" of teleology).

(Do these paths take care both of mortal sins [which end in Hell] and venial sins [purga table in Purgatory]?)

For Buddha (563–483 BCE), the world is a burning boat that we must escape. For Socrates (469–399 BC), the body is the tomb of the soul (the seat of character and consciousness), imprisoning it with our senses.

(For prophets like Jesus the body is its temple and for Jim Jones it is a shell to be discarded in voluntary genocide. Like other philosophers, Buddha does not include fornication as reproduction in his formulation. Theologians, of course, view sex as temptation.)

Luther's spirit was liberated in a latrine (the cloaca of Europe before the bidet and urinal was invented), where his bowels released their hold on what he hoarded longer than he should have.

("Enlightened" inside, he saw dispensations as indulgences for sale as mediation by bribery and sought to eliminate the middlemen by direct and immediate communion with a personal God. That would cut Papal income.)

Marx (1818–1883) saw religion as a device to preserve the politico-economic status quo.

We lost Jesus to Caesar, Popes to emperors, emperors to ayatollahs, and priests to gurus. All of the four great religions (Sino-Taoism,

Indo-Buddhism, Judeo-Christian, and Arabic-Islamic) have lost worshippers to the followers of Lenin-Marxism. Without exception, all produced prophets, messiahs, and reformers.

Only Buddhism has remained free of fanaticism, to become the ultimate exemplar of a non-violent love-in, sit-down strike: quality of (**A**) love is not a question of (**B**) performance.

As we develop instruments to test whether we err, we have gone from worshipping our Maker and changing Him to suit our needs, to becoming skeptics about Marx, to testing the reality that we had been prone or content to accept.

Of course we can test our doubts beyond the limits to which His Marxist creatures or their surrogates or our rivals would submit, and therewith eventually explode ourselves to smithereens. But even then, the universe will only be decimated and not annihilated.

> (Politics has become a secular religion and therefore faces the same hazards that religious crusades once presented in their campaigns to convert the ignorant, indifferent, or dissident infidel. Those crusades are history, will politics be?)

The separation between Church and State guarantees that neither will abuse the other or the people but—separately or together, throughout history—either or both can be good or bad, right or wrong, and neither true nor false. ("True faith" and "political science" are oxymoronic.)

> Frazer in the *Golden Bough* (1890) studied and demanded a different explanation for ritual kingship (**G**), fertility rites [to serve (**H**)], and human sacrifice [ignoring (**I**)]. He substituted ethnography for Comte's historical approach as Teilhard de Chardin (Pierre) would later substitute archeology (paleontology) for both.

G. POLITICAL HISTORY

> (Whatever is politicized in our social development breeds the attack dog mentality of the demagogue.)

What was originally an unsentimental pecking order has evolved into: hero-worship -> tribal pride -> city-statehood -> nationalism (old politics).

1. Even righteous religious crusaders tire of turning the other cheek. After Gandhi expelled the British, his death turned Hindus against Muslims. (Only aliens, including extra-terrestrials, can re-unite India and Pakistan.)
2. The Armenian holocaust was only a dress rehearsal for the German repetition of tribal cruelty.
3. The Koran itself is devoted to conflict and religious conquest, not to peace but lawfulness in the conduct of war.

Political freedom is not a right that one can claim against the state; the right to hold free elections must be fought for. And then, it is political equality that results in a populist government, not territorial equality or equity.

The more centralized the policy decisions, the less leverage the voter has even in a non-totalitarian government, especially where an electoral college can choose a president (Kennedy) other than the winner at the polls (Nixon, who lost Chicago but did not want a divisive recounting).

The "beltway" problem of Washington, D.C. with the rest of the country is that the national budget is allocated according to political clout, not economic needs.

Age of Politics (Political Movements)

> The principal foundation of all states
> is in good laws and good arms.
>
> —Machiavelli

Spain and Portugal once divided the world between their Catholic kings.

Secession in the U. S. civil war was secession from abolitionist churches who threatened slave-owners' peace of mind.

The American Revolution did not have a Reign of Terror, the French, Russian and Chinese Cultural Revolutions did. Why not? Was M. Robespierre (1758–1794)—the French counterpart to England's O. Cromwell—more ideologically extreme? Is it because the Americans successfully fought abroad against foreign imperialists and had only to cope with marauders and carpet baggers after its civil war and with ethnic urban terrorists in its metropolitan centers today?

MAGNO J. ORTEGA, M.D.

Was the Reconstruction Period of carpetbaggers after the Civil War our version of political terrorism or economic imperialism? Was it our kind of serial terrorism or urban guerrilla warfare over earlier frustrations rampant among dictatorial South American banana republics? Does it also explain why Japan was not terrorized by victorious GI's under Gen. MacArthur as an absolute but benign despot?

Are our historians so enamoured of their ideologies that they cannot ask the questions that need answers, but only those they have ready answers for?

(Without a Marshall Plan, how did Hitler rearm?)

H. ECONOMIC HISTORY

Political equality, which ensures equal justice, is a sine qua non if economic equality, not freedom or prosperity, is to be achieved. Nor either during cyclical or structural "crises" does economic equality equalize social privileges.

(Did the North have anti-Negro riots before Alabama used police dogs against blacks? Historians differentiate the French revolution for a classless society from the American Revolution for economic equality (no taxation without representation) among the wealthy.)

1. Labor unity is a must for powerless workers in closed societies. America, unlike Europe (which has finishing schools instead of higher public education), has 51 per cent of women working. The unemployed black (or male adolescent) is the victim, not of racial discrimination, but of our community colleges. [In other countries, trade schools prepare the boys who are ineligible for "public" (parent, not tax-, paid) prep schools.]
2. a. Adolescent competition in capitalist enclaves reduces the economic influence of the establishment.
    b. Child labor laws and compulsory education are therefore resorted to, ostensibly for the sake of the society of the future.

Is it coincidence that above groups of laborers, soldiers, and scholars correspond to castes above the servant class (or slaves who are domesticated like animals of burden under a yoke)?

And that scholarly priests (now chanting rituals in their native tongue) declare themselves servants of a god, and that patriotic politicians (the new untouchables) compete to become public servants?

Is it also coincidence that both mandarin and samurai (literally, servant) are obsolete? And that czars and centurions still exist like "capos" and *"mafiosos"* in ex-Tsarist Russia and our "banana republics"? *(q/5)*

Capitalists believe in the cybernetics of the marketplace until it refuses to correct itself for their benefit. Communists think that what does not suit the masses must be controlled.

(To be toilet-trained to "hoard odorless yellow gold" on top of being a child during the depression makes economics (**H**) a distraction in every decision (**B**).)

(Shared accidents of history and family may influence choice of policy makers who are committed to "allocative efficiency" and "distributive equality".)

3. Now we have workers against automation.

(We should be able to retire earlier with all our labor-saving devices, but we do not even have more leisure time to enjoy along with our higher standards of living.)

(In the past, the elders did not retire until the young can take over. Now both generations compete to exploit scarce resources.)

Age of Barter (Economic Adventurism)

What this country needs is a good five-cent nickel.
—Ed Wynn

Whoever wants to invest a dollar to make two, instead of spending it, is counting his chickens before the eggs hatch.

Reader: Roosevelt abolished the gold standard in 1933. Churchill lost leverage in Britain trying to preserve it.

Author: George Bush frittered away his political capital as commander-in-chief during the Gulf War over capital gains that did not save his job.

| Editor: | Now we barter our services (menial, social or know-how), our goods (gathered, herded, or produced), and our knowledge (gossip, news, know-what). |
| Student: | And in the process try to evade paying taxes on "income." |

Ortega y Gasset was right even in 1930, *Revolt of the Masses*, that the elite must lead the masses but only until successful communists came along to upset the applecart, and then the opposition to tradition came, not from an upwardly mobile middle class, but from the poor and the joyless.

Lenin needed Marx's creative leap that "labor is capital" to overthrow Russian royalty.

I. PSYCHOLOGICAL ROOTS (Egocentricity)

Affluence (**H**) may feed ambition (**B**), not security (**A**) nor self-reliance (**I**). Decrease in either may motivate (**B**) or dismay (**A'**).

1. Ambition (motivation) may move the affluent towards, without genuflecting before, the center of power.
2. Insecurity may bring the rich to their knees before the altars of surrogate fathers (God or fatherland) or the temple (body) of surrogate mothers (women).
3. Earlier economic emancipation (from odd jobs in the summer to working a regular paper route, etc.) allows the juvenile to rise above materialism and even become an "individualist" with an ax to grind in the politics of the "New Right"
4. Identification with the dismay of the insecure or dependent may make social security the rallying flag for rich liberals who are not libertarians.
   a. It is at this level of economic progress that equality of opportunity produces conflict between liberty and equity.
   b. Such a standoff is characteristic of capitalism more than of communism or socialism.

Age of Introspection (Psychological Preoccupations)

Everything without tells the individual that he is nothing;
everything within persuades him that he is everything.
—X. Doudan

Introspection (or consulting one's self) became institutionalized when Rene Descartes (1596–1650) discovered doubting to be universal (it is doubtful if there is anything that cannot be doubted), and found cogitation to be the engine for thinking at all, and therefore the unassailable basis for proving that we exist and the only solid ground for being unique among animals. *(q/6)*

Philosophers who misread cogitation for cognition proceeded as amateur biologists to separate the mind from the body that feeds the thinking brain, and psychologists as amateur philosophers began to study reasoning. Thusly was born the study of mental epiphenomena (excuses, intention, motivation) ahead of observable and/or neuromuscular activity, etc., as behavior.

(Such psychological pre-occupation is just like believing political promises and excusing the politician because they are just campaign promises.)

We did not even want to transplant hearts, and we still do not want to transplant brains. Why?

Those who see man as made in God's image would only consent to touch what is clearly not God-like in him and would refuse to tamper with his "individuality", since that indivisibility is our own mirror image of monotheism.

But is a person not a group of selves, unique in permutation, but as divisible as an atom?

Immanuel Kant (1724–1804) compounded the difficulty of Cartesian dualism by grounding ethics on intention and those who are not motivated enough are now accused of wasting human potential.

To deflate these balloons of hot air, we separate what is personal (virtues) from what is social (values), and what grows (virtuosity) from what is acquired (skills) by tracing their separate evolution and development.

We have learned much from Pinel (1745–1826) and moral treatment (unchaining the insane), Freud (1856–1939) and the will to pleasure (he may as well have asked, "Am I obligated to my father, who cannot stand up to other men?) as well as from Adler (1870–1937) and the will to power (and birth order).

> (If Freud's father had a stronger will (more personal courage), would psychoanalysis have been less passive?)

J. SOCIAL CONSCIOUSNESS

Economic equality of opportunity does not equalize social standing. It merely permits the opportunist to move up in social class.

Equal justice guarantees social justice (**J**) but not class mobility (from motivated initiative or **B** x **I**) nor personal security (**A**).

There are therefore
1. those who watch out to be safe (**A**) from
2. those who watch for opportunities to move in (**B**) as bounty hunters (**G'H'**) who are
   a. superstitious (**C'F'**) about signs as omens at the outset, and/or
   b. more scientific (**D**) about symbols as content in their professional or techno-industrial training and practice.

Age of Altruism (Social Activism)

> Men would not live long in society if they were not the
> dupes of each other.
> > —Rochefoucauld

If Big Brother is a dictator, Big Sister is a special interest group [shepherd to the sheepish)

Socialists are gradualists rather than revolutionaries, like communists.

> (Only twice have revolutions replaced evolution, in technology and electronics.)

Social promises are now more and more backed by power or wealth, not by beliefs in the spirit, autonomy, science or humanity.

(What we called propaganda in USSR is abbreviated to PR in the United States.)

The Universal Declaration of Human Rights states, "It is essential, if man is not to be compelled to have a recourse, as a last resort, to rebellion against tyranny and oppression, that human rights be protected by the rule of law." The first human rights law ever enacted by the UN is the Convention on the Prevention and Punishment of the Crime of Genocide the day before ratifying voting rights, fair housing, and sexual equality.

(Reservation Indians have less freedom in their daily lives, less control over their property, less access to the courts.)

Those with sheepdog mentality (Tories) are protective of their sheep against shepherd pretenders (time-servers). (They are now the New Democrats, Republicans are the old Whigs.)

(To a Tory, "there is no wealth but life": "Life is the possession of the valuable by the valiant.")

The American Constitution had to be amended to include a Bill of Rights. The First Amendment was censorship of censors who interfere with our right to report.

It evolved from the decline of back-fence gossip and should have been limited to the right to choose one's friends in a fight, not protect the scope to evangelize by those who have nothing to contribute themselves.

(In Russia, the definition of a pessimist is an optimist who reads newspapers.)

(Reagan confused (**G**) political democracy with (**A**) moral goodness and (**H**) economic communism with (**F'**) devilish darkness.)

Some also mistakenly equate (1) democracy with freedom, (2) the tyranny of (a) the majority, (b) the proletariat, or (c) the *status quo* in capitalist or socialist republics with the time-tested and naturally lawful precedents of the past, and (3) equality of opportunity to be unequal with territoriality or the pecking order.

(Only the domesticated will accept the judgment of a judiciary according to the law a majority legislated to preserve the *status quo*. Is it to their credit or discredit that the untamed will not?)

K. TECHNOCRATIC REVOLUTION

From hoary superstitions to methodical objectivity, we gained a new technocracy (socio-scientific or -medical and -technological: domestic and military), more atheistic after Sputnik and since, until recently. (The pendulum then swings to the "Religious Right" of *Homo domesticus*.)

All scientific breakthroughs (**K**), perverted with: (1) **G** (politics) can become (a) industrial slavery but, combined with it, may become (b) the military industrial complex, (2) **H** (economics), it will breed (a) the multi-national conglomerates, and/or (b) economic democracy (which, by itself, explains why communism loses converts to socialism). (3) **I** (individualism), it has produced (a) medicine for profit and, (4) **J** (populism), produced (b) socialized medicine.

(What science did was to dethrone hereditary monarchs and elevate the creactive more than the opinionated. (An intellectual is defined as one who is intelligently opinionated.)

1. James Joyce (arguably the most significant writer of the 20th century) discovered that before he can be a true artist, as *Homo sapiens*, he must cast off the shackles of religion and politics and the bigotry they engendered.
2. Psychoanalysis sought to replace the philosopher's ivory tower with the introspectionist's couch.

(With science, priests, politicians, economists, individualists and sociologists became pawns, whether or not they agreed with humanists, ecologists or ethologists (with proof processed by more infallible computers). We may think of computers as artificially intelligent but we might not reject a brain transplant if ours was damaged by disease, drugs, or other miscalculations.)

Age of Technocracy (Heavy Industrialization)

> Modern Man is the victim of the very
> instruments he values most.
> —Lewis Mumford

The combination of public sector bureaucrats and private sector technocrats chronically produced cost over-runs in the military-industrial complex that Ike did not like.

(Russia invented the dum-dum bullet in 1867 and initiated a convention to outlaw it.)

We have since built machines in our image and named them after us, e.g., typewriter, calculator, computer. None of these, of course, without us, can type, calculate, or compute.

Electricity once promised decentralization of power and wealth: early communists promised to electrify the countryside, FDR had a rural electrification program. Can electronics deliver that promise of power (energy as information) on demand?

L. HUMANISTIC PROGRESS

In 1959, C. P. Snow claimed that there is an unbridgeable gap between the cultures of science and of the humanities. We hope that in the intervening years the abyss is not as divisive except between advocates of scientism and "me-too" humanism.

The evolution of (1) senso-socio-sexual behavior and (2) the absolute relativity of nature, life and civilization in the development of rare talent (human or not, can build a bridge between the Two Cultures and between (a) the reductionism of introspectionists and/or of experimental psychology, sociobiology and the physical sciences, and (b) the over-inclusiveness of "holistic" humanism.

From ancient agnosticism among *Homo sapiens* came anonymous altruism. The undisillusioned *Homo domesticus* is convinced that the prayers of the less fortunate are heard, and that the unheard answer is "No". Among disillusioned believers (*Homo metropolus*) the trend is conspicuous consumerism (me, too), if -> since God is deaf -> dead.

(From the easily frightened and the disillusioned, the lap- and attack-dog who have not "burn-out" can evolve to that of the watch-dog mentality. Thusly may *Homo domesticus* and *Homo metropolus* venture back to be "reborn" as a more alert, *Homo sapiens*.)

Not a crybaby among them are **FF**- types (with a colonial mentality) who quietly postulate an unflappable and unfathomable nobility of divine purpose behind all personal misfortune. Its victims disagree.

1. The printing press has reduced reliance on religious missions to spread the "word" by mouth or in a monk's handwriting. The "news" is now.
2. a. Oral prayers (wishful thinking) and free speech cannot be protected or proscribed by community school boards but
   b. censorship of pornography (fantasy) on processed paper or plastic is singled out to be decided by community consensual standards.

Paternalism has been replaced by popularity polls, which also accounts for the activism of our accredited Supreme Court. Thusly has our history evolved from the un-caused Cause waiting to pass last judgment to the court of last resort, all subject to the winds of change. We shall follow where they lead, to the unknown or poorly known to see if/where they become fearsome, get misunderstood or offered as a substitute for (**I-III**) our humanimal nature.

Age of Humanists (Secular Orientation)

> As there is much beast and some devil in man, so there is
> some angel and some God in him.
>
> —Coleridge

Vico asked, "Is society ours?", Sartre wrote about existence *ad nauseam*, and Tillich expounded on ecstatic naturalism.

Are we society's pawns or are we its parents? Which came first, the chicken or secular abstraction?

(Norman O. Brown ended his *Apocalypse* with a quotation from William Blake (1757–1827) which begins: "Two-fold always . . ." This volume may well have been prefaced with "A trinity at least", or nothing at all.)

M. ECOLOGICAL HISTORY

Old nature-worship is now the new religion aimed at galvanizing political action against pollution and pesticides (poisoning food more than pests).

The first environmentalists were animistic inter-actionists. The term "ecology" was proposed in 1866 by Haeckel as the science dealing with "the household of nature".

The term "resource" (partitioning of, competing for it) had no equivalent in German until it was Germanized to "ressourcen".

> (Haeckel also popularized the now obsolete theory of evolutionary biology that ontogeny in any embryo recapitulates phylogeny (when gills were used for breathing). If "recapitulation" is changed to "approximation", and behavior is mediated by biology, this old theory can be extended to read: all history recycles as observable behavior in similar circumstances.)

Ecologists are probably the last subculture to evolve only to play God at safeguarding nature, but also for pure self-amplification, including indulging their love for all His creatures. (At least they are not as greedy as heavy industry.) But ecology has the makings of a double "-ism", which doubles its appeal: puritanism as environmentalism. (Its advocates forget that their guru, Thoreau, was a scavenger who used old factory-fabricated wood and nails to build his rustic cottage in the woods.)

Purists (**B'**) at heart if not in personal hygiene have replaced Fundamentalists (**C'**) among Puritans (**F**).

Today, there are growing demands (**B -> G**) to draft a Technological Bill of Rights. It will demand environmental impact studies (**M**) for robots (**O**) that might eventually replace less dependable workers (**H**).

> (In Japan, management now pays union dues for robots on the job.)

Thusly does (**ii**) society go on from (**G**) political to (**H**) economic to (**K**) technological equality.

Age of Ecology (Recycling/Scavenging +/- Abstention/Conservation)

> Nature is commanded by obeying her.
>
> —Bacon

The nearest to Paradise we can come on earth is an aquarium, with us playing God as maintenance man.

"Insight" into nature became perverted to demand sacrifice of human genes which had been held in check by acts of God (drought or deluge, etc.) or greed (genocide, pesticides, etc.). Voluntary feticide and active euthanasia are no longer anathema.

With ecology, the caste system called human racism (**L**) is beginning to give way to interdependence which demands, not decisions (**B**), but planning (**D**) or improvising in advance (**E**), based on know-how (**K + O**) and know-what (**N**), not know-why (**C + F**):

1. a. Our fitness for survival depends on awareness of natural laws that govern cosmic evolution. We cannot just ask the equivalent of "If there are a billion planets, why not another earth?"

   b. Obviously, the only answer is, "In a stretch of beach of as many grains of sand, do you expect to find an uncut diamond?" In biology, survival of the fittest means fitting into a niche in the future.

   Modern Puritans (like those waiting in Heaven's Gate to hitch-hike on a comet, on a planned pilgrimage to another and "cleaner" New World in outer space to escape Old Mother Earth, are engaged in infantile (**A'**) self-exile rather than (**B'**) childish tantrums or a post- pubescent (**E**) voyage of discovery. Outer space, like our living space, is crowded with toxic litter.

2. The heritage that we leave behind, whether by established adaptation or mutation, cannot be wishfully or teleologically programmed:

   a. What "hardware" is inherited genetically as mental potential is "know how" or "know what" (e.g., that dark surrounds an exit or window, which animals and kids know but is hard to communicate to robots) which will affect, not the present, but the future.

   b. To "know why," believe it or not, is not transmissible by DNA.

3. The more we know "what", the less we need to know "why".

    a.   All that it is up to us to decide is "when", if at all.

    b.   In raising animals, it is called imprinting, or bonding.

    c.   Like using our eyes or ears, it must take place before we can think.

4.   Our senses must be taught without editing, if they are to monitor a different world from what our elders inhabit and now strive to influence with their biases.

5.   Or the opportunity right here and now to build a better one on the past will be forever lost.

N. ETHOLOGICAL RECORD

From a new ethics (identification with endangered species) can come the realization that comparative behavioral biology is the proper study of mankind.

The first published professional ethologist was Darwin (1859). Before him, natural theologists worshipfully studied menageries to divine the Grand Design for unicorns, centaurs, androgynes, etc.

We study cross-cultural trends and children instead, using identical twins, to show the difference elective Cesarean section makes without genital abuse of the neonate by ritual circumcision, etc. (With circumcision of the helpless comes circumspection in *Homo domestici*.)

    (Pubescent slitting of prepuce can be dorsal not circumferential.)

1.   Believers in both animism (**F**) and its antithesis, atheistic human racism (**L**), by "embracing" (**i, A-C**) morality and (**ii**) ideology, are too heavily burdened and staggering on their last legs.

2.   Darwin died a century ago, but his theory of inherited fitness for continued reproductive success in animals and Homo sapiens lives on, whether civilization builds or deserts its centers of culture and "develops" them into a wasteland of inhospitable cities for *Homo metropolus* or suburban ghost towns for *Homo domesticus*.

For the humanimal to survive (domestication/breeding = -1), we must act now: Domestication, no; Breeding, yes.

PROPOSITION: We are more different from other animals in our habitual sexual behavior than we are in our daily communication.

When a gentle gorilla (Washoe) by sign language proved that primates can combine symbols for water and fruit to baptize a watermelon, language ceased to be man's last claim to uniqueness.

Can we see numbers and letters as simply con-familiar signals that only temporarily separate Snow's Two Cultures, like any exclusive bureaucratic in-breeding of scientists and of artists can?

Age of Animalism (Humanimalism -> Ethopsychiatry)

> Worse than our uncles among the apes, we almost eagerly
> prey on our own.
> —Ortega y Jacinto

In this century, despite Darwin, humans still disown their animality, and despite Freud, we still deny that our options are not our choices. Why do we distrust our instincts and insist on reassuring ourselves by chanting ritual clichés that we did not invent?

Sensitive stewardship of this planet with respectful dominion over animals is self-appointed, no matter how much better it may be than thoughtless exploitation of the environment. *(q/7)*

1. Darwin was harder than Aristotle (literate but ignorant) to forgive with his discovery of how we evolved like other animals. After him, we had to be satisfied just with thinking of our-selves as the only animals capable of symbolism.

    Few men have ever been so damned as Darwin, and yet fewer have won scientific support in record time (10 years from publication of the *Origin of the Species* in 1859, 20 years after he finished writing it).

2. Freud later disillusioned us further by proving that our symbols are unconsciously arrived at. And that our religion is the institutionalization of certain symbols. (Can chimpanzees learn holy water is special and carpets inviolate in the same way that we have?)

3. We can now see that our symbols had to come from somewhere and have already begun to wonder if their evolution can be retraced, like that of ours as a species. But we still claim that we are the only animals capable of magical thinking!

    a. Strutting around while beating his chest, like Tarzan, after driving away overhead noise (from aircraft) by rattling his cage, a chimp would be suspected of harboring delusions of adequacy, had it been human.

b. Does its behavior render more obsolete the myth of Eden and Eve's role as a scapegoat to explain the "human condition" from the beginning of time? (Rules, work and suffering, like gas in empty chambers, expand to occupy idle time or workers, like lawyers, and taskmasters under Parkinson's Law.)

c. Does the chimp's ability to believe mean that it can handle abstractions and therefore employ symbols without speech (just like music which soothes the savage breast, and premonitions of chaos that awe catatonics into silence)? (Is not magical thinking the basis of animism?)

4. In fact, not only can we retrace our organic evolution from matter scattered in space but also our cultural development in the delusions of paranoids who are more intractable the more primitive their false beliefs; i.e., religious fanatics are likely to be more chronic than jingoists.

5. Evolution without social Darwinism illuminates and explains the eventual successful occupation of a niche by a species (organic), group (social), patient (personal), or idea (God, nationalism, etc.). (Sex itself evolved to ensure a niche for some species.)

a. Teilhard's theology ignores everything but what evolved from clay to instinct to awareness to self-awareness to cosmic consciousness to Godhead in his journey to Omega point, variously called "It" or One's is-ness, such-ness or so-ness, or the void among Buddhists, "being" among Hindus, which is ever-changing among Taoists, and ever-lasting among Christians. (God's name is legion because His creators are unsure. He is also known to Muslims who read the Koran as the "Trickster".)

b. Hegel's philosophy envisioned an earlier world-soul that developed out of the logic of dialectics: ("to supersede is to negate and to preserve"), but neglected to mention that each advance carries its own risks which, as they materialize, become side-effects that detract from linear progression and produce a saw-toothed or wave-like ebb and flow. We call it "Absolute Relativity."

O. ELECTRONIC REVOLUTION

From old assembly lines came new suburbia and inevitably fatherless weekdays and school lunches, and commuter pollution except in clean Silicon Valley industries of networking computerized cottage conglomerates forging towards supranational post-industrial automation.

Computers can instantaneously digest information received on our instruction from other data banks and correlate them with what we have stored in memory, electronically or on file in our brain or on paper at our convenience. Data can spread faster over a super-highway network in cyberspace.

Mathematician Seymour Papert of the Massachusetts Institute of Technology was quoted in the New York Times (which publishes everything fit to print) as saying that "the effect of the computer on learning and thinking is comparable to that of the invention of writing".

Like God, our infant invention recasts the world after our own image into bits and pieces of data for processing as "yes or no", until programmable "fuzzy sets" softened rigid dichotomies.

(Lofti Zadeh in U.C., Berkeley, tries to program "smart" computers like we solve problems, with "fuzzy logic".)

Later, like ourselves, it will be able to reproduce, also by saying "yes, no, or not yet" as soon as we learn to recombine DNA with silicone.

Age of Robotics (Electronic Progress)

> We can clone cleverness but not wisdom.
> —Ortega y Jacinto

Are we emotionally ready to live out this revolutionary century before it rolls over into history?

We are all partly domesticated, but computers are more cost-efficient. Yet, like pets who are jealous of new arrivals as rivals, we don't like robots inching their way into our domesticated lives and relationships. That is the reason we hate robots, because they're like us, only better.

Computers are lightning-fast "idiot savants" in need of instruction and supervision, just like all of us more sluggish dolts.

(Light and electrical signals in micro-circuits travel a foot/ billionth of a second.)

The reason robots cannot as yet out-think animals is because programmers have to design their function in logical steps, in order to correct any malfunctions. The next breakthrough will come when "smart" computers can be post-logical in design, yet functional and repairable even if not reprogrammable.

(The elite of the electronic age are computer systems programmers. The "fuzzier" their logic, the better for us.)

Computer technocrats can tap sources of information and of power, but only if knowledge is power (or information moves muscles).
1. Mega-bureaucracies are now being replaced by microcomputers:
    a. Obsolescent bureaucrats thus become compuphobic: Government minions placed in charge of processing requests for computer capability are not averse to demanding more paper work to document projected tax-savings in the early dawn of a paper-poor future.
    b. "Anal" agencies (governed by regular annual budget movements) are quicker to approve purely passive copying machines, which means increased control over the distribution of information.

(Bureaucracy is as much a support system as glial cells in the brain which outnumber neurons 10 to 1. Their name is derived from "glue", their function is that of providing a "blood-brain barrier" for self-protection.)

2. a. Powercrats among bureaucrats know where the important "memos" (memories) are buried under a paper mountain and their tenure is thus protected.
    b. What is buried alive has always been a threat throughout history. That is why graves have headstones like those which closed the mouth of caves where the dead were interred before we had tools for digging.
       (Seventy thousand to thirty-five thousand years before Christ's rising from the dead, Neanderthals buried their

dead. (Brain size was 1,500 c.c., or slightly larger than ours. Dead by 40, some reach grandparenthood.)

(We still attend funerals to make sure that whoever haunted us alive rests in peace forever. Even in modern times, no other church without a confessional can compete with the Vatican in power by being privy to state secrets. [The sacrament of reconciliation is unique to Catholic doctrine.])

3. It is not power, but secret power that corrupts, not the powerful, but the corruptible—and total secrecy in totalitarian hands corrupts absolutely all its subjects that can be corrupted secretly.

4. Industrial technology increased manpower by replacing muscle, post-industrial electronics increased brainpower by processing information which, as memory with muscle, becomes power that becomes corrupt with secrecy.

5. What might spell the end of centralization of power is direct communication between computers by modem and fax machines.

ARTIFICIAL SELECTION -> MISCEGENOPHILIA

We will not desist until we can make nature's by-products more artificially intelligent. Fitness to adapt is not just a well-built machine but a fail-safe program. Evolution continues as a process of acquiring and modifying a blueprint for survival.

We can already be re-combined with domestic animal transplants (e.g., pig's liver) and, de-individuated, will soon be recombined with genes from even lower plants and bacteria cultivated in tandem with silicone as bio-chips.

Our hierarchy of God's creatures as a given will then give way to a hierarchy of fitness that guarantees survival by artificial selection and combination with the same organisms that we once felt needed a special explanation to justify co-existence with us.

We will, with biochips, have come a long way from mixed feelings about mixed marriages even with our own kind. Even now, socially motivated mating is more like artificial breeding than natural mating. But if history teaches us anything, it is that society protects itself at the expense of the young.

The male is meant to service the female, the mother the young, the father the brood, both to insure that their genes survive. (Prostitutes deal with impotence more than pornographers have to, male or female.)

The most important difference between wives and their rivals, whether free-lancers or professionals, is that wives are more verbal (argumentative) than oral (receptive). Animals during sex are more vocal than oral.

Interdependence of "mind" and "matter" will also give way to inter-relationships as the key, not only to the cultural evolution of our species, but to the social evolution of personal behavior and its potential for change (relative) in all of us without exception (absolute), including professionals and patients:

Basic to the New Clinical Psychiatry is this axiom: If (C) abstraction is the only evil, each case must be decided by the doctor—not the dear departed theorist by proxy—guided by the history unfolded by the patient for hir (*sic*) to see.

In our New Psychiatry, we can (D) compare and contrast clinical cases as well as collective cultural climates. We can (E) connect political and economic with religious history and see how an artificial prism can usefully and elegantly separate them as ideologies usefully, even in helping patients who have delusions based on these early stages of our evolution as a modern civilization.

The prism of ideological evolution, not the philosophy of history, can have the various "best-friend" mentalities as primary colors: lap-, attack-, sheep-, watch-, seeing-, hearing-, and hunting dog mentalities. *(q/8)*

The pastel colors of living and dead civilizations that tend to run into each other are the ten (F-O) ideological stages of social evolution.

The juxtaposition of the hues of historical eras can highlight the "unholy alliance" between Portugal and Spain for geo-religious colonization, as well as the "balance of terror" for later geo-politico-economic imperialism which tends to blur the distinctions that we want to re-establish. *(q/9)*

We must also compare, in contrast to partnerships for power and profit, classic confrontations that emphasize the alleged differences but not the themes behind media-abetted pyrotechnics, capitalist or communist.

(Are reporters frustrated sportscasters for live blow-by-blow bouts? Or jealous of the successful in pursuits that they can only observe?)

We only have to be artful and competent without necessarily being literate to be an evangelist, politician or trader. We have to be literate and artful to be a psychologist, sociologist and humanist.

We have to be both literate and trained to be a technician, ecologist, ethologist and computer programmer. We also have to be a biologist to be an ecologist, a zoologist to be an ethologist.

We can be an amateur or professional to proclaim cultural values. An amateur does only what (s)he enjoys by hir own standards. A professional does what needs to be done, and does it ethically as demanded by hir profession. Both can be skillful as well as untalented but persistent/ insistent.

The amateur is conscientious only insofar as (s)he is moral. Only the evangelist, politician, and economist can be a professional moralist.

(The ecologist is sometimes a puritan.)

Behavior that is cultural is more historical or consensual than sensual or personal, even if institutionalized as supra-personal (spiritual) or interpersonal (psychosocial). What is interpersonal can be more inter-genital (psychosexual). All human behavior, normal or abnormal, is senso-socio-sexual and natural. Culturally, society evolves just like everything else, without culture itself being the wiser.

We started by saying that history is a laundry list of reasoned errors that kept repeating itself. We can now confidently claim that it is a record of profound hypocrisies by slogan makers aimed at a particular audience, from the Bible for literate men, to the Constitution about self-evident equality for British anti-colonialists, to anti-slavery for cheap labor like children (excluded by compulsory education) and black or brown illegal immigrants competing with Negroes, to anti-affirmative action for rivals, inferior or equal. When affirmative action succeeds, sexual harassment charges by the unequal can dislodge their betters. When doubts about white masculinity (genital hypochondriasis) find expression in rejection of affirmative action by contrived charges of sexual harassment against successful aliens by subordinates suborning failed male or female sex objects, then xenophobia joins miscegenophobia even against naturalized citizens whose cultural diversity threatens the Establishment's traditional values and moral authority.

17.00 q/SOCIETY

q/Chapter Notes

[q/1] We should be better mammals (at nursing) before aspiring to primatehood (by standing). Aristotle was the first to insult the human race by calling man a political animal. Because he did not have data to prove that he knew what he was talking about, we are quick to forgive him. Did his protégé, Alexander the Great, lead him to jump to this conclusion?

[q2] It is commonplace to think of evolution as history, when it is a process that did not stop with Darwin (three stars are born in the Milky Way every year) and continues to this day of antibiotics and pesticides.

The naive (1) grieve over man-mediated extinction of unnumbered and unnamed and unknown species, (2) accuse scientists and profiteers of criminal neglect or malicious ignorance and (3) remind the gullible that creatures of yore are irreplaceable. All may be tenable only if there is no cloning of plant and animal cells. Mutation did not cease when God went on the first Sabbatical. Not all mutants are procreative, but many can multiply on their own without meiosis or sex.

(Ethologists must be intuitive, psychiatrists counter-intuitive.)

[q3] "Ask not what your country can do for you. Ask yourself what you can do for your country." The speaker, John Fitzgerald Kennedy, was a Catholic politician, not a Marxist demagogue.

For the less religiously dogmatic, President Kennedy's clarion call for material, not spiritual, sacrifice can be made in the name of military, economic, civilian, civic and educational equality.

[q4] Professional:	That's why religious wars continued in the Middle East, Northern Ireland, and between Hindus and Pakistanis.
Author:	Our religious, political (from polls), economic, etc. acculturation sometimes become social reflexes before we can be personally "creactive".
Generalist:	Even the cult of "psychological maturity" is almost socialist (Marxist) in denigration of the joys of beholding "stately oaks" who have dwarfed tiny saplings (the proletariat) to reach out to the stars.
Author:	And instead of creactivity (energetic ingenuity), we become righteous and desperate yet wary, and start thinking like lawyers along the lines of the domino theory.
Specialist:	Lawyers must survive in classrooms whose teachers are over-critical to trigger "worst scenario" thinking on cue.
Generalist:	If our generals were also lawyers, we would have had a third world war already where human judgment would be superseded by the algorithms of technology without our knowing the doer from the done, and both from the best that we could have been.

[q/5] Our trainees once complained that I expected them to be samurais. I did not want them to be kamikazes—heroic, perhaps, but not heroes. Instead I wanted all to be more like the Viet-Cong clinically (resourceful in improvising for better patient care).

[q/6] "Everything can be doubted" characterizes open-mindedness, "anything is possible" closure-proneness.

[q/7] George F. Will, Jr., righteous human racist, once claimed for himself "We are the responsible portion of creation." (Does his last name impel taking greater responsibility under a borrowed legacy?) Columnists nag (communicate old news). Novelty, the essence of information and creativity, is the antithesis of communication (repetition).

[q/8] The "Optics" of Humanimal Behavior

My self-assigned task in bio-cosmic senso-socio-sexual rationalysis from **A** to **Z** as a natural, part-time experimental, scientist—observer and student, not philosopher—is to
1. posit discontinuities in ordinary behavior, and
2. discover the sequence of their emergence:
    a. as tangible as primary colors when visible light traverses a prism and
    b. as undistorted as the colors of the rainbow by their artificially induced separation.

You are welcome to insert new colors beyond and between intervals **A** -> **Z**, since we all know there are wavelengths not visible to the eye of the beholder. Distinctive characteristics must go beyond detailed descriptions, as they do in spectroscopy, where the different colors emerge out of a prism in a definite sequence.

Otherwise, all we have is a philosophy of history, e.g., the "great men" theory (starring Freud, Hitler, Jung, Lincoln, etc.), not a science of behavior.

[q/9] 1. In the twentieth century, Americans became imperialists with the annexation of Hawaii, Puerto Rico, the Philippines, Guam, Alaska, and Guantanamo, Cuba, and thus became a colonial power in both the Pacific Ocean and the Caribbean Basin.
2. In modern geopolitics, Hitler and Stalin divided Poland and Stalin and Roosevelt divided Europe and Germany.
3. In our geo-economic times, Germany and Japan almost succeeded in subdividing the world market that was 60 per cent American after defeating them in war, but has since dwindled to 20 per cent.
4. The Moral Majority of *Homo domesticus* is willing to submerge religious interdenominational differences in order to wield greater political clout, just as *Homo metropolus* businessmen will bury their political biases in pursuit of

profit in multinational conglomerates. Power and profits produce the strangest bedfellows among hungry bigots of both subspecies and a blurring of territorial (institutional) boundaries that *Homo sapiens* find artificial for being more political than economic.

("Bias" to Catholic choirboy Bill Buckley is simply a hierarchy of values. The simple Moral Majority believes in one man-one wife, private enterprise, and public prayer in schools for unsuspecting children.)

(After writing "Nearer My God" in the twilight of his life—which began around the time of the Scopes "monkey trial" in the "buckle" or belly button of the Bible Belt—Buckley continues to inveigh against evolutionists on his TV "Firing Line" debates.

(M. Bethe, was one of his loyal guests. Darwinism is touted as based on materialism, creationism a viable alternative when there are gaps in the fossil evidence, without considering that fossils are "created" by "Acts of God", which is not always on time, hence confirmation of Stephen Gould's "punctuate equilibrium" is unearthed only after climactic changes maximize fossilization.)

(Controversial though Gould's alternative view was, in Tennessee of the twenties, instead of the descent of man, apes were claimed to have "devolved" from man. In the 80's, I suggested that man and African apes descended from orangutans of the Orient. (In the 90's, "devolution" of central federal authority over welfare subsidies to the state also came from Southerners fearful for states' sovereign rights (e.g., to own and trade Negro slaves), which was invoked against Scope's violating Tennessee's law in the books specifically prohibiting the teaching of evolution. Today, Scope's lawyer would counter-sue in federal court for academic freedom and his basic human right to worship materialism and against censorship for religious blasphemy.)

Until recently, firebombing of atheist Viet Cong and nuclear attack on the "yellow peril" (in Imperial Japan by order of President Truman, barely aborted with his dismissal of General MacArthur against the Chinese in North Korea) have been our ready answer to all whose religious delusions are different from ours. Is this the first good sign for *Homo sapiens* that should be welcomed by *Homo domesticus* and *Homo metropolus*?

18.00 r/Sex: BREEDING/TAMING

AXIOM (i.e., still unquestioned): It is better to love the one
you "know" (in the biblical sense) than to know the one you
love (in the romantic sense).

DOMESTICITY and/or CARNALITY

Caesarean section without circumcision would make newborn infants less inferior to animals who are not injured by natural birth. Is circumcision not as unnatural as Cesarean section to assist infants? Our biosexual evolution and growth for breeding purposes as a WoMan is unique unto itself, and separate for each gender, unlike our personal and social development towards becoming a more domesticated couple/people. (Men who offer women flowers and jewelries may be wimps. Women who accept flowers as compliments and receive jewelry as investment are likely to be "pushovers".)

In Germany of the Protestant Reformation, the Kaiser took precedent over the church, the church over the children and then the kitchen over the women: Kaiser, Kirche, Kinder, Kuche (ruler, church, children and kitchen). Before Germany, only young men and women and animals were sacrificed to the gods. In Hitler's Germany, women were treated as breeders of Aryan men.

EXTINCTION or SURVIVAL

Not all species are equally capable of exploiting what they accidentally discover, nor are all of us equally resourceful when our resources are limited.

Editor: The unimaginative among us tend to blame others who
           have more talent for inventing what they do not use.

Author: Blaming is a loser's recourse. Losers don't press on but
           retreat, whether in debate or a fight. Winners surrender
           only to escape annihilation, to insure their return to the
           fray. To lose may be a regrettable event, to be a loser is
           self-defeating.

Ed.:   If there are enough of them, we will lose our special
           niche.

Au.:   Like other species who have become extinct for being
           unequal to the competition.

Our survival as a species like all others with two genders depends
on our full sexual development as males and females, whether or not we
are personally or socially advanced, since some of the early stages of our
gender differentiation are unique to humankind. *(r/1)*

MALE AND FEMALE EROTICISM AND SEXUALITY

What is sexual (**P-Y**) is whatever is privately erotic or genitally
mediated, and differs according to gender until (**Z**) grandparenthood
(virtual androgyny).

iii. BIO-SEXUAL GENDER DIFFERENTIATION

	Male	Female

Pregenital, tactile (visual, or vocal):

	Male	Female
P)	autoerotic	narcissistic
Q)	fetishistic	assertive
R)	voyeuristic	homo-erotic

Genital (primary or secondary):

S)	exhibitionistic	flirtatious
T)	pedophilic	seductive
U)	homosexual	heterosexual
V)	bestial	abortive

Procreative (with or without love):

W)	rapacious	adoptive
X)	monogamous	adulterous
Y)	paternal	menopausal

Each gender before grandparenthood can get arrested in or undergo up to ten transitions which are either not identical or do not co-evolve together in any family or society.

P.	Playing with or loving one's self:	"Is my body mine to please me?"
Q.	Quivering fetishism or assertiveness:	"Are what I want anybody's business?"
R.	Restrained sexuality or voyeurism:	"Are bodies created to be hidden?"
S.	Stripteasing or exhibitionism:	"Don't you think my body is better?"
T.	Temptress or tempter of children:	"Can love ever be enough to satisfy?"
U.	Udder urgency (maternal/ homosexual):	"Do I have to share whomever I love?"
V.	Vacillation between petting/ abortion:	"Does sex deserve to be punished?"
W.	Willingness to adopt or to rape:	"Why not do whatever you can do?"
X.	X-purgated monogamy or adultery:	"Do you have to limit your loving?"

Y.	Yen for youth (paternal/ menopausal):	"Does aging exclude loving anyone?"
Z.	Zenith in asexual grandparenthood:	"Are the young not ours to cherish?"

(The question becomes not whether to retire but whether to go on working after grandchildren arrive. What one does as a professional should not be continued for the money but because one is good at it, what one does as an amateur certainly should not be paid for. Those who are neither professionals nor amateurs who get paid are employees or servants of their masters, private or public.)

Time (timing), more than space (crowding), accounts for the covert battle between the sexes because the penis and nipples (in androgynes) will go erect without embarrassment according to their own agendas.

Only mothering (even by fathers) requires both time (for nursing) and space (for nesting and nursing homes).

Historically masculine or not, men separately evolve serially through, if not stuck in

P.	autoeroticism,
Q.	fetishism,
R.	voyeurism,
S.	exhibitionism,
T.	"pedophilia" while "playing doctor,"
U.	prurient homosexuality,
V.	bestiality,
W.	natural rapaciousness,
X.	sensuous coitus, and
Y.	midlife metapause (second adolescent crisis) or fatherhood.

Romantically feminine or not, women can transit through

P.	narcissism,
Q.	tomboy assertiveness,
R.	innocent homosexuality,

S.   heterosexual curiosity, as in "playing house,"

T.   earnest spouse-shopping,

U.   child-swapping or baby-sitting with clingers or clients,

V.   child-bearing, child-saving or child-raising

W.   child-losing from emptied womb or "empty nest",

X.   mate-switching (serial and/or sexual), and

Y.   menopause or May–Decemberhood.

Brief ONTOGENY OF EROTICISM

Autofellatio in animals, our "bestial" tomcat humping the arm of his mistress, snuggling, etc., must have roots that are far-reaching.

Autoeroticism is the first experience of "autonomy" for many. Farm boys have both hands and handy sex objects (proximity is Dr. Samuel Johnson's vaunted excuse for incest indoors according to Boswell's biography of a kindred spirit). *(r/2)*

Were those who hated piano lessons with a passion started on them after being caught with "idle hands in the workshop of the Devil"?

After pubescence, do discovered masturbators belatedly stake territorial claims on their own body and insist that what they do with it is their business and nobody else's, as long as it is between consenting adults of either sex or against the unborn?

Are single-parent/problem-child conflicts less prominent during latchkey urchinhood?

1.   Adam at his God's behest tried bestiality and neither found it "suitable."

When semen intended for breeding or other body fluids gets deposited in the wrong orifice (wound or mucosa), the receiver runs more risks of contracting AIDS from sexually irresponsible or responsive and/but promiscuous partners. The more promiscuous the same-sex non-breeding repository, the higher the risks.

(African primates/patients may be lab subjects improperly managed.)

2. Did Adam father his grandchildren and his sons his wife's? Or did Abel and Cain have sisters, and did Cain's genes produce "black sheep"?

   a. Is father-daughter incest not more permissible in nature than the Oedipal triangle since the sperm is always young and Mongolian idiocy in the offspring thus less probable and therefore unlikely to handicap reproductive efficiency?

   b. Is serial spermatogenesis (which makes male [**P, m**] masturbation and [**W, m**] rapaciousness the physiological norm) also an argument against mother-son incest, even among chimpanzees, because her ovum is as old as his mother?

   (Babysitter/boy and mother/son "grooming behavior" often remains their secret, but is rediscovered as "foreplay" between husband/daughter or /female stepchild.)

   c. Is rapaciousness towards one's "sister" even in the kibbutzim inhibited by (**i**) familiarity breeding contempt (which also explains spouse abuse, divorce with longevity and generation gaps in nuclear families)?

   d) Is active incest more (**i**) a personal decision, or (**ii**) a social risk, or (**iii**) a sexual temptation, or (**Z**) a genetic fail-safe mechanism? (For a man, surrogate daughters/mothers can now stand in for what he cannot keep.)

3. Are "flashers" exhibitionistic or atavistic (chimps court by displaying their erections). Is the shock of the displayed erection a problem of the unaroused female or of the flasher's need to violate her civilized sensibilities?

   In other animals the males are more colorful and compete with each other in sexual display as part of their courting. The unspectacular female becomes a drab mother who can avoid calling attention to herself when hovering over her young.

4. What sexual athletes all fear in common is that it is easier for legitimately married "swinging" couples to go "straight" in/to the closet during sexually repressive social cycles.

   For declared gays and lesbians, true bisexuality—as behavioral, nonorganic androgyny—becomes easy to suspect as closet heterosexuality. Closet bisexuals in turn are the equivalent of homophobes among heterosexuals.

5. Men can become, if only vestigially, "mammarian" with gynecomastia after "metapause" (Stage **Y**).
Because menopause is metabolic and mammalian and therefore con-natural, being captured by career demands at an earlier stage (without infertility) is the equivalent of "perversion"—i.e., sexual arrest or retardation.

Only medicine heretofore has distinguished the sexes by separate specialties in gynecology and urology. Even sociology in studying industry studied only male behavior.

New Psychiatrists will not make the same mistake of ignoring *la difference*.

Our erogenous zones are not different from other animals (even what is touted as "oro-anal" dominance is more mental than sensual), except for our bigger breasts and penises (per unit weight). But though we have analogous erogenous zones, male and female organs also serve different reproductive, with or without urinary, functions, even if their origins are homologous.

1. Our sexual life cycle is different for males and females (who have less skin-covering yet more nerve-endings per pound).
2. It is even more divergent between women and other females: our DNA keeps the human vagina tilted forward and 'infantile' by primate standards.

The ethologically infantile forward tilt of the vagina in human females makes all rape victims no different from sexually abused children. And one out of every four are raped by two or more assailants. *(r/3)*

(A friend wrote of her attempted rape by an orangutan [did he smell "oestrus"?] but gang bangs and statutory rape are unknown among pygmy chimps [*Pan paniscus*] of Zaire and in hippie communes with their liberated women and flower children. [Desmond Morris's *Naked Ape* is now Jared Diamond's *Third Chimpanzee*, the other being the ordinary Pan troglodyte.])

Does this explain why we protect "victims" as helpless children rather than as fertile women? (Abortion may be allowed after incest.)

And why women can be raped at all, when all other animals have to be courted, even when in heat? And why a handicapped female is not neglected by eager tomcats? And why a gang bang may be uniquely human but "wham, bang, thank you, ma'am" after animal courtship or foreplay is not? (Only humans and pygmy chimps of Zaire dally in their fornication. "To dally" is to "f—— around.") And why recidivist rapists, unlike violence-prone felons, may not be victims of child abuse, sexual or physical?

(We went from "Third Chimpanzee" to Neanderthal to Cro-Magnon to *Homo domesticus* and *Homo metropolus*:

(If the evolution of con-vivial and con-familiar "perversions" and "eroticism" is unclear to you, so has its implications escaped our ancestors and may well continue to be incomprehensible to our inheritors.) *(r/4)*

WHICH IS WORSE, INCEST OR SEXUAL ABUSE?

Physical abuse is more "physical" and bruising (unphysiological), sexual abuse more "courting" though coercive (physiologically driven). Perpetrators have different childhood experiences of sexual and physical violence from adult expressions of vengefulness for their own earlier helplessness and victimization.

"Incest," which is not given a separate (Oedipal) developmental niche in this impersonal and asocial theory of sexuality, was rarely observed in the wilds between siblings, never between mother and mature chimp, nor has any sub-primate homosexuality ever been reported. *(r/5)*

Urban homosexuality (e.g., in prisons), may be as opportunistic as rural or laboratory "bestiality" (even among birds, male or female, who are neither man nor beast but were raised by bird-lovers or "imprinted" by bird-watching students).

Can incest between mutants destroy the species?

Miosis = cell division. Meiosis = to diminish. Sex is the way we inject half of the double helix of DNA. Chromosomal meiosis guarantees that no mutation can spread unmodified.

Multiplication without meiosis will weaken mutants.

SEPARABLE SOCIAL AND SEXUAL DEVELOPMENT
(Clinical > Chronological Sequences)

Asymmetrical in the timing of their gender-specific stages of erotogenital maturation, males and females can each enjoy or not, and never equally, any of (iii) ten forms of sexual expression (**P** to **Y**), between the unisex of conception and the androgyny of (**Z**) grandparenthood.

Our biosexual development into Wo-Manhood is separate (XX and XY) and unequal: more advanced in females (the "weaker" sex who survives her older mate):

Female genital anatomy separates reproductive from urinary channels (her vagina from the urethra), whereas males continue to micturate and ejaculate through a common orifice which, in less evolved species like fishes, reptiles and birds, is called a cloaca for passing urine and feces.

1. There is probably an engineering rather than an epigenetic explanation for *"le difference"*. Which is why there are separate specialists for urology and for obstetrics and gynecology.

2. Females will constitute virtually another species once they can reproduce by themselves virginally, which may come sooner than men can accept.

SEXUAL PHYSIOLOGY, SOCIAL ANATOMY

Does physiology (processing of energy), not anatomy (or genitalia), direct our destiny?

> (Men hunt big game; women shelter the defenseless. The patricentric, no matter how small, identifies with the aggressor, e.g., the bullfighter; the matricentric with the underdog, no matter how big, e.g., Russian bear or the bull.
>
> (Anxiety and its expression differs depending on the sex of the anxious. Part of it comes from the readiness to feel trapped [in men by what the gentler sex calls/sells as "commitment"].)

Can anatomy dictate our destiny? Sometimes.

Talent and energy, inherited separately with the XX and/or XY chromosomes from our parents (which were also all they separately inherited from theirs) can decide ours.

(Virtuosity (creactive performance, **B** + **E**) is achieved, creativity (**E**) is genetic, handed down to us by our grandparents (**Z**).)

Will temporary arrest of ovulation during stress allow women with upward mobility or anorexia nervosa to postpone procreation without penalties to their progeny?

Or does social competition demand sexual abdication in asphalt jungles of corporate giants?

In a world nobody owns, surrounded by traditional moral dogma, conventional social demagoguery and fantasied gender symmetry, only our (**Z**) animal nature, inherited talent and sexual stamina can jointly enable us fully to enjoy (**i**) the freedom to (**A**) feel, (**B**) act, (**C**) conceive, and (**D**) correlate, even to (**E**) create, and to savor (**ii**) the errors in the cultural evolution of equality for all souls ("psyche") and all intelligence ("logos"), and to (**iii**) procreate more of our kind.

Thus, (**A-E**) sensual freedom, (**F-O**) ideal equality, and (**f, m**) gender-differentiated (**P-Y**) erotic preferences evolve from (**iii, Z**) heredity, (**i**) passion and action, and (**ii**) bias and beliefs (ideology).

Values, unlike virtues, can be sold as beliefs or developed as social skills. Our ideologies are no less an instrument than our senses. If talented and energetic by virtue of birth, our virtuosity and animality will make us socially superior to our peers.

We have little borrowed time to develop versatility as precocious naked apes under family and social pressures. (A chimp is an old dog unable to learn new tricks by the time we start teaching it to use sign language or computer symbols. Even our children have to start early to become competently bilingual.)

Can we also be personally convincing but not convinced (persuasive but skeptical) and grow to be more of an ideagogue talking than an idealist dreaming.

Are we any wiser for having become less ignorant?

1. Can we feel universal kinship with other animals and with machines, whether metal or synthetic, that we have endowed with the talents that we admire in ourselves?

2. Can we find separate sensual, social, and sexual functions within us that reflect the uses of the different organ systems that we are born with, instead of the differences between the various races or other domesticated species?

3. In fact are there two sexual subspecies of *Homo sapiens sapiens*, the male "manimachineroticus", still an experimental model, and its evolutionary superior in anatomy and physiology, the female "womanimachineroticus"?

Our history is an inelegant record of the domestication of man, trying to tame the beast of a unicorn in us in the name of God in our version of human husbandry, and cultivating the best of the half-human centaur in us in the name of culture for selfless teamwork.

Human domestication is no different from turning the female into a domestic, to help in housekeeping, at home or in the office.

(No new animal has been domesticated in the last millennium. To sexist men or women, the opposite sex is the last among animals to require taming: attending and obeying is called being vulnerable, sensitive and committed. To be sensitive is accepted as substitute for lack of curiosity. The curious is more aware than concerned.)

In peace or in war, domestication always involves brainwashing the captive and the dependent as well as brain-stuffing the active and the curious. Advocates of both claim they can help us cope better. (What preachers profess are echoes from parrots recorded in our libraries. Both preachers and professors, like reporters, are notorious name-droppers rather than constructive critics.)

GETTING DOWN TO CASES

For many, what is sexual is not necessarily genital but may be oral demand for love, anal ambition or urethral competition, penis- or testis-envy *(r/5)* or latency, phallic or procreative, with or without love, exhibitionistic (assertive) or penetrating (rapacious).

My 3-year-old grandson who had announced that he needed to empty his bladder in no uncertain terms was followed by his sister who was half his age to the bathroom. As he hung his penis over the edge of the toilet bowl, so did she her belly, while fully clothed. Did she feel "penis envy"? Neither seemed to think that they had done anything out of the ordinary or achieved anything to crow about. (As teenagers, they still compete as siblings, not socially or sexually.)

In an open society, everyone, whether engaged in one-upsmanship or not, is entitled to form one's own opinion (and therefore be secretly motivated, personally, socially, or sexually), and enjoy an affordable, nondangerous even if intoxicating opiate for the powerless. *(r/6)*

"Sexist" Stereotyping ("p" to "y")

We can now identify a person by a series of initials from (**i-iii**) separate (**A-E**) sensual, (**F-O**) social, (**P-Y, m** or **f**) sexual, (**p** to **y**) "sexist" and (**Z**) androgynous subcategories. In making comparisons, the following translations of different assigned roles may be useful for cross-sexual classification. The letters can be substituted for the paragraphs, like social security numbers for names.

(Other animals manage to find a place in the sun irrespective of sex, race, age or species. Only human couples compare their partners with parents and peers. Partnerships should begin with more "f——ing" than loving, end with more "l——ing.")

p)	S/G	= Male chauvinistic "piglet":	"My wife does not obey me."
q)	G/W	= Male chauvinistic "pig":	"My mother always obeyed me."
r)	G/Y	= Female chauvinistic "hen":	"My husband should obey me or leave me."
s)	Y/A	= Female chauvinistic "chick":	"My father always loved me."
t)	V/T	= "Fecha" (chick's daughter):	"Beach boys are fun."
u)	R/V	= "Macho" (son of a pig):	"Party girls are better."
v)	Y/W	= "Macha" (hen's daughter):	"I think so too."
w)	U/A	= "Fecho" (son of a hen):	"Choice is a must."
x)	A/W	= "Hen-pecked" husband (piglet's son):	"I need my wife."
y)	W/A	= "Oppressed" wife:	"My family needs me."

(Excerpted from "A Psychiatric Odyssey of Personal Discoveries," VOICES, *The Art and Science of Psychotherapy*, Summer, 1974.)

Of all male chauvinists today, the king of beasts has no peer (except perhaps among self-sufficient Mormons). His pride (of concubines) feeds him in exchange for his securing the boundaries of their hunting territory even if lionesses would rather be scavengers (shoppers for dead meat) than huntresses.

The lioness and the mother are more nurturing, and the lion and the father more expectant than our men and women are alike. Girls who are nice to each other should be compared with cubs at play, and neither with either of their own den mothers.

Among "viviparous" animals, the lion's was the first happy harem (no one getting pregnant for many years some of the time). Ahead of all "mammals", his were the first totally committed den mothers for cub care centers (they are willing "wet nurses" for each other's young). (Is "wet" from milk overflow? "Oviparous" birds lay their eggs and cannot milk their breasts.)

For lions as for women whose social consciousness has been raised, the group (their pride, our society) is more important than the youngsters (their cubs, our kids).

It was the success in coping with the New Poor (idled husband living hand-to-mouth on poorly paid but competent working wife's income) that led to the following formulation: "The redundant has to get laid or mothered or both."

Laid off work, (**B'**) layabouts must be (**A**) both indulged and looked after like a child, and not be required to be (**X, m**) the father and (**W, m**) a mother, even if (**u W**) a "father", because that function (**x Y**) is ethologically superfluous: Fathers are only expected by mothers to mind their children in order to tame them. *(For the use or meaning of italicized letters, see Sexist Stereotyping, above.)*

After the last world war overcame the last great economic depression on the home front, many undaunted American mothers (**U, f**) found themselves back to the feudal ages when their labor (H) contributed to the family income. *(r/7)*

In recurrent periods of recession in public consumption of (**K**) assembly line products since then, their men who have returned from war to become (**Y, m**) their family provider again got (**B'**) laid off more regularly.

And just as regularly, they got admitted to mental hospitals in proportion to the depth of economic recession. The worse it is, the higher the suicide rate for the unemployed (**H'**) and helpless (unmothered, **A'**) who feel hopeless (trapped, **B'**).

> In one case, on my recommendation, the wife bought a "leisure suit" as a present, to make her husband more comfortable instead of feeling underfoot all the time. Told she is now keeping a "gigolo", she smiled and said he had been behaving like a child who had just learned that he was adopted from an orphanage, rejected and abandoned. On follow-up, their home life and sex life had improved, their young are again rambunctious instead of morose or aggravating to parents with reversed priorities, and not yelled at oftener than before their father was "demobilized".

1. Being there is all that a lion ever does. His pride of competent females feeds him, if his Afro-like mane of hair interferes with chasing lighter prey, although it intimidates larger predators.
2. He protects the females and their young in his pride and is kept by several "bread-winners" as a mate on demand during oestrus and as a bodyguard on rare occasions. *(r/8)*

NEW DESIGNATIONS FOR COMBINATIONS OF COUPLES

To compare historical with contemporary figures, deities and celebrities with friends or acquaintances, we can convert their initials into pseudonyms.

We grow by leaving one stage of development for another and return to an earlier one when sick or aging.

Bertrand Russell is a good all-around senso-socio-sexual exemplar, and asocio-sexual Emily Dickinson and post-polygamous Gautama Buddha are sensual exemplars par excellence.

But few are influenced by example. Voltaire as social exemplar cannot take credit for the shift away from (**F**) pilgrimage and (**G**) crusades to (**H**) tourism. (Is Jesus also a "sugar-daddy"?)

In general, leaders must keep up with questions asked by followers in their advancing (**A** - **E**) mental development (What, Why not, Why, Why now, and How, respectively). Social hangers-on continue to mislead with (**F** - **O**) acceptable answers (God, power, money, insight, progress, togetherness, fellowship, conservation, coexistence, computers). To disdain stage-specific (male or female) erotic experiences is to signal retardation (**P** - **Z**) in sexual development (*self-abuse" or narcissism, fetishism or self-assertion, voyeurism or homo-eroticism, exhibitionism or strip-teasing, pedophilia or flirting, homosexuality or baby-sitting, bestiality or abortion, "self-insertion" or motherhood, monogamy or divorce, fatherhood or bar-hopping, and grandparenthood).

Instead of social security numbers, or unverifiable horoscope-like Rorschach readings, persons already dead or still alive can be known by a series of senso-socio-sexual initials (**A** to **Z**), with italicized letters **p** to **y**, (above): You can (1) ask what kind of a unicorn (**A-E**), centaur (**F-O**) and androgyne (**P-Z**) they are and (2) have their partner supply their stereotypical sexist initial (**p -y**).

> (Freud, for instance would be **EIq Y**. Author is at least **DNq Z**. **EIqY** is more creative in resolving paradoxes posed by fewer facts. **DOqZ** is more refractive in diffusing the white light of seductive reductionism in the less experienced, including **EIq Y**, who never let his favorite daughter move out to look after a family of her own.)

Are you or yours more emotional than motivated (**A** > **B**), more religious than patriotic (**F** > **G**), more narcissistic than assertive (**P** > **Q**), more rapacious than monogamous (**W** > **Y**), etc.? Partnerships, homosexual or heterosexual, can now be assessed as to longevity (complementarity) by each partner. Paired ratings can be computed and compared with other couples to predict probabilities and thus reduce uncertainty.

> Are the abortive (**V**) the second failures of the planful (**H** + **I**), and is the adoptive (**W**) the vindication of the reproductive (**iii**)? The powerful do not bother with purpose.

18.00 r/SEX

r/Chapter Notes

[r/1] God, like the Magi, evicted the unfit. (Misfits He accepts, like we do: They fit a little or a lot, but not completely.)

Inequality of the races and the "four sexes" in the military is served by fantasies of sexual superiority of the blacks, and moral inferiority of the perverse.

[r/2] First started wearing shorts to go to kindergarten. Earliest interactive erection followed with a pre-school niece who reached in. (Her family couldn't keep a maid because her father also molests them sexually. He was a cousin whose father married much earlier than mine. My contemporaries therefore called me "Uncle"!)

[r/3] Women are unique in their vulnerability to rape because the vagina is tilted forward. Animals cannot be spread-eagled. Escape is possible when there is zero gravity or space suits, and erections fail during the chase.

[r/4] Student: In the musical "La Cage aux Folles" about homosexuals, a transvestite ruefully observed that "Snakes live as males and females".

> St = Student
> Ed = Editor
> Au = Author
> Sp = Specialist
> Gn = Generalist
> Pr = Professional

Ed: In "Cats" they lived as males and females, too.

St: His point was that human beings are free not to do so. He said, "We should know better. But our son (his lover's) is getting married. Where have we gone wrong?"

Au: Open communication keeps one repeating what is as yet not understood.

Sp: Lust is orgasm-seeking behavior, unlike sex, which seeks to reproduce.

Ed: In the Orient they chant, "There is no fire like lust, no grip like hate, no net like delusion, no river like craving."

Gn: It is not whether you are on fire or drowning, gripped or fallen: Obsessions have noth¬ing to do with devotion, denial with love, nor sacrifice with paradise. Flaunting in animals become sexploitation in man, envied by "peers" as "adultery " in presidential hopefuls like Sen. Gary Hart. (His paramour had breast implants.)

Sp: Born leaders like MacArthur, Nixon, Kennedy, Roosevelt and Ike are not just hus¬bands, like Truman.

Pr: The male is dispensable. That is why after coitus, it can be killed in defense of the mother and off-spring without risk to the species as a whole. The cost is variation in its membership, which must be do¬mesticated if the species is puny.

Au: It is interesting that we do not feel as vengeful with mothers who love their sons more, than we do with fathers who love their daughters less.

[r/5] UNMIXING MIXED-UP IDEAS

Sp: It is important to separate (1) incest between a minor and an adult of different sexes who are related, from (2) an oedipal triangle which can include stepchildren.

Au: It is also important to separate oedipal conflict from (3) castration anxiety which has nothing to do with (a) sterilization or even with (b) amputation but as (c) a metaphor for early circumcision.

Ed: Freud "forgot" that Oedipus was not circumcised but he himself had been so traumatized very early (pre-oedipally or pre-genitally), and so he just divided "psycho-sexual" development into oral and anal (pre-oedipal), phallic (oedipal) and, regardless of gender, genital.

Sp: Male development can be divided into pre and postcircumcision if circumcision does not coincide with puberty.

Au: The shorter the pre-circumcision phase, the more problematical the post-circumcision adjustment.

Gn: It is equally important to remember that many victims of the holocaust were circumcised before they knew what was going on, and that the Aryans knew what they were doing. But it is not just the un-circumcised who are more if not fully responsible. All those who had (4) more or less strict toilet training are also more or less domesticated by early programming to obey authority and are not free enough to be culpable.

Au: Also as important to remember is that domesticated Aryans have contributed more great music and mathematics to Western culture than the Greeks. But simple toilet training is not as critical to (5) cruelty as (6) desperation among others who tend to obey their masters and commit war crimes, e.g., the well-drilled Japanese against fellow Asians.

Pr: Their civilians were not victimized by toilet-trained victors who were not desperate, though General MacArthur had more absolute power than any potentate, including the Emperor of Japan.

Ed: Once we succeed in domesticating man to be attack dogs, then we can breed for tame men (harmless "humanists", not trained "masochists") just as we can breed hornless cows.

Sp: We should also think of as simply "cruel" those whom we tend to call "sadistic", which have no counterpart among other animals, if only because we had to be toilet-trained when most rebellious and therefore more instinctively prone to temper tantrums when our territory is threatened.

Pr: Those who have (7) "penis envy" but not "anal" can be content to be in the shadow of their superiors, remain compliant and accept their "amputated" anatomy. If anal but not greedy ("oral"), they work overtime on demand, or stay home to mother their children, including their husbands, of whom they are in awe.

Gn: Women who were "tomboyish" as toddlers become more competitive with (8) "testis envy." They like to wear pants and heavily padded jackets to compensate for lack of androgens as they protest against masculine dominance.

Au: We should therefore separate (5) "cruelty" from (4) "competitiveness" and "compliance" and (6) "efficiency" from "effectiveness". Cruelty comes from frustration of temper tantrums during toilet training, compliance from efficient toilet training, competitiveness from deprivation during periods of scarcity, effectiveness from absence of awe in whatever we do because we know how to cope.

Ed: We tend to worship (a) in silence what is ideal that we feel possessive about, and (b) to fight further deprivation when we are desperate, in (c) crises or during (d) catharsis through confrontation to unlock the bowels of the unconscious in the emotionally constipated. (Cathartics produce diarrhea, crisis fluidity.)

Gn: Men and women with (9) "breast envy" are those who felt deprived when another sibling won the rivalry for what "was not enough to go around". Men who perform better sexually with prostitutes than with wives have their counterpart in men who fantasy as their ideal other women who had bigger breasts than their mothers and in their (10) "breast worship" never go beyond oral foreplay in words and action.

Au: (11) "Phallus worship" among daughters who have no penis envy of their brothers can take the form of "feelings of repulsion on the night of their honeymoon" towards their partners once these become legitimate husbands like their fathers, even if they had been satisfactory sexual partners before they got married.

Ed: Phallic worshipping daughter-wives remain married, find sexual satisfaction outside marriage, but, quite often, when their satisfactory partner gets divorced and demands that they make the same sacrifice, they part from them.

Sp: They are usually older than the brother whom they did not envy for his "extra digit" or "sixth finger," because they "had always felt normal" in the eyes of their father until he came along. If they did not compete for their mother, "breast envy" would not be a problem for either sib.

Gn: Their counterpart among men are more common, and carry the diagnosis of (12) "Mariolatry."

Pr: Where Mariolatry is an integral part of religious ritual, there is greater tolerance of male homosexuality.

Au: In the Philippines and other predominantly Catholic nations, being "gay" is not seen as anti-female.

[r/6] 1. We simply monitored very closely a "sexist" but otherwise acceptable candidate who thought of rapists as nonpersons (the democratic version of the unperson in totalitarian states) because we did not have a token "insane" rapist in our patient population when he came for his screening interview. Ideology alone (including sexual "preferences") cannot disqualify any trainee unless clinical performance suffers.

2. We have turned down psychiatric residency applicants whose femin "ism" gets in the way of establishing rapport with "sexist" patients, e.g., a short, black, unemployed male sporting a military uniform with medals, whose minority status he denies by authoritarian attire:

Recommendations from his superiors that he "deigned to offer" the applicant to document "macho" claims of potential solvency was received with sublime indifference by her. She was turned down herself as a potential resident. (She carried her coffee mug, like an identifying badge or status symbol or security blanket, wherever we went.)

[r/7]   When it comes to (i) personal morality we concern ourselves only with mothers (and loving sisters), sibs (brothers who are pals), and grandparents (who are friendly). Not with fathers.

Au: Between leaders and clingers, there is (**ii**) social ethics by consensus of the leaders. (The erect penis or clitoris has no morality or ethics.)

Ed: Big Brother is for those who do not believe in a Father Almighty. Neither or whether to be loved or befriended, they are admired and feared. The truly totalitarian state must conceive of the family and personal relations of (**A**) love and (**B**) friendship as its rivals.

Au: The nation-state started as playful men's clubs (like street gangs) that quickly became rivals as their territoriality is threatened. Breeding should never be a patriotic act of citizenship but an intuited instinct that our species is fit to survive. Those who refrain from breeding, even as patriots, do not agree that their breed is necessary.

[r/8] The difference between lions and human beings is that couples adopt and then the wife gets pregnant, while lions get new mates into *oestrus* sooner if they eat the deposed rival's cubs.

19.00 s/PREPARING PSYCHIATRISTS for the FUTURE

At the University of Santo Tomas, which is more hoary with age than Harvard, we dissected frogs and cats, but did not study their behavior. Are they more like us dead than alive? Our lectures in psychiatry were on rational psychology, which was an illegitimate child of Aristotelian and scholastic thinking. But this is only to be expected wherever St. Thomas, the ideal Sunday school teacher, is still taken seriously outside philosophy.

We have come a long way from the soul to the mind to the brain to the basic science of chemistry whose advances in the field of neurotransmitters have now bridged the gap between nerves that we call synapses. If the treatment of mental illness is to be mediated by neurotransmitters, then those that relay messages to small muscles (e.g., in anxious finger-tapping), to larger muscle bundles (e.g., in depressive hand-wringing and agitated pacing) and to the whole body (e.g., in fight or flight panic reactions) should be the object of more intensive investigation.

Beyond that, I also want to bridge the gap between science and art, starting with mind and matter, by showing that what we mind always matters, but essentially and existentially only to us rather than to the world of matter that surrounds all of us. (Art makes do with what is at hand, science discovers what more there is to hand.) Then we can begin a culture-free ("transcultural") science of psychiatry with the study of nature, then of life, then of us, dead or alive.

"HISTORICAL" HIGHLIGHTS and SORTING the RECORD THROUGH TIME

Dinosaurs reigned for 100 million years 70 million years ago! Their opposable thumb and ours make both of us superior to mammals with proportionately larger brains, like dolphins.

Roughly 18,000 years after we became dominant, we domesticated animals (in 12,000 BC) and started farming two to four millennia later (around 8–10,000 BC).

Four centuries later, writing was invented (around 5–3,500 BC), then the calendar before the next millennium (in 2,800 BC), and the seven-day week before the next (in 1500 BC). The alphabet followed 200 years later and monotheism in the next century: "In the beginning was the Word, ... and the word was God" ... and on Sabbath God rested? Or, first there was Sabbath (1500 BC), then the Word (1300 BC), then God (around 1200 BC)?

In less than a millennia, divine possession of epileptics was disproved (around 420 BC) by Hippocrates.

There are two kinds of mammalian intelligence, terrestrial (e.g., among cats) and aquatic (e.g., among dolphins). The differences in their habitat can better explain any difference in behavior without crediting their manager of muscles called the brain. *(s/1)*

There are two kinds of unshakable beliefs that distort reality, one shows us in a better light and they are called grandiose delusions, and the other shows us in a worse light, and they are called delusions of guilt despite spiritual amnesty and repeal of the Ten Commandments. Both delusions are encouraged in the gullible by two growth industries called religion and cosmetology: Original sin and potential body odor create need for salvation and under-arm deodorants.

[*Homo sapiens* do not need either, *H domesticus* is guilt-prone, *H metropolus* more grandiose *(Table 16).*

What makes each of us different is (i) the family that produced us, (ii) its traditions that we honor or disown, and (iii) our sexual activity, shared or not, to "immortalize" or bury with us half of the double helix of our DNA that our children can inherit and pass on.

Senso-socio-sexual subcycles, can also be visualized as tri-color strands (red for the war-like "centaur", yellow for the freedom-loving "unicorn" and green for the secretly eager "androgyne" in all of us) roughly wrapped around a more conical or pyramidal than cylindrical barber-pole, slicing which gives us the levels of development reached at that level.

Where we are at any time indicates both where we have been and where we are headed. *(s/2)*

What is not (**i**) personal or (**iii**) private is (**ii**) public. Moral virtues and sensual virtuosities are personal attributes, social values and group ethics are consensual judgments, conventional or perverted eroticism and sexuality are private affairs, even if shared. *(s/3)*

All young animals start with (**A**) assistance in becoming free, and with (**P**) playful autoeroticism. Chimpanzees are capable of (**F**) fantastically magical thinking, other bipeds including birds are also (**G**) governed by pecking orders, and others (**H**) hoard nest decorations and trade lab tokens for sexual favors. We go on to (**F**) Father Almighty in our theology, (**G**) group together to govern and fight as political animals, and enthrone (**H**) High Finance to achieve conspicuous consumption.

Our life cycle is not unlike that of germ layers, e.g., the lining of the uterus. It goes through phases for which it cannot be blamed. Thus, the psychiatrist cannot prefer one stage over others but, like the gynecologist, he must be able to recognize each one.

Does each day repeat some struggle to be (**i**) more free than, (**ii**) at least equal to, or (**iii**) as erotic as, another? [Between parents who are not also (**Z**) grandparents, the greater the discrepancy in (**i**) and/or (**ii**), the more fulfilling (**iii**) must be for both, if the marriage is to survive.

Ratios between sensual autonomy (liberty), social adequacy (parity) and sexual ambition (carnality) influence levels of personal, public, or private harmony. Beyond that, they ultimately affect our planet earth, but not our sun or galaxy.

With the drive for sexual equality, American matrons have gone from being the most beautiful to the angriest women in the world. (Only two that I know, of disparate age, can be angry and stay beautiful: Elizabeth Taylor and my younger daughter.) *(s/4)*

PEOPLE IN THEIR PLACES/PHASES OVER TIME

Many and mischievous paraphrases resulted from originally misreading Lamarck's "besoin" as "decision" instead of "need" (to adapt but only to new environmental demands). This error delayed the easy explanation of unexpected discontinuities in the fossil record that Darwin's theory of evolution had wrongly predicted would logically show smooth progression.

> Ed.:   Scientific predictions, as in genetic counseling, can still go unheeded for being inexact. Einstein himself suspected that "So far as mathematics refer to reality, they are not precise, and so far as they are precise they do not refer to reality."
>
> Au.:   That's how Einstein, a theist to the end, unwittingly betrays his ambivalent readiness to accept that the principle of uncertainty in particle physics makes God a gambler and relativity absolute, even in deist Newton's tangible universe.

It is to avert any accidental mistranslation that we have changed the names of our exemplars to illustrate what they exemplify, with the stage names that we have assigned to them.

We have fabulized exemplars in (i) unicorns, (ii) centaurs, and (iii) androgynes, and (A to Z) "individual" exemplars. Pseudonyms preserve anonymity when cases are reported to strangers.

> (Because "birds of a feather flock together", we can even give names to the places where people of similar preoccupations gravitate, e.g., civic centers for statists, think-tanks for futurists, etc.)
>
> Special names for sensual, social, and sexual "samplers" can prevent misunderstanding of the details of our theory and avoid what happened to Descartes, whose "cogito" (cogitation or doubting) was carelessly thought of as "cognito" (cognition or thinking).
>
> Would we now have "mind-body" duality without such a misconception?

(To the child, the "mind" is just a word, like "God", until it combines both in trying to resolve adolescent dilemmas. We can therefore suspect what stage of development we've reached by the words or statements we use [even in this book] to explain the world we live in. ["Choice", for instance, is also a toddler's choice expression: "That's what I want!"])

Sensual, Social, and Sexual Samplers

Which of these developmental phases/exemplary people would you soon like to work on, with, or for? Which is yours, yours' (*sic*), the author's, your favorite authors', etc.

i. Stages of SENSUAL DEVELOPMENT (Sensual Exemplars)

A: Assistance-/nurture-/support-taking: "How do I feel? Where is my mother?"

> Abby (ABE) a virtual animal at birth, was untamed and rebellious, but eventually learned what was taught with consistency when it was timely, and repaid her debt by training others who were temporarily disabled by pessimism.

B: Bashful or willful experimentation: "What can I do and get away with?"

> Bob (BABETTE) is a "privateer" whose mobility (glibness) eluded capture (exposure) by those he plundered charmingly. His descendants are among the best of lawyer-mercenaries (debaters).

C: Cognitive seeking for true meaning: "What will I find, is it the Answer?"

> Cat (CATHY) valued reason and philosophy, and believed that the highest form of intellectual activity is the study of dogma or the metaphysics of existence.

D: Disproving/comparing specific claims: "What is proved and who verified it?"

> Deke (DOT) believed in the neutrality of numbers, which facilitates armchair research of discovered data to explore their

significance in relation to what is already accepted, in library shelves arranged according to the Dewey decimal system.

E: Excellent or precocious creativity: "What can I synthesize ahead of all?"

Emil (EMMY) is an erudite scholar who also attempted a synthesis of Greek philosophy and the Scripture (as a literal, ethical and allegorical exegesis) which resulted in a recondite blending of pagan thought and Christian theology.

ii: SOCIAL (ASEXUAL) EXEMPLARS

F: Faith in spiritual rebirth, rewards: "Am I alone? Where is my Father?"

Fess (FERN) is a sculptor who believed in a master planner, and worshipped the golden calf he created.

G: Government-offered assistance user: "What is my party and who is my patron?"

George (GINA) was a leader and war hero who sacrificed youthful believers in his cause for his own glorification. He would rather plot than plan.

H: High finance finagling or derision: "Who is my provider and competitor?"

Hew (HEDDA) was a merchant and trader and head of his family business firm. He traded as he played.

[Greed is the sum total of (1) hunger ("oral") plus (2) material deprivation ("anal"), with or without (a) malnutrition during economic recessions or (b) dehydration with fluid loss from diarrhea, plus (3) chronic rejection or (4) extended inattention to *Homo domesticus*. With (3) or (4) among *Homo metropolus*, even mild hunger pangs produce bulimia from an immediate sense of instinctive entitlement in the face of any mild threat of (a) scarcity or (b) morbidity, which in turn scares even the muscular to exercise or the flabby to diet, but without risking "anorexia nervosa" (more common among *Homo domesticus* and a tested defense against early maternal stuffing with excess food and a compromise solution to adolescent ambivalence about procreation and pregnancy, often complicated by amenorrhea).

Au.: Good will is preserved by paper transactions which tend to reduce the temptation to cheat one another, and thusly prevent the risk of recrimination. Contracts may also be written with protective clauses in small print which shelter the seller against Acts of God that may delay delivery of goods. Bad debts can be documented and written off with ease for purposes of reckoning at some later date, and in order to claim allowable deductions for commercial losses. Clerical overhead is thus minimized.

I: Individualistic ego-centricity: "Who am I? Who will play with me?"
Isa (IZA) is an individualist who disowned her divisiveness by devising elegant collages but dabbled seriously in psychobabble.

J: Joint ethno-centric advocacy: "Who are we? Who are our friends?"
Joyce (JAY) believes in joining her self-anointed group in fighting against sexist self-serving enemies of the public interest.

K: Kinesthetic mechanical prosthetics: "What can we do? Or man produce?"
Kane (KAY) was a self-taught factory technologist in a mass assembly line of skilled workers.

L: Lover of mankind (human racism): "What are we doing against ourselves?
Les (LIL) is a poll-taker of the civilized expression of popular human prejudices.

M: Mother Nature worshipper, conserver: "What do we risk losing by overkill?"
Micki (MAC) is an environmental safety engineer, above- and below-ground as well as underwater, interested in oil, geology and seismology.

N: Native habitat protector of animals: "Who is our kin under the skin?"
Nat (NITA) was a student of more physically superior species whose feats he wanted to duplicate. He did not live to see the day when man-powered flight over watery depths surpassed

the apocryphal miracle of walking on water without suffering seasickness.

O: Over-awed by artificial intelligence: "What can we use to teach ourselves?"

> Otto (ODETTE) is a computer expert who rejects being classified with either essentialists or existentialists and only concerns himself, like a computer, with the concrete, in order to transcend the limitations and avoid the temptations of abstract concepts.

iii: MALE AND FEMALE EROTICISM AND SEXUALITY Exemplars

Pete (PIPPA) was self-absorbed and almost self-sufficient in fantasy, like Narcissus:

> "Masturbation is a private perversion." (Peter Portnoy y Philcox)
> "Narcissism is a form of fidelity." (Pippa Peacock y Penny)

Queenie (QUINBY) was almost self-sufficient until she discovered an object to love as well as to cherish with great anticipation, and attempted to assert her claims for the first time:

> "Assertiveness is territoriality." (Querida Quigly y Quinlan)
> "Fetishism is erotic stamp-collecting." (Quinby Quincy y Quickman)

Rena (ROD) frigidly looked and listened but refused to go further and remained in the closet, unwed but not unwanted or unwanting:

> "Aesthetics is better than sex." (Regina Reinart y Razilli)
> "Voyeurism is a victimless crime." (Randy Rather y Ramsey)

Sal (SONYA) managed to keep his self-suspected ignorance a secret by allowing others to reveal theirs first:

> "Exhibitionism threatens the envious." (Simon Shaw y Segal)
> "Teasing safely tests one's skills." (Sonya Sinclair y Seefeldt)

Terry (TESS) eventually seduced a child-bride who was just barely learning to flirt:

> "Pedophilia keeps one young at heart." (Tyrone Turner y Tucker)
> "Coquetry opens doors of opportunity." (Trixie Tourney y Tischler)

Una (ULA) needed another to love/suckle:

"Mamma means mammary." (Ulyana Unger y Ubaldi)
"Homosexuality is safe contraception." (Ulrich Ullman y Unzicker)

Vi (VITO) had several affairs after initially almost capitulating to the lure of safe and secure monogamy:
"Promiscuity is non-discriminatory." (Viola Vaillant y Vaughn)
"What you get is what you're good at." (Victor Vessey y Vetter)

Will (WILLA) was later glad to provide for his bastard daughter from a youthful liaison:
"Rape can be a kindly close encounter." (William Waelder y Wolfson)
"Killing the innocent is too convenient." (Wilhelmina Wilson y Weinman)

Xavier (XENIA) kept his spouse monogamous by virtual social isolation:
"Adultery is word-of-mouth publicity." (Xenia Xerxes y Xanthippe)
"Divorce is easier than coping harder." (Xavier Xavier y Xavier)
Xenia lives for the time when "it takes two to tango.

Yoko (YUL) a lyric poet, did not attempt family life until very late:
"Man needs mates, has to want heirs." (Yusef Young y Yeager)
"Kids have time, the old too little." (Yoko Younger y Yates)
Yoko yearns for "what might have been," now that she is menopausal.

Are children easier to raise and therefore more enjoyable to domesticate, even without being needed as farm hands, because we are forewarned about what to expect of our progeny and can see our own version of ourselves in them as they grow?

Au.:   And are bastards thereby harder to socialize and therefore less acceptable except among the strong for the same reason? The irony is that the weak who are starved for love beget more bastards.

Z. SHARED ASOCIAL CHILD-LIKE SENSUALITY: grandparents adore genes

Zena's (and ZENO's) forebears divided metaphysics into logic, psychology, and ethics, which is not served by study and science ("Beyond the Mind" and "Beyond Beliefs"):

Zenaida Zimmerman y Zareb and Zeno Zecariah y Zylinski: "Kids will be kids."

As grandparents, Zena and Zeno have bridged their gender gap and survived the battle between the sexes that sometimes seem to arise around asexual issues—(A) emotional, (B) volitional, (C) intellectual, (F) spiritual, (G) political, (H) financial, etc.— that all children seem to trigger. To arrive at the aristocracy of grandparenthood, they have also seen different facets of life separately with great clarity.

> Au.: Both have reached the truncated peak of life's pyramid, ascending it as untamed unicorns, yoked together as concerned centaurs, and now united as asocial androgynes, unconcerned about what people think of them or of the world they live in, with their sensual powers beginning to wane. **Z** as *Homo sapiens* will not "burn out".

As untamed unicorns they felt the hand of Big Brother, as concerned centaurs the embrace of Big Sister, as asocial androgynes they are growing confident of their progeny and have only their ancestors to thank for their genes. They have thus reverted to private ancestral sun-worship, personal and communal (when they follow the sun in the winters of their lives like other retirees whose blood runs cold and thin with aging).

Their only fear now is that in their second childhood, they will be treated as dinosaurs who have outlived their usefulness. And that neither can outlive the other for very long. And so, feeling intimidated by what lies ahead of both of them, their intimacy now seems more vulnerable. Can they last till death doth part them?

CAST of CHARACTERS REVISITED: Developmental Levels in Parentheses

The following happened to be the first case where (**A**) good and (**B**) right and (**F**) Godly had needed to be separated and is now compared with the next case, that of Xera (**X**, a widow), which was reported many years later.

These Ladies Are Not for Burning

Criminals accused of arson are usually male. Displaced psychoanalysts more Freudian than Freud and who also believe that women should concentrate on the three Ks (kuchen, kirsch, and kindergarten), explain their taking over backyard barbecues by claiming to be volunteer firefighters with fail-safe equipment: Their wives cannot easily prevent the spread of fire from forgotten embers without being singed!

1. Christopher Fry who is an aptly named religious playwright wrote *The Lady's Not for Burning*. Was he also a feminist, a "small fry" (prey to bigger fish), or fearful he would fry? *Homo domesticus* or *metropolus*?

2. The clinical challenge that triggered early exposition and later elaboration of our New Psychiatry was posed by a young, (**A'** + **B'**) unhappy and untidy homemaker: Her husband had chronically compared her unfavorably and invidiously with his "un-liberated" but happy (**A** + **B**) mother-heroine of a housekeeper. She divorced him, but worried that the apartment which they had shared and given up still contained residues of (**B'**) unrinsed suds.

3. Tess (**T, f**) seduced Bobby, an ex-con (**B'**), who had a prison record for arson, to burn the apartment, not to replace Xavier (**X, m**), her husband. Naturally, the fire died quickly on reaching still moist surfaces from her repeated rinsing. Also expectably, instead of going to prison, she was sent to us for our expert medical opinion. Our treatment recommendations were implemented without first sharing the underlying analyses in detail with Jay and George (**J** + **G**, socio-centric authorities).

4. Fortuitously, there was a similar incident reported by the news services many years later: Xera, a 63-year old widow, saw her living room as (**A' + B'**) a hopeless mess and set fire to it. She then went to the movies, and on return, assaulted the firemen who were trying to put out the fire. "I told them to stop, that the house was dirty." It was a total loss and the 'hopeless' housekeeper (**A' + B'**) was arraigned for arson. Unfortunately, we did not hear more about the "con-sequences" (*sic*) in Xera's case. It was probably not newsworthy, except locally.

But from comparative analyses, we can boldly make one comprehensive recommendation. (It may be unwelcome to all socio-centric law enforcers.) Both "arsonists" were using fire as (**F**) the ultimate purifier. What is adjudged as not (**A**) good enough by family standards prompted (**B'**) wrong-doing, thus sacrificing (**I**) personal autonomy and (**H**) property values. It also suggests that burning flame purifies, extreme heat punishes—in prison camp isolation holes as well as in hell—freezing hell will numb any feelings of pain.

Neither "arsonist" sought punishment or pain, nor felt any guilt. They (**A**) sought and (**B**) decided to be (**I**) "autonomous", emancipated by (**F**) all-consuming fire. Their value systems (**ii: F, G', H'. I**), not their virtues (**i: A, B**), were the crucial issues.

Neither (**K**) antidepressants nor (**G**) incarceration of the righteous but unrepentant "arsonists" will help them. Nor will either option change (**i**) family virtues or protect (**ii**) society's values (already secured by the police or fire department).

Both "arsonists" felt (**A**) the "need" to flee from the impasse (**F'**, if cleanliness is godly). Tess invited society's enemy to help, Xera took it upon herself to "liberate" herself. Tess found the "prudent" means (a convicted arsonist), our widow a "prudish" strength to cope with the impasse.

The "decision" (**B**) did away with the paralysis (**B'**) imposed by the impasse (**F'**) and enabled them to act.

Activity (**B**) made e-motion (**A**) superfluous until they were thwarted. a) Xera should have part-time help (**H**, if provident) and confidant (**A**, if accepting) when overwhelmed. b) Tess should be encouraged to make "imprudent" moves (**B'**).

Tess felt better (**A**) just dancing with abandon to rock music. Disco music that moves your feet (**B**) is almost as potent as sweet music that appeals directly to your heart (**A**), both bypassing deliberate thought (**C**).

Is it surprising that we (**iii**) "twist" or "rock and roll" when young? Or "toss and turn" when older but still cannot decide (**B'**)?

Would sharing the foregoing clinical analyses make bureaucratic authorities enthusiastic about our recommendations?

Does being (A) good or feeling good make you happy?

Not if yours is a jealous/righteous mother-in-law or God.

[Were the above attributes awarded by a jealous and righteous creature of His? If Christopher Fry's first (given) name tended him towards religious plays and "atavistic" means "ancestral", then this author is a "throwback" to the cave-man, though more grandfatherly (unconditionally loving, **A**) than God-fatherly (unconditionally forceful, **B**) as a therapist with dysfunctional people and families.]

Does being (**B**) right or (**F**) in the right make you happy?

Extended TREATMENT Review

The following case study illustrates how stages or levels of human senso-socio-sexual development (from **A** to **Z**) - can be used to illuminate clinical issues.

It is based on material presented to Dr. Otto Kernberg by Dr. Una A. Foreman-Isaiah for a symposium on "Narcissistic and Borderline Disorders" at UCLA, in the fall of 1982.

All names come from the initials assigned to different developmental stages. Should all psychiatrists be exemplars par excellence of A, C, D, F (or witch doctor), I, J, K, N, and Z?

Case History:
(Developmental levels in parenthesis)

(Added to original record)

Sonya X. Turner, is a 63-year old Caucasian actress, divorced, small-framed (5 ft., 100 lbs.), attractive and intelligent (I.Q. 130), born to travelling vaudeville performers, the older of two (junior's whereabouts unknown). Her early memories were unending lessons in preparation for a future stage career. She recalls loneliness, a sense of futility, and always a vague "depression".

Our diagnosis is indicated by the fictitious names and middle initial that we have given her: Sonya X. Turner-*Adams* *(Senso-socio-sexual Samplers)*. Kernberg might accept "borderline." (Kohut would opt for narcissism.)

Sonya has outgrown men like Turner but not all men or all children. Her life's odyssey has still in store for her a sexy (**Y**) May–Decemberhood and/or asexual (**Z**) grandparenthood.

Part of her future depends on a male Dr. Y. who can be Mr. Turner in transference and then, neither Freudian or Eriksonian, accept X. Under treatment, our case analysis becomes like family diagnosis, with the dyad of care-taker (S) and caregiver (Dr. Una A. F.-I. as "Mrs. Adams." her keeper) constituting our primary unit of observation. (The doctor's name was picked by the author.)

In her sexual development, Sonya (S) is the antithesis of **X**, though already older than **Y**. In her sensual development she is inferior to **A** (e.g., Abe blessed with his loyal keeper), had tried moving out for good like **B** and eventually failed, ending up "shocked" by **K** (during electro-"convulsive" therapy). In her social development, she never quite reached **I**'s, because her parents could not succeed like **H**, her father being a Turner.]

She remembers her father as effervescent, good-natured, but lacking in practical financial ability (unlike **H**), her mother as well-disciplined, interested in details and correctness, worried about such matters as financial security and the proper education of children (like **H**, unlike **X**). They may have originally been two people of similar spirit, but they seemed to have a complementary, asymmetrical relationship; he was the mover (like **B**), she was the nagger, the container (like **A**).

S. always felt transient, something apart, and was aware of the fact that their reason for being was to please an audience.

When S. was 11, her mother's urgent need for stability won, and the family settled down, father managing a theater, and mother keeping the books. The three of them had a radio show on the stage in the morning. Father began drinking and staying away from home more and more; her mother was more and more "alone, barren, angry and lost".

S. cannot recall being held, gazed at tenderly, or merely existing in peace with her mother. She warned S. that she should base her life on her career, her talents and her own wits (like **B**), and not trust men because they were all inadequate (like **T**) and not supportive (like **I**).

Other animals chose mates for sex, not companionship or partnership for farm chores, etc.

When S. could not decide between a blue or pink dress, her father's solution was buying them both (like **T**). One example, which to her is an ultimate symbol of love and life in a visceral sense was "when my dad lifted me up before he went to the theater, and I curled up to him resting my face on his shoulder, and I could feel the touch of his cheek on my face, and I could smell the after-shave cologne—such a secure and clean smell".

S. left home to work and study on a drama scholarship and began a successful acting career in her early 20's.

She married a wealthy, narcissistic, "immature" man (like **T**), had two sons by him and divorced him because of his excessive drinking.

Left with their baby-sitter, her 2-year-old son came down the stairs where his 5-year-old brother was playing with a toy gun just as S. was returning from grocery shopping. "An accident resulted", he lost his eye and "wears a patch to this day".

S.'s struggle to save his eye or provide him with a glass one so that he does not feel "insufficient" parallels her mother's frantic training of her daughter for the stage.

S.'s second marriage lasted 20 years. Five years after the wedding, when she was 39 (but more like **X**), her husband (like **T**) was involved with another woman.

S. was hospitalized due to depression and agitation, and again 19 years later for short periods, the last with dramatic results from electroconvulsive therapy. She was readmitted 3 years later in 1981, when her doctor (Una A.) started her on intensive, long-term, modified psychoanalytic and integrative individual psychotherapy. Her medication included Sinequan, Librium, and Valium with varying effectiveness. Her diagnoses at different times have been reactive psychosis, dependent, borderline and obsessive-compulsive personality, and involutional melancholia.

Progress during Treatment

(Comments by Author)

"On admission to a receiving ward where I am the staff psychologist, Sonya looked chronic and deteriorated, . . . moaning and groaning, grunting, burping, gasping and gulping, barking in a low guttural voice, body folding forward and suddenly jerking backwards, wringing her hands, scratching and pulling, gestures of clawing and gouging her eye . . . In marked contrast to her outward appearance, I was astounded by the intelligence with which she articulated her perceptions . . .

Sonya's sensual and social behavior are separable, as was her off and onstage life.

"In the Women's Group which I led, I was impressed by her ability to command the absorbed attention and interest of the members, who were usually distractible, irritable and intolerant of each other. I made this observation aloud. I further reflected that S.'s breathing and movement difficulties seemed to be of two types: one, a sucking and gulping in of air as though she was afraid that she had not had enough sustenance; and the other, the partial letting out of profound wailing and/or rage."

S. can still make her stage presence felt.

S. has become potentially one of careful Dr. Una's care-taking clients.

"S. then made eye-contact with me, and she began to pour out her anger toward her second husband who, after 25 years of marriage, had left her for a younger woman."

Dr. Una as "Mrs. A." was introduced to care-less "son-in-law," T.

Mothers-in-law tend to identify with abandoned daughters if they had also been abandoned. Has Dr. U been abandoned for a younger woman by her partner?]

"... 'I hate being old ... myself because I still love him, and am not enough for myself. My life means nothing without him ... I can't even hurt him because I have nothing which he wants. It is too late, it is too late. I can't make a go of it. I tried, but everything I did was only temporary, before I fell apart.'"

In fact, it is too soon. S. is not ready to be an ex-wife, much less to be different as X .

"... In addition to the naked terror and helpless pleading in her eyes, one eye, or a separate person within her, watched my reaction steadily in a cool, commanding manner."

S. has accepted her caregiver and now watches, as an actress, how her emotions affect her audience, just like the helpless, silently monitoring their rescue, or the child its babysitter. "Mrs. A." is not yet S.'s keeper but a role model as "Ms. U." waiting for Mr. Right.

"... Should I allow her to continue in the Women's Group?"

"Ms. U." is not yet "pregnant" with Sonya.

"... I told her ... that we would definitely make time soon for her ..."

"Ms. U" is pregnant, but not married. Will she "abort" or raise S. as a single parent?

"... 'If I met you one year ago, maybe even three months ago, I might have been saved, but now it's too late.'"

S. is not sure about being "Ms. U."'s bastard child.

"I then asked her ... if she felt necessary to warn me about her. I said that her perception of my kindness and innocence must worry her in the event I was seduced by her plight ... Without making a well-thought out, or conscious commitment on my part, and with unresolved ambivalences and ponderings, I realized that I had already committed myself to her, and her restoration."

"Ms. U." is now S.'s keeper.

"Ms. U." is now "Mrs. A."

"I had been touched by her anguish, her ability to feel things wholeheartedly with abandon, and by her refusal to be defeated by life ... Her hatred of the man who had wounded her in such a devastating way and her disillusion with herself because of her inability to extricate herself made this commitment obvious to me. I admired her, and her cry resonated with mine."

"... Many examples of sudden shifts in her mental activities were related to the emotions or regressive shifts ... Once, while Sonya walked beside me, she suddenly looked dazed, her face softening with suffused emotion, her voice and talk that of a small girl saying, 'Daddy, Daddy ... Daddy, I need you ...' When questioned she said she had seen the green 'Exit' sign of the ward and instantly thought she was in the theatre which her father managed when she was 11 years old ..."

S. is still yearning for the first Mr. T. and not yet ready to be the ex–Mrs. T. or to exchange him for "Mrs. A.'s" Mr. Right.

"... However, I wondered if her father's love, and father's person, were strong and substantial enough ...

"Mrs. A." thinks S. needs her own Mr. Right.

"Or was even this sole love-base contaminated by traumatic disappointments?"

". . . Her attempt at restoration was all through urgent actions . . . I decided that every contact and every act I made with her must be a movement toward hope and legitimacy for her existence . . . The rest would then come."

"Mrs. A.'s" Mr. Right will be all (?) that is necessary.

"Six weeks after admission, S. was transferred, as planned, to an open ward . . . When she came to my office four days later, she looked like a different woman. When she saw me, there was a momentary unsure look . . ."

S., the lifelong exhibitionist thought she had lost her best fan.

". . . 'I am the sickest person there . . . I know they are all thinking I don't belong there . . .

S. is wondering if she is worth keeping, and seeking reassurance as a care-taker from her care-giver.

". . . I encouraged her to sense out someone on the ward, with whom she could feel at ease, and express her fears."

"Mrs. A." tells her caretaker to look for a second caregiver.

". . . As she no longer saw me every day, I increased our sessions to four times a week . . .

"The partial fragmentation lasted one month before she could take hold of herself. She began to adapt to the ward routines."

The "narcissistic" (Kohut's special clientele) are often misdiagnosed as "borderline" by "narcissistic" Kernberg after "decompensating" during his short absences to talk about them in conferences.

". . ." She discussed how she can't ever remember being herself, and that she doesn't know who she really is. She feels that she has always been a 'personality kid', and has done everything by playing roles."

This is perhaps literally a peerless case of human domestication to entertain adults like a trained dog performing tricks to please.

". . . Even though S. had no idea what she truly (sic) was, she was absolutely certain that if the truth be known, she would be totally unacceptable by (sic) anyone, and she shall be really alone permanently . . ."

This is why some celebrities need lots of applause, not out of hungry narcissism, but only when they briefly impersonate short lived fictional characters.

"After a calm and enjoyable two weeks, she fell off her bike and hit her right shoulder and nose on the grass. She said that she wasn't injured, but it shook her up . . ."

Just as a performing artist might, like a violinist who sprains either hand.

"By the time she came to her next therapy session, she was just as badly off as the day she was admitted four months previously... 'I am slipping back, I was doing so well but a girl made a nasty remark and it hurt my feelings. She said, 'You should have a face lift because you have so many wrinkles." She also told me that I was too old to ride a bike.'"

S. is thinking (i) sensually of her aging skin and how her mind manages her muscles (kinesthesia, proprioception).

"'It made me think how old I was, and how I have to start all over again and find a routine job and make a new life for myself, alone.'"

S. is worrying (ii) socially about a career.

"'I may never find a man I could love. There will be no enchantment in my life ever.'"

S. is now (iii) sexually ripe to be Turner's ex-wife but not yet ready to be Ms. Xerxes.

"... I also knew that I was about to go on a vacation for three and a half weeks... S. was distressed about the anticipated separation... 'I shall have no friend at all. There will be no one for me. I don't think I could make it. Even now I am barely holding myself between the times I see you . . . Something terrible is going to happen to me. I am afraid to see you go . . .' I felt helpless."

This is literally so and S.'s "mother" had no one for her to help with her daughter.

". . . I was saying to myself that she had other staff on the ward who were devoted to her, who were in fact stronger than I . . . She will be all right once I am gone."

If Kernberg shares this rationalization, it explains his surprise at the decompensation that greets him on his return from speaking tours.

"I even discounted my intuitive sense of alarm that S. was actually warning me of something, and my presence was essential . . . as my inflated sense of self-importance. I even went so far as to conclude that she might even be better off without me, and that our relationship may be weakening her. I hoped that I would find a stronger person on my return."

If the hope that one may be dispensable is self-destructive in the long run, Kernberg tests such rationalization repeatedly to prove himself wrong.

(Where constancy helps Kohut's clients, Kernberg consistently withdraws farther from his "borderlines".)

"Since then I have learned afresh, never to be forgotten, something I had known all along... One person's sensitive devotion and constancy can save another by offering an experience of unity, continuity, and meaning to one's existence."

Questing "identities" plus contiguity = continuity -> constant though discontinuous interdependence

". . . For three weeks she deteriorated progressively . . . her finger nails were clipped to prevent injuries to her eyes and face, etc."

Did the ward wonder about her one-eyed son or about Oedipus plucking his eyes?

(Freud probably was projecting (thinking of himself) and therefore called their conflict "oedipal," before he finally concluded—after the death of his own father—that his patients were not deflorated by their fathers.)

". . . I returned a few days earlier than planned. When she saw me her face lightened with relief and pleasure... and she was smiling and calm during the entire 60 minutes."

S. is a seasoned trouper, a professional actress, which means she doesn't have to like the face she puts on for effect as demanded by the role that she is playing. Alcoholics can speak their lines without hesitating even when intoxicated.

". . . But I noticed something quite uncharacteristic, which made me feel disturbed. Her flow of thought was more halting than ever before. Even when she was most disturbed, the flow had been fluid and smooth."

S. is treading the border between compensated and decompensated function (not physical but mental or sensual [or **C'**] and not psychological nor social).

(She is in a "borderline state of mind" (Schmideberg's version), bordering on psychosis, which is different from being a borderline personality (or Kernberg's attempted denial of culpability for absenting himself from his "borderline patients" to lead seminars about them). Melitta Schimedeberg was Melanie Klein's daughter. (Against all expectations, Dr. Klein was the first to see depression and paranoid tendencies in infants.)]

". . . After the last session when (we) began anew, she showed a sudden and almost miraculous change in her stability."

This indicates resiliency or lability (organic but not necessarily irreversible structural instability).

". . . Unfortunately, however, her next appointment had to be cancelled as I had to appear in court. When she came to my office the following day, all her physiological symptoms were upon her again."

The unscheduled absence of the keeper/caregiver was the proverbial "last straw" to break the back of the caretaker.

". . . She explained, 'There is a "crack" in the absolute love I have had for you. I hate myself for it. Rationally, I know about a therapist needing a vacation. I am glad that you had a rest from me. Did you spend some time with your son?' (Her face softening.) . . ."

S. wants to be acknowledged not only as a caretaker but as a caregiver to her own sons.

"... 'Even though I felt deserted by you, the problem isn't that I doubted your love. I do know you care about me. But that doesn't help because it's not in me to forget and mend once I am wounded.' I wasn't sure whether she was grieving more for herself or apologizing to me ..."

S. was talking about the son she cannot mend.

"... My sadness was indescribable. I saw a profoundly wounded, tragic woman who had sustained so many traumatic disappointments, rebuffs, and betrayals in her search for love that—in order to give herself a semblance of any dignity—it was imperative that she took action on her behalf against someone who had violated and injured her if she were to have any hope of living with herself ... I told her that her tragic dignity humbled me."

Is this role reversal, with lines that can be spoken by either protagonist or antagonist?

"Subsequently, her agitation and physiological symptoms increased, even to the point of 'hitting her head on the floor and pulling out clumps of her hair.'"

For differential diagnosis, this is more somesthetic violence (**B'**), in the absence of her father's caresses (**A**), than kinesthetic (more sexual).

"(She) never missed a session, and she continually expressed, 'I don't feel the same. You don't look the same. It is too late. I am hopeless.'... The question of E.C.T. was raised ... I thought of adding a male therapist.

"... She saw Dr. Y. eight times over the next month, while keeping her usual appointments with me. She drew some comfort from this relationship, and repeatedly said how fine and understanding a man he was."

I would have seen her conjointly, since S. had no past experience of parents working harmoniously. The time to see her separately is when she can stand on her own two feet and needs to see an example of someone single but stronger to imitate, then emulate.

"... One day she said, her face softening (again), 'I love you, you are a lovely person, you would go to any extent for me. Please don't let me give you up.'"

"Mrs. A." is both S. and the son they must not desert.

"All the crinkled wrinkles on her face smoothed away for a few moments . . ."

Not only our voices, but our faces change, with any memory crossing our minds. Distant memories make us look younger and feel as old as we think.

". . . and yet, her physiological distress did not diminish. If anything, she became ill. I began to see her daily . . . She talked of her sons."

Her sons are now motherless as she is fatherless.

". . . She worried about my loneliness, and she felt that I was alone and did not have enough of (a) man's love. She could not get this thought out of her mind."

Is she thinking of herself as well, and as a daughter?

"Even though her worry for my fatigue and loneliness had tenderness, and these softened her overall tension, this did not stay the progressive physical deterioration to the point of developing temperatures and being incontinent of urine and stool at times.

"She had more difficulty in swallowing. The worst kind of growling began. She began gasping, pulling her hair, yelling, 'I have gone crazy'."

She has become her sons, with the labile physiology of the very young. Growling and hair-pulling is her atavistic self (primates groom each other in a manner not unlike foreplay, and infants put themselves to sleep pulling on their hair).

"She said she was having an 'epileptic fit'. She urinated on the ward, she passed gas during a session, which is most uncharacteristic of her, and for which she was both deeply ashamed and frightened."

S. is indirectly asking for ECT (electroconvulsive therapy) and angry that she is not heard with her body language.

". . . She said, 'I can't control my body. My body is changing. It is turning to stone. I am becoming an animal.'"

I don't know what "turning to stone" means unless it is loss of animation. But it is negated immediately. (Did she go from connatural to convivial, from mineral or vegetable to animal?)

"After three months since her relapse, she had lost 20 pounds, her weight reaching an all time low of 85 pounds . . ."

Is she "stone cold", unexcitable, anhedonic and unerotic? Patients suffering from 'anorexia nervosa' bring down their weight to pre-pubescent levels to defend psychosocially against getting pregnant. Their ovaries cooperate hormonally and physiologically and they cease menstruating.

[But there is no recorded case of "anorexia nervosa" after menopause. (Nor of "borderline personality", either.)]

". . . No matter where she started now, all thoughts were centered around one theme - her 'imperfection', her shortcomings, and her failing herself . . . Then she developed the obsessional rumination: 'If I came five minutes earlier from shopping, my son David would not have lost his eye. My beautiful son lost his eye, and it ruined his character and his happiness . . .'"

At least, her son is now separate from her no matter how much pain the separation cost her. If they had stayed together, mother and ovum, he would not yet be "imperfect".

". . . Secondarily, she focused on her perception of my depression for which she felt responsible . . . She thought that I was absolutely without a man, and I was poor as a woman, and this was due to her insatiable need for me."

This is projective identification "par excellence". She is talking of herself.

"She felt responsible for her mother losing all her vitality. And now this same failure was repeating itself with me. Her final, focal, organizing thought came to rest on having done harm to her son. She became preoccupied with death."

Mrs. A. is going the way of her mother.

S.'s struggling truly dignifies her, and had ennobled her enough to stay married while her sons needed a family, like her mother did with more personal, less maternal success.

"The preparations for E.C.T. were complete... She was afraid that 'her brain would be scrambled'."

She needed reassurance about sensual more than social or sexual integrity.

". . . She began to shake and say she was having convulsions inside, 'like an earthquake', and wanted an autopsy when she died so that 'they'll know' what was going on inside her."

S.'s curiosity will not be dampened by death, since dying is not suicide. She will not kill herself. She is trying to duplicate the motor seizures ECT produces without interfering with sensations.

"Her horror was not only that she didn't know why she was suffering so, but that no one seemed to understand . . ."

The customer is always right. When we are wrong, we call them psychotic, when they are merely out of touch with our reality.

"After endless vacillating, she consented to ECT. She received 14 treatments."

The first is always the hardest to get underway, and the most hazardous, but not to the brain.

Brain death is not likely. Drugs to reduce muscular contractions may affect non-skeletal muscles in the heart and diaphragm.

(Without muscle relaxants that paralyze respiration, the hazard would be confined to weakened bones pulled by stronger muscles.)

"She had a miraculous recovery after the first treatment . . . Within two weeks, . . . she had gained 12 pounds, . . . gone on community trips . . . cheerful, joking and laughing . . . exultant . . . could not believe this 'sudden joyous turn' . . . and how outspoken she had become, etc."

Probably explains why she received lithium on prior admissions, to abort hypomania.

"Then came a day I was shocked to speechlessness. She came to her appointment, ran to me, with joy in her face, and said to me, I am glad to see you, Dr. F-I. I didn't see you since last . . .' (naming the month of my return from vacation five months ago)."

ECT produces retrograde amnesia, and S. had been, in her transference, misidentifying people in the past whom she wants to remember less vividly and painfully.

(Whenever the clinical picture confuses, rule out prior intensive psychotherapy, electrical (e.g., electroconvulsive treatment or ECT) or chemical assault on the brain with drugs or alcohol. Then consider possible early relapse or acute (*sic*) convalescence.)

". . . She talked of her golden years in Hollywood, of what she did and with whom… (They) 'were received by others as "tall stories", "bragging" . . . These responses by others wounded her. She felt ashamed and ugly'."

Only the depressed feel ugly, only when you are not depressed can you act ugly.

". . . She began to express her irritations and anger openly. '. . . Some staff members yelled at me and told me "we want your old self back. You were sweeter and more considerate before. Now you are so bossy and obnoxious we can't stand you."'"

This is a good test and early treatment for relapsing depression in the hands of professionals. If the patient talks back, not to worry.

". . . She withdrew and again became fearful and hyperventilating."

Only the anxious hyperventilates, not the depressed.

". . . She experienced the authorities in her life as demanding, resolutely and bellicosely stripping her of pleasant illusions, dreams, sparkles, imaginations and hope, the very stuff which had been keeping her afloat, which gave her reason for continuing."

She is speaking against house arrest. Not to worry yet.

"Her new assertiveness was paper-thin when faced with the well-practiced rigidity of some people in the real world. She raged against her weakness, which burst forth in her consciousness, and she felt that she would really go crazy."

Now start worrying. The customer may just be right again. Especially if she had been proven to be so once before.

(Await further developments to clarify the clinical picture.)

"In her panicky and desperate effort to hold her ground and assert her position she saw in herself a raging and raving woman just like her own mother, whose angry and strained desperation she had so feared and hated. Now her despair was complete, and her 'lowest bottom' seemed endless."

If she identifies with her mother, she'd survive like her.

"By the beginning of . . . (the next month), she began pulling out clumps of hair, wringing her hands, hyperventilating, and being incontinent of urine."

If her appetite goes, think again of ECT.

"'I don't want ECT, I hate to have it done again.'"

This is different from being afraid of it. You can only hate if you're not depressed from hating only yourself. Suicides murder themselves.

"By now her emotional tie with me and her lucidity were fully restored... I told her that an "emotional upset" has its own container... I asked (her) to give attention to her glandular system, allow it to feel her emotions... and to allow the water to flow in her body. To this day, I do not know why this worked, but she began to sweat, and she kept sweating for the entire session, wiping her face again and again. She said, 'I am all wet'."

S. no longer had to piss (or fart) in anger at her mother-keeper.

". . . (She) continued to sweat during the next three sessions . . . She began to dream, almost nightly, for a while."

Were they "wet dreams"?

Is she getting younger herself?

"The theme was mostly her relationship with husband with traumatic ruptures involving 'other younger women'."

"She began to recall endlessly, many details about her 'transient' days, . . . their perpetual struggle in pleasing the human multitude called, 'audience'."

Listen to the lines, closely.

". . . She is beginning to have more diverse emotions . . . and feel them through, rather than 'spitting them out' . . . She has recovered her old capacity to laugh, to see the ludicrous in life."

She will not only survive, she may yet prevail.

"She has just touched on, and has not yet worked through, . . . the possibility of living alone and living a reduced life, and eventually dying."

The caretaker will face aging, as soon as her keeper/caregiver is ready to risk another transitional crisis because S. is getting stronger. She is getting more reconciled to being the ex-wife with an empty nest (which may be better than Ms. U. emptily waiting for Mr. Right), and might yet find temporary refuge from aging as X., with or without a face-lift.

". . . She now has many relationships with others with varying degrees of intimacy and satisfaction."

Social relationships cannot make up for sensual satisfaction, especially among the hungry, and intimacy allows only sharing of secrets, not sexual fulfillment.

(This is beautiful work, whose artistry is diminished by analysis. In our professional work, it is more important that our heart is in the right place, than that our thoughts are in order. In academic teaching, one has to be more orderly in order not to mislead the receptive.)

"There are personal imperatives in each of us which cannot be ignored or changed without mutilating one's spirit and soul."

Or at least, one's beliefs. That was not "Mrs. A." but Dr. F.-I. agreeing with Dr. Kohut and Maslow behind Dr. Kernberg's back. (Maslow makes sex basic and spirituality (**F**) supreme.)

DISCUSSION

> A great man is one who can turn a paradox (e.g., class
> discrimination in the genteel South) into a platitude
> (e.g., school integration pushed by Boston Brahmins)
> within his lifetime.
>
> —Isaiah Berlin

In Piaget's senso-mental (cognitive) schema, Sonia would vacillate between sensorimotor and concrete operations (pre-conceptual in following the script and intuitive as a performing artist), despite her latent ability to abstract. *[Table 10]* How does knowing this help the patient?

In Erikson's psychosocial "life-cycle" *[Table 9A]*, Sonia would be searching for an identity, but handicapped because she cannot emancipate herself from her loyalties and find trustworthy intimates. Where will she find a different social, not psychological or secret, identity at 63?

In Freud's psychosexual evolution *[Table 8A]*, S. is arrested at the oral biting stage from being oedipally frustrated. How can she stop biting if she is starved?

In our senso-socio-sexual development *[Table 4E]*, we agree with Piaget *[Table 12]* that Sonia is emotional, with Erikson *[Table 14]* that she is individualistic, with Freud that she is trying to be assertive when she cannot be exhibitionistic. How can someone not be exhibitionistic as an actress, assertive or individualistic when frustrated, emotional except when freely mobile, or resigned when exhausted?

The patient fights (**A'**) despair with (**B**) action or (**C'**) fiction. Lies never hurt anyone but the one deceived who is feared, including the punitive self. The guilty self then accepts the penalties for (**B'**) wrongdoing, (**C'**) fantasied or not, and there is no arguing with the fanciful. When the guilt-ridden (**F'**) acts (**B**) on their illusions (**C'**), they (**A'**) hurt themselves.

1. The diagnostic question is whether the patient feels (**F'**) guilty or (**H'**) deprived. Her world started to come apart long after her son lost his eye but soon after her age became a factor in her sexual life. She still looked attractive, but not to her husband with the wandering eye.

2. As to therapeutic stratagem, we disagree with Maslow, in that sex has its own kinetics or schedule throughout life independent of ideology, and with Erikson and Freud. "Menopaused," Sonia cannot—in Maslow's physiosocial, Freud's psychosexual, and Erikson's psychosocial, theories—find hope and happiness with a man younger than her father or husband who does not need a symbolic mother nor a spiritual sister.

Neither Maslow, Erikson, or Freud, nor Piaget, Kernberg, or Kohut will map a separate treatment approach for S. just because she happens to be female. Yet, as they age the problems they face are tougher. Empty nests belong to mothers. Females can safely reproduce only with a limited number of eggs.

Sexist theories of development, by denying gender, fail to see also that the battle between the sexes has nothing to do with equality (some women are "more equal" than men, they are simply less organized even if more numerous).

The gender gap is the difference in age and divergent trends in the separate development of the two sexes, even in the womb.

3. As to prognosis, the next stage in our senso-socio-sexual life cycle, not given to everyone, and therefore poorly studied as yet, is (Z) grandparenthood. That is the least stressful niche of all, if you welcome kids. (There is no mention of this becoming an event in our patient's life. Those afraid of aging do not like being called "grandma.")

CONCLUSION

We travel through time past generations of ancestors in their sacrificial altars of worship and struggle to survive and prevail, eventually to fail and give way to the young growing older every day in their separate ways. In the end all become as one as we had been before, in our noisy but inarticulate beginning. (s/5)

HISTORICAL DYNAMICS vs. KINETICS

In anthropology, there is individuation (sensual, **A-E**), acculturation (social, **F-O**), and reproduction (sexual, **P-Z**). What is sensual, e.g., creativity (**E**) in art or science may become a cultural icon, and so may reproduction be recruited in the service of society. In both cases, domestication takes over the person.

Society is a synthetic concoction like psychoactive drugs. In pharmacology, there is pharmacodynamics and pharmacokinetics. In psychotherapy, there is psychodynamics and psychokinetics like transference neuroses, which is allostatic. In our species, there is homeostasis in *Homo sapiens*, allostasis in *H domesticus* and *H metropolus*.

Like psychoanalysis and psychopharmacology, history has its own dynamics and kinetics. Its dynamics dictate what it does to those under its spell, whether they know it or not.

> (We can no longer pretend that the earth is flat or at the center of the universe even if some still believe there is heaven above and hell below, but only for us. This is necessary to preserve the power of temptation to separate the brain from the body by promising us the freedom to be willful or willing.)

"Kinetics" is what those who know their history do deliberately to vindicate themselves or unwittingly to advance its dynamics.

> A baby thinks its mother is part of itself, and so should it until it separates from her on its own, but not before or it will later "want to make a difference", i.e., pay its dues for membership in another group and create a ripple effect which soon drowns in a host of other ripples after "Andy Warhol's 15 minutes of fame" for all.
>
> (Time as a dimension is a human invention to offset the reach of determinism on a scale beyond life itself. Traditions enthrone time and end up as superstitions that allow followers to hide their own redundancy.)

Science tends to frown on randomness, even if validated by numbers that make pure coincidence suspect. The numbers may raise valid hypothesis but disproving it requires more than analogy, which only helps us understand what is new: e.g., DNA as entwined snakes was an inspired idea out of a dream, but how DNA informs our lives required working out how we are different yet not random.

Consider this about food and sex chains: Plants preceded us. Once they have produced enough oxygen, we began to spread. We started to spread their seeds wherever we went. Is this what is behind our mobility that plants do not enjoy? Do they vegetate so that we can have the energy to move around, or the other way around? And are we around to keep viruses virtually immortal? Do we spend most of our lives in virtual rehabilitation from the handicaps which we are born with that other animals outgrow earlier in their youth? Are there other species who abuse their young and old dependents and mates as badly as we do?

Our tomcat eats nurslings that he did not sire in order for their mothers to stop nursing and go into heat sooner. Praying mantids and black widows kill their dispensable male partners (and some men light a cigarette or urinate after coitus to verify that nothing is missing). Both are not provoked by familiarity that drives the contemptuous to kill. Soldier ants like all animals kill for territory, not over beliefs. If all who kill eat their victims, there will be no war without epidemics of bulimia.

The first thing we need to know about any phenomenon is its history (all will be context-sensitive), even that of human consciousness (content-selective), which begins as self-consciousness when an infant accidentally bites its toe.

> [This reminder might be of interest to Dr. Penrose and readers of his Shadows of the Mind as well as to others of similar persuasion who see consciousness as the crux of our humanity, and the basis as well as the bias that allows information to spread: But there is no "mind", there is only "minding", nor "free will" but just being willing or unwilling (willful).]

Contextual (lateral, rather than critical (linear), thinking also eliminates consciousness of guilt for all but original sin, which funds churches. English bulldogs and human beings are the only species who, without elective Cesarean section, are born with a headache worse than any hang-over after each New Year's Eve carousing to forget or remind us how serious our recurring resolutions for the future were. Our evolution has required almost routine surgery to release our head (that has grown bigger than our mothers' breeches) without permanently damaging the vaginal walls holding it back during normal delivery. No helmet can protect already damaged goods or take the place of eggshells.

[Original sin until now satisfactorily explains the pain of childbirth for both uneducated mother and child. The less satisfactory it is to explain suffering, the shorter our list of New Year resolutions and the less we need drug dealers. One also cannot be responsible for any neighborhood which invites either reformers and "fun" lovers.

[But, unlike animal ingenuity which does not burden its owner, human creativity makes us feel additionally irresponsible if we cannot change direction. Yet, talented or not, the child is still father to the man and no man is an island. (A ship's captain may steer the soul's vessel without a compass or strings attached, but not towards any destination he can take personal credit for inventing.)]

Parroting what others have written betrays our ancestry, intellectual as well as social. From these seeds planted in the past come the fruits which we harvest in the present. A pair of believers makes it a "*folie a deux.*" New recruits may transform it into a gossip circle or mutual admiration society and become the nucleus of a gang or political party.

Rationalysis of sensual, social and sexual endowments and developments cannot just be separated into discreet and separate stages, but transitions in-between as they co-evolve must also be studied. (Is this con-vivial thermokinetics as opposed to con-natural thermodynamics?)

A discontinuous fossil record from so-called "Acts of God" like flash floods or volcanic eruptions did not disprove natural selection. Senso-socio-sexual transitions depend on the diagnostic skills of the clinician.

NATURAL "EXPERIMENTS": EXPERIENTIAL AND CLINICAL

[This section contains very unorthodox and therefore challenging findings to guide inexperienced practitioners. Like most medical students, post-graduate trainees see in patients or themselves everything described in print that they recently read.

Thus we need to look harder for subtle differences rather than more obvious similarities. In the following sub-sections, try to pinpoint the differences, and formulate them according to the stages of development involved.

[Disconfirm any of the author's formulation whenever possible: Whether you succeed or not, your understanding will increase so that the next "dissection" does not intimidate, deter, or frustrate. (In clinical training, the author deliberately excludes the last theory the residents swallowed and had not digested but with instant relief regurgitates to explain the next patient's predicament. Even scientists must also believe when unsure, even if only in science as Science. It is not so much that we should not impose our values, but that we cannot do without a few.)]

Random (unselected) experiences have intrinsic validity rather than proven certainty, and high probability rather than exact replicability (from selected sampling). They are widely rather than uniformly applicable for practical use.

Clinical diagnosis that is more than merely descriptive requires comprehensive understanding, not just nodding acquaintance. Otherwise, any yield will be more rhetorical (intellectual, **C**) than additionally applicable (potentially effective, **B**). If (**A'**) emotionally disturbing, the gain will be even less.

It is also a cumulative process: the more carefully you read about actual cases, the richer the yield even in the absence of the patient, everyone of whom is a book unto hirself (*sic*).

FAMILY THERAPY FINDINGS, CORRELATIONS

1. Touching is better than talking for healing wounds, candor leaves them gaping without draining abscesses.

2. Before we acquired a "backbone", our "sympathetic" nervous system made us fight or flee, willing or not. The willful in chronic danger risks "stomach" ulcers. Feeding (digestion) and the fourth "f" (successful sex) depend on the "parasympathetic" system. Any threat of violence in the vicinity precludes sex. (His partner can enjoy the lion's supremacy, undisturbed by my presence. That is what makes power the best aphrodisiac.) To

"know" more, today's Adam and Eve still hide behind bushes or between bed sheets. You, too?

FAMILY POLITICS Testable (D, 2 and 3) or Usable (creactive, B + E, 6 and 7):

(Unlike *Homo domesticus* whose soul is always at risk, for *Homo metropolus* and the New Woman, everything that (s)he perceives takes a political coloring, and therefore becomes very personal and unerotic (and no longer romantic and sexual). Fertility is squandered in both subspecies, unlike among Homo sapiens.) *[Table 16]*

1. Love and sincerity may not be enough when lust is lost.

2. Sex is more senso-muscular (kinesthetic, than talking and touching.

   When lust is lost, there is less fornication (parasympathetic, like eating) and more aggression (sympathetic fighting and fleeing).

   (Those who postulate fusion of sex and aggression are confused (*sic*) by the noise and violence of the primal scene that they may have audited or visualized as children outside the master bedroom. Secrecy fosters fantasies.)

3. There is deafness to or flight from complaints, and fighting demands for explanation.

   (In order to reduce distractibility in family therapy, the author usually holds the youngest in his lap until it feels drawn to a particular member of its natural family.)
   (Almost invariably it goes to whomever is hurting the most.)

4. Aggressive verbiage is more literal (specific) and legalistic (prudish and prim) than seductive, which is more lyrical or cryptic. (Fundamentalists and constructionists go by the letter of Biblical ghost-writers or Constitutional forefathers as their rusty but heavy anchor to reality.)

    a. In dysfunctional families, words are used with precision as ammunition with vehemence but without *gusto*. They distinguish us from inarticulate animals or discotheque dancers whose proprioception is stimulated by lust and whose non-verbal signals are quite unmistakable for being more pelvic than cerebral.

    b. All communication (redundancies) becomes more verbal and there is less communion (body language).

5. Because (**A+J**) charity and (**B+F**) forgiveness must start at home, it can fail as the only sanctuary outside mental asylums where one need not be one's (**A**) sweet or (**C**) reasonable self and can truly be (**I**) one's own "Wo-Man" (unlike churches which expect those seeking sanctuary to behave inside, even if they have committed wrong-doing outside).

(Out of this experience, I have derived a new group ethos without which a leader cannot be a healer: All members must have the freedom to feel (**A**) like a child, the freedom to choose (**B**) like a toddler, or the freedom to think (**C**) like a juvenile, and the freedom to compare (**D**) like an adult. All groups must be given equal time, seniority has no priority. Creativity (**E**), of course, may be precocious.)

(Psychiatrists listen to combinations of (**A**) feelings and (**C**) meanings, intellectuals only hear meanings, intuitionists only feel feelings. Psychiatrists have to be anti-intellectual and counterintuitive.)

Latent Domestic Aggression

Where once family togetherness was trendy, personal relationships have recently been emphasized and lately replaced by interpersonal communication. The result is to blur the differences between parenting and togetherness, sexual relations and relationships, and information (non-redundant) and communication (repetition).

6. Some families break-up because a member wants others to be (**A**) good who are only willing to be (**B**) fair.

7. Family therapy also helps clarify jealousy, whether vengeful from envy (talomania) or not (cf. Ortega, "Delusions of Jealousy," *Psychoanalysis and the Psychoanalytic Review*, vol. 46, No. 4, Winter 1959).

   a. As is both necessary and useful separately for the jealous or the envious, monogamy (suspicious spouse) and monotheism (grudging God), respectively, both also promise to punish the infidel and reward the faithful in the foreseeable future.

   b. It is this promise rather than the seductive analogy of the unwatched "watch-maker" that makes the homologous animistic faith powerful and fascinating for both lonely human or captive chimp.

   (Here for the first time can we connect monolithic faith and monotonous sex [unlisted even as a perversion] with dogmatic incuriousity or hidden fantasies [sexual or satanic].)

8. A house-bound wife who was well-provided for (1) but does not want (a) to fight boredom with adultery, nor (b) their child to take her husband's place—unlike the caged and "kept" chimpanzee who smothers her offspring at leisure when there is nothing better to do—(2) can resort to hypnosis-resistant subterfuge to keep her provident husband home. For the child's sake, this is preferable, but for the adults, silent to violent rage may punctuate family harmony (cf. 3 [e], below).

RAGE REACTIONS

Without classifying their clinical characteristics, it would be difficult to influence the differing patterns in emergence and/or nonappearance of rage.

1. Normal (potentially explosive, verbal or otherwise):

    a. Passive-receptive women (often taken for granted) $= A - Q', f.$

    b. Strong silent men (entrapment -> discovered weakness -> potentially "e-motional," sometimes lonely and hungry; includes professional listeners silently scorning equally hungry and scorned "children") $= W, m (B/A') - A'V,$ f or $AU, m.$

2. Potentially violent nonverbally:

    c) Scorned adults, wanting to be dominated by a partner, straight or gay $= A/V, f$ or $A/U, m$

    (respectively)

    d) Rejected adolescents, wanting to be independent $= B' \times I$

3. Unprovocative (passive-dependent):

    e. Clinging-controlling (hypnotherapy resistant) $= A \times G$
    f. Obedient-expectant (compliance begets cooperation) $= B \times J$

4. "Borderline":

    g. Submissive-subversive (pathological liars: "Doctor should know without having to be told.") $= A \times I'$
    h. Cloying-castrating type $= A + T', f$

5. Provocative:

    i. Caustic-contrary (pathologically honest but hostile) $= C - G$
    j. Impetuous-imperious $= B' \times G$

6. Defensive offenders:

    k. Stubborn (true territoriality in "humanimals") $= B \times G$
    l. Rigid (absent in animals) $= C \times G$
    m. Apologetic (appeasement gestures in animistic "manimals") $= A' \times F$
    n. Suicidal (absent among animals) $= B' \times F$

(In New Guinea, when sick persons can no longer talk, they are buried alive, because it is thought that the soul resides in the throat, and once it is silent, the person must be dead.) Such myths explain a lot of suicide and assisted suicide in modern societies.)

(Excerpted from Ortega, "A Psychiatric Odyssey of Personal Discoveries," VOICES, *The Art and Science of Psychotherapy*, Summer, 1974.)

NEW DIAGNOSES FOR COMMON DISCOMFITURES

Albert Einstein claims that "it is the theory which decides what can be observed." That may be true for near-invisible particles in theoretical physics. However, the following diagnoses were made before senso-socio-sexual rationalysis could simplify their classification.

Out of different world experiences, we have slowly developed context-specific, content-independent categories (below) from modern dilemmas *[k/Violence]* which slide sideways into transitional phases within adjacent stages of development in the **ABZ**'s of life. It is more spatial (topological) than linear (narrow).

(Thus this book grew almost organically, like we do or most enterprises have, not according to an agenda, which we often establish and abandon with equal frequency.)

These are separate people's "hang-ups" which must be treated differently. Not everyone should be encouraged to "let it all hang out." Nor should anyone be ridiculed even when invited to do so: Never take away another's song and leave him without a lullaby.

None of the following have comparable labels even in popular literature on human behavior. The Psychopathology of everyday life is of limited value as nosology. For practical use, a classification of Common Discomfitures allows intervention to be tailored to the conflict.

(Clinical diagnoses serve statistical tables, but problems have to be solved on a case-by-case basis, with or without using mythical figures like Oedipus or unicorns, etc., as a springboard for discussion. Senso-socio-sexual exemplars illustrate the core issues.)

The following discoveries are veritable mutations (combinations of segmented groups from the **ABZ**'s of Life), either context-free (in-vulnerable) or -sensitive (fragile or friable).

Suffix of "-chondriasis" for context-sensitive psycho-socio-pathology signify vulnerability that is popular among kindred spirits with chronically "bleeding hearts."

(In screening applicants who want to be specialists in psychiatry, author would rather they had not decided on becoming a psychiatrist before entering medical school. Changing one's "mind" afterwards is more realistic.)

CONTEXT-SENSITIVE Diagnoses

1. The worried well who become neurotic (worried sick) are fearful that what they are afraid of will *not* happen. This is the reason why reassurance does not pay them or their caregivers any dividends.
2. Forcing them to accept that it will not happen—an implosive tactic (e.g., that the plane will not plummet when the fearful fly), strategically titrated—sometimes works, e.g., with phobo-chondriac clients, usually in the hands of non-phobo-chondriac caregivers with a different domestication diagnosis by triangulation. (Are your doctors *Homo sapiens*, *Homo domesticus* or *Homo metropolus*?)

    The implosive approach to phobic patients is like taking their breath away with a solar plexus blow when hyperventilating, instead of forcing them to breathe into a paper bag to collect and re-cycle hot air.

Otherwise, be gentle, especially with professionals (better treated as extrasensitive paranoid "porcupines") whose patienthood is disowned if not projected.

(Notice that context-sensitive diagnoses (below) multiplies or confronts (subtracts) coevolving expectations of family and/with social development of domesticity.)

3. These new context (-"chondriasis") -sensitive diagnoses symbolically and figuratively invite options to strike or stroke the patient's extra-soft "underbelly":

a) hyperchondriasias   **(B × I)**   perfectionism from precocious toilet training

b) hypochondriasis   **(B × F)**   near fulfillment with the joy of almost living

c) socio-chondriasis   **(A - H)**   near fulfillment in almost earning

d) schizo-chondriasis **(D - F)**   near fulfillment of nearly yearning

e) cyclo-chondriasis   **(I - A)**   fear of the joy of almost hating

f) para-chondriasis   **(F - A)**   fear of the joy of just trusting

g) hysto-chondriasis   **(B - A)**   fear of the joy of nearly winning

h) phobo-chondriasis   **(G - B)**   fear of the joy of not winning

Strategically "situated" behind the cartilaginous false ribs (chondrocostal), each conflict in the pit of their "soft-belly" reminds the doctor to allow the patient to catch his breath while suffering from mental stress, without strenuous measures (extra strain produces hyperventilation, which serves as a signal to desist).

(We do not crawl on our belly as much as we are serpentine in our mind in deceiving ourselves about reality. Why are we the only species who needs swaddling clothes after we leave our mother's womb, and genital abuse soon after?)

(Animals are conscious of their surroundings without acute self-consciousness that "having one's fly open" brings. Fear of exposure can bring stage-fright that is forgotten when one visualizes everyone in the audience as naked.)

CONTEXT-FREE DIAGNOSES

1. Context-sensitive domesticity may reduce the surprise from the first group of new diagnoses of common discomfitures in the vulnerable.

2. The following context-free diagnoses may start out to be startling but their relative invulnerability (for being dogmatic in what seems to be purely arbitrary contexts) may prove more disquieting for those who need (beyond mere desire) to be needed:

a) chastimentia $(A \times F)$:   the flesh is weak

b) demosthenia $(D \times J)$:   consensus is the cop-out

c) digniphrenia $(B \times L)$:   elegance is all

d) freedophilia $(B \times I)$:   emancipation liberates

e) honestitis $(B \times F)$:   "So help me, God."

f) morobsession $(D \times L)$:   less is not more

g) naturiasis $(A \times M)$:   what feels good is best

h) opporanoia $(B \times H)$:   apathy is opposition

i) phobikenia $(A \times H)$:   better "red" than dead

j) planetism $(B \times M)$:   the earth is "our" hearth

k) powerobia $(B \times J)$:   "It's nobody else's business."

l) privalysis $(B \times G)$:   "What's hidden in your closet?"

m) progressteria $(B \times K)$:   "Look at my GNP!"

n) sciencegression $(C \times K)$:   scientism by osmosis

o) soulitosis $(C \times F)$:   "The spirit must be cleansed."

z) talomania $(B \times G)$:   vengeance is divine

(To reduce the non-clinical novel appeal or idiosyncratic shock value of context-free domestication disturbances, each diagnosis (a-o, z) is plotted below, but not set in concrete.)

(Lower case letters—a–o, z—can be added to p-y sexist stereotypes as needed.)

3. Because this new formulation is also an exercise in self-assessment, construction of another or further triangulation of other behavioral discontinuities (religious, political, economic, social, etc.) are recommended to interested readers.

TRIANGULATION OF DOMESTICATION (Diagnosis = Data > Dogma)

CONTEXT-FREE DIAGNOSES

Socio-"Moral" Cycles

	1	2	3	4	5	6	7	8	9	10	9	8	7	6	5	4	3	2	1
i:																			
1		a	i						g	A									
2		e	z	h	d	k	m	c	j	B									
3		o					n			C									
4					b		f			D									
5										E									
ii:		F	G	H	I	J	K	L	M	N'	M'	L'	K'	J'	I'	H'	G'	F'	
5										E'									
4										D'									
3										C'									
2										B'									
1										A'									
	1	2	3	4	5	6	7	8	9	10	9	8	7	6	5	4	3	2	1

INSTANT INSIGHTS: PRECEPTORSHIPS in RESIDENCY TRAINING (SORTING after DOING and READING)

Resident (R)
Preceptor (P)

R: How can psychiatry depend on words so much?

P: Words may be cathartic, emetic or purgative, and thus trigger physiologic reactions (crying, vomiting or diarrhea). They may be slogans and trigger social reactions. Thus they serve as stimuli in the sense of signals (releasers). When they serve as symbols for sharing what is absent, understanding is sharpened.

R: Are words absolutely necessary for human understanding?

P: For human relationships, even among the deaf. But when a ventriloquist's audience forgets his puppet is not human just because it talks, we have gone too far in worshipping language. Language serves as a lubricant, as well as for camouflage, confession, confrontation, or celebration.

R: That is our art, not the science that spells survival?

P: Science only means understanding things in terms of things. Even
      art merely reveals the mystery without unraveling it. Psychiatry
      ought not concern itself with survival or "quality of life" but
      should, as art and science, swing slowly between both, trying
      to understand things and learning about what mystifies whom.
      I went to medical school to find out. The primary function of
      education is to make us fearless.

R: You mean independent?

P: Helen Keller's teacher first established a minimum but total
      dependency on her. She did not confuse the process with the
      product.

R: Does independence always mean emancipation?

P: In the history of nations, yes. But for persons, the "I" is always
      located in a relationship, never outside it. Even a ray of light never
      stands alone, and a light beam is surrounded by relative semi-
      darkness, just as the sound of one hand clapping is surrounded
      by silence broken by air currents.

R: The fearless is free?

P: Uneducated or not, we have the right to make choices, but not
      free to change the range of options. There is no free will. There
      is always our past when we were taught to be more willing than
      willful, which limited our options. Among living things, animals
      are freer than plants. In man the past afflicts the sick more than
      the normal, and the weak and retarded more than the strong and
      intelligent.

R: What about insight?

P: It leads nowhere but to another in-sight, if thinking is not
      translated into action. Action changes activity, and therefore
      behavior. Reading may afford more clues that must be sorted out.

R: What do you mean?

P: When we are self-conscious, we are in the middle of a stream
      of awareness that meanders, even if the song sounds exactly
      the same no matter how the acoustics change. We have to go
      beyond wool-gathering (humming the melody) to stock-taking
      (remembering the rhymes), then memory inventory (singing the
      lyrics), then feeling (nostalgia) and then activity (sending flowers,
      etc.). What we do should not go against the fail-safe mechanism
      of our unconscious autonomic nervous system, or we will have
      a civil war and need a psychiatrist to negotiate the terms of a
      cease-fire to achieve "peace in our time." To achieve it does not
      involve philosophy or finding meaning in our life. We can see
      the shape of our "three lives" and find what ratios gave them that
      shape sensually, socially and sexually, by clinical rationalysis.
      And decide what subspecies we have joined, without conscious
      choice.) *[Table 16]*

IMMEDIATE and REMOTE IMPLICATIONS (1–10)

1. NORM vs. NORMAL

(Norms are the mores of professionals, or the average expectation
of the reasonable, prudent person in legal fiction. Normal is what
keeps the animal going effortlessly and is usually unnoticed.)

CLING or TRUST or v.v. The clutch reflex in the infant fades with
familiarity with the family, whether trustworthy or not. For the child,
it then becomes "acquire or be fair", and for the adolescent "believe
or despair." Only afterwards can one compare (a matter of ratios, not
either-or). One has to be talented (precocious) to begin inventing without
waiting.

Only the fear of falling precipitously as infants makes us see violence
as akin to sudden death for which we are not ready even as adults. (This
fear *[s/6]* and sudden loud noises make us cower in thunderstorms and/
or at the closed door to master bedrooms.)

GROUP ETHOS should include the freedom to feel (good or bad)
like an infant (affective, **A**), the freedom to choose (right or wrong) like
a child (conative, **B**), and the freedom to think (true or false) like an
adolescent (cognitive, **C**).

Groupies search for a surrogate family to replace those that failed them or that they failed with. Leaders can become mothers, then fathers, then gurus, then guides, then grandparents [silently applauding any tentative steps of the toddler from (**A**) e-motion to (**B**) motility].

We also imitate absent models (rumors about them are reported by gossips and sold as news, sometimes ending up as bestsellers) and trust others differentially.

The cult leader must be democratic for its middle-class clientele, and authoritative for the lower classes. The upper classes don't go in for groups unless they are elevated into cults.

Did President Kennedy opt for equality because his father felt that his older brother was more deserving? Did his successor, President Johnson of Texas, who passed civil rights legislation against Southern opposition, also feel inferior to the Eastern Establishment liberals whom JFK left behind?

We can find new solutions to old problems by (**B**) trial and error. The process itself—whatever its purpose or goal, which is novel only to children—can be creative in not being bound by rules.

We can group objects by shape or by homology (morphology, **D**) or by color (analogy, **C**). What is more superficial and not structural can be the harbinger of bigotry (e.g., based on skin-deep pigmentation).

We hoard with our mouth or under one arm, while reaching for more, and can give up toys on request by the powerful or have tantrums (true territoriality or/with imperious greed).

(Among other species, altruism is a group characteristic only where dimorphism is pronounced between the sexes, when the size differential is not taken advantage of.)

When we are negativistic (**B'**, which is based on fear, **A'**), we refuse naps, eating (early diet faddists) or new foods, and avoid strange places ("preferring" cages in agoraphobia) or disorienting expanses of space (and developing claustrophobia).

Distressed by separation from caregiver, we become affectionate (**A**) towards relatives or clothing or stuffed toys (identification with mother) and other transitional objects (icons in religious art).

Thusly have we set the stage for becoming "civilized." By now already much different from other animals, our troubles have just begun. Trying to belong becomes a need to be needed.

> (The author has modified his previous formulation of "loyalty" as "need for leadership", and enlarges it to include "allegiance" and need for allies. One can, however, be "true" to "friends" [standing by them and thus reinforcing their stressed "self-esteem" with "personal esteem"], even as their popularity [public esteem from fans or "fair weather friends"] drops [without corresponding loss of self-respect].)
>
> (He sees human society as corrupted by money accumulated by the elderly to hire muscles to victimize the young whom they envy. Among social animals, might makes right for the mighty, not the wealthy. Thusly, animal fitness survives.)

Human groupings become defined by shared armbands. Sharing becomes sanction to excuse what consensus dictates. Heretics are vilified, nullified, and then sometimes deified by consensus.

2. PAIN AND FEAR OF HURTING

Severe pain is self-limited by eventual loss of consciousness. It is a signal to desist, not a sign of divine displeasure. Less severe distress is relieved by drugs in those who also feel guilty.

At least, with humans but not with our pets who cannot object, we confer with and consult those in distress, and never coerce our relatives to die. Yet their deathbed initiative or assent is not the answer either. Their rationalization is the reason and therefore the question.

> (The author claims more active euthanasia is likewise also more economical than imperative, like putting a horse out of its misery when it breaks a leg. To defend it by saying the whole is more than just the sum of its parts is trite. [Only in fiction is it debatable: Dying takes life away from the total of whatever is left!])

When we try merely to cope (instead of take control, which is worse, or exercise some influence, which is better), we tend passively to self-destruct, e.g., with limited post-war genocide (zero population growth).

3. CAN WE CHOOSE?

Those who marry for love need each other rather than children. Relations used to mean relatives, and sexual relations outside marriages of convenience begot unwanted bastards. Children are even less in demand now that people search not for love but for relationships, and, instead of relatives, prefer friendship. Mankind would presently much rather be kind or kindly treated—or, even worse, feel pity for those who are potentially pitiable, sought after as "vulnerable", since children are less available—instead of reproducing mankind.

If kids are an endangered subgroup, try to understand them as evolving like we all did, and maybe their extinction will not precede ours.

Personal virtues (A -> C) depend on our parents. Creactivity (B + E), compareactivity (B + D), and (VWf, $WXYm$) procreative ability are more animal and congenital or genetic (from our grandparents) than familial (parental) or cultural (social).

Excessive doubting about the ability to make (B) the right choices is what distresses and even freezes catatonics, who are afraid that any movement might destroy the only world they know. (Handcuffed, they relax, as if relieved of the responsibility for the range of "choices" open to them.)

Did you decide where you want to live as a child or even as to your immediate neighbors as an adult? Did you have a choice of dormitory or fraternity or sorority and roommates and classmates to learn from or with in college, in essential preparation for your existential future?

Advocates of "choice" about their bodies in later life are likely to be those who were prevented from choosing to masturbate anywhere, anytime. They are still fighting the same battle, waged in the battlefield of their bodies, not their minds (as "freedom to think" which is free precisely because one can secretly change one's mind anytime, anywhere). Unless you can freely choose your own DNA, what differentiates the illusion of "choice" from "options" is biological time intervals.

There can be neither direction nor motion without friction (physical) or resistance (emotional), which must in-form (shape) any "decision", whether it is (A) good or bad for someone and/or (B) fair or not to another.

Its momentum (direction instead of choice) follows a pattern (movement instead of action) that might disclose its "meaning" (**C**, not purpose), whether significant or not, to anyone interested.

When pressure (familial or official) is uniform on both sides and from behind, direction is incontestably forward and movement is unimpeded.

When friction is alternating but from both sides, progress is slow and serpentine.

1. Whether we believe it or not, the "decisions" we make about earth-shaking events are neutralized by the countless numbers making "uninformed" (biased) decisions unbeknownst to us.

    This is the secrecy of power which corrupts, not its power for good or evil itself, for which accountability may be assigned and assassinations arbitrarily arranged.

2. The decisions that we ourselves make to change our predicament—not our reactions post facto—are very few indeed, as are the predicaments subject to our direct influence.

    Only our acknowledgment or disowning of responsibility is up to us alone.

4. PERCEPTION and IMAGINATION: MENTOR or MASTER?

Thoughts are like hallucinations. Only when they are unclear are we aware of their presence (memory fails or light is too faint). Otherwise, just the product of the process of thinking or seeing reaches our consciousness and only then can they be shared without sacrificing veracity.

Reason and illusion thus clarify or cloud but do not illuminate or engineer our activity.

Perceptions are not turned off, even during sleep, even if unattended to (by overtly responding to accumulating data), unless of immediate significance, e.g. to a mother hearing her infant whimper.

Thus, editing is concurrent and operative (consciously in confessions, which are therefore useless for the uptight), even in dreaming, wetly or dryly (virtually uncontrolled fantasies about wakeful perceptions).

Were our muscles operative, instead of virtually paralyzed, the consequences would be unequivocally fascinating.

It is only because our dry dreams are edited so much that the dreamer/reporter must not censor any associations to their contents— not at all because the consequences of disinhibition are salutary (denied by Confucius, claimed by Socrates, and sold by Shakespeare, none of whom are clinicians to begin with).

Thus does psychoanalysis treasure truth more than treatment. But reporting shows traces of editing with imagination: Dream content changes when informally exchanged during psychoanalytic seminars.

(Postpubescence, dry dreams displace as conversational gambits the wet dreams that adolescents still compare in locker rooms.)

Our wakeful dreams, on the other hand, remain hidden because, once shared, they are more easily shattered, unlike dry dreams, to be replaced by another, also secret, if less rosy. As our dream approximates the unrealized reality that triggered it, our contentment increases, and vice versa.

Waking or wet or dry dreams, whether their meaning be uncovered or not, signify discontent, their different versions a sure sign of our struggle to accept what earlier dreams cannot offer.

(We often, in fact, maybe even right now, rise above objectivity or activity to inhabit the higher realms of hope, and thus abdicate control of our muscles and let our eyelids droop as our eyes wander—in their REM or rapid eye movement—from these pages to scan more vivid scenarios scripted by our imagination.)

5. DREAMS and PLANNING

When daydreams lead to foreseeable realization, then the wool-gathering becomes a blueprint for action instead of just a wish-fulfilling fantasy (like a wet dream).

Worry may then enter the drafting room as inability to plan for all-important contingencies. Hypochondriasis is worry over statistical improbabilities and, as bureaucratic hypochondriasis, characterizes insecure administrators, policy-makers and legislators who, like menopausal women, draw up "worst-case" scenarios with corresponding rules, regulations and laws to cover all loopholes.

Worry's opposite is pragmatism. The pragmatist is himself day-dreaming if he expects a dream of a plan not to miscarry.

Decisions are shaped by events (data) that we have sensed (clearly or peripherally or even outside conscious awareness)—rather than by reason itself consciously in-forming (shaping) them, especially when desire (e-motion, **A**) is the significant datum—whereupon we become resourceful to survive as a humanimal.

Darkness produces dark moods, because we cannot move with confidence. Kids who fear the dark are fearless as toddlers at the break of dawn.

Is incertitude the lot only of those left in the dark about data on which decision-makers depend? Or the reason for loneliness at the top of the heap? Are our "fearless" leaders' strong convictions a mask of confidence rather than a sign of competence? Are we more interested in staged performances than in substance? (Reporters are often caught off-guard by important developments.)

All who are spooked by darkness see devilish ghosts and superstitiously invoke higher powers to intercede or themselves assiduously acquire the power to overcome. They fervently believe that (**A** and **F'**) good and evil are in a life and death struggle that must be won at the expense of life itself.

(I expect to be similarly spooked in my deathbed. Death makes believers even of those not inclined to superstition. Desperation produces trust or superstitions, even about science.)

[President Reagan fervently believed that "To flee from the fight for good against evil and between right and wrong is folly." He is appreciated as predictable by those who do not want to be surprised by decision-makers.]

"Believing (**A** + **C** -> **ii**) is lying to one's self until the next rude awakening", e.g., in a mid-life crisis or metapause (second adolescence) or senescence (second childhood when retired to a nursing home or bed-ridden in another rail-enclosed crib).

Biophilia is overcome by pre terminal euthanasia, with or without self-castration.

6. FEEL-INGS (*sic*) and DREAMS

The eyelids (previously transparent as a nictitating membrane) evolved from our skin much later than the eyes, which are our window to the world and to its wonders, not to our soul. It is our ears which produce awe.

> (The fascination of horror movies may be in the visual special effects, but the spine-tingling is evoked by the sound track, which allows our imagination to go beyond what is displayed on the screen and impel us to reach for our date. Money-grubbers exploit this tendency.)

Not just because (1) the eyes are our only windows to the world, but when we are asleep, dreaming can carry heavy e-motional baggage also because (2) the eyeball can float around from side to side rapidly in its socket without waking us up from REM sleep, since it allows no movement except of the eyes. This may also explain why animals whose eye-sockets are built like ours can dream or show Rapid Eye Movements, even if their brains are less exercised by memories recorded in libraries or by current events massaged by the media. (Art assists memories among fellow travelers.)

Because feelings are contagious (which is why they are called "affect"), they infect groups. The fury from groups of the puny is more lethal than that of the strong who is solitary. The group in over-developed countries is the middle-class equivalent of spiritual cults which their converts worship and from which they expect miracles. Contact with spirits/other people is a way of getting in touch with forgotten experiences and enriching one's memory bank. Depletion of memory (emotional bankruptcy) demands establishing contact as often as necessary, or we "go bananas."

7. FIGHTING FIRE WITH FIRE

(We re-cycle back to the time we learned of hellfire. Was this the knowledge that Eve should have abstained from?)

1. Heretics were burned at the stake. Even lately, firebombing against atheist Viet Cong and nuclear attack on the yellow peril in Imperial Japan (aborted when threatened against the Chinese

allies of North Korea) have been our ready answer to those whose political delusions are different from ours. (South Koreans and South Vietnamese were Christians, North Koreans and North Vietnamese were Communists.)

2. Their (**B**) territorial (**C**) rhetoric and ours do not meet on the same ground (cognitive or **C**, religious or **F**, political or **G**, and economic or **H**) for leaders to hear each other and (**A**) e-mote at the same time while their hands are tied by their constituents from being raised against each other.

3. The most righteous (**BB**) among us are (**C'**) deluded, and the longer the history of cultural conviction (from **F** to **O** or fear of God to awe of computers), the more intractable the paranoid patient: Belief in primal Satanic possession (original sin) fades ever more slowly than illusory satellite surveillance of the paranoid's every move, and (**G**) nationalism makes the jingoist harder to treat than (**H**) left/right wing communists/reactionaries.

To be (**O**) electronically watched all the time by a super-power is more of a self-serving protest than being possessed by the Devil (**F'**). But it recapitulates the typical pattern of mythical evolution.

The first puzzling fact that prompted deeper probing was the relative difficulty of helping patients with religious delusions, compared with those who were jingoistic. He who believes that he is persecuted because of a divine (**F**) mission gives up his delusion more slowly than he who thinks that the FBI (**G**) or CIA (**H**, anti-communist) has given him a special assignment.

Patients of all three persuasions (**F'**, **G'**, and **H'**) were very common in my in-hospital years of post-graduate training as a psychiatrist.

God, by definition, can exist but is not alive nor involved, or else He can die, like His Son before Him, who got involved. Alive like us, He will also be subject to the risk of believing only in what exists, if only in the mind.

(A tongue-in-cheek serio-comic quip that sons can use as an excuse to save their mother from being accused of incest, divine or not, is never to call whom she calls Father by the same name, unless they are orphans or bastards and need one to call their own. [For my part, I just made it easier for my mother to meet her Father at early morning mass without mishap by building a ramp to eliminate the risk of her falling downstairs in the dark.])

4. Vigilance in the more paranoid jingoist endures longer than in the militant who are, regardless of gender, personally as well as socially, simply self-serving (chauvinistic and sexist, respectively).

5. At a higher price than other political animals pay, we have evolved from the Trojan horse to the blitzkrieg of Warsaw and Pearl Harbor and preemptive strikes against Hiroshima and Nagasaki, to shaking hands to disarming enemies by verifiable arms limitation agreements or sanctions.

6. Weapons of mass destruction make any enemy legitimate (as the Devil's assistant). Such enemies establish our claim for special consideration while denying that we may just be unenlightened cosmic bastards. If only we can find "intelligence" like ours elsewhere, we can convert them into even better enemies.

7. Armageddon survives as the answer to potential perdition of our immortal soul in the hands of unbelievers. The less attractive alternative is intelligent acknowledgement of total interdependence in our planet and throughout the universe.
   a. Radioactive fall-out may produce better mutants than ourselves.
   b. This probability threatens our self-impressed sense of how essential we are, and drives existentialism out of sun-drenched enlightenment back to the dark gloom of Plato's cave.
      (The author decompartmentalizes science and the humanities to unite all behavior, absolutely without exception, as natural phenomena: In bio-socio-cosmic terms, if "Nature abhors a vacuum", and "No man is an island", is behavior a reaction or transaction between units of nature, whether electromagnetic or gravitational or alive or human? If stardust can become insects, quantum physics applies to both, only the rate of entropy [decay] can be different.)

If human, is behavior a vector that is decided by our sense of past reactions, present transactions and what they portend for our future as a unit of (**i**) nature or as (**ii**) child of God (**F**), or citizen (**G**), consumer (**H**), etc., or (**iii**) sexual partner or loner, man or woman or pervert?

What started me thinking along these lines was a loaded inquiry. A homosexual already accepted for post-graduate training in psychiatry once asked me what makes him different.

The question behind the query was why were there no homosexuals among their consultants. I replied that there were twice as many nipples as breasts in my faculty.

We used to have litters, or some would not have supernumerary nipples even at this stage in our evolution. And then we had extended families. Now we have nuclear families, broken households, and scattered children.

Between couples, lust is enough. In families, even God's, love is a must.

8. WHAT MAKES CAPITALISM GROW while COMMUNISM SELF-DESTRUCTS?

Like the yellow pages, it pays to cover all questions that may be asked of a new approach.

It is not capitalism as ideology, just adult "sibling rivalry"—even with near-total strangers (including new customs inspectors tracking smugglers who travel by air)—that moves consumer goods, increases trade, and earns venture capital for heavy industry. In the beginning, even subliminal window-shopping on TV screens can galvanize ambition in the inert.

But in order to be sold, consumer goods must be sampled by those without them (and slip through their hands before their very eyes to be addictive, as with drugs that promote delusions of equality with the users' superiors. [Ambassador Paula Harriman died after a woman was confirmed as Secretary of State instead of her]).

The old Marshall Plan had nothing to do with (**A**) emotional counter-phobic altruism or (**F**) the blessedness of giving, nor (**G**) Big Brother's dirty politics, nor (**H**) the coercive economics of reparation, nor with (**I**) divisive individualism or (**J**) socialism in the pursuit of equality.

Epic in scope, the Marshall Plan embodied the simple biology of semi-permeability between adjacent and incompletely fenced-in territories, translated into social biochemistry by a military mind: the salt of the earth must distribute itself equally among the world's inter-connected oceans, including the blood in our veins.

Timed just right, we supported the Marshall Plan because we can, because it is something to do, not because it is the thing to do: We did not know if it was, although some American Indian tribes and early American philanthropists knew that sharing is surviving. (Gen. George Marshall was neither a social worker nor an anthropologist but a soldier.)

We are unique among animals in generously sharing what we have with outsiders in order to establish our pre-eminence, even if only by conspicuous consumption at cocktail parties. (Wakes also keep company around longer in case the dead rise from the grave, and weddings serve as public denial of Oedipal fantasies between father and bride.)

9. A DATING SYSTEM FOR CULTURES FOR ALL TIME

Only the Chinese count the days of our lives from the moment of conception ("A>C>"). Most of us count birthdays from the moment of birth ("A.B."). Scholastics (monastic scholars) started the practice of dividing history into BC (before Christ was born) and AD (Anno Domini or the Master's Years from four years before the first Christmas). (1997 should have been AD 2001)

I think it is time to replace Jesus Our Lord in Anno Domini, with Dinosaurs whose reptilian image reappears in our wrinkled necks with aging. [Are Cain and automation in the form of Egyptian waterclocks contemporaneous?]

When the old get sent to old people's homes by their own children from their homes, is it because human adults fear life among reptiles and the aged? Animals do not care whether we are young or old.

My older grandson prizes a pet lizard. (Psychoanalysts would suggest that he is struggling with oedipal fantasies.)

I like children visiting my geriatric patients because they fondly trace the web of wrinkles on the old faces with their tiny fingers, and make the elderly no longer feel unloved by the young. Only those who have lost their youth dislike the aged.

As long as we think in terms of before the Child was born (BC) and the years of His reign (AD or Anno Domini), it will be a struggle to change our focus or our pre-occupation with the promise of old prophets. (It is very much like reckoning the months of the year by astrological signs.) To use BD (before dinosaurs), and ADD (after the arrival of dinosaurs) is better science. It reduces our importance but improves our perspective of biological vicissitudes, including the origins of life.

10. Emergent/Emergency MERGERS

Values (ii) based on any stage of our historical evolution is an inflationary exaggeration of what we already accept as well as an esoteric excuse for remaining ignorant of the rest.

Ethologists (N) look to animals for different leads (B). Computers (O) collate data for correlations (D) but also search for hidden connections (E).

(I myself started making house calls when I began treating families instead of "individuals" as a psychiatrist. This is precisely the approach field workers use to study other animals in their natural habitat. A family therapist must be an etho-psychiatrist to heal and learn, not from what is said but by what their behavior reveals.)

(It is interesting that family psychiatrists often failures in marriage, unless we grant St. Paul, who never married but was an early *Homo domesticus*, authority to speak about love for married couples. Love itself for one's neighbors (Leviticus 19:18) was not mentioned before male nocturnal emissions (Leviticus 15:16). They were deemed unclean, if not (F') evil. Is this where "Cleanliness is next to Godliness" came from?)

(Why do men wash their hands after, instead of before, they "Free Willy" from hiding under their underwear, unless they think "sex is dirty"?)

From working intensively with families and extrapolating data, many stereotypes can be better understood as more familial than cultural or sexual in origin: The rich, of course, see the world differently and react to what they see. Even as children, their world was differently organized and meeting their universal needs was attended to differently. Proud and pampered, they get what they want, while the humble and hungry scramble for what they need. It is how needs are unmet that makes the poor and rich alike, just as tuberculosis has the same end-result in manors or hovels.

>(It is easier for rich aristocrats without a chip on their shoulder—like FDR and JFK, who are celebrities in their own right—to keep the media on their side, than proud, self-made "peers" who must keep proving that they can make a difference. They are seen as rivals by reporters who can only score with "scoops.")
>
>(Is it better to be different or to make a difference?)

We need comfort and/or authority (the Chinese went with Mao without modern conveniences and creature comforts). The domesticated need both (among the Moral Majority), the untamed (humanimals) rely only their own authority.

Man is anti-managerial to the extent that he is left untamed, and will choose Barabbas over Christ, mistakenly or not.

(But there were enough centurions to crucify Christ, and enough "centaurs" around for riot control during his uphill climb to Calvary.)

If our morality derives from our need for security, our values must serve to reassure us in our puniness (compared to other natural predators). The first stage of (ii) believing that matters is attempting (F) to please Santa Claus, then progressively preferring what is (G) effective, (H) efficient, (I) self-elected (*sic*), (J) mutual, (K) productive, (L) humane, (M) conservative, (N) convivial, and lately what is (O) rapidly communicable.

A conformist is domesticated. Conformists would agree about him.

Non-conformists are untamed. Non-conformists would disagree about each other.

Comparative study of animals with whom we share nature, instincts, and tradition (as unwritten natural law, moral law, and common law, e.g., squatters' rights) illuminates many dark corners of our past. There is (I) con-naturality and (**II**) conviviality, and (**III**) con-familiar (**i**) morality and (**ii**) consensual ethics and (**iii**) conventional sex.

SQUATTER'S PRIVILEGES

There is an unwritten law that in polite society we should not discuss (**G**) politics or (**F**) religion or (**iii**) sex except (**X, f**) infidelity, even in the Clinton years. And scientists may discuss politics only on socio-moral grounds (**i** and **ii**), and religion only to support ethical preoccupations among evangelistic (**F**) and/or humanistic (**L**) anthropologists and/or archeologists.

These cultural taboos are observed with (**G**) nobility and (**L**) sentimentality

The political crown (**G**), commercial town (**H**), and academic gown (**K**) are now inseparable. Thus does classical "virtue" (or asexual territoriality and territorial equity) team up with old-fashioned "values" (respectively symbolized by the cross, the crown, the town, and the gown). And "EveryWoMan" (convert, subject, peon, and technician) looks on while the un-mastered is hunted.

> Are the best examples of (**B**) territoriality (perverted by imperialists) the Great Wall of China and the Monroe Doctrine?
>
> Was the Berlin Wall itself just another (**G'**) sovereign temper tantrum when (**C'**) the dogmatic are threatened with (**BB'**) dispossession of, and desertion or defection by, their locally trained (**K**) cadre of technicians and professionals? Or must the contest be ceded or won?

Not **A'** (ill-feeling) but (**B'**) "bad manners" may be due to (**H'**) scarcity of goods, but (**iii**) breeding cannot be reserved for the rich even if they have inherited the fitness of their forebears as (**BB'**) robber **H** barons.

Because (**C**) thought and logic developed later than our (**A**) emotions and (**B**) motility, they are more dependent on co-evolving vocabulary (e.g., from "bad manners" to (**G**) "jingoism") than on the fact of our perceptions and collisions with unthinking but reactive "reality."

19.00 s/PREPARING PSYCHIATRISTS for the FUTURE

s/Chapter Notes

[s/1] A dolphin who has been bullied by a gang would return with his own to bully another, but because they have not invented weapons, nobody gets killed.

Despite hemispheric photographs of our planet taken from outer space, flat-earthers still deny its shape. (The Great Deluge cannot have been global at the time of the Biblical ghost-writers.) That is the inertia of logic that reasons out what it cannot verify long before there were "candid" cameras to take pictures of what happened that can be shown to those absent but interested. Between post-logical technology and thinking logically, logic (that holds there must be supernatural perfection in an imperfect natural world) loses eventually.

[s/2] The height of intellectual arrogance is to claim that if we know history, we would not repeat the same mistakes. Knowing where we or the wind came from does not solve much of anything. But what we, with our opposable thumb, or the wind with its load of moisture, do is measurably more advantageous to know.

[s/3] For instance, all involved with the judiciary confirmation hearings of Clarence Thomas for the U.S. Supreme Court may be stuck in stages **C** and **G**. (The polygraph test taken by Anita Hill, the sole audience to lurid sexual importunations, does not verify the story being retold, but only confirms how convinced she was that it actually happened.)

Science has found that only what has been disproved (by the "null hypotheses") can be held to be untrue. Myths lead to mistakes. Yet even the CIA lobby greets visitors to this spy headquarters with "and ye shall know the truth, and the truth shall set you free" (John 8:32).

[s/4] Personal morals may be defined by parental constraints on the freedoms enjoyed by their children and limited to them and, - expectably yet sometimes surprisingly - by their children to theirs. Social ethics may be narrowly defined by the rights and responsibilities of the guild: In professional ethics, it is often simply the rights, privileges and obligations of the members of the profession.

Morality and ethics domesticate the weak by reward and punishment of cowards. The strong and sensual surrenders only to sensation, the socially ambitious always to superiors, while the sexually fearless can kill or die to copulate.

[s/5] (Tongue in cheek, so to speak, author has a very simple explanation for the theology of original sin which needed a spectacular sacrifice to erase with a crucifixion and resurrection. He thinks our heads just got much bigger for our mother's breeches [sic] than that of any other species, and so must thereafter deny that we suffered more brain damage than other animals at birth by placing our ideas on a pedestal. At the same time, we long to return to the Eden of our mother's womb, but this time under the governance of another parent who has changed His mind about expelling us from the first paradise that He originally intended only for Adam and other animals.)

(The first exiles were limit-testing pubescents (Adam and Eve) who had to cover their genitals and work. Paradise regained is where laundry is free and work, like sex and fighting, is playful and satisfying. My father wanted me to study and not work at all. I was post-pubescent before I "worked," but only at what I wanted to occupy myself with. Thusly did I regain Eden during my second and third adolescence, as an intern in America and on the staff in an English hospital.

(The author's equally simple alternative to the longing for the time before natural birth and traumatic expulsion from the womb is an elective Caesarean section and prolonged stay afloat in a warm incubator with tape recordings of uterine sounds. That is our sensual moratorium which is equivalent to the social moratorium of extended education [cultural cloning] during adolescence before we may reproduce sexually.)

(The ability to remain (i) free will then replace the residual need to be (ii) equal to compensate for the sense of earlier deprivation, even in (iii) eroticism, in some cultures where mothers abandon their young to be with their mates at night. Is the first absentee parent our role model for a seasonal Santa Claus and an invisible God Almighty? And we identify with the aggressors so that He will not also turn on us who are twice handicapped/evicted, peri and postnatally?)

[s/6] Birds do not share our fear of falling that we must have acquired when we (1) stopped climbing as primates or (2) started evolving to equal another master race that ruled the skies in the Age of Dinosaurs.

We now make do (1) with jumping with our ankles anchored to a treetop or bridge railing, or (2) from an airplane, or (3) with mastering hang gliding.

20.00 t/SUMMATION CONCLUSIONS

(Can we now organize what we have learned from parents, patients, students, colleagues, clients, pets and masters, untamed friends and dead strangers? Can we systematize our discoveries and findings into a testable theory and thereby enlarge our clinically verifiable body of knowledge? Does rationalysis and absolute relativity lead to bio-anthropology and away from cultural relativism? The challenge is how comprehensive as well as comprehensible.)

Any summary would naturally include restatements (envoi) that are necessary to clarify and emphasize the points in our subcycles (as well as anticipated parallel development in subdivisions of the species) that it must make for it to be conclusive. Conclusions are usually exercises in deduction. Not this post-logical, data-based summation (predominantly induction and abduction). Verification will take at least a generation.

Clinicians find continuing trends as we go through life from **A** to **Z**. We call them senso-socio-sexual patterns of becoming, believing and begetting. Life seems to subdivide through time within each person species. A preliterate subculture is common to children and other primates. Cohabitation characterizes certain ages in both sexes. It is therefore not surprising that human beings become, believe and beget in similar ways.

Believing we are special makes our depredations of nature acceptable. Believing we are not animals makes it easier to define what is not natural as human, and what is natural as not preferable. But we also believe that what is human is what we were taught to believe, which is different from place to place. What is human then becomes purely parochial and may be un-American or American, or legal and just for jingoists. (California itself used to be part of Mexico. Native Americans "americanized" Europeans by resisting expropriation of their "squatters' rights", now regained centuries later, to run plush gambling casinos under special legal dispensations on their reservations!)

We cannot be perfect with only five senses, no matter how advanced our technology. We live with a sense of quiet desperation because we believe we deserve better simply because we are human. But we have not learned how to be human, and we do not like being like an animal. Which means we were probably raised where there are no animals to admire. Expectably, instead of living as *Homo sapiens*, we try to become *Homo domesticus* or *Homo metropolus*.

As metropolitan areas develop suburbias where commuters sleep, its skies get smudged with smog. Stars disappear from the heavens in a cloud of hydrocarbons. Is this a mixed blessing that hides the firmament above and keeps our dreams earth-bound?

What can we do? First we must find out what is wrong with *Homo domesticus* and *Homo metropolus* in our modern civilization.

There are disagreements in the hard sciences, but they agree on what they have disagreed. Their reality is described precisely enough without words to produce predictions, with or without understandable implications. The information that they rely on is not subject to modification, only to misinterpretation by the ignorant and verbose ("opinionated").

In human discourse called communication, we do not merely transmit or repeat but we also modify or misinterpret the sense of what we mishear or do not understand about the data that we report, not necessarily to be able to predict better but just to achieve greater understanding.

Information is better transmitted (1) chemically as in genetics (our brain also relies on neurochemical transmission), (2) electronically as in automation (or intelligence gathering by orbiting satellites), or by (3) written numeral or musical symbols, than by (4) animal vocalization, which can be used to mislead predators, or (5) oral verbalization and, least well, by (6) every backyard gossip, including investigative reports (by/for faceless strangers) which need only submit to the test of legal fiction for veracity or plausibility: Testified beliefs [originally recited while holding the testes, count as court evidence and all precedent opinions as justified decisions!

There is both a reason and a remedy for communication being mistaken for information. We can diagnose and cure ourselves of, this predilection for, and addiction to, unexamined redundancies as facts ("faction").

Born as sensual "unicorns" we become social "centaurs" with (i) brain-washing and (ii) brain-stuffing. We become less *Homo sapiens* and more *H domesticus* or, worse, *H metropolus*.

> (The first domesticated pet is the dog, the last the cat until we got hen-pecked husbands. Dog foxes can be thrown out by pregnant vixens but come back to feed her. Should husbands also give way to, at least, the newborn?)

We need to find the ratio of sensual, social and sexual development in everyone who minds instead of minding.

Transcultural psychiatry must then begin with the business of spelling out what we mean by "mind." Literally cross-cultural psychology should change its spelling to "mynd" or "myths of my mind" that cannot be tested. Ethopsychiatrists are better off thinking of it as "minding" what is going on and how it affects behavior.

Whatever we share with healthy animals is not sick or uniquely human but adaptive. What is not, is man-made, and has not been tested long enough in the crucible of time to be depended on for survival.

Cross-species comparisons can show us where we have erred because we are human. To control nature, exploit animals and domesticate children is to abuse them to realize our dreams.

The "battle of the sexes" is both human and recent. With sexual inhibition and genital hypochondriasis, the brain compensates as another erogenous zone. But that is more intended for recreation, not for procreation.

How did we go astray? People tend to look down on themselves or up to others, even to God.

> I was once taken for a miracle-worker when I relieved a boy's distended bladder by immersing his hand in cold water.

Scientists try harder to look out for the unexpected, and around for what is taken on faith. (We now know that birds start out as males and some become hens. Contrary to most creation myths, we all started out ourselves as "Eve" and, by the grace of dice or chance or God, some of us in the first trimester became "Adam." Nor did we or they have any choice, either, in what happens to any of our or their heirs.)

How special are we in our emotions (**A**), violence (**BB'**) and creativity (**E**)?

Instead of confusing (**C**) critical thinking with (**D**) constructive criticism, conceptions with perceptions, and reasoning with fact-finding, can we separate virtues (**i**) from values (**ii**), sensations from sex (**iii**), and freedom from equality?

Without a star or rhetoric of short and catchy sound bites to guide us on our journey to our destiny or destination, can we slowly if painfully be more context-centered, content-conscious, and conclusion-cautious, through tough times and over rough terrain in the next century? Only to find that we are not special as a species?

Can we show that we are not a singular aberration? We must forget everything that was taught before we learned about zero, all about the soul before we learned about the cell, all slogans before we learned about organs, and all about selfhood before we learned about life cycles.

Psychiatric practice that is limited to one specific group or cult or culture is a form of tribal medicine with its own magicians and vocabulary of incantations. We can leave this Ivory Tower of Babel of words with a better alphabet for coding behavior in the next century.

The **ABZ**'s of life started out as a modern periodic table of elements of behavior to go with Mendeleev's and Meyer's independent but similar revolutionary discoveries in chemistry. Our **ABZ** is an alphabet for non-genetic transmission of information.

DNA forms the organism, senso-socio-sexual development shapes its own legacy. Can senso-socio-sexual ratios now be used to understand us, just like the four codons of Crick and Watson's DNA in basic biochemistry can explain how life continues from generation to generation?

Our (**E**) discovered non-linear, ratio-driven patterns do not differ from other natural verifiable patterns that (**A**, e-motional) non-ambulatory (**C**, logical) reductionism has not (**B**) tried to (**D**) explore.

Human life cycles can be seen as the "ontogeny" of the phylogeny represented by the periodic elements of chemistry. It can then be plotted in the same way. Why it has escaped earlier discovery may be due to serendipitous and non-deterministic accidents. In that, it repeats the phylogeny of mutations followed by variations undreamed of in self-serving philosophies or religions.

Beyond all these, "to be or not to be" is a variable but non-random combination of becoming, believing and begetting, our book's subtitle.

Continuing education for professionals is like a secular purgatory, where one can purge what is not essential. But we may not always succeed. (Oscar Wilde claims that given a choice to go to heaven or attend a lecture about heaven, there would be more going to a lecture hall.)

Faithful laymen would argue that the soul is no more invisible than the electron. Heisenberg's Principle of Uncertainty and quantum theory can be perverted into solipsism and teleology. Darwinian theory is used as a wedge to teach creationism as another "theory" children must also learn. Only our shared but now visible DNA escapes controversy about our "ascent from the apes."

I came from a feudal family in the country all the way to America, but not because it is industrialized. Now the blight of industry has our cities hidden under a toxic fog of smog and a mist of acid rain.

I can see the change from rural to urban civilization in all its advantages and disadvantages. It is not just a question of increasing and decreasing standards of living. There is a drift away from basic ethology and native intelligence. We are rushing forward towards post-industrial electronics and artificial intelligence.

No one learns from history, we just keep repeating its well-reasoned errors. Personally, we also keep recycling to early stages of social development in our own life cycle, back to another adolescence in mid-life and a second childhood in senility. Which reverses Haeckel's biogenetic law.

Without intending to, we have now created an ontogeny of behavior that, as cultural embryology, replaces what was discredited in Haeckel's bio-genetics as recapitulation *in utero* of adult amphibious organs, like gills. Haeckel's recapitulation exalted our embryology as evidence of human ascension to superior animalhood. We now think "neoteny" (prolonged asexual maturation) explains the data on which he theorized.

Our neo-Haeckelian "recapitulation" is the social extension of ontogeny repeating phylogeny, except that what we keep repeating are the birth defects of society. This is also the exact opposite of Lamarck's social Darwinism.

Human society, by cosmic reckoning, is also still in its embryonic stages of development. And this is where the theory of absolute relativity—not between God and man, but between cosmology and biology and between biology and anthropology—becomes critical in transcultural psychiatry. "No man is an island" is too narrowly anthropocentric.

Social tolerance is no substitute for science or it becomes condescension. Science does not need to apologize to the tolerant or intolerant for whatever it discovers.

Beyond cultural relativism, the **ABZ**'s of life can pinpoint and explain the focus of studied indifference (*ignorabissimus*) in closed minds. Each letter stands for a stage of development that may be progressive or regressive.

For a truly transcultural psychiatry, no cultural values should supersede universally valid findings in our new science of absolute relativity in anthropology, biology and cosmology.

To practice our New Psychiatry without alchemy, we offer this post-industrial periodic table of elements of behavior from **A** to **Z** to go with Mendeleev's and Meyer's discoveries in chemistry during the industrial revolution.

This post-industrial alphabet for non-genetic transmission of information also complements Crick and Watson's DNA codons of adenine, cytosine, guanine, and thymine, three of which in different combinations with cytosine form the DNA alphabet for genetic "fingerprinting."

MERGING/DIVERGING DOMESTICATION/BREEDING

(To call procreation "breeding" and see indoctrination in morality and ethics as personal and social domestication respectively is to integrate the evolution of behavior in animals and man. *Homo sapiens sapiensis* can then be subdivided into *H. sapiens*, *H. domesticus*, and *H. metropolus*.)

We can think of senso-socio-sexual rationalysis as tri-color ratios of sensuality's "Maybe" in yellow, society's "No" in red, and carnality's "Yes" in green. Our cultural development retraces the behavior of social animals. Just as ontogeny (intrauterine development) recapitulates phylogeny (the evolution of our species) in a new approximation of Haeckel's bio-genesis, so does the history of humanity repeating itself illuminate how change depends on our limitations as well as inherited ingenuities.

If the past is prologue, can we, like Picasso, treat "individuality" as just a metaphor, unlike singularity, e.g., of black holes or a Big Bang?

There are only two paintings I want to own, the last self-portrait of Van Gogh and Picasso's war-torn *Guernica*. How will Picasso have portrayed the civil war of animal, moral and ethical impulses?

Almost a century ago, Picasso shocked the art world by his powerful portrayal of the fragmentation of "individuals" into disparate pieces. With us, his imitation of life was a challenge to fit the fragments together in some recognizable form.

Today, without distaste, we can accept Picasso's *Les Demoiselles d' Avignon*, not so much as abstract art but as asymmetrical, post-logical portraiture of our separate personal and cultural evolution and racial (bio-sexual) re-evolution as WoMAnimal. Neither always neuter nor unisexual nor androgynous, we are not special at all except as a sub-specialist like others, living or radioactive or not, in the rest of our universe.

Just as there are transitions between sub-stages of sensuality, including learning what is new, so are there transitional stages between the sub-cycles of moral, ethical, and erotic development.

Socrates claimed that an unexamined life is not worth living. True to his word as always, he gave his own life a final examination, and then drank hemlock, a potent poison. He had convinced himself, through *reductio absurdum*, which underlies all supernatural notions, that he could have better conversations with those already dead! (If he had "ascended" to heaven, he might have found the righteousness of its populace quite deadening.) The same absurd but unrelenting logic produced the Inquisition "proved" that the earth was flat to all afraid of falling off its edge straight down to hell.

If (1) the critical faculty and the creative faculty develop differently and are not necessarily interdependent nor age-dependent, and because (2) most critics compare creators but creators seldom bother to, - only those (a) insecure in their talent (b) evaluate their contribution, and

(c) seek consensus if not applause from critics - we have to be (**B** x **D**) "compreactive" beyond simple comparison (**D**), and (**B** x **E**) "creativative" beyond clever innovation in motivating the energetic (**B**) and inventive (**E**).

BRIEF SUMMARY

We are different from the rest of creation in only a few things:

We do not have the biggest brains except among land-locked mammals.

Dolphins have proportionately bigger brains but they don't have opposable thumbs.

Dinosaurs did and, as they are not land-locked but aquatic and air-borne as well, they bested their rivals.

One hundred million years ago, Gigantosaurus inhabited Argentina.

Two and a half million years ago, smaller animals had entirely supplanted dinosaurs and lived in the Stone Age.

A million years ago, we started using fire, and sun worshippers—like the followers of Zoroaster—thought it represented their God on earth. This later made Jehovah jealous. This Self-assigned jealousy made His claims to perfection questionable.

Fifty thousand years ago, recognizable art expression started to appear.

Ten thousand years ago, we invented agriculture, cultivated coffee after three thousand years, and brewed beer a millennium later.

We also began domesticating other animals and, in another millennium, started domesticating ourselves with the invention of papyrus in Egypt.

A thousand years later, China excluded barbarian hordes with 1700 miles of its Great Wall.

Two thousand years later, we invented wheels and carts.

A millennium later, the Chinese invented gunpowder

The invention of the compass is 200 years got other barbarians into China from the sea.

Another millenium later, China supplanted papyrus with paper.

In five hundred years, Copernicus took the earth away from the center of cosmos. (What Ptolemy was to Copernicus (1543),

Aristotle was to Galileo (1600). Kant (1787) complained that "... since Aristotle, logic has not been able to take a single step ahead ...")

Galileo verified what Copernicus suspected, with the invention of the telescope.

The new science of optics (Holland also produced the microscope) fascinated Newton (1642–1727), who elaborated the three laws of motion and validated what Galileo did to logic by discovering gravity. (Galileo, who died when Newton was born, found that objects fell uniformly irrespective of weight: For university women guests, a ping-pong and a tennis ball dropped from the cat-walk above our living room hit each other at the bottom.)

The following century saw the steam engine and the Industrial Revolution, hot air balloons over land and steamboats over water.

The next century brought steam locomotives and Darwin who took creationists for the ride of their lives.

The twentieth century gave birth to Mendel and heredity, DNA and genes transmitting information better than telephones by wires or through the airwaves.

160,000,000 have died in this century's wars. This is like killing off all Americans in the continental United Sates just before Alaska and Hawaii became parts of the union.

The air we breathe is impure, not from using carts yoked to animals whose leavings smell bad, but because of *Homo metropolus* commuters yoked to single-passenger cars.

Is achievement different from success? Is it more personal than social?

We end up with a global and clinical analysis of ratios that shift with (i) morality and sensual liberty, (ii) ethics and social equality and (iii) erotic and sexual pursuits in human beings. Over-emphasis in what is ethical (religious, political, fiduciary, etc.) or erotic skews ratios in the direction of what is missing and overcompensated for.

With absolute relativity, which is more natural than cultural, life can then be seen as **iii/(i/ii)**. Without such culture-free rationalysis, life can only be studied or remain unexamined after kindergarten as an inglorious collection of habits of thinking and compromises with contrived excuses (rationalizations without ratiocination).

CLINICAL RATIONALYSIS of BECOMING, BELIEVING and BEGETTING

Of becoming, believing and begetting, the middle is still evolving. Becoming and begetting have been going on since the beginning of time, only now is believing interfering with both. Is disbelieving and begetting unbecoming?

The earliest beliefs interfered less with begetting, i.e., beliefs in (**F**) God, divine (**G**) rule of kings, or inherited (**H**) wealth. Later ideologies about (**I**) individualism, (**J**) ethnicity, (**K**) technocracy, (**L**) humanism, (**M**) conservation, and (**N**) "neo-totemism" for scarce species started to interfere more and more with begetting. Awe of computers as Big Brother replacing an omniscient God side-tracks becoming more than begetting. *(t/1)*

It is time to look anew at the old and new enemies of, and remedies for, health. When we graduated there were miracle drugs against infection. When I started psychiatry, they had just discovered miracle drugs for severe mental illness. Do we need to go beyond drugs in medicine and psychiatry? We still have schizophrenics. Newer drugs are being tried for manic-depressive, anxiety, phobic and panic disorders. I know that in psychiatry we must progress beyond what was depended on before there were drugs, and look at our socio-ethology as well as our biochemistry.

Only since our exploitation of fire are we different from other animals. Only because of our thumbs have we surpassed porpoises.

If the link from chimpanzees to champion humans like Einstein is an Olympic gymnast, then *Homo sapiens* is the missing link to *Homo sapiens sapiens*. *Homo domesticus* and *Homo metropolus* are not humanimal enough.

Our society is also more violent and more sexual than other animals. We have bigger penises and breasts than any other beast, pound for pound. Is our violence then a product of our brain?

Homo domesticus, male or female, is more pompous (from indoctrination) than the pugnacious *Homo metropolus* (from intimidation).

THE BASIC ABCs OF GLOBAL BEHAVIOR THROUGHOUT HISTORY

We want to offer a more systematized thesis from a quarter century of clinical experience among people of different colors who are color-blind only until confronted by a different culture.

Out of Anthropology, Biology and Cosmology, for a culture-free, gender-weighted (i-iii) senso-socio-sexual rationalysis: (iii/i)/(ii) we have mapped out the relationship between biophysics (I: Universal galactic, planetary, atomic and nuclear con-naturality), etho-biology (II: General viral, bacterial, plant, animal and human con-viviality) and socio-ethology (III: Specific con-familiarity).

The more (I) natural you are and the more (II) animal you are, the better. That life may or may not have been intended by nature need not imply that to hang on with artificial life support systems is wrong. Life, like the human brain, creates its own bureaucracy. To be unhealthy for long is not bad but merely unhealthy.

SENSUALITY, SOCIETY and SEX in GLOBAL VILLAGE PSYCHIATRY

Between being born and getting old, we become (A) emotional and passionate while passive or immobilized, (B) mobile and active or intuitive and decisive, (C) reactively reflective (mirror-like) or deliberative, then more objective or (D) comparative and, at any stage if free and talented, (E) inventive or innovative.

Do barnyard fowls who can "talk" without pointing all employ the magnetic north as their reference point? Do they use nouns without reverence or piety?

A to E: Sensually, we are unique in our ability to go from vocalization to verbalization. To do this, we developed the ability to pronounce other sounds. To vowels which animals and infants can utter and master, we added consonants.

For ease of speech, we use some of the letters oftener. And write ETAOINSHRDLU in that order of frequency more than the other consonants in our alphabet. I wish we stopped there, but from verbalization we went on to the idolatry of nouns we call abstractions.

We also thought that thought itself involves using consonants when, in fact, the right brain can think as well as, if not better than, the left. All the left brain has, after handedness acquired the motor centers, are the speech centers.

F to O: Socially, we are unique in our taboos against sex and violence and in needing to believe in order to belong. Before leaving home, all animals belong with those they knew from birth, and do not need to do more to be counted among the herd. Many humans disown those who gave them a start in life, and end up becoming first generation immigrants wherever they happen to settle down.

(In China, the dead emperor's retinue of outsiders who have become his courtiers gets buried alive with him.)

P to Z: Sexually, women are unique in their vulnerability to rape because their vagina is tilted forward. "Lower" animals cannot be held down and spread-eagled.

Unaided escape from a rapist with a high sperm count is possible only in outer space. When there is zero gravity or space suits, erections can fail during prolonged chase.

A vagina that is separate from the urethra makes women biologically more advanced and superior to man. Males use one orifice for sex and liquid wastes. In frogs such multi-purpose openings are called "cloacas."

Yet women depend on using another multi-purpose orifice to achieve equality with words. (Outside verbal foreplay, who prefers conversation to fornication? Seals of both sexes "scratch each other's back" and each *alpha* male mates with his "harem" a hundred times a season.)

Speech makes another "cloaca" of our mouth, which accepts food and emits sound. Other animals use other organs to communicate, like rubbing their legs for insects like crickets. Only Marilyn Monroe has mastered "tail-talk" on which deer in our hill depend.

As the fittest, insects, bacteria and viruses are the dominant life-forms in our planet. A quarter of all mammals are bats and more species are appearing. ("Creation" is not just a one-time event, even for stars.) They also create their own echoes, while we only echo our idols.

The struggle to be equal to others is a confession of perceived inferiority. To catch up, the inferior tries to undo or discount evolution, even depend on another cloaca. Their superiors, male or female, who are not guilty of endorsing such a failed strategy, do not battle for equality.

Only after we have outgrown the uniquely human battle of the sexes in this new sexology can we be what other animals never get to enjoy. We can begin to enjoy grandparenthood. (The best arranged marriages had grandchildren in mind.) And develop a New Psychiatry.

From above obvious considerations came senso-socio-sexual rationalysis in the transcultural art and science of living from **A** to **Z**.

(i) SENSO-MORAL DEVELOPMENT of VIRTUES and VIRTUOSITIES:

We gave up the infant's freedom to feel (**A**) good or (**A'**) bad so as to be free to do what is (**B**) right or (**B'**) wrong, and being right or wrong to see what is (**C**) true or (**C'**) false or to (**D**) sort out facts from fancies, as adults, or (**E**) invent theories or tools with (**Z**) inherited talents.

(ii) SOCIO-ETHICAL DEVELOPMENT of VALUES and BIASES (BELIEFS):

F.	Religion	(all souls must be saved)
G.	Politics	(rights guarantee freedoms)
H.	Economics	(playing fields must be level)
I.	Psychology	(individuals always count)
J.	Sociology	(diversity is more desirable)
K.	Technology	(tools should be shared)
L.	Humanism	(mankind is one family)
M.	Ecology	(the planet is for all of us)
N.	Ethology	(animals have equal rights)
O.	Electronics	(artificial intelligence helps)

(iii) EROTO-SEXUAL STAGES of GENDER DEVELOPMENT w/ or w/o PERVERSIONS:

	Male	Female
	Male	Female
(P)	autoeroticism	narcissism
(Q)	fetishism	boy-aping
(R)	voyeurism	homoeroticism
(S)	exhibitionism	stripteasing
(T)	pedophilia	flirting
(U)	homosexuality	babysitting
(V)	bestiality	heavy petting
(W)	rapacity	mothering
(X)	monogamy	empty-nesting
(Y)	fatherhood	adultery

Z: A social SENSO-SEXUAL (Z)enith of HUMAN DEVELOPMENT: Grandparenting

Our SENSES = SENSE of REALITY

Awful, scratchy sounds make our skins crawl even if they don't qualify as awesome.

A child who cries unappeasably irritates violence-prone adults who were themselves injured as children for the same reason and learned but too well the value of peace (confused with quietude) at any price, including physical measures to stop the noise.

Sudden, loud noises more than even very bright lights make young animals, especially infants, shrink away from their source.

The first time I sneezed near my granddaughter, she cried in alarm. Now used to it, she just turns her head in my direction and waits for the next sneeze.

Thunderclaps scare even adults whom lightning does not reach. Our senses, invented to monitor our environment, prompt different responses from the same event.

Without them and/or imagination we are bored or lost. The bored are unimaginative.

(Except in the dark, animals and children on their own are never bored. But in the darkness of a van taking us to dinner, two kids—who had just met and played side by side silently indoors—startled us when they started "talking" to each other in their own "language", probably because they need sounds around them when they cannot see what is going on.)

Utopians go from perception to imagination, from reality to fantasy. Scientists reverse the process.

Like Machiavelli, I don't mind appearing either wise or wicked or both.

1. "To be" or "to act" is sensual if, in being or acting, we know our being and our acts.

"Sensual" means "touch me," "catch me," "teach me." Without someone to touch it, the infant will (P) "groom" itself autoerotically or narcissistically. Without someone to catch or/and teach it without preaching, the toddler may remain (Q) a packrat (future fetishist) or a tomboy (assertive feminist). As juveniles or adolescents, other "learned" sensual experiences become erotized despite parental preaching, and we become what adults call (R) voyeurs or lesbians, (S) "flashers" or "teasers", (T) molesters or flirts, (U) gay or maternal, and (V) bestial or abortive. Erotized and reproductive, we become (W) rapacious or adoptive, and (X) monogamous or adulterous. Later we become (Y) paternal or menopausal, until what is sexual becomes (Z) familial.

(Some of those who were "caught" and stopped from masturbating as children now insist that what they do with their bodies is their business, though not always their choice, and nobody else's. Sometimes, not even the father of the "abortus" (the embryo is always female in the first trimester among mammals), or "stillborn" (a short-lived fetus), finds out.)

2. As (A) infants we are inescapably adualistic (pre-Cartesian), as (B) children very curious (experimental or operational and pre-logical), as (C) adolescents eagerly autonomous (dichotomy-driven, still pre-Cartesian but logical), and (D) as adults more doubtful (Cartesian) and comparative (post-logical), less

utopian or metaphysical as contradictions become paradoxes (post-Cartesian).

Throughout life, precociously or not, inherited (**E**) creativity (post-logical) and animality shape our self-expression (cathartic) and unevenly sublimate in art or science our divined discontent.

A, **B**, and **C** are stages where, respectively, good or bad, right or wrong, and true or false are primary pre-occupations. Those stuck in one of them may never (**D**) test or (**E**) create. *(t/1)*

3. Our values (**F** to **O**) are always congruent with our virtues, but that is not the whole story behind our personal development and our social evolution. Congruencies are compromises with overt contingencies. Thusly do our virtues and values tell more about concurrent circumstances and lesser-evil options than they do about us.

"Value" is a fetish and object of blind reverence, like "democracy", for habitual reductionists or whatever is regarded with awe by existentialists in anguish. Values are newer than "virtues", and more power-invested or equality-sensitive and less morally informed or liberty-conscious.

You can be happy with a fetish (work or fiction). Those without one can make the pursuit of happiness a fetish in itself and, unlike obsessed "weight-watchers", hunger without starving.

(Instead of its being a happening, happiness becomes the Holy Grail against despair.)

But scientists are also captive if relentless taskmasters. Our concern about gods and computers repeats the sequence of our personal development. We decide whether our God and/or computers, etc. are good or bad, right or wrong, true or false, testable or not, and creative or not.

4. There are sensorimotor stages and serendipity, neither equitable nor equal. Then there is bio-sexual asymmetry and gender-differentiated "chosen" cronies and synchrony that are

just as serendipitous. With sexual partners, distance between developmental "preferences" (stasis) may disclose duration of dissonance or pregnant silences, present and future. Through no fault of theirs, though they tend to blame each other or their teachers.

(Contrast the Duke and Duchess of Windsor with Adolf Hitler and Eva Braun. Which partner of each pair had higher dominance? [Is dominance an obsolete notion for our species? In others, the dominant wins but never annihilates.])

Are you
(**A**) affectionate and (**F**) God-fearing or (**G**) hero worshipping;
(**B**) bashful or willful and (**H**) barter-minded or (**I**) individualistic;
(**C**) seeking answers and (**J**) civic-minded or (**K**) mechanical;
(**D**) discriminating and (**L**) lonely, a loner, or (**M**) Mother Nature's lover; and/or
(**E**) endowed with talent and appreciative of (**N**) natural or (**O**) artificial intelligence?

Will you revert to old habits with aging (**A** -> **E** -> **A'** or **F** -> **O** -> **F'**)?

Can consensual or traditional and professional or confraternal ethics equalize the imbalance of power (divine or secular) between the elite and the unwashed (sinner or supplicant)?

When your work does not change your life, then your job is not needed to survive. Therefore, that you have prevailed is a fact.

5. To regress is to reverse our program. During regression, by definition emerging unconsciously (unchosen), we become more childlike, as when we get sick.

Note that progressive fits and starts always imply (1) transitory "regression" (reversion to old, or already unconscious, habits of resistance or offence), and (2) a concerted defense against (a) any novelty (like this transcultural, sex-linked but not time-bound synthesis), and (b) the changes which it invites.

BASICS in BUILDING BEHAVIOR

Because our brain got bigger to gain advantage, our infants are damaged on delivery and then sometimes are sexually, mentally and physically abused as children by "well-meaning" but similarly handicapped kin and "baby doctors" or lay "surgeons" who engage in ritual (unquestioningly accepted) circumcision and clitoridectomy.

What—beyond postnatal bruising of our brain that has grown bigger than its mother's breeches and its subsequent over-scheduling to cope with contingencies which it has impractically multiplied—is unique about us that we must all cultivate and await, Thoreau-like, to blossom, or else domesticate and then surrender to society?

Setting aside anything for later retrieval in contingency planning has given us larger brains for banking memories longer than any headlong pursuit requires. Prudence is just procrastination of what comes naturally. But, for internal harmony to be maintained, attention span cannot be exceeded by imposed time span in animals, young or old, with undeveloped brains.

> (Or harmony with nature takes a backseat to harmony with society or its deity when we seek success or salvation more than survival: For instance, we cannot slow down if we must outrun acquired rivals and, instead of perceiving nature as neutral and animals as single-minded (but not greedy,) we believe both are here on earth for us to enslave.)

Bigger human brains under collapsible "fontanelles" (soft spots in the infant's skull) get battered at birth and violence-prone when frustrated or provoked.

Only a violence-prone human brain finds "love" in "mercy killing", and excitement in hunting with weapons which, intermixed in the same people, make us a problem for some target species that we domesticate or treat as pets or prey.

Besides being brain-damaged on delivery, we are also bodily less able than other animals to survive on our own. Might our inhumanity arise from surviving and thriving only by over-compensating for (a) both disabilities and/or (b) early genital trauma—from enduring either circumcision or clitoridectomy in some cultures without consent or anesthesia—for reasons that have to be learned but not probed?

(Future harm from infection or self-indulgence are not any more fanciful as excuses for traditional sexual abuse of any child after the Stone Age than the fear of smothering an infant who sleeps with its mother that prompts her to abandon it all night! Crib deaths occur in isolated nurseries.

ENVOI

Personal morality may be defined by parental constraints on the freedoms enjoyed by their children and limited to them and—expectably yet sometimes surprisingly—by their children to theirs. Social ethics may be narrowly defined by the rights and responsibilities of the guild: in professional ethics, that is often simply the rights, privileges and obligations of the members of the profession.

Morality and ethics domesticate the weak by reward and punishment of cowards. The strong and sensual surrender only to sensation, the socially ambitious always to superiors, while the sexually fearless can kill or die to copulate.

Without self-consciousness except perhaps belatedly as rare hindsight, we grow as (**i**) persons by (**A**) feeling for animals and those like us, (**B**) trying, "willing" or "choosing" sides, (**C**) speculating by polarities and "teasing" to pieces what we think, (**D**) "sizing up", "sorting out" and (**E**) connecting anew—precociously, if our grandparents were talented— to invent and synthesize prostheses or tear up and build other theories.

Old but not senescent, we can enjoy **A** to **E** also as (**Z**) grandparents. We age in reverse order (**E'** -> **A'**), by ceasing to create, compare, reflect, select, and expect.

Sensual (**A** to **E** and **Z** for zenith of personal development) is what we do with all real or imaginary age groups, including leading, teaching, testing, and "sexual" foreplay in the infant-mother dyad. Love, including love of old deities and new celebrities, is sensual, before it becomes a cult or grows into lust.

People often confuse (**A**) good with (**B**) right and/or (**C**) true, or (**A'**) bad with (**B'**) wrong and/or (**C'**) false, before they could (**D**) compare and (**E**) connect good with beneficiary, right with arbiter, and true with reporter. *(t/2)*

Wrong or misdeed and false or misleading do not have to be prisons because they can be corrected or verified, if one is free to be disloyal or unfaithful.

Historically we have claimed to be (**ii**) "civilized" by being (**F**) "holier than thou", (**G**) powerful, (**H**) wealthy, (**I**) self-conscious, (**J**) civic-minded, (**K**) technical, (**L**) humanistic, (**M**) puritan about pollution, (**N**) protective of endangered lives, and (**O**) artificially intelligent, proudly and predictably.

> Americans who are (**I**) individualistic have been directly challenged by a (**J**) group-conscious Japanese (**H**) economy. (Islanders sometimes behave like sub-mariners sharing limited and vulnerable space requiring collective vigilance to ensure survival. Large land-mass inhabitants can be like test pilots who can break sound barriers without fear of jeopardizing comrades.)

Social (**F to O**) is what we believe with our age group, like following any teaching, even about God. What is social, like bias or hate, which has to be learned but not scrutinized or compared, is neither sensual nor sexual.

As ideology, **F to O** were created to stop questions about (**F**) God ("true faith" is the first known oxymoron), (**G**) government, (**H**) money, (**I**) persons, (**J**) groups, (**K**) machines, (**L**) humanity, (**M**) environment, (**N**) animals, and (**O**) robots.

> The poorest countries are deluged with (**F**) religious missionaries and (**G**) military consultants, and spend more on traditional rituals and conventional arms than the affluent (**H**). *(t/3)*

Sexual (**P to Y**) is what we erotically do alone or with another to procreate or not. Consensus is social; co-habiting is carnal. What is sensual grows with freedom, procreation is sexual and comes with puberty, with or without romance. Auto-, homo-, and hetero-erotic orientation or "preference" may be but only very rarely freely "chosen" and yet oftener more loudly proclaimed than hidden.

P to Z comes from large multitudes with private experiences of (**P**) autoeroticism or narcissism, (**Q**) pack-rats or tom-boys, (**R**) peepers or lesbians, (**S**) flashers or "strippers", (**T**) child-molesters or flirts, (**U**) gays or baby-sitters, (**V**) "animal-" or "baby-lovers", (**W**) lover-boys or "baby-losers", (**Y**) heir-seekers or youth-fanciers, and (**Z**) grandparents.

Beliefs in self-selected myths allow the righteous to feel good about reproducing or not. Believers who do not become what they can be for fear of falling off the edge—like "flat-earthers" or advocates of "Earth first"—inevitably narrow the range of behavior that suits them. "Grand-orphanhood" is the result. *(t/4)*

BEYOND THE MIND

William James (who separated psychology from philosophy): "The word 'dog' does not bite."

M. Ortega: "Behavior betrays what hides behind abstractions: hearts throb to pump, brains build bureaucracies to suit, minds mind or monitor and consciously rehearse what to reveal."

Nouns, e.g., "mind," are more toxic and intoxicating than gerunds, e.g., "minding," unless replaced by a better one, i.e. "mynd" for "myths in my mind."

Like traces of our ancestral heritage reappearing in the human fetus in the order that they evolved, cultural cliches are the milestones in the embryology of civilization which decide our cultural legacy to our descendants: from (**F**) divine purpose or rule or spiritual-mindedness to (**G**) political and (**H**) economic democracy, to (**I**) individualism for the affluent and (**J**) civic-mindedness for neglected minority groups, etc. *(t/5)* Social slogans also shape us—if somewhat irregularly—in the order in which they appeared in history, asking to be taken seriously as the last word until a better slogan comes along: (**F**, as theology, the evangelical "science") "God is great", (**G**, as politics, the "tragic science") "The State is sovereign", (**H**, as economics, the dismal science) "Money makes the world go round", (**I**, as psychology, the "self-important" science) *"Homo sapiens sapiensis* is wise", (**J**, as sociology, the soft science) "The greatest good for the greatest number", (**K**, as engineering, the applicable science) "Progress is our most important product", etc. *(t/6)*

METAPSYCHIATRY

In "meta-psychiatry", the concepts of "soul" and "sin" are seen as no different from other self-serving biases that set up one group above another and make subjects observing related but different rituals open to unwarranted and unyielding criticism from the prejudiced.

Muslims teach that the pain of childbirth was Eve's punishment for listening to the serpent. Other animals do not cry while giving birth or on being born. Are our inauspicious tearful beginnings the true original sin that we "visit" on our children? *(t/7)*

(Birth trauma has been used by Otto Rank (1884–1939) to explain primal anxiety without reference to acute brain injury.)

To blame everything on (1) God's short attention span or "foot-dragging" or (2) early upbringing by struggling parents is to keep one end of the tunnel lighted, but not the cave.

Does "original sin" (stealing from a tree) constitute or include the imposition and substitution of symbols (abstractions and verbalizations) for signals (signs and vocalization)? Has original sin made us congenital cripples clutching at the cross or sword or word as crutches? (Animals do not fret that "In the Beginning was the Word and the word was God . . . His name is legion", including the "Watchmaker" a la Rube Goldberg.) *(t/8)*

Except for Eve plucking the apple, there is no Biblical record of hunters and gatherers, only herding and farming. Cain founded Enoch, the first city in history, in his lifetime. (Dinosaurs are also conspicuous by their absence. Africa was below the equator 3 million years ago.) *(t/9)*

Original Bible stories are still better histories than edited prophecies. *(t/10)* The Dead Sea Scrolls have Jesus telling the Jews that the world would end with their generation. *(t/11)* Myths breed doubts about or beliefs in miracles and martyrs. Is martyrdom just another utopian rescue fantasy? Is parental self-sacrifice less necessary because of martyrs? Is Earth itself merely God's waiting room or holding cell while his assistants fight among themselves for followers?

Opinions that become convictions are delusions by definition. (Can you tell what I actually know quite matter-of-factly from matters of belief?) *(t/12)* Those who believe in believing will confidently use their beliefs to decide what they are not sure about. (Those who are convinced are not lying nor detectable liars on polygraph testing.) Only believers vote or gamble (to see if they are right. That is why church bingo draws religious laggards back to the fold.)

BEYOND BELIEFS

"Education, unlike persuasion, is not poker, which depends on how well you hide your hand or agenda. Philosophy, history and literature, like insanity, have buried drives and hidden agendas." --Ortega

Scientifically speaking, our "behavior" is the reaction or output of the brain and the body working together, whatever their respective states may be, well or ill or dying. With this fact, psychiatrists do not need to factor in "soul" and "sin" (sickness of the soul which never dies, by definition) in their theorizing.

To replace the "soul" that promised continuity to the Jesuits, we have our DNA to outlast us.

"Mind" (the verb) is what the brain does with its environment. The environment that the brain minds or monitors includes its external, physical or social, and internal material surroundings—liquid, soft, and hard—healthy or toxic, benign or malignant. Minding is more selective; monitoring is simply attentive.

Because most plants are physically stationary, their "minds" are also set,—like most of us who are sedentary—and their behavior does not vary much.

Without the new solipsism of an anthropic principle, the fact that the cosmos is comprehensible to us does not make our mind pre-eminent. It only proves that our senses approximate reality enough for us to be able to rely on our perceptions and feel confident that they will be as dependable as the sun rising in the morn.

Pure animal awareness that compares, classifies and tests its perceptions is complicated by vainglorious self-consciousness in our species. (Julius Caesar welcomed the honor of wearing a laurel wreath around his forehead to hide his baldness.) Should we congratulate ourselves for consciously bending our science to understand the world even if the world on its own can go on, as it has done without us or, perhaps more smoothly, without science?

Our nervous system is both old (decentralized) and new (more centralized) mega-ganglia (or special clusters of neurons), the old providing us with memories on which we build responses to our environment that are "instinctual" (autonomic) or "intuitive" (reptilian) rather than thought out by our newer brain (neo-cortex). The old feeling (limbic) and the newer thinking (hemispheric) brains are also the repository of experiences that the talking brain (Broca's and Wernicke's areas in the left hemisphere) may not yet have words or ready excuses for, in which case we cannot easily articulate or remember some of those that are externally shameful or internally sinful (evoking self-centered guilt).

Our increasingly selective mind is therefore better spelled as "mynd", since it is made up of memories or myths to resolve doubts in our own mind. Older unfalsified memories may be ancestral in the animal "collective unconscious" or archipallium (olfactory cortex) that may be more intuitive (what smells may be putrid) than instinctive. Newer memories show up in our uniquely human mythology (in which case they may be recalled in dreams or unconsciously stored, individually or racially, respectively). Racial archetypes in myths (still intuitive) and recurring (old and uncreative) individual dreams (limbic) are easier to retrieve personally or culturally, especially if they still serve purposes which created or inspired and then hid them to begin with. (Or is that another, new, fantasy?)

To demystify "mynd" would allow the brain to monitor its external and internal world in order for our "body" to verify what had been perceived. The body, growing or aging, is left out when verification is feared. Without verification, self-deception is guaranteed. Our body, which makes it possible for us to test what we think, was also bequeathed to us by distant ancestors whose legacy we may be honoring briefly by looking like them while inside the womb (ontogeny roughly retracing phylogeny).

Without testing, we can play with our mind and come up with philosophy and solipsism (as in "the anthropic principle", rather than art or science. Logical thinking is mental rehearsal, not reality testing. Even computer simulation is simply dress rehearsal, to be tested by actual performance.

Our senses enable us to learn by testing. Without them, we can simply believe without learning to compare myths or slogans ("God is great", "Our country, right or wrong", etc.) *(t/13)*

EVOLUTION of (i) SELF, (ii) CLAN and (iii) KIN

To "know thyself" or examine the "quality of life" that we have, it is more revealing if (**i**) the self or (**A-E**) personal sensomoral development of family virtues and familial virtuosity can be analyzed separately from (**ii**) the clan or (**F-O**) public socio-ethical values and group ideologies, and both from (**iii**) our kin or (**P-Y**) private erotosexual "preferences" according to gender (**m** or **f**) until (**Z**) grandparenthood.

> Beliefs produce more "stepchildren" (neglected "orphans") than divorce or working mothers. (Parents who do not want to be grandparents produce "social welfare-dependent unwed teen-agers" with children without fathers.)

We can then compute the various senso-socio-sexual ratios to discover where we are at any age, compared with peers from any era. Additionally, we now have the means to see what ratios are more or less conducive to the survival of our species than to personal prosperity or social success with or without the burden of responsibility imposed by those more likely to be inconvenienced: rulers rule with restrictions enforced with power to expand their privileges.

More than most species, human beings need communities to thrive in a broader band of habitats. Desert plants and animals cannot migrate to colder climes. It is as if each person is an organ in a more evolved organism, fed by arterial highways and defended by soldier specialists against invaders, large or small. Is this stage of evolution to be desired or encouraged for whom/which: *Homo sapiens, H domesticus,* or *H metropolus*?

Must we become what those who begot us are? Do we become what we believe we are? Do we beget because of our beliefs? Or can believing excuse ignorance in the incurious? (From and for what we already know, believing is unnecessary.)

As we all grow at our own speed from **A** to **E** and **Z** (for Zenith), we leave what we had been to become what we can be. ("Being" was "presence" for the Greeks, and "existence" for Sartre, who was childless but not celibate. ("Being" for Ortega is what we momentarily are.) In believing, from **F** to **O**, we think like others (e.g., Jew or Jesuit, fascist or populist, communist or capitalist, etc.) to keep from doubting too much. From **P** to **Y** (always more gender-determined), we do what we can to beget or not, yet another.

In metaphysics, ontology studies "being" as "essence." Aging intellectuals who confine "theo-ontology" to "becoming human" reserve the right to "beget" for those past their prime. In any herd or flock, animal or human, "becoming" must lead to "begetting." But it cannot be doubted that "believing" (others) delays "becoming" (separate) and puts off "begetting" (our kind).

To get a better idea of how we change, we need to know what it is that undergoes change. One of the inevitable changes is that we grow. But what is it that we grow out of?

We never outgrow what we inherit from our grandparents. We may outgrow what our parents tried to turn us into, if what we had to begin with from our grandparents can offset what our parents demand from us.

When we were very young, we trusted without needing to believe. Blind faith (a redundancy) is trusting without knowing and believing without rituals. If our parents are trustworthy, faith will not require belief in or graven images of (**F**) savior-martyrs, (**G**) master-protectors, and/or (**H**) underwriter-sponsors. Like other well-mothered animals, we will not hesitate to beget.

Doubts which might create (**B**) suspicious skeptics can breed (**C**) gullible believers who postpone becoming what they can be and begetting when they can. (Instead, they then defend second-hand beliefs in utopia as their "favorite children" against their critics.)

Children value the dress code dictated by peers of the same sex even if it offends their parents' sensibilities. (Compulsory education surrounds them with their own age group.) What are virtuous or moral changes from parent to parent, what is valuable or ethical from peer group to peer group, and what is exciting or erotic from partner to partner.

This is why history keeps repeating itself, truly newsworthy media coverage lags behind every new generation, and we cannot legislate morality for adults (even in court, one does not have to be truthful to be believed as long as one does not lie.) Social guilds can only punish public dissent and we must still leave consenting adults alone, provided their sexual deviations remain private.

Values should not be left to parents, virtues should not be left to society. Otherwise, cultists or bigots can be raised at home, and what is bad, wrong or false can be decreed by society (e.g., during the Grand Inquisition).

You can think of raising your parents only if you were loved enough. Love by itself can make them do what you want done. You cannot make them do what they won't. If they refuse, you end up waiting until you can do them yourself, instead of enjoying each day to the full.

Waiting to enjoy yourself makes you look back longingly later for your lost chances or missed opportunities, and because looking back is hard, you try to look harder at what's ahead. If you look hard enough, you can find a reason for going on, but that is just an excuse not to cry for missing out before.

Children can, like other animals, now disown fathers—who may have made them feel insignificant as a "runt"—in the bosom of a new extended family. They could then survive artificial grand-orphanhood in a mobile industrial society, and enjoy a rich post-industrial multi-generational but purely sensual, not social or sexual, family life linked in real time by electronic networks.

It is better to have our children born by elective Cesarean section under hypnosis and to forego surgery of their genitals until they can understand why anyone needs it. *(t/15)*

> All animals inspect a newborn's genitals, but we are the only ones whose infant offspring get theirs cut, whether male or female, by circumcision or clitoridectomy, respectively. *(t/14)*

And then make sure that babies thereafter feel that their home is not just their base for exploring the world but also their sanctuary when hurt, until they have a hearth of their own for their children to huddle around at any age.

> Some cultures keep the newborn from its mother in a strange nursery on arriving "home" from isolation in a hospital nursery. No study of cross-cultural prevalence of crib deaths has reduced this enforced isolation. In adulthood, it continues in the secret nursery of

a car for commuting *Homo m*etropolus in ever-increasing numbers. These same neglected adults, at the expense of their own children, seek to be No. 1 as husbands, or "Queen of the Day" at elaborate weddings.

Kids should be able to play to their hearts' content without risking punishment by/or starvation.

All births that start and end with pain and fear should stop. Safer elective (non-emergency) Cesarean section of the mother without surgical "ethnic cleansing" (to prevent itching?) of the infants' genitals is a simple solution if, like plants interested in cross-pollination, our procreative goal is multiplication. (Sex is cross-pollination, people also romanticize it for recreation or mythologize it as divine procreation.) DNA is shared in non-teleologic teleonomy.

Eventually, we can have universal "immaculate conception" with chemical or electrical stimulation of the egg to start cell division. The one disadvantage is that it can only produce an exact image or "clone." The best cloning method may prevail over others, although only sexual reproduction ensures variation for non-deterministic survival of the fittest in a changing world.

But before attempting wholesale cloning, we have to understand and explain our cruelty to animals and our inhumanity towards each other, as well as our extraordinary kindnesses and achievements. (t/16)

We therefore have to study if

1. the damage from natural childbirth to our over-sized brain makes us, unlike animals, violence-prone or considerate of victims of any violence, including all "Acts of God";

2. life in our nuclear family triangle virtually makes each of us a "runt" at birth;

3. genital abuse soon after makes us afraid of the unknown and keen to control what happens as soon as we can escape unhurt;

4. our motor handicaps and sensory deprivations make what is often trivial to animals seem pregnant with mysterious meaning for us;

5. such search for meaning make murderers of believers in their own myths, like Hitler; and/or

6. the same handicaps and deprivations either (a) force us to concentrate our energies better to become an over-achiever like Helen Keller or, after failing, (b) prompt us to congratulate ourselves for our obsessions and/or convictions. (Animals pay for failing.)

To answer all these, can we study the children of identical twins, one of whom delivers by elective Caesarean section, refuses surgical sexual abuse of, sleeps with, and breast-feeds her infant on demand, does not prematurely delegate grooming and educating it by early toilet training or kindergarten schooling, and supplements bed-time stories of goblins, fairy god-mothers and absentee guardians with user-friendly computer instruction, without emphasizing logic or rhetoric and virtues or values, so that they can beget without believing with others, even in God? *(t/17)*

Our heritage shapes our legacy. Can a new mutation correct any imbalances that we may already have wrought, wittingly or unwittingly, but cannot ever reverse? Or must a Messiah arrive in time to save our souls, if not our skin? *(t/18)*

Cultures without the necessary tools to master stronger animals have worshipped their graven images as totems and then eaten their principal organs, as do the vulnerable among us who need to partake of the body and blood of their designated martyr in order to be saved by His sacrifice. (Must we give up living like all animals in our place under the sun for the promise to sit at His table after we die?)

We cannot depend on "good" and "bad" vibrations to change course like bats can, or on UFO reports that may only foreshadow our need for another Star of Bethlehem (which was not even a star at that). *(t/19)*

Where Western theologians use miracles and mysteries to convert their unschooled missionaries to their logically derived notion of an orderly universe, Eastern "gurus" lose the simple-minded by using paradoxes to illustrate complementary reciprocities in their theory. They also meditate or communicate unity in silence and do not pray or praise to advance their reincarnation or to deserve salvation by sincere flattery or attempts at bribery.

The chasm between (1) linear "cause and effect" thinking for believers in a "Final Cause" and (2) non-linear "inter-relatedness" for disbelievers can be bridged by demonstrating that we all share our roots regardless of our myths or reservations.

An orphan, even after adoption, expects to be reclaimed by its distinguished parents as soon as they complete a very important mission.

Does yearning for divine parenthood imply mental reservations about our own parents or, Jesus-like, just about our mother's husband? (t/20)

Neither the Holy Trinity of Christian monotheism nor Freud's patricidal Oedipus is comprehensible to Trobriand Islanders in the Pacific who live with their mothers and maternal uncles. (Fathers don't count!) They cannot identify with a son who kills his father to monopolize his mother, or a Child who dies by the hands of His social superiors in order to return to His Father's side.

Many who believe that there is no "mental illness" and expect patients to take responsibility for their deeds are also equally convinced that they know what it takes to be "human", but even the best and worst examples of either start by having been not as good or somewhat better in the past and changing for the worse or for good later on. Such "irritability" proves that changes are real and unintentional, welcome or not, stigmatized or pedestalized or not.

Belief systems, whether idiosyncratic as in paranoid delusions, or shared as in social delusions, say to each believer, "I'm O.K., others are not!"

Beliefs ultimately divide, intentionally or not; science ultimately unifies, even as it clarifies: A recurrent theme may be discovered that unites disparate elements, even delusions, into a comprehensible unity:

In the beginning was either a Bang or a Word, that nobody heard. What makes both important are the adjectives used in connection with them, the Big Bang or Father Almighty ("and the word was God"). Their importance cannot be measured, except subjectively.

The Children's Manifesto

We have a manifesto for children these abuses that must be prevented: natural childbirth even with episiotomy, circumcision and clitoridectomy, silencing their cries by battering the source of incoherent or annoying noise, premature denial of vocalization to replace it with verbalization and emphasis on common nouns to de-individualize their experience.

As long as children cannot choose their parents, every child should be a "love-child", unburdened by expectations that were born before its talents have emerged. Toilet and language training (replacing vocalization with verbalization) should not be regimented. Every child should have a guaranteed annual income, a parent and at least two grandparents. With its grandparents as its *ombudsmen* or advocate and its parent's junior, but older, partners, it ought just please only one bossy adult animal.

Are Cesarean section and circumcision unnatural? Which is better for infants mentally and physically? All children can be born by elective Cesarean section, without genital abuse, and breast-fed on demand by mother or surrogate who sleeps with them until they can acquire their own roommate and/or be circumcised, whichever comes first. Only then should the artificial nuclear family take over. Thus, most men can expect only to be grandfathers.

(Testosterone-linked maleness needs no role models, but mothering does. Only men have killed the young without regret, women historically keep them alive.) (t/21)

We have to make sure that children can question what to believe before indoctrination with blind faith, because the sole antidote for indoctrination is decortication. Only those whose doubts are stilled by what they assume without challenge find their mental safety net less secure and become perceptibly uncomfortable with questions about their forgotten doubts. *(t/22)*

Why are human beings the only animals who abuse their mates and their own offspring? (Sometimes I love my wife more when she is asleep, and adults are fonder of children when they are quiet.)

Why do only human beings kill strangers for other strangers, even invisible ones whom they believe in, like God or Queen. (Fathers, not mothers, sacrifice their sons to strangers.)

(And why do human beings grant these strangers' their magical qualities? Lower primates only deceive themselves by believing that they can actually do things from a distance by and for themselves.)

If we are less like other social animals who do not fight with their females or abuse their own offspring—some tomcats get rid of those of another's to secure their nursing mother sooner as a "sex object"—can we outlive peer pressure for parity (post-adolescent equality) without limiting our liberty and fertility, through socio-medical (condoms are unwritten pre-nuptial agreements) or surgical contraception and the technotronics of mass murder? One frees oneself, not to be equal, but to be masterless.

THE BIO-ANTHROPOLOGY of/from CLINICAL RATIONALYSIS

(The author sees psychiatry as reconciling the order of science with the exceptions that exist in nature. His expositions in art unite the aesthetics of abstract forms with natural beauty in snowflakes. He does not therefore discount the discoveries of Freud and Jung.)

Freud's psychoanalysis enriched culture with the psychopathology of everyday life, and Jung's archetypes illuminated the collective unconscious. Our rationalysis of sub-cycles in life also produced the subspecies of *Homo sapiens, H domesticus* and *H metropolus*, almost from the time we engaged in herding and farming, merchandising and manufacturing, to the computer and space age. *[Table 16]*

Today, motorized *Homo sapiens*, who think they deserve the best, hog the left lane; *Homo domesticus*, who think they are undeserving, leave it even if there are no cars wanting to pass; *Homo metropolus*, who think they deserve better, tries to pass every car or shoot at those who drive by and cut across their secret, private nursery.

Domestication with agriculture aided by farm animals started in Southeast Asia about ten thousand years BC. Goddesses reigned in Southeast Europe from 7000 BC. The Near East produced the first cities. Jericho was founded between five and 6000 BC.

(Marija Gimbutas of UCLA wrote of gods and goddesses. India had 108 names for its goddesses. Where goddesses reigned supreme, as in the first 25 verses of Genesis, the world was more harmonious with nature.)

Five thousand BC produced the earliest writing. The Bible was written long afterwards.

(If the first word was God, it must have been derived from "Help!" Words evolve from conversation, not by immaculate conception.)

Nature deities were supplanted by ceremonial deities (**F**) but beyond tribal feuds, ceremonial wars were followed by wars of conquests, (**G**), even now preceded by warriors' prayers.

Primates also enjoy magical thinking.

CONCLUSIONS

One cannot be free as a unicorn unless independently wealthy, no matter how high the income, especially if it cannot erase all debts, even in this age of timesaving technology for centaurs. To be happy, instead of just complacent, all one needs is a demanding sport, a compatible partner in bed, a satisfying profession and a challenging problem, in that order.

(In surroundings unspoiled by human ambition, animal appetites are easier to satiate. Surrounded by domesticated, status-conscious "yuppies", all I need, in order to be content, is one woman, two books on different sides of the same subject, and three new tennis balls.)

One of the first things scientists have come to accept about our species is that words cannot compensate for sensory deprivations which shape our thoughts.

Dogs can hear, bees smell, bats avoid obstacles, and birds, who share our ear for music, see better than we do. (Teamwork was discovered by insects, architecture practiced by termites, engineering started by beavers, and shelter invented by nesters.)

Neither "To be or not to be?" nor "TV or not TV?" for a short life under the spotlight are the important questions. Better questions are: (**i**) "To be or to become?", (**ii**) "To believe or disbelieve?", and (**iii**) "To beget or not?"

"Becoming" is not becoming unless it means becoming free to be one's own self.

"Believing" is merely sharing gossip (public opinion if widespread) unless it means believing with one's clan that its members are special or at least equal to those of others.

"Begetting" does not get one more than another kin who shares one's genes.

We have grown up as soon as (i) being free means being masterless, not masterful, (ii) believing we are all equal gives way to the discovery that we are all different, and (iii) begetting is simply multiplying our kin, not necessarily kindred to us in spirit or to our kind of people in shared interests.

What makes us different (alienated) from other life-forms, domesticated or not, in our universe? Whatever it is does not make us unique or special, except in our eyes. But we cannot ask how time, even before we evolved, ties into our behavior if we insist on thinking that we are unique and special—e.g., as (J) ethnocentric Nazi Aryan racist or Zionist xenophobic Jew or (L) anthropocentric humanist or "white-collar racist", etc.—instead of just different; i.e., (II) humanimal, even if (iii') "sexist," like a lion with his pride or a queen bee with her drones.

Are we the Helen Kellers of the cosmos or the Adolf Hitlers of the animal kingdom, or inextricably both simultaneously, unlike their "children"? (More controversial editions of Helen Keller and Adolf Hitler are Franklin Roosevelt and the KKK.)

A zealot will deny some of the following and their denial is a confession of zeal for what is not denied.

The children of monolithic zealots are seldom serially free to (A) feel, (B) try, (C) think, (D) compare, and (E) be different.

Scientists are kibitzers in a contest whose rules are not obvious to all. Even specialists in our field can talk confidently only of the part of the "human elephant" nearest to them.

(I was lucky to be born of a free-thinking Mason and a devout Catholic and to be raised by both and a maiden aunt who was a spiritualist. They could doubt each other's belief without disrespect. We did not need consensus to enjoy our blessings.)

[Anoxia from nearly drowning when I was nine years old may also have destroyed traces of indoctrination when still gullible (virtually undefended). Without gills for breathing, did it also cause me to try using my old reptilian brain underwater? (Amphibians have survived for 200 million years, outliving dinosaurs and outlasting the Ice Ages. Hydrophilic rhinoceros are near extinction because of alleged aphrodisiac properties in the chemistry of their upstanding tusks. Will the recent discovery of Viagra for erectile dysfunctions save them?)]

Those who only value what is not denied may or may not die for what they value. They may not refuse to die for their country (while serving as medical corpsmen in the battlefront), yet refuse to kill for it as a conscientious objector.

The value placed on an ideology may not be priceless, and betrayal can be bought with promised privileges or threatened retaliation from competing ideologists [who (**F**) pray convincingly, (**G**) terrorize fearlessly, (**H**) barter persuasively, etc.]

To be "civilized," we have serially swallowed many a theological, political, economic, psychological, sociologic, technological, humanistic, ecological, ethologic, and even electronic fiction without demanding data (which we here provide). Those who conform are afraid to be on their own.

We are taught, in varying ratios and with varying success, that the Church (**F**) is the spirit of the body politic (our psyche has its own soul), the state (**G**) the sword or shield, business (**H**) the gold, psychology (**I**) the mind, society (**J**) the child, technology (**K**) the hand, humanism (**L**) the aim, ecology (**M**) the truth, ethology (**N**) the test, and electronics (**O**) the intelligence.

(Victor Frankl who was victorious in the end is a product of **C** × **F'** (search for meaning during spiritual distress), Alfred Adler of **C'** × **G** (will to power during mental conflict), Adam Smith of **B** × **H** [will to riches in the marketplace].)

Is God the Joker a pre-eminent taskmaster who must be obeyed or has the state superseded God in its claim on the citizen? Or is money the better master? Whom/which do you trust?

Whom will you work harder to please, your Creator, your country, or your creditors? Or do you wish for the Heavenly Father, Dear Motherland or the Almighty Dollar to leave you alone at peace with simple creature comforts?

Can we probe the reciprocal ratio between enjoying and dreaming according to our belief in magic (animism), a creator (deism), a clock-maker (monotheism) or our own creation (pantheism)?

We can enjoy the unidimensional protagonists of fiction just as we enjoy the heroes of fairy tales and Westerns, without clothing them with regal raiment as symbols of truth and beauty.

We can enjoy a royal parade and its glitter and pomp without attributing divinity to the procession or the participants or wishing that the emperor had dressed for it. Or wishing that the prince would change places with paupers (antiheroes).

We can now be more precise in triangulating antecedent and immediate trends of concurrent "disease" and predict and influence "direct" consequences (destinations or ports of call in its course):

1. Provided we develop better strategies of diagnosis and intervention, not by measurement, but in the elision of what is trivial, which only experts in ethology, including human behavior, can decide (about abstractions, debate, institutions, marriage, opinions, ritual, scores, success, values, etc.)
2. Otherwise, we would correlate garbage with trash and sink in sewage worse than wasted words: numbers are harder to consign to "the round file." With computers, interrelationships are easier to sort out. The basic science of ethology will assist in and be facilitated by the study of human behavior.

What high technology can do that is new is to plot where significant relationships intersect and where reciprocity does not exist.

Unless value-ridden ourselves, we can personalize or tailor our attitude to patients who respond as persons whether the patient in them grudgingly consents or not. We can think of them, not as individuals, but as patiently awaiting the emergence of other selves from the family closet.

The "battle of the sexes" is both human and recent. It brings a rival into the mother-child dyad. With sexual inhibition and genital hypochondriasis, the brain compensates as an erogenous zone.

When it comes to love, your first must be someone you did not dream you could even touch and the last someone you could not see living without. With both, you must get along in at least two positions, not including kneeling. Couples who play together last longer than those who pray together:

> My wife and I are well matched in tennis but/and do not agree on anything we can do sitting down except in what to order in a restaurant. [Socially, she's more of a yuppie than I am a hippie. (She shined my dress shoes even after I told her clean boots only means one has horses, and decided against going braless to my 16-year-old granddaughter's cotillion where I wore tails for her first dance.) She believes in reward and responsibility, I believe nothing except what I learn from experience but even that cannot foretell what the future holds.)

We only need three things from life, parents who love us more than they love themselves, a good mate, and grandchildren.

It is said that children and grandparents get along because they have a common enemy in the children's parents. It is now timely to issue a separate manifesto for those who have survived married life to graduate as grandparents: They have to ensure that the helpless are not taken advantage of.

If the net effect of disbelieving is like that of a wet blanket on one's enthusiasms, it may be both sad and timely. Which it is matters a lot.

20.00 t/SUMMATION

t/Chapter Notes

[t/1] How many grandparents build treehouses? (Its 8 levels on 8 trees which grew around one that I planted 20 years ago - to provide summer shade for a three-story-high window, - were made of materials that I can lift and haul atop the roof of an old car that I knew was strong enough to carry its own weight.

Moreover, how many psychiatrists design habitats? Do you know of any?

In my case, both were signs of aging, the first a return to nest-building by the original female with which all mammals start fetal life. [Ostensibly, building for patients was to re-route indoor traffic in troubled homes: I had a family therapy session once that centered around a teenage daughter needing a bra for graduation, and her father being surprised that she had breasts, when they were clearly better developed than his wife's. Contrast this self-imposed blindness with unabashedly asking my braless daughter once to change to something less distracting than a T-shirt when she came to the dinner table. (I found subsequently that there was less need for denial or confrontation when the ambivalent or quarrelsome guardians are out of sight or hearing of the adolescent or retiree. Tension used to increase on school or work holidays when the student or commuter is under-foot. Before then, I had always wondered why more money is spent on cars than in homes when corrected for time spent in both. *Homo metropolus* also needs the privacy of a secret nursery in a single-passenger car.]

The second sign of aging was a return to an earlier life-style as a primate. (We can now go from the tree-house to the master bedroom by walking across a suspension bridge or swinging from a glider on a steel cable without touching the floor, or down to the ground on a fireman's pole!) Once we leave the hillside for the seashore, I will have completed the cycle back to amphibian life.

[t/2] Young girls are taught that sex is" better" when it is "right", which results in some finding it more exciting when it is "wrong." "Truth" is also a byword among those who impersonate characters on stage or screen. Is acting according to their nature their goal?

[t/3] After Eden (where there was no freedom of information), there was only one wholesale successful attempt (Soviet) to deny a particular ideology (**F**) for generations. This is just as wrong as people denying (**A**) feelings or disdaining (**P**) masturbation.

As (**iii**) male or female, we evolve (**P** to **Y**) separately and asymmetrically whether we are loners or lovers: The decided "gender gap" is biologically based and not due to inculcated virtues (**A, B, C**), nor to indoctrinated values or ideology (**F** to **O**). Unexamined virtues and values may make us moral automatons and social robots.

[t/4] Grandparenthood (**Z**) may be foolishly or uselessly sacrificed— to (**F**) Father Almighty, (**G**) Little Father or czar or Caesar, etc.)—on the altar or comforting sanctuary of changing (**F** to **O**) mythology (religious, political, economic, psychological, sociological, technical, anthropological, ecological, ethological or electronic).

[t/5] So seen, when Russia first became more involved in (**H**) economics than (**F**) religion, it forged ahead and drew even with the Western military-industrial complex (**G** x **K**). But when the state (**G**) became its new religion, Russia retrogressed, like "born-again" convicts who undergo tardy (**F'**) religious conversion while incarcerated.

[t/6] Only when power from converted energy (**K**) and politics (**G**) become personalized (**I**) in an energetic leader (**B**) who develops inordinate appetite (**AA**), does economic imperialism (**HH**) reign supreme. Totalitarianism ensures the destruction of all that stands in its way (**A, B, F, G, H, I** as in Hitler's Germany, Mussolini's Italy and Stalin's Russia). (But is this also true of theocracies?)

[t/7] The King James' edition of our Bible is rated PG-13 for parental guidance of pre-pubescent children. The X-rated version reserved in Harvard's archives for scholars allows Adam two wives (seen on the door of St. John's chapel in the Greek island of Patmos, where he was buried), Eve and Lilith (who preferred God as her consort: only Eve was evicted from Eden).

[t/8] "God", who was great, if only in the first week, was the answer to how everything got started until "zero" appeared as an equally logical, and "evolution" as a verifiable, explanation. If we speak of time warp from the time the universe began with a Bang, it has been argued that God took the cosmic equivalent of "six earth days" to create us, after which he rested, slept or died. Yet the seven-day week came—late on the seventh "earth day"—from the Sumerian calendar that the Semites had taken over along with their land. To explain this, divine omniscience is required. But omniscience makes omnipotence redundant. So we end up with divine redundancy. (Nonetheless, self-serving creationism can still be reassuring, if the study of evolution is disturbing to our pride or insulting to the human spirit.)

[t/9] Without God, how can the faithful find new converts with stories of a global (bipolar?) flood that is outlived by a bigamous, drunken Noah when we still debate how dinosaurs died? And why choose a deluge instead of a Messiah to declare religious amnesty (and make Moses and the Ten Commandments obsolete)?

[t/10] Eden, of course, which was often deluged by rain- and sand-storms, cannot claim to be the paradise of the Old Testament which was written after Sumerians taught the Semites to write when they took over Mesopotamia.

Bali, on an island without flashfloods, now called the Last Paradise, was and is more idyllic and enduring than Eden. It still worships blacksmiths who use meteorites from outer space and volcanic fire from the core of the earth to produce "gems" of near-perfection (which have inspired my youngest to design jewelry in their idiom). (Why are over-priced cut stones called "gems"?)

[t/11] Did the Jews, and not the Romans lose with the crucifixion of Jesus, because the Jews chose Barabbas over Jesus? (They are still waiting for the coming of the Messiah, Redeemer from Sin and Savior of Souls.

Did Heisenberg, who won the Nobel Prize for discovering that we cannot ever be absolutely sure, grant Hitler, like self-taught Jesus His Father, the presumption that the Nazis and their land have been chosen by destiny over all others? Were the Jews gassed because a super-race cannot abide the thought that a God had selected another to love more?

[t/12] A single cell would have been enough to clone innumerable Steves. (Or God must be a hermaphrodite to have "impregnated a Virgin.") Can a unicorn have come from a horse and a caribou, a centaur from Adam and an ass, and an androgyne from a forgiven Adam and Eve in Paradise regained after Resurrection of a crucified sacrificial lamb/ Shepherd?

[t/13] In the last war, it was thought that because the Japanese were carried on their mother's back, their pilots cannot counter-attack and, instead of getting into a dog-fight in mid-air, would dive and die in kamikaze attacks on surface vessels.

Believing is a social disease in need of judicious injections of doubt as an antidote. Socially, when our senses do not satisfy our curiosity, we believe in, but do not gain knowledge from those who teach, preach, profess, or parrot what they have not tested. (Sexually, we can also play with ourselves and never or later join another to reproduce.)

[t/14] Harems (now replaced by mistresses for the wealthy, groupies for celebrities, and hangers-on for politicians) were guarded by eunuchs, but castration-anxious neurotics fear harm from fathers and wives or surrogates, not to their ability to procreate (from pending testicular excision) but to penetrate, not from penile amputation but out of unresolved fears around an un-consented post-natal incision called circumcision. [Catholics also, for domestication/acculturation purposes, ritually baptize their kids before the age of consent, but that is easier partly to undo, though permanent emotional if partial scarring (**A'**) will still be unavoidable.]

[t/15] In a quarter century of surveying patients randomly assigned for training - at least 2 each week to more than 200 physicians over their four-year, post-graduate program in psychiatry - I was unable to find but a single admission who had been born by elective Cesarean section or was an accomplished trumpet player: Ronnie Scott had a history of "nervous break-downs and finally killed himself.") Both groups presumably had no breathing difficulties to handicap them. Relaxed breathing is characteristic of those who meditate or terrorize successfully

As the full term baby's oversize head exits, obstetricians routinely, - by "episiotomy" under local anesthesia, - cut the vulva to have a clean-cut wound instead of ragged edges to stitch together. (I have taught auto-hypnosis to make birth and routine episiotomy painless and the process orgiastic, but this only helps the mother to finally let go.)

[t/16] Other animals take strays as members of their family, but never indulge them like we do our pets, lavishing on them the affection that we had enjoyed, or deserved but never received. Following a dog with a "poop-scoop" for its sidewalk droppings is similar to what mother cats do for their kittens, to keep their lair unsoiled.

[t/17] The last logical and therefore appealing utopian dream was to free mothers to be citizens. Instead of "poor me, first" or "Earth first", can we put our "kids first"? Then wanting to be "Queen for a Day" (the star in a grand wedding ceremony) or "Miss America" or "King of the Hill" will seem less necessary or compensatory.

[t/18] Our earliest ancestors could not have seemed superior to other animals. Native Americans drove stampeding buffaloes – which can panic like lemmings and sheep – over cliffs when they could not overpower them.

Some birds who had no land enemies gave up flying and cannot cope with deadly newcomers. Those who rule the air are the most majestic still. Uprooted, we cannot shirk our job to help the wind spread plant seeds.

[t/19] Who disposed of the gifts of the Magi (Greek for "magician")? (All were perishable goods except the gold.) There are still some islands where warplanes landed whose natives continue to search the skies for the "second coming" of generous soldiers. Prostheses e.g., space ships can give us greater range so that we do not have to be earth-bound (i.e., moon-struck). Can you imagine the thinking that overlooks hibernation because it is not present in desert life? (No teddy bears for gifts!)

The Biblical scribes were chosen from those who could read and write but, like us, they did not know that the information they have in their heads can be dated. What is in Genesis is Bronze Age lifestyle.

[t/20] Jesus was thought to be a mulatto because of his hair and skin color, which could explain much of his social and sexual history. He lived the life reserved for bastards but never grew closer to His mother. (Did His rescue of Mary Magdalene an adulteress also signify His forgiveness for her namesake?) Dead, is He the right Mr. Right for nuns? Or a Santa Claus for all seasons for children of all ages. "Married", like Santa, is he an ideal Sugar Daddy for the hungry to fantasize about *in absentia*?)

At any time, are there more sincere believers in Santa than in God? Both are probably equal as commercial opportunities most likely to succeed without paid ads.

[t/21] I am the exception that validates the Children's Manifesto. I did not have grandparents and was delivered by forceps, but my mother obeyed me as the firstborn son, and so did my wet nurse.

By dealing with psychiatry's most disturbing patients with whom my predecessors have failed, no one could boss me around. As director of training, I did not exert extra effort during accreditation visits but always exceeded the expectations of accreditors which were lower than mine.

(Nor have I ever submitted a budget but on the basis of my reputation as a "big spender" received calls towards the end of each fiscal year from federal agencies with unspent money who must show that each penny of their budget was spent before they can ask for more. Thus, my training program expanded while state, county and city budget cuts trimmed those of others. This disgruntled local bureaucrats no end.)

[t/22] There are more Mohammedans than Catholics and Mohammad and Newton surpass Jesus in personal popularity.

What do we teach our children in Sunday school? We tell them that Jesus loves them. Where does that leave them? It implies that whoever loves them can get crucified for doing so.

There was religion and gods and goddesses before zero was invented centuries after the crucifixion. (It did not make Roman numerals obsolete right away.) Children before Sunday school count back to zero After brain-washing about Genesis with a capital G, they can only count back to God.

(Our children are no match for evangelists who can make even gullible adults salivate over old twists of soap opera plots.)

Orthodox religion also warns its followers against tasting the fruit of the Tree of Knowledge. The more Sunday schools there are the lower their science scores on testing. Their studies concentrate on pre-Galilean, pre-Darwinian subjects and their graduates are expected to learn Socratic and critical, instead of scientific thinking.

The outstanding scientist who was also a deist was Sir Isaac Newton, who died boasting he remained a virgin and, like Jesus, did not dally with the opposite sex. (Self-castration may be behavioral or surgical. Can abstinence and absence of distraction or his genetic inheritance explain his intellectual powers? Or is their common disinterest in sex the result of low testosterone levels in Newton and Jesus?

(Albert Einstein, a theist, also maintained that God does not gamble. Einstein himself did not gamble. Is his conviction the result of his own disposition?)

Not very long ago, my younger granddaughter was boasting about her ability to count backwards from ten. When challenged, she ended her count with "zero."

Asked what "zero" meant, she exclaimed "Nothing." To why "Nothing" should have a name, she said it was to end her counting.

I said, for many our name for the beginning was "God" until zero was invented, but she was too young to appreciate that.

Adults, including God, would rather we believe as children in dogma to answer our questions.

A child once objected to a New York museum acquiring a meteor that had fallen in Oregon because God had made it come down in Oregon, not New York!

Their teachers are still in the Dark Ages, waiting to pounce on those who refuse to be domesticated.

The Middle Ages was a huge Sunday school.

21.00 u/Postscript:
BEYOND THEATER and RHETORIC,
PHILOSOPHY and METAPHYSICS

(The author, without planning, is at the end of his third life, having enjoyed a second childhood after near-drowning, and a third adolescence of sowing wild oats in another near-paradise abroad. He wants to add Dr. Roger Penrose's twistor to string theory, and include Y. Ne'eman and M. Gell-Mann's periodic table for subatomic particles in quantum physics among pioneers of this cladistic approach to science.)

What in PSYCHIATRY IS and IS NOT PHILOSOPHY, ART, or SCIENCE?

About the time of this writing, I developed internal bleeding from using aspirin as an analgesic to reduce allergic itching in my eyes. I lost a quarter of my total blood volume, which I have since slowly recovered without transfusion.

Once I nearly died, I began to appreciate what the dying share with the very young. Both are not ruled by stereotypes that dominate the life of the no longer young yet not quite old enough to see the difference each person represents beyond the usual stereotypes.

Stereotyping does not only occur with strangers, it also occurs within families.

Parents, especially those who looked forward to having children, are incompetent insofar as they live in the past with their parents. To be without grandchildren is to be handicapped or to be trapped in a world without surprises or reminders. (The verbs [live, be] are crucial.)

747

Everyone is more than an example, all are different persons who elude capture by ingenious or torturous use of words by believers in abstractions. The right to believe is inversely related to the freedom to think and separate from the ability to sort through facts. But to be unique as a person does not mean to be singular or above natural law.

> Personal "uniqueness" is a confession of our ignorance of important ratios, mostly due to an urgent need for closure in order to be true to our beliefs. No other animal would find believing so demanding. Social diversity in human history is not as necessary as planetary biosexual diversity.

Not unexpectedly, this book is like the universe it writes about. There are no points in it that cannot be seen from another vantage point (pinpointed in the chapter notes). And any illumination that each point provides influences the path of light traversing the region. (Everything is related and matters.) There are clusters (the main chapters) that throw more light, like galaxies will, but they are never in total isolation. Reflections are deflected in different directions. (What we don't know may be as important.)

After we mastered fire we could fashion better tools for studying our world and ourselves, just as once we saw "the light" we can measure more accurately, and photographers capture what "is" better than if the best editors, painters or philosophers rearrange the scene.

We can now return to what I have entitled the "**ABZ**'s of Life." It is about life in nature, itself both inanimate and alive. Even the life-less, like crystals, grow according to rules that we call instincts in animals and that grow into habits in the three human subspecies: *H. sapiens*, *domesticus* and *metropolus*.

> DNA differences separate species because they shape the range of adaptations that can be used under identical surroundings. Not DNA but habits divide our species into, at least, three sub-species of different ranges of flexible adaptations. Inflexibility results from garbage they swallowed as kids to fight normal instincts. Pat answers can stifle curiosity, doubts are settled by exploration, not by an act of faith.

We have gone beyond irritability, which is the biological definition of life even among "immortal" viruses. We see seeds or the ability to multiply as common to all life that has evolved since. But plants do not have to move to spread their seeds, although when threatened they send signals of distress to their kind at a distance.

We also feel (**A**) "emotional" when we cannot move away, and this is the literal source of the word "e-motion." But unlike plants, animals can (**B**) move and change their life by what they can do by moving, including making tools to better their standard of living, if not the quality of their lives. What human beings do that both plants and animals cannot is spread their seeds and recognize the fruits beyond the second generation. And this is the "**Z**" of grandparenthood in the "**ABZ**'s of Life":

"**A**" is "e-motion", "**B**" is "motility", and "**Z**" is conscious enjoyment of the fruits of motility beyond the traditional "oak-acorn" and mother-child dyads. But it is grandparenting, not the consciousness of "**Z**", that counts.

Consciousness itself is our claim to superiority over animals and plants who do not need it, absent a sense of inferiority from acceptance of "original sin" or awareness of handicaps not shared by other species, e.g., brain cells that cannot regenerate like those of fishes, amphibians and birds.

The quest for equality is the burden of society, just as pursuit of liberty is for all who were born unable to run, and just as sexual compatibility is for those who were told to wait for Mr. Right, etc. Out of this separate needs came rationalysis of our (**i**) sensual, (**ii**) social and (**iii**) sexual development, to identify where we stagnate or excel, alone or collectively.

Genital hypochondriasis resulted in (1) denial of academic freedom to impart carnal knowledge for training experts in living and loving and (2) rejection of affirmative action by contrived charges of sexual harassment from subordinates suborning failed sex objects.

Beyond all this, to be or not to be is a variable but non-random combination of becoming, believing and begetting.

This book was originally subtitled *Bible of Behavior in Becoming, Belonging, and Begetting*. It contains both a prophecy and a revelation. It is only a prophecy if you cannot unravel the mystery in its cryptic statements and symbols. It becomes a revelation after all is explained and your questions answered. The intent is to encourage exploration and even trigger discoveries for those who are not mired in a deep rut or who have been trying hard to leave it.

Like a cardiologist who thinks the heart is a pump even if it beats faster at the sight of beauty or danger, so must a psychiatrist think of the mind as a clearing house for shame and a locked cabinet for memories that open up when close to overflowing, by dreaming or inventing, while mindful of the reality all around it, with varying degrees of success.

Unwittingly repressing your animal instincts or returning to nature as scientists is not an exercise of free will but its abdication. Over-indulgence of your acquired taste in art or science as an intellectual or in food as a gourmet or gourmand may not meet your natural or metabolic needs. Moderation in all but sex and love is more conducive to health. (In love, it is better to love than be loved.)

Stopping before being satiated with food for thought or fuel will allow "postprandial" somnolence to rest mind and stomach. Satiety is for the starving. So is overachieving. Pride in striving is needed only by the poor, rich or not, who have nothing else to be proud of. Over-exertion without crisis is deadly.

In life, the only things one used to be able to buy without strong strings attached are sex (before the AIDS epidemic), space and time. No one can steal them from you without your connivance. If you are busy, you may be distracted, but not free. If you feel trapped or cramped, you are a prisoner even in a gilded cage.

The search for meaning by the unfree on parole is distorted by the need to explain why the innocent suffers from the time it is extruded from the womb in fear and in pain. Disbelief in a Messiah, departed or coming, makes one an atheist. One of the worst predicaments is to be an atheist but addicted to order. An atheist who can be an artist is better. An agnostic who can be a scientist is even better. Those who can live with disorder without doing any thing about it are the healthiest and happiest.

An artist or scientist always tries to re-arrange what is given. Those addicted to order try to keep the world from changing. Those who do not care to keep change from happening can live with chaos better than all who cannot help themselves. Those around people seeking to find meaning have the worst time.

ART AND THE THEATER

Art, more than science, means nothing if it does not enhance the art of living and loving. The performing artist then, necessarily, goes through stages of development through life. Precocity is given to only a very few who are called gifted. Many of us do not become artists because we were not given talented grandparents.

Creativity, Wit (mental agility), and Self-Expression (psychological acrobatics)

If freedom to think is inversely related to the right to believe, abuse of the right to believe kills creativity. That's why Albert Einstein left Germany before, like Russia, it repressed non-utilitarian art and science that humanists now frown upon.

The less excess baggage from the past that the talented brings to the present, the more creative does one become.

Excess baggage includes all learning that came before zero got included in scientific discourse. Such a drag on thinking includes theology, philosophy and logic. Discussions in which any of these three cognitive anachronisms predominate today tend to be the opposite of bright conversation, which is playful and tolerant of imagination and exaggeration, which closed minds abhor. Exaggeration, of course, includes gross understatements.

My father who was a farmer insisted that in life, there is only the natural and the contingent compensatory strategy, like building dikes to contain flash floods. For Freud's daughter Anna, there is ego and defenses to keep it afloat. My wife is a wine connoisseur. I like to eat grapes as soon as they are ripe. I did not appreciate what made man try to improve on nature until I discovered that all who are handicapped compensated for their handicaps.

I am more minimalist than reductionist. Without "decorations" that are not intrinsically structural, our house that I designed is not stark but full of the play of light almost overcoming darkness, and of spaces interpenetrating each other, with great economy. (Many houses are still at a technological stage equivalent to the "inner tube" even in this age of "tubeless tires.")

Unlike Hawking who is reductionist, I am more contextualist. His sense of time is more linear, in the image of an arrow. Mine is of a wave that rolls, or a ripple that spreads. Both wave and ripple may visibly dissipate, but cannot vanish. An arrow can rise and fall with greater initial and terminal velocity, depending on the archer and the target revealed by his trajectory. Is God an archer or a ripple? Are we His target or His aquatic playground? (Or is He a ticket-scalper or trickster-puppeteer?)

The arrow has a linear trajectory, the ripple a more lateral dimension that produces subtle changes in, as it is changed by, all that it touches. "Free will" may simply be a confession of ignorance of some permutations. Does entropy (linear thermodynamics or Newton's "original sin") and negentropy (non-linear thermokinetics) always add up to zero? The Principle of Uncertainty allows variation and enough variation creates a new Darwinian mutation.

Creativity, which, by definition, must result in something new, novel, original and surprising, may be artistic or scientific, wit is intellectual agility, and self-expression mental acrobatics. When witticism is facetious, it may earn laughter but not confidence or credibility. Opinions, like all forms of self-expression, are confessions from prison cells.

Soap operas in America present stereotyping that is emotionally satisfying, TV talking heads on BBC provide stereotyping that is more intellectually satisfying. Soap operas are more intelligent (in the sense that they are drawn from data, which is what all intelligence agencies require); BBC talking heads have more headstrong opinions than hard facts.

> There is a bumper sticker that says, "Everybody is entitled to my opinion." What I want to share with you are not parroted opinions but personal findings. Do not swallow any, especially if you find them indigestible.

Using one season of London theater to attempt to understand theater as an art form:

1. Creativity which immediately resonates with its consumers is not as original as that which must be incubated to hatch in its own good time before gaining universal acceptance or achieving commercial success. Incubation period for self-expression is shorter for the gifted and/or witty.

Theater productions are good indices of prevailing expectations or tolerance. "Plays" are even better suited than musicals. We have seen the British production of "Smokey Joe's Cafe" which merely rendered old popular songs, and of "Lady in the Dark", another American musical that had not been produced in New York in quite a long time. The latter will have greater staying power because it deals with "ugly ducklings" and asks whether fathers must help make daughters feel sexually desirable if they are overshadowed by beautiful mothers.

Of the "plays", two are revivals of old classics and the audience now yawns at the dialogue. They are Oscar Wilde's *Lady Windermere's Fan* and Jean Baptiste Moliere's *School for Wives*. (In both, some "play-goers" did not bother to return to their seats after intermission.)

2. Three plays were better received: "Censors", "Art" and "Skylight." Like "Lady in the Dark", "Skylight" deals with relationships and holds the audience spellbound. "Art" and "Censors" examine art and its uses. "Art" would probably die aborning if its three protagonists had good-humored women to distract them from talking at great length about their relationships that swirl around buying and appreciating an abstract painting. "Censors" makes the point that all art is the sharing of secret shame (or "wounds from failed intimacy").

(While acidheads turn to mathematics for certitude, epileptics like St. Paul tend towards religion more than art. Do artists and addicts share the same world of shame, and are artists less self-destructive because they are talented? Was Edgar Allan Poe's death while drunk decided by the depth of shame that he could not erase with alcohol or express with his poems?)

3. "The Herbal Bed" plays with the legal recourse to libel suits for accusations of adultery. In it what is fervently sought to be hidden is both the shame of venery and the mode of transmission of syphilis from Shakespeare to his daughter.

In a way, it recalls Oscar Wilde's prosecution for libel by a father whose son had been seduced by him and who accused him of being a "sodomite," which he denied ever having been, whether because of its curious spelling or out of overconfidence in his wit. (His greatest ambition was to win in a legal contest with the state, like his father did who only had to pay his accuser a nominal sum for her alleged rape. This was overlooked in "Judas Kiss" where he refused to exile himself and desert his lover.) His wit did not keep him from being sentenced to two years in prison for corrupting the young, whom he adored more than art.

Real art is more original and enduring than self-expression, which is no more than a convoluted confession or the postponed sharing of secret shame. If previously successful plays like Moliere's "School for Wives" are cryptobiographies, who was the victim in Oscar Wilde's "Lady Windermere's Fan" which brought him instant fame as a playwright? And who was vindicated? Her mother abandoned her but saved her marriage. If Oscar Wilde wanted to re-enact his father's life, did he just change the sex of later objects of his affection? As well as the sex of the child in "Lady Windermere's Fan", but not its deserter? (Is "Fan" a lighter version of Tennessee Williams' "A Street Car Named Desire"?)

Oscar's own mother wanted a girl after his older brother was born, and had one two years after Oscar's birth but lost it 10 years later. There are pictures of Oscar as a child dressed as a girl. (This is not unremarkable in England but more noteworthy in Ireland. And there are other biographers who, in praise, write, "there could seldom have existed a couple more avid for culture than Mr. and Mrs. William Wilde. (Sir William was, in fact, knighted for service to royalty as a specialist for ear and eye afflictions.)

Were children this family's second love until the young could share their cultural interests? For all mammals, closeness to the mother is more important than supplementing the "daily breast" with eating "cake" late at night in the company of the cultural elite.

> (Children who are not breast-fed on demand are the human equivalent of a runt in a litter. Is "Lady in the Dark" [above] lyricized by a "runt"?)

4. "Censor" was forthright in portraying explicit sexual behavior and probing the reasons for paying censors as middle-men or pimps in reverse to give the fastidious only what is not unseemly. (With technology, those who are to be protected can now be titillated by the work-products of puritans who envy Bill Clinton.)

5. Prophetically, "Popcorn" is uninhibited in portraying raw violence and demanding that those to whom it appeals should stand up and be counted. In this, it revolutionizes theater in cleverly not ending the play before the audience applauds by adding an epilogue after a standing ovation. Such originality makes this art form for immediate consumption a creative activity beyond just a convoluted confession from Oscar Wilde or an alibiography from Moliere. [But it still uses the cortex to curb or "mind" the sympathetic nervous system.]

TWO SCIENCES (Galileo Galilei, 1638)

Civil life being maintained through the mutual and growing aid of men to one another, and this end being principally served by the employment of arts and sciences, their inventors have always been held in great esteem . . . Similarly, those are worthy of great praise and admiration who, by the acuity of their minds (intuitive knowledge is on a level with definition) have improved things previously discovered, revealing the fallacies and errors of many propositions put forth by distinguished men and received as truth for many ages.

For such exposure is praiseworthy even if the discoverers themselves have but removed something false without introducing the truth, which is hard to acquire. Thus the prince of orators (Cicero) declares: 'Oh, that we could get at truth as easily as we refute falsehood!'

. . . Of these two new sciences (full of phenomena and theorems not previously noticed) the outer gates are opened in this book, wherein with many demonstrated propositions, the way and path is shown to an infinitude of others, as men of understanding will easily see and acknowledge." (Excerpt, FROM THE PRINTER TO THE READER)

(Galileo was supposed to have authored above introduction to *Two Sciences*. His Latin writing style is not unlike the author's convoluted English.)

Galileo Galilei held that "causal inquiries might be well abandoned in physics." His Aristotelian interlocutor/philosopher (probing the extent of Galileo's deviation from church dogma) was poorly versed in mathematics, much less in new physics and astronomy.

> A reader can gain more from another's words by forcing himself to arrive at the best which he can conceive." [Though its principal conclusions have been worked out three decades earlier, Galileo had become blind before he received the printed book at age 74. He died in 1642, when Isaac Newton was born, exactly 300 years before Stephen Hawking was.]
> . . . (T)here will be opened a gateway and a road to a large and excellent science of which these labours of ours shall be the elements into which minds more piercing than mine shall penetrate recesses still deeper." (Galileo Galilei)

BEYOND PHILOSOPHY

Is classical philosophy mutual mental masturbation with the already dead? And semantic analysis which replaced it oro-anal masturbation?

It does not require the dedicated study that philosophy demands, just an ability to articulate what can be digested and retained from the pages of the dictionary, e.g., accepted definitions and conventions in style and syntax.

There are several misconceptions about philosophy: that it is about truth rather than beliefs, that it is basic rather than a window-dressing for lies and that, (a) if truth can set you free, (b) then philosophy is the door to freedom, both of which are untrue.

> (Truth is an impostor behind noble sentiments. There are two good reasons for telling the truth: (1) you are afraid or (2) your memory is not good enough to sustain a lie. There are two good reasons for telling a lie: (1) you can get away with it and (2) your imagination is equal to the task. Trustworthiness is needed only by the desperate, not the gullible believer.)

a. The truth does not set you free because there is no truth, only approximations of the reality that we process with less than perfect senses.

(Those who habitually tell the truth are called "realists" and their number is decimated by well-lighted photographs, even in court. Those who distil the truth unseen or unappreciated by others are called "reductionists" in philosophy and "abstractionists" in art. Those who combine the literal truth with photographs produce documentaries, not commentaries. Those who abstract and reduce with sound and pictures are called animators. Their products sell almost as well as "action pictures", by-passing the cortex to stimulate reactions and reflexes, bamboozling the audience without their conscious consent. The "truth" can also be told without photographs or consonants and vowels by cartoonists.)

b. And despite the stubborn gullibility of truth-seekers (who are quite literal in interpreting ancient texts but distrust high-fidelity tape recorders), there is no passkey for the door to freedom for *Homo sapiens*, only the need to defend against domestication into social slavery by the powerful who are otherwise one's inferiors.

(Domestication, as with animals, is the denial of sensual freedom for social privileges. It has to start early, depending on how domesticated the child needs to be, which urban life demands of *Homo metropolus* more than villages of *Homo domesticus*. Early abuse of its animal rights make domestication easy. If, on its first day, the mother leaves it to sleep alone without her smell and warmth to reassure it of its safety, it will learn what to do to earn greater security.

(Early circumcision and clitoridectomy also guarantees compliance with adult demands. Toilet training teaches orderliness and punctuality. Forcing children to give up their vocal skills for better verbalization makes them educable. Nouns make them gullible. *Homo sapiens* can develop into *Homo domesticus* or, worse, *Homo metropolus*.

Webster's Dictionary defines philosophy as inquiry into the nature of things based on logical reasoning rather than empirical methods.

At its best it is a critique of fundamental beliefs as they came to be conceptualized and formulated. ("Empirical" means relying on experiment or observation.)

Some people cherish logic, some treasure magic. (There is also science and superstition, as well as superstitious scientists and scientific superstition, e.g., the truth is elegant, not uncouth.) Absence of playfulness and imagination separate both from others. Those who believe in logic have no imagination or playfulness even when they acknowledge logic as tautologic, like mathematics. Those who believe in magic are too serious to entertain doubts contrary to their beliefs. They do not see magic as imaginative.

Philosophy is paradoxically useless if all it means is the art of persuading one to believe it, which is the newest discovered paradox. I believe it is the newest because I discovered it myself. No one has ever written of philosophy in this way. But that is what it is.

To show that what one does not know can be seen as trivial, one has to lie to one's self. Those who use logic to do so are the best at lying to themselves. (Science tries never to subtract from reality and well-fed artists who sell well are all trying to reach out.)

Truly lying is true believerism in social don'ts and do's: Die, kill for your God, country, money, etc. No animal would sacrifice life or its young for them.

("Hippies" also do not believe in God, Queen or money. They like goods, queens and charities.)

If we can track "true beliefs" with radioactive tags, we'll see no randomness in their distribution.

Philosophy studies a system of belief that relies heavily on tautology or linear reasoning rather than data.

1. Tautology is best illustrated by some self-evident statement like "A is not not A."

People who say something like that make it sound as if they said something very important. Not having listened to the inanity of what they have just uttered, if you asked them to explain it, they would not be able to tell you more without being rhetorical.

From *Arrow of Time* authors Peter Coveney and Roger Highfield's *Frontiers of Complexity*:

> Only in the 20th century did logicians . . . realize that they could formulate logical systems different from Aristotle's. They rejected the law of the excluded middle (which says that any proposition is either true or false), permitting statements that could either be true or false or undecided.

> Lotfi Zadeh of U.C., Berkeley: "Most of human reasoning, however, is approximate rather than exact . . . (H)umans have a remarkable ability to make rational decisions in an environment of uncertainty and imprecision. We can understand distorted speech, . . . poetry . . . fuzzy patterns without sharply defined boundaries . . .' The key concept is a linguistic variable ('more or less') . . . This is at the heart of most practical applications of fuzzy logic."

2. Besides tautology, philosophy's only claim to fame is the use of linear reasoning to make data more digestible. But data do not have to be tenderized to be digestible. It is better to let data alone than to make them fit.

    There are two kinds of linear reasoning. They are also the basis of either existentialist philosophy or essentialist philosophy. The worse kind is more used in essentialism. Existentialism at least provides the data (e.g., "that man gets sick because he is not perfect") which the essentialists beg for in the question "why is man mortal?" Essentialism was Aristotle's mono-centric reductionism.
    Jean-Paul Sartre credits Descartes with giving existentialism a good start: "Whatever I know, I know intuitively that I am." [The Latin for "know", as distinguished from (A) emotion and (B) volition, is (C) "Cognitio" (as in "cognosco" for "scientific knowledge" and "cognoscente" for those who understand, recognize, identify or reconnoiter, as in unagitated meditation), not (B') "Cogito" as in cogitation. Descartes was misquoted.]

"Cogito, ergo sum" comes directly from Descartes' "Discourse on Method" (1637): "I saw that from the normal fact of doubting ("cogito" or "cogitare" for cogitate), it followed quite evidently that I existed."

All of Cartesian philosophical propositions co-exist contemporaneously and comfortably with modern scientific experiments (like Galileo's). In fact, it is Cartesian analytic geometry, which could not have been developed without "zero", and led Newton and Leibnitz independently to discover calculus, which is basic to modern physics that enabled epidemiologists like Florence Nightingale (1820–1910) to graph statistics.

She demonstrated faulty clinical practices in treating the sick and the wounded. Even her reasoning is noteworthy for being data- rather than premise-driven. She re-interpreted "free will" as "the will to be free" (to be tempted, to be ourselves: "The greatest freedom is to surrender to our nature."

(I found "free will" among animals in the form of willfulness at play: our first cat forcing us to play "hide and seek" and always winning hands down, birds teasing cats to catch them and then flying to a higher perch.)

With the freedom to feel, try, think, compare and invent, feelings ("e-motions") only say you are trapped (immobilized). [Feminists seek the freedom to choose, yet they did not even choose to be female. It is the luck of the draw. In cosmology, it is called "coincidence." Florence Nightingale calls it "necessity." (Carl Jung calls it "synchronicity.")]

Before science, the sole acid test for free will was temptation to which Eve gave in. Her original sin was visited on the uncircumcised sons of all fathers and explained the labor of childbirth among their mostly illiterate sisters according to the ghostwriters and translators of the Bible and the Koran. And then anthropocentrism came under rapid fire from Copernicus, Galileo Kepler, Descartes, Darwin, Pavlov, Freud and Heisenberg in the "Old West." (In the Orient and among Native Americans in the "New World", there was no special relationship between persons only between tribal groups and totemic species, and their Maker.) Newton (better known in the East than Jesus) continued to believe in his soul and triumphed over certain temptations (he never "knew" a woman), Einstein insisted to the end against Heisenberg's Quantum principle of Uncertainty that God does not condone gambling. Even scientists of Einstein's stature, precocious or not, can be as human as those less gifted, in seeking old sanctuaries and safe harbors, illusory or real now or in the hereafter. Once more, love of science is lost in shadows of the mind that believing creates. Incertitude about nature falls, not through logic, but only with more data.

Some would limit the exercise of free will to areas of uncertainty that won the Nobel Prize for Heisenberg. But that is by definition a prodromal state, whereas willing is implementing and only prodromally planning. Both phases are illusory but people take responsibility for the consequences, nonetheless. Blind faith in the Bible and the Constitution have ramifications for the idea of sin (esp. in its origin as original sin) and the politics of meaning (which is an acknowledgment of what is valued). Whenever self-serving, neither document should be worshipped nor defended.

Without original sin there would be no rhumba (seduction), tango (negotiation), samba (rape), mambo (foreplay), or lambada (coitus). (Some dance steps like the conga or the twist, are for group or solo performance, and do not need original sin, just willingness and willfulness. "Aerobic dancing" is just exercise.)

Because Florence Nightingale used her personal experience (away from safer traditional roles expected of her social class) to bolster her professional reasoning, epidemiology, born in the 1830s, is the mother of modern medicine, Florence Nightingale was widely sought after for practical advice, even during the American civil war.

(But even consultees who insist on being consulted cannot decide on their own, and consultants often merely suggest options. "Choosing" and "deciding" are heavy responsibilities for those who feel responsible but do not want to be held accountable.

(Those who decide unilaterally are impatient about waiting for more data. Data make decisiveness unnecessary by illuminating the series of steps necessary that must be taken in harmony with what is happening. Pre-emptive action [crime prevention, pro-active censorship, or "prior restraint"] nullifies or distorts data-gathering to serve one's own ends. Their "closed minds" flee from surprise ["serendipity"].)

A Nightingale model of nursing has developed. As has Freudian psychoanalysis in psychology. Can an Ortega type of postlogical, postindustrial, transcultural, value-free, sex-aware rationalysis likewise take root?

ACADEMIA

Historically, polytheistic Aristotle's "anima" was misunderstood by monotheistic Aquinas to mean "soul", which made the Grand Inquisition inevitable. Thusly did the kinetics of reasoned errors in philosophy and logic delay the dynamic advance of science past the dark Middle Ages until low and high technology took over.

There are believers who read, listen and profess, explorers who learn to follow pioneers, and pioneers who lead.

A professor communicates by trying to make what is old seem fresh and refreshing.

A teacher who must lead in order to educate makes what is new less strange and alarming.

A speaker who expects listeners to remember uses novel means to make important points memorable.

Fighting increases fitness. (Even harmless "straw man" challenges one's ingenuity.) Killing is bad teaching. Spoon-feeding is necessary for "mentanorexics":

A middle-aged uncreative "atheist" who has no fond memories of his teachers—and cannot compute how many marbles a boy has if it is five times that in another's hand who says he has twenty four less—badly wanted to debate whether the "Big Bang" is, by simple definition, beyond the reach of science.

Before there was zero or the big "O", there was only "No" for those enamored of logic and symmetry.

THE BIG "O" BEFORE THE BIG BANG

Philosophy can try to catch up with natural science by discarding what it taught before (1) "zero" came into general use (and now, as "nought", in binary computations), (2) "up" and "down" lost their meaning except in conversation, and (3) "center" was found to be non-existent in an expanding cosmos.

Knowing only Zeus and nothing about zero had handicapped Aristotle's pedestrian speculation about "final cause" which is still thoughtlessly parroted in theology or thinly disguised as philosophy. (The Mayans were familiar with zero by AD 500, and had a more human image of an insatiable god.) Philosophers and prophets before Roman numerals became obsolete are scientific duds. In I Kings 7:25, pi = 3 (a diameter of 10 units was circumscribed by 30!).

(The Chinese were also using pi = 3 in their calculations around twelfth century BC. Also around AD 500, astronomer Tsu found pi to be 3.14159+. (Would we have a different number if we did not use 10, which our fingers offer to us, as a base for counting?)

"God", who was great, if only in the first week, was the answer to how everything got started until "zero" appeared as an equally logical, and "evolution" as a verifiable, explanation. If we speak of time warp from the time the universe began with a Bang, it has been argued that God took the cosmic equivalent of "six earth days" to create us, after which he rested, slept or died. Yet the seven-day week came—late on the seventh "earth day"—from the Sumerian calendar that the Semites had taken over along with their land. (But self-serving creationism can still be reassuring, if the study of evolution is disturbing to our pride or insulting to the human spirit.)

Without God, how can the faithful find new converts with stories of a global (bipolar?) flood that is outlived by a bigamous, drunken Noah when we still debate how dinosaurs died? (Polytheistic Babylon had a comparable flood tale in the Epic of Gilgamesh.) And why choose a deluge instead of an Old Testament Messiah to declare religious amnesty and make Moses and the Ten Commandments obsolete? (The Magi visiting Jesus in Bethlehem came from followers of Zoroaster, Jehovah's old rival.)

Zero: crucial in dismissing "causes" conceived of before Roman numerals became obsolete: Nothingness is a vacuum. Modern quantum theory sees empty space as an energy field that has an average value of zero. Once in a while, a random particle will pop up (according to the Principle of Uncertainty: simply as an alternative event rather than as a mathematical probability). Why not a whole universe out of empty space, without an uncaused Cause?

> If the Invisible Presence has made Itself felt directly and the convert feels magnified, so be it. It is no different from one meeting (in the same city) the only partner meant for a lasting marriage. It is not coincidence that both are occasions of relative deprivation screaming for surcease. And that one succumbs to contemptuous familiarity but absence makes the heart grow fonder in the other.

The Vatican, where the first Christians (whom Nero blamed for burning Rome) were sacrificed, has recently conceded that the world may have started with a Big Bang that nobody heard, and that evolution is acceptable to it as a theory. Until Darwin, there was no alternative to the singularity of creation. Until Hawking, there was no alternative to the singularity of black holes that he and Penrose postulated. Darwin disposed of creation as a singularity and offered natural selection as a testable alternative to a supernatural entity playing God. Now, Hawking is willing to theorize that physical laws cannot hold once singularity is allowed.

> (But biology reduces entropy without violating the Second Law of Thermodynamics. Are we not more comprehensible "black holes" without the singularity that was once known as "élan vital"?)

From the Big Bang to Black Holes: "A Brief History of Time"

The discovery that the universe is expanding (published by Edwin Hubble in 1929) was one of the great intellectual revolutions of the 20th century . . . This behavior of the universe could have been predicted from Newton's theory of gravity . . . in the late 17th . . . century. Yet . . . (e)ven Einstein, when he formulated the general theory of relativity in 1915, was so sure that the universe had to be static that he modified his theory to make this possible . . . Only one man, Alexander Friedmann, a Russian physicist and mathematician was willing to take general relativity at face value . . . In fact, in 1922, . . . Friedmann predicted exactly what Hubble found!

    . . . The Catholic church had made a bad mistake with Galileo (who would not blindly accept dogma) . . . Now, (four) centuries later, . . . (the pope) told (cosmologists) that it was all right to study the evolution of the universe after the big bang, but we should not inquire into the big bang itself because that was the moment of Creation and therefore the work of God. (He) did not know . . . that I (Stephen Hawking) had raised the possibility that space-time was finite but had no boundary, which means that it had no beginning, no moment of Creation" (by a flawed First Cause, jealous Father and xenophobic Son).

    (The author went to see Dr. Roger Penrose [author of *Shadows of the Mind*] who saw the shortcomings of general relativity inside singularities, like the black hole. He gave Dr. Penrose a recording of a parrot mimicking household voices, including the dog's, almost as an impersonator would, and therefore with great sensitivity to the nuances it heard. Dr. Penrose now concedes, in his *The Large, the Small and the Human Mind* that animals "also have some kind of understanding, and so also must have awareness.")

Words are more misleading than numbers. The cortex is a bureau of critical disinformation, pigeon-holing reality with abstractions and metaphors.

The relationship between juxtaposed particles in the cosmos is more complicated as they become more crowded together, often overstated as "chaotic" (asymmetrical), when it is merely inelegant for being absolutely relative (contextual) and therefore non-reducible (non-linear, like quantum mechanics).

From Mitchell Waldrop's "Complexity (. . . at the edge of Order and Chaos)": "In example after example, the message was the same: everything is connected . . . All that was required was a little bit of non-linearity."

The modern transcultural conflict is not between religion or art and science, but between science and philosophy. Thinking involves doubting and reasoning, and science comes with doubts, while philosophy depends on reason to resolve doubts. To the extent that it does, philosophy holds science back from facts. With facts, science makes philosophy obsolete.

In the beginning, there was nothing to see. Newton showed us that we can filter light into different shades but, without a prism, we cannot see light in all its glory.

Once we could begin to see, we were not content unless the evidence was before our eyes. All else is debatable without hope of resolution. There was only hot air without illumination. We cannot see beyond our nose because there was no light to see with. But with light on the small cell or the vast universe, we can feel confident that there is matter to reflect light into our eyes or instrument.

From reflection to recognition with our neurological equipment comes illumination of what is murky in our "mind's eye", whether blinded by dogma or not about the vaunted invisibility of the mysterious, Who is also deaf to our pleas and dumb about whether deafness or death has befallen It.

If nouns spell doom, verbs in combination may be a testable solution: kill and eat, help or pay, fornicate or wait, nurse and train, fight or flee, prevail or fail, etc.

THE ALPHABET OF CREATIVITY, INSANITY, AND SURVIVAL

A to **E** is the alphabet of creativity in art and science, **F** to **O** is the alphabet of ideology in feticide and genocide, **P** to **Z** is the alphabet of eroticism, procreation and grandparenthood.

We're different from other animals (a) when we are better for being more creative as *Homo sapiens* and (b) when, as *Homo domesticus* and *Homo metropolus*, we become homicidal in our delusions or social insanities. There are golden ages of creativity, two of which produce insanities. The first to be abused is the creativity that produced monotheism. The second is the centralization of power in the envious and ingenious. Both produced "true believers" and their ideologies produced widespread insanity.

Laws enforce institutionalized prejudices (dogma) that are thereafter perpetuated by worship of precedents.

Social progress from **F** to O is the history of our hopes and fears (even in the Goferobot created in our image.)

People who are afraid even to ask questions are afraid of rejection. Those who ask do not care whether they are rejected or not.

But centuries after the Grand Inquisition of the Dark Ages stopped persecution based on unprovable premises, question construction is still more of an art than a science. As long as that is the case, answers can amuse but not edify.

I have now become even more like Kepler in cosmology than like Darwin in biology.

Creationism demands a steady state universe, evolution an expanding one. In life, this need to expand is met by social mutations. In clinical practice, everyone is a relative, because everything is relative. This is the ABZ's of womanimalhood.

Only in our species is chaos seen as the result of unconditional sex, unexpected violence, or of death and decay. Since my latest near-death experience, I have been able to focus more on complexity born out of relativity. Even decay is measurable, or else we would not have forensic science.

What is normal is natural (e.g., laws of gravity) and what is normative is cultural (i.e., imposed).

Comparing inferences is more philosophy than science.

Intuitions are memories that remind us without conscious analysis of what to do.

Deists, theists and atheists see the world as friend or foe, agnostics see it as interesting.

If we are animals, then what clearly distinguishes us from plants is our joints. Unhealthy joints anchor us as solidly as roots in plants.

Eyes did not evolve to favor literacy.

CONFLUENCE of LIFE, SCIENCE, and ART

The original **ABC**s of Science in the **ABZ**s of Life is a theory and guide in transcultural rationalysis that connects life with art and science in absolute relativity.

Without artificial boundaries to cross between all life-forms and the creativity of arts, letters and science, "humanimal unity" is a better name for their confluence. All specialists see only the "elephant" that they can examine.

When Bill Clinton finished playing in kindergarten and C. P. Snow was talking about artists and scientists not talking to each other, I found out that psychiatrists cannot even talk to medical students. I am today trying to bridge the gap, not only between art and science, but between psychiatry and medicine.

I'll begin by telling you of the most embarrassing moment in my life. It happened in England while teaching Oxford medical students. One of my more difficult patients was a young girl who was afraid of intimacy (which I define as "love admixed with sex").

Her brother used to make friends by inviting them to molest her. I told the students that she was typical of patients who suffer from "chronic impoverishment of loved objects." One of the students looked up with a slight smile and asked, "Doctor, do you mean she has poor relatives?" (The others suppressed a grin at my expense.)

What I had said would have been easily understood in America without being challenged. This was when I realized that psychiatry, unlike medicine, does not transcend cultures, even if they share the same language.

If I had placed any patient on chemical restraint, all I would have to explain is on what. And if I had prescribed what we call "Thorazine" in America, that it is the same drug that pharmacists here sell as "Largactil."

Ever since then I have tried to practice psychiatry without regard to culture. I started calling my practice "Transcultural

Psychiatry" if it did not include psychopharmacology. And, as in pharmacology, I needed a separate vocabulary. It must sort out common characteristics of behavior at all times and places, like the chemical properties shown in the periodic table of elements during the Industrial Revolution.

It cannot therefore split the mind from the body. The body antedated the mind, the eye our hands, the thumb its manager in the brain. Philosophers still separate the conscious mind from the environment that it minds without knowing. What gives them false courage is a mistranslation of Descartes' dictum, "Cogito, ergo sum."

For Descartes, it is the spirit that is separate from the mind that develops by doubting. (He was at the time trying very hard to forestall any suspicion that he was a heretic like Galileo, who had agreed with Copernicus that the earth itself revolved around the sun, and was placed under house arrest.)

"Cogito, ergo sum" does not mean "I think, therefore I am." What it means is "I doubt, therefore I exist" or "Cogitating, I cannot doubt that I doubt." To doubt is to be indecisive but not closure-prone. To be intuitive is to be sensually decisive in doubting society's certitudes.

Many intellectuals have not thought to question what Descartes intended to deny. Because of that omission, they may be unwittingly pre-modern or pre-scientific. They can only deal with dichotomies of obsolete absolutes (God and evil, etc.), and are content to substitute thinking for predicting and testing.

Some ideas may be old enough to pass the Spanish Inquisition. They can be ancient and pre-Hippocratic, reasoned or pre-Copernican, borrowed or pre-Cartesian and biased or pre-Darwinian. They can be simply humanistic or pre-Pavlovian. We can date such ideas as fanciful superstitions or unvalidated opinions.

One doubt that even post-Darwinian cosmologists cannot face is that we may not be special. They use teleology, instead of solipsism, to say that they are special.

Cosmologists call what is special by a different name. They call it "singular." And what they find most singular in nature is our ability to look around and understand our cosmos. It is singularly meant for us and only for us. There may be alternative universes, but we cannot apprehend or comprehend their laws. Our senses and the prostheses that we have invented to survive in our surroundings cannot find them. What we see is all there is.

The study of unearthly violence started out as the province of cosmologists, who are still mostly male. That is because cosmology begins with mathematics and mathematics appeals to boys earlier in life. Its fascination stays with them longer than among girls.

> Boys tend to appreciate the number 1 when they first get erections. They think that mathematics should start with that digit. Only later do they appreciate zero as the start of everything nice.

> [In the Middle East, erectile tissue at the entry to the vaginal orifice is amputated in clitoridectomy. This is done with impunity and without consent in 50% of the girls. (The orifice itself is sewn together, to be opened postnuptially: Analogy is made to a house whose door cannot be left open to strangers.)

> (Ex-Marxist author of *The Color Purple*, when asked if matriarchies, now her goal, will be censorious, replied that only patriarchies would censor a woman's anatomy by clitoridectomy. Will she ban circumcision?)

Plato thought that a circle is perfect in form and therefore unearthly. From Aristotle's older anima, St. Thomas crafted an immortal, unearthly soul. (In Latin, anima simply means "breath." Does this make concentration on breathing during meditation a transcendental exercise?)

When the circle became an ellipse (from pre-Hippocratic Ptolemy to post Copernican Kepler), we lose the perfect circle (and our soul?) and gain zero. Zero is better than one, for it can be the beginning of less than one (< 1), unlike One (or God) before we found zero.

I found out about the post-Copernican role that "zero" plays right after my younger granddaughter proved that she can count backwards. She stopped counting with "zero." When asked why, she said because she had to end up somewhere. Then I realized that that was where it all began: Einstein's God (Who does not shoot crap) died the year I was born, though I did not know it. That was when Heisenberg won the Nobel Prize for his "Uncertainty Principle."

A quantum universe can start with one or zero. Heisenberg thought that it could or may not, according to his "Uncertainty Principle. Whether there is a God or not is like a child asking if the refrigerator light stays on with the door closed to keep the food inside from spoiling in the dark.

"Amen" or so be it. By starting with zero—or an asymmetric O—instead of 1, you only need to be superior, without any supervision from the Old No. 1. Those who need supervision from God still say "Thy Will (*sic*) be done." That is the greatest escape clause ever invented, better even than "Satan made me do it." (Satan as "virtual antiparticle" model was in on it from the start!)

We should stop teaching everything that dates back before the Mayans discovered zero. We would then have more time for science than for logic. Such a curriculum change will not be acceptable to cosmologists who are numerologists, philosophers who are necrophiliacs, and historians who failed to predict the fall of the Berlin Wall.

BEYOND TRYING TO BELONG

In a new synthesis of "humanimal unity" that I call the **ABC**'s of Absolute Relativity, **ABC** means **A**nthropology, **B**iology and **C**osmology, in ascending order of importance: "Nothing being equal, nothing stands alone, no matter how important or distant or still unseen."

This innovation needs three hyphenated adjectives. The pioneers of Absolute Relativity can be con-natural or (**I**) universal, convivial or (**II**) global, and con-familial, or (**III**) human family, specialists, as follows:

I. Universal (cosmic or con-natural): Copernicus, Newton, Einstein, Planck, Bohr, Heisenberg

II. General (biological or con-vivial): Mendel, Pasteur, Darwin, Lorenz, Crick, Miller, Goodall

III. Specific (human or con-familial): Pavlov, Freud, Jung, Piaget, Maslow, Erikson, Ortega

The **ABZ**s of rationalysis evolved from the absolute relativity of cosmology, biology and anthropology in reverse order of clinical relevance. We have, in fact, started, tested and refined it over the last 30 years.

One's own senso-socio-sexual life-cycle serves as its own control for self-diagnosis, and changes in behavior are the only treatment indices in longterm care.

Art as well as science have to reach beyond or transcend time (history) and place (geography) to be universal. Those parts of both that do are reliable guides to what applies to humanimals that we all are.

BEYOND BELIEFS or Cross-Cultural PSYCHOLOGY

My father used to breed fighting cocks like we train boxers. Brains (dreams) without muscles (deeds) are impotent. Comparing us now with animals can help us see if, when and how they are moved to act just like us.

We are the only species who would "choose" national and economic security over life itself.

Politics, as pecking order, was intended to cope with disorder. It has, instead, increased mortality rates. (War killed 170 million in the "enlightened" 20th century.)

What we kill with man-made tools we should dispose of like we did when we first invented tools, for feeding our kin and clan. Otherwise who might enforce gun control and a ban on weapons of mass destruction?

Violence got us here a long time ago, we are hurt when we are born worse than when we die of old age, and sex has kept us going all this time. Where we fail, can psychiatry help?

In the beginning, there was only cell division. Now we call it cloning. Cloning among plants and animals is pure immaculate conception. It is called "apomixis" and "parthenogenesis", respectively.

Plants were the first to discover sex, but because they are rooted to the spot where they sprouted, they needed the wind for cross-pollination before there were birds and bees to help out. Some plants grew taller and bore fruits which drop to the ground when ripe.

Insects and animals, including birds and beasts, then developed sexual organs. At first, they were vegetarians and, if they did not have wings, can only eat what drops to the ground. Eventually, climbers, including us, can pluck fruits from the highest branches even before they are ripe. Now we can scatter the seeds even across the seas as we developed transport to leave home with food from fruits that ripen during our journey. (And to pollinate, we also serve even if we only sneeze.)

This then is the history of how sex evolved, to spread plants away from their native habitat with more and more of us dropping their seeds wherever we go.

We are therefore meant to multiply and, to facilitate that, procreation was made pleasurable. It may be perverted to limit fornication to recreation. When we forget what it is intended to do, we risk not having fun in doing what comes naturally. We worry about not having erections even when our sperm count is low. ("Because they don't ask for directions, many are needed!") We also invite recidivism for rapists when we discount their sperm count.

The praying mantis dies to ejaculate. Bill Clinton risked a lot in doing the exact same thing but not reproductively.

Our own sperm get scattered afar even if only one from each ejaculate is needed to fertilize an egg. In fact, a single or alpha male can ensure a herd's survival, unless he's Spider Man (like Clinton) or he has a Joseph complex (resigned to immaculate conception).

We have an overpopulation of sperm and sperm carriers, who are soon to be replaced by sperm banks. (This would replace natural with artificial selection by those who fit into social niches, who may be the least fit.)

Is oral sex autofellatio that animals and only human contortionists enjoy?

(If risking death to ejaculate and autofellatio are true of other animals, does jumping off an airplane (as President Bush did in his seventies) recall apes leaving trees?)

Clinton is also accused of testifying falsely. For some this is unthinkable, but they do not know why.

It should be noted that, even before oaths were invented, it was called testifying because the witness has to cup his testes or risk losing them if he were found to be untruthful. Has this concern returned when we say "He lost it"?

In the Torah, a rabbi tells of a sinner who died and on being asked by God "Have you kept (**F**) the Torah?", replied "No." "Did you (**A**) pray regularly?" "No." "Have you been (**X**) faithful at least to your wife?" "No." And God says, "Come inside." The sinner asked "How can I, an adulterer (**W**) who does not pray (**A'**) nor observe the Torah (**F'**) ?" And God replied, "Because you told the (**C**) Truth."

In my training program, the inherent right to fail saves those who (**C'**) cheat because they are (**A'**) afraid of (**B'**) failing. Both (**C'**) cheating and lying acknowledge (**B'**) failure to achieve a common goal

Our first sense of separateness comes when we successfully lie to our parents and escape unscathed. Suddenly, we know they are not always looking over our shoulders. Those who believe in God and original sin are still looking over their shoulders.

Did those who have Viagra-resistant castration anxiety, penis envy or homosexual curiosity rush to get details of Clinton's sexual indiscretions?

[His impeachment and defeated Dole's endorsement of Viagra makes American politics a sexual forum about social values and hidden jealousies.

We can now identify where we excel or stagnate.

We have seen TV news anchor-persons deserting the Pope (**F**) during his first visit to communist Cuba (**H**). He was the first Pope to preach pluralism (**J**). Yet more air-time was instead used to broadcast President Clinton's stale or unoriginal extra-marital indiscretions (**W, m**). If coverage of such a sexual scandal is not distracted by a military threat to bomb Iraq to enforce a U.N. ban on weapons of mass destruction, we'd be in good shape.

Sex should always win over (**F**) heaven, (**G**) politics and (**H**) money. (Heaven is occupied by dead people. Politics is practised by envious people who use power as a substitute for sex. The relative lack of sex, power or money may be the root of all evil.) As soon as we can be less and less equality-driven, we'd be much better off.

The economy of acculturation demands that we sublimate our instincts. If we are to feel proud of our culture. Which increases creature comforts but kills more than any natural disaster or "Acts of God." It records repeated genocide from Biblical times (Numbers 31) for those who think differently. No other species but us has killed so many others so wantonly and well.

It is fortunate that the Industrial Revolution had made obedience less required of our muscles. Can we now boost the expansion of ingenuity in our brains?

The **ABC**'s of science (anthropology, biology and cosmology) make the **ABZ**'s of life testable in theory and in clinical work. Comparing senso-socio-sexual behavior among neighboring species makes their rationalysis more biological than ideological. Their interdependence reflects the relationships between juxtaposed particles in the cosmos and how more complicated they become with crowding.

The modern conflict is not between art and science but between science and philosophy. Thinking involves doubting and reasoning, and science comes with doubts while philosophy depends on reason to resolve doubts. To the extent that it does, philosophy holds science back from facts. With facts, science makes philosophy obsolete.

I was raised in an extended family without concerted brain-washing. I nearly drowned after reaching the "age of reason" and washed away what I did not think to question before. I had the equivalent of what would need at least two years of sabbatical sorting out. Then I discovered post-logical thinking that replaces analogy and metaphors with homology.

I have grandchildren who wanted their own separate rooms in a tree house they wanted me to build for them. I enjoyed climbing as much as they did and more than I enjoyed thinking. The tree house was a series of unplanned improvisations.

You only need three things in life: parents who love you more than each other, a good mate, and grandchildren. You cannot love yourself until you believe your parents or God loves you.

There are up to five stages in our professional development: post-Hippocratic, post-Copernican (heliocentric), post-Cartesian (doubt brings thought), post-Freudian (consciousness is selective remembering) and post-Pavlovian (programming is not conscious but conditioned)...

Plato thought the soul is a circle and St. Thomas made of Aristotle's anima an immortal soul. When the circle became an ellipse (from Ptolemy to Kepler), we lose it and gained zero, which is not nothing but better than one, since it can be the beginning of less than nothing.

What we have written explores sensuality, society, sex and violence in the practice of a truly transcultural psychiatry.

22.00 v/GLOSSARY of WORDS and LETTERS A DICTIONARY of DISTINCTIONS and INSIGHTS OVER the LAST 35 YEARS

(Author delights in gerunds, which emphasizes "processing." Index of nouns is for cross-referencing.)

Like Voltaire's dictionary, this glossary is intended to demystify. Definitions only define the definer, (e.g., of God, evil, etc.); they are not facts. But, like fiction, they demand a brief suspension of disbelief. (What may be too radical are separated under "Misleading and Better Words and Phrases) Because words, especially nouns, even when "disembodied", shape perceptions, the following is also an attempt to correct popular preconceptions.

Parentheses enclose pertinent stage of development (**i, ii,** or **iii, A** to **Z, XX** or **f, or XY** or **m**) to which term refers in the text.

absolute relativity. Photon particles traveling as waves means nothing stands alone, is exact, and matters. (Cf. zero) Systematic ratiocination of behavior in (**I**) nature, (**II**) animals, and (**III**) people, sensually (**i, A-E**), socially (**ii, F-O**) and sexually (**iii, P-Z**) helps. Relationships may be reciprocal: the more social equality, the less sensual freedom for everyone (**ii** / **i** = domesticity), domestication / breeding (**iii**) = >1 -> eventual extinction.

abstraction (**C**). Seductive but sterile reduction of web-like relationships (vector-driven) to linear sequences; idealistic or dishonest classification of—or impractical or academic distraction from—observable but not self-evident, properties, e.g., common nouns instead of gerunds: I store my tools, not by name, but by function, e.g., "attaching", "boring", "chipping." Aging makes nouns more forgettable.

acidheads. Intoxicated with LSD, instantaneously responsive to unedited perceptions, e.g., of color shimmering over rug: what we actually see around us are the reflected, un-absorbed colors of each object, yet we attribute to it the color that escapes from it! (To show that "reality" is what is rejected, we use fabulized exemplars and usually depend on joint accounts of events.)

adolescence (**C**). Period right after puberty when perceived chaos is countered by oversimplifying instead of (**D**) comparing (for adults).

a-dualistic (**A**). Pre-Cartesian unity of self-object (outside skin envelope) or of body-mind (relationship between brain and environment, internal and extracranial).

advocate. Intensely interested or highly skilled in specialized pleading.

affect (**A**). E-motion, mood when moved but unable to move others (except to "affect" their mood and produce a reaction), effective only if it motivates audience to act for the actor (and productive or counter-productive only when action proves to be consequential).

agnostics. Post-Copernican nonbelievers; atheists are unbelievers, Copernicus or no Copernicus.

ali-biography. Literate brief or literary apology.

alienist. One who treats the mentally ill, strange, or alienated.

anal (early **B**, lifelong **Q**, **m**). Successor to (**A**) oral primacy as a source of "sensual" pleasure, e.g., in (**Q**) the hoarding of (**H**) odorless "filthy lucre" to cherish; precursor to "urethral", pre-genital and pre-pubescent pre-occupation with bladder function and its expression in public (**S**, exhibitionism) or in competition (not a spectator sport) with peers who are neither (**Q**, **f**) tomboys or (**R**, **m**) voyeurs. Capacity to concentrate rectal excretory contents is comparable to the kidneys', not the bladder's.

analogy (**C**). Self-selected similarities in otherwise dissimilar discrete objects, like apples and oranges.

In biology, analogues are physiologically alike (fruits are functionally oxidizable, regardless of ripeness), but not homologous in structure (anatomy) or development (ontogenesis) or origin (family tree or phylogenesis). Distinguish from the phylogeny of behavior in primates (e.g., aggression) and its ontogeny in (i) the clan (e.g., territoriality), and (ii) the tribe (e.g., imperialism in the naked ape).

androgyny. Not hermaphroditism (with sexual organs of both genders), nor bisexuality ("swinging"), nor submergence of sex-linked or gender-expected characteristics with psychological or social counter-pressure or from aging (hormonal). Niche can be reached after bridging gender gap by parents with fertile offspring.

animistic (F). Habitual displacement of power to unlikely objects, natural or supernatural (invisible).

anthropocentrism. Man is the central referent of all events; compare with "humanistic."

anthropomorphic. Attributing human form (morphology) or qualities (incl. functions) to gods, or things (incl. animals).

antisocial. Against (ii) society, but not only as a macrocosm of (i) the family which cannot be directly attacked by juvenile delinquents (B) without reason (C).

anxiety. Tension in (1) small muscles from fear that what is anticipated will *not* happen, which is why saying it won't does not reassure (in contrast to (2) overactive large muscles in agitation among melancholics, who regret lost opportunities, relieved by pacing or (3) panic in "frozen" catatonics, who have been playing "possum" like animals unable to escape what is terrifying, inducing fleeing or fighting if trapped).

aphrodisiac. Produces erections, usually chemical (Viagra) or herbal, or internal from parasympathetic stimulation with physical relaxation after riots); may be pornographic (mental stimulant) that is not puerile (obscene, **B'**).

apperception (C). "Common-sense" interpretation according to synthesis of self-selected sensual data (actively sorted out of "passive" perceptions).

Armageddon. Final conflict between forces of good and evil ($A \times F'$).

assimilation. Digestion and absorption, or incorporation, not merely integration (which see) or tolerance; hence, even intolerance must be assimilated as developmental, not merely tolerated (condescendingly) as fair (**B**) or forgiven (**F**) as a result of natural human weakness.

associations. Connections, may be (1) loose or tangential in schizophrenic thinking, (2) scattered from distractibility in manic flight of ideas.

atheists. Unbelievers who need to believe there is no God yet longs to belong by bellyaching.

atomistic. Hierarchical organization even inside atoms.

autistic (A'). Not (**A**) dereistic or dreamlike passive wish fulfillment nor (**P**) narcissistic nor (**I**) introverted (which see under "introspective"), nor adualistic, nor (**C'**) schizoid (loner but not lonely) but instead, a precocious and unchildlike shrinking from (**E**) novelty with tendency to predictable rhythms including (**B'**) headbanging (which fades in experimental inebriation with alcohol), and a preference for a constricted status quo instead of attending to demands other than its own, with (**B**) temper tantrums that endure (**B'**) beyond threats to territoriality.

autonomy. Self-government, not sovereignty. Involuntary fail-safe arrangement in our autonomic nervous system when we are unconscious or incapacitated, as during sleep. [Cf. Individuation (undomesticated)].

Unlike autonomy, as in the "interdependent" British Commonwealth, independence is a national issue, freedom a personal one: To mix them up and expect nations to act like persons in the name of human rights is to deny the prerogatives of government in relation to each other.

Bad (A'). What is without merit or is distasteful to our sensibilities, starting with our palate.

bondage. External restraint to render internal control superfluous.

borderline. Whatever is "gray" to those whose prism (clinical experience) cannot distinguish shades of color (clientele self-selected and homogenous).

brachiation. Swinging by the arms from one tree branch to the next.

brain stuffing (ii'). Perverting intelligence to preserve the status quo.

brainwashing (i'). Sensory deprivation (saying no) to distort animal reality.

capitalism (H). "Man must make money to invest for profit." To be distinguished from communism (which see) or (**G**) equal voting rights for slave owners before their civil war.

Cartesian. Dichotomous thinking, from Rene DesCartes, who wanted man to use his own brains to doubt Aristotle (scholasticism) and the Bible (revelation), but dared not publish his *Treatise on Man* (1664) while alive to avoid being accused of heresy: He voted an unpaired "teardrop," the pineal gland, as the seat of the soul, reached by light through the eyes as its windows, and energizing the nerves to move muscles. Thus did Descartes separate himself from God, "a substance infinite," and join body and soul, only to be misinterpreted as separating mind and matter or child and Mater: "I think, therefore I am."

catatonic. Rigid but not stiff like the autistic (which see), inelastic (waxlike positions, when modified under physical pressure, are maintained as modified before, even after release), concerned with what might eventuate, warded off by stereotyped gestures or mannerism and by negativism, which can be overcome by positive demands without offering options. Relaxes when denied "choice."

Centaur. Mythical defender of what is valued.

cladistic. Genealogy, classification based on evolutionary lines of descent, ignoring similarities.

clinician. Personal physician or nonmedical professional caregiver.
    Medical administrators are professional caretakers who minister to the needs of clinical practitioners, like head gardeners in large estates.
    To be precise, in ministering with more (**B**) caution than (**A**) caring (which even the needy sometimes will not seek), administrators can be more ambitious care-takers for care-deniers, but they generally prefer only to look after the needs of care-givers, and sometimes even seek to limit assistance to many care-seekers.

cloaca (**XY**). Common opening from two different cavities for the discharge of their contents (e.g., urine and sperm in men, not the ovum in women).

clone. Asexual product of cell-division, as in a pure (genetically identical) culture of bacteria. Frogs and sheep have been cloned from a single cell: duplication is more exact than in identical twins.

codon. Nonoverlapping code couched in three of four nucleotides (one of every three is never part of either adjacent codon) stored in and transmitted by DNA chains from the parent to be faithfully replicated by RNA in the offspring.

cognitive (**C**). Cognizant after cogitating (to resolve doubts) by "reflexion" (passive even if "co-agitated").

cognoscenti. "In the know," connoisseur as distinguished from dilettante.

compuphobes. Those fearful of artificial intelligence superseding theirs, unable to compare retrievable memories in both, aware only that their processing is not as accurate or rapid.

conative (**B**). Volitional (in children) or voluntary (in adult), whether purposeful or not; active initiative, conscious "choice" between right and wrong (constraint-dictated), or tendency beyond mere inclination (unconscious polarization of desire for "good" and "bad" or **A'**), denied among counter-phobes and bigots, unsuccessfully if agitated, successfully if confident.

con-familiarity (**III**). Nonsexist, true of WoMankind; not monkeyhood, but ape-man-likeness.

con-naturality (**I**). Eco-systemic (not autoecologic) beyond syn-ethology (etho-socio-centric).

con-sequence. Neither "final cause" (teleological) nor effect (incidental) of "efficient cause," but sequence of phenomena serially or simultaneously following upon antecedent (not causal) or contingent events; concomitant at most, not axial ("committed") in the least.

con-viviality (**II**). Syn-ethology, not bestiality; shared biological characteristics as living things.

cosmogeny. Theoretical account of the origin of the universe, neither cosmology (study of the natural order, including physical laws) nor taxonomy (our man-made laws of/and order).

counterphobic. Daring to confront what it fears: disgust becomes solicitude, etc.

creactive (**B+E**). Whoever conceives to full-term and delivers, unlike Buddha but more like St. Augustine, who practiced what he pontificated.

(Socrates only tried to prove the Delphic oracle right, as usual, that he was less ignorant than those he grilled.)

data. "Hard" if one can correct for inaccuracies, e.g., Newton's; "soft" if unreliable, e.g., opinions.

DesCartes. See *Cartesian*.

de-differentiation. Reversion of cells to a more primitive form. Atavistic ("regressive") more than anaplastic (malignant) (cf. *undifferentiated* below.)

de-individuation. "Progressive" rather than "regressive" social homogenization; domestication, not solitary de-differentiation.

deists. Those who believe in God for (**A**) emotional reasons of their own.

delusions. Fixed beliefs, personal or social (shared), regardless of facts.

dialectics. Search for ever higher uncapitalized truths (syntheses) behind paradoxes (contradictions which do not cancel each other out) that ushers every historical change; compare with "Socratic."

dialectical materialism. Official Communist philosophy emphasizing the economic roots of history, society, politics, and literature which had enslaved the individual and will always be dictatorial, even if the proletariat is in power.

differentiation. Specialization, e.g., from the ectoderm to our skin and brain, from the mesoderm to heart and muscles, and from the endoderm to guts and lungs.

dimorphism. Two different sizes or coloring in the same species, e.g., baboons and birds, respectively.

dissonance. Mismatch (in accustomed ratio) between new and stored data (excess quickly kills curiosity, absence produces boredom).

distressed. Stressed too much, but not drained.

DNA. Deoxyribonucleic acid, two strands coiled in a double helix of nucleotides, each containing a sugar (deoxyribose), a phosphate group, and one of four nitrogenous bases (A, G, T, or C), sequences of three of which form a codon (which see) to encode only 20 amino acids out of a possible 64.

domesticated. Brain, tongue, and genitals can be, but not the liver, our most important organ.

dorcision. Slitting without circumferentially excising the skin on top of the glans penis to allow painless erection.

dysfunctional. Disturbed but functioning, with or without structural defect.

dystopia. When utopian fantasies fail to shield us from hard realities.

dyssocial. Disturbing to the social order, but not to the family (**i**); not antisocial or against society at large (**ii**).

eclectic. Screening for the most suitable sources or methods.

ecology (**M**). The interdependence of organisms and their environment; autoecology is humanistic or anthropocentric (we're custodians or beneficiaries), syn-ethology is socioethological.

ecumenical. General, universal, catholic without a capital *C*.

Electra complex. An affinity for mythic spinster-avenger of hero-father's murder by her mother.

embryo. Fetus in the first trimester.

empirical. Autodidactic, self-taught, practical rather than idealistic; see also *scientific empiricism* (and *logical positivism*).

endorphin. Endogenous morphine, produced by the body during extreme stress, and produces a "high" during jogging (for the unskilled) or boxing (for the professional) above ordinary pain thresholds.

enteroceptive. "Gut reactions" (endo-) from other than external sensory stimulation (ecto-) or internal motor activity (meso-dermal).

entropy. Tendency to disorganize.

epigenesis. Mythical tabula rasa–like origin of structures from undifferentiated material (vs. ontogeny recapitulating phylogeny).

equifinality, principle of. "All's well that ends well," whatever the cause (overdetermined) or treatment (determined only by titration) (cf. "initial value, law of").

Erikson. Epigenetic psychologist searching for "individual" identity, absent normative family identification.

ethics. Study of, and adherence to, standards of practice, customary or not, legislated or uncoded; professionally-dictated duty, not chronic peer-review-wariness for self-protection against malpractice: Defensive medical practice is (**H**) profit-oriented or (**J**) social, not (**K** x **N** x **O**) scientific medicine.

ethological. Behavioral study of animals, nesting and courting, contesting and feeding, hunting and learning, etc. started by Darwin and carried on by Lorenz, Tinbergen, Goodall, etc.

Euclidean. Deductive system of thinking mathematically about plane and solid geometry: terms are defined, derived assumptions are postulated but not proved, and then deductions made from definitions and assumptions (logical but linear, not rigorous enough for complex variables on coincident planes or Riemann [curved] surfaces).

euthanasia. Self-serving conspiracy to terminate life in the unworthy or helpless (pets in pain, "non-persons" in death row or death camps, unwanted fetuses and disabled and/or moneyless relatives) by interfering with, or disconnecting, life-support systems.

evangelism. Nonsecular extortion/expropriation by promising protection from or reward for suffering by redemption through superstitious, ritual supplication.

evil (F'). Divine version of what is (**B'**) bad.

existential "guilt" (BB') The anguish or burden of choosing, including opting not to choose. More (**C**) intellectual, less (**A**) affective than true guilt (which see).

Freud, Sigmund Schlomo. Early mother worshipper, father hater until half-orphaned by *his* death, passionate lover, pedestrian husband, soft pornographer, avant-garde neurologist, sublime psychoanalyst, hypnotic writer (cf. *Oedipus, pornography*).

genetic. Gene-determined, not sexual drive "dynamics" (to understand the libidinal economics of underlying hydro-dynamic ego defense "mechanisms" against undomesticated lust in persisting behavior patterns dating back from early object/erotic relationships in psychoanalytic theory).

gestalt. Shape or form whose properties are not derivable from individual parts of the configuration, not *weltanschauung* nor holographic.

good (A). What is tasteful (palatable) or meritorious, sensible rather than reasonable (excusable).

growth. Differentiation from the union of germ cells, in accordance to instructions from parents' sex chromosomes (halved into XX and XY from father, both halves XX from mother), and the halves of their parent's (your grandparents') other chromosomes.

guilt (FA'). Not (**G'**) legal culpability but personal (**A**) emotional conviction of need to expiate for (**BB'**) initiating wrongdoing; readiness to receive (**F'**) divine retribution without anxiety (which see) over "inevitable" outcome.

Heisenberg. Quantum theorist; first to convert physical laws into statements about relative probabilities instead of absolute certainties.

heuristic (E). Discovering for one's self what still remains undercover (-> short bibliographies).

(There is no spontaneous generation or special creations.)

histology. Study of the structure of tissues and its component cells.

history (**ii**). What is recorded.

hologrammatic. Tridimensional recording of objects which can then be examined from different angles even if only fragments of original record is available.

homology. Correspondence in position, structure, origin (bird's wing and our arm are homologous), or ratio (value).

Homo domesticus. Fire cleared vegetation for farming with better tools to reduce nomadic living.

Homo metropolus. Seeker of equality with superiors.

Homo sapiens. Undomesticated and unenvious.

Humanistic (**L**). Denies (**F**) divinity of Jesus and relies on universal human potential more than on over-ambitious interference with nature by (**K**) technocrats; compare with "anthropocentrism" and "human racism."

human "racism." Not anthropocentric, but presumes out of ignorance (as is true of all racists) that human beings are qualitatively superior rather than just different from "other creatures" (so-called in token humility).

hypergamy. Marrying a higher caste (Hindu).

iatrogenic. Diagnosis-provoked unease (hypochondriasis) or treatment-induced disease.

iconoclasts. Antiestablishment icons, including celebrities.

ideagogue. Addicted to ideas.

identity. Secret self (past and present) after weaning, in the process of individuation; mental/body image, including potential for change while the "true" self lives on or as long as it does, instead of suicide as self-murder, there is role confusion in identification with, or mixed loyalties to, (**i**) persons/principles or (**ii**) allies/causes that could change "identity" into a series of "closet" selves, all precious (treasured in hiding) if not equally esteemed and therefore variably vulnerable to "murder."

ideologue. Sold on an ideology.

ideology. Body of opinions, point of view, self-serving study of the evolution of ideas.

imprinting. Bonding at first sight, Lorenz-like.

individuation. Undomesticated differentiation from the herd: (a) involuntary or inherited (sympathetic and parasympathetic) and (b) voluntary or learned ("mind-body" functions are balanced and self-regulating until senescence).

To do with your body only what animals do with theirs is to keep it in good working—not order, which is to enslave it—condition, never simply to stay fit, which begs the question: Fit for what? For living a long life?

To neglect your body (for what?) means you have to put it back in shape, before you can be as animals are. You cannot just sit under a tree as Buddha did, nor at the desk as bureaucrats have done since. Eunochoids only live long years.

In self-indulgence beyond mere survival, to eat more than you will need is (**A**) "oral", to be richer for the sake of your heirs is (**B** × **H** × **Y, m**) "anal" enough to institutionalize fatherhood.

inertia. Resistance against change in direction or acceleration (Newton's second law of motion: the greater the mass, the less the acceleration from a given force).

initial value, law of. "Drugs affect the initial state in the opposite direction inside the extremes of a normal distribution curve. In both extremes, paradoxical reactions may be expected."

integration. Social or secret compromises to preserve integrity (recognizable unity).

intellectualization. Not circumstantiality or compulsive attention to, nor (**Q, m**) "anal" hoarding of, small details; but morose (undistractible) pondering of (**C**) abstractions to escape being drawn into (**B**) action; mood (**A**, e-motion) inescapable from inaction, but criticized as unfeeling by the irritable who may be senescent or (**Q, f**) assertive.

intoxication. To change "reality" as with acidheads or to avoid pain or sinful accountability.

Introspection (I'). Not introversion (preoccupation with one's self instead of the world outside), nor egocentricity (self-aggrandizement even in the extrovert), nor narcissism (withdrawal into self-absorption in one's image), but an examination of one's mental processes: dualistic, if not solipsistic, may be dereistic but not autistic (which see).

intuition. Inherited wisdom, regained soon after recovery from natural birth injury to brain, when softer fontanelles allow head to squeeze ahead of trunk.

Jung. Freud's only gentile disciple, psychiatrist son of a Calvinist minister who eventually rejected infantile sexuality but saw mythology as a repository of ancient insights, in the collective unconscious, probably saurian, in our reptilian brain.
juvenile (B). Period before puberty after infancy.

Kohut. Controversial psychoanalyst who enlarged **(Z)** inherited, conflict-free functions (intelligence, coordination, etc.) to include **(i)** nontraumatic learning, not **(ii)** indoctrination.

lability. Variable emotional state.
limbic system. Linked midline brain areas responsible for emotion in man and other mammals.
literati. Wordsmith or consumer of output filtered with variable forgetfulness or misunderstanding.
logic. Methodical (*methodos*, which see) or systematic argument by syllogism: validation of reality by inference or language; contrast with pre-scientific experimentation by children and "postlogical" exploration of incertitude after adolescence.
1. William of Occam: the structure of language and logic corresponds only to the structure of the mind, not to reality
2. Bertrand Russell: knowledge depends on the data of original experience, i.e., the logical independence of individual facts.

logical positivism. Scientific empiricism: treats ideas like chess pieces, confined entirely to what has already been conceded to them; inferences are not truths; compare with Wittgenstein (Russell's disciple):
1. What is logical is not necessarily real.
2. Metaphysical speculation is nonsensical.
3. Mathematical propositions are tautological.
4. Values and morals are merely emotive.

logos. Intelligence or information (cf. *methodos*).

Lorenz, Konrad. Ethologist dogged by geese.

love. Invariably linked with commitment, instinctual or romantic.

machismo. Male sexism.

Maophilia. Love of power that comes from the end of a revolver.

mariolatry. Worship as an icon of "Virgin" Mary or as an intermediary with her Son, who repeatedly rebuked her before, Kamikaze-like, dying for his faith in an imperial godhead ("rational" euthanasia, no less lethal than suicide). (Some biblical scholars suspect that he pardoned adulterous Magdalene as Mary's proxy.)

Marx. History (**ii**) is economic evolution (**H**), ripe for labor unions.

Maslow. Psychologist whose personality theory focused on the healthy person rather than concentrate on psychopathology.

masochism. Moral need for (**i**) sensual punishment among (**F**) martyrs and counter-phobic (**G**) patriots, sexual release with bondage or induced itching without bleeding (crossing the pain threshold or blood platelet destruction automatically mobilizes fight or flight reactions and inhibits erection or erotization).

matriot. What to Mother Earth is patriot to the Fatherland, synethology without species-ism (humanistic environmentalism or autoecology). Cf. *Con-naturality, ecology*.

memory. Early and forgotten but influential, remote but remembered, and recent (spotty if aged).

mental (**i**). Sensual as a function of specialized skin (invaginated ectoderm); functional (or social, **ii**), not structural (or organic, which see) or (**I**) "psychological" or cultural ("sociological", **J**) but trained or trainable skill like other neurological adaptations with or without initial handicaps; more than (**A**) emotional, may be pathological (characterologic, neurotic or psychotic) like other dysfunctions (non-organic) or diseases (with structural change, reversible or not). Also see "milieu," "mind," "neuroses," "psychoses."

"mentanorexia." Distaste for novelty.

metaphysics. Speculative philosophy to grapple with the non-physical (immaterial or nonsensical or intangible).

methodos. Armchair substitute for extramural exploration to sort out information or intelligence.

milieu. Environment, internal (somatic, intra or extracranial) or external (socio-cultural attitudes and expectations, **ii**); includes internal (mental, **i**) and external bureaucracy from human perversions called "principles" (moral reflexes, **i'**) and "policies" (rules and regulations).

mind. Not an abstraction (the psyche or "black box") but the stimulating or responding relationship between brain, minding, and environment, somatic (intra or extracranial) or social.

miscegenophobia. Fear, hidden or not, of mixed marriages or alliances; what homophobic fascination for gays or lesbians of the same sex is to racist social chauvinists.

morality (**i**). Fashionable mores or customs or conduct already internalized as virtues but / and validated by external reference to a recognizable (con-sensual) ladder of values. New morality is non-traditional values. The "immoral" nonconformist has unorthodox "virtues" internalized from "dyssocial" upbringing.

natural selection. What survives the demands of daily life that is reproduced in the offspring: there is no continued change in one direction by discoverable design (orthogenesis, which see) or dinosaurs would not have been displaced by social insects who "very nearly took over the world" (Edmund Wilson, Harvard Museum of Comparative Zoology).

negentropy. Success in forestalling maximum entropy.

neo-Haeckelian. Social equivalent of the embryology of mankind as history repeating itself in our cultural development and as self-expression in our sensual and sexual lives.

neologism. Invented word, before in-crowd exploitation, e.g., con-familiar, con-natural (v. autoecology and bio-social syn-ethology), con-vivial, compeering, creactive, crea-teasing, crea-tickling, crea-trying, circu-centric (cybernetic), e-motion (absence of motion with passionate passivity), EveryWoMan, hirs, Hum-Ani-Machin-Erotic, ideagogue, jingo-centric, Maophilia, matriot, meta-psychiatry, miscegenophobia, philosophist, post-logical, rationalysis, scienethics (which see).

neoteny. Prolonged maturation except sexually (common among salamanders). Insect larvae can mate if environment inhibits metamorphosis and mature when conditions improve; in some species, daughter consumes mother larva to continue the process as paedogenesis (precocious re-production, pediatric obstetrics).

Unlike pygmies who don't prolong youth, overdeveloped countries increase incidence of (a) violent rape with social ambivalence about *oestrus*, (b) illegitimate teenage pregnancies in those un-ambivalent or unable to keep up, (c) early use of contraception, and (d) abortion as the last resort.

neuroses. Mental dysfunction with symptoms (unease, not disease, though sometimes severe and/or prolonged unacceptable to patient, unlike in characterologic disorders where personality disdains or denies chronic patienthood). See also *mental, psychoses*.

nihilistic. Rejects contemporary notions, without offering alternative options; more empty than pessimistic (uniformly glum about alternatives).

noise. Nonsense that is not useless, uninformative but highlights what is.

normal. Not norms or averages (not even useful for betting on horses), nor mores, but what works for the organism, sound or handicapped.

obscenity. Scatological more than pornographic (which see), appeals to the anal (**B'**, **H** or **Q**).

Oedipus. Exiled mythical son of King Laius of Thebes (he feared and suffered patricide) who returned and married his mother (Queen Jocasta) and then blinded himself.

Freud's "choice" instead of Electra to universalize what is happening to his female clientele: He similarly "blinded" himself about coveting his mother, denying paternal lechery towards daughters only after his father died, before he realized that he was incestuously-inclined and wished to replace a father whom he did not respect.

oestrus. Mating period in females, marked by intense sexual urge, annual or semi-annual in most birds and mammals, monthly in primates (monkeys and apes), outside which period fertilization cannot take place; more frequent when male eats his rival's young when mother is not vigilant, and her lactation stops.

ontogenesis. Evolution of individual organisms (developmental history approximating that of the animal kingdom in man).

open system. Exchanges matter and energy with its surroundings.

operant conditioning. Reinforcing spontaneous activities by immediate rewards, including praise. Unacceptable habits can be extinguished by immediate punishment: screening of slide transparencies of *inamorata* can save a marriage if showing each slide is synchronized with mild electric shock to philanderer's fingertip.

oral (A). Continued primacy of the mouth as a source of pleasure.

organic. Not functional disability but demonstrably anatomical or structural defect, like narrowing of blood vessels in the elderly or even earlier, as in pre-senile dementia. With disorientation (not expected in non-organic psychoses), forgetfulness of recent events (remote memory loss is neurotic amnesia), irritability from both or denial of either by delusions (convictions) or confabulation (examiner offers fables for confirmation), and/or vivid hallucinations.

organismic. Not individual organs but the organism as a unit.

original sin. Partaking of the forbidden fruit of knowledge, theological equivalent of the mythical Pandora's box, and of the lethal quality of curiosity, the danger of a little knowledge, and of the bliss of ignorance.

orthogenesis. Eugenics.

overachiever. Driven to succeed, successful workaholic.

overdeterminism. Freud's *fortissimo:* there is no uncaused cause, but several simultaneously; supersedes germ theory of disease.

paranoid. Not suspicious (skeptical) but convinced (deluded) but/and projects conviction(s) about self to others and/or, oftener, one's betters: 'scapegoats' (which see) must survive blameworthiness in order to serve better and longer than Satan.

parthenogenesis. Asexual method of reproduction in nature without benefit of fertilization by a spermatozoon, or experimentally by chemical or mechanical stimulation of the unfertilized egg.

Pavlov. Russian scientist whose dogs salivated with sounds associated with mealtime; classified his experimental animals into classic Hippocratic types: sanguine, phlegmatic, choleric, and melancholic, the first two being more immune to chronic neuroses: their therapeutic response to "uppers" and "downers" when inhibited or excited parallel their masters'. ("Negative reinforcement" is not "negative feedback," nor is "positive reinforcement" "positive feed-back" [which can gather momentum and self-destruct].)

periodic table of chemical elements. A map of their main properties which vary smoothly and predictably from neighbor to neighbor.

perversion. Erotic fulfillment without vaginal penetration.

Peter principle. Promoting from within the organization as long as competence is demonstrated, until the last promotion; implications include (1) current position does not imply competence, only seniority, unless there is rapid mobilization, or office holder was recruited from outside and (2) if from a similar job, his new subordinates have been adjudged incompetent for further promotion, and he might have to move again if not demonstrably superior to them.

phallic. Pertaining to the penis, e.g., penile narcissism (hidden hypochondriasis in the macho who protests too much).

pheromones. An external secretion or subliminal odor that elicits a specific response, sexual or not.

phylogenesis. Evolution of primary divisions of organic life.

Piaget. Epigenetic child psychologist, early cognitive observer and later fatherly protector of his daughters: delay or absence of ability to abstract not a handicap to women in science (his idealistic norms are biological or adaptive, not ideological).

Pinel. French psychiatrist who first unchained the insane male inmates of Bicetre and based "moral treatment" on environmental manipulation, including coercion, to balance all passions (more precisely, emotions), which were considered the link between body and mind (or animals and mankind).

pornography. Whatever produces erections conducive to breeding (**iii**), not exciting scatology (puerile analysis of fecal preoccupation:) Compare with "aphrodisiac."

postlogical (**D**). Postpubescent disdain of logic as a scientific method for testing.

postpubescent (**D**). From puberty to (**D'**) the Indian summer or late autumn of a second adolescence (mid-life aping of the young in manners, demeanor, and attire).

pregenital. Concentration on pleasure that does not require use of genitalia for reproduction.

presenescent (**E**). Kids of all ages before their second childhood.

prognosis. Likely outcome from intervention.

projective. Disowning by blaming or scapegoating, "fleeing from one's conscience" (incompatible with depression, which insists on blameworthiness). Used throughout life, by sibs and by the old and forgetful who have misplaced their prostheses (eye-glasses or walking canes). Emphatic and effective projection from the stage makes theater audiences "compassionate" about actor's plight (sympathy more than empathy or pitiless understanding), which tempts literate clinicians to depend on playwrights to bring abstractions to life beyond the footlights.

proprioception. Nonexternal stimulation (more motor than sensory).

psychedelic. Hallucinogenic drug effect from use, abuse or misuse of mini-doses of LSD, mescaline, etc., but not macro-doses of opiates, cocaine, etc. Psychosis more toxic (disorienting) than schizophrenic-like (no confusion as to time, place or person in schizophrenia).

psychobabble: Colloquial double-talk in professional jargon.

psychosis. Loss of contact with past reality, not social orientation (**J**), but (**i**) personal or (**ii**) historical ("This is not me"), with withdrawal from peers, but without disorientation ("Where am I?") or loss of recent memory or amnesia ("Who am I?") unless associated with injury or intoxication.

Ptolemy's symmetry. Neat geocentric theory, with all orbits centered around the earth, including the sun's.

pudendum (**L**: shameful). External (secondary) genitalia.

rational. Appeal to (**C**) reason instead of (**A**) emotion: what is reasonable may be emotionally unacceptable if not agreeable; if (**B**) willingness to act is expected, reason also must be supported by (**G**) duress.

ratiocination. The use of ratios to establish *rationale* (data based policy justification) without implied apology.

rationalization. Reasonable excuse, usually an unconscious apology for irrationality, not conscious ratiocination.

rationalysis. Formulation of ratios between sensual, social, and sexual selves among participants who cope according to achieved stage of development of inherited endowments.

re-cycle. Not "regress" (which see); return to previous state.

redundancy. Repetitiveness which distinguishes communication (reiteration of shared data: "You know") from information (brand new data: "studies show"). Not tautology (most philosophy and all mathematics).

reductionistic. Any philosophy which holds that everything must or can be explained in terms of simple elemental components, e.g., "drives" ("trieb" or impulse) in psychoanalytic theory, "final cause" in philosophy, "original sin" in theology.

regression. Return to more familiar levels of adaptation (previous "fixation," e.g., father fixation), as repression fails to defend against current stress.

REM sleep. Brain "awake" (according to electronic monitors) but only eyeballs and penis move (erect but involuntarily, as usual (even when fully aware): Involuntary erection is a better test in the waking state than for arbiters of taste to distinguish between erotica (**iii**) and "puerile" obscenity (**B'**)—of material "gazed" upon by potent males).

Riemann. Post-Euclidean theorist of elliptical space and differential geometry, which were basic to the mathematics of general relativity.

right (**B**). What is fair (or lawful to the powerful, **G**).

scapegoat. Villain, not victim; strong, not weak; to survive projected attributes.

schizoid. Not shy but aloof, superior by self-estimate, not lonely but a loner, marching to a different drum-beat without the lyrics of the deluded, psychotic or not

schizophrenia. Not precocious dementia (forgetfulness). Splitting of mental functions (affect or **A** from thought or **C**), not of personality (neurotic "persona" or masks, as in the "faces of Eve"). Psychotic but without "organic" defect.

scienethics. Ethical practice derived from data, not dogma, desire, tradition or group consent.

scientistic. Out to prove, not disprove.

Scopes, J. Tried for teaching evolution in 1925.

self. Subject according to subject, present and future "identity" (more subject to change than the "self" itself).

separation/individuation. Waning away from early attachments (**A**), including transitional objects, towards self-reliance without leaning on peers (**B**) or professional colleagues (**D**) or conspicuous consumption (**H**) to impress them.

sexuality (**iii**). Reproductive stages or potential.

social sibling rivalry. Women dressing for other women, men outdoing rivals in ostentatiousness.

socialization. Make fit for living with and around (**ii**) historical contemporaries by (**i'**) early domestication.

society. Time-sharing company.

Socratic. Search for flaws to establish superiority (not "Truth"); compare with "dialectical."

solipsism. "The self is the only existing object of real knowledge."

speciesism. Humanistic environmentalism, human racism.

strain. When reserves are drained; compare with "distress."

stranger anxiety. Childish fear induced by anxious mother, not by novelty.

stress. Challenge to our resources.

syncitium. Fusion of several cells resulting in a single large one with many nuclei.

synergistic. Harmony beyond mutual tolerance between constituent parts.

tabula rasa. A clean slate, unmarked by another's mistakes (which are usually iatrogenic in the case of intractable clinical syndromes, lethal or sublethal in the fantasy of the seeker of easy answers).

tautology. Unnecessary reiteration (A is A, not B), not redundancy (excess employment) nor repetition (extra wordiness).

taxonomy. Principles of classification, systematic categorization into a coherent scheme of natural organization (artificial if flowers were classified by color, instead of by their genealogical relationships).

technocratic (**K**). Control of resources by "experts," esp. in industry; contrast with "humanistic" and "anthropocentric."

techno-tronic (**K-O**): combined machine and computer technology

teleology. Doctrine of fulfillment of divine design (as in astrology); contrast with "teleonomy."

teleonomy (as in astronomy). "Goal-directedness" controlled by DNA programming.

theists. Those who believe in God for more logical (**C**) than (**A**) emotional reasons.

theopathic. Overenthusiastic.

titration. Addition or subtraction of enough to what already exists to produce a desired change. Usually a chemical reagent, a change in medication or dosage to stimulate or sedate, a different attitude that provokes or pacifies, seldom simply catalytic (itself unchanged, unchanging, or unchangeable).

totem. Ideal model object for group.

transference psychoses. Hallucinations and delusions beyond neurotic preoccupation with psychotherapist.

transitional objects. Substitutes for earlier attachments, e.g., security blanket for a mother's lap, or a bedtime story.

triage. Old quality control -> emergency allocation of resources.

triangulation. Pinpointing location by angle of convergence from two sources, e.g., by approximating (probable) distance (elapsed time x average speed) a ship has travelled (in space) towards one direction (or psycho-moral stage of development, **i**) and its angle in relation to a visible landmark (or pet ideology, **ii**) or star ("shooting the sun"). (Cf. Heisenberg's probability theory).

unconscious. Not accessible for immediate recall.

undifferentiated. Primitive cell organization.

unicorn. Legendary lover of liberty.

urethral. Successor to anal primacy as a source of pleasure, e.g., in competition among peers (**B**) to see who can "piss" the farthest, or professional colleagues (**D**) for social acceptance.

valence. Power or capacity of certain elements or atoms to combine with or displace definite proportions of each other.

vitalistic. Not vital organs, but the notion that a vital (immaterial) principle underlies the behavior of living things.

weltanschauung. Apperceptive worldview of God and His creation or the cosmos and comets.

Whiggish. Mournful of the inertia of eras and those "-isms" that they don't like: The Whigs of old are the puritan prigs of the present who will eventually be the pricks of the past (entrenched interests who paralyze "progress."

Wilson, Allan. Berkeley biochemist.

Wilson, E. O. Harvard sociobiologist.

WoMAniMalectronic. Scientific prosthetic progress that allows mankind to outdo and outwit unencumbered and undomesticated animals.

wrong (B'). What may be unfair (intolerable in the view of the mighty).

xenophobia (G'). Shrinking from strangers among adults (in children from the unfamiliar among the autistic, and in the domesticated from novelty among the anal, less in the urethral, both post-oral but pre-genital), more (**FF'**) theo-"pathic" (*sic*) as in Jesus calling Greeks "dogs" than (**A'**) emotionally disturbing, (**B**) motivating or (**E**) inspiring.

yuppie. Status-seeking overachiever.

zero. Crucial in dismissing "causes" conceived of before Roman numerals became obsolete: Nothingness is a vacuum. Modern quantum theory sees empty space as an energy field that has an average value of zero. Once in a while, a random particle will pop up [according to the Principle of Uncertainty (intimately linked with the concept of chance in quantum physics): simply as an alternative event rather than as a mathematical probability]. Non-zero does not have to be 1. Why not a whole universe out of empty space, without an uncaused Cause?

INSIGHTS ABOUT MISLEADING and BETTER WORDS and PHRASES

acute = overreactive (chronic = habitual)

afterlife = promise to keep the powerless meek by lying to themselves about this life, denied fanatic Marxists, unnecessary for soul-less Buddhists (cf. "psyche" below)

beliefs = born of weakness and denial, resulting in bondage, like smoking and gambling; only when beliefs are defended like territory are they likely to result in genocide

cause-effect = factors and consequences simply overemphasized in linear thinking

choice = option, otherwise pure caprice (never free or as free as "free fall") or mulish will-fulness ("free will"); lies about free will make original sin and evil undeniable

codependent = symbiotic partner in maintaining "status quo"

communicative = repetitious (informative = unfamiliar)

conformity = bowing to pressure when outnumbered, rationalized as "discretion"

creation = serial evolution of random mutation by natural selection of chance variations

divine = benign (demonic = malignant)

fetocide = abortion in the first six weeks affecting only females before fetus changes sex

genocide = homicide of all males of all ages

hero = killed or died without eating or being eaten

individuation = finding out how far one can go from home, where it is safer to test limits

instinct = what our technology copies by programming our appliances to work on cue; guilt-free instinctive reactions are an index of freedom, health and strength. With mutation (accidental variation), materialism and determinism become irrelevant.

intimacy = sharing of shame, disavowal of secrets, untimid union of body and mind

life, full = better than a good life; with good food (dieting is not), good sex (if you don't do it every day, you can't do it every-day), and grandchildren

logical = methodical (Western logic = Aristotle's syllogism)

love = always blind, like faith or trust, never true or false but a symptom of the need to cling and an alacrity to prove rather than the rigor to disprove

martyrdom = dying done by strangers to save others whom they feel responsible for

mental hygiene = active sex, right to fail and freedom to be disloyal (breaking ties)

natural childbirth = makes human beings the most lethal of species from early brain trauma: sex is sinful, circumcision cleanses, animals are inferior to the domesticated (indoctrinated, or toilet-trained, etc.), gerunds replaced by nouns to persuade

noble savage = free to kill to eat without excusing murder as pious or patriotic (*Homo sapiens* also free to fornicate.)

normal = functional (abnormal = rigid "parrot", paranormal = stuck "pervert")

opinion = must be persuasive (palatable) but not as compelling as unpalatable fact

original sinners = congenital cripples clutching at the Cross as a crutch

personal commitment = social entrapment

pessinic = a cynic who cannot get started because the only outcome is bound to disappoint

(P)syche = Cupid's earthly lover, TV's Edith Bunker, Aristotle's earthy spirit, St. Thomas Aquinas's immortal soul that separates from the mind when it cannot mind itself

rebirth = spiritual (to Father in resurrection) or physical (from a mother in re-incarnation)

rescue = selfless struggle to avert imminent tragedy; fantasies include rebirth after dying

responsibility = blameworthiness

section, Caesarean (elective) = Buddha birth (by repute; sedentary life = rotundity) for lifelong equanimity, without asking or promising reward or reprieve

skeptomist = a skeptic who is not outcome-oriented but optimistic enough to find out

truth (C) = ratio of known to unknown, uncouth or elegant, symmetrical or feared to be chaotic

23/w Curriculum vitae: Professional experience

I have been published on both sides of the Atlantic. Below is my *curriculum vitae*. (I was the youngest to be certified as a specialist in psychiatry before I became a citizen and then applied for and was recertified after I became a citizen.)

Ortega, Magno Jacinto: Special Certificate in Psychiatry and Neurology, 1959
Recertified, Psychiatry, 1965

b. Aliaga, Nueva Ecija, Philippines
MD, '52 (University of Santo Tomas, Manila)

Intern, '52–'53 (St. Joseph Hospital, Elmira, NY)
Resident in Internal Med, '53–'54 (Cornell University Infirmary, Ithaca, NY)
> (I got six months credit in lieu of experience toward eligibility for special certification examination as a noncitizen, which I passed in 1959)

Resident '54–'55 (Howard State Hospital, Providence, RI)
Resident '55–'56 (Trenton State Hospital, Trenton, NJ)
Resident '56–'57 (Pinel Foundation Hosp, Seattle, WA)

Chief of Service, '57–'58 (Central State Hospital. Norman, OK)
> Published first professional article: *Mental Hospitals*: "Bio-social Approach to Long-Term Hospitalization"

Staff Faculty Appointment: 1958–59: Wayne County General Hospital, Eloise, Michigan

Published *Psychoanalysis*: "Delusions of Jealousy"

Rsgistrar '59–'60 (Littlemore Hospital, Oxford, England)
        Published: *Mental Hygiene*, Vol. 16, No. 1, 1962: "Open-door
        management of disturbed patients of both sexes" (unreplicated
        in America)
Registrar '60–'61 (Warlingham Park Hospital, Surrey, England)

Director of Training '61–'64 (Wayne County General Hospital, Eloise, MI)
Chief Professional Education '64–'81 (Napa State Hospital, Imola, CA)
Associate Clinical Professor (UC San Francisco, CA) 1978-2009
PT-Private Practice Solo (stepfamilies by referral only)
PT Academic Faculty (UCSF)

As chief of professional education, I was the director of a four-year
training program for doctors from all over the world who wanted to
be psychiatrists (we need them in California). Their fourth year of
training is spent in electives in UCSF or Stanford or abroad, the only
state program which does not keep trainees under one roof (we cannot
teach everything).

Change in challenges keeps curiosity alive. Creative response can be
measured by the struggle to invent new words to delay "mentanorexia."

Publications

Books:

Shneidman, PhD, Edwin S. and Magno J. Ortega, MD. *Aspects of
Depression*. International Psychiatric Clinics, Vol.6, No.2, Boston, Little,
Brown and Co., 1969.

Articles:

Ortega, Magno J., MD. "Principles in Practice or the Problem of Values,"
        "Playful/Useful Definitions,"
        "Freud Revised: Paths to Art, Religion & Science,"

"Unitary Biosocial Systems."
The Napa Quarterly, Spring, 1980.

Ortega, Magno J., MD. "Styles and Standards of Psychiatric Practice." "Issues & Answers in Residency Training' Napa Quarterly, Winter, 1976.

Ortega, Magno J., M.D. "Dialogue on Violence between M.J. Ortega and Joyce Sutton." Napa Quarterly, Imola, Ca., Spring, 1975.

Ortega, Magno J., M.D. "Identity without Belligerence." Napa Quarterly, Spring, 1975.

Ortega, Magno J., M.D. "Editorial. Required writings in Residency Training."
         "Twenty Years' Perspective in the Family Practice of Psychiatry." Napa Quarterly, special issue, Spring, 1974.

Ortega, Magno J., M.D. "A Psychiatric Odyssey of Personal Discoveries." *Voices: the art and science of psychotherapy.* A journal published by the American Academy of Psychotherapists. Potpourri VI, Volume 10, No.2, Issue 36, Potpourri IV, Summer, 1974.

Ortega, Magno J., M.D. "Transcultural Aspects of Adolescence and Senescence." The Napa Quarterly, Imola, Ca., Special issue, Spring, 1972.

Ortega, Magno J., M.D. "A Psychiatric Odyssey of Personal Discoveries - Things my Patients Taught Me." Napa Quarterly, Winter, 1972.

Ortega, M. J., M.D. 'Thinking Process Disturbances, Clinical Characteristics' Napa Quarterly, Imola, CA, Winter, 71–72.

Ortega, M. J., M.D. "Controversy Over Normalcy" Napa Quarterly, Spring, 1971

Ortega, M. "Editorial. Required writings in Residency Training."
         "Controversy over Normalcy."
Napa Quarterly, Special issue, Spring, 1971.

Ortega, M.J., M.D. "Depression, Loneliness, and Unhappiness." International Psychiatry Clinics.Volume 6, No.2, Little, Brown and Co., Boston, Mass., 1969.

Ortega, M.J., M.D. "Editorial."
       "Biosocial Psychiatry."
The Napa Quarterly, Special issue, Imola, Ca., Spring, 1969.

Ortega, M.J., M.D. "Schizophrenia or the Groups of Schizophasic Reactions." Journal of Schizophrenia, Vol. 1, No.2, Elias Publications, 1967.

Ortega, M.J., M.D. "Editorial." *The Napa Quarterly*. Imola, Ca., Fall, 1967.

Ortega, M.J., M.D. "Introductory Remarks. Community Approach to Mental Health." *The Napa Quarterly*. Imola, Ca., Spring, 1965.

Ortega, M.J., M.D. "Instant Day Hospital." *The Napa Quarterly.Journal of the NSH*, Imola, Ca., Spring, 1965.

Ortega, M.J., M.D. "Psychiatric Residency Training at Napa State Hospital." *The Napa Quarterly*. Imola, Ca., Fall, 1964.

Ortega, M.J., M.D. "Editorial." "Why Patients Get Well" *The Napa Quarterly*. Imola, Ca., Summer, 1964.

Ortega, M.J., M.D. "Open-ward Management of Disturbed Mental Patients of Both Sexes." Mental Hygiene., Vol.46, No.1, Jan., 1962.

Ortega, M.J., M.D. "Delusions of Jealousy." *Pyschoanalysis and the Psychoanalytic Review*, Volume 46, No.4, Winter, 1959.

Ortega, M.J., M.D. "A Service-Centered Plan for a Therapeutic Community." *Mental Hospitals.*, Dec., 1958.

Editor:

The Napa Quarterly. Journal of the Napa State Hospital, published 4x/ yr, 1964–1980.

Letters to the Editor:
Lancet, "Psychoanalysis"
Schizophrenia Bulletin. Oxford journals, "chronic schizophrenia –
readers" opinion, 1974
1990 Psychiatric Times

Abstracts:

"Mind & Matter, Body & Behavior. A Global Perspective." No. 1963,
Psychiatry Today, Accomplishments and Promises, VIII World Congress
of Psychiatry Abstracts, Excerpta Medica, International Congress Series
899, The Netherlands, 1989.

Pamphlets/Monographs:
The ABCs of Sensuality, Society, and Sex, Abstract for VII World
Congress of Psychiatry, Athens, 1989.

Absolute Relativity. Beyond the Mind.
Beyond the Mind = From Computers to Sex for a New Psychiatry.
Handbook of Human Behavior

PUBLICATIONS

Books:

Shneidman, Ph.D., Edwin S. & Magno J. Ortega, M.D. *Aspects of
Depression.* International Psychiatric Clinics, Vol.6, No.2, Boston, Little,
Brown and Co., 1969.

Articles:

Ortega, Magno J., M.D. "Principles in Practice or the Problem of Values,"
          "Playful/Useful Definitions,"
              "Freud Revised: Paths to Art, Religion & Science,"
              "Unitary Biosocial Systems."

The Napa Quarterly, Spring, 1980.

Ortega, Magno J., M.D. "Styles and Standards of Psychiatric Practice." "Issues & Answers in Residency Training' Napa Quarterly, Winter, 1976.

Ortega, Magno J., M.D. "Dialogue on Violence between M.J. Ortega and Joyce Sutton." Napa Quarterly, Imola, Ca., Spring, 1975.

Ortega, Magno J., M.D. "Identity without Belligerence." Napa Quarterly, Spring, 1975.

Ortega, Magno J., M.D. "Editorial. Required writings in Residency Training."

"Twenty Years' Perspective in the Family Practice of Psychiatry." Napa Quarterly, special issue, Spring, 1974.

Ortega, Magno J., M.D. "A Psychiatric Odyssey of Personal Discoveries. *"Voices: the art and science of psychotherapy.* A journal published by the American Academy of Psychotherapists. Potpourri VI, Volume 10, No.2, Issue 36, Potpourri IV, Summer, 1974.

Ortega, Magno J., M.D. "Transcultural Aspects of Adolescence and Senescence." The Napa Quarterly, Imola, Ca., Special issue, Spring, 1972.

Ortega, Magno J., M.D. "A Psychiatric Odyssey of Personal Discoveries - Things my Patients Taught Me." Napa Quarterly, Winter, 1972.

Ortega, M. J., M.D. 'Thinking Process Disturbances, Clinical Characteristics' Napa Quarterly, Imola, CA, Winter, 71–72.

Ortega, M. J., M.D. "Controversy Over Normalcy" Napa Quarterly, Spring, 1971

Ortega, M. "Editorial. Required writings in Residency Training."
        "Controversy over Normalcy."
Napa Quarterly, Special issue, Spring, 1971.

Ortega, M.J., M.D. "Depression, Loneliness, and Unhappiness." International Psychiatry Clinics.Volume 6, No.2, Little, Brown and Co., Boston, Mass., 1969.

Ortega, M.J., M.D. "Editorial."
          "Biosocial Psychiatry."
The Napa Quarterly, Special issue, Imola, Ca., Spring, 1969.

Ortega, M.J., M.D. "Schizophrenia or the Groups of Schizophasic Reactions." Journal of Schizophrenia, Vol. 1, No.2, Elias Publications, 1967.

Ortega, M.J., M.D. "Editorial." *The Napa Quarterly*. Imola, Ca., Fall, 1967.

Ortega, M.J., M.D. "Introductory Remarks. Community Approach to Mental Health." *The Napa Quarterly*. Imola, Ca., Spring, 1965.

Ortega, M.J., M.D. "Instant Day Hospital." *The Napa Quarterly.Journal of the NSH*, Imola, Ca., Spring, 1965.

Ortega, M.J., M.D. "Psychiatric Residency Training at Napa State Hospital." *The Napa Quarterly*. Imola, Ca., Fall, 1964.

Ortega, M.J., M.D. "Editorial." "Why Patients Get Well" *The Napa Quarterly*. Imola, Ca., Summer, 1964.

Ortega, M.J., M.D. "Open-ward Management of Disturbed Mental Patients of Both Sexes." Mental Hygiene., Vol.46, No.1, Jan., 1962.

Ortega, M.J., M.D. "Delusions of Jealousy." *Pyschoanalysis and the Psychoanalytic Review*, Volume 46, No.4, Winter, 1959.

Ortega, M.J., M.D. "A Service-Centered Plan for a Therapeutic Community." *Mental Hospitals.*, Dec., 1958.

Editor:

The Napa Quarterly. Journal of the Napa State Hospital, published 4x/ yr, 1964–1980.

Letters to the Editor:
Lancet, "Psychoanalysis"
Schizophrenia Bulletin. Oxford journals, "chronic schizophrenia – readers" opinion, 1974
1990 Psychiatric Times

Abstracts:

"Mind & Matter, Body & Behavior. A Global Perspective." No. 1963, Psychiatry Today, Accomplishments and Promises, VIII World Congress of Psychiatry Abstracts, Excerpta Medica, International Congress Series 899, The Netherlands, 1989.

Pamphlets/Monographs:
The ABCs of Sensuality, Society, and Sex, Abstract for VII World Congress of Psychiatry, Athens, 1989.

Absolute Relativity. Beyond the Mind.
Beyond the Mind = From Computers to Sex for a New Psychiatry.
Handbook of Human Behavior

Bayor inter-university forum for educators in community psychiatry, Harvard, NIMH, 1967–71
First Session, Evolving Theory and Practice in Community Psychiatry, Houston, Texas, 10/31–11/10/67
Second Session, member, Program Committee, 4/16-4/26/68
Third Session, Administration and Communication, Houston, Texas, 10/14–25/68i
Fourth Session, Contributions of Research to a Conceptual Foundation of Community Psychiatry, Houston Texas, 4/14-25/69

Fifth Session, Preventive aspects of Community Psychiatry, Houston, Texas, 10/13-24/69
1971, Host, program, Silverado, Napa, CA
Final program, Detroit Michigan, 6/14-17/73

PRESENTATIONS

"A Psychiatrist's Perspective on Humanity, Sex and Violence, Domestic and Social" UST Dept. Neurology and Psychiatry, 12/11/02

"A Psychiatrist's Perspective on Humanity, Sex and Violence, Domestic and Social" De La Salle University, College of Liberal Arts Psychology Department, 12/2/02.

World Forum for Mental Health. The 5th World Congress on "Innovations in Psychiatry, 1998, London, England, May 19-22, 1998, 2 presentations; The ABC's of Sex and Violence" "A New Transcultural Psychiatry."

"The ABZ's of Life" The Maudsley, Croydon Mental Health Services, Warlingham Park Hospital, Summer Academic Programme for Junior Dotors, 6/26/95

"Creativity, Ideology, and Madness." at conference "Creativity and Madness. Psychological Studies of Art and Artists." The American Institute of Medical Education., Burbank, Ca., Athens, Delphi, Olympia, Naphthio, Aegean Cruise, 9/17-10/1/94, (22 hours Category 1 credit).

"Stages of Development of Creative Talent." at conference "Emotional Growth and Creativity in Adult Life For the General Health Care Community." The American Institute of Medical Education, Burbank, Ca., The Inn at Loretto, Santa Fe, NM, 2/21-25/94, (18 hours CME Category 1).

CME Panel: Bioethics for the Thomasian Physician (The Physician's commitment to the Terminally Ill.) 11th Dr. Mariano M. Alimurung Memorial Postgraduate Course, A Scientific Programme in Conjunction with the USTMAA general homecoming, 12/13-15/92, 12/14/92

Zanax Interactive Panel Discussion: Panic Disorder, 4/9/91, SF

"Our Life through Time", UST, 38th class of 52 Reunion cruise to Mexico, Long Beach, CA, Stanford U., Palo Alto, 8/24-27/90

"Human Senso-socio-sexual behavior in our longer second half of life" Stanford U, 1990

"Mind & Matter, Body & Behavior. A Global Perspective." Session 00296 Philosophy and Psychiatry. 8th World Congress of Psychiatry., Athens, 10/12-19/89.

UST class, "52, lunch in Napa, 9/15/89

"Evolution of Human Behavior." Post graduate alumni homecoming, Far Eastern University, Manila, Phil., 12/19/87.

"Evolution of Human Behavior." Scientific Program of UST Class of 52 Reunion, Veterans' Memorial Hospital, Quezon City, Phil., 12/11/87.

"Cross Cultural Considerations in Psychiatry, "Second Pacific Congress of Psychiatry, Manila, Philippines, 5/12-16/80

"German contributions to Psychology." Panel Discussion, Napa Valley College TV program, 222/79

Symposium: "Violence" NSH, SFUC, Program Chairman, 5/4-5/74

Symposium: "Senescence and Adolescence" UCSF, NSH, 4/8/72.

Symposium: "Family Process", Moderator, NSH, UCSF, NSH, 3/31/73

Symposium: "Autism and Mental Retardation", UCSF, NHS, 3/11/72

Symposium: "Drug Dependence" UCSF, NSH, 3/13/71.

Normalcy as a Transcultural Entity. Deprssion, Unhappiness, and Lonliness, Schizophrenia since Bleuler, Chronic Scchizophrenia, Milieu Therapy and Day Hospitals, Difficult patients, 1970

Symposium: Community and Mental Health: Prevention, Treatment and Relevance. Program Chairman and Panel Discussion Moderator. NSH, 10/3-4/70.

Symposium" "The Archepelago of Psychotherapy" NSH, UCSF, 5/16-17/70

"A Fresh Look at Mental Retardation" Program Chair and Panel Discussion. NSH, UCSF, 3/15-16/69

"Suicide Symptoms and Handling Potential Suicide Cases." Public Offering, NVC, Napa College with Dr. Carol Wilcox 4/6/68 (4 hours)

"Personality Disorders and Sexual Disturbances, NSH, UCSF, Program Chair, 10/26-27/68

A Symposium on Neurotic and Neurotic-like Disturbances: "Neurotic-like Disturbances", moderator, panel discussion, speaker, NSH, UCSF, 3/16-17/68

A Symposium on Depression: "psychopathology of Depression" "Loneliness, Unhappiness and Depression "Moderator, panel discussion participant, speaker. NSH, UCSF, 4/15-16/67

"Schizophrenia" Program Chair, Moderator, presentation: "Psychopathology in Schizophrenia", NSH, UCSF, 9/24-25/66.

Symposium: "Working with Groups in a Mental Hospital" NSH, 5/20/66

"Hypnosis in Yesteryears and Today" (Why Freud abandoned hypnosis) Symposium: "Hypnosis: A Critical Evaluation" NSH, UCSF, 5/14-15/66

Symposium: "Child Psychiatry" Program Chairman, "Approaches to emotionally disturbed children in Great Britain" and "Hospital Treatment of Adolescents" NSH and UCSF, 9/25-26/65.

"Instant Day Hospitals" at "The Community Approach to Mental Health" NSH, UCSF, 2/13-14/65.

"Resources an Facilities for Community Mental Health." Panelist. Community Health Education Series: Community Goals in Mental Health. Inkster, Mich., Monday evenings. 7/15-8/5/63.

"Instant Day Hospitals" Michigan Assoc. of Neuropsychiatric Hospitals and clinic physicians. 6/14/63.

"The Future of the Emotionally Disturbed Teenager in our Hospitals" 25th Annual Conference Michigan Society for Mental Health, Inc., Assignment: Community Action for the Mentally Ill, panel arranged by Psychiatric Attendant Nurse Association of Michigan, speaker, panelist, Detroit, 10/5/62

"Day Hospitals", Michigan Society for Mental Health, 5/62

"Philosophy of Mental Health, AAUW, Shawnee, OK. 1/19/59

Edwards Brothers Malloy
Thorofare, NJ USA
March 28, 2016